SUMMARY OF WATFIV STATEMENTS AND FUNCTIONS USED IN THIS TEXT

STATEMENT	DESCRIPTION (TEXT PAGE)	EXECUT-ABLE?	EXAMPLES
ELSE	Defines ELSE-block in IF-THEN-ELSE structure; see block IF (143)	Yes	ELSE
ELSE IF	Tests logical expression and defines ELSE-IF-block in multiple alternative decision structures (201)	Yes	ELSE IF (AGE .GE. 30 .AND. AGE .LT. 40) THEN
END	Defines end of program unit (38)	No	END
END AT END	Defines end of block that gets executed at end-of-file condition; see AT END (178)	Yes	END AT END
END BLOCK	Defines end of remote block; see REMOTE BLOCK (527)	Yes	END BLOCK
END CASE	Defines end of CASE structure; see DO CASE (208)	Yes	END CASE
END IF	Corresponds to particular block IF statement; see block IF (143, 153)	Yes	END IF
ENDFILE	Places endfile record on sequential-access file (408)	Yes	END FILE 10
END LOOP	Defines end of generalized loop; see LOOP (173)	Yes	END LOOP
END WHILE	Defines end of WHILE structure; see WHILE (165)	Yes	END WHILE
EQUIVALENCE	Specifies sharing of storage locations by two or more entities in same program unit (356)	No	EQUIVALENCE(A,B,C),(D,ARRAY(5))
EXECUTE	Calls or invokes remote block (526)	Yes	EXECUTE PLANS
FORMAT	Provides format specification (445, 470)	No	90 FORMAT('1',T9,'NAMES'/('0',A20)) 92 FORMAT(2I5,F10.2,E15.6,20X,D20.10)
FUNCTION	Defines beginning of function subprogram (361)	No	FUNCTION MINI(M,N,G) . . . END
GO TO	Transfers control to labeled statement unconditionally (211)	Yes	GO TO 50
IF	Tests logical expression and executes statement to right if result is true, when form is that of *logical* IF statement (155)	Yes	IF (A .GT. B) MAX = A IF (A .LE. B) MAX = B

IF	Tests logical expression and defines IF-block in IF-THEN, IF-THEN-ELSE and multiple alternative decision structures, when form is that of *block* IF statement (143, 153, 200)	Yes	IF (A .GT. B) THEN
			  MAX = A
			ELSE
			  MAX = B
			END IF

Applied Structured

WATFIV

ROY AGELOFF
University of Rhode Island

RICHARD MOJENA
University of Rhode Island

WADSWORTH PUBLISHING COMPANY
Belmont, California
A division of Wadsworth, Inc.

Signing Representaive: Rich Giggey
Computer Science Editor: Frank Ruggirello
Editorial production services by Cobb/Dunlop Publisher Services, Inc.

Cover: Computer graphics image courtesy of Metheus Corporation.

Printed in the United States of America

 2 3 4 5 6 7 8 9 10———88 87 86 85 84

Library of Congress Cataloging in Publication Data

Ageloff, Roy, 1943–
  Applied structured WATFIV.

  Includes index.
  1. FORTRAN (Computer program language)   2. Structured
programming.   I. Mojena, Richard.   II. Title.   III. Title:
Applied structured W.A.T.F.I.V.
QA76.73.F25A336   1984   001.64′24   84-2392
ISBN 9-534-03079-3

ISBN 0-534-03079-3

To Our Students,
for what they have taught us

Preface

This textbook is designed for a first course in FORTRAN programming using the WATFIV dialect. No prerequisites are required other than a willingness to develop problem-solving skills.

The combination of features described below distinguishes this book from others in the field.

WATFIV implementation. WATFIV is the basis of the FORTRAN material. Statements and functions used in this book are summarized and illustrated inside the front and back covers. This version of WATFIV is very similar to ANSI FORTRAN 77. Key differences between these two versions of FORTRAN are summarized in Module H at the back of the textbook.

Evolutionary design. Following a comprehensive overview of the field in Chapter 1, coverage of programming proceeds from simple to difficult, with the student writing complete programs by the end of Chapter 2 and running programs by the end of Chapter 3.

By design, the pace of Chapters 2–4 builds slowly, to encourage confidence and to develop a sound foundation. This approach necessarily discards the complete treatment of a topic in one place. For example, loop structures are first overviewed in Chapter 4, and a DO-loop implementation is illustrated. General WHILE, UNTIL, and Last-Record-Check loops, however, are not implemented until Chapter 5.

Structured programming. The structured programming philosophy is presented early in Chapter 4, elaborated upon in Chapters 4–6, and adhered to throughout the book. All programs use well-defined control structures (IF-THEN-ELSE, CASE, pretest loop, etc.) and GOTO-less programming.

Chapter 4 implements the loop structure through DO/CONTINUE statements. The early implementation of the loop structure based on DO/CONTINUE statements has two advantages: it allows the early introduction of realistic problems and the power of repetitive processing, and it minimizes breadth of coverage (thereby student confusion) in one chapter by postponing the introduction of logical expressions and a variety of looping statements (LOOP, ENDLOOP, WHILE, UNTIL, AT END, and QUIT).

Program design and style. Good program design and style are emphasized throughout the book. For example, in Chapter 2 we present a four-step program-writing procedure that includes problem analysis and design of algorithms through flowcharts and pseudocode. Other design and style considerations include documentation (from Chapter 3 on), indentation (from Chapter 4 on), structured programming (Chapters 4–11), structured charts (Module A), the "proper" use of GO TO statements (Section 6.4), top-down design (Module E), and modular programming (Module F).

Additionally, Module G summarizes a number of issues in good program design, including the interrelationships among structured, top-down, and modular programming; the readability versus efficiency tradeoff; the design of general versus specific programs; the use of documentation aids; and considerations regarding debugging, transportability, reliability, and management practices.

Use of modules.   We have attempted to design flexibility into the use of this book by placing certain topics in modules at the book's end. Structured charts (Module A) can be assigned as early as Chapter 4; I/O with formats (Modules B–D) is not used specifically until Chapter 7, but can be assigned at any time after Chapter 4; top-down design, including stepwise refinement (Module E), can be assigned either during or after Chapter 5; modular programming (Module F) can be assigned at the end of Chapter 9; and Module G (On Designing Better Programs) can be assigned any time after Chapter 6.

Emphasis on meaningful applications.   The word "applied" in the title of the book is used to suggest our emphasis throughout on meaningful applications of the computer. Applications include those relating to *information processing* and those relating to *mathematical modeling*. They are described in a wide variety of contexts, including areas in business, economics, mathematics, statistics, and the sciences, as well as emerging areas in the public sector (such as health care delivery, emergency response systems, and allocation of public resources).

Table A summarizes and references the applications described in the book through examples and exercises. This table clearly illustrates our philosophy that problems should be presented in an *evolutionary* context. As new material is learned, many examples and exercises improve upon previous versions of the same problem. This approach not only is pedagogically sound but also is consistent with (but not identical to) the evolutionary nature of program design in the "real world."

Extensive examples and exercises.   The learning of FORTRAN is greatly facilitated by numerous and carefully designed examples and exercises. More than 60 *complete* programs are illustrated in this book; entirely new programs are accompanied by flowcharts and/or pseudocode. Exercises are found both within chapters (Follow-up Exercises) and at the end of chapters (Additional Exercises). The book has approximately 500 exercises, many with multiple parts. The chapters on programming (Chapters 2–11) average better than 40 exercises per chapter.

Follow-up exercises serve to reinforce, integrate, and extend preceding material. This feature gives the book a "programmed learning" flavor without the regimentation of such an approach. Additionally, we have found that such exercises create an excellent basis for planning many classroom lectures. *Answers to selected follow-up exercises are provided at the back of the textbook.* Solutions to those follow-up exercises identified by either a single or double asterisk are given in the *Instructor's Manual*.

TABLE A   Page Reference for Application Programs

Information Processing

student billing 30, 44, 61–63, 65, 68, 83, 92, 97, 113, 119, 443, 466

form letter 137, 397

sales bonus 145, 159, 175, 179, 194, 441

finding minimum value 153

computerized matching—a file search 187, 318, 431

credit billing 188, 432

personnel benefits budget 191

tuition schedule 194

microcomputer discount schedule 201

class report 204

traffic court fines 209

property tax assessment 223, 279

mailing list 223, 318, 431

telephone company billing 225

checking account report 226

analysis of bank deposits 235, 250, 253, 258, 289, 303

direct access to array element—SAT scores 263

table look-up: life insurance premium 267

sorting 273, 347

crime data summary 279, 320

revenue sharing 281, 431

exam grading 283

stock portfolio valuation 284

income tax 309

projected enrollments 314

interactive airline reservation system 320, 431

personnel salary budget 322

questionnaire analysis 323

electric bill 371, 432

text editing 390

text analysis 398

text processing 399

cryptography 399–400

personnel file 410, 417, 420

Index file 422

hashing algorithm 422

computerized blood donor system 424, 431

payroll 432

class grades 434

Government Printing Office orders 499

Mathematical Modeling

bank savings 71, 117, 128, 138

area 51, 73, 100, 134, 185

microeconomics 53, 73, 100, 135

temperature conversion 55, 73, 100, 133

blood bank inventory 73, 100, 135, 185

forecasting population growth 74, 100, 184

automobile financing 74, 101, 136

mean exam scores 124

exponential CDF 136

retirement contribution 139

optimal cost per credit 140

inflation curse 167, 171, 173

Poisson probability function 185

factorials 186

quadratic roots 187

police car replacement 190

root bisection algorithm 216, 368

crew selection—a combination problem 228, 342

Newton's approximation method 229

numerical integration 231

polynomial plot 270

support facility for oil drilling platforms 280

sales forecasts 282

vector representation of a matrix 306

Poisson-distributed electronic failures 321

matrix multiplication 325

combinations 329, 359

mean of one-dimensional array 343, 348

exponential function 365

statistical analyses 373

automobile rental decision 516, 527

The chapter-end exercises offer opportunities for review and the development of new programming problems. *All programming problems include test data.* Examples and exercises are generally framed in a "real world" context that will interest and motivate the student. Exercises are ordered from least difficult to most difficult. The more difficult exercises are designed to challenge the good student, and are identified by a double asterisk. The *Instructor's Manual* gives answers to all chapter-end exercises.

Common errors.   The necessary process of debugging is time-consuming, frustrating, and difficult to master by beginning programmers. In our experience, students commit certain programming errors more commonly than others. Accordingly, the book features sections on debugging procedures and common errors at the end of *each* programming chapter, beginning with Chapter 3 and ending with Chapter 11.

I/O with formats.   Our treatment of I/O with formats is carefully designed to give instructors as much flexibility as possible regarding the choice of list-directed I/O versus format-directed I/O. The topic (I/O with formats) is set off in modules (B–D), which can be assigned as early as the end of Chapter 4. Within chapters, the use of format specifications is postponed until Chapter 7; thereafter the use of format specifications is either clearly labeled (and easily skipped) or incidental to the material.

In effect, the book is essentially independent of I/O with formats, but is designed to facilitate timing and integration of the topic. Our own preference is to delay its introduction until after Chapter 6, to provide ample time first for algorithmic design.

Batch and remote batch.   Since the computer systems at institutions of higher education vary, we illustrate both batch (card) and remote batch (online terminal) approaches to computing. Remote batch is given more than a superficial treatment in keeping with its increased use in universities, governmental agencies, and companies.

To accommodate both card and online users, most programs and discussions of FORTRAN are independent of processing environments. For example, we consciously use the term input record instead of card.

Camera-ready programs.   All complete programs and their input/output are reproduced by camera rather than typeset. This increases the realism of the programming material and ensures the reliability of programs. Moreover, many of the programs include pedagogic shading and margin notes to enhance student understanding.

A book on programming and problem solving, not a programming manual.   We believe that a FORTRAN course should be much more than just a course that teaches the FORTRAN language. It should teach the process of programming as a creative activity, from conceptualization of the problem to implementation of the computer program.

In keeping with this belief, we sacrifice some scope in the FORTRAN language by devoting more space to pedagogy through patient explanations and extensive examples and exercises. Additionally, we emphasize problem analysis and program development by formalizing the writing of programs through a four-step procedure first introduced in Chapter 2, which subsequently is integrated with top-down design and modular programming.

A programming course also should broaden a student's perspective. Accordingly, Chapter 1 presents a more thorough overview of the field than does the typical introductory chapter; Module G summarizes style issues of keen topical interest; and Module H compares WATFIV and FORTRAN 77 dialects.

ACKNOWLEDGMENTS

We wish to express our deep appreciation to many who have contributed to this project: to Frank Ruggirello, our editor, for unflagging humor, support, and expert advice; to Lila M. Gardner of Cobb/Dunlop Publisher Services and Jerry Holloway of Wadsworth for editorial/ production magic and liaison par excellence; to Richard R. Weeks, Dean, University of Rhode Island, for administrative support; to the Computer Laboratory at the University of Rhode Island for obvious reasons; to our reviewers, R. W. Elliot, University of Florida; Donald Ewing, University of Toledo; Ronald Lancaster, Bowling Green State University; Orlando Madrigal, California State University, Chico; James Marr, University of Alabama at Huntsville; Charles Neblock, Western Illinois University; and Glenn Thomas, Kent State University, who provided invaluable corrections and suggestions for manuscript revisions; to Joe Daly, Sharon Masters, and Chris Guglietti for "grunt" work on programs; to Fran Mojena who finally learned to "word process" in typing parts of the manuscript on our IBM PC; to our students, who always teach us something about teaching; and to our immediate families, who are still wondering when it will all end.

Kingston, Rhode Island   ROY AGELOFF

                                                            RICHARD MOJENA

Contents

CHAPTER 1

Orientation

The electronic computer is one of our foremost technological inventions; for good or for bad, its presence affects each of us, and its future holds even more potential to affect our lives.

This chapter is an orientation to the course you are about to take. We first define the computer and discuss its impact. Thereafter we provide a relatively complete, nontechnical overview of what makes up a computer system and a preview of how to communicate with the computer. Finally, we outline how you will benefit from this course.

If you are warm-blooded and living in the twentieth century, then we suspect that you are curious about the computer. By the time this course is over we hope that we (together with your instructor) will have helped you translate that curiosity into a continuing, productive, and rewarding experience.

1.1
WHAT IS A COMPUTER?

An electronic **computer** is defined most generally as *an electronic device that is capable of manipulating data to achieve some task.* Given this definition, electronic cash registers, electronic gasoline pumps, and electronic calculators all qualify as simple computers. The machine we usually think of as a computer, however, has three significant characteristics.

1. It's fast.
2. It stores large amounts of data.
3. It executes alterable, stored instructions.

Characteristics of Electronic Computers

The great speed of today's electronic computers is a direct result of miniaturization in solid-state electronics. To give you a rough idea of the speed capabilities of large electronic computers, consider the following estimates. One minute of computer time is equivalent to approximately 6700 hours of skilled labor by a person using a calculator. In other words, a person using a calculator would take one hour to accomplish what a computer can accomplish in less than one hundredth of a second. In fact, the electronic transfers within computers are so fast that computer designers use a basic unit of time equal to one billionth of a second (called a *nanosecond*)—quite a feat when you consider that the basic unit of time for us mortals is one second.

Another significant characteristic of electronic computers is their capacity to store large amounts of data and instructions for later recall. In other words, much like the human brain, the computer has "memory." For example, computers at most universities store several million characters of data in primary storage and hundreds of millions of characters in secondary storage.

Finally, an electronic computer is differentiated from most other computing devices by its ability to store and obey instructions in memory. Moreover, these instructions are easily programmable (can be altered or changed). In other words, the computer executes instructions from different users without interference from human beings. This characteristic makes the computer flexible and efficient: it carries out multiple tasks automatically while we do something else. Of course, the computer cannot do without us completely, but more about that later.

Computer Classifications

To distinguish among different types of electronic computers, we make the following comparisons: analog versus digital computers, special-purpose versus general-purpose computers, and mainframes versus minicomputers versus microcomputers.

The **analog computer** manipulates data representing continuous physical processes such as temperature, pressure, and voltage. The fuel injection system of an automobile, for example, deals with physical processes as it regulates the fuel/air ratio on the basis of engine speed, temperature, and pressure; the gasoline pump converts the flow of fuel into price (dollars and cents) and volume (gallons or liters to the nearest tenth).

You will be using the **digital computer,** which operates by counting digits. This type of computer manipulates data (numbers in our decimal system, letters in our alphabet, and special characters such as the comma and dollar sign) by counting binary (two-state or 0–1) digits. **Hybrid computers,** which combine the features of digital and analog computers, have been designed for certain types of applications. For example, hybrid computers control the production of products such as steel and gasoline, provide on-board guidance for aircraft and spacecraft, regulate the peak energy demands of large office buildings or factories, and monitor the vital life signs of patients in critical condition.

Computers are classified not only by how they process data as in analog versus digital, but also by the function they serve. **Special-purpose computers** are designed to accomplish a single task, whereas **general-purpose computers** are designed to accept programs of instruction for carrying out different tasks. For example, one special-purpose computer has been designed strictly to do navigational calculations for ships and aircraft. The instructions for carrying out this task are built into the electronic circuitry of the machine so that the navigator simply keys in data and receives the answer. Other special-purpose computers include **word processors** for preparing, storing, and printing letters, documents, reports, manuscripts, and anything else previously typed; those used in color television sets to improve color reception; those used in PBX (Private Branch Exchange) telephones to perform various functions, such as automatic placement of a call at a preset time and simplified dialing of frequently used telephone numbers; and those used in automobiles to calculate such items as "miles of fuel left" and "time of destination," and to monitor and read out instantaneously the status of oil level, gasoline level, engine temperature, brake lining wear, and other operating conditions.

In contrast, a general-purpose computer used by a corporation might accomplish tasks relating to the preparation of payrolls and production schedules and the analyses of financial, marketing, and engineering data all in one day. Similarly, the academic computer you are about to use might run a management simulation one minute and analyze the results of a psychology experiment the next minute, or it might even accomplish both of these tasks (and more) concurrently.

In general, compared with the special-purpose computer, the general-purpose computer has the flexibility of satisfying the needs of a variety of users, but at the expense of speed and economy. In this textbook, we focus strictly on the *electronic, digital, general-purpose computer.*

Another useful distinction among computers is based on size, which generally translates into storage capacity, speed, and cost. **Mainframe** computers are physically large, process huge amounts of data at incredibly fast speeds, and strain data processing budgets. Control Data Corporation (CDC), International Business Machines (IBM), and Burroughs are typical manufacturers. **Minicomputers** range in size from a filing cabinet to a closet, process large amounts of data at very high speeds, and are moderately priced. Digital Equipment Corporation (DEC), Hewlett-Packard (HP), IBM, and Prime are popular suppliers. **Microcomputers** come in sizes that fit pockets to desktops, with correspondingly lower storage capacities, processing speeds, and prices. Apple Computer, Commodore Business Machines, DEC, HP, IBM, Radio Shack, and Texas Instruments are common suppliers.

1.2
IMPACT OF THE COMPUTER

Since the first sale of an electronic computer by Remington Rand in 1951, the computer industry has become a worldwide giant, both in terms of sales and jobs. The computer has revolutionized the operations of many governmental agencies, private enterprises, and public institutions, and many experts agree that the computer industry is a "young child," if not still an "infant." In this section we present a brief historical sketch of the development of the computer, provide you with a sample of computer applications, and end with an assessment of the computer's impact.

Historical Sketch

Many conceptions and inventions dating back to the early nineteenth century were necessary precedents to the development of the computer. The first electronic digital computer was built in the late 1930s by John V. Atanasoff and his assistant Clifford Berry at Iowa State College. Named the **ABC** (for Atanasoff-Berry Computer), it was a small computer that performed mathematical operations for graudate student work.

The first *large-scale* digital general-purpose computer was completed in 1944 when Howard Aiken at Harvard University designed the **Mark I** to generate mathematical tables. Unlike electronic computers, the Mark I was a mechanical computer that operated by a system of telephone relays, mechanized wheels, and tabulating equipment. By current standards, it was *very* large, *very* unreliable, *very* slow, and *very* limited in its scope of applications.

In 1946 the team of J. W. Mauchly and J. P. Eckert, Jr., from the University of Pennsylvania, completed the first *large-scale electronic* computer. This computer was named **ENIAC,** for the intimidating title Electronic Numerical Integrator And Calculator. Essentially, ENIAC was an electronic version of Mark I, in which vacuum tubes replaced the function of telephone relays; this replacement resulted in an increase of computing speed by a factor of nearly 200. Commissioned by the U.S. Army, it did an incomparable job (for the times) of generating artillery trajectory tables, but weighed 30 tons, filled a 150-square-meter room, and had over 18,000 vacuum tubes that failed at the rate of one every 7 minutes.

UNIVAC I (Universal Automatic Computer), developed by Remington (now Sperry) Rand in 1951, was the first commercial computer. Unlike its predecessors, it computed using binary arithmetic and allowed the storage of instructions in internal computer memory. During this **first-generation** period computers were developed by RCA, Philco, GE, Burroughs, Honeywell, NCR, and IBM. The first computer to achieve dominance in the industry was the IBM 650, which became the commercial leader during the period 1954–1959. These first-generation machines used vacuum tubes, required air conditioning, had relatively small amounts of internal memory, and were slow by today's standards.

Subsequent generations of computers resulted in dramatic reductions in *size* and relative *cost* and increases in *speed, reliability,* and the capacity for *storage.* **Second-generation** computers from the late 1950s to the mid-1960s replaced the vacuum tubes of the first-generation computers with transistors. The most widely used second-generation computers were the IBM 1620, the IBM 1401, and the IBM 7094.

The **third-generation** computers from the mid-1960s to about 1970 made use of the emerging field of microelectronics (miniaturized circuits). The use of solid logic technology (SLT) allowed the placement of transistorized circuits on small "chips," which increased the packing densities of transistorized circuits by a factor of 100. The third-generation computers were more reliable, faster, and more sophisticated than earlier computers. They also had the ability to handle several programs concurrently (*multiprogramming*), resulting in a more efficient use of the computer. The most prominent family of computers in this generation was the IBM System/360.

During the 1970s and early 1980s a series of refinements and improvements to third-generation machines were marketed. These **fourth-generation** computers utilized large-scale integrated circuitry (LSI) and other microminiaturization features, resulting in further reductions in size and power requirements as compared with earlier computers.

Another significant development in the 1970s was the use of small (in physical size and memory capacity), inexpensive, yet powerful computers called *minicomputers* and *microcomputers*. The use of minicomputers is common in small to medium companies, colleges, hospitals, governmental agencies, and other organizations. In the past decade many organizations have decentralized their computer processing activities by implementing what is called *distributed processing,* whereby a network of computers links together geographically remote locations. A typical configuration is a minicomputer at each location for either local processing tasks or communication to a large central computer for major processing tasks.

Microcomputers, which are smaller than minicomputers, currently are marketed by consumer retail outlets such as Radio Shack, Sears, and Computerland. Today's desk-top microcomputers are 20 times faster, have larger memory, are thousands of times more reliable, consume the power of a light bulb rather than a locomotive, occupy one 30,000th of the volume and cost one 10,000th ($500 versus $5 million) as much as the massive first-generation machines that filled an entire room. Their use in organizations and homes is expected to increase dramatically during the 1980s.

Applications

The computer represents a revolutionary technological tool for extending our applied capabilities. The diversity of the sample applications listed in Table 1.1 should give you an idea of the increasing influence of computers. Users of the computer include all facets of our society: individuals; private organizations such as industrial companies and banks; and public institutions such as hospitals, universities, and governmental agencies.

Basic information processing such as updating customer accounts, preparing payrolls, and generating status reports on personnel, sales, production, and inventories was a common early use of the computer. Although these automated approaches were more effective than hours of "hand-crunching" effort by an "army" of clerks, they failed to integrate adequately the sources and uses of information in complex organizations. Today, users are calling for the design and implementation of **management information systems** (**MIS**) that can integrate, aggregate, and analyze timely information for use by management in their decision-making activities.

Engineers, scientists, and mathematicians have used computers since their introduction for extensive mathematical calculations. In recent years, managers and social scientists have increasingly emphasized mathematical modeling in their decision-making activities. For example, disciplines such as *operations research* and *management science* develop and apply quantitative techniques (mathematics, probability, statistics) to help solve problems faced by managers of public and private organizations.

The second part of Table 1.1 gives you an idea of the types of problems that lend them-

---

TABLE 1.1   Sample Applications of the Computer

Information Processing

Preparation of payroll and billings
Maintenance of inventory information
Maintenance of customer accounts
Technical processing of reference information by media and public libraries
Calculation of income taxes by the IRS
Maintenance of student records by universities
Maintenance of flight and reservation information by airlines
Cataloguing of blood supplies by regional blood banks
Maintenance of checking accounts by banks
Editing and reproduction of typed manuscripts
Maintenance of criminal records by the FBI
Maintenance of property tax records by a municipality
Budgeting by organizations and individuals
Recording of monetary distributions by state and federal welfare agencies

Mathematical Modeling

Statistical analyses of census data, biological data, engineering data, etc.
Production scheduling and inventory control
Medical diagnosis
Orbital analysis for satellites
Management of financial portfolios
Location of fire stations in an urban area
Simulation of economic decay in a city
Dietary meal planning in institutions
Statistical forecasting
Educational planning and school bus scheduling
Design of airway and highway traffic systems
Chemical analysis
Design of solar energy systems
Planning, scheduling, and controlling of complex projects (such as construction of a submarine,
   office building, or sports stadium)

---

selves to mathematical modeling. In many cases the data required for these quantitative approaches to decision making are best provided by an MIS, which effectively integrates our two broad classes of applications. Systems that combine elements of MIS and quantitative modeling are often called **decision support systems (DSS).**

Inevitably, the following question is asked: Can computers think? The computer cannot think in the usual sense, for it can accomplish only what people instruct it to accomplish through written programs of instruction. It is best at solving problems that are well structured—that is, problems whose solutions can be determind on a step-by-step basis that is quite explicit. Problems that require ill-defined or spontaneous actions to cope with complex or entirely new situations do not lend themselves as well to computer solution. For example, an executive can reorganize a company better than a computer can; a composer writes music better than does a computer; a chess master plays better chess than a computer does; and an inventor is more capable of inventing than is a computer.

As scientists come to understand better the thinking processes behind creativity, adaptation, and judgment, programs of instruction for solving ill-structured problems will improve. This area of research, called **artificial intelligence,** has made some progress as computers have been programmed to compose music, play chess, prove theorems, and solve puzzles. Success, however, has been limited, and future progress in this area is uncertain.

Assessment

Any task that can be performed by a general-purpose digital computer can also be performed by a human being (given enough time). Of course, when it comes to the amount of data that can be stored and the speed with which these data can be manipulated, the computer is in a class by itself. In effect, therefore, the computer magnifies our own capacities. This results in both advantages and disadvantages, which we now summarize.

ADVANTAGES

1. *Power of analysis and technological advancement.* The computer performs massive amounts of scientific calculation in a short span of time and controls complex processes such as steel making, automatic guidance of spacecraft, and air–ground traffic control.
2. *Career opportunities.* The computer upgrades the skill requirements of jobs and creates new career opportunities both for labor and management; the current (and projected) supply of skilled people in this area is short of demand.
3. *Information needs.* As a society becomes more complex (and the individuals become more numerous), the computer provides a means to satisfy the society's information needs.
4. *Level of service.* The computer provides faster and better quality service to members of society; examples include airline reservation systems, health care delivery systems, bank accounts, and preregistration of classes for university students. To illustrate the scale of service that the computer makes possible, consider this:

   The U.S. Department of Health and Human Services provides round-the-clock services that go directly to 115 million Americans and indirectly touch just about everybody in the nation. It is an empire, moreover, of 1,125,000 bureaucrats augmented by computers. Without its electronic marvels, [its] accomplishments would be unthinkable. While most of the departments programs are administered from its huge Washington headquarters, Social Security data are processed in a building outside Baltimore by the most extensive computer system in the world. Every day an average of 20,000 claims are filed; every night the complete Social Security wage file, contained on 220,000 reels of tape, is run through the computers to provide information on the claimants. Next day off go the forms that bring life-sustaining checks to the nation's aged and disabled.[1]

5. *Cost savings to society.* The computer results in a more efficient delivery of services when used in applications where it is more productive than alternative approaches.

[1] "The Beneficient Monster," *Time Magazine,* June 12, 1978, p. 24.

DISADVANTAGES

1. *Mistakes.*   Surveys of the public have indicated that a significant percentage of those surveyed have had a problem because of the computer, with billing problems accounting for the majority of reported mistakes insofar as the public is concerned. In recent years, however, channels of communication for correcting errors have been improved. *The source of such mistakes is typically traced to computer personnel rather than to the computer equipment.*

2. *Privacy and crime.*   Invasion of privacy and safeguards to programs of instruction and data have become major issues of national concern. The increasing centralization of files that contain information about individuals requires the legal protection of accuracy and confidentiality. Moreover, computer crime has been one of the fastest growing categories of crime; examples of such crimes include the $2 billion Equity Funding Corporation fraud of the early 1970s, bank embezzlements that average $500,000 per swindle, and the theft of computer data tapes for ransom.[2]

3. *Regulatory problems.*   Federal and state agencies have an increasing problem in regulatory issues relating to computer product pricing policies, protection of copyrights and patents, and quality of data transmission over telephone lines.

4. *Job displacement.*   The creation of new jobs by the computer has resulted in the displacement of old jobs, a result that is typical of all new technologies (automobiles, airplanes, electricity, and so on); inevitably this causes psychological trauma, social displacement, and economic deprivation for the affected segment of the population.

5. *Dependence.*   Our increasing dependence on the computer raises philosophical and practical issues regarding security—for example, backup systems are needed in airport traffic control should the main computer become disabled; and duplicate copies of critical data files should be maintained in case the original files are destroyed.

On balance, the positive aspects of the computer far outweigh its negative aspects. As with all new technologies, however, those in positions of responsibility must strive toward correcting existing problems and, more important, toward preventing potential problems.

1.3
ORGANIZATION OF A COMPUTER

Figure 1.1 should give you a "feel" for the makeup of a digital general-purpose computer. As you can see, six components are identified by the nature of their functions. But before describing each of these components, we define two terms that we use often.

An **instruction** represents a specific task for the computer to accomplish. For example, the following represents three instructions.

1. Read and store the name of a student and the grades received for the school term.
2. Calculate and store the grade point average.
3. Print the student's name and grade point average.

Data represent facts or observations that the computer is to input, manipulate, and/or output. In the above example, the student's name, grades, and grade point average all represent data.

---

[2] See, for example, Don Parker, *Crime by Computer,* New York: Scribner's, 1976.

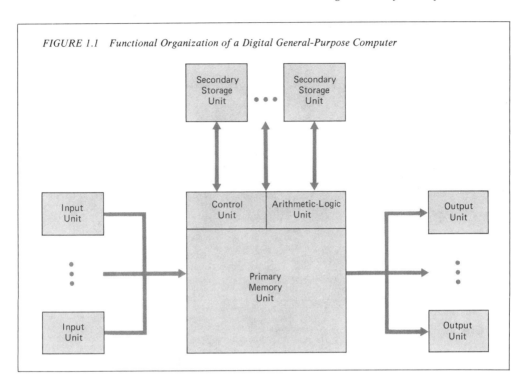

FIGURE 1.1 Functional Organization of a Digital General-Purpose Computer

As you read through the remainder of this section you might find it useful to look frequently at Figures 1.1 and 1.2. The first illustration relates components functionally, and the second shows specific components.

Input Units

The input function of the computer brings data and instructions from the "outside world" to the computer's memory. To accomplish this transfer process the data and instructions must be converted into a machine-readable input medium. The more commonly used **input media** are punched cards, magnetic tapes, magnetic disks, punched paper tape, optical characters, and magnetic ink characters.

These media require **data preparation devices** to convert data from source documents (bills, invoices) to the desired medium. For example, the *keypunch machine* (Figure 1.2B) is a data preparation device for converting data on source documents to punched cards; a *key-to-tape machine* transfers data from source documents to magnetic tapes.

Data, once in machine-readable form, are transferred to the computer through an **input unit.** This device "reads" the coded data on the input medium and converts them into electric impulses, which are transferred to the memory unit of the computer. For example, the holes in a punched card are sensed by a *punched card reader* (Figure 1.2E) and converted to appropriate electric signals, which are submitted to the computer's memory for storage. Table 1.2 lists some input units used with specific input media. By the way, MICR units are used by banks to process checks, and OCR units are widely used by universities for processing student records and grading exams.

FIGURE 1.2A   Functional Components of a Computer System (IBM 370) (Courtesy of IBM.)

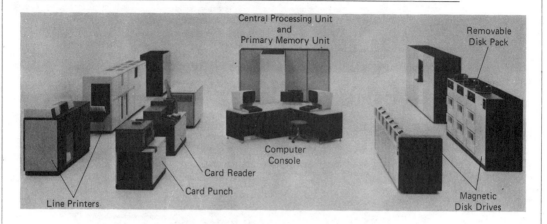

FIGURE 1.2B   IBM 059 Keypunch Machine. (Courtesy of IBM.)

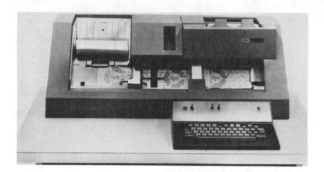

FIGURE 1.2C   NCR 798-401 Video (CRT) Terminal. (Courtesy of NCR.)

FIGURE 1.2D   Xerox 1760 Typewriter Terminal. (Courtesy of Xerox Corporation.)

FIGURE 1.2E   IBM 3505 Card
Reader Unitl (Courtesy of IBM.)

FIGURE 1.2F   IBM 3420 Magnetic
Tape Drive. (Courtesy of IBM.)

FIGURE 1.2G   IBM 3211·Line Printer. (Courtesy
of IBM.)

FIGURE 1.2H   An Integrated Circuit.
(Courtesy of IBM.)

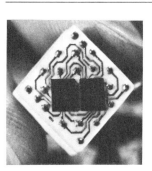

FIGURE 1.2I   Radio Shack TRS-80 Microcomputer System. (Courtesy of Radio Shack Division of Tandy Corporation.)

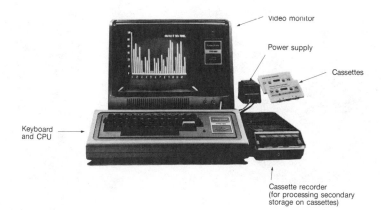

FIGURE 1.2J   HP 300 (left) and HP 3000 Series 33 Minicomputer Systems. (Courtesy of Hewlett-Packard Corporation.)

TABLE 1.2 *Input Units and Input Media*

MEDIUM	CORRESPONDING INPUT UNIT
Punched card	Punched card reader (Figure 1.2A,E)
Punched paper tape	Paper tape reader
Optical characters	Optical character reader (OCR)
Magnetic ink characters	Magnetic ink character reader (MICR)
Magnetic tape	Tape drive (Figure 1.2F)
Magnetic disk	Disk drive (Figure 1.2A)
Cassette	Cassette recorder (Figure 1.2I)
Keyboard	Online terminal (Figure 1.2C,D)

Data and instructions also may be entered into a computer through **online terminals** (Figure 1.2C,D). The terminals are connected directly to the computer (the meaning of online) by either cable or telephone lines. Terminals have a keyboard for entering data and instructions, and either a visual (video) display or teleprinter for viewing.

In general, a computer system will have more than one input unit. The mix of input units in any one computer system, however, will depend on factors such as cost, the amount of data to be processed, and the method by which data originate.

Primary Memory Unit

The **primary (internal) memory** unit of the computer stores instructions and data. Sometimes this unit is called *core storage,* because in earlier computers primary memory was made up of thousands of doughnut-shaped magnetic cores strung like beads on wire. More recent computer models use *semiconductor memory,* where the basic memory component is the microelectronic (silicon) chip, two of which are illustrated in Figure 1.2H. These units are cheaper, faster, and more compact than core memory. Incidentally, in the early 1960s engineers could place eight transistors on a chip; by 1982 they could manage nearly half a million transistors on a $\frac{1}{4}$-in. square chip. On microcomputers, primary memory is called *random-access memory* (**RAM**), to distinguish it from *read-only memory* (**ROM**), where data and instructions are "hard wired" at the factory.

Another recent type of primary memory is called *bubble memory.* This technology creates and manipulates tiny magnetic fields in a crystalline or semiconductor material. These fields appear as little black specks or bubbles under a microscope, hence the name "bubble" memory.

Regardless of the technology used to construct memory units, primary memory consists of storage locations that have numerical designations called addresses. Figure 1.3 represents a means of visualizing the storage locations of primary memory. Each storage location is assigned a number (**address**) that is used to reference the location whenever the item of data stored within that location (**contents**) is to be accessed. For example, in Figure 1.3 the character R is stored in location 1 and the character 8 is stored in location 2.

Figure 1.3 illustrates what is called a *byte-addressable* organization, a method of addressing storage that is common to many computers. It means that each address stores a single **character** (a letter, one of the digits 0 through 9, a comma, etc.), usually called a **byte.**

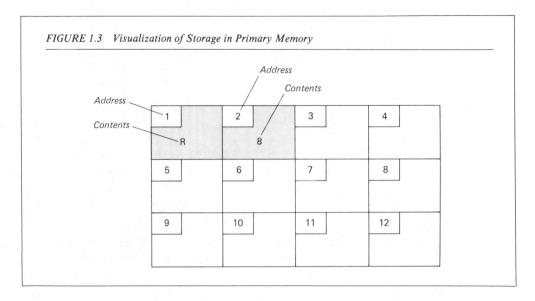

FIGURE 1.3   *Visualization of Storage in Primary Memory*

At the machine level, a byte is a packet or grouping of **binary digits.** A binary digit, or **bit** for short, takes on one of two possible values: 0 or 1 from a mathematical point of view; off or on from a mechanical perspective; and low voltage or high voltage from an electronic viewpoint.

A common coding scheme abbreviated as *EBCDIC* (for Extended Binary Coded Decimal Interchange Code) uses 8 bits to represent a byte or character. For example, in Figure 1.3 the letter R would be coded and stored as 11011001 and the digit 8 would be coded and stored as 11111000. A seven-bit code that is widely used in data communications is called American Standard Code for Information Interchange, or *ASCII*. A common procedure is the internal storage and processing of characters based on EBCDIC and their conversion to ASCII equivalents for transmission to online terminals. It's also common, as in the IBM Personal Computer, to enhance the ASCII code to eight bits, thereby expanding the character set with graphics, Greek, foreign language, and other characters. As a result, *the usual assumption is that a byte is eight bits.*

The storage capacity of computer memory usually is expressed as the number of characters (bytes) that can be stored. Because of the way memory units are constructed, storage capacity is often expressed as some multiple of 1024, where the number 1024 is represented by the letter K. For example, many home computers have quoted memory capacities of 64KB (or 64 Kilo Bytes), which means that each can store 65,536 (that is, 64 × 1024) bytes of data. Primary memory units usually range in storage capacity from 4KB for some pocket computers to 16 megabytes (or 16MB) for some mainframes, where a *megabyte* is one million bytes.

Central Processing Unit (CPU)

The arithmetic-logic unit and the control unit together make up what is called the **central processing unit** (CPU), or simply **processor.** (See Figures 1.1 and 1.2A.) The processor, together with primary memory, is what most professionals think of as *the* computer. Input and output units, secondary storage, and other components that attach to the CPU are called **peripherals.** These are not thought of as the "computer" since they are peripheral or external to the computer.

Data stored in primary storage are transferred to the **arithmetic-logic unit** whenever processing of data is required. Basic arithmetic operations such as addition, subtraction, multiplication, and division are performed within the arithmetic-logic unit. Moreover, logical operations such as comparison of values can be made. This capability permits the testing of various conditions, for example, whether an employee is entitled to receive overtime pay.

The **control unit** of a computer directs the operation of all other units associated with the computer, including peripheral devices (input/output units, external memory, and others). The control unit obtains instructions from primary memory, interprets these instructions, and then transmits directions to the appropriate computer components. For example, suppose the instruction "read and store student's name and grades" is obtained from memory and interpreted by the control unit; the input unit would be directed to read these data into memory. The next instruction might be "calculate and store the grade point average"; the control unit would direct the memory unit to provide the arithmetic-logic unit with the data; then the arithmetic-logic unit would be directed to perform the calculations and to transmit the result to primary memory.

Interestingly, current technology can place an entire CPU on a single microelectronic chip that is less than one quarter of an inch square. These so-called **microprocessors** are as effective as small second-generation computers in terms of calculating and storage capabilities. In effect, a microprocessor that you can balance on the tip of your finger is equivalent to an early-1960s computer with a CPU as large as an office desk.

Output Units

The function of an **output unit** is exactly opposite that of an input unit; that is, an output unit receives data from the computer in the form of electronic signals and converts these data into a form that can be used by either humans or computers. The list below summarizes output units; of these, most likely you will use line printers and online terminals.

Line Printers.   If output of data is meant for human "consumption," then the line printer may be used. The *impact line printer* illustrated in Figure 1.2G is capable of printing 2000 lines per minute, each line having up to 132 characters. Picture yourself standing in front of such a printer. At 65 lines per page, you would see approximately 31 pages of printed output whiz by you in the time span of one minute. More recent nonimpact printers produce printed pages at stunning speeds. For example, *laser printers* operate at about 20,000 lines per minute and *ink jet printers* sprint at approximately 45,000 lines per minute!

Online Terminals.   If you are using either a video or teleprinter terminal as an input unit, then most likely you are also using the terminal as an output unit. This is convenient, but compared with a line printer the speed of output is slow. Many computer systems, however, allow input through terminals and output on line printers, a feature that is advantageous if a particular job requires a high volume of printed output on paper.

Other Output Units.   Other output units include *magnetic tape drives,* which have both read (input) and write (output) capabilities using the magnetic tape medium (Figure 1.2F); *paper tape units,* some of which can be attached to remote, online terminals for the purpose of both input from and output to punched paper tape; *magnetic disk drives,* which allow both input from and output to magnetized disks that resemble a stack of LP phonograph records (Figure 1.2A); *card punch units,* which allow output onto punched cards (Figure 1.2A); and *voice response units,* which process verbal output. Voice response units have been used by telephone companies for many years. Most likely you have listened to the computer give you someone's new telephone number.

Secondary Storage Units

Secondary storage (**auxiliary** or **external storage**) is memory that is housed outside the central processing unit. Instructions and data not currently in use are kept on secondary storage media and read into primary storage when needed. Magnetic tapes, disks, drums, and data cells are commonly used media for secondary storage. Secondary storage units such as tape drives and disk drives (Figure 1.2A,F) are used to process specific media. Compared with primary storage, secondary storage has greater capacity (billions of bytes) at much less cost per byte, but the amount of time it takes to access data is greater.

1.4
COMMUNICATING WITH THE COMPUTER

If we wish to solve a problem using a computer, we must communicate our instructions to the computer through a language. A *language* can be defined as patterns that have meaning. To a computer, these patterns are electronic; to a human being, they are symbolic (letters, numbers, punctuation). Unfortunately, no computer can understand any of the some 4000 languages practiced on earth. It was necessary, therefore, to invent **computer languages** for the express purpose of person–machine communication. These are classified into the three categories shown in Figure 1.4. The designation **high-level** refers to a computer language that is far removed from the patterns "understood" directly by the computer. A **low-level** language, therefore, deals with patterns that are more nearly compatible with the electronic patterns of the machine.

Procedure- and Problem-Oriented Languages

Any language is distinguishable from any other language by its **syntax,** that is, by the rules for arranging a specified set of symbols into recognizable patterns. You will be communicating your instructions to the computer using the **WATFIV** version of a language called **FOR-TRAN.**[3] This is one of many so-called **procedure-oriented languages.** In general, these computer languages are easily understood by us humans (after some education, of course) and are relatively *machine-independent,* which means that they can be used across a wide variety of computers. FORTRAN is the most popular high-level language used for solving algebraic or scientific-type problems. By this we mean that FORTRAN is an excellent language for solving the types of problems that we described earlier as "mathematical modeling." Moreover, FORTRAN is used for "information processing" applications as well, although COBOL

---

[3] FORTRAN stands for FORmula TRANslation. It was originally developed by IBM in the 1950s. WATFIV was especially developed for the educational market by the Computer Systems Group at the University of Waterloo in Canada. The original version was called WATFOR, which stands for WATerloo FORtran. The present version has been cleverly given a numerical increment from four (FOR) to five (FIV); hence, WATFIV.

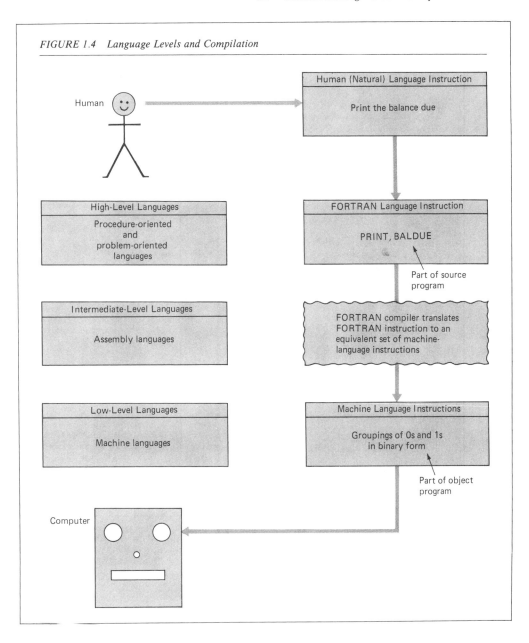

FIGURE 1.4   Language Levels and Compilation

(COmmon Business Oriented Language) is a more widely used language for such applications. BASIC (Beginner's All-purpose Symbolic Instruction Code) is another popular procedure-oriented language that is commonly implemented on microcomputers.

   Problem-oriented languages usually refer to a set of high-level languages that have been developed for solving certain special-purpose problems, such as the simulation of traffic flows in a city or the computer editing of newspaper articles.

TABLE 1.3 *FORTRAN (WATFIV) Program for Calculating and Printing the Balance ($) Due a University Based on a Student's Tuition and Fees*

FORTRAN (WATFIV) PROGRAM	HOW THE COMPUTER EXECUTES EACH INSTRUCTION (AND WHAT IT MEANS IN ENGLISH)
REAL CREDIT, TUIT, BALDUE	Inform the computer that the storage locations called CREDIT, TUIT, and BALDUE are to store "real" or decimal values.
CREDIT = 15.0	Store a value of 15.0 as the contents of a storage location addressed or identified as CREDIT. (The 15.0 represents the number of credits taken during the school term.)
TUIT = CREDIT *100.0	Multiply the contents of the storage location known as CREDIT by 100.0 and store this result in the location called TUIT. [In other words, the tuition is the number of credits (15) times the cost per credit ($100), or $1500.]
BALDUE = TUIT + 250.0	Take the contents of the address known as TUIT, add 250.0, and store this result in the address known as BALDUE. (The balance due the university is tuition plus $250 in fees, or $1750.)
PRINT, BALDUE	Print the contents of the address known as BALDUE. (The number 1750 is printed by either the line printer or the online terminal.)
STOP	Stop execution of the program.
END	This instruction defines the end of the program.

A **computer program** *is a complete set of instructions written in a computer language for solving a specific problem.* Table 1.3 illustrates and describes a FORTRAN or WATFIV program having exactly seven statements. **Statement** is another term for instruction. In the next chapter, we examine this program in detail (so don't be concerned about it yet).

Assembly and Machine Languages

Each type of computer has associated with it an assembly language and a machine language. An **assembly language** is specifically designed for a particular type of computer; hence it can accomplish more detailed tasks for that computer than could a high-level language. Such a language, however, requires more specialized training for persons who would use it. In other words, it is more difficult for us to learn an assembly language than to learn a high-level language. To illustrate, consider the following assembly language instruction for the IBM 370 computer:

S2,COST

In plain English this instructs the computer to subtract the contents of the location named COST from the value currently in register 2 and store the result back in register 2. A *register* is a memory location within the arithmetic-logic unit.

Another disadvantage of assembly languages is that they vary from one computer type to another. Thus, if we were restricted to programming only in assembly languages, we would need to learn a new assembly language for each computer type we might use—and worse yet, every computer program written for one computer would have to be rewritten for use on another computer.

After all this, you might be surprised to learn that computers do not directly "understand" either high-level or assembly languages! Computers understand only machine language. An instruction in **machine language** is written either in *binary* form as a series of 0s and 1s or in one of the "shortcut" notations for binary forms such as *hexadecimal* (base 16) or *octal* (base 8), as these schemes conform to the electronic circuitry in binary computers. For example, the hexadecimal instruction 5A20C01A says "Add the constant 14 to register 2 and store the result in register 2." Of course, this hexadecimal form would be stored in binary form within the computer itself. Needless to say, programming in machine language is tedious, which is one reason why high-level languages were developed.

The Compiler

How is it possible for the computer to understand the FORTRAN program that we write? Well, each computer manufacturer provides the means for that computer to translate our FORTRAN-language program into an equivalent program in machine language. This translation of a high-level language into its equivalent machine language is accomplished by a computer program called a **compiler.** In other words, the compiler acts as the language interpreter between you and the computer, much as a foreign language interpreter would translate from English into, say, Spanish.

The compiler resides as a separate program in primary memory. It first translates all instructions line by line. If a particular instruction violates syntax, then the compiler does not "understand" the instruction and prints an error message to that effect. When there are no syntax errors, the compilation process generates a separate program in machine language, called the **object program.** The instructions in the object program are then *executed,* or carried out, by the computer. In this case, the program written in the high-level language is called the **source program** (see Figure 1.4).

Each manufacturer of a general-purpose computer provides its own FORTRAN compiler. Most FORTRAN compilers conform to a standard form of FORTRAN developed by the American National Standards Institute (**ANSI**); however, some manufacturers may also provide certain extensions of *ANSI FORTRAN* that differ from the prescribed standard. In 1978 ANSI finalized its latest version of FORTRAN in a document labeled ANSI X3.9-1978. This version of the language, called **FORTRAN 77,** is a significant revision of the 1966 version. Although *WATFIV is the basis of the FORTRAN material in this textbook,* it has many similarities to FORTRAN 77. Module H at the end of the textbook summarizes key differences between these two versions of FORTRAN.

1.5
COMPUTER SYSTEMS

Your interactions with the computer involve much more than a simple communication between you and the CPU. In fact, you will be dealing with a comprehensive computer system.

Hardware and Software

The **computer system** is a collection of related hardware and software. As the name implies, **hardware** refers to the physical equipment: input/output (I/O) units, CPU, secondary storage, and other specialized machinery. The term **software** refers to computer programs, procedures, and specialized aids that contribute to the operation of a computer system. In general, software is classified as either systems software or applications software.

Systems software is a term for programs that are designed to facilitate the use of hardware. The **operating system** of a computer (supplied by the computer manufacturer) is the most important piece of systems software. This software, which is often called the "manager," "monitor," or "supervisor," consists of a number of specialized programs for operating the computer efficiently. Among others, the following important functions are performed by the operating system.

1. Scheduling the sequence of jobs within the computer[4]
2. Supplying the appropriate compiler
3. Allocating storage for programs and data
4. Controlling input and output operations
5. Performing "housekeeping" chores, such as accounting for the amount of CPU time used by each user

Applications software are programs written in either high-level or assembly languages to solve specific types of problems. These programs are often developed "in-house" (by the organization's systems analysts and programmers) to process applications such as payroll, inventories, billing, and accounts receivable.

Many computer manufacturers and independent software companies prepare generalized applications packages ("canned" software) for widely used applications. The cost of these packages ranges from a few hundred dollars to amounts in excess of $100,000. For example, the MRP (Materials Requirement Planning) package provided by IBM is designed to assist a manufacturing company in managing its labor force, machines, materials, and money; VisiCalc, by VisiCorp, is the original electronic spreadsheet program for microcomputers; it is one of the biggest selling software packages; Information Associates, Inc., has developed a package called "Students Records System" for generating class rosters, grade reports, and student transcripts; and SAS (Statistical Analysis System), SPSS (Statistical Package for the Social Sciences), and BMD (BioMeDical) are three statistical packages widely used by

---

[4] Each computer program to be run (executed) is called a "job."

researchers. The types of programs that you will be writing in your computer class are examples of applications programs.

Processing Environments

The specific configuration of hardware and software in a computer system is determined by the needs of that organization. For example, many small- to medium-sized organizations use minicomputers for all of their data processing needs. Microcomputers in particular are becoming commonplace in businesses and in homes. More recently, communications networks that link various types of computers and other office equipment are increasingly used. In this section we summarize the major processing environments.

Batch Processing.   This method of processing periodically accumulates jobs in groups or "batches." Typical jobs include weekly payrolls, monthly billings, and periodic financial reports. Jobs that require many computations or large amounts of input or output are best processed by batch methods. Those of you who will be punching programs on cards will be submitting jobs by the batch method. After you have punched your program onto cards, you submit your job to the computing center personnel in order to have your program compiled and executed. In this mode of operation, programs are grouped and executed at the computing center according to job priorities eatablished by computing center personnel. Alternatively, if *remote batch* is available, then *you* input your own job to a Remote Job Entry (RJE) unit (a combination input unit and line printer) and receive your output at the same location. In some batch environments, each program is run serially, that is, one program at a time. In more sophisticated systems, with *multiprogramming* capabilities, several programs may be executed "simultaneously" under the control of the operating system. In either case, it may take from a few minutes to several hours before the results of your program are available to you. When you pick up your job, errors may exist. These errors must be identified and corrected, and the job must be resubmitted. This cycle continues until you are satisfied with the results.

Time-Shared Processing.   In a time-sharing environment many users working at online terminals have "simultaneous" utilization of the computer system. In this mode of processing jobs, you send data and instructions to the computer via terminals, and the computer responds within seconds. This dialogue between you and the computer continues until you complete your task. Thus you code, execute, and correct programs at a terminal that is connected directly to the computer. While sitting at a terminal you may believe you have the computer to yourself. Actually, you and others who use terminals are sharing the computer's CPU in rotation under the control of the operating system (thus the term "time sharing").

Online Processing.   This type of *interactive processing* is achieved by linking either a terminal or keyboard to the processor and directly communicating with the CPU through the operating system. Common examples include online processing to a microcomputer using a keyboard and to a mainframe using a terminal. Time-shared processing, of course, is a form of online processing. Online processing is common in automated banking systems, in airline reservations and other inquiry systems, and in MIS and DSS environments to implement "What if . . .?" interactive analyses. Online processing on mainframes also includes *batch interface,* whereby we bypass the use of cards altogether by entering our program at a terminal into the batch "stream" and receiving our output on either a line printer or the online terminal. This method of batch processing is superior to the use of cards for two reasons: it's convenient to submit and receive jobs at the terminal and the system's editing and help (SOS) facilities are immediately available. In particular, we can alter programs and data by moving the cursor around the screen and by using the powerful commands of a text editor, which we demonstrate in Chapter 3. Many of you will use a batch interface system, as we do for all jobs in this textbook.

Distributed Processing.   Communications networks that link various computers and automated office equipment (such as word processors, copying machines, electronic mail and tele-conferencing equipment) at scattered locations are called distributed processing systems. A typical system at universities includes a centralized mainframe computer linked to satellite minicomputers and microcomputers at different locations on and off campus. Key advantages of this type of system include greater reliability (any one computer can "crash" and the others continue to operate); greater convenience, custom-tailoring of jobs and software, and more timely information at the local level where each computer is located; and systemwide access to specialized software packages and databases.

1.6
BEFORE YOU LEAP

Before you "leap" into your course in FORTRAN, we offer some objectives for you to think about, and some advice that we believe is sound.

Objectives

By now we should have convinced you that the computer is used increasingly as an indispensable tool for clerical purposes, to satisfy information needs, and to make decisions. Increasingly, people have jobs that require either direct or indirect contact with a computer. Moreover, the job market in computer-related fields looks quite promising for years to come.[5]

What does all of this mean to you? Well, we feel that if you don't accomplish the two objectives stated below, then you are shortchanging what will prove to be a very relevant part of your education.

Objective 1. Achieving a modest level of programming and problem-solving skills
Objective 2. Acquiring a basic knowledge of computer concepts, uses, and limitations

The first objective is intended to develop your ability to access, utilize, and exploit the computer for the purpose of more effectively analyzing problems and making decisions, both in subsequent academic courses and in your career. The second objective should serve to dispel the mystique and misconceptions surrounding computers—and to aid you in feeling "comfortable" and in operating effectively in a computerized environment.

Advice

Some of you have a great aptitude for the material that follows. We hope you will get "turned on" to do fine things in this field. Others of you are less inclined to absorb this type of material

[5] Estimates by the Bureau of Labor Statistics show over 50,000 new openings annually for programmers and systems analysts.

readily. If you feel that you are in the latter category, then you should take the following advice seriously.

1. Pay close attention to *written detail*. The computer is not very permissive. For example, if you spell REID instead of READ, the computer will not understand.
2. Pay close attention to *logical detail*. The computer is a machine. Therefore, you must tell it what to do in rather precise detail, which is broken down into logical steps.
3. Develop *good habits*. Work consistently (not constantly!). Try to rely on others as little as possible in order to sharpen your own inherent problem-solving skills. Try to solve the "Follow-up Exercises"—before looking up answers in the back of the book.
4. Take note of an interesting *paradox* in the act of programming. On the one hand, good programming requires the type of "scientific method" outlined in items 1–3 immediately above; on the other hand, "art" and creativity distinguish great programs from average programs. Look upon your programming as a written composition, and let your creative "juices" flow.
5. Be *patient*. Don't become frustrated by your mistakes. Don't get angry at the computer if it breaks down (after all, it also works hard). Finally, give yourself time. Our years of teaching this course show that many students take about six to eight weeks before the material crystallizes.

EXERCISES

1. Can you define the following terms?

computer	byte
analog computer	character
digital computer	binary digit
hybrid computer	bit
special-purpose computer	CPU
general-purpose computer	processor
word processor	peripherals
mainframe	arithmetic-logic unit
minicomputer	control unit
microcomputer	microprocessor
MIS	output unit
DSS	line printer
artificial intelligence	secondary storage
instruction	computer language
data	high-level language
input media	low-level language
data preparation devices	procedure-oriented language
input unit	problem-oriented language
online terminal	FORTRAN
primary or internal memory	WATFIV
RAM	computer program
ROM	statement
address	assembly language
contents	machine language

compiler	systems software
object program	applications software
source program	operating system
FORTRAN 77	batch processing
computer system	time-shared processing
hardware	online processing
software	distributed processing

2. Identify and briefly discuss the three outstanding characteristics of electronic computers.
3. Identify two broad areas of computer applications. Give a sample application in each area.
4. Cite some advantages and disadvantages of the widespread use of computers. (Don't necessarily restrict yourself to what we said.)
5. Sketch the organization of a digital general-purpose computer. Briefly describe the functions of each component.
6. Briefly describe the functions of the operating system.
7. Briefly describe the functions of the compiler.
8. Compare processing environments with respect to various features and criteria.
9. How are you doing?

Fundamentals of FORTRAN

This chapter shows you how to write a computer program and provides you with some fundamentals of the FORTRAN language. By the end of this chapter, you will be able to write a complete (although simple) FORTRAN program; by the end of the next chapter, you will be able to run such a computer program on either a batch or an online system.

2.1
STEPS IN WRITING COMPUTER PROGRAMS

As you might recall from Chapter 1, a **computer program** is a complete set of instructions written in a computer language; its purpose is to solve a problem that has been defined by the programmer. This problem is solved when the computer program is executed in a logical sequence by the computer.

Writing a computer program involves the following **four-step procedure.**

1. Problem statement and analysis
2. Design of algorithm (flowchart/pseudocode versions)
3. Specification of code (FORTRAN version)
4. Debugging process

Step 1: Problem Statement and Analysis

First, we need to state and analyze the problem. A common approach is to specify

a. The data we will provide the computer
b. The output we wish to receive as the solution to the problem
c. The computations and/or logical processes by which the computer converts the provided data to the output data

As an illustration, suppose that State College is in the process of converting its student billing system from a manual to a computerized system. The total student bill or balance due the college is made up of charges for tuition and fees. The tuition charge at the college varies depending on the number of credits for which a student is enrolled. The present charge is $100 per credit. Other fees include an activity fee, a union fee, and a health fee, for a total of $250.

In our problem statement we need to specify clearly three aspects of this problem.

a. *Provided data*
   Cost of tuition per credit ($100)
   Cost of fees ($250)
   Number of credits for which a student is enrolled (15 as a test case)
b. *Output data*
   Balance due State College
c. *Computations*
   Multiply the number of credits for which the student is enrolled (15) by the cost of tuition per credit ($100) to determine the tuition charge. Add the tuition charge to the fees ($250) to determine the balance due the college.

TABLE 2.1 *Flowcharting Symbols*

SYMBOL	NAME	MEANING
	Terminal	Indicates the start or end of the program.
	Input/output	Indicates when an input or output operation is to be performed.
	Process	Indicates calculations or data manipulation.
	Flowline	Represents the flow of logic.
	Decision	Represents a decision point or question that requires a choice of which logical path to follow.
	Connector	Connects parts of the flowchart.
	Preparation	Indicates a preparation step as in describing a DO-loop (Chapter 4).
	Predefined process	Indicates a predefined process or step where the details are not shown in this flowchart, as in calling a subprogram (Chapter 9).

Step 2: Design of Algorithm (Flowchart/ Pseudocode Versions)

An **algorithm** is the sequence of instructions that solves the problem. Its design includes the logical sequence by which data are provided, manipulated, and output. In effect it is an elaboration of the problem statement in the preceding step. The manner in which we specify the algorithm, however, is closer to the problem-solving logic of the computer than to the type of prose statement in our preceding step. Throughout this textbook we use flowcharts and pseudocode to specify the algorithm.

A **flowchart** is a drawing of the algorithm. It has two primary uses: to help us write the computer program by serving as a "blueprint" and to document the logic of the computer program for future review.

Flowcharts use specific symbols to represent different activities and a written message within each symbol to explain each activity. Table 2.1 shows the "traditional" flowcharting

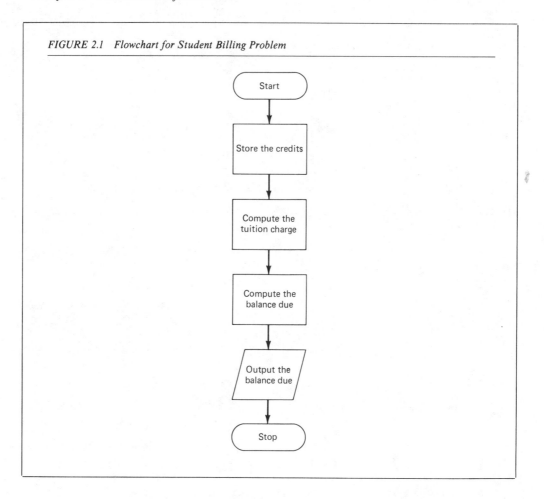

FIGURE 2.1   *Flowchart for Student Billing Problem*

symbols we use in this textbook, and Figure 2.1 illustrates the flowchart for the student billing problem.[1]

The flowchart in Figure 2.1 breaks the problem down into several steps.

1. Store the number of credits in a memory location.
2. Calculate tuition.
3. Calculate balance due the college.
4. Print the output.
5. Stop processing.

Note that this flowchart uses only the first four symbols in Table 2.1. The other symbols are introduced in later chapters, as your programming becomes more sophisticated.

---

[1] Module A at the end of the text presents a more recent alternative (and more sophisticated) method of flow-charting. Try it, but not until after Chapter 4 or 5!

In general, a flowchart must indicate a "Start" and must have at least one "Stop." The flow generally runs from top to bottom and from left to right. As an option, you can use arrowheads to indicate the direction of flow, which is our preference.

A flowchart is one way of diagramming the logic of a program. Many professional programmers and systems analysts use them regularly; others do not. One reason for not using flowcharts is the difficulty in revising the flowchart once a program has been modified.

In the past few years, a program design tool called either **pseudocode** or **program design language** has been gaining acceptance among professional programmers. Pseudocode expresses the logic required in the solution of a program using English-like phrases. A key reason for the growing acceptance of pseudocode is its compatibility with the thinking processes of the programmer. Unfortunately, pseudocode has not been standardized; as a result there are many variations. The example that follows, however, should give you some idea of its syntax and structure.

Before writing the student billing program we can map out its structure by using a "false" (pseudo) code, as follows:

```
Number of credits = 15
Tuition = number of credits × $100
Balance due = tuition + $250
PRINT balance due
Stop
```

In general, a program written in pseudocode is similar to a program written in a higher-level language such as FORTRAN. The major difference is the emphasis placed on content versus syntax. Pseudocode primarily concentrates on mapping out the algorithmic logic of a program, with little regard for the syntax of the actual programming language to be used. Thus we are free to concentrate on the design of the program by expressing its logic using ordinary English, including abbreviations, symbols, and formulas. The word PRINT appears in capital letters in the above pseudocode because this word—called a keyword—is used in the FORTRAN program in the next step.

Either flowcharts or pseudocode can be used to design and document programs. The simplicity and compactness of pseudocode, however, may tip the balance in its favor, particularly for documenting programs that are likely to undergo frequent modification.

We prefer pseudocode to flowcharts in designing and documenting programs, but believe that flowcharts are useful as a pedagogical tool for teaching a programming language. Thus, in this textbook we use both flowcharts and pseudocode.

Although the above flowchart and pseudocode are rather simple, and you may be tempted not to use them for such a simple problem, *we strongly suggest that you get in the habit of using either pseudocode or flowcharts now.* As programs become more complex, you will find these design tools increasingly helpful.

Step 3: Specification of Code (FORTRAN Version)

Coding is the translation of our problem-solving logic from the flowchart or pseudocode into a computer program. In other words, we use the flowchart or pseudocode as a guide for writing instructions to the computer.

The computer language that our instructions are to be written in must be decided by this step in the procedure. (Quite often the same flowchart or pseudocode can be used with any computer language.) Some languages are more suitable than others, depending on the application.

In this textbook we use a version of FORTRAN called WATFIV. The "relative" ease of learning FORTRAN and its excellent mathematical capabilities are two reasons for the widespread use of this language.

FORTRAN code for the student billing program is shown below. Note the correspondence between the program and its flowchart/pseudocode predecessors.

FORTRAN (WATFIV)	Comments
REAL CREDIT,TUIT,BALDUE	Declare three real (as opposed to integer) variables.
CREDIT = 15.0	Assign 15.0 to a memory location named CREDIT.
TUIT = CREDIT*100.0	Compute the tuition. (The * represents multiplication.)
BALDUE = TUIT + 250.0	Compute the balance due by adding fees to tuition.
PRINT, BALDUE	Print the balance due.
STOP	Instructs computer to stop the execution of the program.
END	Last FORTRAN instruction in the program.

For simple programs, this correspondence is *almost* one for one; that is, each symbol in the flowchart (except for "Start") or line in the pseudocode will have a corresponding instruction in the program. As problems grow in length and complexity, however, the number of symbols in the flowchart or lines in the pseudocode will be less than the number of instructions in the program, for two reasons.

1. Symbols in the flowchart or lines in the pseudocode can be used to summarize related groups of instructions in a program. For example, "Compute the tuition charge" and "Compute the balance due" in Figure 2.1 can be combined into a single rectangle that reads "Compute the tuition charge and the balance due."
2. Not all instructions need be represented in flowchart/pseudocode versions. We need only represent what we call executable instructions. We take up this topic later in the chapter.

At this point you need not worry about the exact meaning of each instruction in the program, for we will discuss them further throughout the chapter. However, the program should make some sense to you.

Typically, we first write our code on either a regular sheet of paper or on special paper called FORTRAN *coding form*. After we are reasonably sure the program is correct, we place the code on the appropriate input medium for our system. As a beginning programmer you will most likely use either a keypunch for punched cards or a computer terminal. Details on these procedures are presented in Chapter 3.

Step 4: Debugging Process

The next step is to run or execute the program on the computer. By **run** or **execute** we mean that the instructions that make up the program code are processed (carried out) by the computer. Our purpose in this case is to detect and correct errors.

You will often write programs that fail to run or will run improperly. (It happens to all of us.) **Debugging** is the process of locating and correcting errors, or "getting out the bugs." Types of bugs and methods of correcting them are illustrated in the next chapter.

2.2
ELEMENTS OF FORTRAN

Nine elements describe the structure of the FORTRAN language. These are briefly described here for the purpose of perspective and are elaborated upon in the remainder of this chapter and other chapters.

1. Character Set

Forty-nine characters can be used in FORTRAN: 26 alphabetic characters (the letters of the alphabet), 10 numeric characters (the digits 0 through 9), and 13 special characters (plus sign, minus sign, asterisk, slash, equal sign, left parenthesis, right parenthesis, comma, decimal point, apostrophe, dollar sign, colon, and blank space). These characters represent the most fundamental element of the language, since they are used to construct the other eight elements.

2. Data Types

FORTRAN allows the representation of six types of data. We will regularly use the following three types.

   a. *Integer type.* Used to represent exactly an integer (integral or whole-number) value, such as 80 and −705; these can be positive, negative, or zero.
   b. *Real type.* Used to represent approximately a real (decimal) value, such as 250.0, 6.14, and −0.157; these can be positive, negative, or zero.
   c. *Character type.* Used to represent a *string* (sequence) of characters, such as CLARK S. KENT; the *length* of a character datum is the number of characters in the string (13 in the above example), including the two blank characters surrounding the middle initial. Character data can include any of the 49 characters in the character set.

FORTRAN also includes three other data types: *double precision* to increase the number of digits stored in a real value; *logical* to represent the logical values "true" and "false"; and *complex* to represent complex (imaginary) numbers.

3. Constants and Variables

Constants and variables are used to reference arithmetic (integer, real, double precision, and complex), logical, and character data within programs. For example, the real constants 15.0, 100.0, and 250.0, and the real variable names CREDIT, TUIT, and BALDUE are used in the student billing program on page 30. These we discuss fully in the next section.

4. Keywords

Certain words, called **keywords,** are used either to describe an operation that is to be performed by the computer or to communicate certain information to the computer. PRINT and END are keywords in the student billing program. We introduce other keywords throughout the remainder of the book.

5. *Function Names*

Certain operations can be performed by using what are called function names. For example, we can use SQRT to take square roots and ALOG10 to find base 10 logarithms. These and other functions are discussed in Section 2.6.

6. *Expressions*

Expressions are combinations of variable names, constants, function names, and special characters. They are used to express arithmetic calculations, character data, and logical comparisons. For example, CREDIT*100.0 is an arithmetic expression in the program on page 30. We introduce arithmetic and character expressions in Section 2.5 and relational/logical expressions in Chapter 5.

7. *Statements*

A **statement** is an instruction that either directs the computer to perform a specific task or declares certain information that the computer needs. FORTRAN statements are combinations of characters, variables, constants, keywords, function names, and expressions. Thus they utilize the first six elements of FORTRAN. The program on page 30 contains seven statements. We introduce the various types of FORTRAN statements in Section 2.4 and discuss them in detail throughout the book.

8. *Statement Numbers (Labels)*

Individual statements may be labeled by preceding the statement with a statement number. We discuss statement numbers when first used in Chapter 4.

9. *Lines*

A **line** is a sequence of 72 characters, including blanks. Programs contain three types of lines: initial lines, continuation lines, and comment lines. *Initial lines* are those that initiate a statement. If a particular statement is too long to fit within the initial line, it can be continued on one or more *continuation lines. Comment lines* are used to document programs. The program on page 30 contains seven initial lines and no continuation or comment lines. Continuation and comment lines are illustrated later in the book.

2.3
FORTRAN VARIABLES AND CONSTANTS

Programmers use **symbolic names** to reference either certain procedures (in Chapter 9 and Module F) or to specify memory locations. For example, BALDUE in the student billing program is a symbolic name that clearly indicates that the balance due the college is stored in this location.

In FORTRAN a symbolic name that represents a single storage location is called a **variable name,** or simply a **variable.** A variable name therefore identifies a location in memory where a particular item of data is stored (found). The student billing program used three variables: TUIT, which represents "tuition charge"; CREDIT, which represents "number of credits for which the student is enrolled"; and BALDUE, which represents "balance due the college." In choosing a variable name, you can use a combination of letters and/or numbers;

however, it is best to choose meaningful names to help you remember what values you are storing in the memory locations.

FORTRAN has three rules for forming a variable name.

1. A variable name must have six characters or fewer.
2. The first character of a variable name must be a letter (WATFIV also allows the dollar sign symbol, $).
3. The remaining characters can be letters, digits, or a combination of both. No special characters such as plus (+), slash (/), asterisk (∗), or comma (,) are permitted, except for the $ sign. Blanks are ignored by the compiler. For example, TAXDUE and TAX DUE are interpreted as the same memory location.

In the remainder of this section we focus on variables and constants that represent integer, real, and character data types. Later in this chapter we introduce variables and constants for double-precision and logical data types. Throughout we omit and make no further mention of complex data types.

EXAMPLE 2.1

The following list illustrates both acceptable and unacceptable variable names in FORTRAN.

Variable Name	Comment
VELOCITY	Unacceptable. Too many characters.
VEL	Acceptable.
1EXAM	Unacceptable. Does not begin with a letter.
EXAM1	Acceptable.
X + Y	Unacceptable. Special character not allowed.
$AMT	Acceptable.
AMT$	Acceptable.
XPY	Acceptable.
MALESEX.	Unacceptable. Too many characters and use of period.
M SEX	Acceptable, but not recommended.
MSEX	Acceptable.

Follow-up Exercise

1. Tell whether each of the following variable names is acceptable or unacceptable. If a name is unacceptable, indicate why.

   a. X
   b. IX
   c. 3Y
   d. Y3
   e. AGE/35
   f. AGE35
   g. $RATE
   h. ACCELERATION
   i. ACCEL
   j. SET-UPCOST
   k. SU COST
   l. SUCOST

Integer, Real, and Character Variables

Two common types of numeric values that can be stored in memory locations are integer values and real values. *Integer values* are whole numbers with no decimal point, such as 25, 175, −42, or 24; *real values* are numbers with a decimal point, such as 25.3, −7.26, 1234567., or 24.0.

The distinction between real and integer data types is necessary because the computer stores integer values differently from real values. Moreover, this distinction allows certain advantages and efficiencies, which we discuss later.

Because both integer and real values can be stored in a memory location, the computer needs to know which type of value (integer or real) a particular location is going to hold. We indicate which type of value the memory location holds in one of two ways, implicit typing and explicit typing.

Implicit typing determines the data type (integer or real) of a variable by the first letter of the variable name. To tell the computer we wish to store an integer value, we select a variable name beginning with a letter I through N; the variable is referred to as an **integer variable.** For example, INDEX, MONEY, and NUMBER are storage locations in which integers are stored.

If we begin a variable name with the letters A through H, O through Z, or $, we are telling the computer to store real values, and the variable is called a **real variable.** RATE, PAY, and BALDUE are all examples of real variables.

Explicit typing uses certain statements to declare the data type of a variable. We discuss these statements in Section 2.4.

Character variables store character data. These variables are primarily used to store names, addresses, text, and other nonnumeric data. The typing or identification of a character variable is best accomplished by explicit typing, as discussed in the next section.

Integer, Real, and Character Constants

Not all data in a computer program need to be stored in memory locations that are referenced by names. In some situations it is best to use a *constant* (unchanging) value, such as the constant π in the computation πr^2. In this case, we can write the number 3.141593 directly into a FORTRAN program.

In the student billing program the instruction

```
BALDUE = TUIT + 250.0
```

consists of two real variables, BALDUE and TUIT, and the constant 250.0. The values stored in the variable may change whenever the computer executes an instruction, but the value 250.0 is not subject to change. A **constant,** therefore, represents a fixed, unvarying value that does not change during the execution of a program.

As with variables, FORTRAN makes a distinction between integer and real constants. An **integer constant** represents a whole-number value and does not include a decimal point. For example, in the instruction

```
KOUNT = KOUNT + 1
```

the "1" is an integer constant. An integer constant is written as a sign (− or optional +), followed by a string of digits. Thus,

15   −100   6000   123046

are all examples of integer constants.

A **real constant** represents a real value and is generally written as a sign (− or optional +), an integer part, a decimal point, and an optional fractional part, in that order. For example,

250.1   −1.645   0.7074   650.01

are all real constants.

Very small or very large real constants can be represented by using scientific or **E-notation,** as follows:

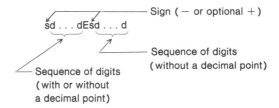

Table 2.2 shows several examples of E-notation used in the FORTRAN language and equivalent conventional scientific notation. Thus, E represents "times 10 to the power given by the digits following." In other words, E6 in the constant −0.845E6 says to multiply −0.845 by 10 raised to the power 6, or multiply −0.845 by 10^6, giving −0.845 × 1,000,000 or −845,000. In "plain English," E6 simply denotes move the decimal point 6 places to the right and E−8 says move the decimal point 8 places to the left.

TABLE 2.2   E-Notation Examples

E-NOTATION	SCIENTIFIC NOTATION	STANDARD NOTATION	COMMENT
7.2E+12 7.2E12 +7.2E12	7.2×10^{12}	7,200,000,000,000.	Move decimal point 12 places to the right (multiply by 10^{12}).
−0.845E06 −0.845E6 −0.845E+06 −0.845E+6	-0.845×10^6	−845,000.	Move decimal point 6 places to the right (multiply by 10^6).
5E−8 5.E−8	5×10^{-8}	0.00000005	Move decimal point 8 places to the left (divide by 10^8).
0.5E−7	0.5×10^{-7}	0.00000005	This constant is identical to the preceding.

Most likely you will first see E-notation when reading computer output, since some systems print real values using this convention. Thus, an understanding of E-notation facilitates the reading of computer output.

You should be aware of the following issues when using numeric constants.

1. Commas and other special characters are not permissible within a numeric constant. For example, both the constants 6,000 and $54.50 would provoke errors from a FORTRAN compiler.

2. All computers have a limit to the number of digits used to represent a value. This is referred to as the **precision** of the computer. A real number typically can have no more than seven significant digits, although this limit varies from system to system. For example, when the precision is seven digits, the real constant 500.6182 is retained as is; the value 50027.629 is retained as 50027.62 or 50027.63; and the value 98765432.1 is retained as 98765430.

3. The maximum and minimum values (magnitudes) allowed for a number differ from system to system. Integer values on the IBM 370 range from $-2,147,483,648$ to $2,147,483,647$ (-2^{31} to $2^{31} - 1$) while on the CDC CYBER series they range from $-(2^{59} - 1)$ to $2^{59} - 1$. Thus the integer constant 12345678 is within the range of acceptable integer values on both these machines; however, the integer constant 123456789012 is beyond the range (cannot be retained) on the IBM machine but is acceptable on the CDC machine. Real values on the IBM 370 range from 10^{-78} to 10^{75} and on the CDC CYBER from 10^{-293} to 10^{322}. Thus a value such as 2.5E82 is too large on the IBM machine but acceptable on the CDC machine. *Ask your instructor about the limits on your system.*

A **character constant** is a string of characters enclosed in apostrophes. Thus,

'CLARK S. KENT'
'BALANCE DUE IS $'
'JULY 4, 1776'

are all legitimate character constants. Note that character constants can include letters, digits, and special characters such as blanks, commas, and dollar signs.

The maximum length for a character constant varies from system to system. For example, if you are using IBM-compatible machines, the limit is 255 characters; on a Honeywell Series 60 or 6000 machine, the limit is 511 characters.

We use character constants to store data within character variables (Section 2.5), to print labels, report headings, messages, and other text (Section 2.6), and to effect logical comparisons (Chapter 5).

Follow-up Exercises

2. Identify each of the following as integer constant, real constant, or unacceptable constant.

a. 5,000	d. −0.05	g. 7.351E03
b. 5000	e. +0.05	h. 7,351
c. 5000.0	f. 0.050	i. 7351

3. Identify each of the following as an integer variable, real variable, or unacceptable variable.

   a. YEAR   e. AGE
   b. NYEAR   f. JAGE
   c. K   g. 72P
   d. XK   h. $72

4. Express the following constants using E-notation.

   a. -6.142×10^{15}
   b. -6142×10^{12}
   c. 0.0000000007
   d. 7×10^{-10}
   e. 0.167×10^{125}

5. Express the following constants using standard notation.

   a. 123E4
   b. 0.123E7
   c. 456E−8
   d. 0.456E−5

6. Identify what is wrong, if anything, with each of the following character constants.

   a. 'DELTA WING
   b. "ENCOUNTERS OF THE 3RD KIND"
   c. 'YOU'RE OK, I'M OK'

2.4
FORTRAN STATEMENTS

The statments in a FORTRAN program can be classified as those that are executable and those that are not executable.

Executable versus Nonexecutable Statements

An **executable statement** is one that causes activity within the CPU *during execution of the program.* Table 2.3 indicates five types of executable statements and the activities they represent.

We discuss termination statements in this section, the assignment statement in the next section, simple versions of input and output statements later in this chapter, and transfer of control in Chapter 4.

TABLE 2.3 Types of Executable Statements

TYPE	ACTIVITY
1. Assignment	Computes and/or stores data
2. Output	Causes output unit to print stored data
3. Input	Causes input unit to accept data for storage
4. Termination	Causes control unit to stop execution
5. Transfer of control	Alters sequence of execution in the program

A **nonexecutable statement** is used to provide or declare certain information to the computer during compilation of the program. *Nonexecutable statements are ignored during execution of the program.* We introduce six types of nonexecutable statements in this section and others throughout the book.

END and STOP Statements

Look at the student billing program on page 30. The statement

```
STOP
```

is an *executable* statement that terminates the execution of a program. Typically, you will place this statement just before the END statement, although one or more STOP statements can be placed anywhere in the program.

This statement

```
END
```

is a *nonexecutable* statement that identifies the last physical line in a FORTRAN program. It simply tells the compiler this is the last instruction of the program.[2] Once this instruction is compiled, execution of the program begins, provided that rules of the FORTRAN language have not been violated. Don't forget to include the END statement in every program you write.

INTEGER, REAL, DOUBLE PRECISION, LOGICAL, and CHARACTER Statements

In Section 2.3 we illustrated how integer and real variables can be typed implicitly, and altogether glossed over the typing of character variables. A **type statement** is used to *explicitly* type names, which supersedes any implicit typing. In this section we discuss the three type statements that correspond to integer, real, and character names; present a fourth type statement that approximately doubles the precision of real values; and introduce a fifth type statement that declares logical names.

The statement

```
INTEGER list of names
```

explicitly informs the compiler that the names in the list are to be typed as integers. For example,

```
INTEGER YEAR,AGE
```

causes the compiler to treat YEAR and AGE as integer variables. This means that YEAR and AGE will store integer numbers and will be treated as integer variables. The fact that they begin with letters other than I through N is ignored in determining data type.

---

[2] More precisely, the END statement defines the end of a "program unit." We discuss this in Chapter 9.

The INTEGER statement improves the description of names. For example, if AGE is to store whole numbers only and is to be used only in integer arithmetic, then it should be treated as an integer variable. The name AGE is more descriptive than, say, JAGE, so we select AGE and use the INTEGER statement to ensure integer type.

As a matter of good programming style, we recommend that you use the INTEGER statement to type all integer names explicitly.[3]

The statement

> **REAL** *list of names*

explicitly informs the compiler that the names in the list are to be typed as real. For example,

    REAL INC,LOAD,NARC

causes the compiler to treat the variables INC, LOAD, and NARC as if they were real variables. In other words, the fact that they begin with letters in the range I through N is not used by the compiler to determine type. Thus, these variables will store real numbers and will be treated by the computer as real variables.

Use the REAL statement to type all real symbolic names in a program, as this improves the selection of names and clearly indicates which names in the program are typed real.

The statement

> **DOUBLE PRECISION** *list of names*

explicitly declares to the compiler that the names in the list are to be typed as double precision. For example,

    DOUBLE PRECISION INC,LOAD,NARC

specifies that the variables INC, LOAD, and NARC are to store real values having approximately double the number of digits as the usual (single) precision of the computer. To illustrate, if LOAD is typed real, then it stores real values with, say, 7 digits; however, if LOAD is typed double precision, then it usually stores slightly more than double the number of digits in real values, say, 15 or 16 digits. Double-precision variables are useful in circumventing certain roundoff error problems, which we discuss at different points later in the book.

The statement

> **LOGICAL** *list of names*

explicitly declares that names in the list are to be typed as logical. For example,

    LOGICAL SWITCH,FINIS

---

[3] Later in the book we make minor exceptions to explicit typing of integer variables when using the variables I, J, K, L, M, and N. We might also note that the list of names in type statements can include not only variable names but also other symbolic names: array names and array declarators (Chapters 7, 8), and function names (Chapter 9).

identifies SWITCH and FINIS as **logical variables,** that is, variables that store either the logical value *true* or the logical value *false*. Incidentally, the forms .TRUE. and .FALSE. represent **logical constants.** We illustrate the use of logical values in Chapters 5 and 6.

The statement

> **CHARACTER** *name∗length,name∗length, . . .*

or

> **CHARACTER**∗*length,name,name, . . .*

explicitly declares character names and their respective lengths. By length we mean the number of characters in the string that can be stored within the storage location identified by the character variable. For example,

```
                                                    ┌──── Assumed length of 1
CHARACTER NAME∗18,ITEM∗10,ANSWER∗70,CODE
```

instructs the compiler that character strings of lengths of 18 characters, 10 characters, and 70 characters are to be stored in the respective character variables NAME, ITEM, and ANSWER. Alternatively, this statement could be written as

```
CHARACTER∗18 NAME
CHARACTER∗10 ITEM
CHARACTER∗70 ANSWER
CHARACTER    CODE
```

We also could write

```
CHARACTER∗20 CAR1,CAR2,CAR3
```

should we wish to declare the *same* length for each of a series of variable names.

The 13-character string CLARK S. KENT would appear within the 18-character storage location NAME as follows:

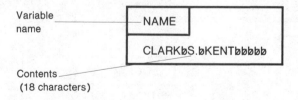

Variable name — NAME

CLARKƀS.ƀKENTƀƀƀƀƀ

Contents (18 characters)

We use the symbol ƀ to represent the blank space character (space bar on the keyboard of a keypunch or terminal). Note that the computer pads in five blanks at the end of the data item, since the specified length is 18 and the data item only contains 13 characters. Just how we get the computer to store this string in the character variable is a topic in the next section. *If the length specification is omitted, then a length of 1 is assumed,* as illustrated by the variable CODE in the example.

All type statements are *nonexecutable,* and must appear in the program before all executable statements and DATA statements (Section 2.8).

In designing your programs you will have to decide both the type of each variable and its name. *Decide type on the basis of the data needs of the problem.* For example, if the number of credits in the student billing problem is to include half credits, then the variable that represents credits should be real, and its name should suggest what it represents. Thus we selected the name CREDIT and explicitly typed it as real.

From this point on, *each program in the book will use type statements for all key names in the program.* Although it is not necessary to type explicitly, this practice minimizes confusion with respect to type, thereby improving programming style.

2.5 ASSIGNMENT STATEMENTS

An **assignment statement** is used (1) to perform and store calculations, (2) to assign a constant to a storage location, or (3) to copy the contents of one storage location to another. In the student billing program, we computed the balance due using the following assignment statement.

```
BALDUE = TUIT + 250.0
```

This statement adds the value stored in TUIT to the constant 250.0 and stores the result in the storage location named BALDUE.

Structure

In more general terms, the assignment statement in FORTRAN is structured as follows:

```
name = expression
```

On the left-hand side of the equal sign, a single variable name identifies a storage location in internal computer memory.[4] The right-hand side of the equal sign is a character expression, an arithmetic expression, or a logical expression (Chapter 5).

Character Expression. A **character expression** can include either a character constant or a character variable. For example, if we define the character variables R and S by

```
CHARACTER R*20,S*20
```

then execution of

```
R = 'IbLOVEbFORTRAN'
```

would store the following in memory.

---

[4] The only other names permitted to the left of the equal sign are array element names (Chapters 7, 8) and function names (Chapter 9).

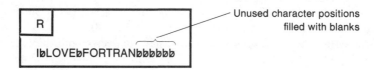

where again the symbol Ƅ is our way of representing the blank space character. In this case the character expression is a character constant of length 14, including the two blanks surrounding LOVE but excluding the apostrophes.

The assignment statement thus tells the computer to "replace the contents of R by the expression to the right of the equal sign."

Note that the length of 14 for the constant is six characters less than the specified length of 20 for R in the CHARACTER statement. As a result, the computer left-justified the character value in storage by filling in the rightmost unused character positions with six blanks. *In general, if the number of characters we attempt to store in the character variable is less than the length specified in the CHARACTER statement, then the computer fills in the remaining (rightmost) character storage positions with blanks. Alternatively, if we attempt to store more characters than the length we have specified in storage, then the computer fills up storage by truncating the righmost characters.* For example, if we had only specified a length of 6 for R in the CHARACTER statement, then IƄLOVE would have been stored in R.

If the computer next executes

    S = R

then memory for these two character variables would appear as follows:

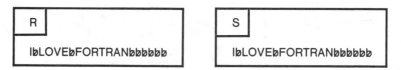

In this case the character expression to the right of the equal sign is the character variable R. Note that the assignment statement simply copies the contents of R into S, *leaving the contents of R unaffected.*

If the computer next executes

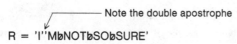

    R = 'I''MƄNOTƄSOƄSURE'

then memory would appear as follows:

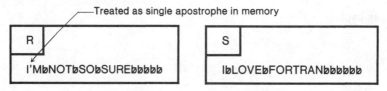

Note that the apostrophe in the contraction I'M requires a double apostrophe in the character expression in order for the compiler to distinguish between embedded apostrophes and the apostrophe that ends the constant.

TABLE 2.4   *Arithmetic Operators*

OPERATOR	ARITHMETIC OPERATION
+	Addition
−	Subtraction
/	Division
*	Multiplication
**	Exponentiation (raise to a power)

You should clearly realize that *the equal sign in an assignment statement dictates that the storage content of the variable to the left of the equal sign is to be replaced by the value of the expression to the right of the equal sign.*

Follow-up Exercise

7. Write down the necessary statements to store the string CLARK S. KENT within the 20-character memory location called NAME. Draw the memory box and clearly indicate its contents. How would the memory box look if only 15 characters were reserved in NAME? Only 10 characters?

Arithmetic Expressions.   A simple **arithmetic expression** is used to express a numeric computation and can consist of a single numeric constant, a single numeric variable, or a combination of numeric constants and numeric variables separated by parentheses and arithmetic operators.[5] An **arithmetic operator** indicates the type of computation that is desired. Five arithmetic operators are used in the FORTRAN language to indicate the type of arithmetic operation, as described in Table 2.4.

Table 2.5 illustrates three sample uses of assignment statements. In the first illustration the real constant 5000.0 is placed in the storage location identified by VOL. In the second

---

TABLE 2.5   *Sample Arithmetic Assignment Statements*

variable name = arithmetic expression

TYPE	ILLUSTRATION
Variable = constant	VOL = 5000.0
Variable = variable	COST = MONEY
Variable = combination of constants and variables	PROF = 7.0*VOL − COST

---

[5]More generally, arithmetic expressions also can include numeric array elements (Chapters 7, 8), and numeric functions (Section 2.6 and Chapter 9).

case, the contents of the storage location called MONEY are copied by the storage location called COST. Note, however, that this transfer is electronic; that is, whatever is in MONEY remains there, but whatever was in COST gets replaced by whatever is in MONEY. Finally, the third illustration places the computational result of 7.0∗VOL − COST in the storage location called PROF. This means that the contents of COST will be subtracted from seven times the contents of VOL and the result will be stored in PROF. Note that an asterisk (∗) *must* be used for multiplication; implied multiplication such as 7VOL would give a syntax error since the compiler takes this to be an illegal variable name.

Again you should carefully note the meaning of the equal sign (=) in FORTRAN. It means "place the value indicated by the expression on the right in the storage location indicated by the name on the left." Because of this meaning, an assignment such as

KOUNT = KOUNT + 1

makes sense in FORTRAN but not in algebra. Note that each time this statement is executed by the computer, the content (value) of KOUNT gets increased by 1. In other words, this statement instructs the computer to "add 1 to the contents of KOUNT and place this result in KOUNT." This type of statement is used quite often in FORTRAN programs for the purpose of "counting," as you will see in the chapters that follow.

Try to avoid the following two language violations. *Two arithmetic operators must never appear adjacent to one another,* as this would cause a syntax error.[6] Thus, the expression

B∗ − 6

is not permitted. Instead we could write − 6∗B.

Avoid raising a *negative value to a nonintegral power,* as this would cause an error during execution. For example, finding the square root of −25 from

(−25)∗∗0.5

is incorrect. Negative values may be raised only to whole-number powers (see Exercise 8).

EXAMPLE 2.2   Assignment Statements in Student Billing Program

In the student billing program, three assignment statement were used:

```
CREDIT = 15.0
TUIT   = CREDIT*100.0
BALDUE = TUIT + 250.0
```

In the first assignment statement the expression is a single constant; hence the value 15.0 is simply stored in the memory location named CREDIT, as indicated below.

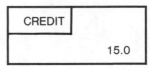

---

[6]Note that the double asterisk (∗∗) is treated as a single operator for exponentiation.

The second statement instructs the computer to multiply the constant 100 by the contents of the memory location named CREDIT, and to store the result in the memory location TUIT. After this calculation, the memory locations appear as follows:

The third instruction tells the computer to add the constant 250.0 to the contents of the memory location TUIT, and to store the result in the memory location BALDUE. After this calculation, the memory locations appear as follows:

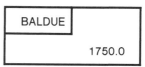

Follow-up Exercises

8. Identify what is wrong (if anything) with each of the following assignment statements.
   a. B + C = A
   b. D = 4.0* − X
   c. 5. = AGE
   d. X = Y = Z = 5.3
   e. K = J**3.2 where J stores a negative value
   f. K = J**3 where J stores a negative value
9. Consider the following sequence of instructions
   A = 37.0/C
   B = A + 1.6
   D = B**2
   and the current contents of the specified storage locations given below.

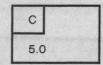
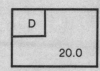

   Indicate the new contents following the execution of the above instructions.
10. Given the instructions

       KOUNT = KOUNT + 1
       SUM = SUM + X

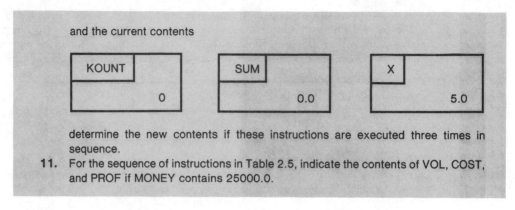

and the current contents

KOUNT
          0

SUM
          0.0

X
          5.0

determine the new contents if these instructions are executed three times in sequence.

11. For the sequence of instructions in Table 2.5, indicate the contents of VOL, COST, and PROF if MONEY contains 25000.0.

Integer and Real Arithmetic Expressions

There are four types of arithmetic expressions, two of which are used routinely: integer and real.[7] An expression is an **integer expression** if *all* of its data elements (constants and symbolic names) are of type integer. The shaded right-hand sides of the following assignment statements are examples of integer expressions.

```
INTEGER NUM,KOUNT,INVEST,MATERL,LABOR,TCOST,NUM,UCOST
NUM    = 50
KOUNT  = KOUNT + 1
INVEST = MATERL + LABOR
MONEY  = NUMSLD*ITMCST + 5000
TCOST  = NUM*UCOST + 5000
```

An integer expression performs *integer arithmetic;* that is, the results will be integer values. Awareness of this is particularly important in *integer division,* where an integer quantity is divided by another integer quantity. In this case, the "whole number" portion of the result is retained and the fractional portion is lost. This procedure is called **truncation;** the result is not rounded, as illustrated next.

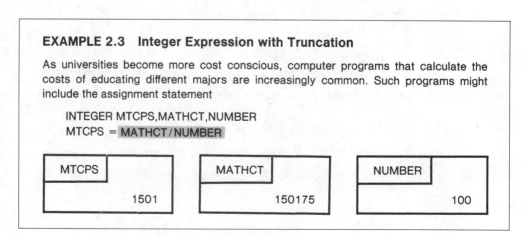

EXAMPLE 2.3   Integer Expression with Truncation

As universities become more cost conscious, computer programs that calculate the costs of educating different majors are increasingly common. Such programs might include the assignment statement

```
INTEGER MTCPS,MATHCT,NUMBER
MTCPS = MATHCT / NUMBER
```

MTCPS
          1501

MATHCT
          150175

NUMBER
          100

---

[7] The other two types are double precision (see page 49) and complex (not covered in this book).

where MTCPS represents the "cost per student for the Math Department," MATHCT
represents the "total cost for the Math Department," and NUMBER represents the
"number of majors in the Math Department."

   If 150175 is stored in MATHCT and 100 is stored in NUMBER, then 1501 will be
stored in MTCPS. Note that the numerical result is not rounded up to 1502; rather, the
fractional value (.75) is truncated, since MATHCT / NUMBER is an integer expression.

An expression is a **real expression** if all of its data elements (constants and symbolic
names) are of type real. The shaded right-hand sides of the following statements are examples
of real expressions.

```
REAL BALDUE,TUIT,CREDIT,PAY,HOURS,RATE,WAGE,VEL,LENGTH,TIME
BALDUE = TUIT + 250.0
CREDIT  = 15.0
PAY     = HOURS*RATE
WAGE    = PAY
VEL     = LENGTH/TIME
```

A real expression performs real arithmetic. That is, the result will be a real value.

EXAMPLE 2.4   Real Expressions

A student received an 85 and a 94 on two exams. The average can be found by using
the following assignment statements.

```
REAL SUM,EXAM1,EXAM2,AVG
   ⋮
SUM = EXAM1 + EXAM2
```

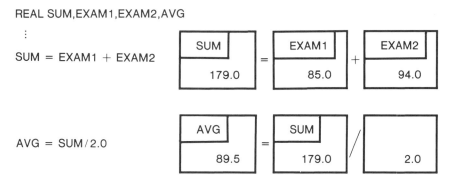

```
AVG = SUM/2.0
```

If EXAM1 has the value 85.0 and EXAM2 has the value 94.0 then SUM has the value
179.0 and AVG the value 89.5. Note that both expressions are real since EXAM1,
EXAM2, and SUM are typed as real and 2.0 is a real constant.

If numeric data types are combined in an expression, *the exception being a real value
raised to an integer power,* then the expression is known as a **mixed-type expression.** The
following are examples of mixed-type expressions. (Assume T and SUM are type real and J
and N are type integer.)

Mixed-Type Expression	Comment
T + 2	T is a real variable and 2 is an integer constant. The result is a real value.
50.5*J	J is an integer variable and 50.5 is a real constant. The result is a real value.
SUM/N	SUM is a real variable and N is an integer variable. The result is a real value.

As a programmer you must pay close attention to mixed-type expressions for two reasons. First, *integer values in a mixed-type expression are converted to real type during pairwise computations, and the final result will be a real value;* however, the exact value of the final result may differ, depending on the sequence of computations. A "pairwise computation" is one that involves a single arithmetic operator, as illustrated by the evaluation of each of the three mixed-type expressions above. (We elaborate on this issue later in Example 2.10.)

A second reason for you to pay close attention to the use of mixed-type expressions is that you may get an incorrect or undesirable result. To illustrate, the cost per student in Example 2.3 is actually $1501.75. If truncation is undesirable for a particular computation, then a real expression should be used. *When truncation is of no concern integer arithmetic is preferred to real arithmetic because it is faster.*

In our definitions of integer, real, and mixed-type expressions we omitted one complicating factor. *Any expression (positive or negative) may be raised to a (positive or negative) integer power, but only (positive) real expressions may be raised to real powers. Expressions having negative values can be raised only to integer powers.* Study Example 2.5 to make sure you understand this condition.

EXAMPLE 2.5   Expressions as Powers and Mixed Typing

Expression Raised to a Power	Comment (Assume X and A Are Real; J, K, and L Are Integer)
X**K	Real expression (X) may be raised to integer power (K); X is simply multiplied by itself a total of K times. For example, if 5.0 is in X and 3 is in K, then the result is 5.0 × 5.0 × 5.0 or 125.0.
J**8	Integer expression (J) may be raised to integer power (8). J is multiplied by itself eight times.
J**8.0	Considered mixed type. J is treated as real for this calculation and the computer evaluates antilog of 8.0 log (J). Whenever a real power is used, the computer uses logarithms in the evaluation. J**8 is preferred for greater efficiency and precision.
K**X	Considered mixed type. Same treatment as preceding case.

Expression Raised to a Power	Comment (Assume X and A Are Real; J, K, and L Are Integer)
$(-4.0)**L$	Use of parentheses causes treatment of 4.0 as a negative number. This is permissible since the power is integer. If 2 is in L, then the result is $(-4.0) \times (-4.0)$, or 16.0. If 3 is in L, then the result is -64.0.
$A**3.0$	This is permissible if A stores a positive value, but $A**3$ is preferred.
$(-A)**3.0$	This is not allowed since the expression is negative (assuming A stores a positive value) and the power is real. The computer attempts to evaluate this as the antilog of $3\log(-A)$, but the log of a negative number is undefined.

In general, *it is good programming practice to avoid complicated mixed-type expressions,* since the process of conversion is inefficient and follows complicated rules. We use simple mixed-type expressions when it is convenient to do so, as illustrated in various examples throughout the book.

Precision Revisited

For many computers, the maximum number of digits retained in integer arithmetic is ten;[8] the maximum number of significant digits in real arithmetic is generally seven, although double-precision declarations approximately double this figure. Thus, for example, a computational result having an actual real value given by 575.45248 is either rounded to 575.4525 or truncated to 575.4524, and one having an actual value of 98765432.1 is retained as 98765430.

If greater precision is required, then double-precision variables and constants can be used. An expression is a **double-precision expression** if all of its data type constituents are of type double precision. A **double-precision variable** is declared by using the DOUBLE PRECISION statement and a **double-precision constant** is written in the manner of a real constant in E-notation, except that E is replaced by D. For example, in the statements

```
DOUBLE PRECISION RADIUS,AREA
AREA = 0.3141592654D01*RADIUS**2
```

the expression

```
0.3141592654D01*RADIUS**2
```

is a double-precision expression; the value 0.12566370616D02 retained in AREA is stored with greater precision than an equivalent real expression. Without the DOUBLE PRECISION statement the value in AREA would be 12.56637.

---

[8] More specifically, machines that use 32 *bits* (0 or 1 digit) in a *word* (a single unit of storage that holds data or instructions) can retain integer values in the range -2^{31} to $2^{31} - 1$ or $-2,147,483,648$ to $2,147,483,647$; a 16-bit word machine stores a maximum integer value of $2^{15} - 1$, or 32,767.

A vexing problem called **roundoff error** is caused by the computer's *precision* (digit retention limitations). Assuming a computer that stores seven digits in real arithmetic, we can illustrate the problem by evaluating the expression 1.0/3.0, which of course has the actual value 0.3333333333. ... Since the computer stores 0.3333333, the sum 1.0/3.0 + 1.0/3.0 + 1.0/3.0 would yield 0.9999999 rather than exactly 1. While this may seem insignificant, roundoff error is a serious problem for many applications, as in the computation of trajectories in space flight or interest computations for a large savings account.

Finally, note the following:

1. A mixed-type expression also includes the mixture of double precision names and constants with integer or real names and constants. For example, the expression PI∗DIA is mixed type if PI is double precision and DIA is real. In this case, the resulting value is double precision.
2. If a numeric value exceeds the upper limit allowed by the computer, then **overflow** has occurred; values smaller than the lower limit cause **underflow.** For example, an actual value such as 0.15E85 would cause overflow on most computers. The computer usually prints an error message whenever overflow or underflow occurs during execution, as we illustrate in the next chapter.

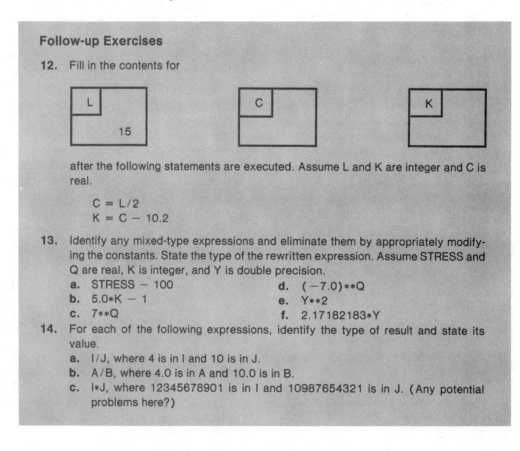

Follow-up Exercises

12. Fill in the contents for

after the following statements are executed. Assume L and K are integer and C is real.

```
C = L/2
K = C − 10.2
```

13. Identify any mixed-type expressions and eliminate them by appropriately modifying the constants. State the type of the rewritten expression. Assume STRESS and Q are real, K is integer, and Y is double precision.
     a. STRESS − 100
     b. 5.0∗K − 1
     c. 7∗∗Q
     d. (−7.0)∗∗Q
     e. Y∗∗2
     f. 2.17182183∗Y
14. For each of the following expressions, identify the type of result and state its value.
     a. I/J, where 4 is in I and 10 is in J.
     b. A/B, where 4.0 is in A and 10.0 is in B.
     c. I∗J, where 12345678901 is in I and 10987654321 is in J. (Any potential problems here?)

d. A∗B, where 2E50 is in A and 4E70 is in B. (Any potential problems here?)
e. A∗B, where 2D50 is in A and 4E70 is in B.
15. Are the following considered mixed-type expressions? (Assume CREDIT and COST are real and MONEY is integer.)

CREDIT = 15
COST   = MONEY

Comment on how you think the computer handles these.

Arithmetic Hierarchy

Computers do arithmetic on only one arithmetic operation at a time, called **pairwise arithmetic.** Therefore, an arithmetic expression involving several computations must be computed in a certain sequence.

In FORTRAN the sequence for performing arithmetic operations is

First: All exponentiation is performed.
Second: All multiplication and division is completed.
Third: All addition and subtraction is performed.

We illustrate this so-called **arithmetic hierarchy** through examples.

EXAMPLE 2.6   Student Billing Revisited

The calculation of amount due for tuition and fees in the student billing program can be combined into one assignment statement, as follows:

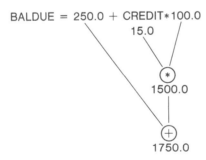

If CREDIT has a value of 15.0, then 1750.0 is stored in BALDUE. The value 1750.0 is determined by the following sequence.

Step 1. CREDIT is multiplied by 100.0 because multiplication is completed before addition. The result is 1500.0.

Step 2. 250.0 is added to 1500.0. The result is 1750.0.

EXAMPLE 2.7   Area Problem

An analyst for Prangles Potato Chips, a competitor of Pringles, wishes to determine the area of the top that would be required on a super-economy-size cylindrical container of radius 5 inches. As you might recall, the area of a circle is computed by using the formula *area* $= \pi r^2$, where *r* is the radius. This can be written in FORTRAN (assuming all variables are real) as follows:

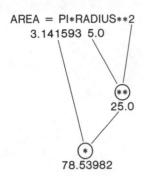

AREA = PI∗RADIUS∗∗2

If the variable RADIUS has the value 5.0 and PI is the symbolic name of a constant with a value of 3.141593, then 78.53982 is stored in AREA. This result is achieved in the following way.

Step 1. RADIUS is raised to the second power because exponentiation is performed before multiplication. The result is 25.0.

Step 2. 3.141593 is multiplied by 25.0. The result is 78.53982.

Left-to-Right Rule

The exact order of computation when two or more operations are at the same level of arithmetic hierarchy will differ depending on the complexity of the arithmetic expression and the particular computer system. If you avoid intricate mixed-type expressions, however, then *the computational result will be consistent with a left-to-right scan of the arithmetic expression,* as the following examples illustrate.

EXAMPLE 2.8   Percentages

The percentage of engineering students relative to the university enrollment is calculated using the following assignment statement, where all variables are typed real:

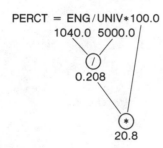

PERCT = ENG/UNIV∗100.0

If 1040.0 is stored in ENG and 5000.0 is stored in UNIV, then 20.8 is stored in PERCT. The value of 20.8 is determined by the following sequence.

Step 1. ENG is divided by UNIV because division and multiplication are at the same level, so operations are from left to right. The result is 0.208.

Step 2. 0.208 is multiplied by 100.0. The result is 20.8.

Note that the left-to-right rule prevents the wrong sequence of first multiplying UNIV by 100.0 (giving 500000.0) and then dividing this result into ENG (giving 0.00208 for PERCT).

If PERCT had been typed integer, then the result 20.8 would have been truncated to 20 for storage in PERCT. To *round* a real value for storage in an integer variable, simply add 0.5 to the real value. For example,

PERCT = ENG/UNIV*100.0 + 0.5

would give a value of 20.8 + 0.5 = 21.3 for the real expression, which is subsequently stored as 21 in integer PERCT (the fractional part .3 is truncated). In effect, we rounded 20.8 up to 21.

EXAMPLE 2.9 Microeconomics Problem

The daily cost in dollars (c) of operating a small manufacturing firm is described by the equation

$$c = u^3 - 6u^2 + 250$$

where u represents the number of units produced by the firm per day. The equivalent assignment statement in FORTRAN is (all variables real):

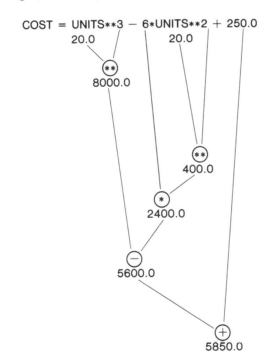

If UNITS has the value 20.0, then 5850.0 will be stored in COST. The value 5850.0 is determined as follows:

Step 1. UNITS is raised to the third power because exponentiation is the first operation performed, and UNITS**3 appears to the *left* of UNITS**2. The result is 8000.0.

Step 2. UNITS is raised to the second power. The result is 400.0.

Step 3. 6.0 is multiplied by 400.0 because multiplication is performed before addition and subtraction. The result is 2400.0.

Step 4. 2400.0 is subtracted from 8000.0 because the subtraction operation is found to the left of the addition operation. The result is 5600.0.

Step 5. 250.0 is added to 5600.0, giving 5850.0.

EXAMPLE 2.10 Pairwise Integer to Real Conversions

Let's take a look at mixed-type expressions again to illustrate better the pairwise nature of integer to real conversions. Consider the expression below and the sequence of computational steps, where 2.1 is in real A, 6 is in integer N, 10 is in integer K, and 3 is in integer J. X is typed real.

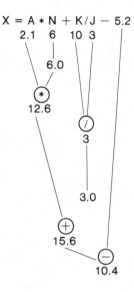

Step 1. 6 converted to 6.0 since we have mixed type in this pairwise multiplication.

Step 2. 12.6 placed in intermediate storage.

Step 3. Integer division truncates this result. Note that this pairwise division is not mixed type, so integer arithmetic is used.

Step 4. 3 converted to 3.0 in preparation for pairwise mixed-type addition.

Step 5. 15.6 placed in intermediate storage.

Step 6. The value of this mixed-type expression is 10.4.

Note that *type real takes precedence in an integer-real mixed-type pairwise computation;* that is, the integer value is converted to real and the value of the result is real. Similarly, *double-precision data types take precedence over both integer and real data types when pairwise arithmetic is performed.*

Use of Parentheses

The insertion of parentheses within arithmetic expressions changes the order of computation according to the following rules.

1. The operations enclosed within parentheses are computed before operations not included in parentheses.
2. Parentheses may be embedded inside other parentheses in complicated expressions.
3. The innermost set of parentheses contains the computations done first.

We might note that within parentheses themselves the hierarchy and left-to-right rules apply.

EXAMPLE 2.11   Temperature Conversion

Conversion of temperatures from Fahrenheit to Celsius is given by the formula

$$Celsius = \tfrac{5}{9}(Fahrenheit - 32)$$

In FORTRAN the formula is written (all variables real)

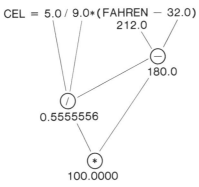

CEL = 5.0 / 9.0*(FAHREN − 32.0)

If 212.0 is stored in FAHREN, then 100.0000 will be stored in CEL according to the following steps:

Step 1. 32.0 is subtracted from FAHREN because this operation is enclosed in parentheses. The result is 180.0.

Step 2. 5.0 is divided by 9.0 because the division operation is found to the left of the multiplication operation. The result is 0.5555556.

Step 3. 0.5555556 is multiplied by 180.0. The result is 100.0000.

Note: Dividing 5 by 9 actually gives the irrational number 0.555555555 . . . , that is, the 5s never end. We expressed the result to 7 significant digits according to our discussion on page 49. When this 7-digit number is multiplied by 180, the precise result is 100.000008, which we have expressed to 7 digits as 100.0000.

EXAMPLE 2.12   Potpourri

In the preceding example, *parentheses were used as a means of improving the readability of the arithmetic expression,* since we could have written the mathematically equivalent but less readable

CEL = 5.0/9.0*FAHREN − 5.0/9.0*32.0

Similarly, readability plays a role in expressing the algebraic expression $x \cdot (-y)$ as

X*(−Y)

rather than as

−X*Y

Note that we would not express this as

X* − Y

since it violates the rule that two arithmetic operators must not be adjacent.

In many cases, however, parentheses must be used. For example, an expression for a statistic called variance is given by

$$\frac{s^2}{p - 1}$$

In FORTRAN we would write this as

S**2/(P — 1.0)

The square root of variance, called the standard deviation, is algebraically given by

$$\left(\frac{s^2}{p - 1}\right)^{1/2} \quad \text{or} \quad \sqrt{\frac{s^2}{p - 1}}$$

In FORTRAN we can write this by *nesting the parentheses* as follows:

(S**2/(P — 1.0))**0.5

One final point: *When nesting parentheses, take care that the number of left parentheses equals the number of right parentheses, as a mismatch in these numbers is a common error.*

Follow-up Exercises

It is very important that you pay close attention to hierarchy, left-to-right, and parentheses rules when you are writing FORTRAN expressions. Inattention to these rules is a leading cause of logic errors. The following exercises emphasize this point.

16. To simplify the computation of average in Example 2.4 a student developed the following assignment statement

        AVG = EXAM1 + EXAM2/2.0

     What is stored in AVG? Correct the expression.

17. In Example 2.11, what would be stored in CEL for each case below?
     a. CEL = 5.0/9.0*FAHREN — 32.0   (CEL and FAHREN real)
     b. CEL = 5.0/9.0*(FAHREN — 32)   (CEL and FAHREN integer)
     c. CEL = 5/9*(FAHREN — 32)   (CEL and FAHREN integer)

18. Suppose *all* variables were typed integer in Example 2.8. What would be stored in PERCT? Modify the expression to give a legitimate integer result.

19. Indicate what would be stored in real A for each of the following, given that 3.0 is in real B and 2.0 is in real C:
     a. A = (4.0 + B**3 — C)*C**2
     b. A = (4.0 + B**(3.0 — C))*C**2
     c. A = (4.0 + B**(3.0 — C))*(C**2)
     d. A = 9.0/B*C + 5.0/C
     e. A = 9.0/(B*C) + 5.0/C
     f. A = 9.0/B/C + 5.0/C

20. Write FORTRAN arithmetic expressions for each of the following algebraic expressions. Assume all variables are real except for *K*. Avoid mixed typing.

   a. x^{k+1}

   b. $x^k + 1$

   c. $\dfrac{(x-a)^2}{s+4}$

   d. $\sqrt{\dfrac{(x-a)^2}{s+4}}$

   e. $(7-x)^{1/2}$

   f. $\left(y - \dfrac{5}{x \cdot t} + 2\right) \cdot (-4)$

   g. $(y - 3^{x-1} + 2)^3$

   h. $\left(\dfrac{x-y}{100}\right) \cdot \left(\dfrac{1}{a+b}\right)$

21. Find values for the following expressions, assuming 2.5 is in real X and 20 is in integer K.

   a. K/7 − X/K

   b. X**(K − 18)/K

2.6
LIBRARY FUNCTIONS

Suppose we wish to determine the square root of the arithmetic expression

$$b^2 - 4 \cdot a \cdot c$$

and to store it in the address labeled Y. As you know, we simply could use the assignment statement

   Y = (B**2 − 4.0*A*C)**0.5

An alternative approach in this case is to use the following:

   Y = SQRT(B**2 − 4.0*A*C)

The right-hand side of this statement is called a **library function**,[9] which is of the following general type:

> **function name (argument list)**

The **argument list** is either a single arithmetic expression or a list of arithmetic expressions separated by commas. As before, an arithmetic expression also includes either a single constant or a single variable. In the above example, SQRT is the function name and B**2 −

[9] Other commonly used terms are **built-in function** and **intrinsic function**. In actual practice there are technical distinctions between these two terms, but we need not be concerned for our purposes.

TABLE 2.6 Selected* Library Functions

FUNCTION NAME	PURPOSE	NUMBER OF ARGUMENTS	TYPE OF ARGUMENT(S)	TYPE OF RESULT	EXAMPLE NUMBER	ALGEBRAIC EXAMPLES	CORRESPONDING FORTRAN EXAMPLES
ABS	Absolute value of argument	1	Real	Real	1.	$z = \lvert x - y \rvert$	Z = ABS(X − Y)
IABS		1	Integer	Integer	2.	$k = j \cdot \lvert 1 - m/n \rvert$	K = J*IABS(1 − M/N)
ALOG	Base e log of argument	1	Real	Real	3.	$p = q \cdot \ln 5$	P = Q*ALOG(5.0)
ALOG10	Base 10 log of argument	1	Real	Real	4.	$t = \log(a + 2 \cdot b)$	T = ALOG10(A + 2.0*B)
EXP	Exponentiation; base e raised to the argument	1	Real	Real	5.	$y = ae^{-2t}$	Y = A*EXP(−2.0*T)
FLOAT	Real version of integer argument	1	Integer	Real	6.	$\bar{x} = s/n$	XBAR = S/FLOAT(N)
INT	Integer version of real argument	1	Real	Integer	7.	$m = k \cdot [p]$	M = K*INT(P)
AMIN0	Smallest value in argument list	2+	Integer	Real	8.	$s = \min(i,j,k)$	S = AMIN0(I,J,K)
AMIN1		2+	Real	Real	9.	$s = \min(7,x)$	S = AMIN1(7.0,X)
MIN0		2+	Integer	Integer	10.	$m = \min(i,j)$	M = MIN0(I,J)
MIN1		2+	Real	Integer	11.	$m = \min(p,r,q,s)$	M = MIN1(P,R,Q,S)
AMAX0	Largest value in argument list	2+	Integer	Real	12.	$b = \max(50,n)$	B = AMAX0(50,N)
AMAX1		2+	Real	Real	13.	$b = \max(5x,y,z)$	B = AMAX1(5.0*X,Y,Z)
MAX0		2+	Integer	Integer	14.	$l = \max(2i,j,k)$	L = MAX0(2*I,J,K)
MAX1		2+	Real	Integer	15.	$l = \max(y,p)$	L = MAX1(Y,P)
SQRT	Square root of argument	1	Real	Real	16.	$r = \sqrt{s}$	R = SQRT(S)

*These functions represent a subset from among roughly 50 functions that are available on many FORTRAN compilers.

4.0*A*C is the single argument. The purpose of this function, of course, is to determine the square root of the argument.

Other commonly used library functions are listed in Table 2.6. Study these examples and note the following points:

1. The function is implemented by using its name in an arithmetic expression. When this expression is compiled, the machine language instructions for performing the function are provided by the compiler. For example, to find the logarithm of a number as in Example 3 of Table 2.6, the compiler utilizes a set of instructions (a subprogram) which calculates logarithms. This saves us the trouble of having to "reinvent the wheel" (write these instructions ourselves) each time we wish to evaluate a logarithm.

2. The **argument** is any arithmetic expression, including either a single constant or a single variable. Commas must be used to separate multiple arguments. In all cases, arguments must be enclosed in parentheses following the name of the function.

3. Functions can be used within functions; that is, a function can call another function. For example, the statement

        Y = SQRT(ABS(A − B))

   is legitimate. In this case, the main program calls the function SQRT; the function SQRT then calls the function ABS. Thus if 6.0 is stored in A and 10.0 is stored in B, then A − B is evaluated, giving −4.0; next, the absolute value is taken giving +4.0; finally, the square root is taken, giving 2.0, and this result is stored under Y.

4. Note *that the first letter in the name of a function implicitly types the function* according to the usual convention for variable names. Thus, AMIN0 yields a real result and MIN0 yields an integer result. Also note the restrictions on the mode of the argument. For example, the "0" suffix on AMIN, MIN, AMAX, and MAX refers to *integer arguments;* the "1" suffix refers to *real arguments;* and the logarithm and square root functions require *real arguments* in all cases.

5. Finally, note that the INT function "truncates" rather than "rounds." For example, INT(8.7) gives 8 and INT(−5.6) gives −5. To get a rounded result we simply add 0.5 to the argument. For example, INT(X + 0.5) gives 9 when X stores 8.7.

Follow-up Exercises

22. In Table 2.6, look at the column headed "Corresponding FORTRAN Examples" and answer the following:
    a. Examples 1, 2. What is stored in Z if 5.4 is in X and 6.0 is in Y? Suppose 7.0 is in X and 5.2 is in Y? What value is stored in K if 10 is stored in J, 7 in M, and 2 in N?
    b. Examples 3, 4. What value is stored in P if 0.1 is stored in Q? What is stored in T if −4.0 is in A and 3.0 is in B?
    c. Example 5. What value is stored in Y if 50.1 is in A and 4.0 is in T?
    d. Examples 6, 7. What would you say is the purpose of "floating" N? Of treating P as an integer in the arithmetic expression?
    e. Example 9. What is stored in S if 10.2 is in X?
    f. Example 14. What is stored in L if 5 is in I, 10 is in J, and 7 is in K?

> **23.** Indicate what would be stored in real A for each of the following, given that 3.0 is in real B, 2.0 is in real C, and 10 is in integer K.
>
> **a.** A = INT(B/C)*5 − 1
> **b.** A = FLOAT(INT(B/C)*5 − 1)
> **c.** A = SQRT(FLOAT(INT(B/C)*5 − 1))
> **d.** A = INT(C)/INT(B) + 5.4
> **e.** A = INT(C/B) + 5.4
> **f.** A = 1.2 + FLOAT(K)/4.0
> **g.** A = 1.2 + K/4.0
> **h.** A = 1.2 + K/4
> **i.** A = 1.2 + FLOAT(K/4)

2.7
LIST-DIRECTED INPUT/OUTPUT (I/O)

In this section we present simplified input and output statements that do not require us to specify formats for exactly how data are to appear on input and output media. This type of I/O is termed *list-directed* because we need only specify the "list" of items that we wish to input or output.[10]

The PRINT Statement

The PRINT statement is used to transmit or output the values of constants, variables, or expressions to an output unit such as a line printer or terminal. PRINT statements enable us to observe the results of programs on media such as printed paper or video screens.

A general form of the **list-directed PRINT statement** is given by

PRINT,*list*

where *list* refers to

1. A constant (numeric or character)
2. A variable (numeric or character)
3. An expression (numeric or character)
4. Any combination of constants, variables, and expressions separated by commas

For example, execution of

PRINT,BALDUE

in the student billing program on page 30 results in a printed real value of either

1750.0000000

---

[10] Modules B, C, and D present formatted I/O, whereby the programmer controls the exact placement of data.

or in E-notation

    0.1750000E 04

depending on the system. Some compilers print all list-directed real values in E-notation.

In the next example we show that: The items listed in the PRINT statement are specified in the sequence in which you want the items to appear in your output; each item in the list is separated from the previous item by a comma; each PRINT statement initiates a new line of output.

EXAMPLE 2.13 Student Billing with Output Variations

Consider the following version of the student billing program.

```
REAL CREDIT,TUIT,BALDUE
CREDIT = 15.0
TUIT   = CREDIT*100.0
BALDUE = TUIT + 250.0
PRINT, CREDIT,TUIT,BALDUE
STOP
END
```

One print line

When this program is executed the following line is printed.

```
15.0000000        1500.0000000         1750.0000000
```

Note that the output appears on one print line; that the sequence of numbers in the output corresponds to the sequence of variables in the list; and that each number contains a decimal point, since each variable in the list is a real variable. Again, some systems will print these values using E-notation.

Now, suppose we replace the PRINT statement by the following sequence of PRINT statements.

```
REAL CREDIT,TUIT,BALDUE
CREDIT = 15.0
TUIT   = CREDIT*100.0
BALDUE = TUIT + 250.0
PRINT,CREDIT
PRINT,TUIT
PRINT,BALDUE
STOP
END
```

Three print lines

In this case the output would appear as follows:

```
  15.0000000
1500.0000000
1750.0000000
```

Note that numeric output is *right-justified* (aligned to the right).

Note that each PRINT statement has one variable in its list; hence each print line has a single value. Further note that *a new print line is printed each time a new PRINT statement is executed.*

Most programs include labels for numeric output in order to improve the readability of output. For example, the three output values above would be meaningless to a person not familiar with the program. From this point forward, *all of our programs will include labeled output.*

Output is labeled by enclosing character strings (constants) within apostrophes directly in the PRINT statement. The character string is displayed exactly as typed (with the apostrophes removed).

EXAMPLE 2.14   Labeled Output

To label the student billing output we might use the following PRINT statements.

```
REAL CREDIT,TUIT,BALDUE
CREDIT = 15.0
TUIT   = CREDIT*100.0
BALDUE = TUIT + 250.0
PRINT, 'NUMBER OF CREDITS: ',CREDIT
PRINT, 'TUITION           : ',TUIT
PRINT, 'BALANCE DUE        : ',BALDUE
STOP
END
```

Now the printed output would appear as follows:

```
NUMBER OF CREDITS:          15.0000000
TUITION          :        1500.0000000
BALANCE DUE      :        1750.0000000
```

Thus, output can be labeled by using character constants.

Did you notice how nicely we aligned the labels? *Good program design dictates thoughtful design of output to ensure its readability.*

Finally, consider the following version of the program.

```
INTEGER     ID
REAL        CREDIT,TUIT,BALDUE
CHARACTER   NAME*15
NAME   = 'W. MITTY'
ID     = 266612463
CREDIT = 15.0
TUIT   = CREDIT * 100.0
BALDUE = TUIT + 250.0
PRINT, 'NAME              : ',NAME
PRINT, 'ID NUMBER         : ',ID
PRINT, ' '
PRINT, 'NUMBER OF CREDITS: ',CREDIT
PRINT, 'TUITION           : ',TUIT
PRINT, 'BALANCE DUE        : ',BALDUE
STOP
END
```

```
NAME             :    W. MITTY
ID NUMBER        :    266612463

NUMBER OF CREDITS:          15.0000000
TUITION          :        1500.0000000
BALANCE DUE      :        1750.0000000
```

Notice that we have included the output of the character variable NAME and the integer variable ID. Also note that we can insert blank lines into the output to control vertical spacing by using a single blank character (the symbol ƀ represents a blank character) in the list of a PRINT statement. Thus the statement

   PRINT,'ƀ'

following the statement that prints ID has the effect of printing a blank line immediately following the print line for ID.[11]

Follow-up Exercises

24. Modify the last program in Example 2.14 so that CREDIT, TUIT, and BALDUE are treated as integer variables. How would the output change? What advantages do you see in using integer variables? Disadvantages?

*25. Modify the last program in Example 2.14 so as to print the following output.

```
NAME            :        W. MITTY
ID NUMBER       :        266-61-2463
NUMBER OF CREDITS:       15.0000000
                  ←─────────────── Two blank lines

FEES..........................$    250.0000000
TUITION.....................$   1500.0000000
                  ─ ─ ─ ─ ─ ─ ─ ─ ─
BALANCE DUE..........$    1750.0000000
```

*26. Create two versions of the *first* program in Example 2.13 such that
   a. All assignment statements are eliminated in favor of one PRINT statement that prints the number of credits, the tuition charge, and the balance due.
   b. The cost per credit of $100 is stored in a real variable named CPC and the fee of $250 is stored in a real variable named FEES.
   Can you state advantages and disadvantages of each approach?

27. **Computer as Hand Calculator.**   The computer can be used as an expensive hand calculator by writing short programs that include all calculations in the list of PRINT statements. Specify a PRINT statement for each of the following.
   a. $\dfrac{-6.5 + \sqrt{(6.5)^2 - (4) \cdot (-3.4) \cdot (50)}}{(2) \cdot (-3.4)}$
   b. The square, cube, square root, and cube root of the number 100.56
   c. The base 10 logarithm of 100 and 10 raised to the base 10 logarithm of 100
   d. The quantity $e^{6.21461}$, the base e logarithm of 50, and the base e logarithm of $e^{6.21461}$

---

[11] WATFIV uses 12 positions to output each list-directed integer value, 20 positions to output each list-directed real value (7 of the 20 positions are for decimal positions), and as many character positions as specified in the CHARACTER statement to output each list-directed character value. Numeric output is right-justified and character output is left-justified.
* Answers to exercises marked with a single or double asterisk are not given at the end of the text. Ask your instructor for these answers.

28. WRITE Statement. The following list-directed WRITE statement is an alternative to the PRINT statement.

> **WRITE** (*output unit number*, ∗) *list*

where "output unit number" is an integer number that identifies the output unit for that system. For example, IBM 370 systems use

WRITE(6,∗)list

for output to a line printer or terminal. Find the output unit number for your system and rewrite the first program in Example 2.13 using the WRITE statement.

The READ Statement

You need to make an important distinction between your computer program (that is, the instructions that tell the computer what to do) and your input data (that is, the data that you want processed through an input unit). For example, an employer has data on the number of hours worked and the rate of pay for each employee. The employer has recorded these data on an appropriate input medium such as cards or magnetic tape, and uses these to compute each employee's pay. The hours worked and rate of pay for each employee are considered input data; the FORTRAN instructions to determine each employee's pay represent the computer program.

In the student billing program, three items of data were provided: cost of tuition per credit ($100), cost of fees ($250), and number of credits (15). By definition, these are not input data, since they represent constants in the computer program. For example, the assignment statement

CREDIT = 15.0

was used to store 15.0 in CREDIT and the 100.0 and 250.0 were incorporated in the assignment statements

TUIT = CREDIT∗100.0

and

BALDUE = TUIT + 250.0

The READ statement is an alternative approach to storing data in memory locations and *is preferred to the assignment statement whenever data have a high likelihood of changing values each time the program is executed*. The READ statement enables the computer to transfer the data from some source, such as punched card or terminal, to the appropriate storage locations in computer memory.

A common form of the **list-directed READ statement** is

> **READ,** *list of names*

where the *list of names* contains variable names (separated by commas).

EXAMPLE 2.15   Student Billing with Input

The following version of the student billing program treats NAME, ID, and CREDIT as input variables that are to be read in by a single READ statement.

```
INTEGER    ID
REAL       CREDIT,TUIT,BALDUE
CHARACTER  NAME*15
READ, NAME,ID,CREDIT
TUIT    = CREDIT*100.0
BALDUE  = TUIT + 250.0
PRINT, 'NAME             :    ',NAME
PRINT, 'ID NUMBER        : ',ID
PRINT, ' '
PRINT, 'NUMBER OF CREDITS: ',CREDIT
PRINT, 'TUITION          : ',TUIT
PRINT, 'BALANCE DUE       : ',BALDUE
STOP
END
```

The only difference between this version and the one in Example 2.14 on page 62 is that the single statement

```
READ, NAME,ID,CREDIT
```

replaces the three assignment statements

```
NAME   = 'W. MITTY'
ID     = 266612463
CREDIT = 15.0
```

For now, assume that the data items W. MITTY for NAME, 266612463 for ID, and 15.0 for CREDIT are on a single punched card (or terminal input line) for batch processing. The READ instruction activates the appropriate input unit and transfers the values on the input medium (punched card or input line) to the memory locations NAME, ID, and CREDIT as illustrated below.

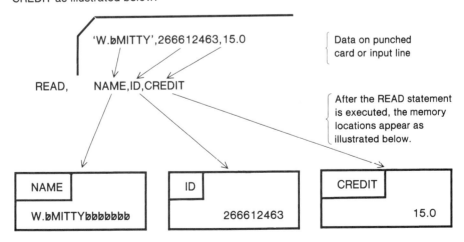

Note that each value on the card or input line is a constant list in *the same sequence and of the same data type* as the list of variables in the READ statement. Also notice that character values must be enclosed in apostrophes and that each data value is separated by a comma.

Each time the computer executes a READ statement, a new data card or line is processed. The computer reads as many lines or cards as necessary to supply values for each variable in the list. For example, if the READ statements were arranged as

```
READ,NAME
READ,ID
READ,CREDIT
```

then the data would be arranged as

```
'W.ЬMITTY'
266612463
15.0
```

The use of a READ statement for NAME, ID, and CREDIT is preferred to the use of assignment statements, since the values of NAME, ID, and CREDIT will change for each student who is processed. If a READ statement were not used, then the assignment statements would have to be changed for each student, which is both cumbersome and more costly than the use of input data.

Follow-up Exercises

*29. Change the program in Example 2.15 in each of the following ways.
  a. Treat the "cost of tuition per credit" (CPC) and the "cost of fees" (FEES) as input variables. Use a single READ statement for these two variables, separate from the other READ statement.
  b. Instead of defining CPC and FEES as input variables, use assignment statements.
  Under what conditions might any one of the above approaches be preferred to the others?

30. Alternative READ Statement. The following READ statement is an alternative to the READ statement used earlier.

> **READ(** *input unit number,* * **)** *list of names*

where the "input unit number" refers to a specific input unit such as a card reader or a terminal; the asterisk identifies this input statement as list-directed; and the "list" contains variable names separated by commas.

The input unit number varies from system to system. For example, IBM 370 systems use the number 5 for the card reader or terminal, as follows:

```
READ(5,*)list of names
```

Ask your instructor about this number on your system and modify the program in Example 2.15 to use this version of the READ statement.

2.8
DATA STATEMENT

We have already introduced two ways to place values in memory cells: the assignment statement and the READ statement. Another method, the **DATA statement,** instructs the compiler to put initial values into specific memory locations.

A simple form of the DATA statement is given by

> **DATA** *list of names / list of constants /*

For example,

    DATA ID / 266612463 /

is a nonexecutable statement that declares to the compiler that 266612463 is stored in ID.

Several variables can be initialized in the same data statement. Thus in Example 2.14, the following DATA statement could replace the three assignment statements

    DATA NAME,ID,CREDIT / 'W.bMITTY',266612463,15.0 /

This stores W.bMITTY in NAME, 266612463 in ID and 15.0 in CREDIT. This DATA statement has the same effect as

    NAME   = 'W.bMITTY'
    ID   = 266612463
    CREDIT = 15.0

Both approaches are termed **initialization** of variables: however, there is an important difference that should not escape you: The DATA statement initializes when the program is *compiled* and the assignment statements initialize when the program is *executed*.

If more than one variable needs to be initialized to the same value, as in

    DATA S1,S2,S3 / 0.0,0.0,0.0 /

then the list of three constants can be written in the form 3*0., as follows:

    DATA S1,S2,S3 / 3*0.0 /

We recommend using the DATA statement whenever the initialized variable does *not* need to be reinitialized to its former value during the execution of the program.

The DATA statement may appear anywhere after type statements such as INTEGER, REAL, and CHARACTER, but before the END statement. Data statements usually are placed immediately after all type statements.

Alternatively, WATFIV allows the initialization of variables within type statements such as REAL, INTEGER, and CHARACTER, as the following illustrates.

Traditional (ANSI) Alternative		WATFIV Alternative
CHARACTER NAME*15		CHARACTER NAME*15 /'W. MITTY'/
INTEGER ID		INTEGER ID /266612463/
REAL CREDIT,TUIT,BALDUE		REAL CREDIT /15.0/,TUIT,BALDUE
DATA NAME/'W. MITTY'/	or combined	
DATA ID /266612463/	into one	
DATA CREDIT /15.0/	statement	

The WATFIV alternative is more convenient, with little or no sacrifice in readability. See Module H at the end of the book for other current differences between WATFIV and the most recent ANSI FORTRAN.

EXAMPLE 2.16   Initialization of Parameters

In the student billing program, cost per credit (CPC) and student fees (FEES) are called **parameters** because in reality they represent values that remain constant *while the program executes.* Parameters in programs are represented in any of the following ways.

1. As constants

```
REAL CREDIT,TUIT,BALDUE
READ, CREDIT
TUIT   = CREDIT* 100.0
BALDUE = TUIT +  250.0
PRINT, CREDIT,TUIT,BALDUE
STOP
END
```

Input data

```
15.0
```

2. As variables initialized through assignment statements

```
REAL CREDIT,TUIT,BALDUE,CPC,FEES
CPC    = 100.0
FEES   = 250.0
READ, CREDIT
TUIT   = CREDIT*CPC
BALDUE = TUIT + FEES
PRINT, CREDIT,TUIT,BALDUE
STOP
END
```

Input data

```
15.0
```

3. As variables initialized through READ statements

```
REAL CREDIT,TUIT,BALDUE,CPC,FEES
READ, CPC,FEES
READ, CREDIT

TUIT   = CREDIT*CPC
BALDUE = TUIT + FEES
PRINT, CREDIT,TUIT,BALDUE
STOP
END
```

Input data

```
100.0,250.0
15.0
```

4. **As variables initialized through DATA statements**

```
REAL CREDIT,TUIT,BALDUE,CPC,FEES
DATA CPC,FEES/100.0,250.0/
READ, CREDIT
TUIT   = CREDIT*CPC
BALDUE = TUIT + FEES
PRINT, CREDIT,TUIT,BALDUE
STOP
END
```

Input data

```
15.0
```

Each program gives the following identical output:

```
15.0000000        1500.0000000        1750.0000000
```

If parameters have descriptive meanings, as in the above examples, then it's a matter of good programming style to use names, as in options 3 and 4. This practice improves your understanding of the parameters when reviewing the program, since names suggest contextual meaning and (presumably) are defined as part of the program's documentation.

More important, the use of names for parameters reduces software maintenance costs in environments where parameters are likely to change values over time. For example, if CPC and FEES change values each year, then option 3 requires a simple change in a single data input line, whereas option 1 requires access to the program and changes in two lines of code. For simple programs like our student billing program, this consideration is insignificant (except in principle). However, in a commercial environment where programs are thousands of lines long, perhaps with parameters in hundreds of lines, we can begin to appreciate this design consideration.

Generally, we don't recommend option 1 for the reasons outlined earlier. Option 2 is cumbersome, and generally not preferred to options 3 and 4. Option 3 is desirable if the values of the parameters change often over time. If values don't change often, then we recommend option 4.

Follow-up Exercise

31. a. Specify a DATA statement to initialize A, B, C, D, and E to 0.0, F to 100.0, and R1, R2, R3 to YES.

b. Initialize the variables in part a using type statements.

2.9
BANK SAVINGS PROBLEM

To complete your introduction to fundamentals of FORTRAN we present one more problem scenario for which we write a complete FORTRAN program.

Suppose that we have $1000 to invest in a savings account that yields interest of 0.015

($1\frac{1}{2}$ percent) per quarter (every three months). If we deposit the $1000 now, then one quarter from now we have our original $1000 plus $15 interest (1000 × 0.015), or a total of $1015. This calculation can be written as follows:

$$1015 = 1000 + 1000 \times (0.015)$$
$$= 1000 \times (1 + 0.015)$$

Now, consider how much we would have two quarters from now: the $1015 at the end of the first quarter plus the new interest of $15.22 on this amount (1015 × 0.015), or a total of $1030.22. In other words,

$$1030.22 = 1015 + 1015 \times (0.015)$$
$$= 1015 \times (1 + 0.015)$$

But we already know that

$$1015 = 1000 \times (1 + 0.015)$$

Thus,

$$1030.22 = 1015 \times (1 + 0.015)$$
$$= 1000 \times (1 + 0.015) \times (1 + 0.015)$$
$$= 1000 \times (1 + 0.015)^2$$

Do you see an emerging pattern? In general, if A represents our accumulated funds, N represents the number of quarters into the future, P represents the principal we start off with, and R represents the quarterly interest rate, then

$$A = P \cdot (1 + R)^N$$

Today's banks have computerized virtually all computational aspects dealing with savings and checking accounts, mortgages, loans, and investments. The following four-step procedure illustrates a simple program for determining accumulated funds in a savings account.

Step 1: *Analysis*

Bank savings account program that determines accumulated funds given the principal, quarterly interest rate, and number of quarters.

a. *Input data*
   Principal
   Quarterly interest rate
   Number of quarters
b. *Output data*
   All input data
   Accumulated funds
c. *Computations*
   Accumulated funds = Principal × (1 + Rate)$^{\text{Number of quarters}}$

Step 2: *Design*

Flowchart and pseudocode representations of the algorithm are illustrated in Figure 2.2.

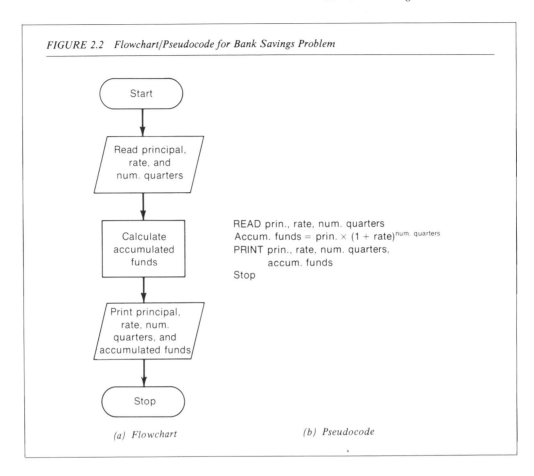

FIGURE 2.2   Flowchart/Pseudocode for Bank Savings Problem

READ prin., rate, num. quarters
Accum. funds = prin. × (1 + rate)$^{num. quarters}$
PRINT prin., rate, num. quarters,
          accum. funds
Stop

(a) Flowchart   *(b) Pseudocode*

Step 3: Code

```
C-- --------------- --------------
C    BANK SAVINGS PROGRAM
C
C    KEY:
C      PRIN  = PRINCIPAL
C      RATE  = QUARTERLY INTEREST RATE
C      ACCUM = ACCUMULATED FUNDS
C      NUM   = NUMBER OF QUARTERS
C-- --------------- --------------
     INTEGER NUM
     REAL    PRIN,RATE,ACCUM
C-- --------------- --------------
     READ, PRIN,RATE,NUM
C-- --------------- --------------
     ACCUM = PRIN*(1.0 + RATE)**NUM
C-- --------------- --------------
     PRINT, 'PRINCIPAL = ',PRIN
     PRINT, 'RATE      = ',RATE
     PRINT, 'QUARTERS  = ',NUM
     PRINT, 'AMOUNT    = ',ACCUM
C-- --------------- --------------
     STOP
     END
```

These **comment lines** show simplified program documentation. Note their use for describing programs, defining variables, and segmenting programs into ''blocks'' of related statements. For greater detail see the next chapter.

Step 4: Debugging

For the input data

```
1000.0,0.015,2
```

we get the following output:

```
PRINCIPAL  =          1000.0000000
RATE       =             0.0150000
QUARTERS   =          2
AMOUNT     =          1030.2220000
```

Just how we go about running this program is the topic for the next chapter.

Follow-up Exercises

32. Why is it best to use a READ statement rather than assignment statements for storing values in PRIN, RATE, and NUM?

33. Write down expected printed output if 1000.0 is stored in PRIN, 0.02 in RATE, and 2 in NUM. Be specific by showing the print lines.

34. Modify the program to input the customer's name (20 characters), street address (20 characters), and city-state-zip (30 characters). Print these data just before the output of PRIN, making sure that two blank lines separate the print line for city-state-zip from the print line for PRIN.

ADDITIONAL EXERCISES

35. Define the terms below. For each, where appropriate, include FORTRAN rules for its use and state its purpose or function.

computer program	integer variable
four-step procedure	real variable
algorithm	character variable
flowchart	implicit typing
pseudocode	explicit typing
program design language	constant
coding	integer constant
run	real constant
execute	E-notation
debugging	precision
FORTRAN character set	character constant
data types	executable statement
keywords	nonexecutable statement
function names	END statement
statement	STOP statement
line	type statement
symbolic name	INTEGER statement
variable name	REAL statement

DOUBLE PRECISION statement
LOGICAL statement
logical variable
logical constant
CHARACTER statement
assignment statement
character expression
arithmetic expression
arithmetic operators
integer expression
real expression
mixed-type expression
truncation
double-precision expression
double-precision variable

double-precision constant
roundoff error
overflow
underflow
pairwise arithmetic
arithmetic hierarchy
library function
argument
list-directed PRINT statement
list-directed READ statement
input data
DATA statement
initialization
parameters
comment lines

36. **Temperature Conversion.** Write a program that accepts degrees Fahrenheit as input and outputs degrees Celsius. (See Example 2.11 on page 55.) Don't forget to specify the first three steps in the four-step procedure. *Note:* Input data for this problem are provided in Exercise 12 of the next chapter.

37. **Area Problem.** Consider the scenario in Example 2.7 on page 51. Suppose that each top costs C dollars per square inch of surface and X containers are needed. Write a computer program which determines the total cost of X containers. Treat RADIUS, C, and X as input variables. Don't forget to specify the first three steps in the four-step procedure. *Note:* Input data for this problem are provided in Exercise 13 of the next chapter.

38. **Microeconomics Problem.** Consider the scenario in Example 2.9 on page 53. Suppose that all units produced can be sold at a constant price of $100 per unit. Noting that daily revenue is price times the number of units produced and sold in one day and that daily profit is daily revenue less daily cost, write a program that calculates daily profit. Treat UNITS as an input variable, and print the daily revenue, daily cost, and daily profit. Don't forget to specify the first three steps in the four-step procedure. *Note:* Input data for this problem are provided in Exercise 14 of the next chapter.

39. **Blood Bank Inventory Problem.** Decision making relating to the management of physical inventories is an established area in the management sciences, which, in recent years has been applied increasingly in semiprivate and public organizations.

Suppose that whenever a hospital replenishes its supply of a certain type of blood, it orders from a regional blood bank the amount indicated by the formula

$$q = \sqrt{2 \cdot c \cdot d / h}$$

where q is the number of pints of blood to order, c is the administrative and shipping cost (in dollars) of placing the order, d is the average weekly demand (usage) for this type of blood, and h is the cost (dollars per pint per week) of refrigerating the blood.

Also, it can be shown that the cost per week of this inventory policy is given by the formula

$$e = \sqrt{2 \cdot c \cdot h \cdot d}$$

where *e* is the expected cost (dollars) per week. Write a computer program that inputs values of *c*, *h*, and *d*, and determines how much blood to order and the cost of such a policy. Don't forget to specify the first three steps in the four-step procedure. *Note:* Input data for this problem are provided in Exercise 15 of the next chapter.

40. Forecasting Population Growth.   In recent years, the prediction of world population levels into the next century has been a concern of many political, environmental, and agricultural planners. The following equation can be used to predict future levels of world population.

$$p = c \cdot (1 + b - d)^n$$

where *p* is the predicted level of future population, *b* is the birthrate, *c* is the current level of population, *d* is the death rate, and *n* is the number of years into the future.

Write a program that can be used to predict future population level given the current level, the birthrate, the death rate, and the number of years into the future as input data. Don't forget to specify the first three steps in the four-step procedure. *Note:* Input data for this problem are provided in Exercise 16 of the next chapter.

41. Automobile Financing Problem.   Many consumer automobile loans require the borrower to pay the same amount of money to the lending institution each month throughout the life of the loan. The monthly payment is based on the amount borrowed (purchase price − trade-in of used car − down payment), the time required for repayment, and the interest rate. A lending institution uses the following formula to determine the car buyer's monthly payment.

$$a = i \cdot (p - d - t) \cdot \left(\frac{(1 + i)^m}{(1 + i)^m - 1} \right)$$

where *a* = monthly payments
   p = purchase price of car
   d = down payment
   t = trade-in allowance
   i = monthly interest rate
   m = total number of monthly payments

If the interest rate is expressed on an annual basis, then *i* in the above formula is replaced by *i*/12. Note that (*p* − *d* − *t*) is the amount to be borrowed.

a.   Write a program that determines monthly payments given purchase price, down payment, trade-in allowance, *annual* interest rate, and total number of monthly payments as input data. Include amount borrowed, total number of months, and annual *percent* interest rate in your output, along with the monthly payment. Also include the make and model of the automobile as part of your I/O.

b.   Design your program to also calculate and print:
   total amount paid over the life of the loan
   total interest paid over the life of the loan
   the ratio of total interest to total amount paid

Don't forget to specify the first three steps in the four-step procedure. *Note:* Input data for this problem are provided in Exercise 17 of the next chapter.

Running the Complete Computer Program

By now you should have written on paper at least one program from the problems at the end of the last chapter, which, presumably, you are impatient to run on the computer. In this chapter we give you that opportunity by describing and illustrating procedures for running FORTRAN programs in batch and remote-batch environments. *Note:* If you use a terminal to interface with the batch environment, you should study both Section 3.1 and Section 3.2.

3.1 RUNNING A FORTRAN PROGRAM IN A BATCH ENVIRONMENT

If you are using a terminal to interface with the batch environment, then this section and the next still apply to you. In this case, treat lines on the screen or paper as if they were the "image" of a punched card. Your instructor should explain this procedure.

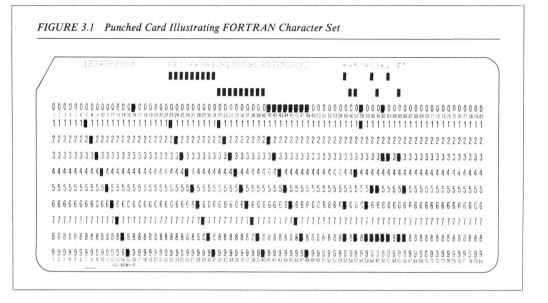

FIGURE 3.1   *Punched Card Illustrating FORTRAN Character Set*

Punched Cards

Computer programs run in a batch environment may use punched cards to transmit both the computer program and the input data to the computer.

The **punched card** illustrated in Figure 3.1 has 80 columns. Each column is capable of holding one character (a digit, a letter, or a special character). Rectangular holes punched in specific positions on the card represent a code of the different characters. Observe that a single hole is used for numbers (0–9), two holes for letters (A–Z), and one, two, or three holes for special characters.

As mentioned in Chapter 1, a *keypunch machine* is used to enter characters onto a punched card. Your instructor should give you a brief introduction to operating the type of keypunch available to you. Then find a keypunch machine and try your hand at it.

The Card Deck

To submit a FORTRAN program to a batch environment you need to prepare a **card deck,** which generally consists of four different types of punched cards.

1. Cards for FORTRAN instructions
2. Cards for comments
3. Cards for control
4. Cards for data

Each of these uses the standard 80-column punched card, but differs with respect to subject matter, purpose, and layout.

Instruction Cards. Each FORTRAN instruction is punched on one or more cards according to a prescribed set of rules that specify how the instruction is to be placed on the punched card. Figure 3.2 summarizes these rules, and Figure 3.3 illustrates the appearance of the FORTRAN *instruction cards* within the card deck for a revised student billing program. Notice that each statement must be punched anywhere between column 7 and column 72 inclusive. At this point, you should begin each statement in column 7, which avoids wasted space and is visually appealing. Later, we will show you how certain indentations further improve the appearance of a program.

FIGURE 3.2   *Rules for Placement of FORTRAN Instruction on Punched Card*

Columns on Punched Card	Use	Explanation
1–5	Statement number field	These may contain an unsigned, nonzero, integer constant that serves as a statement number.
6	Continuation field	This is used when a statement is too long to fit on the preceding card. Any character other than a blank or zero in column 6 identifies this card as a continuation of the preceding card.
7–72	Statement field	These contain the FORTRAN statement, except for the statement number.
73–80	Identification/ sequence field	These are used either to identify a particular program or to sequence cards within the program so that if cards are dropped, the deck can be reordered correctly. The contents of this field are ignored by the compiler.

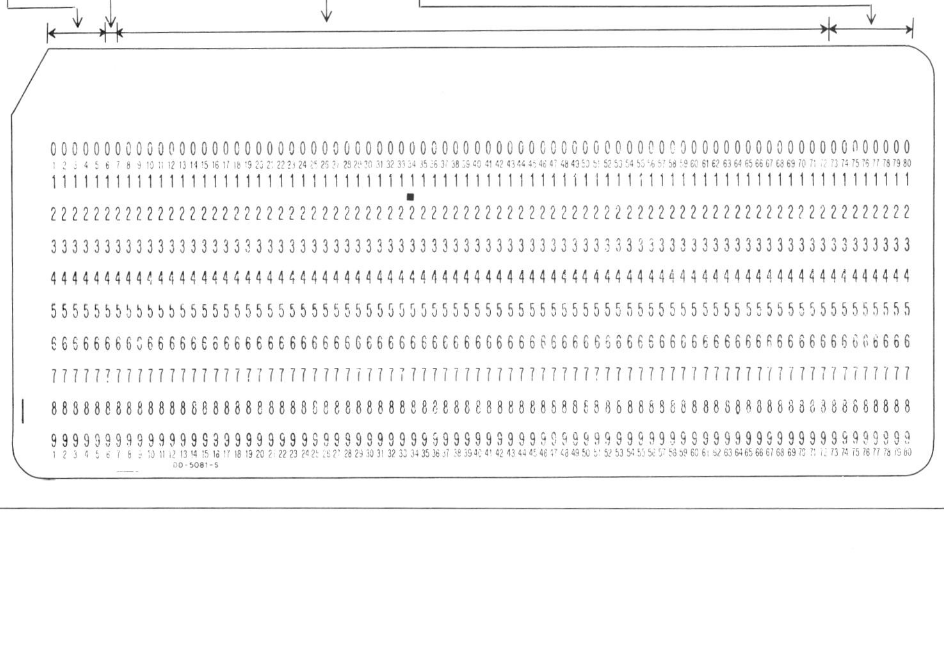

FIGURE 3.3   Complete Card Deck for Running the Revised Student Billing Program

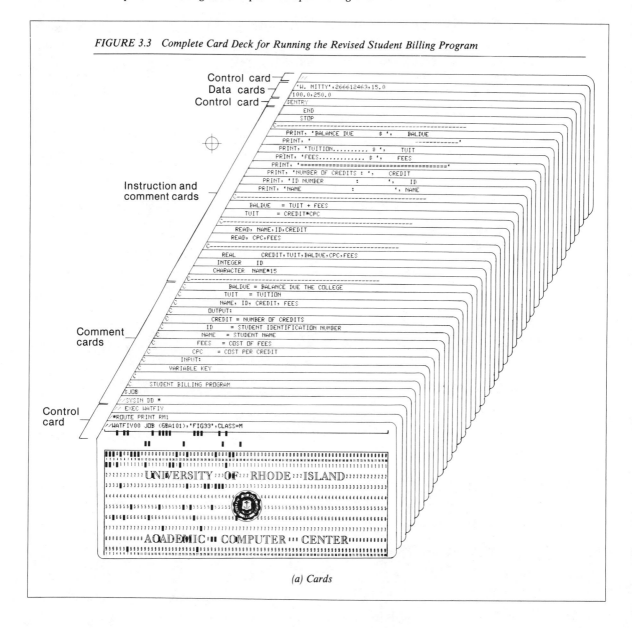

(a) Cards

The statement number field is used for labeling statements. The instruction cards in Figure 3.3 do not use this field, as we do not have a need for statement numbers until the next chapter.

The continuation field described in Figure 3.2 is not utilized by the instruction cards in Figure 3.3, since no statement is too long for one card. WATFIV allows up to 5 successive continuation lines (cards), unless changed by your computing center.

Finally, columns 73 through 80 of Figure 3.3 are left blank. The use of this identifica-

FIGURE 3.3   *Continued*

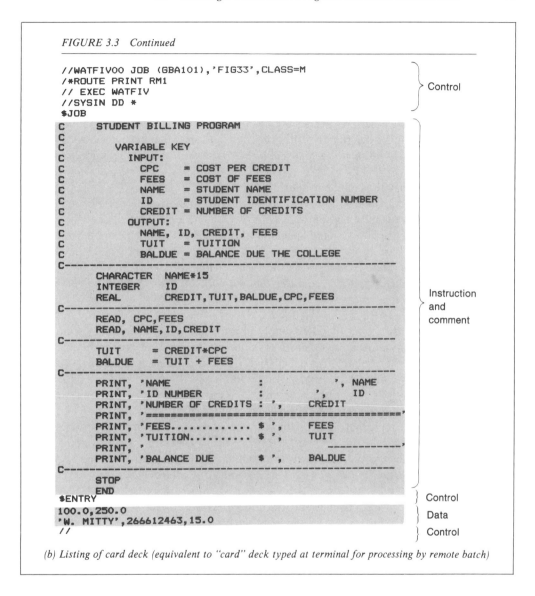

```
//WATFIV00 JOB (GBA101),'FIG33',CLASS=M      ⎫
/*ROUTE PRINT RM1                            ⎬ Control
// EXEC WATFIV                               ⎪
//SYSIN DD *                                 ⎭
$JOB
C       STUDENT BILLING PROGRAM
C
C
C       VARIABLE KEY
C         INPUT:
C           CPC    = COST PER CREDIT
C           FEES   = COST OF FEES
C           NAME   = STUDENT NAME
C           ID     = STUDENT IDENTIFICATION NUMBER
C           CREDIT = NUMBER OF CREDITS
C         OUTPUT:
C           NAME, ID, CREDIT, FEES
C           TUIT   = TUITION
C           BALDUE = BALANCE DUE THE COLLEGE
C-----------------------------------------------------------
        CHARACTER   NAME*15
        INTEGER     ID
        REAL        CREDIT,TUIT,BALDUE,CPC,FEES
C-----------------------------------------------------------
        READ, CPC,FEES
        READ, NAME,ID,CREDIT
C-----------------------------------------------------------
        TUIT      = CREDIT*CPC
        BALDUE    = TUIT + FEES
C-----------------------------------------------------------
        PRINT, 'NAME               :            ', NAME
        PRINT, 'ID NUMBER          :          ',   ID
        PRINT, 'NUMBER OF CREDITS : ',    CREDIT
        PRINT, '==========================================='
        PRINT, 'FEES............. $ ',    FEES
        PRINT, 'TUITION.......... $ ',    TUIT
        PRINT, '                         --------------'
        PRINT, 'BALANCE DUE       $ ',    BALDUE
C-----------------------------------------------------------
        STOP
        END
$ENTRY
100.0,250.0
'W. MITTY',266612463,15.0
//
```

Instruction
and
comment

Control

Data

Control

(b) Listing of card deck (equivalent to "card" deck typed at terminal for processing by remote batch)

tion/sequence field is optional; in most cases, you probably will not require it. Many commercial programs use it, but you should have no need for it.

Have you been wondering about the *use of blank spaces in FORTRAN statements?* With the exception of blanks within character constants, the compiler ignores blank spaces. For example, you need not be concerned about the number of blank spaces between NAME, ID, and CREDIT in the READ list, or around equal signs and arithmetic operators in assignment statements. *Use blank spaces simply to improve readability.* It's even permissible to embed blank spaces within key words, such as RE AD, but we don't recommend it since it detracts from readability.

Comment Cards.   Each card that has a C punched in column 1 is known as a *comment card* or *comment line.* Thus the comment cards in Figure 3.3 identify this program as "Student Billing Program," describe the variables, and segment the FORTRAN code for better readability.

Comment lines are useful for program **documentation.** This means that they can be used to describe programs, identify sections of programs, explain logic, and define variables. In fact, the entire description under Step 1 in the four-step procedure and the pseudocode version in Step 2 can be incorporated in a program by using comment lines. At a minimum, *each program you write should include comment lines that identify the program and describe symbolic names.*

Note that the comment lines made up of dashes effectively segment the program into "blocks" of related instructions. This small effort improves the style of the program, which facilitates readability and any subsequent maintenance (changes). See the listing in Figure 3.3(b) to realize how visually appealing this is, since it's difficult to appreciate this point by looking at a card deck.

You can place comment cards anywhere within the set of instruction cards, as they are ignored by the compiler. Also, *after the first column, the remaining 79 columns of the comment card can be used.*

Control Cards.   *Control cards* supply information to the operating system regarding user identification number, user name, expected processing time, programming language, and other factors. These are often called **JCL** (job control language) **cards.**

Control cards are *not* part of the FORTRAN language: moreover, the specific control cards necessary to run a program vary from computer center to computer center. All computer centers, however, require the use of control cards; otherwise, the essential information they supply would not be available for the operating system to do its job. Typically, two WATFIV control cards are included in the deck. They are the $JOB and $ENTRY cards, which precede the WATFIV program and card data, respectively. *Your instructor will provide you with additional information concerning the control cards for your computer center.*

Data Cards.   Most computer programs are designed to "read" data from an external source such as punched cards. For example, in the program of Figure 3.3, the data for NAME, ID, and CREDIT are not part of the FORTRAN program. Instead, the program contains a READ instruction to transfer the student data from a punched card to computer memory. In general, cards that contain data for processing by a READ statement are called *data cards.*

The placement of data on a punched card does not follow the rules specified for placing a FORTRAN instruction on a punched card. *Data may be punched in columns 1 through 80.*

Data cards must physically follow the instruction cards that make up the entire FORTRAN program, since the instruction cards must be processed first by the card reader in order for the program to *compile.* If the program compiles without errors, then the computer begins *executing* or "running" the program; that is, it carries out your executable instructions in the same sequence given by the cards.

Once again, notice how data items are processed. First, look at the two READ statements and two lines of data in Figure 3.3(b). Now, execution of the first READ statement stores 100.0 in CPC and 250.0 in FEES. Execution of the second READ statement stores W. MITTY in NAME, 266612463 in ID, and 15.0 in CREDIT. Note that the comma sep-

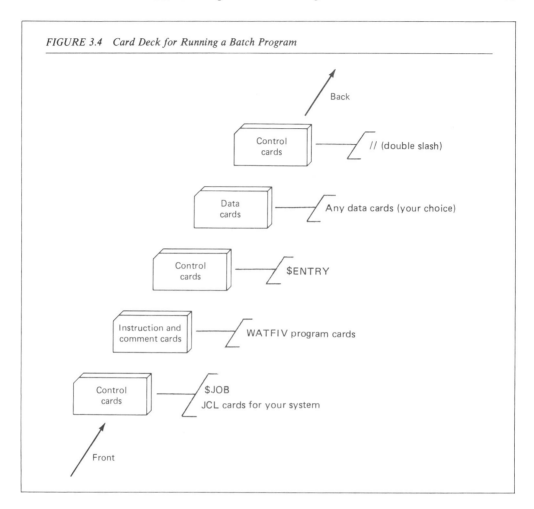

FIGURE 3.4   *Card Deck for Running a Batch Program*

arates two successive data items within the same data card. *Besides the comma, one or more blanks can be used to separate data items that are to be input through a list-directed READ statement. Note that character values must be enclosed in apostrophes when input through list-directed READ statements. Also, each time the computer executes a READ statement, a new data card is processed.*

Process of Running the Program

The general setup for a card deck is illustrated by Figure 3.4. Once again, however, we remind you that the nature and placement of control cards is specific to each system. Figure 3.5 describes the process of running a FORTRAN program in a batch environment. Figure 3.6 illustrates **computer printouts** when the card deck of Figure 3.3 is submitted to a computer.[1]

---

[1] Most likely your computer is different. Read on, however, since the general discussion still applies to you.

FIGURE 3.5 *Process of Running a FORTRAN Program in a Batch Environment*

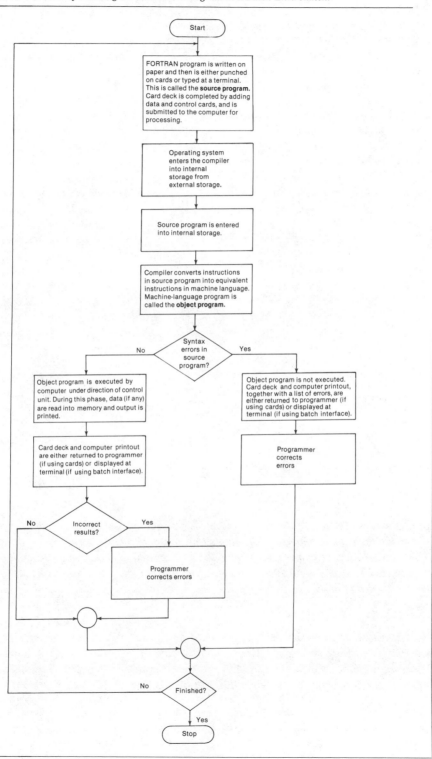

FIGURE 3.6   Computer Printout for Card Deck of Figure 3.3

```
        $JOB
        C        STUDENT BILLING PROGRAM
        C
        C            VARIABLE KEY
        C            INPUT:
        C               CPC    = COST PER CREDIT
        C               FEES   = COST OF FEES
        C               NAME   = STUDENT NAME
        C               ID     = STUDENT IDENTIFICATION NUMBER
        C               CREDIT = NUMBER OF CREDITS
        C            OUTPUT:
        C               NAME, ID, CREDIT, FEES
        C               TUIT   = TUITION
        C               BALDUE = BALANCE DUE THE COLLEGE
        C--------------------------------------------------------
      1         CHARACTER   NAME*15
      2         INTEGER    ID
      3         REAL        CREDIT,TUIT,BALDUE,CPC,FEES
        C--------------------------------------------------------
      4         READ, CPC,FEES
      5         READ, NAME,ID,CREDIT
        C--------------------------------------------------------
      6         TUIT    = CREDIT*CPC
      7         BALDUE  = TUIT + FEES
        C--------------------------------------------------------
      8         PRINT, 'NAME                 :            ', NAME
      9         PRINT, 'ID NUMBER            :          ',    ID
     10         PRINT, 'NUMBER OF CREDITS : ',    CREDIT
     11         PRINT, '================================='
     12         PRINT, 'FEES.............. $ ',    FEES
     13         PRINT, 'TUITION........... $ ',    TUIT
     14         PRINT, '               ------------'
     15         PRINT, 'BALANCE DUE       $ ',    BALDUE
        C--------------------------------------------------------
     16         STOP
     17         END
        $ENTRY
```

Line numbers added by system →

(brace) Listing

```
NAME        :           W. MITTY
ID NUMBER   :           266612463
NUMBER OF CREDITS :     15.0000000
==================================
FEES.............. $      250.0000000
TUITION........... $     1500.0000000
                        ------------
BALANCE DUE       $     1750.0000000
```

(brace) Output

```
STATEMENTS EXECUTED=       12
CORE USAGE          OBJECT CODE=     1008 BYTES,ARRAY AREA=        0 BYTES
TOTAL AREA AVAILABLE= 100352  BYTES
DIAGNOSTICS         NUMBER OF ERRORS=        0, NUMBER OF WARNINGS=      0
NUMBER OF EXTENSIONS=      0
COMPILE TIME=     0.05 SEC,EXECUTION TIME=      0.01 SEC,     13.31.32
        C$STOP
```

(brace) Technical matter

In general, computer printouts have three distinct segments, assuming that errors are absent.

1. Listing
2. Output
3. Technical matter

The **listing** is a printed copy of the FORTRAN program. This is simply a convenience which is especially useful when you are debugging or modifying a program. The **output** is printed matter based on the execution of PRINT statements in the program. **Technical matter** includes the technical information on control cards and other information, such as amount of memory and CPU time that was utilized. For example, the program in Figure 3.6 used 0.06 second of CPU time to compile and execute.

Note that the value of the integer variable ID is printed without a decimal point, whereas the values of the real variables CREDIT, FEES, TUIT, and BALDUE are printed with decimal points. You should confirm that all output values are correct.

Also, note how we aligned the output of disparate data types (NAME, ID, and CREDIT) by varying the blank spaces within the single quotes in lines 8–10 of the program. Try to design attractive output, as it enhances readability (and most likely your grade). Doing so will take some trial-and-error effort on your part. Later on, Module B will facilitate this process for you (we think).

Finally, note that the input data punched on data cards do not directly appear anywhere on the computer printout. These data can be printed out only through PRINT statements, which is what we did with NAME, ID, CREDIT, and FEES.

Multiple Statements per Card

WATFIV allows the placement of more than one statement per card or line, where statements are separated by semicolons and appear within columns 7 to 72. For example, in Figure 3.6 we could have replaced lines 4 and 5 by

```
READ, CPC,FEES ;   READ, NAME,ID,CREDIT
```

All other factors equal, a program with multiple statements realizes some compile time and storage efficiencies over equivalent programs that strictly use one statement per card or line; however, the readability of programs with multiple statements is often compromised. For this reason, we suggest the use of multiple statements only under situations where readability is either enhanced or unaffected, as in

```
STOP ;   END
```

or

```
S1 = 0 ;   S2 = 0 ;   ANS = 'YES'
```

or

```
S1 = S2 = 0 ;   ANS = 'YES'
```

Follow-up Exercises

Prepare and submit a card deck on your particular batch system for the exercises below.

1. **Student Billing Program.**   First submit the job in part a; then make the necessary changes and submit the job in part b.
    a. Prepare the same program as that in Figure 3.3, but input 18.5 credits and whatever name and ID number you wish. Confirm that your output is correct.
    b. Prepare the same program as that in Figure 3.3, but type CREDIT and all other numeric variables as integer. Use the same data input as the example, with one change: Include dashes in the student identification (Social Security) number, that is, 266-61-2463. How must you type ID? What are the advantages of typing the computational variables integer? The disadvantages?
2. **Bank Savings Program.**   Prepare and submit the same program as in Section 2.9 on page 71. Use 1000.0 for PRIN, 0.015 for RATE, and 4 for NUM. Confirm that your output is correct by hand calculation. Repeat for the same PRIN and RATE values but change NUM to 20.

3.2
RUNNING A FORTRAN PROGRAM IN A REMOTE-BATCH ENVIRONMENT

The term **remote batch** refers to a computer system that allows the entry of programs and data, their submission for execution, and their output at a location that is physically removed from the computer center. Typically, this is accomplished via terminals, card readers, and line printers. For example, if a remote job entry (RJE) unit is available, you could prepare your card deck at a keypunch, walk over to a card reader and load the deck yourself, press a button, and await printout at the attached line printer.

The use of an RJE unit is little different from the traditional submission and retrieval of jobs at the dispatch desk of a computer center. For our purposes, we will use the term *remote batch* or **batch interface** to mean the following procedure:

We access the computer through a (hard-copy or video display) terminal.
We key in the "card deck" (control lines, program lines, and data lines) at the terminal as if each line is the 80-column image of a card.
We type certain "system commands" to get our job executed and to receive printout either at the same terminal or at a nearby line printer.

In fact, with your own microcomputer or terminal and a modem (a device for transmission of computer signals over telephone lines), you could submit remote-batch jobs from the comfort of your home. As you will see, this approach to batch processing is superior to the use of keypunches and cards, particularly with respect to the preparation, submission, and editing of programs.

System Commands

In remote batch you communicate with the computer by entering your program at a terminal, through which information is transmitted over either a telephone line or a cable to the computer. To interact with the operating system when you are at the terminal requires the use of a set of commands called **system commands.** Among other things, system commands allow you to run the program, list the program, and save the program for future recall. Therefore, when you develop and run programs in a remote-batch environment, you will have a set of system commands to learn in addition to the FORTRAN instructions and JCL.

Unfortunately, system commands are not universal, which means that they differ from one system to another. *Your instructor, therefore, must provide you with the system commands that are specific to your system.*

Work Area versus Secondary Storage Area

The first step in using a remote-batch system is "signing on." This means that you must type your assigned identification (user) code, which is then validated by the operating system. If your identification code is acceptable, *the operating* system assigns you a portion of memory, which we call the **work area** or **workspace.** In fact, each user currently utilizing the system is assigned a separate work area. The purpose of the work area is to enter and modify your FORTRAN program.

Once you "sign off" the system, the program in your work area is "erased." For this reason, each user also has access to **secondary storage** (usually magnetic disk), to save programs from the work area. These "saved" programs are stored in your **library.** In other words, your library saves you the trouble of having to retype programs that you previously entered into your work area.

Illustration

In this section we illustrate a remote-batch session on IBM's CALL-MVS operating system. *If you use a different system, your system will not operate exactly as shown in the illustration.* In this case, just pay attention to the principles, since these are universal. *Your instructor will discuss the appropriate modifications for your system.*

The program we use is an abbreviated version of the student billing program on page 79.

In what follows on page 88, boxed segments indicate the computer run and marginal notes describe the corresponding boxed segment. To point out clearly the interactions between the user and the computer, all information typed by the computer is shaded; information typed by the user is not shaded.

Line Numbers.   Note that, as the "card deck" is entered at the terminal, each line (whether control, FORTRAN instruction, comment, or data) is preceded by a **line number.** These numbers, which typically run from one to five digits in length, are used to sequence the card images. After a program is entered and before it is executed, the operating system rearranges the lines in the work area from lowest to highest number. In other words, the lines can be entered "out of order," but the computer executes in the desired sequence according to the line numbers. This feature makes it convenient to insert lines into an existing program. For example, suppose we inadvertently omit the REAL statement in the illustration and realize this once the END statement has been typed. We can simply "insert" the REAL statement by typing it after the END statement and giving it a line number that numerically falls between the line numbers of the INTEGER statement and the next statement (between 190 and 200). Also note that we have incremented line numbers by at least 10, that is, each line number changes by no less than 10. This allows room to insert new lines at some future time, should it be necessary to do so. Finally, at least one blank space must separate your line from your line number.

More on System Commands. The system commands we have illustrated represent a small subset of the many commands available for a typical system. For example, variations of edit commands exist for simultaneously making changes in different parts of the program, for merging two or more program files, for relocating portions of a program within the same program, and for finding the occurrence of specific text within a program. Ask your instructor about the system commands on your system.

Follow-up Exercises

Prepare and submit a job program on your particular remote-batch system for the exercises below.

3. **Student Billing Program.** First submit the job in part a; then make the necessary changes and submit the job in part b.
   a. Duplicate our illustration, but input 18.5 credits and whatever name and ID number you wish. Confirm that your output is correct.
   b. Submit the same program as in the illustration but type CREDIT and all other numeric variables as integer. Use the same data input as the example, with one change: Include dashes in the student identification (Social Security) number, that is, 266-61-2463, and print this number as part of the output. How must you type ID? What are the advantages of typing the computational variables integer? The disadvantages?
4. **Bank Savings Program.** Prepare and submit the same program as in Section 2.9 on page 71. Use 1000.0 for PRIN, 0.015 for RATE, and 4 for NUM. Confirm that your output is correct by hand calculation. Repeat for the same PRIN and RATE values but change NUM to 20.

3.3
DEBUGGING PROGRAMS

Debugging is the process of detecting and correcting errors. Much of your time, in fact, will be spent on this process. To help you along, we now define general types of errors and indicate how you go about debugging such errors.

1.

Entry of user identification and password for signing on. Password entry is printed over by the computer for security purposes. *Note:* Each time you finish typing a line, you must depress the carriage return key on the terminal.

The computer types READY to indicate that it has accepted our entry and is ready for us to do something next.

```
USER NUMBER, PASSWORD---
gba101, ᴴᴴᴴᴴᴴᴴᴴ
READY
```

2.

The entire "job program" (control lines, FORTRAN program, and data lines) is entered. Generally, we follow the same "placement rules" used for punching cards, except we begin each line with a line number followed by a space. The second position following the line number defines column 1 of the "card." Thus, the C in line 260 is located in column 1 and PRINT in line 270 begins in column 7.

```
100 //WATFIVOO JOB (GBA101),'HARVEY CORE',CLASS=M
110 /*ROUTE PRINT RM1
120 // EXEC WATFIV
130 //SYSIN DD *
140 $JOB
150 C    STUDENT BILLING PROGRAM
160 C
170 C
180       CHARACTER NAME*15
190       INTEGER  ID
200 C
210       READ, CPC,FEES
220       REED, NAME,ID,CREDIT
230 C
240       TUIT   = CREDIT*CPC
250       BALDUE = TUIT + FEES
260 C
270       PRINT, 'NAME              :          ', NAME
280       PRINT, 'ID NUMBER         :          ', ID
290       PRINT, 'NUMBER OF CREDITS :          ', CREDIT
300       PRINT, '======================================='
310       PRINT, 'FEES.............. $ ', FEES
320       PRINT, 'TUITION........... $ ', TUIT
330       PRINT, '
340       PRINT, 'BALANCE DUE        $ ', BALDUE
350 C
360       STOP
370       END
380 $ENTRY
390 100.0,250.0
400 'W. MITTY',266612463,15.0
410 //
```

3.

System command for creating in the library a duplicate copy of job program in work area; job program now has been saved under the name FEE for recall at a later time.

```
save fee
```

4. Signing off system.

```
off
OFF AT 14:04
PROC. TIME....    0 SEC.
TERM. TIME....   20 MIN.
```

5. Logging on system at a later data.

```
USER NUMBER, PASSWORD----
gba101, ########
READY
```

6. System command for loading a copy of program FEE, which is taken from library and placed in work area.

```
load fee
READY
```

7. System command for listing at the terminal the job program that currently resides in the work area. Variations of the LIST command allow the listing of single lines and groupings of lines.

```
list
FEE    14:05   MON  13 JUN 83
100 //WATFIV00 JOB (GBA101),'HARVEY CORE',CLASS=M
110 /*ROUTE PRINT RM1
120 // EXEC WATFIV
130 //SYSIN DD *
140 $JOB
150 C      STUDENT BILLING PROGRAM
160 C
170 C
180        CHARACTER NAME*15
190        INTEGER   ID
200 C
210        READ, CPC,FEES
220        REED, NAME,ID,CREDIT
230 C
240        TUIT   = CREDIT*CPC
250        BALDUE = TUIT + FEES
260 C
270        PRINT, 'NAME                    :', ', NAME
280        PRINT, 'ID NUMBER                            ID
290        PRINT, 'NUMBER OF CREDITS :', ',     CREDIT
300        PRINT, '=======================   :
310        PRINT, 'FEES.............. $ ',    FEES
320        PRINT, 'TUITION........... $ ',    TUIT
330        PRINT, '====================
340        PRINT, 'BALANCE DUE       $ ',   BALDUE
350 C
360        STOP
370        END
380 $ENTRY
390 100.0,250.0
400 'W. MITTY',26661246 3,15.0
410 //
```

8.

```
195     real credit,tuit,baldue,cpc,fees
```

To edit a job program, the job program must be in the work area. We can add a statement simply by typing a line. The line number determines where it will be inserted.

9.

```
rep 220/reed/read
REPLACED 1
```

To change a line that has an error, the entire line can be retyped. The new line replaces the old lines within the work area. Alternatively, we can use editing commands to replace portions of one or more lines without having to retype entire lines. The command at left replaces REED with READ in line 220.

10.

```
delete 280 t 290
READY
```

We can delete a line simply by typing the appropriate line number immediately followed by a carriage return. Alternatively, we can use a system command to delete one or more lines (or a group of lines). At left we delete lines 280 through 290.

11.

```
list

FEE   14:09   MON  13 JUN 83
100 /WATFIVOO JOB (GBA101),'HARVEY CORE',CLASS=M
110 /*ROUTE PRINT RM1
120 // EXEC WATFIV
130 //SYSIN DD *
140 $JOB
150 C       STUDENT BILLING PROGRAM
160 C
170 C----
180     CHARACTER NAME*15
190     INTEGER  ID
195     REAL CREDIT,TUIT,BALDUE,CPC,FEES
200 C----
210     READ, CPC,FEES
220     READ, NAME,ID,CREDIT
```

This shows a listing of the job program currently residing in the work area, as edited in Boxes 8–10. Compared to the version in Box 7, this version includes line 195 (from Box 8), a correct line 220 (from Box 9), and deleted lines 280–290 (from Box 10).

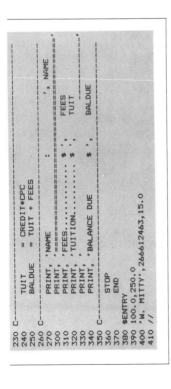

```
230 C------     TUIT    = CREDIT*CPC
240            BALDUE  = TUIT + FEES
250 C------
260 C------
270        PRINT,  'NAME            :              ', NAME
300        PRINT,  '=================================='
310        PRINT,  'FEES..........  $ ',  FEES
320        PRINT,  'TUITION.......  $ ',  TUIT
330        PRINT,  '------------------------------'
340        PRINT,  'BALANCE DUE     $ ',  BALDUE
350 C------
360        STOP
370        END
380 *ENTRY
390 100.0,250.0
400 'W. MITTY',266612463,15.0
410 //
```

The current version of FEE (the one in the work area) now replaces the old version in the library. A common mistake is to edit a program and then forget to save it. Also, to run a batch job, the program must have been saved in the library.

12.

```
save fee
READY
```

System command for submitting the job program to the batch system for execution. P1 is a parameter to request the computer printout as output to the terminal; otherwise, the printout is routed to the line printer. The operating system (OS) responds with a jobnumber and jobname.

13.

```
sub fee/p1
JOB #06 SUBMITTED WITH JOBNAME #GBA1016
```

System command to inquire about the status of a job. The OS responds that the job is completed.

14.

```
job 6

JOB  FILENAME  DATE     TIME   JOBNAME   JOB STATUS
#06  FEE       13JUN83  14:10  #GBA1016  COMPLETED
READY
```

15.

A special variation of the LOAD command retrieves the remote batch job from a disk file into the work area.

```
load 6,p1

LOAD COMPLETE
```

16.

The LIST command is used to print both the FORTRAN program listing and the output from the batch run. This is equivalent to Figure 3.6 (except for our modifications).

```
list

14:12  MON  13 JUN 83
00001        $JOB
00002  C
00003  C      STUDENT BILLING PROGRAM
00004  C
00005   1        CHARACTER  NAME*15
00006   2        INTEGER    ID
00007   3        REAL  CREDIT,TUIT,BALDUE,CPC,FEES
00008  C
00009   4        READ, CPC,FEES
00010   5        READ, NAME,ID,CREDIT
00011  C
00012   6        TUIT   = CREDIT*CPC
00013   7        BALDUE = TUIT + FEES
00014  C
00015   8        PRINT, "NAME          :        ", NAME
00016   9        PRINT,
00017  10        PRINT, "FEES.........: $ ", FEES
00018  11        PRINT, "TUITION......: $ ", TUIT
00019  12        PRINT,
00020  13        PRINT, "BALANCE DUE    $ ", BALDUE
00021  C
00022  14        STOP
00023  15        END
00024        $ENTRY
00025  NAME     :          W. MITTY
00026
00027  FEES.........: $     250.0000000
00028  TUITION......: $    1500.0000000
00029
00030  BALANCE DUE    $   1750.0000000
00031  STATEMENTS EXECUTED=        10
00032  CORE USAGE   OBJECT CODE=  100352 BYTES,TOTAL AREA AVAILABLE=  856 BYTES,ARRAY AREA=    0 BY
00033  DIAGNOSTICS  NUMBER OF ERRORS=       0,  NUMBER OF WARNINGS=
0, NUMBER OF EXTENSIONS=       0
   COMPILE TIME=   0.04 SEC,EXECUTION TIME=    0.01 SEC,    14.11
.00  MONDAY  13 JUN 83   WATFIV - MAR 1980 V2L0
00035          C$STOP
```

Output

17.

Session is over. Now it's your turn (after you have studied the commands for your system).

```
off

OFF AT 14:14
PROC. TIME...   0 SEC.
TERM. TIME...   9 MIN.
```

Error Detection and Correction

Any programming error can be classified into one of the following three categories.

1. Syntax error
2. Execution error
3. Logic error

A **syntax error** occurs when a FORTRAN instruction violates a rule of the FORTRAN language. When you make this type of error, your program will fail to compile, and the compiler will identify the incorrect instruction by an appropriate diagnostic message. Thus syntax errors are detected by the compiler during the compilation of the program. If a syntax error is found, it follows that the program never enters the execution phase.

Common syntax errors at this point in your programming development include the following.

1. Typing error, as when READ is typed as REED.
2. Variable name that exceeds the allowable number of characters (six in WATFIV). *Note:* A separate error message will be printed for each statement that contains this variable name.
3. Imbalance between the number of left parentheses and the number of right parentheses in an arithmetic expression.
4. Missing equal sign (=) in an assignment statement.
5. Arithmetic expression to the left of the equal sign in an assignment statement.
6. A violation of the rules for placing a statement on a card, as when the keyword END is punched within the first six columns of a card.
7. Forgetting to include an END statement.
8. Forgetting to use an asterisk for multiplication. (This one might get by the compiler but will then show up as either an execution or logic error.)
9. Omitting required commas in READ and PRINT statements.

Once you determine the exact nature of your syntax error (with the help of the error message), you simply replace the incorrect instruction with a syntactically correct instruction.

Your program begins executing only after it is free of syntax errors. Unfortunately, a second type of error can occur after the compilation phase: An **execution error** is one that takes place during the execution of your program. Typically, when an execution error is encountered, an error message or code is printed and the computer terminates execution. Common execution errors include the following.

1. Incorrect data input, as when a letter is typed for numeric data input.
2. End-of-file condition, as when the computer attempts to execute a READ statement and a data item is not provided.
3. Improper numeric condition during the evaluation of an arithmetic expression; for example, you might attempt to divide by a variable that has the value zero in its storage location, or you might attempt to raise a negative real number to a real power, or you might attempt to take the square root of a negative value, or the value might exceed the range of values allowed (underflow or overflow). In the last case, some systems continue exe-

cution by assigning machine "infinity" (largest possible value) to the value that overflows and machine zero to the value that underflows, whereas other systems stop execution. WATFIV jobs get terminated for each of the above errors.

4. Initialization of variables, where **initialization** is a term that refers to the initial value taken on by a variable. Just before execution, some systems assign arbitrary values to all variables, whereas other systems initialize all variables to zero. To illustrate the possible difficulties, consider the following statement.

        N = N + 1

Now, suppose that prior to this statement you have not *explicitly* assigned a value to N. One of three things will happen when the system executes this statement.

  a. An arbitrary (wrong) value is used for the N to the right of the equal sign.
  b. A value of zero is used for the N to the right of the equal sign.
  c. The system treats the initial contents of N as undefined and aborts execution. (This is the usual WATFIV job response.)

Thus whenever a variable is used in an arithmetic expression it needs to have been previously defined (explicitly assigned a value) either through an assignment statement or through an input statement. For example, if we want N to have an initial value of zero, then earlier in the program we should write

        N = 0

Generally, it is more difficult to determine the exact location and nature of an execution error than of a syntax error, for several reasons: Execution errors tend to be system-dependent; execution error messages may be more ambiguous than syntax error messages in locating and diagnosing errors; and the cause of an execution error may be due to faulty program logic, which is related to the third category of errors.

If your program runs but gives you unexpected, unwanted, or erroneous output, then you may assume that a **logic error** exists. Common logic errors include the following.

1. No output. Did you forget to include PRINT statements?
2. Wrong numeric results.
  a. Are the input data correct?
  b. Are the arithmetic expressions and assignment statements correct? In particular, check the sequence of arithmetic calculations within arithmetic expressions.
  c. Is the program logic correct? For example, are the statements in proper sequence?
  d. Have any statements been omitted?
3. Unintentional, displeasing, or unaligned output. Output from a program should be labeled, easy to read, and visually appealing. Before writing down your PRINT statements, you should map out your output on a sheet of paper. You might be surprised at how much effort will be saved by this practice. By the way, once you're assigned Modules B and D, you will (theoretically) be able to control the placement of output exactly.

Here is some emphatic advice: *Just because your program runs (that is, you get results) it does not mean your program is correct—check your results for logic errors against a set of known results.* We cannot overemphasize the importance of this advice. In Step 4 of the four-step procedure, *always* validate your program under varying conditions using a set of test data for which you already know the correct results.

Classic Debugging Techniques

In your efforts to debug execution and logic errors, you might try the following **classic debugging techniques.**

1. *Roleplaying the computer.* Pretend that you're the computer and begin "executing" your program line by line. As you do this, enter data into boxes that represent storage locations. You will be surprised at how many errors you can find this way. Really. You should do this with every program you write.

2. *Mirror or echo printing.* To check your data input for errors, place a PRINT statement immediately after each READ statement. The paired READ and PRINT statements must have identical variable lists. Once you have confirmed that the input data are correct, remove these statements.

3. *Diagnostic PRINT (trace) statements.* Place temporary PRINT statements at strategic points in your program. These should print the values of important variables as the calculating sequence evolves. In other words, these PRINT statements provide you intermediate results that may be helpful in tracing what, where, and when something went wrong. When the error is corrected, remove these PRINT statements.

4. *Programming technique.* You will avoid many errors if you carefully develop the first three steps of our four-step procedure. Get in the habit now.

5. *Experience.* Learn by your mistakes. Experience is a classic teacher.

6. *Attitude.* Debugging can be fun. Finding errors and correcting them can be a very satisfying experience. Perhaps you will become the greatest debugging sleuth in computer history.

Illustration

Figure 3.7 shows a listing for the student billing program that purposely incorporates syntax, execution, and logic errors. The syntax error messages are those given by the compiler.[2] The compiler has printed several syntax error messages, each of which begins with ***ERROR***. Note that each error message is printed immediately following the incorrect line of instruction.

As you can see, some error messages are helpful, whereas others are either ambiguous or misleading. The following description should clarify the nature of these errors.

Line	Syntax Error
1–3	No syntax errors
4	READ misspelled as REED
5–6	No syntax errors
7	Arithmetic expression to left of equal sign
8–10	No syntax errors
11	Missing comma following PRINT
12–16	No syntax errors
17	END punched in columns 1–3 instead of columns 7–9. Note that this last error generated both error and warning messages.

---

[2] It's also possible to make an error in preparing your control cards, in which case your program will not execute. **Control card errors** are specific to the system you're using, so carefully review the instructions you received for preparing control cards.

FIGURE 3.7   Illustration of Syntax Errors

```
      C       STUDENT BILLING PROGRAM (WITH SYNTAX ERRORS)
      C
      C       VARIABLE KEY
      C         INPUT:
      C           CPC    = COST PER CREDIT
      C           FEES   = COST OF FEES
      C           NAME   = STUDENT NAME
      C           ID     = STUDENT IDENTIFICATION NUMBER
      C           CREDIT = NUMBER OF CREDITS
      C         OUTPUT:
      C           NAME, ID, CREDIT, FEES
      C           TUIT   = TUITION
      C           BALDUE = BALANCE DUE THE COLLEGE
      C ----------------------------------------------------
    1       CHARACTER   NAME*15
    2       INTEGER     ID
    3       REAL        CREDIT,TUIT,BALDUE,CPC,FEES
      C ----------------------------------------------------
    4       REED, CPC,FEES
***ERROR***  UNDECODEABLE STATEMENT
    5       READ, NAME,ID,CREDIT
      C ----------------------------------------------------
    6       TUIT    = CREDIT**CPC
    7       TUIT - FEES = BALDUE
      C ----------------------------------------------------
***ERROR***  ILLEGAL QUANTITY ON LEFT OF EQUALS SIGN
    8       PRINT, 'NAME              :         ', NAME
    9       PRINT, 'ID NUMBER         :         ',    ID
   10       PRINT, 'NUMBER OF CREDITS : ',      CREDIT
   11       PRINT '============================================'
***ERROR***  EXPECTING OPERATOR BUT '==== WAS FOUND
   12       PRINT, 'FEES.............. $ ',     FEES
   13       PRINT, 'TUITION........... $ ',     TUIT
   14       PRINT, '                             ------------'
   15       PRINT, 'BALANCE DUE       $ ',      BALDUE
      C ----------------------------------------------------
   16       STOP
   17  END
***ERROR***  INVALID CHARACTERS IN COL 1-5. STATEMENT NUMBER
IGNORED.PROBABLE CAUSE:STATEMENT PUNCHED TO LEFT OF COLUMN 7
**WARNING**  MISSING END STATEMENT;END STATEMENT GENERATED
```

The above syntax errors were corrected by repunching a new card for each statement in error and then resubmitting the job.[3] This time the program compiled without syntax errors; however, an execution error was encountered, as illustrated in Figure 3.8. The message "X .GT. 174.673" indicates that the computation of a real value exceeds the maximum value permitted by this computer (overflow). Line 6 in the listing illustrates the problem: we have mistakenly used exponentiation instead of multiplication. This error was corrected and the job was resubmitted once again.

Figure 3.9 illustrates a run with no syntax or execution errors, but with two logic errors. Note that the output for BALDUE is $14750, instead of the expected $1750. The first logic

---

[3] If you're using a terminal to submit batch jobs (as we actually are), then errors are corrected at the terminal by replacing incorrect lines with correct lines, and the job is resubmitted at the terminal. Ask your instructor about your system's editing capabilities, which greatly simplify program modifications.

FIGURE 3.8   *Illustration of Execution Error*

```
            C        STUDENT BILLING PROGRAM (wITH EXECUTICN ERRCR)
            C
            C        VARIABLE KEY
            C          INPUT:
            C            CPC    = COST PER CREDIT
            C            FEES   = COST OF FEES
            C            NAME   = STUDENT NAME
            C            ID     = STUDENT IDENTIFICATION NUMBER
            C            CREDIT = NUMBER CF CREDITS
            C          OUTPUT:
            C            NAME, ID, CREDIT, FEES
            C            TUIT   = TUITION
            C            BALDUE = BALANCE DUE THE CCLLEGE
            C-------------------------------------------------------
   1                 CHARACTER   NAME*15
   2                 INTEGER     ID
   3                 REAL        CREDIT,TUIT,BALDUE,CPC,FEES
            C-------------------------------------------------------
   4                 READ, CPC,FEES
   5                 READ, NAME,ID,CREDIT            Cause of execution error
            C-------------------------------------------------------
   6                 TUIT      = CREDIT**CPC
   7                 BALDUE    = TUIT - FEES
            C-------------------------------------------------------
   8                 PRINT, 'NAME                 :            ', NAME
   9                 PRINT, 'ID NUMBER            :            ',    ID
   10                PRINT, 'NUMBER OF CREDITS : ',        CREDIT
   11                PRINT, '================================='
   12                PRINT, 'FEES.............. $ ',      FEES
   13                PRINT, 'TUITION........... $ ',      TUIT
   14                PRINT, '                   ------------'
   15                PRINT, 'BALANCE DUE        $ ',    BALDUE
            C-------------------------------------------------------
   16                STOP
   17                END                              Execution error message
                 $ENTRY
   ***ERROR***   X .GT. 174.673 FOR EXP CR DEXP OF X
                 PROGRAM WAS EXECUTING LINE      6 IN ROUTINE M/PROG WHEN
   TERMINATION OCCURRED
```

---

error is easily uncovered by the echo print in line 5 for CPC and FEES. It appears that the value for FEES was input properly, but 1000.0 instead of 100.0 was input for CPC, which can be further confirmed by examining the input data (not shown). The second logic error is identified by noting that FEES was subtracted rather than added to TUIT in the assignment statement for BALDUE. Correcting these two errors and removing the echo print results in the run illustrated by Figure 3.6 on page 83.

Follow-up Exercises

5. Duplicate our debugging illustration on your system, noting any differences.
6. Create your own debugging illustration by experimenting with the Bank Savings Program in Section 2.9, page 71. Try some of the syntax, execution, and logic errors described on pages 93 and 94.

FIGURE 3.9   *Illustration of Logic Errors*

```
C          STUDENT BILLING PROGRAM (WITH LOGIC ERRORS)
C
C             VARIABLE KEY
C               INPUT:
C                 CPC    = COST PER CREDIT
C                 FEES   = COST OF FEES
C                 NAME   = STUDENT NAME
C                 ID     = STUDENT IDENTIFICATION NUMBER
C                 CREDIT = NUMBER OF CREDITS
C               OUTPUT:
C                 NAME, ID, CREDIT, FEES
C                 TUIT   = TUITION
C                 BALDUE = BALANCE DUE THE COLLEGE
C ---------------------------------------------------------
1          CHARACTER   NAME*15
2          INTEGER     ID
3          REAL        CREDIT,TUIT,BALDUE,CPC,FEES
C ---------------------------------------------------------
4          READ, CPC,FEES
5          PRINT, 'ECHO---> CPC =',CPC,' FEES =',FEES          <--
6          READ, NAME,ID,CREDIT
C ---------------------------------------------------------
7          TUIT     = CREDIT*CPC
8          BALDUE   = TUIT - FEES    --- Cause of second logic error
C ---------------------------------------------------------
9          PRINT, 'NAME               :         ', NAME
10         PRINT, 'ID NUMBER          :         ',   ID
11         PRINT, 'NUMBER OF CREDITS  : ',        CREDIT
12         PRINT, '=================================='              Echo
13         PRINT, 'FEES............. $ ',         FEES               print
14         PRINT, 'TUITION.......... $ ',         TUIT
15         PRINT, '               ------------'
16         PRINT, 'BALANCE DUE      $ ',          BALDUE
C ---------------------------------------------------------
17         STOP
18         END                    --- Cause of first logic error
     $ENTRY
ECHO--->   CPC =        1000.0000000  FEES =        250.0000000  <--
NAME                 :      W. MITTY
ID NUMBER            :      266612463
NUMBER OF CREDITS    :      15.0000000
====================================
FEES............. $         250.0000000             Incorrect values
TUITION.......... $       15000.0000000
                  ------------
BALANCE DUE       $       14750.0000000
```

ADDITIONAL EXERCISES

7. Define or explain each of the following terms associated with batch environments.

punched card	computer printout
card deck	listing
instruction cards	source program
comment cards	object program
control cards	rules for placing instructions,
JCL cards	data, and comments
data cards	on punched cards

8. Define or explain each of the following terms associated with remote-batch environments.

remote batch
batch interface
system commands
work area
workspace
secondary storage area

library
line numbers
control (JCL) line
instruction line
comment line
data line

9. Define or explain each of the following terms.

execution
compilation
use of the blank character
documentation
debugging
syntax error
execution error

logic error
initialization
roleplaying the computer
mirror printing
echo printing
diagnostic PRINT
trace statement

10. **Debugging Problem.** Run the program below on your system *exactly* as shown. On the first run let the compiler identify syntax errors and then make the necessary corrections. On the second run let the operating system identify execution errors and then make the necessary corrections. Finish with an error-free run. Use the following data input: First try 4.2 for X and 0.0. for Y; next try −4.2 for X and 0.1 for Y; finally, try 4.2 for X and 0.1 for Y.

PROGRAM THAT ADDS, SUBTRACTS, MULTIPLIES, DIVIDES, AND EXPONEN-TIATES TWO NUMBERS

```
READ X,Y
SUMMATION = X + Y
SUB = X − Y
X•Y = MULT
DIV + X/Y
EXP = X••Y
PRINT,SUMMATION,SUB,MULT,DIV,EXP
```

11. **Precision.** Determine your system's precision by solving the exercises below.
    a. Write a simple program to determine how accurately you can express the value for pi (3.141592654 . . .) on your system. In the same program, store and output PI1 as a real variable and PI2 as a double-precision variable.
    b. Run the following program on your system using the following values for X: 50, 70, and 90; and for N: 15, 31, and 47.

```
READ, X,N
PRINT,10.0••X,2••N − 1
END
```

What are your system's limits for real and integer values?

c. Run the following program on your system:

```
INTEGER I,J,K
REAL A,B,C
DOUBLE PRECISION D,E,F
A = 500.6182
B = 500.618273
C = 9876543.26
PRINT, A,B,C,B•C
D = 500.6182
E = 500.618273
F = 9876543.26
PRINT, D,E,F,E•F
PRINT, A•C,A•F
I = 1234567890
J = 9876543210
K = 1234567890123
PRINT, I,J,K,I•J
END
```

Comment on the roundoff error associated with real arithmetic versus double-precision arithmetic. Did you get integer overflow on your system?

12. Temperature Conversion. Run the program of Exercise 36 in Chapter 2 on page 73. Determine the degree Celsius equivalents of -10, 0, 32, and 80 degrees Fahrenheit.

13. Area Problem. Run the program of Exercise 37 in Chapter 2 on page 73. What is the total cost of 500,000 container tops, where each top has a radius of 5 inches and costs $0.02 per square inch? What if the cost is $0.005 per square inch, all other things being the same?

14. Microeconomics Problem. Run the program of Exercise 38 in Chapter 2 on page 73. How many units should be produced to maximize profit? *Hint:* Try input values of 1, 2, 3, . . . , 10 for UNITS.

15. Blood Bank Inventory Problem. Run the program of Exercise 39 in Chapter 2 on page 73. How many units of blood should be ordered if it costs $50 to place an order, weekly demand averages 3000 pints, and it costs $0.20 per week per pint of blood to refrigerate? How much should be ordered if the refrigeration cost increases to $0.30? What is the expected cost per week for each of the above?

16. Forecasting Population Growth. Run the program of Exercise 40 in Chapter 2 on page 73. Predict the earth's population in the year 2000. The population in 1976 was approximately 4 billion.

   a. Assume a birthrate of 0.025 (2.5 percent) per year and a death rate of 0.009 (0.9 percent), both of which are expected to remain constant until the year 2000.

   b. How would your prediction change if the birthrate fell to 0.02? *Suggestion:* Input the 1976 population as a real constant having one digit (that is, as 4.). Why did we make this suggestion?

   c. How many years before the earth's population doubles? Use the birth and death rates given in part a. *Hint:* Try different input values for *n* and observe the output values for *p*.

**d. Go to your library and look up comparable current population level, birthrate, and death rate figures for a country or state. Make some predictions.

17.   Automobile Financing Problem.   Run the program of Exercise 41 in Chapter 2 on page 74 for a car costing $7200, with a down payment of $1000, a trade-in allowance of $1200, a financing life of 60 months, and an *annual* interest rate of 0.15. What are the effects if the down payment is increased to $2000? What if the life of the loan changes to 36 months, the interest rate drops one percentage point (0.01), and the down payment remains at $1000?

Control Structures and the DO-Loop

Programmers often consider the programs they write their own creations without regard for others who have to modify them. The programs work, but they may include confusing or tricky logic that may be understood only by the original programmer. This increases the costs and creates difficulties whenever it's necessary to modify the programs. In addition, without a standard method of solving a problem, a programmer may spend more time than necessary in determining the appropriate solution and developing the program. To counter these trends a concept known as structured programming has received widespread acceptance.

Structured programming is an approach to designing, coding, and testing programs that is based on a body of principles that promotes well-thought-out, readable code and reliable execution. The basic foundation of structured programming is that any program can be written using three logical structures.

1. Sequence structure
2. Decision structure
3. Loop structure

These so-called **control structures** can be used to describe the logic of any program completely, as we illustrate in the next four sections.

4.1 SEQUENCE STRUCTURE

The **sequence structure** consists of a sequence of instructions that occur one after the other *without* any transfer of control. When **transfer of control** or **branching** occurs, the computer interrupts the normal sequential execution of a program and branches (jumps or transfers control) to some other *executable* statement in the program that is not necessarily the next instruction in the normal sequence.

Figure 4.1 illustrates the concept of the sequence structure for the student billing program. Up to now, the sequence structure is the only type of control structure we have presented.

The connectors (circle symbols) in the flowchart allow us to focus on the structure of interest. *The first connector defines the beginning of or entry point to the structure; the second connector defines the end of or exit point from the structure.*

4.2 DECISION STRUCTURES

Decision structures consist of choices among alternatives based on the testing of *conditions*. In the two-alternative case, either a particular **block** (sequence of one or more statements) is to be executed if the condition is true, or an alternative block is to be executed if the condition is false. Figure 4.2a–b illustrates this two-choice structure or **IF-THEN-ELSE structure.** Note that the pseudocode version directly incorporates the terms IF, THEN, and ELSE; the flowchart version uses the *diamond symbol* to represent the test of a stated condition.

Sometimes we have a situation in which, if a condition is true, we execute a particular block; otherwise we continue in the program sequence. This is called the single-choice or **IF-THEN structure,** as illustrated in Figure 4.2c–d.

One example of the IF-THEN-ELSE structure is the calculation of tuition based on part-time (less than a cutoff of, say, 12 credits) versus full-time (12 credits or more) student status, as illustrated in Figure 4.3. The term *counter* refers to the fact that each block counts the number of students that are processed through that block. Note that the *pseudocode version indents the statements in each block to improve readability.*

More complicated decision structures are possible when more than two choices need to be made or more than one condition needs to be tested. We discuss these decision structures in the next chapter, together with methods of coding all decision structures in FORTRAN.

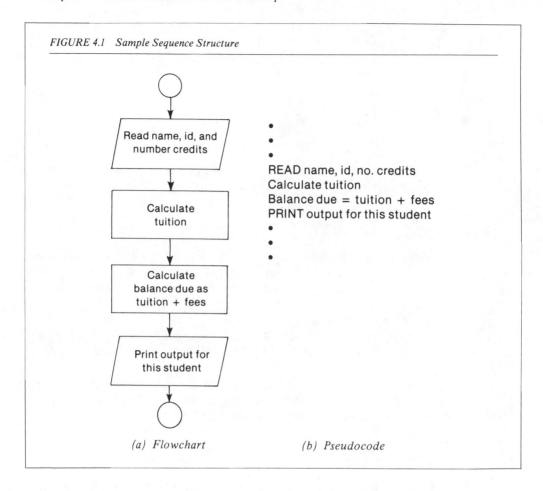

FIGURE 4.1   Sample Sequence Structure

Read name, id, and number credits

Calculate tuition

Calculate balance due as tuition + fees

Print output for this student

•
•
•
READ name, id, no. credits
Calculate tuition
Balance due = tuition + fees
PRINT output for this student
•
•
•

(a) Flowchart   *(b) Pseudocode*

4.3
LOOP STRUCTURES

The **loop structure** refers to the repeated execution of a sequence of instructions. This structure consists of two parts.

1. A **loop body,** which represents the sequence of statements that are to be repeated
2. A **loop control,** which specifies either the number of times a loop must be executed or the test condition under which the loop is to be terminated

Figure 4.4 represents the logic of the loop structure. In the **WHILE structure,** shown in Figure 4.4a, the first action is to test whether or not the body of the loop is to be executed. If the condition is true, then control passes to the body of the loop. After the statements within the body have been executed, control goes back to the test statement preceding the loop body. When the test indicates a false condition, the statements in the loop body are skipped and

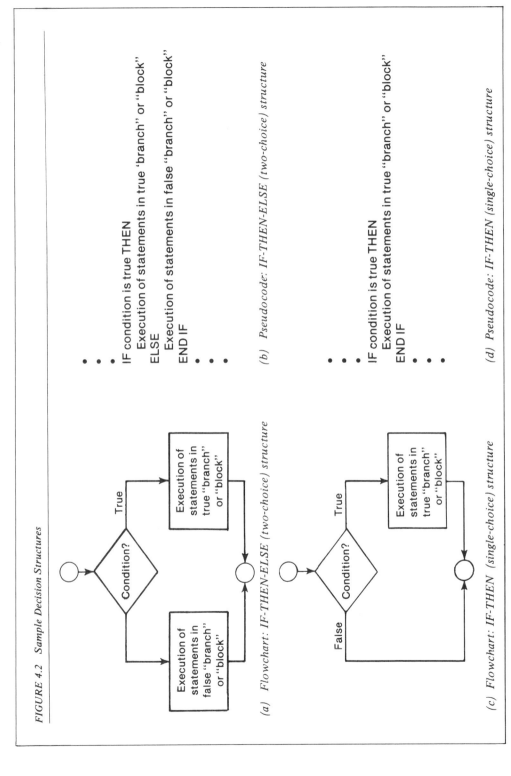

FIGURE 4.2 Sample Decision Structures

(a) Flowchart: IF-THEN-ELSE (two-choice) structure

```
.  .  .  .
IF condition is true THEN
    Execution of statements in true 'branch'' or "block''
ELSE
    Execution of statements in false "branch'' or "block''
END IF
.  .  .  .
```

(b) Pseudocode: IF-THEN-ELSE (two-choice) structure

(c) Flowchart: IF-THEN (single-choice) structure

```
.  .  .  .
IF condition is true THEN
    Execution of statements in true "branch'' or "block''
END IF
.  .  .  .
```

(d) Pseudocode: IF-THEN (single-choice) structure

FIGURE 4.3   IF-THEN-ELSE Structure for Student Billing Problem

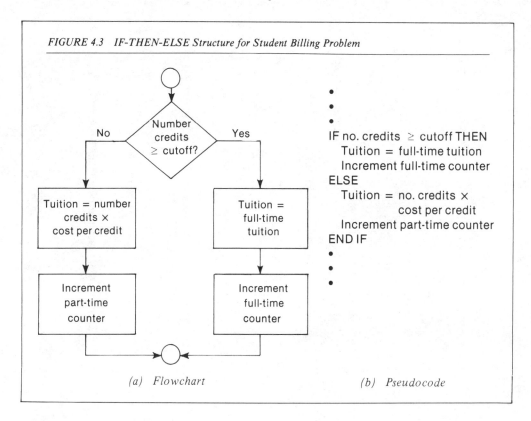

(a)   Flowchart

(b)   Pseudocode

control passes to the next statement outside the loop. Thus *looping continues WHILE the condition is true.*

A variation of the loop structure is the **UNTIL structure,** illustrated in Figure 4.4b. This structure ensures that the body of the loop is executed at least once. In this case, the test for the end of the loop is made after the loop body is executed. Thus *looping continues UNTIL the condition is true.*

The major difference between these two loop structures is that the test precedes the body in a WHILE loop whereas the body precedes the test in an UNTIL loop. The WHILE structure is an example of a **pre-test loop,** since the test for loop termination (loop control) *precedes* the loop body. Similarly, the UNTIL structure illustrates a **post-test loop** because the loop test *follows* the loop body.

Loop structures are powerful features of programming languages because they enable the automatic processing of large amounts of similar data. For example, any realistic version of the student billing program must include a loop for processing all students at the college in one computer run, as illustrated in Figure 4.5. Note that *the pseudocode version indents the body of the loop for better readability.*

We present one popular version of FORTRAN coding for the loop structure in Section 4.5 and conclude the treatment of loops in the next chapter.

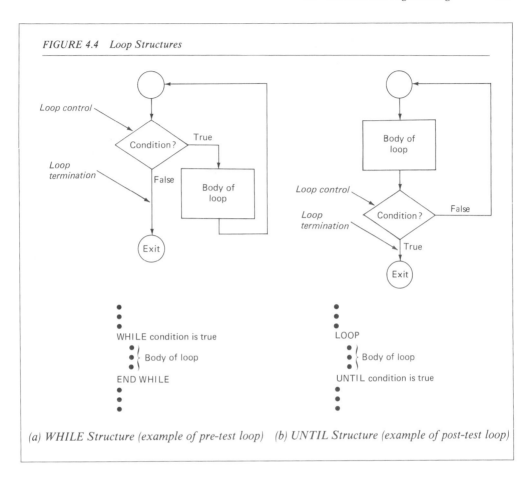

FIGURE 4.4   Loop Structures

(a) WHILE Structure (example of pre-test loop)   *(b) UNTIL Structure (example of post-test loop)*

4.4
STRUCTURED PROGRAMMING

Let's define a **structured program** as one that is written strictly in terms of sequence, decision, and loop structures. The flowchart that corresponds to a structured program is defined as a **structured flowchart.** Pseudocode itself reflects a structured design when it is based strictly on sequence, decision (IF-THEN-ELSE, IF-THEN, etc.), and loop (pre-test and post-test) structures.

If you look back at Figures 4.1 to 4.5, you should realize that *each control structure has a single entry point and a single exit point,* as denoted by the circle symbol (O). In effect, a structured program is simply a set of these control structures put together in some meaningful fashion. For example, the IF-THEN-ELSE structure in Figure 4.3 includes a sequence structure within each of its branches, and the loop structure in Figure 4.5 contains a sequence structure as its body. Are you ready for this? If we were to replace "Calculate tuition" in Figure 4.5 by the IF-THEN-ELSE structure in Figure 4.3, the revised Figure 4.5 would be

FIGURE 4.5   Loop Structures for Student Billing Problem

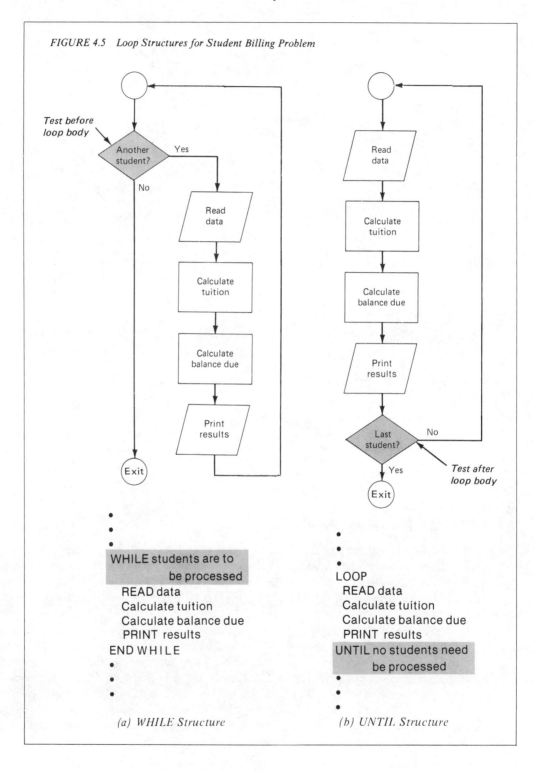

(a) WHILE Structure

(b) UNTIL Structure

a loop structure having a body made up of a sequence structure with an embedded IF-THEN-ELSE structure.[1]

Structured programs utilize a concept called "modular programming," which breaks down a complex problem into a set of modules, where each performs a specific function within the overall solution of the problem. In the present context, each control structure is a module.[2]

Structured programming is also associated with "top-down design" of programs in the sense that execution enters the "top" of a structure and proceeds "down" and out through the bottom of the structure. This approach to the development of programs (software) reduces the time it takes to write a program and produces a more readable and reliable program in the process.[3]

Follow-up Exercise

1. Incorporate Figure 4.3 into Figure 4.5 by reworking the following.
   a. Flowchart version in Figure 4.5
   b. Pseudocode version in Figure 4.5

4.5
DO/CONTINUE STATEMENTS

In this section we present a common type of loop structure called the DO-loop. Looping by this method is used when we know beforehand the number of **loop iterations,** that is, the number of times the body of the loop is to be repeated. In this case, the DO and CONTINUE statements are used to handle automatically all details of looping.

Loop Mechanics

A DO-loop is best defined by a DO statement at the beginning of the loop and by a CONTINUE statement at the end of the loop. For example, the statements

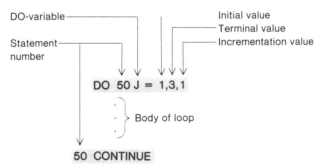

define a DO-loop that iterates three times.

---

[1] Other legitimate decision structures are presented in the next two chapters. An alternative approach to designing structured flowcharts is described in Module A, which we don't recommend reading until after Chapter 5.

[2] Module F includes a detailed discussion of modular programming, which is best covered at the end of Chapter 9.

[3] Top-down design is fully discussed in Module E, which we recommend reading at the end of Chapter 5.

The general form of the **DO statement** is

$$\boxed{\textbf{DO}\ \ ^{statement}_{number}\ \ DO\text{-}variable\ =\ ^{initial}_{value,}\ ^{terminal}_{value,}\ ^{incrementation}_{value}}$$

The **CONTINUE statement** that is paired with a DO statement has the following general form.

$$\boxed{^{statement}_{number}\ \textbf{CONTINUE}}$$

In the DO statement you must

1. Indicate the range of the DO statement. The statements that are to be repeated as part of the loop are those *executable* statements beginning with the statement *immediately following* the DO and ending with the statement specified by the *statement number* in the DO. These statements are called the **body** or **range** of the DO-loop. Statement number 50 in the instruction

    ```
    DO 50 J = 1,3,1
    ```

    indicates that the last executable statement in the loop is the one labeled 50, the CONTINUE statement. A **statement number** is a sequence of one to five digits. When used as a statement label, as in

    ```
    50 CONTINUE
    ```

    it must precede the statement on the same line. The statement number must be placed in columns 1–5, preferably right-justified (up against column 5). By the way, the CONTINUE statement need not end a DO-loop, but we recommend this practice as it visually facilitates DO-loop identification and neatly bypasses our having to remember what statements may *not* end a DO-loop.
2. Specify the **DO-variable,** which must be an integer variable. In the above example, J is the DO-variable.
3. Specify the initial value of the DO-variable as an integer constant or variable. For example, J is first set to 1 in the sample DO statement, since 1 is the value of the initial value.
4. Specify the terminal value of the DO-variable as an integer constant or variable. In this example, 3 is the terminal value. The value of the DO-variable must exceed the terminal value before the loop is terminated. In our example, when J first exceeds 3, looping terminates.
5. Specify the incrementation value as an integer constant or variable. The value of the DO-variable changes by the incrementation value at each iteration of the DO-loop. Thus, each time our sample DO-loop iterates, the value of J increases by 1. *The incrementation value can be omitted, in which case the computer assumes it has a value of 1.* For example,

    ```
    DO 50 J = 1,3
    ```

    is equivalent to our earlier version. Note the omission of the comma following the 3.

6. The initial, terminal, and incrementation values must be positive.

To illustrate better the mechanics of the DO-loop consider the loop structure

```
DO  100 KOUNT = 1,5,1
  .  ⎫
  .  ⎬ Loop body
  .  ⎭
100 CONTINUE
```

When the DO statement is executed, the DO-loop is activated and the DO-variable KOUNT is thereby initialized to 1. Next, the body of the loop is processed for the first time. After each loop body is executed, according to Figure 4.6, the value of the DO-variable is automatically increased by the incrementation value. Now the current value of KOUNT is 2. Next, the loop control test is performed. When the DO-variable becomes greater than the terminal value repetition of the loop body is terminated and control is transferred to the first statement following the CONTINUE statement. Since the current value of KOUNT (2) is less than the terminal value (5), the body of the loop is processed for a second time. KOUNT is again increased by its incrementation value (1) and the loop control test is performed. This process continues until the DO-variable is incremented to 6. Now that the DO-variable exceeds the terminal value, control is transferred to the next executable statement following the DO-loop. At this time the DO-loop is said to be *inactive*. Note that this loop iterates five times, which means that the body is sequentially processed five times.

In general, the number of iterations for a DO-loop having initial and incrementation values of 1 is given by the terminal value. In this case, the DO-variable is said to be a **counter** and the loop is called a **counter-controlled loop.**

To make sure you understand loop iterations, confirm Table 4.1 given the following DO-loop.

```
DO  200 K = 3,10,2
  .
  .
  .
200 CONTINUE
```

Note that the DO-loop in WATFIV is a post-test structure, since the loop control test follows the body of the loop.

Follow-up Exercise

2. What values get printed for each of the loops below? How many times does each loop iterate?

a. DO 75 K = 1,7
      PRINT,K
   75 CONTINUE
b. Same as part a except
      DO 75 K = 1,7,3
c. DO 85 L = 2,5
      PRINT,L
   85 CONTINUE
d. Same as part c except
      DO 85 L = 5,5
e. Same as part c except
      DO 85 L = 6,5

FIGURE 4.6   Logic of WATFIV DO-Loop

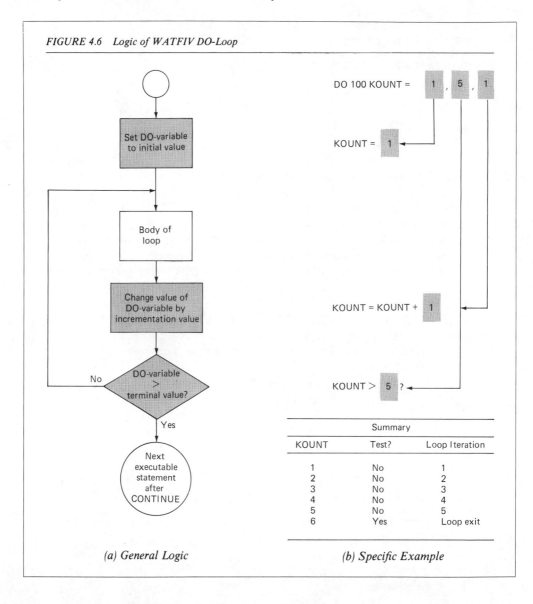

(a) General Logic

(b) Specific Example

Summary

KOUNT	Test?	Loop Iteration
1	No	1
2	No	2
3	No	3
4	No	4
5	No	5
6	Yes	Loop exit

TABLE 4.1   DO-Loop Mechanics Based on Figure 4.6a: Four Iterations when Using
DO 200 K = 3,10,2

K	EXIT-LOOP?	ITERATION
3	No	1
5	No	2
7	No	3
9	No	4
11	Yes	Loop exit

EXAMPLE 4.1   Student Billing with DO-Loop

Consider the following version of the student billing problem.

```
C----------------------------------------------------------------
C      STUDENT BILLING PROGRAM
C
C         VARIABLE KEY
C          INPUT:
C            CPC    = COST PER CREDIT
C            FEES   = COST OF FEES
C            N      = NUMBER OF STUDENTS
C            NAME   = STUDENT NAME
C            ID     = STUDENT IDENTIFICATION NUMBER
C            CREDIT = NUMBER OF CREDITS
C          OUTPUT:
C            NAME, ID, CREDIT, FEES
C            TUIT   = TUITION
C            BALDUE = BALANCE DUE THE COLLEGE
C----------------------------------------------------------------
       CHARACTER   NAME*15
       INTEGER     ID,N
       REAL        CREDIT,TUIT,BALDUE,CPC,FEES
C----------------------------------------------------------------
       READ, CPC,FEES
       READ, N
C----------------------------------------------------------------
       PRINT, 'STUDENT NAME    IDENTIFICATION      BALANCE DUE'
       PRINT, '----------------------------------------------------'
C----------------------------------------------------------------
       DO 50 J = 1,N
          READ, NAME,ID,CREDIT
          TUIT     = CREDIT*CPC
          BALDUE   = TUIT + FEES
          PRINT, NAME,ID,BALDUE
   50  CONTINUE
C----------------------------------------------------------------
       PRINT, '----------------------------------------------------'
C----------------------------------------------------------------
       STOP
       END
```

These print report headings. See output part A.

This prints report lines. See output part B.

This prints report ending. See output part C.

Input data appear as follows:

```
100.0,250.0
3
'W. MITTY',266612463,15.0
'X. MITTY',266612464,18.5
'Y. MITTY',266612465,12.0
```

Output from this program would appear as follows:

STUDENT NAME	IDENTIFICATION	BALANCE DUE	
			Part A

W. MITTY	266612463	1750.0000000	
X. MITTY	266612464	2100.0000000	Part B
Y. MITTY	266612465	1450.0000000	
---			Part C

Note the following points.

1. The number of students to be processed is read in under the variable N. Its value of 3 in the input data is consistent with the fact that three students are to be processed.

2. The terminal value in the DO statement is given by N. Since this is effectively a counter-controlled loop, it follows that the value of 3 in N is the number of loop iterations, that is, the loop will process three students. Note that *the use of the variable N instead of the constant 3 in the DO statement promotes the generality of the program.* In other words, the program itself need not be changed to process a different number of students; only the input data need be changed. This design reduces the cost of programming, which is an important consideration in actual programming environments.

3. The DO and CONTINUE statements act as "visual brackets" for the loop, thereby improving the readability of the program. We also indent the body of the loop to make it stand out further. *We will follow the convention of indenting the body of loops to identify them better visually.* Although it is not necessary to do this, it is yet another programming practice that promotes good program design.

4. The body of the loop iterates three times, which gives the following successive values in memory as if a "snapshot" were taken just before the CONTINUE statement is executed (see Table 4.2).

TABLE 4.2   Successive Values in Memory

CPC	FEES	N	J	NAME	ID	CREDIT	TUIT	BALDUE
100.0	250.0	3	1	W. MITTY	266612463	15.0	1500.0	1750.0
↓	↓		2	X. MITTY	266612464	18.5	1850.0	2100.0
			3	Y. MITTY	266612465	12.0	1200.0	1450.0

5. Finally, note that output values within the loop for NAME, ID, and BALDUE give the appearance of a "table," and that column headings for this table must be printed *before* the loop.

Follow-up Exercises

3. Suppose we have to process 4562 students. What changes need to be made in the program and data of Example 4.1?

4. What would the output look like if the statement

        PRINT,'STUDENT NAME   IDENTIFICATION   BALANCE DUE'

were placed between the DO and READ statements?

5. Anything wrong with the following loop? Explain.

```
      DO 50 J = 1,N
      READ,NAME,ID,CREDIT
      TUIT = CREDIT*CPC
      BALDUE = TUIT + FEES
   50 PRINT,NAME,ID,BALDUE
```

The Fine Points

Try to keep in mind the following points when using DO-loops.

1. If the initial value is equal to or greater than the terminal value, the loop body is executed once.
2. The DO-variable can be utilized within the body of the loop, as illustrated in the program segment

```
     DO 10 J = 1,4
        PRINT, J
 10  CONTINUE
```

However, the value of the DO-variable may not be redefined within the body. For example, the program segment

```
     DO 10 J = 1,4
        J = J + 1
        PRINT,J
 10  CONTINUE
```

would "abort" execution. Also, none of the variables appearing as loop parameters may be altered in the loop body.

3. Branching within the body of a DO-loop is allowed, but not directly to the DO statement itself. Branching out of an active DO-loop is also allowed. This causes the DO-loop to become inactive and preserves the current value of the DO-variable. *Branching into the body of a DO-loop from outside the loop is not permissible.* At any rate, either branching into the body or branching out of the body of a DO-loop is not a good programming practice since *it violates the single-entry single-exit philosophy of a control structure.* We come back to these issues later in the book, at a point when you are capable of making these errors.

4. There is no standard notation for specifying a DO-loop either in a flowchart or in pseudocode. One common flowcharting approach is to use the hexagon-shaped symbol to define the start of the loop (DO statement) and the circle symbol to define the end of the loop (CONTINUE statement). Figure 4.7 illustrates this approach for Example 4.1. Note that the loop returns to the first executable statement following the DO statement, not to the DO statement itself. Alternative approaches to flowcharting the DO-loop are illustrated in Figures 4.4b and 4.6.

Follow-up Exercises

6. Why are the following DO-loops invalid?
   a.   DO 50 X = 1.5,4.5,0.0

```
            .
            .
            .
    50 CONTINUE
```

FIGURE 4.7   Flowchart/Pseudocode for Example 4.1

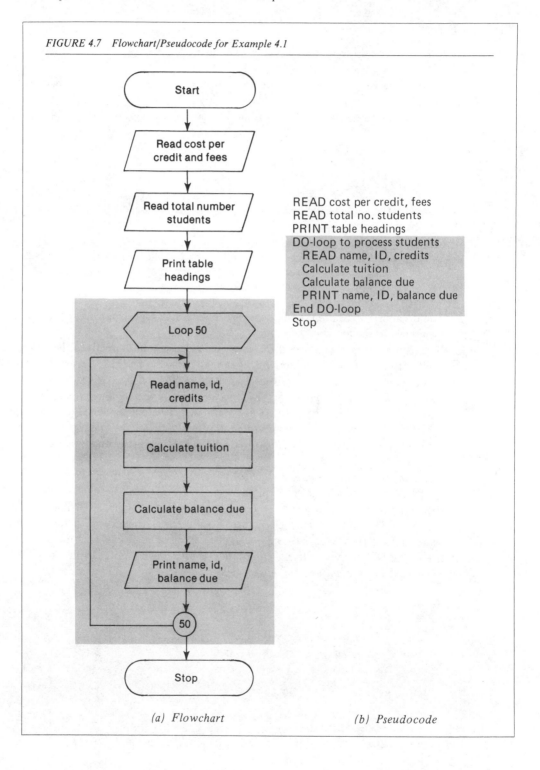

READ cost per credit, fees
READ total no. students
PRINT table headings
DO-loop to process students
    READ name, ID, credits
    Calculate tuition
    Calculate balance due
    PRINT name, ID, balance due
End DO-loop
Stop

(a) Flowchart   (b) Pseudocode

b.   DO J = 1,10
              .
              .
              .
              CONTINUE

c.   DO 100 K = 10,0
              .
              .
              .
         100 CONTINUE

d.   DO 100 K = 10,0,−1
                  K = N − 1
         100 CONTINUE

*7. Bank Savings Problem. Modify the program in Section 2.7 (page 71) as follows:

a. Use the input variables NUM1, NUM2, and NUM3 as loop parameters that specify a sequence of values for NUM.

b. Design a DO-loop to print a table as shown below.

```
PRINCIPAL  =          $  5000.0000000
RATE       =             0.0200000


QUARTERS                     AMOUNT
-----------------------------------------
   17                      7001.1100000
   18                      7141.1200000
   19                      7283.9400000
   20                      7429.6100000
-----------------------------------------
```

Specify the required input data for the output above and show either a flowchart or pseudocode.

4.6
INITIALIZATIONS AND SUMS

Accumulating and printing sums for one or more variables is a common computation in programming. For example, a payroll program computes gross pay, deductions, and net pay for each employee and also computes the total gross pay, total deductions, and total net pay for all employees. To illustrate how the computer can accumulate a sum, we return to our tuition and fee problem.

EXAMPLE 4.2   Student Billing Program with Sum

The Financial Vice-President of State College needs to know the total amount of money that State College will collect in tuition and fees. Conceptually, we set aside a memory location (that is, assign a variable) which represents the sum. Each time the computer computes the amount owed by a student, the sum is increased by the amount the student owes. In effect the sum can be thought of as a running total whose final value is not known until all the student data are read in and processed. For our test data in Example 4.1, the amounts due from each student are $1750, $2100, and $1450. As the program is computing, the sum will be:

After the first student,	$0 + 1750 = 1750$
After the second student,	$1750 + 2100 = 3850$
After the third student,	$3850 + 1450 = 5300$

Thus a running total accumulates.

The shaded portions in the pseudocode of Figure 4.8 illustrate the incorporation of a sum in the version of Figure 4.7. Note that the only changes are the initialization of the accumulator (sum variable) to zero before the loop, the incorporation of the accumulator in the loop to compute the running total, and output of the accumulator following the loop.

FIGURE 4.8   *Incorporating a Sum in the Student Billing Loop*

```
READ cost per credit, fees
READ total no. students
PRINT table headings
Accumulator = 0
DO-loop to process students
    READ name, ID, credits
    Calculate tuition
    Calculate balance due
    PRINT name, ID, balance due

    Accumulator = accumulator +
                    balance due
End DO-loop
PRINT accumulator
Stop
```

The program is as follows:

```
C-------------------------------------------------------------
C       STUDENT BILLING PROGRAM WITH SUM
C
C           VARIABLE KEY
C            INPUT:
C             CPC    = COST PER CREDIT
C             FEES   = COST OF FEES
C             N      = NUMBER OF STUDENTS
C             NAME   = STUDENT NAME
C             ID     = STUDENT IDENTIFICATION NUMBER
C             CREDIT = NUMBER OF CREDITS
```

```
C           OUTPUT:
C              NAME, ID, CREDIT, FEES
C              TUIT   = TUITION
C              BALDUE = BALANCE DUE THE COLLEGE
C              SUM    = TOTAL BALANCE DUE
C------------------------------------------------------------
        CHARACTER   NAME*15
        INTEGER     ID,N
        REAL        CREDIT,TUIT,BALDUE,CPC,FEES, SUM
C------------------------------------------------------------
        READ, CPC,FEES
        READ, N
C------------------------------------------------------------
        PRINT, 'STUDENT NAME    IDENTIFICATION       BALANCE DUE'
        PRINT, '---------------------------------------------------'
C------------------------------------------------------------
        SUM = 0.0   ◄─────────────── Initialize sum to zero to avoid execution error
C------------------------------------------------------------
        DO 50 J = 1,N
           READ, NAME,ID,CREDIT
           TUIT    = CREDIT*CPC
           BALDUE  = TUIT + FEES
           PRINT, NAME,ID,BALDUE
           SUM     = SUM + BALDUE
   50   CONTINUE
C------------------------------------------------------------
        PRINT, '---------------------------------------------------'
        PRINT, 'TOTAL BALANCE DUE:        $',SUM   ◄───
C------------------------------------------------------------
        STOP
        END
```

Each time the computer calculates
the balance due for a student,
the location for SUM is increased
by the value stored in BALDUE.

SUM is printed
following the loop.

Input

```
100.0,250.0
3
'W. MITTY',266612463,15.0
'X. MITTY',266612464,18.5
'Y. MITTY',266612465,12.0
```

Output

```
STUDENT NAME       IDENTIFICATION       BALANCE DUE
---------------------------------------------------
W. MITTY            266612463            1750.0000000
X. MITTY            266612464            2100.0000000
Y. MITTY            266612465            1450.0000000
---------------------------------------------------
TOTAL BALANCE DUE:          $           5300.0000000
```

In the program, SUM is the variable that stores the accumulated amount due from all students. Changes from the program in Example 4.1 are shaded.

First, we explicitly initialize SUM to zero for the reasons outlined on page 94 of Chapter 3. Even though some systems initialize all variables to zero, *it is a good programming practice to explicitly initialize variables that need zero initialization.* This makes programs more "portable," since they would also work on systems that don't initialize variables to zero. In other cases, as we illustrate later in this chapter, sums must be explicitly initialized to zero to avoid logic errors.

By placing the instruction

SUM = SUM + BALDUE

within the loop the value stored in BALDUE is added to the value stored in SUM, and the result of the addition is stored in SUM, replacing the value previously stored in SUM.

As the program is executed, the contents of memory locations for CREDIT, BAL-DUE, and SUM change in the following way.

After initialization:

SUM
0.0

After the first student is processed:

CREDIT		BALDUE		SUM
15.0		1750.0		1750.0

After the second student is processed:

CREDIT		BALDUE		SUM
18.5		2100.0		3850.0

After the third student is processed:

CREDIT		BALDUE		SUM
12.0		1450.0		5300.0

Follow-up Exercises

8. With respect to Example 4.2:
   a. Would the output change if the instructions

      PRINT,NAME,ID,BALDUE

      and

      SUM = SUM + BALDUE

      were reversed?
   b. Would the output change if the instruction

      SUM = SUM + BALDUE

were placed before

   BALDUE = TUIT + FEES

c. Describe the output if the statement that prints SUM were placed just before the CONTINUE statement.

d. Describe the output if the statement

   SUM = 0.0

   were omitted from the program.

9. Prepare a flowchart for Example 4.2.

10. Modify the program of Example 4.2 to calculate and print the average balance due, AVE. Print AVE immediately after the output of SUM.

11. Specify a DATA statement to initialize SUM.

*12. Modify the program in Example 4.2 to accumulate and print three sums: cumulative tuition, cumulative fees, and cumulative balance due. *Hint:* You need a separate variable to accumulate each total. Can you think of simplifications in the program that make use of the fact that once you have two of these sums you automatically have the third?

4.7
NESTED DO-LOOPS

As problems become more complex, the solution may require the programmer to embed one loop inside another. For every iteration of an outside loop, the inside loop iterates through a complete cycle. The inside loop is said to be **nested** within the outside loop. DO-loops are nested when one DO-loop lies entirely within another DO-loop, as illustrated below.

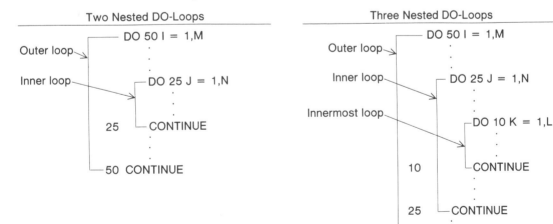

Two Nested DO-Loops	Three Nested DO-Loops
Outer loop ⟶ ┌── DO 50 I = 1,M	Outer loop ⟶ ┌── DO 50 I = 1,M
Inner loop ⟶ │ ┌─ DO 25 J = 1,N	Inner loop ⟶ │ ┌─ DO 25 J = 1,N
25 └─ CONTINUE	Innermost loop ⟶ │ │ ┌─ DO 10 K = 1,L
└─ 50 CONTINUE	10 └─ CONTINUE
	25 └─ CONTINUE
	└─ 50 CONTINUE

Nested DO-loops must not cross over or overlap, as illustrated below.

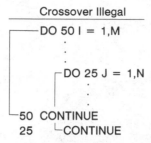

To understand nested DO-loops you must pay careful attention to iterations and the values assigned to DO-variables. For example, in the program segment

```
     DO 200 I = 1,2
         DO 100 J = 1,3
             PRINT, I,J
100      CONTINUE
200  CONTINUE
```

the inner loop 100 gets "exhausted" for each value of the outer loop's DO-variable I; that is, J changes from 1 to 2 to 3 to 4 (at 4 the inner loop becomes inactive) before I is incremented to its next value. Thus the inner loop is said to "vary the fastest." Each time the inner loop is exhausted, its DO-variable J is reset to its initial value, since the statement

```
     DO  100 J = 1,3
```

gets executed for each new value of I. For example, the output from the above segment would appear as follows:

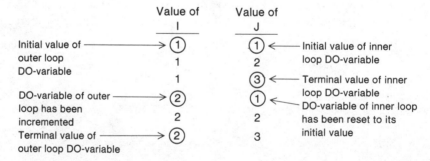

Notice that this double loop iterates a total of six times (2×3), or the product of the total iterations of the outer loop and the total iterations of the inner loop.

EXAMPLE 4.3   Mean Exam Scores by Section

Consider Figure 4.9 for calculating the mean or average exam score for *each* section of a multisection academic course. Note the treatment of nested loops in the flowchart and pseudocode versions, particularly the indentation in the pseudocode version.

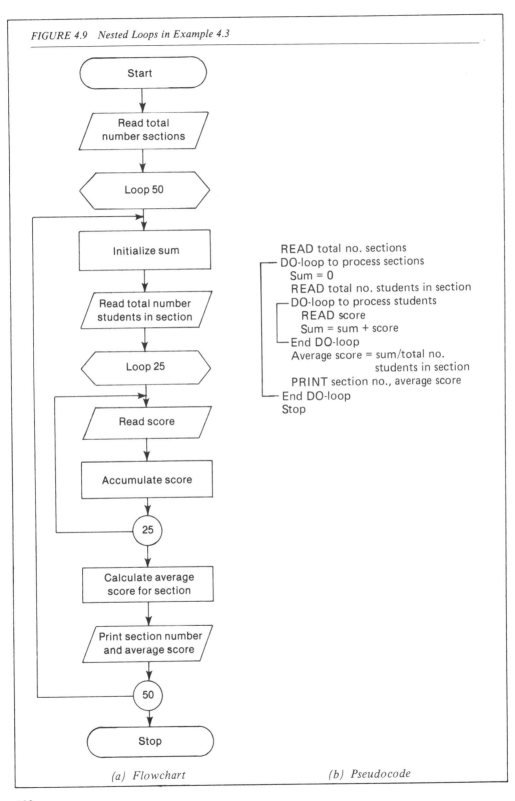

FIGURE 4.9 Nested Loops in Example 4.3

Start

Read total
number sections

Loop 50

Initialize sum

Read total number
students in section

Loop 25

Read score

Accumulate score

25

Calculate average
score for section

Print section number
and average score

50

Stop

READ total no. sections
DO-loop to process sections
    Sum = 0
    READ total no. students in section
    DO-loop to process students
        READ score
        Sum = sum + score
    End DO-loop
    Average score = sum/total no.
                        students in section
    PRINT section no., average score
End DO-loop
Stop

(a) Flowchart   (b) Pseudocode

In this example the inner loop processes the scores for a specific section and the outer loop processes sections. In particular note (1) that the sum is reinitialized each time the inner loop is reactivated or each time a new section is processed, (2) that the scores for a section are summed within the inner loop, and (3) that the average score is calculated and printed immediately following the inner loop.

The program below reflects this design.

```
C---------------------------------------------------
C    EXAM AVERAGING PROGRAM
C
C    KEY:
C      N     = NUMBER OF STUDENTS IN A SECTION
C      M     = NUMBER OF SECTIONS
C      SCORE = EXAM SCORE FOR A STUDENT
C      SUM   = SUM OF SCORES IN A SECTION
C      AVE   = MEAN EXAM SCORE FOR A SECTION
C---------------------------------------------------
       INTEGER N,M
       REAL    SCORE,SUM,AVE
C---------------------------------------------------
       READ, M
C---------------------------------------------------
       DO 50 I = 1,M
          SUM = 0.0
          READ, N
          DO 25 J = 1,N
             READ, SCORE
             SUM = SUM + SCORE
25        CONTINUE
          AVE = SUM/N
          PRINT, 'MEAN SCORE FOR SECTION',I,'=',AVE
50     CONTINUE
C---------------------------------------------------
       STOP
       END
```

For example, given two sections with the scores

	Scores	
Section 1		Section 2
90		50
70		90
80		

Input data would be prepared as

```
2  ←———————— Number of sections, M
3  ←———————— Number of scores in first section, N
90.0⎫
70.0⎬ ←———— Scores in first section
80.0⎭
2  ←———————— Number of scores in second section, N
50.0⎫
90.0⎭ ←———— Scores in second section
```

and output would appear as

```
MEAN SCORE FOR SECTICN          1 =          80.0000000
MEAN SCORE FOR SECTICN          2 =          70.0000000
```

You should solve Exercise 13 to make sure you understand the mechanics of this program.

Follow-up Exercises

13. Roleplay computer for Example 4.3 by filling in values in the following memory locations, as if the snapshot of memory were taken just before execution of *each* CONTINUE statement.

M	N	I	J	SCORE	SUM	AVE

14. Modify the input/output data in Example 4.3 to process the scores 20, 90 for Section 1; 40, 100, 70, 80 for Section 2; and 60, 80, 70 for Section 3.
15. What would happen in Example 4.3 if

    DATA SUM/0.0/

    were used instead of

    SUM = 0.0

    Be specific.
*16. Modify Figure 4.9 and the program in Example 4.3 to compute and print the average for all sections combined (COMAVE) in addition to the average for each section.
17. **Standard Deviation. Modify Figure 4.9 and the program in Example 4.3 to compute and print the standard deviation (a measure of variation about the mean) for each section, in addition to the average.

$$s = \sqrt{\frac{n\Sigma x^2 - (\Sigma x)^2}{n(n-1)}}$$

where
   n = number of scores
   x = score
   Σx = sum of scores for a section
   Σx^2 = sum of squared scores for a section

** Double-starred exercises are somewhat more difficult and/or tedious than other exercises. Answers to these exercises are not given in the back of the book.

18. Specify printed output and number of iterations for each of the following nested loops.

a.
```
        DO 500 J = 1,4
            DO 300 K = 1,2
                PRINT,J,K
300     CONTINUE
500 CONTINUE
```

b.
```
        DO 300 I = 1,2
            PRINT,I
            DO 200 J = 1,3
                PRINT,'ʙ',J
                DO 100 K = 1,4
                    PRINT,'ʙ','ʙ',K
100         CONTINUE
200     CONTINUE
300 CONTINUE
```

c.
```
        M = 0
        DO 100 I = 1,10
         J = I
         DO 50 K = 1,5
          L = K
          M = M + 1
50   CONTINUE
100 CONTINUE
    PRINT,J,L,M
    PRINT,I,K
```

19. What is wrong, if anything, in each segment?

a.
```
        DO 100 X = 1.,P
            DO 200 Y = R,S
                PRINT,'I LOVE NESTED LOOPS'
100     CONTINUE
200 CONTINUE
```

b.
```
        DO 300 I = 1,3
        DO 200 J = 1,4
        DO 100 K = 1,5
        PRINT,'NOT ME'
100 CONTINUE
200 CONTINUE
300 CONTINUE
```

4.8
BANK SAVINGS PROBLEM REVISITED

The bank savings program first introduced in Chapter 2 (page 69) is now modified to include a DO-loop for processing the effects of changing the quarterly interest rate from 0.02 to 0.04 in steps of 0.005. The principal (amount we deposit in the account) is $1000 and the number of quarters over which interest is earned is 20.

Step 1: Analysis

A bank savings program that determines the effect of changing the quarterly interest rate on the accumulated funds given the principal, number of quarters, initial interest rate, terminal interest rate and incrementation interest rate.

a.   *Input data*
     Principal
     Quarterly interest rate
     Number of quarters
     Initial rate of interest
     Terminal rate of interest
     Incrementation rate of interest
b.   *Output data*
     Principal
     Number of quarters
     Quarterly interest rate
     Accumulated funds
c.   Computations

$$\text{Accumulated funds} = \text{principal} \times (1 + \text{rate})^{\text{number of quarters}}$$

$$\text{Number of loops} = \left[\frac{\text{terminal rate} - \text{initial rate} + \text{incrementation rate}}{\text{incrementation rate}} \right]$$

Step 2: Design

The pseudocode representation of the algorithm is illustrated in Figure 4.10.

FIGURE 4.10   *Pseudocode for Expanded Bank Savings Problem*

```
READ   principal, number of quarters
READ   initial rate, terminal rate, incrementation rate
PRINT headings
Calculate   number of loops
Rate = initial rate
DO-loop to process rates
    Accumulated funds = principal × ( 1 + rate)^(number of quarters)
    PRINT interest rate, accumulated funds
    Rate = rate + incrementation rate
End DO-loop
Stop
```

Step 3: Code

```
C-------- -- ---------------------------------------------
C    BANK SAVINGS PROGRAM
C
C    KEY:
C      PRIN  = PRINCIPAL
C      RATE  = QUARTERLY INTEREST RATE
C      R1    = INITIAL RATE
C      R2    = TERMINAL RATE
C      R3    = INCREMENTATION RATE
C      LOOPS = NUMBER OF LOOPS
C      NUM   = NUMBER OF QUARTERS
C      ACCUM = ACCUMULATED FUNDS AFTER NUM QUARTERS
```

```
C------------------------------------------------------------
      INTEGER I, NUM, LOOPS
      REAL      PRIN,RATE, ACCUM,R1,R2,R3
C------------------------------------------------------------
      READ, PRIN,NUM
      READ, R1,R2,R3
C------------------------------------------------------------
      PRINT, '           PRINCIPAL =',PRIN
      PRINT, '           QUARTERS  =',NUM
      PRINT, ' '
      PRINT, '                RATE           ACCUM. FUNDS'
      PRINT, '           -------------------------------'
C------------------------------------------------------------
      LOOPS = INT((R2 - R1 + R3)/R3 + 0.5)
      LOOPS = MAX0(LOOPS,1)
      RATE  = R1
C------------------------------------------------------------
      DO 100 I = 1, LOOPS
        ACCUM = PRIN*(1.0 + RATE)**NUM
        PRINT, RATE,ACCUM
        RATE  = RATE + R3
  100 CONTINUE
C------------------------------------------------------------
      STOP
      END
```

Step 4: Debugging

Input

```
1000.0,20
0.02,0.04,0.005  <------------------------+
```

Output

```
PRINCIPAL =           1000.0000000
QUARTERS  =                20
     RATE           ACCUM. FUNDS
     ------------------------------
    0.0200000         1485.9320000  )
    0.0250000         1638.6040000   |
    0.0300000         1806.1010000   }  5 iterations
    0.0350000         1989.7820000   |
    0.0400000         2191.1210000  )
```

Discussion

After reading in the initial parameters and printing heading lines for the output, the program calculates the number of interest calculations desired. This number represents the number of times (iterations) we want to perform the interest rate calculation. The number of iterations is based on what is called an **iteration count,** as given either by the *integer part* of the expression

$$\left[\frac{\text{terminal value} - \text{initial value} + \text{incrementation value}}{\text{incrementation value}} \right]$$

or by one, whichever is greater.

In this program the number of loop iterations is five; that is,

$$\left[\frac{0.04 - 0.02 + 0.005}{0.005} \right] = [5]$$

Within the program, this value is calculated by the assignment statements for LOOPS, where we use a 0.5 adjustment to avoid roundoff error problems (as discussed in Section 4.9). Then, the number of iterations is determined as the value of this expression or 1, whichever is greater. (Note the use of the INT and MAX0 functions from Table 2.6 on page 58.) Next, RATE is initialized to its initial value, R1. The DO statement is set to iterate (loop) the number of times given by the value of LOOPS, and RATE is accumulated within the loop by the incrementation value R3 according to

$$\text{RATE} = \text{RATE} + \text{R3}$$

To make sure you understand this procedure, solve Exercise 20.

Follow-up Exercises

20. **a.** Roleplay computer by filling in a memory table for the bank savings run as done in Table 4.2 on page 114.
   b. Describe the output if your input data for R1,R2,R3 were 0.01, 0.02, 0.002.
*21. What changes need to be made in the banking program if R1, R2, and R3 are defined as *annual* rates instead of quarterly rates? Note that RATE still must be defined on a quarterly basis; the input data now appear as

   1000.0,20
   0.08,0.16,0.02

   The rate to be output should be on an annual basis.

4.9
COMMON ERRORS

Beginning programmers are likely to make at least one of the following errors when applying the material in this chapter. Will you?

Statement Number Errors

Two types of syntax errors seem to occur often here: *multiple* statement numbers and *missing* statement numbers. In the first case, two or more statements have the same statement number. So, as you're writing your program, *make it a habit to scan your existing statement numbers prior to assigning a new statement number*. In the second case, a control statement references a statement number that does not exist. For example, if you have the statement DO 50 J = 1,N and no executable statement is labeled 50, then you have a missing statement-number error.

DO-Loop Errors

1. *DO-variable redefined within loop*

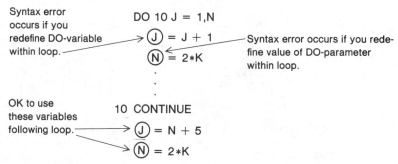

Syntax error occurs if you redefine DO-variable within loop.

DO 10 J = 1,N

Syntax error occurs if you redefine value of DO-parameter within loop.

OK to use these variables following loop.

10 CONTINUE

2. *Improper DO-values*

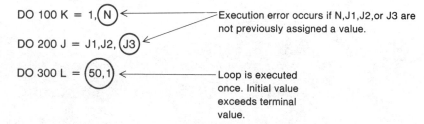

DO 100 K = 1, N ← Execution error occurs if N,J1,J2,or J3 are not previously assigned a value.

DO 200 J = J1,J2, J3 ←

DO 300 L = 50,1 ← Loop is executed once. Initial value exceeds terminal value.

3. *Improper nesting.* Watch out for crossovers like the following:

```
      DO 50 J = 1,L
      DO 40 K = 1,N
         .
         .
         .
   50 CONTINUE
   40 CONTINUE
```

and use of the same DO-variable for nested DO-loops:

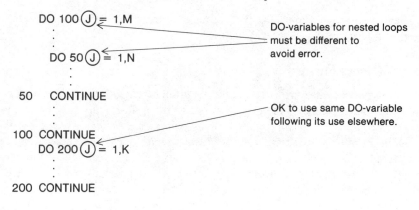

DO 100 J = 1,M

DO-variables for nested loops must be different to avoid error.

DO 50 J = 1,N

50   CONTINUE

OK to use same DO-variable following its use elsewhere.

100 CONTINUE
DO 200 J = 1,K

200 CONTINUE

4. *Branching errors.*   A transfer of control to the DO statement is not permitted while the DO-loop defined by that DO statement is active; branching into the body of a DO-loop from outside the loop is not permitted. At this time it's not possible for you to commit these errors since we have not yet discussed other branching statements. We mention these errors for the sake of completeness.

Initialization Errors

If you forget to initialize S in the assignment statement

    S = S + X

and the system treats S as undefined, then an execution error results when this assignment statement is executed. It is good programming practice to initialize S through an assignment statement such as

    S = 0.0

through a DATA statement such as

    DATA S/0.0/

or through a READ statement such as

    READ,S

Caution: If S needs to be initialized more than once during the same computer run, then avoid use of the DATA statement, since this statement is nonexecutable (see Exercise 15).

**Roundoff Errors

As discussed in earlier chapters, roundoff error is a vexing computer problem. Not only does precision limit the representation of a value such as 1.0/3.0, but also the use of a binary computer to represent decimal (real) values automatically introduces roundoff error. Thus, a real value such as 1.0/10.0 cannot be represented *exactly* in a binary (0–1) system; it can only be *approximated*. For example, it's possible for a machine with seven-digit precision to compute the result 0.9999996 instead of 1.000000 when 1.0/10.0 is added 10 times.[4]

The roundoff problem is compounded if many *recursive calculations* are performed. (A recursive calculation is a calculation whose value is in part determined by a preceding calculation.) The use of DO-loops makes possible large numbers of recursive calculations, as illustrated by the following program.

```
        READ,N
        S = 0.0
        DO 100 J = 1,N
          S = S + 2.0/3.0
100  CONTINUE
        PRINT,S
        STOP
        END
```

---

[4] Only fractional values given by $\frac{1}{2}$ to an integer power can be represented exactly, such as $\frac{1}{2}$, $\frac{1}{4}$, $\frac{1}{8}$, $\frac{1}{16}$, etc.

TABLE 4.3   Roundoff Errors for Recursive Calculations with Seven-Digit Precision

NUMBER OF LOOP ITERATIONS N	PRINTED VALUE OF S	INTENDED VALUE OF S	ABSOLUTE ROUNDOFF ERROR	PERCENT ABSOLUTE ROUNDOFF ERROR
3000	1999.571	2000.	0.429	0.02
12000	7983.813	8000.	16.187	0.20
48000	31890.06	32000.	109.94	0.34
192000	123869.2	128000.	4130.8	3.23

This program was run on an NAS/7 computer[5] for various values of N, giving the results in Table 4.3. For example, when 2.0/3.0 is summed 12,000 times, the intended value is (12,000) · (2.0/3.0), or 8,000; the printed value was 7983.813, which gives a roundoff error of 16.188, or 0.20 percent.

Note that the roundoff error increases as the number of iterations increases, *which clearly shows the magnification of roundoff error as the number of recursive calculations increases.* In some applications, particularly in engineering and the sciences, roundoff error of this magnitude can render the results useless. For such cases, special algorithmic procedures must be implemented that reduce the magnitudes of roundoff errors.[6]

Also note that roundofff error is affecting the value of the DO-variable itself. In effect, the computed values of the DO-variable will increasingly diverge from their intended values, since these values are determined recursively. As in our earlier illustration, this roundoff error will increase as the number of iterations increases.

A simple way of postponing roundoff error problems is to use double-precision variables. In this case, roundoff error is shifted to the extreme right set of digits, thereby having little effect on the first seven digits, unless the number of iterations is very large. For example, Table 4.4 is a modification of the run in Table 4.3, where S is declared as a double-precision variable.

TABLE 4.4   Roundoff Errors for Recursive Calculations with 16-Digit Precision

NUMBER OF LOOP ITERATIONS N	PRINTED VALUE OF S (16 DIGITS)	PRINTED VALUE OF S (ROUNDED TO 7 DIGITS)	INTENDED VALUE OF S
3000	1999.999880790710	2000.000	2000.
12000	7999.999523162842	8000.000	8000.
48000	31999.99809265137	32000.00	32000.
192000	127999.9923706055	128000.0	128000.

[5] NAS stands for National Advanced Systems. This is one of many "plug-compatible machines" that utilize IBM systems software.
[6] These procedures are treated in a field of study called numerical analysis.

Note that calculated values of S to 7 digits are identical to corresponding intended values. Double-precision arithmetic should be used sparingly, however, since it dramatically increases the computational burden on the computer.

For the most part, the effective treatment of roundoff error requires specialized knowledge not covered in this textbook. You should be aware of the problem, however, and recognize it when it occurs.[7]

ADDITIONAL EXERCISES

Please Note

End-of-chapter assignments in this and other chapters generally require you to prepare and submit the following

1. Flowchart and / or pseudocode
2. Listing of the program
3. Sample run showing test data and results

To be sure, ask your instructor.

---

22. Define or explain each of the following terms.

structured programming	post-test loop
control structures	structured program
sequence structure	structured flowchart
transfer of control	loop iterations
branching	DO-loop
decision structures	DO statement
block	CONTINUE statement
IF-THEN-ELSE structure	body or range of DO-loop
IF-THEN structure	statement number
loop structure	DO-variable
loop body	counter
loop control	counter-controlled loop
WHILE structure	nested DO-loops
UNTIL structure	iteration count
pre-test loop	

23. **Temperature Conversion.** Modify the algorithm and program in Exercise 36 of Chapter 2 (page 73) as follows.
    a. Convert degrees Fahrenheit to degrees Celsius by using a DO-loop that varies degrees Fahrenheit from its initial value (F1) to its terminal value (F2) in increments of F3. Run the program for the following sets of values.

---

[7] One of the exercises at the end of this chapter (we won't say which) has potential roundoff error problems.

F1	F2	F3
20	40	1
−30	120	5

Note that we are treating degrees Fahrenheit as integer. For example, your output for the first run should look like this.

	DEGREES FAHRENHEIT	DEGREES CELSIUS
21 rows {	20	−6.67
	21	−6.11
	22	−5.56
	.	.
	.	.
	.	.
	40	4.44

b. Include an outer loop that processes as many sets of data as desired (two sets for the above data). Note that the loop of part a is completely within this outer loop.

24. Area Problem. Modify the algorithm and program in Exercise 37 of Chapter 2 (page 73) as follows.

a. Calculate and output total cost based on different values of cost per square inch (C). Use a DO-loop that varies C from its initial value (C1) to its terminal value (C2) in increments of C3. Run the program for the following three sets of values.

C1	C2	C3	RADIUS	X
0.005	0.100	0.005	5.0	500000
0.005	0.100	0.005	5.2	500000
0.010	0.150	0.010	5.2	650000

For example, your output for the first run should look like this.

	COST PER SQUARE INCH	TOTAL COST
20 rows {	0.005	196349
	0.010	392699
	0.015	589048
	.	.
	.	.
	.	.
	0.100	3926991

b. Include an outer loop that processes as many sets of data as desired (three sets for the above data). Note that the loop of part a is completely within this outer loop.

25. **Microeconomics Problem.** Modify the algorithm and program in Exercise 38 of Chapter 2 (page 73) as follows.

   a. Calculate and print daily revenue, daily cost, and daily profit based on different values of UNITS. Use a DO-loop that varies UNITS from 1 to a maximum (MAX) in increments of 1. Input MAX for the following four sets of data.

MAX	Price
15	80
15	100
15	120
15	140

   For example, your output for the first run should look like this.

UNITS PRODUCED	DAILY REVENUE	DAILY COST	DAILY PROFIT
1	80	245	−165
2	160	234	−74
3	240	223	17
.	.	.	.
.	.	.	.
.	.	.	.
15	1200	2275	−1075

   b. Include an outer loop that varies price. In other words, the loop in part a is completely within this outer loop. Define initial (P1), terminal (P2), and incremental (P3) prices as input variables, along with MAX. The above input data now appear as follows.

P1	P2	P3	MAX
80	140	20	15

   The computer now prints all four tables in one run. Note that the computer run terminates after the price variable reaches P2. Just before each table, print the price that corresponds to that table.

26. **Blood Bank Inventory Problem.** Modify the algorithm and program in Exercise 39 of Chapter 2 (page 73) as follows.

   a. Calculate and print the number of pints to order (Q) and the expected cost per week (E) based on different values of cost of refrigeration (H). Use a DO-loop to vary H from its initial value ($H1$) to its terminal value ($H2$) in increments of $H3$. Input $H1$, $H2$, $H3$, administrative and shipping costs (C), and average weekly demand (D) for the following three sets of values.

H1	H2	H3	C	D
0.20	0.30	0.01	50.	2500.
0.20	0.30	0.01	50.	3000.
0.20	0.30	0.01	50.	3500.

For example, your output for the first run should look like this.

	COST OF REFRIGERATION	ORDER QUANTITY	COST PER WEEK
	0.20	1118	223.61
	0.21	1091	229.13
11 rows	.	.	.
	.	.	.
	.	.	.
	0.30	913	273.86

Draw conclusions with respect to the behavior of Q and E as H and D change.

b. Include an outer loop that varies D. In other words, the loop in part a is completely within this outer loop. Define initial ($D1$), terminal ($D2$), and incremental ($D3$) demands as input variables, along with $H1$, $H2$, $H3$, and C. The above input data now appear as follows:

H1	H2	H3	C	D1	D2	D3
0.20	0.30	0.01	50	2500	3500	500

The computer now prints all three tables in one run. Note that the computer run terminates after the demand variable reaches $D2$. Just before each table, print the demand that corresponds to that table.

27. Automobile Financing. Modify the algorithm and program in Exercise 41 of Chapter 2 (page 74) to include a DO-loop that processes as many sets of input data as specified by the user. Run this program to process the three sets of data suggested in Exercise 17 of Chapter 3 (page 101).

28. Exponential Cumulative Distribution Function. The function

$$p = 1 - e^{-x/a}$$

describes the probability (p) that a random (chance) variable takes on a value less than or equal to x, where a is the expected (average) value of the random variable and e is the base of natural logarithms (see Table 2.6). For example, if the random variable "number of hours an electronic component operates until failure (life)" is distributed exponentially and average life is known to be 8000 hours, then the probability this component lasts 5000 hours or less is

$$\begin{aligned} p &= 1 - e^{-5000/8000} \\ &= 1 - e^{-0.625} \\ &= 1 - 0.5352614 \\ &= 0.4647386 \end{aligned}$$

that is, approximately 46 percent of these components will last 5000 hours or less.

a. Design a program that inputs average life (a), initial value for x, terminal value for x, and incremental value for x, and outputs a table of x-values and corresponding probabilities. For example, if we wish to run x from 1000 to 12,000 in increments of 1000, then output might appear as follows:

LIFE	PROBABILITY
1000	0.1175030
2000	0.2211992
3000	0.3127107
.	.
.	.
.	.
12000	0.7768698

Run your program for the above test data.

b. Include an outer loop that processes N different values for average life *a*. Now, the loop in part a is completely within this outer loop. Run this program for the following input data.

a	Initial x	Terminal x	Incremental x
8000	1000	12000	1000
10000	1000	15000	1000
11000	1000	25000	500

29. Form Letter. Write a program that prints the following personalized form letter.

MS. JANE BUDWICK
10 NORTH ROAD
KINGSTON, RI 02881

DEAR MS. BUDWICK,
    YOU ARE INDEED ONE OF THE FORTUNATE FEW WHOM WE HAVE SELECTED FOR OUR GALA PRIZE DRAWING. ALL YOU NEED TO DO, JANE, IS FILL IN THE ENCLOSED HANDY MAGAZINE ORDER FORM, WHICH MAKES YOU ELIGIBLE FOR ONE OF OUR MANY GALA PRIZES. INDEED, THE BUDWICK RESIDENCE AT 10 NORTH ROAD MAY BE LUCKY ENOUGH TO RECEIVE THE MOST GALA PRIZE, A FREE SET OF ENCYCLOPEDIAS AT A MAINTENANCE COST OF ONLY 10 CENTS PER DAY FOR 30 YEARS.

GOOD LUCK!
HOODWINK G. FOX, MANAGER
DILL COMIC BOOK CO., INC.

In one computer run, print the letter for each of the following.

Name	Address	
MS. JANE BUDWICK	10 NORTH ROAD	KINGSTON, RI 02881
MR. AL BELLA BITTA	20 BIRCH ST.	CINCINNATI, OH 44451
DR. H. DOOLITTLE	10 DOWNING	LONDON, UK

Make sure that each letter fits nicely within an $8\frac{1}{2}$-inch width and takes up 11 inches in length.

30.   Bank Savings with Multiple Compounding.   Consider the formula

$$A = P \cdot (1 + R/M)^{N \cdot M}$$

where

A = accumulated funds
P = principal (amount we first invest)
R = annual interest rate
N = number of years
M = number of times per year the account is compounded (for example, if the account is compounded quarterly, then $M = 4$, or interest is added in four times a year)

To illustrate, if we start with $1000 ($P = 1000$) at 6 percent per year ($R = 0.06$) compounded once a year ($M = 1$), then after two years ($N = 2$) we end up with

$$A = 1000 \cdot (1 + 0.06/1)^{2 \cdot 1}$$
$$= \$1123.60$$

However, if we compound quarterly ($M = 4$), then in two years we end up with

$$A = 1000 \cdot (1 + 0.06/4)^{2 \cdot 4}$$
$$= \$1126.49$$

which is $2.89 better than under annual compounding.

In recent years banks have competitively increased the number of compounding periods to attract customers. For example, under daily compounding ($M = 365$) your account earns interest daily, which is preferred to, say, monthly compounding ($M = 12$).

a.   Design and run a program that processes the following input data in one run.

P	R	N	M
1000	0.06	10	1
1000	0.06	10	4
1000	0.06	10	12
1000	0.06	10	52
1000	0.06	10	365

As output, print the above table together with a new column for A. Comment on the behavior of A.

b.   The "ultimate" account compounds continuously according to the formula

$$A = P \cdot e^{R \cdot N}$$

where e is the base of natural logarithms (see Table 2.6). For example, if we start with $1000 and compound continuously at 6 percent per year, then after two years we end up with

$$A = 1000 \cdot e^{(0.06) \cdot (2)}$$
$$= 1000 \cdot e^{0.12}$$
$$= (1000) \cdot (1.127496)$$
$$= \$1127.50$$

which is $1.01 better than under quarterly compounding. Wouldn't you rather earn money even as you read this? Modify the output in part a to include a last row in the table for continuous compounding. Comment on the behavior of A.

31. Retirement Contribution. The personnel department of a large corporation is offering a new pension plan to its employees that works as follows. The employee contributes an amount C that is deducted from each biweekly paycheck. The company then matches this amount (also contributes C) and invests the money at an annual interest rate R. At the end of Y years, when it is time for the employee to retire, the employee can withdraw a tidy sum S. The necessary biweekly employee contribution to achieve S after Y years when the fund is compounded biweekly at rate R per year is given by

$$C = \left(\frac{S}{2}\right) \cdot \left(\frac{R/26}{(1 + R/26)^{26Y} - 1}\right)$$

Thus, if the interest rate is 0.07 per year, 30 years remain toward retirement, and the employee desires $40,000 at retirement, then the employee must contribute

$$C = \left(\frac{40000}{2}\right) \cdot \left(\frac{.07/26}{(1 + .07/26)^{(26) \cdot (30)} - 1}\right)$$
$$= \$7.54$$

every two weeks.

a. Design and run a program that processes the input data

Name	Y	S
Tahiti Joe	30	$ 40,000
Jet-Set Sal	40	200,000
Too-Late Leroy	5	10,000

and prints the following output.

NAME	YEARS TO RETIREMENT	RETIREMENT SUM	BIWEEKLY CONTRIBUTION
XXXXXXXXXXX	XX	XXXXXX	XX.XX
.	.	.	.
.	.	.	.
.	.	.	.

What would be the effect of an increase in the interest rate to 9 percent per year?

b. Include a loop that processes interest rates from an initial value $R1$ to a terminal value $R2$ in increments of $R3$. Process the data in part a by varying the interest rate from 7 percent to 10 percent in increments of 1 percent. Thus, this run prints four output tables, or one table per interest rate. Precede the output of each table by printing the appropriate interest rate. Is the interest rate effect significant?

32. Optimal Cost per Credit.   Suppose that the cost per credit charged by a college directly affects student enrollment according to the following *demand curve.*

$$S = D1 - D2 \cdot C$$

where
  S = number of students enrolled
  C = cost ($) per credit
  $D1$ = first parameter in demand curve
  $D2$ = second parameter in demand curve
For example, if the tuition charge is $80 per credit, $D1$ is 14,000, and $D2$ is 100, then the number of students that will enroll is estimated by

$$S = 14000 - (100) \cdot (80)$$
$$= 6000$$

If the cost per credit is increased to $90, then the estimated enrollment drops to

$$S = 14000 - (100) \cdot (90)$$
$$= 5000$$

The average balance due the college is given by

$$B = A \cdot C + F$$

where
  B = average balance due the college
  A = average number of credit hours for the college
  C = cost per credit
  F = average fee for the college
For example, if the average number of credit hours taken by students is 14, the cost per credit is $80, and average fees are $250, then the average bill per student is

$$B = (14) \cdot (80) + 250$$
$$= \$1370$$

Since projected enrollment is 6000 students when the per-credit charge is $80, it follows that the college would realize a projected revenue of ($1370 per student) · (6000 students), or $8,220,000.

a.   Design and run a program that includes a DO-loop for varying C from $C1$ to $C2$ in increments of $C3$. Process the following input data.

$D1$	$D2$	A	F	$C1$	$C2$	$C3$
14000	100	14	250	50	80	1

Print an output table headed by four columns: Cost per Credit, Average Bill, Expected Enrollment, and Expected Revenue. On the basis of this output, what cost per credit maximizes expected revenue for the college?

b.   Add an outer DO-loop that processes N colleges in a statewide system. Run the following test data through your program.

College Name	D1	D2	A	F	C1	C2	C3
Test 1	14000	100	14	250	50	80	1
Test 2	14000	25	14	250	200	300	5
Test 3	30000	250	13.5	500	10	60	1

Just before each output table print the name of the college, *D1, D2, A,* and *F.*

What tuition (cost per credit) should be charged at each college in order to maximize revenue? Would you say there's a flaw in the algorithmic logic if students freely change colleges within the system on the basis of tuition?

c. Solve this problem by calculus. Do your analytic and computer results agree?

CHAPTER 5

Simple Decision and Loop Structures

The **decision structure** expresses the logic by which one or more conditions are tested to determine which group of statements (from among alternatives) is to be executed next. In this chapter we implement the IF-THEN-ELSE structure first discussed in the last chapter. We also conclude our presentation of the loop structure by showing several variations of pre-test and post-test loops.

5.1
BLOCK IF, ELSE, AND END IF STATEMENTS

Each decision structure in this chapter begins with the block IF statement and ends with the END IF statement. These two statements enclose the body of the structure. If the ELSE statement is enclosed within this body, then an IF-THEN-ELSE structure is defined.

IF-THEN-ELSE Structure

The two-choice or **IF-THEN-ELSE structure** is generally implemented as follows:

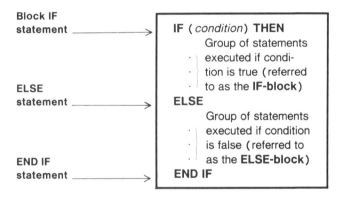

When the block IF statement is executed, the condition within parentheses is tested. If the result is true (the condition holds), then the *IF-block* (block of statements following the keyword THEN up to but not including the ELSE statement) is executed, after which control passes to the END IF statement (which has the same effect as passing control to the first executable statement following the END IF statement). If the condition is false (the condition does not hold), the IF-block is skipped and the *ELSE-block* (block of statements following the ELSE statement up to but not including the END IF statement) is executed, after which control passes to the END IF statement (that is, the first executable statement following the END IF statement).

EXAMPLE 5.1   Sales Bonus Problem

Suppose sales personnel earn a weekly base salary of $350 plus a $100 bonus if weekly sales are above $5000; otherwise no bonus is added to the base salary. Figure 5.1 illustrates the algorithm for the program below, where all data are expressed in whole dollars.

FIGURE 5.1   Sales Bonus Algorithm

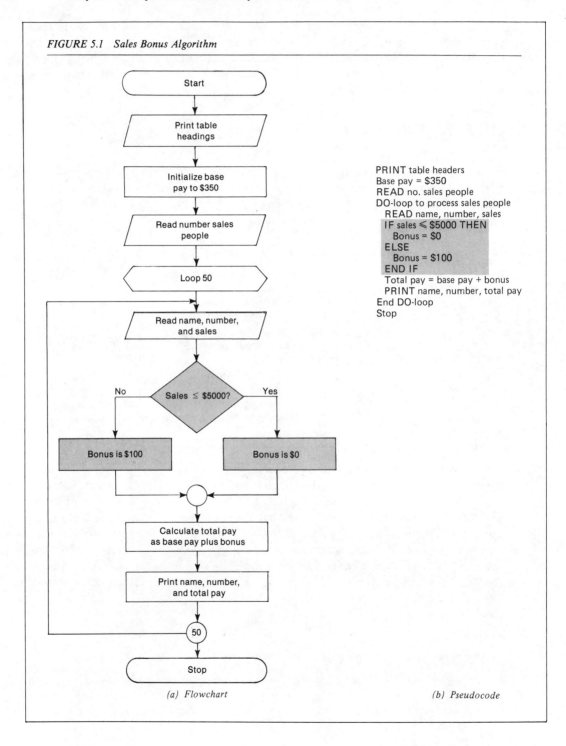

PRINT table headers
Base pay = $350
READ no. sales people
DO-loop to process sales people
  READ name, number, sales
  IF sales ≤ $5000 THEN
    Bonus = $0
  ELSE
    Bonus = $100
  END IF
  Total pay = base pay + bonus
  PRINT name, number, total pay
End DO-loop
Stop

(a) Flowchart

(b) Pseudocode

```
C-----------------------------------------------------------
C    SALES BONUS PROGRAM
C
C    KEY:
C      BASE   = BASE SALARY
C      N      = NUMBER OF SALESPERSONS
C      NAME   = SALESPERSON'S NAME
C      SSN    = SOCIAL SECURITY NUMBER
C      SALES  = WEEKLY SALES
C      BONUS  = SALES BONUS
C      TOTPAY = TOTAL PAY
C-----------------------------------------------------------
       CHARACTER NAME*15
       INTEGER   BASE,N,SSN,SALES,BONUS,TOTPAY
C-----------------------------------------------------------
       PRINT, 'EMPLOYEE NAME      SS NUMBER      TOTAL PAY'
       PRINT, '-----------------------------------------'
C-----------------------------------------------------------
       BASE = 350
       READ, N
C-----------------------------------------------------------
       DO 50 I = 1,N
         READ, NAME,SSN,SALES
C-----------------------------------------------------------
         IF (SALES .LE. 5000) THEN
            BONUS = 0
         ELSE
            BONUS = 100
         END IF
C-----------------------------------------------------------
         TOTPAY = BASE + BONUS
         PRINT, NAME,SSN,TOTPAY
 50    CONTINUE
C-----------------------------------------------------------
       STOP
       END
```

A test run for three salespeople given the input data

```
3
'W. LOMAN',123456789,4500
'X. LOMAN',432198765,6500
'Y. LOMAN',987654321,5100
```

would result in the output

```
EMPLOYEE NAME      SS NUMBER      TOTAL PAY
-------------------------------------------
W. LOMAN           123456789         350
X. LOMAN           432198765         450
Y. LOMAN           987654321         450
```

The salesperson's base salary of $350 is stored in a variable named BASE and the IF-THEN-ELSE structure determines whether or not the salesperson receives the $100 bonus.

The expression "SALES .LE. 5000" is called a "relational expression"; it represents the condition "sales less than or equal to $5000," where .LE. stands for "less than or equal to." When executed, the block IF statement tests this condition, giving one of two results: true or false. If the value in SALES is less than or equal to 5000, then the result of the test is true and the statements within the IF-block are executed. In other words, the computer executes

    BONUS = 0

However, if the result of the test is false, control immediately goes to the ELSE-block. In this case the statement

    BONUS = 100

is executed.

A simple condition in the block IF statement is expressed by a relational expression. The relational expression can compare either numeric or character values. Every **relational expression** takes the form of an (arithmetic or character) expression, then a relational operator, and then another arithmetic or character expression. A **relational operator** indicates a mathematical comparison such as less than, equal to, or greater than. FORTRAN uses six relational operators, as indicated in Table 5.1. *Notice that the periods that surround the letters are part of the relational operator.* To test a condition, we use one of these relational operators "wedged" between the two arithmetic or character expressions, as follows.

Relational Expressions

arithmetic expression or character expression	relational operator	arithmetic expression or character expression

When evaluated, a relational expression will have either the value true or the value false. This determines which group of statements (IF-block or ELSE-block) is executed next.

As in Chapter 2, *arithmetic expressions* may consist of a single variable, a single constant, or a combination of variables, constants, parentheses, functions, and arithmetic operators. As in our previous work with arithmetic expressions, it is good programming practice not to mix type when coding a relational expression; that is, *the arithmetic expression to the*

TABLE 5.1 *Relational Operators in FORTRAN*

MATHEMATICAL COMPARISON	RELATIONAL OPERATOR	MEANING
=	.EQ.	Equal to
≠	.NE.	Not equal to
<	.LT.	Less than
≤	.LE.	Less than or equal to
>	.GT.	Greater than
≥	.GE.	Greater than or equal to

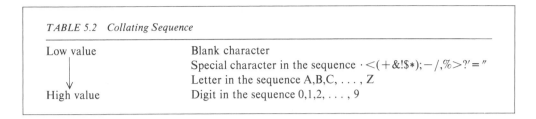

TABLE 5.2   *Collating Sequence*

Low value	Blank character
	Special character in the sequence $\cdot < (+\&!\$*);-/,\%>?'="$
	Letter in the sequence A,B,C, . . . , Z
High value	Digit in the sequence 0,1,2, . . . , 9

left of the relational operator should be the same type as the arithmetic expression to the right. A *character expression* usually includes either a character variable or a character constant.

Notice in Figure 5.1 that the diamond-shaped (◇) flowcharting symbol is used whenever a decision or test is made. The test is described within the diamond, and the arrows show the alternative paths that your program may take from that decision point. The circle symbol (○) indicates transfer of control points in the program.

Did you notice in the pseudocode and program of Example 5.1 that statements in the IF-block and ELSE-block are indented? *Although indentation is not required, it improves the readability of the IF-THEN-ELSE structure.*

Example 5.2 further illustrates the use of the IF-THEN-ELSE structure for testing numeric conditions within programs.

A relational expression also can compare two character expressions (strings). As you know, the computer internally stores all characters as binary numbers. Thus we can view the comparison of two character strings as a comparison between the values of two binary numbers, where one value (string) is less than, equal to, or greater than the other value (string).

The comparison of two strings is actually carried out from left to right, one character at a time. This comparison ends in one of two ways: (1) The character in one string has a lower value than its corresponding character in the other string; or (2) the end of each string is reached, in which case the two strings have equal value.[1] In WATFIV the sequence in Table 5.2 (called the **collating sequence**) is used to order characters by value. Example 5.3 illustrates this method of evaluating string-based conditions.

Follow-up Exercises

1. Indicate whether the relational expression is valid or not. If valid, indicate whether a true or false condition exists for each relational expression.

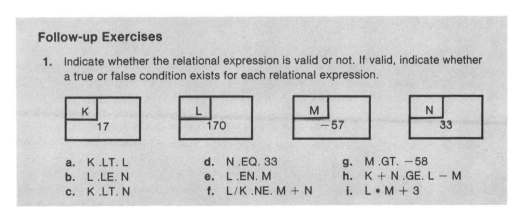

a. K .LT. L	**d.** N .EQ. 33	**g.** M .GT. −58
b. L .LE. N	**e.** L .EN. M	**h.** K + N .GE. L − M
c. K .LT. N	**f.** L/K .NE. M + N	**i.** L * M + 3

[1] Usually the two strings to be compared have different *lengths,* so before the comparison the computer pads the shorter string with blanks on the right until both strings have the same length.

EXAMPLE 5.2 Illustrations of IF-THEN-ELSE Structure

Flowchart	Pseudocode	FORTRAN	Explanation

a.

Pseudocode:

```
IF Hours Worked ≤ 40 THEN
    Regular pay = hours
        worked × rate of
        pay

    Overtime pay = 0
ELSE
    Regular pay = 40 × rate of pay
    Overtime pay = (hours − 40)
        × rate of pay
        × 1.5

END IF
```

FORTRAN:

```
IF (HOURS .LE. 40.0) THEN
    REGPAY = HOURS*RATE
    OVRTM  = 0.0

ELSE
    REGPAY = 40.0*RATE
    OVRTM  = (HOURS − 40.0)
        *RATE * 1.5

END IF
```

Explanation:

If the value stored in HOURS is less than or equal to 40.0 then the statements
REGPAY = HOURS*RATE
OVRTM = 0.0
are executed.
If the value stored in HOURS exceeds 40.0, then the program executes the statements
REGPAY = 40.0*RATE
OVRTM = (HOURS − 40)
*RATE*1.5

b.

Pseudocode:

```
IF distance/time > critical
        velocity  THEN
    Acceleration = 0.9 ×
        acceleration

ELSE
    Acceleration = 1.02 ×
        acceleration

END IF
```

FORTRAN:

```
IF (DIST/TIME .GT. VELCRI) THEN
    ACCEL = 0.9*ACCEL

ELSE
    ACCEL = 1.02*ACCEL

END IF
```

Explanation:

If the value stored in DIST divided by the value stored in TIME is greater than the value stored in VELCRI, then execute
ACCEL = 0.9*ACCEL
otherwise execute
ACCEL = 1.02*ACCEL

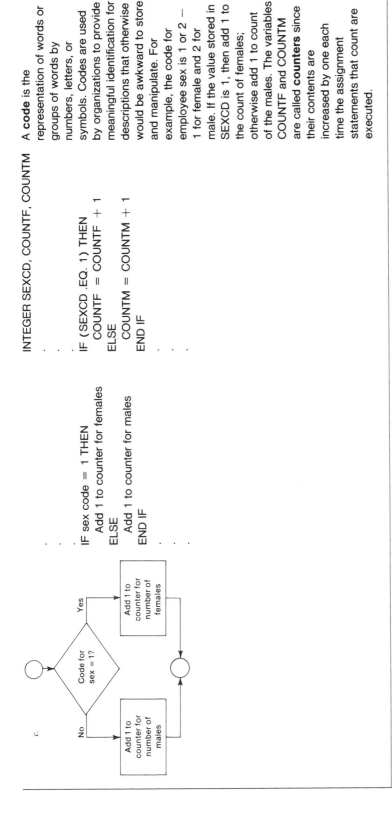

c.

IF sex code = 1 THEN
    Add 1 to counter for females
ELSE
    Add 1 to counter for males
END IF

```
INTEGER SEXCD, COUNTF, COUNTM
 .
 .
IF (SEXCD .EQ. 1) THEN
   COUNTF = COUNTF + 1
ELSE
   COUNTM = COUNTM + 1
END IF
 .
 .
```

A **code** is the representation of words or groups of words by numbers, letters, or symbols. Codes are used by organizations to provide meaningful identification for descriptions that otherwise would be awkward to store and manipulate. For example, the code for employee sex is 1 or 2 – 1 for female and 2 for male. If the value stored in SEXCD is 1, then add 1 to the count of females; otherwise add 1 to count of the males. The variables COUNTF and COUNTM are called **counters** since their contents are increased by one each time the assignment statements that count are executed.

EXAMPLE 5.3   IF-THEN-ELSE Structures Using Character Strings

Program Segment	Value Stored in A	Value Stored in B	Output	Comment

a. CHARACTER A*5,B*5
IF (A .GT. B) THEN
  PRINT, A
ELSE
  PRINT, B
END IF
	HAPPY	SMOKE	SMOKE	S is greater than H; thus SMOKE is greater than HAPPY.

b. CHARACTER A*4,B*8
IF (A .LT. B) THEN
  PRINT, A
ELSE
  PRINT, B
END IF
	KING	KINGSTON	KING	The character string in A is padded to KING𝒷𝒷𝒷𝒷 and then compared to KINGSTON. Blank (𝒷) is less than S; thus KING𝒷𝒷𝒷𝒷 is less than KINGSTON.

c. CHARACTER A*4,B*4
IF (A .EQ. B) THEN
  PRINT, 'EQUAL'
ELSE
  PRINT, 'NOT EQUAL'
END IF
	750A	A750	NOT EQUAL	Letters are lower in the collating sequence than digits; hence A is less than 7, and A750 is less than 750A.

2. Indicate the output from each program segment.
    a. CHARACTER A∗4, B∗4
        A = '123'
        B = 'HELP'
        IF (A .LT. B) THEN
            PRINT,A
        ELSE
            PRINT,B
        END IF

    b. CHARACTER A∗6, B∗6
        A = 'O''HARE'
        B = 'OHARE'
        IF (A .LT. B) THEN
            PRINT,A
        ELSE
            PRINT,B
        END IF

3. Modify Figure 5.1 and the program in Example 5.1 using the test "sales greater than 5000" instead of "sales less than or equal to 5000."

4. Modify the program of Example 5.1 to calculate and print the number of people who do not receive a bonus and the number of people who do receive a bonus.

*5. Modify the program of Example 5.1 to incorporate the fact that base pay varies from salesperson to salesperson. Also assume that the current bonus of $100 and the cutoff of $5000 are likely to change often in the life of the program. As a result, we wish to treat these values under the names CURBON and CUTOFF.

6. Write IF-THEN-ELSE structures for each situation below. Include flowchart or pseudocode along with FORTRAN code.
    a. If credits taken are 12 or more, then tuition is $1200; otherwise tuition is $100 times the number of credits.
    b. If fixed costs plus variable costs are less than sales revenue, then compute profit as sales revenue minus (fixed costs plus variable costs) and output the message PROFIT = · · · ; otherwise, compute loss as fixed plus variable costs minus sales revenue and output the message LOSS = · · · .
    c. A department store has the following minimum payment policy for its customers. When the balance owed (BAL) is under $50, the customer pays (PAYS) the full balance owed. When the amount owed is $50 or more, the customer pays according to the formula $50 + 10 percent (balance owed − $50).
    d. If sex is male, then print the message "SEX = MALE"; otherwise print the message "SEX = FEMALE."

7. Code each flowchart into a segment of a FORTRAN program.

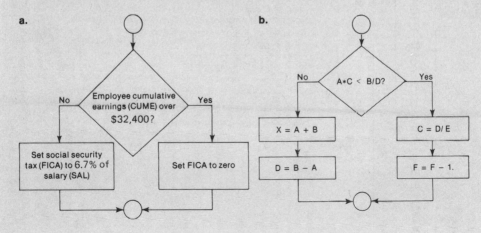

EXAMPLE 5.4 Illustrations of IF-THEN Structure

Flowchart	Pseudocode	FORTRAN	Comments
a.			

	IF age ≥ 65 THEN
	   Increment dependents counter
	END IF
		IF(AGE .GE. 65)THEN
		   DEP = DEP + 1
		END IF
			If the value stored in AGE is 65 or more, then the statement DEP = DEP + 1 is executed; otherwise, this statement is skipped and control goes to the statement following END IF.

b.	READ name and phone number
	IF name = 'Smith' THEN
	   PRINT name and phone number
	END IF
		READ, NAME, PHONE
		IF(NAME .EQ. 'SMITH')THEN
		   PRINT, 'NAME:',NAME
		   PRINT, 'PHONE NUMBER:', PHONE
		END IF
			If the name 'Smith' is found, then the name and telephone number are printed; otherwise, execution continues with the statement following END IF.

IF-THEN Structure

The block IF and END IF statements can be used to code the single-choice or **IF-THEN structure.** In this case the ELSE segment of the IF-THEN-ELSE structure is omitted, as the following variation indicates.

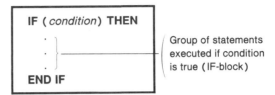

Thus, if the condition tested is true, the IF-block is executed, after which control passes to the first executable statement following the END IF statement. If the condition is false, control passes directly to the first executable statement following the END IF statement, without executing the statements within the IF-block. (See Examples 5.4 and 5.5.)

EXAMPLE 5.5   Finding the Minimum Value

The Department of Health and Human Services has a data file that includes the per capita income (that is, total income divided by total number of people) for each standard metropolitan statistical area (SMSA) in the country. An administrator wishes to determine the SMSA code that has the smallest per capita income. The program below illustrates the determination of this minimum and its associated SMSA.

```
C----------------------------------------------------------------
C    MINIMUM VALUE PROGRAM
C
C    KEY:
C       N      = TOTAL NUMBER OF SMSA'S
C       SMSA   = CODE ASSIGNED TO STANDARD METROPOLITAN
C                STATISTICAL AREA
C       PCI    = PER CAPITA INCOME OF SMSA
C       MINSMS = SMSA WITH MINIMUM PCI
C       MINPCI = SMALLEST PCI
C----------------------------------------------------------------
       INTEGER N,SMSA,MINSMS
       REAL    PCI,MINPCI
C----------------------------------------------------------------
       MINPCI = 1E30
       READ, N
C----------------------------------------------------------------
       DO 100 I = 1,N
         READ, SMSA,PCI
C      --------------------------------------MINIMUM VALUE LOGIC
         IF (PCI .LT. MINPCI) THEN
            MINPCI = PCI
            MINSMS = SMSA
         END IF
C      ---------------------------------------
   100 CONTINUE
C----------------------------------------------------------------
       PRINT, 'SMSA NUMBER      ',MINSMS
       PRINT, 'HAS MINIMUM PCI OF',MINPCI
C----------------------------------------------------------------
       STOP
       END
```

Input	Output	
5		
147,5165.0	SMSA NUMBER	41
56,7860.0	HAS MINIMUM PCI OF	4293.0000000
75,6350.0		
41,4293.0		
105,5415.0		

Note that the variable that stores the minimum value (MINPCI) is initialized to a very large value (1E30). This assures that one of the data items for PCI will be the minimum value. The IF-block is executed whenever a per capita income (value in PCI) is smaller than the minimum value up to that point (value in MINPCI). This means we have found a new minimum value and its associated SMSA.

Follow-up Exercises

8. Draw a flowchart or pseudocode for the program of Example 5.5. Check the logic by roleplaying (with you as computer) through the provided test data. Indicate below the values stored successively, where the "snapshot" of memory is taken at each iteration just before the execution of the CONTINUE statement.

N	I	SMSA	PCI	MINPCI	MINSMS

9. Modify the program of Example 5.5 to find and output the largest per capita income (MAXPCI) and its associated SMSA (MAXSMS), in addition to MINPCI and MINSMS. First draw the flowchart or pseudocode.

10. Write IF-THEN structures for each situation below. Include flowchart or pseudocode along with FORTRAN code.
    a. If sales for week (SALES) are above $10,000 add $150 to pay for week (PAY); otherwise go on to the next statement.
    b. If part name (PART) equals "WRENCH," output the quantity on hand (QOH); otherwise go on to the next statement.

11. Code this flowchart into a segment of a FORTRAN program.

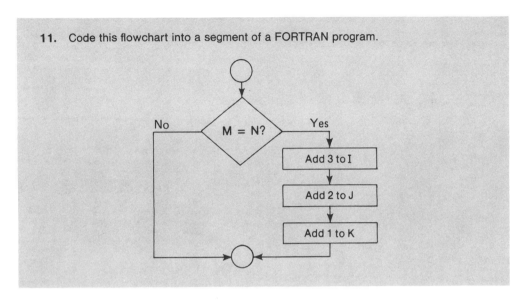

Logical IF Statement

There are many situations where an IF-block has a single statement. In this case, the logical IF statement is a convenient way of establishing an IF-THEN structure.

The **logical IF statement** requires the computer to test a condition and then, based on one of two possible results, to take a proper transfer of control action.

The general form of this statement is

IF (*condition*) *executable statement*

The result of this test is either "true" or "false." If the result is true, then the executable statement to the right of the parentheses is executed. (Only one statement can follow the condition.) If the result is false, the executable statement to the right of the condition is skipped, and the next executable statement following the logical IF statement is executed. In general, the statement to the right of the parentheses can be any executable statement (such as assignment, PRINT, READ, STOP) except for another logical IF, block IF, ELSE IF, ELSE, END IF, END, or DO statement.

Note that the END IF statement is not paired with the logical IF statement.

EXAMPLE 5.6 IF-THEN Structure Using Logical IF Statement

In the calculation of number of dependents for income tax declarations, one additional dependent can be added to the count if the taxpayer or any dependent is 65 or older. This logic was illustrated in Example 5.4a using the block IF statement and is now rewritten using the logical IF statement.

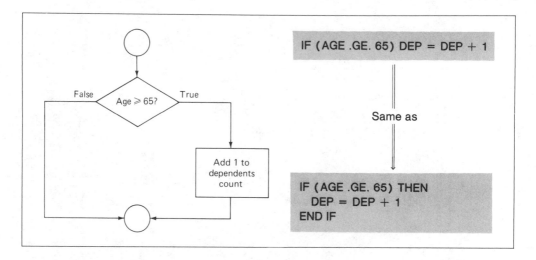

Follow-up Exercises

12. Indicate what is wrong (if anything) with each of the following.
    a. IF (A .GT. B) END
    b. IF (MAJOR .EQ. 'ECN') PRINT,NAME,GPA
    c. IF (A LT 10) A = A+1
13. Rewrite Example 5.4b using logical IF statements.

5.2
LOGICAL EXPRESSIONS

A logical expression is an expression that, when evaluated, is either true or false. Relational expressions are one kind of logical expression. In this section we discuss other variations of logical expressions.

Logical Variables

As you may recall from Chapter 2, page 39, the logical values .TRUE. and .FALSE. are stored in logical variables in the same way numeric values are stored in real or integer variables and strings in character variables. A logical variable first must be typed by using a LOGICAL statement. For example,

    LOGICAL YES, NO, MALE

types YES, NO, and MALE as logical variables.

Logical variables can be assigned values through assignment statements

    logical variable = logical expression

where the **logical expression** can be a *logical constant* as in

YES = .TRUE.

or a *logical variable* as in

NO = YES

or a *relational expression* as in

MALE = SEXCD .EQ. 1

or a *compound logical expression,* which we discuss in the next subsection.

Logical variables are commonly used within IF statements in a variety of situations, as illustrated in the next example.

EXAMPLE 5.7 Logical Variables

Code	Comments
a. LOGICAL MATH INTEGER MAJOR CHARACTER NAME * 30 . . . MATH = MAJOR .EQ. 22 . . IF (MATH) PRINT, NAME . . .	The logical variable, MATH, is used to simplify the understanding of a condition within the IF statement. In this case, MAJOR stores an integer code for a student's major subject area, where code 22 refers to a major in mathematics. Whenever MAJOR stores 22, the logical expression MAJOR .EQ. 22 evaluates as .TRUE., MATH stores the value .TRUE., and the logical IF statement prints the name of the student.

b.   LOGICAL   ERROR
CHARACTER   CODE *1
.
.
.
DO 50 J = 1, N
ERROR = .FALSE.
READ, CODE
IF (CODE .LT. 'A') ERROR = .TRUE.
IF (CODE .GT. 'E') ERROR = .TRUE.
.
.
.
50 CONTINUE
	The logical variable, ERROR, is used as a **flag** or **switch.** A flag identifies whether or not some condition (error, end of data, etc.) has occurred during the processing of a program. In this case a flag is used to signal that an error report is needed whenever code values are outside the range A through E. The flag is usually initialized to .FALSE., meaning the condition has not occurred. At an appropriate point in the program

```
              .
              .
              .
     IF (ERROR) THEN                    the condition is checked, and if
         PRINT, 'ERROR REPORT'          present the flag is assigned a value
              .                         .TRUE.
              .
              .
     END IF
     END
```

Compound Logical Expressions

Up to now we have used a single logical variable or a relational expression made up of a relational operator (.EQ., .NE., .LT., .LE., .GE., .GT.) wedged between two arithmetic or character expressions to test one condition at a time. In many cases complex decisions involving two or more conditions can be expressed by combining relational expressions and or logical variables into a single logical expression. We can accomplish this by using the **logical operators** .AND., .OR., and .NOT. to connect these logical expressions. The resulting expression is called a **compound logical expression.** For example, the relational expression B .GT. A can be combined with the relational expression B .LT. C using the logical operator .AND. as follows:

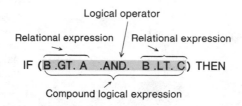

The entire expression within the parentheses is a compound logical expression, which when tested will be either true or false. Note that the first relational expression is the first condition to be tested and the second relational expression is the second condition to be tested. Thus compound logical expressions can be used to test multiple conditions within one block IF statement by applying the following scheme:

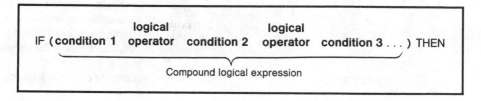

Logical Operator .AND.

When using the operator .AND., if *each* of the conditions is true, then the logical expression is true, and the statements within the IF-block are executed. IF, however, any condition is false, the statements within the IF-block are skipped, and control is transferred either to the ELSE-block (if used) or the END IF statement (if the ELSE-block is not used).

EXAMPLE 5.8   Sales Bonus Problem with Compound Logical Expression

The decision structure in Example 5.1 is modified to reflect the policy that a salesperson receives a bonus of $100 if sales are above $5000 *and* travel expenses are below $600; otherwise the bonus is set to $0.

```
IF (SALES .GT. 5000 .AND. TRAVEL .LT. 600) THEN
   BONUS = 100
ELSE
   BONUS = 0
END IF
```

Logical Operator .OR.

When using the operator .OR., if *any* condition is true, then the logical expression is true and the statements within the IF-block are executed; however, if *all* the conditions are false, then the IF-block is skipped and control is transferred to either the ELSE-block (if used) or the END IF statement.

EXAMPLE 5.9   Use of .OR.

An employer is interested in interviewing students with an economics (ECN) or mathematics (MTH) major. A search routine to find such persons might include the following statements.

```
IF (MAJOR .EQ. 'ECN' .OR. MAJOR .EQ. 'MTH') THEN
   PRINT, NAME, MAJOR
END IF
```

Logical Operator .NOT.

The logical operator .NOT. reverses the logical value to which it is applied. For example, if .NOT. is applied to a false relational expression, then .NOT. makes the logical expression true. If the relational expression is true, then .NOT. causes a false logical expression.

EXAMPLE 5.10   Use of .NOT.

To count the number of programmers who *don't* program in FORTRAN the following statements can be used:

```
CHARACTER  LANG*10, JOB*15
LOGICAL  FORTRN
   .
   .
   .
FORTRN = LANG  .EQ.  'FORTRAN'
   .
   .
   .
IF (JOB .EQ. 'PROGRAMMER'  .AND. .NOT. FORTRN) THEN
   COUNT = COUNT + 1
END IF
```

Hierarchy

To represent more than two conditions we can use more than one logical operator within a logical expression. For logical expressions of this type there is a hierarchy among the logical operators that determines the order in which the operators are evaluated, unless the order is changed by using parentheses. Logical operators are evaluated according to the following hierarchy.

Operator	Order
.NOT.	Highest priority
.AND.	⇓
.OR.	Lowest priority

EXAMPLE 5.11   Hierarchy Rules and Use of Parentheses

If the following values are stored

then the logical expression in

```
IF (I .EQ. J  .OR.  I .GT. K  .AND.  AG .LE. 5.1) THEN
   SUM = SUM + AG
END IF
```

is true and the IF-block

    SUM = SUM + AG

is executed. This logical expression is evaluated in the following manner.

1. According to the hierarchy, .AND. is evaluated before .OR., which means that we should focus on the shaded portion below.

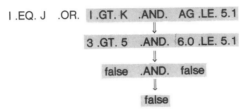

2. We are now left with

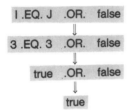

Thus the logical expression itself has the value true.

As in arithemetic expressions, parentheses can be used to modify the order of evaluation within logical expressions. For example, assuming the same values for I, J, K, and AG, the logical expression in

    IF ((I .EQ. J .OR. I .GT. K) .AND. AG .LE. 5.1) THEN
       SUM = SUM + AG
    END IF

is false and control goes directly to the END IF statement without executing the IF-block. Now the expression is evaluated in the following manner.

1. Expressions enclosed within parentheses are evaluated before expressions not enclosed within parentheses. Thus the shaded portion below is evaluated first as true.

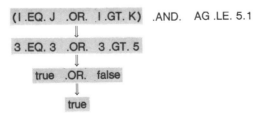

2. We are now left with

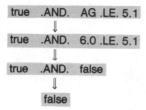

The logical expression therefore is false.

Improving readability is an alternative use of parentheses within logical expressions, as it is in arithmetic expressions. For instance, the clarity of the original block IF statement in this example can be improved as follows.

IF ((I .EQ. J) .OR. (I .GT. K   .AND.   AG .LE. 5.1)) THEN

The value of this logical expression is true, as before; however, it is now quite clear that the operator .AND. is considered before the operator .OR., since .AND. is within parentheses.

Follow-up Exercises

14. Given the type statements

        REAL A, B
        LOGICAL X, Y, Z

which of the following statements are syntactically correct?
a. X = A .LT. B
b. Y = A + B
c. Z = .FALSE.
d. A = .TRUE.

15. Simplify the decision structure conditions for CODE in Example 5.7b by using a compound logical expression. Which version do you prefer?

16. Indicate what is wrong (if anything) with each of the following:
a. IF (VAL .GT. 100   .AND.   .LT. 200) THEN
b. IF (MAJOR .EQ. 'ECN'   .OR.   'MATH') THEN
c. IF (A .EQ. B   .AND.   (C .EQ. D   OR   L .LE. M)) THEN

17. Given the stored values

indicate whether or not the IF-block is executed for each of the following.

   a. IF (.NOT. (L .LT. M)) THEN
   b. IF (L .GT. M .AND. M .EQ. N .OR. L .LE. N .AND. M .LT. 4) THEN
   c. IF (L .GT. M .AND. (M .EQ. N .OR. L .LE. N) .AND. M .LT. 4) THEN
   d. IF ((L .GT. M .AND. M .EQ. N .OR. L .LE. N) .AND. M .LT. 4) THEN
  *e. IF ((L .GT. M .AND. (M .EQ. N .OR. L .LE. N)) .AND. M .LT. 4) THEN

18. Develop code for each flowchart using logical operators.

   a.

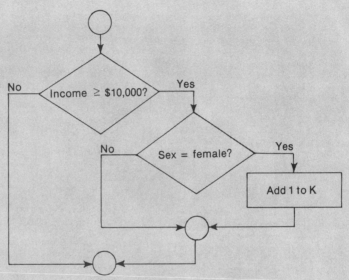

   b.

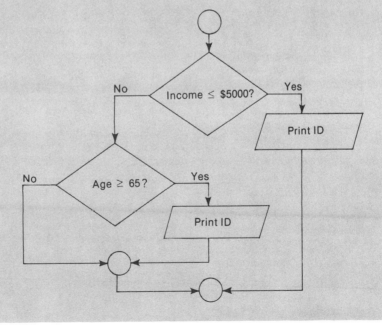

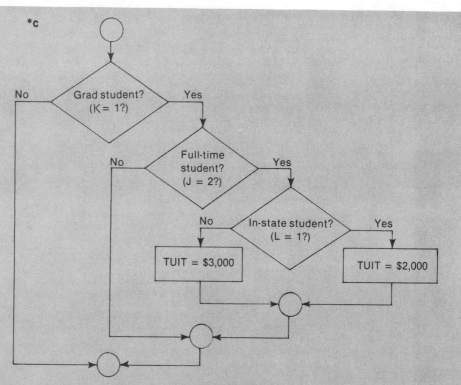

19. Assume that three logical variables LFORT, LCOBOL, and LPASCL are set to indicate whether a programmer can program in FORTRAN, COBOL, or Pascal. A value of .TRUE. for any variable indicates that the programmer can program in that language. Write compound logical expressions to answer the following questions.
    a. Which programmers know COBOL and FORTRAN?
    b. Which programmers know either Pascal or FORTRAN or both?
    c. Which programmers know all three languages?
    d. Which programmers do not know Pascal?

20. Input Data Validation. Modify the program in Example 5.5 on page 153 to include an error routine that validates the input data. Specifically, following the input of SMSA and PCI values, test to make sure that SMSA is between 1 and 200 inclusive and PCI is greater than $1000 and less than $25,000. Program the following versions.
    a. If an error is found, print the input data line number where the error is located, print the corresponding values in SMSA and PCI, and continue processing as if nothing is wrong.
    b. Same as part a, except stop processing as soon as an error message is printed.
    c. Same as part a, except once an error message is printed, bypass the IF-THEN structure that finds the minimum value and go on to process the next input line.

Include a flowchart or pseudocode for each version. Which approach do you prefer and why?

5.3
WHILE STRUCTURE

As you might recall from Chapter 4, the first action in a **WHILE structure** (Figure 5.2) is to test whether or not the loop is to be executed. If the loop is to be executed, control passes to the body of the loop. After the statements within the body have been executed, control returns to the test statement preceding the loop body. When the test indicates that looping is finished, control passes to a statement outside the loop. Thus we are telling the computer to loop "WHILE" the condition tests true. This structure can be used to specify the number of times a loop is to be executed or specify some condition under which the loop is repeated.

WATFIV implements the WHILE structure with the following two statements:

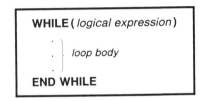

The condition given by the logical expression is tested before entry into the body of the loop. If the condition is false, then control passes to the statement following the END WHILE statement. If the condition is true, then the body of the loop is executed. When the END WHILE statement is reached, control returns to the loop test and the condition in the WHILE statement is tested again. If false, control passes to the statement following the END WHILE; if true, the loop body is executed again. Thus, the WHILE and END WHILE statements represent the loop structure exhibited in Figure 5.2.

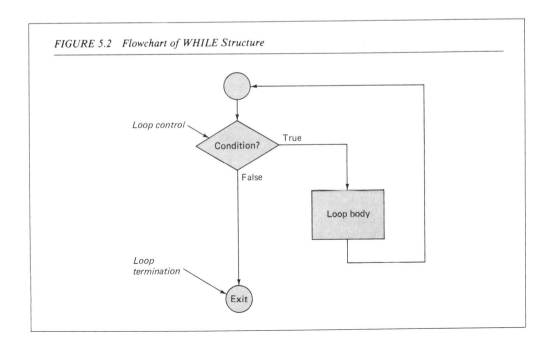

FIGURE 5.2   *Flowchart of WHILE Structure*

In the next example we illustrate how the WHILE statement is used to control loop repetition when the condition tested is based on a value computed within the loop body.

EXAMPLE 5.12   The Inflation Curse: WHILE Version

High rates of inflation in a "free" market economy can have devastating effects. For individuals, particularly those, such as retirees, who live on fixed incomes, purchasing power (the ability to buy goods and services) can erode dramatically over time. For the economy as a whole, it can lead to recession and unemployment as a result of such factors as uncertainty and high interest rates.

To illustrate, suppose an item currently costs $100 and increases in cost at a 10 percent rate of inflation per year. The future cost of this item one year from now would be $110, determined as follows:

$$100 + (100) \cdot (0.1)$$

or

$$100 \cdot (1 + 0.1)$$

Two years from now it would cost $110 plus an additional 10 percent for the price increase in the second year, or

$$110 \cdot (1 + 0.1)$$

which is $121. Thus if we define

C = current cost of item
R = rate of inflation

and

F = future cost of item one year from now

then we have

$$F = C \cdot (1 + R)$$

for the cost at the end of one year and

$$F = (\text{previous year's } F) \cdot (1 + R)$$

for future costs in subsequent years.

Figure 5.3 and the program on page 167 illustrate an algorithm that prints successive future costs by years until the future cost equals or exceeds double the current cost.

FIGURE 5.3   *Algorithm for Inflation Curse Problem*

READ current cost, percent inflation rate
Error routine for inflation rate
Rate = percent rate / 100
PRINT input data and table headers
Future cost = current cost
Year = 0
WHILE future cost < 2 × current cost
   Year = year + 1
   Future cost =   previous future cost ×
                   (1 + inflation rate)
   PRINT year, future cost
END WHILE
Stop

```
C--------------------------------------------
C    INFLATION CURSE PROGRAM:      WHILE VERSION
C
C    KEY:
C       YEAR  = YEARS INTO FUTURE
C       RATE  = RATE OF INFLATION
C       PRI   = PERCENT RATE OF INFLATION
C       COSTC = CURRENT COST
C       COSTF = FUTURE COST
C
C--------------------------------------------
        INTEGER YEAR
        REAL    COSTC,COSTF,RATE,PRI
C--------------------------------------------
        READ, COSTC,PRI
C--------------------------------------------
        IF (PRI .LT. 1.0  .OR. PRI .GT. 100.0) THEN
          PRINT, '*** INPUT ERROR ***'
          PRINT, 'PERCENT RATE OF INTEREST (PRI) MUST BE'
          PRINT, 'IN THE RANGE 1.0 TO 100.0.  YOU INPUT',PRI
          PRINT, 'DEFAULT PRI = 10.0'
          PRI = 10.0
        END IF
C--------------------------------------------
        RATE = PRI/100.0
C--------------------------------------------
        PRINT, '--------------------------------------'
        PRINT, 'CURRENT COST: $',CCSTC
        PRINT, 'INFLATION RATE:',PRI,'%'
        PRINT, '--------------------------------------'
        PRINT, 'YEARS INTO FUTURE      FUTURE COST'
        PRINT, '--------------------------------------'
C--------------------------------------------
        COSTF = COSTC
        YEAR  = 0
C--------------------------------------------
        WHILE (COSTF .LT. 2.0*COSTC)
          YEAR = YEAR + 1
          COSTF = COSTF*(1.0 + RATE)
          PRINT. YEAR,COSTF
        END WHILE
C--------------------------------------------
        PRINT, '--------------------------------------'
        STOP
        END
```

Error
routine

← ———————— Test precedes
loop body

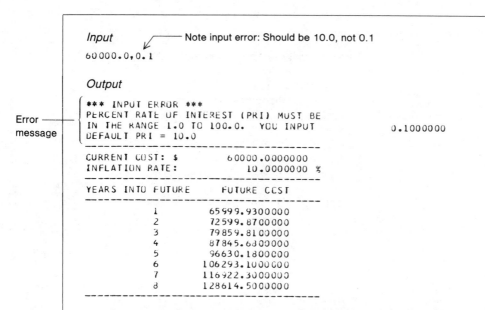

Input   — Note input error: Should be 10.0, not 0.1
60000.0,0.1

Output

Error message
```
*** INPUT ERROR ***
PERCENT RATE OF INTEREST (PRI) MUST BE
IN THE RANGE 1.0 TO 100.0.   YOU INPUT          0.1000000
DEFAULT PRI = 10.0
-----------------------------------------------
CURRENT COST: $       60000.0000000
INFLATION RATE:          10.0000000 %
-----------------------------------------------
YEARS INTO FUTURE       FUTURE COST
-----------------------------------------------
         1            65999.9300000
         2            72599.8700000
         3            79859.8100000
         4            87845.6300000
         5            96630.1800000
         6           106293.1000000
         7           116922.3000000
         8           128614.5000000
-----------------------------------------------
```

The input data assumes an item (say, a house) that costs $60,000 and increases in value at a rate of 10 percent per year. According to the output, the price of the house will double in its eighth year.

The **error routine** in the program and the subsequent error message in the output illustrate the common "defensive" programming procedure of checking the data for common input errors. In this case, the program requires input of the inflation rate as a percent in the range 1 to 100, instead of a proportion in the range 0 to 1. Since we input the proportion 0.1 (purposely, of course), the error routine detects the error, prints an error message, defaults to 10 percent (conveniently), and continues processing. If possible, we generally prefer the use of default values along with an appropriate message and program continuation to the termination of execution whenever an error is detected—it makes for "friendlier," more robust programs.

Now look at the WHILE structure in the program.

COSTF is the loop control variable whose value is tested in the WHILE statement to determine whether the loop body should or should not be executed. As long as the condition "future cost less than twice current cost" is true, the body of the loop is executed. However, the first time the condition is false, the loop body is skipped and control is transferred to the first executable statement after the END WHILE statement.

Thus, just to keep up with inflation, the house must sell at the indicated future costs. In the eighth year, the future cost exceeds double the initial cost, so execution terminates based on a false value for the relational expression in the WHILE statement.

Follow-up Exercises

21. Confirm the output by roleplaying the computer. As you do this, fill in the contents of the indicated storage locations on page 169 as if a "snapshot" of memory were taken just before execution of the END WHILE statement.

	COSTC	RATE	YEAR	COSTF

22. In Example 5.12, what would happen if
    a. The statement

    COSTF = COSTC

    were omitted?
    b. The statement

    COSTF = COSTF*(1.0 + RATE)

    were changed to

    COSTF = COSTC*(1.0 + RATE)

    c. YEAR were initialized to 1? Modify the program to obtain the same output if the year is initialized to 1.
    d. Can you think of a way of improving the computational efficiency within the body of the loop?
23. Modify the program in Example 5.12 so the user specifies as input a multiplicative factor (M). In the example, M has a value of 2 (that is, the loop terminates when the future cost exceeds double the current cost).
24. Modify the program in Example 5.12 to terminate looping either when future cost equals or exceeds double the current cost or when ten years have passed.
25. In Example 5.12,
    a. Modify the program to incorporate a second loop that processes N sets of data.
    b. Run the program for the following sets of values.

COSTC	PRI
60000	5
60000	10
60000	15
100000	10

*26. Rewrite the following examples using WHILE/END WHILE statements instead of DO-Loops. Which approach do you prefer? Why?
    a. Sales bonus program, Example 5.1, page 145.
    b. Minimum value program, Example 5.5, page 153.
    c. Bank savings program, Section 4.8, page 127. (Eliminate the use of variable LOOPS.)

5.4
UNTIL STRUCTURE

The WHILE structure is a popular type of loop structure, but it is not necessarily preferred for all types of looping. Some problems are best served by the type of loop structure first discussed in Chapter 4 and illustrated in Figure 5.4. The **UNTIL structure** first processes the body of the loop, after which a condition (logical expression) is tested to determine if the loop should be repeated. If the result of the test is false, control goes back to the beginning of the loop and the body is processed once more; if the result is true, control is transferred out of the loop. Thus we are telling the computer to loop "UNTIL" the condition tests true. Note that, unlike the WHILE structure, the UNTIL structure ensures that the body is processed at least once.

WATFIV implements the UNTIL structure with the following two statements

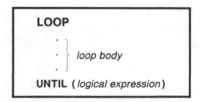

The condition given by the logical expression is tested after the loop body is executed. If the condition is true, control passes to the statement following the UNTIL statement. If the condition is false, then the body of the loop is executed, after which the condition in the UNTIL statement is tested again. If true, there is a loop exit as control passes to the statement following the UNTIL statement; if false, the loop body is executed again . . . (and so on).

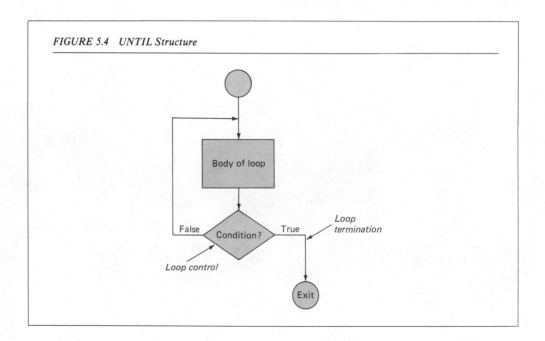

FIGURE 5.4   UNTIL Structure

EXAMPLE 5.13   Inflation Curse Using UNTIL Structure

The inflation curse program using the UNTIL structure is rewritten as follows.

```
C------------------------------------------------
C    INFLATION CURSE PROGRAM:    UNTIL VERSION
C
C    KEY:
C       YEAR  = YEARS INTO FUTURE
C       RATE  = RATE OF INFLATION
C       PRI   = PERCENT RATE OF INFLATION
C       COSTC = CURRENT COST
C       COSTF = FUTURE COST
C
C------------------------------------------------
      INTEGER YEAR
      REAL    COSTC,COSTF,RATE,PRI
C------------------------------------------------
      READ, COSTC,PRI
C------------------------------------------------
      IF (PRI .LT. 1.0  .OR. PRI .GT. 100.0) THEN
         PRINT, '*** INPUT ERROR ***'
         PRINT, 'PERCENT RATE OF INTEREST (PRI) MUST BE'
         PRINT, 'IN THE RANGE 1.0 TO 100.0.  YOU INPUT',PRI
         PRINT, 'DEFAULT PRI = 10.0'
         PRI = 10.0
      END IF
C------------------------------------------------
      RATE = PRI/100.0
C------------------------------------------------
      PRINT, '------------------------------------'
      PRINT, 'CURRENT COST: $',COSTC
      PRINT, 'INFLATION RATE:',PRI,'%'
      PRINT, '------------------------------------'
      PRINT, 'YEARS INTO FUTURE     FUTURE COST'
      PRINT, '------------------------------------'
C------------------------------------------------
      COSTF = COSTC
      YEAR  = 0
C------------------------------------------------
      LOOP
         YEAR = YEAR + 1
         COSTF = COSTF*(1.0 + RATE)             ─── Test
         PRINT, YEAR,COSTF                          follows
      UNTIL (COSTF .GE. 2.0*COSTC)  ←              loop body
C------------------------------------------------
      PRINT, '------------------------------------'
      STOP
      END
```

The I/O for this program is exactly the same as in Example 5.12.

In many cases, the choice of a pre-test or post-test loop design is simply based on the programmer's preference for one style over another. In other cases, the pre-test approach avoids an unnecessary execution of the loop body.[2]

---

[2] This is especially true for LRC loops. See Section 5.6 and "Loop Errors" in Section 5.8.

Follow-up Exercises

27. For the program in Example 5.13
    a. Draw a flowchart.
    b. Write pseudocode.
28. Modify the program in Example 5.13:
    a. To print the message "cost has at least doubled *xx* years from now" instead of printing the entire table.
    b. Add an outer loop to process *N* sets of data.
*29. Revise the following examples using LOOP/UNTIL statements instead of DO-loops. Which approach do you prefer? Why?
    a. Sales bonus program, Example 5.1, page 145.
    b. Minimum value program, Example 5.5, page 153.
    c. Bank savings program, Section 4.8, page 127. (Eliminate the use of variable LOOPS.)
*30. A $4000 bank deposit that is compounded quarterly at the rate of 6 percent per year accumulates as follows:

Quarter	Amount
1	4060.00
2	4120.90
3	4182.71
4	4245.45
.	
.	
.	

Note that the quarterly rate is 0.06 divided by 4. Write code in each of the three ways below to determine and print the balance at the end of the fourth quarter in 1990 if the $4000 is deposited at the beginning of the first quarter in 1980.
    a. Use a DO-loop.
    b. Use a WHILE structure.
    c. Use an UNTIL structure.
Which approach do you prefer and why?

5.5
GENERALIZED LOOP STRUCTURE

Occasionally situations arise where it is inconvenient to specify the loop termination parameters at the beginning or end of the loop. Instead, termination of a loop is specified somewhere in the body of the loop. WATFIV has a **generalized loop structure** to handle pre-test, post-test, or "embedded" test loops. To implement this structure the **LOOP** and **END LOOP** **statements** are used as follows

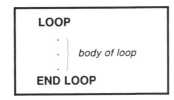

The statements in the loop body are repeated until control is transferred out of the loop, usually by a **QUIT statement.**

The QUIT statement has the format

```
QUIT
```

and can be combined with the logical IF statement as follows

```
IF (condition) QUIT
```

to transfer control out of a loop to the statement following the next END LOOP, END WHILE, or UNTIL statements. Example 5.14 illustrates this generalized loop structure.

EXAMPLE 5.14   Inflation Curse Using Generalized Loop Structure

```
C---------------------------------------------
C    INFLATION CURSE PROGRAM: GENERALIZED LOOP VERSION
C
C    KEY:
C       YEAR  = YEARS INTO FUTURE
C       RATE  = RATE OF INFLATION
C       PRI   = PERCENT RATE OF INFLATION
C       COSTC = CURRENT COST
C       COSTF = FUTURE COST
C
C---------------------------------------------
        INTEGER YEAR
        REAL    COSTC,COSTF,RATE,PRI
C---------------------------------------------
        READ, COSTC,PRI
C---------------------------------------------
        IF (PRI .LT. 1.0  .OR. PRI .GT. 100.0) THEN
          PRINT, '*** INPUT ERROR ***'
          PRINT, 'PERCENT RATE OF INTEREST (PRI) MUST BE'
          PRINT, 'IN THE RANGE 1.0 TO 100.0.  YOU INPUT',PRI
          PRINT, 'DEFAULT PRI = 10.0'
          PRI = 10.0
        END IF
C---------------------------------------------
        RATE = PRI/100.0
C---------------------------------------------
        PRINT, '---------------------------------------'
        PRINT, 'CURRENT COST: $',COSTC
        PRINT, 'INFLATION RATE:',PRI,'%'
        PRINT, '---------------------------------------'
        PRINT, 'YEARS INTO FUTURE     FUTURE COST'
        PRINT, '---------------------------------------'
```

```
C- — -- -- --- --- -- -- --- --------- -- ----------- -
    COSTF = COSTC
    YEAR  = 0
C- — -- -- --- --- -- --------- ----------- -- --------
    LOOP
        YEAR = YEAR + 1
        COSTF = COSTF*(1.0 + RATE)
        PRINT, YEAR,COSTF
            IF (COSTF .GE. 2.0*COSTC) QUIT  <—
    END LOOP
C- — -- -- --- --- -- --------- ----------- -- ------- -
    PRINT, '------------------------------------------'
    STOP
    END
```

Here we place test at end of loop, although it can be placed anywhere within loop

This version of the inflation curse program establishes the beginning, end, and repetition of the loop by using the LOOP and END LOOP statements. The logical IF and QUIT statements take care of loop control. I/O is the same as in Examples 5.12 and 5.13. Note that our placement of the logical IF and QUIT statements makes this loop an UNTIL structure. Thus, when the logical expression tests true, the QUIT statement is executed and control goes to the statement immediately following the END LOOP statement (in this case the PRINT statement).

The following schematic diagram summarizes this loop structure.

Generalized Loop Structure

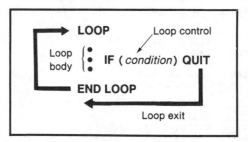

The direct UNTIL structure in Example 5.13 is preferred to the indirect UNTIL structure in Example 5.14; however, the generalized loop structure is more flexible with respect to the placement of the loop control. For example, we could place the logical IF/QUIT statements anywhere within the loop of Example 5.14, which we ask you to do in the follow-up exercises. Whenever possible, however, we prefer the strict use of pre-test and post-test loops, since these are stylistically "clean" with respect to indentation and body/control mechanics.

Follow-up Exercises

31.   Specify output for Example 5.14 if:
      a.   The logical IF/QUIT statements were placed just before the PRINT statement.

> **b.** The logical IF / QUIT statements were placed just after the LOOP statement. The statements IF(COSTF .LT. 2.0 * COSTC)QUIT were placed just after the LOOP statement.
> ***32.** Solve Exercise 30 using a generalized loop structure.

5.6
LAST-RECORD-CHECK (LRC) LOOPS

DO-loops are convenient when we know beforehand the number of desired loop iterations. If we don't wish to specify in advance (or don't know) the exact number of times the loop is to be repeated, the **Last-Record-Check (LRC) loop** may be appropriate. Use of the LRC loop is especially common in data processing applications.[3]

Trailer Number Method

The construction of an LRC loop by the trailer number method requires a special data item that signals the end of the data. This special data item, sometimes called a **sentinel** or **trailer number,** is placed at the end of the data as a "unique" number (or string constant) assigned to one of the input variables. By a "unique" number we mean one that would never be part of normal input data. For example, in the sales bonus program a Social Security number (SSN) of −99 might serve as a trailer number since Social Security numbers are always positive. After a salesperson's data are read in, a test is made to determine whether or not the data just read in contain the trailer number. If the test determines that a particular value of SSN is the trailer number, this indicates that all the data have been read and control branches out of the loop; otherwise, looping continues. Figure 5.5 illustrates this method for the sales bonus problem and Example 5.15 presents the corresponding program.

EXAMPLE 5.15   Sales Bonus Problem with LRC Loop Based on Trailer Number

The following version replaces the DO-loop in Example 5.1 on page 145 with an LRC loop

```
C-------------------------------------------------------------
C     SALES BONUS PROGRAM: TRAILER NUMBER VERSION
C
C     KEY:
C        BASE   = BASE SALARY
C        NAME   = SALESPERSON'S NAME
C        SSN    = SOCIAL SECURITY NUMBER
C        SALES  = WEEKLY SALES
C        BONUS  = SALES BONUS
C        TOTPAY = TOTAL PAY
```

---

[3] For example, see Chapter 11.

FIGURE 5.5   *Sales Bonus Problem with LRC Loop Based on Trailer Number*

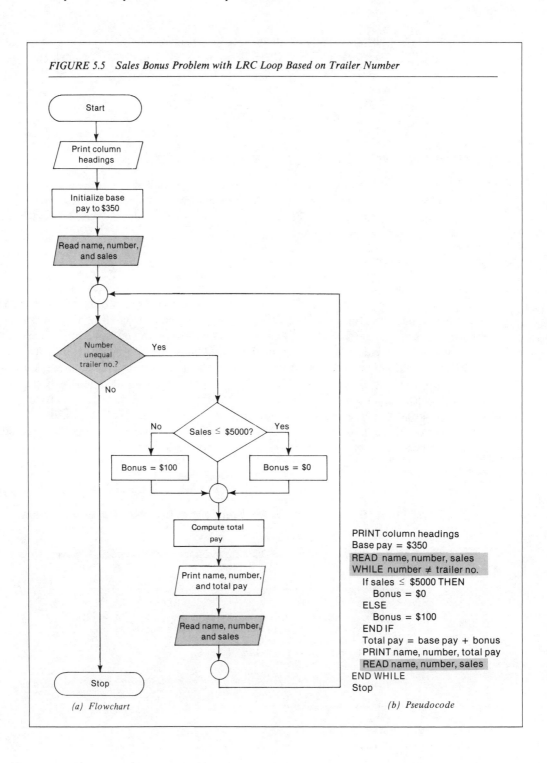

(a) Flowchart

```
PRINT column headings
Base pay = $350
READ name, number, sales
WHILE number ≠ trailer no.
  If sales ≤ $5000 THEN
    Bonus = $0
  ELSE
    Bonus = $100
  END IF
  Total pay = base pay + bonus
  PRINT name, number, total pay
  READ name, number, sales
END WHILE
Stop
```

(b) Pseudocode

```
C- —— —— —— —— —— —— —— —— —— —— —— —— —— —— —— ——— -----
      CHARACTER NAME*15
      INTEGER   BASE,SSN,SALES,BONUS,TOTPAY
C- —— —— —— —— —— —— —— —— —— —— —— —— —— —— —— —— -----
      PRINT, 'EMPLOYEE NAME       SS NUMBER      TOTAL PAY'
      PRINT, '——————————————————————————————————————————'
C- —— —— —— —— —— —— —— —— —— —— —— —— —— —— —— —— -----
      BASE = 350
      READ, NAME,SSN,SALES   ◄————————  This READ statement is used
C- —— —— —— —— —— —— —— —— —— —— —— —— —— —— —— —— -----  only for the first input line
      WHILE (SSN .NE. -99)  ◄————— Loop control
         IF (SALES .LE. 5000) THEN ⌐
            BONUS = 0
         ELSE
            BONUS = 100
         END IF                        ⎬ Body of loop
         TOTPAY = BASE + BONUS
         PRINT, NAME,SSN,TOTPAY
         READ, NAME,SSN,SALES  ◄————— This READ statement is used
      END WHILE                          for all remaining input lines
C- —— —— —— —— —— —— —— —— —— —— —— —— —— —— —— —— -----
      STOP
      END
```

Input

```
'W. LOMAN',123456789,4500
'X. LOMAN',432198765,6500
'Y. LOMAN',987654321,5100
'LRC',-99,0          ◄——————— Trailer record
```

Output

```
EMPLOYEE NAME       SS NUMBER      TOTAL PAY
————————————————————————————————————————————
W. LOMAN            123456789         350
X. LOMAN            432198765         450
Y. LOMAN            987654321         450
```

The **trailer record** or last input line has the trailer number −99 assigned to the salesperson's Social Security number. This record does not represent another salesperson; it's simply placed at the end of the data to indicate no more data. When the computer reads this record, it has already processed data for all salespersons. The statement

   (SSN .NE. −99)

needs further explanation. Immediately after the first READ statement is executed, the computer checks for the trailer number before executing the loop body by testing the value of SSN against −99. After the data for the first salesperson are read in, the location SSN contains the value 123456789, which is not equal to −99. Thus the relational expression ''SSN .NE. −99 ' is evaluated as true. As a result, the computer next computes and prints the total pay, reads in another line of data (using the second READ statement), and returns to the WHILE statement to test for the trailer number. For the second and third sales people the same process is repeated; that is, the loop body is executed. Finally, when the trailer record is processed, the contents of SSN test false against the value −99. As a result, control is transferred outside the loop and processing terminates.

> Note that the loop structure in this example is a WHILE structure, since the loop test precedes the body and looping continues "while" SSN is unequal to -99.
>
> Output from a run of this program is identical to the earlier DO-loop version in Example 5.1.

AT END Method

Another variation of the LRC loop uses the **AT END** and **END AT END statements** combined with the LOOP/END LOOP and QUIT statements first presented in Section 5.5. There are two variations for these statements, as illustrated in Figure 5.6.

First consider the version in Figure 5.6a. In this case, looping continues while data lines remain to be processed by the READ statement. Once data lines are exhausted, the attempt to read a nonexistent data line results in what is called an **end-of-file (EOF) condition**. At this time, the QUIT statement to the right of the AT END statement is executed, and loop exit is achieved. Example 5.16 illustrates this approach.

FIGURE 5.6   AT END LRC Loop Designs

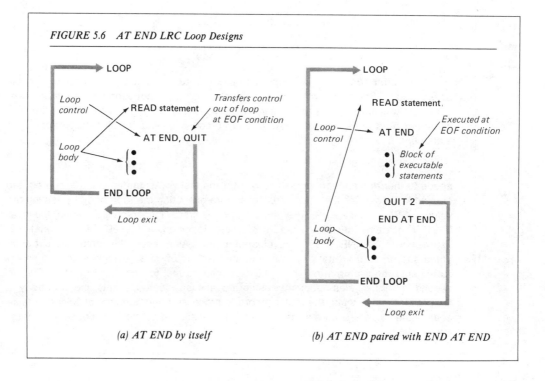

(a) AT END by itself   (b) AT END paired with END AT END

EXAMPLE 5.16 Sales Bonus Problem with AT END LRC Loop

```
C--------------------------------------------------------
C    SALES BONUS PROGRAM:  AT END VERSION
C
C    KEY:
C       BASE  = BASE SALARY
C       NAME  = SALESPERSON'S NAME
C       SSN   = SOCIAL SECURITY NUMBER
C       SALES = WEEKLY SALES
C       BONUS = SALES BONUS
C       TOTPAY = TOTAL PAY
C--------------------------------------------------------
       CHARACTER NAME*15
       INTEGER   BASE,SSN,SALES,BONUS,TOTPAY
C--------------------------------------------------------
       PRINT, 'EMPLOYEE NAME      SS NUMBER      TOTAL PAY'
       PRINT, '-----------------------------------------'
C--------------------------------------------------------
       BASE = 350
C--------------------------------------------------------
       LOOP
          READ, NAME,SSN,SALES
          AT END, QUIT
          IF (SALES .LE. 5000) THEN
             BONUS = 0
          ELSE
             BONUS = 100
          END IF
          TOTPAY = BASE + BONUS
          PRINT, NAME,SSN,TOTPAY
       END LOOP
C--------------------------------------------------------
       STOP
       END
```

Loop control → (points to AT END, QUIT and READ)

Loop body → (points to loop body statements)

Input

```
'W. LOMAN',123456789,4500
'X. LOMAN',432198765,6500
'Y. LOMAN',987654321,5100
```

← Trailer record not necessary;
EOF condition occurs when READ statement
attempts input of nonexistent fourth data line

Output

```
EMPLOYEE NAME      SS NUMBER      TOTAL PAY
-------------------------------------------
W. LOMAN          123456789         350
X. LOMAN          432198765         450
Y. LOMAN          987654321         450
```

The only difference in I/O between this version and the trailer number version in Example 5.15 on page 177 is that the AT END version does not require a trailer record. In this case, an EOF condition is encountered as the loop attempts its fourth execution of the READ statement.

The EOF condition causes the processor to execute the QUIT statement, since it appears to the right of the AT END statement. This in turn transfers execution control to the first statement following END LOOP, which in this example is a STOP statement. In effect, looping continues while the EOF condition is *not* encountered.

The version in Figure 5.6b uses the more elaborate AT END/END AT END block, which gets executed at the EOF condition. This version requires the following variation of the QUIT statement,

QUIT *n*

where *n* is an integer constant that guarantees a transfer of control out to the *n*th *nested* level. In Figure 5.6b we use

QUIT 2

where the "2" gets us past END AT END (first level) to the END LOOP (second level). Exercise 37 illustrates this version of the QUIT statement.[4]

Please note the following two CAUTIONS when using AT END LRC loops:

1. The AT END statement must immediately follow the READ statement.
2. Make sure loop exit is achieved by having a transfer of control statement such as QUIT, STOP, or RETURN (Chapter 9) to the right of END in the Figure 5.6a version or just before END AT END in the Figure 5.6b version; otherwise the loop body is inadvertently processed following the EOF condition.

In general we should use the AT END LRC loop whenever a loop is to process many lines (records) of data whose number is likely to change from run to run. This approach is convenient and reliable since it avoids the error-prone activity of having to specify beforehand the exact number of loop iterations, as in using a DO-loop. This is a key reason why the EOF approach is the method of choice in commercial data processing applications such as payrolls, billings, and inventory control.

The trailer number LRC approach is useful either in interactive systems that don't support the EOF condition or in applications when the EOF condition is undesirable, as when more data need to be read following the LRC loop.

Follow-up Exercises

33. With respect to Example 5.15:
   a. If we were to use zero as the trailer number, how would you change the input data and program? Is there a danger in using zero? Explain.
   b. Do you need data entries for name and sales on the trailer record? Do these have to be "LRC" and zero? Explain.
34. What would happen in Example 5.16 if we were to use the input data from Example 5.15?

---

[4] To be more precise, the QUIT statement transfers control to the end of either a DO-loop or a "structured block" where the latter is defined by any of the following statements: ENDLOOP, ENDWHILE, UNTIL, ENDIF, END-CASE (Chapter 6), or END AT END. If the QUIT statement is "buried" within nested structured blocks, then QUIT *n* exits out to the *n*th level.

35. Change Example 5.15 such that NAME is used to test the last line of data. Use the string constant "EOF" as the trailer "number." How would the trailer record look in this case?

36. Revise Example 5.16 so that the message END OF DATA is printed after the EOF condition. (*Hint:* Try using the END AT END statement.)

37. Specify output.

a.

Program	Input	Output
INTEGER AGE	10	
LOOP	20	
READ, AGE	30	
AT END		
PRINT, 'EOF'		
QUIT 2		
END AT END		
PRINT, AGE		
END LOOP		
PRINT, 'LOOP EXIT'		
STOP		
END		

b. Same as part a, except delete QUIT.

c. Same as part a, except use QUIT instead of QUIT 2.

*38. **Bank Savings Account Program.**   Change the bank savings program of Section 2.9 on page 71 by inserting an LRC loop to process customers. Input customer name (20 characters) and use each of the following methods:

  a. Trailer number method

  b. AT END method

*39. **Student Billing Program.**   Revise Example 4.2 on page 118 by using each of the following LRC loops.

  a. Trailer number method

  b. AT END method

5.7
TOP-DOWN DESIGN

It would be best if you were to study Module E at this time. This not only would introduce you to an important topic called "top-down design," but also would further reinforce decision and loop structures and the four-step procedure within the context of a new scenario.

5.8
COMMON ERRORS

Be alert for the following types of errors.

Errors in Logical Expressions

1. Don't forget that the periods are part of relational and logical operators. If we write

   IF (I .GT. J   AND   I .LT. K) THEN

   we have a syntax error: Having omitted the periods around AND causes the compiler to "think" that J AND I is the variable JANDI. This in itself does not cause a syntax error. The syntax error is provoked when the compiler next encounters the relational operator .LT. instead of a logical operator. This is illegal since the relational expression on the left must be connected by a logical operator to any relational expression on the right.

2. Remember to use the relational operators .LT., .LE., .GT., .GE., .EQ., and .NE. instead of algebraic symbol counterparts. For example, a common error is to use "=" instead of ".EQ.".

3. Do you see what's wrong with the following?

   IF (I .GT. J   .AND.   .LT. K) THEN

   The relational expression on the right is incomplete. We have a tendency to do this because of the way we would state this decision verbally: "If I is greater than J and less than K." To avoid a syntax error it must be written as follows.

   IF (I .GT. J   .AND.   I .LT. K) THEN

4. Pay attention to hierarchy when using more than one logical operator. Reread Example 5.11 and make sure you understand the answers to Exercise 17.

5. If possible avoid using .EQ. when comparing real values, as *roundoff error* may guarantee a false result. For example, the relational expression in

   IF (A/B   .EQ.   0.1) THEN

   may test false even if 1.0 is in A and 10.0 is in B. If the above real values must be tested for equality, we could allow for roundoff error up to ± 0.000001 by writing

   IF ((A/B .GE. 0.999999)   .AND.   (A/B .LE. 1.000001)) THEN

6. Don't forget to type logical variables; otherwise a statement such as

   FOUND = .TRUE.

   will result in a *mixed-mode* syntax error. Also, if a variable is typed LOGICAL, the expression must be logical. Therefore, the statements

   LOGICAL MALE
         .
         .
         .
   MALE = 1

   are inconsistent, the latter giving a mixed-mode syntax error.

END IF and END WHILE Errors

1. Remember that every block IF statement requires a corresponding END IF statement.
    For example, the following code will give a syntax error.

    ```
    IF (J .EQ. 1) THEN
        K = K + 1
    ELSE
        L = L + 1
    ```
    ←————————— Missing END IF

2. Make sure you have WHILE and END WHILE statements at the beginning and end
    of each WHILE structure.
3. Remember to use the correct structure terminator—END IF for block IF statements,
    END LOOP or UNTIL for LOOP statements, END AT END for the second version of
    AT END statements, and END WHILE for WHILE statements.[5] The following code
    results in an execution (run-time) error.

    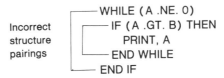

    ```
    Incorrect        WHILE (A .NE. 0)
    structure           IF (A .GT. B) THEN
    pairings               PRINT, A
                        END WHILE
                     END IF
    ```

Loop Errors

1. **Unnecessary processing.**   When designing an LRC loop by the trailer number method,
    beginning programmers often use an UNTIL structure by placing the test at the end of
    the loop rather than at the beginning of the loop. Thus the loop is processed unnecessarily
    one additional time. Although this does not provoke a syntax error, it does promote pro-
    gramming inefficiency and may cause either a logic or an execution error.
2. **Infinite loop.**   In designing the WHILE and UNTIL structures, take care that the loop
    control satisfies the condition sometime during the processing of the loop. If the condition
    is never met, then we have committed a logic error called an **infinite loop.** In this case,
    the body of the loop continues to be processed until execution is stopped by outside inter-
    vention. *One cause of infinite loops is testing for equality of real values.* If the test is
    based on a computational result, roundoff error may prevent the resulting value from
    exactly equaling the test value. If you use a generalized loop (LOOP/END LOOP state-
    ments), don't forget to include a loop control (such as AT END, QUIT), unless you like
    infinite loops.
3. **Loop pairing.**   If you use a LOOP statement, don't forget to define the end of the loop
    by pairing it with either an UNTIL statement or an END LOOP statement. Similarly,
    pair the WHILE statement with an END WHILE statement.

---

[5] UNTIL can also be paired with WHILE, but it makes for a confusing structure.

4.   AT END exit.   If you use either the AT END, or AT END/END AT END statements, don't forget to exit from the loop by using STOP or QUIT. (For example, see Exercise 37b.)

Data Input Errors

If you can't find fault with your algorithm, yet computer output does not validate your hand-calculated results, then (assuming that your hand-calculated results are correct) look for the possibility of faulty input data. For example, sometimes we inadvertently switch two or more values in the input sequence, or mistype values, or place values improperly on the input medium.

We can check any input data visually that are part of the output data to make sure correct values are stored. More generally, we can check for input data errors by inserting an *echo print* immediately after each READ statement, as follows:

```
READ,list
PRINT,list ← Same list as READ statement
```

Most commercial programs anticipate data input errors by using error routines that validate the input data. Example 5.12 (page 166) and Exercise 20 (page 164) illustrate several approaches. We show other approaches in the next chapter.

In general, you should program "defensively" by testing all parts of your program and by training yourself to anticipate potential errors that can be overcome by good program design.

ADDITIONAL EXERCISES

40.   Define or explain the following.

decision structure	logical operators
IF-THEN-ELSE structure	compound logical expression
block IF statement	WHILE structure
ELSE statement	error routine
END IF statement	WHILE/END WHILE statements
IF-block	UNTIL structure
ELSE-block	LOOP/UNTIL statements
relational expression	generalized loop structure
relational operator	LOOP/END LOOP statements
code	QUIT statement
counters	LRC loop
collating sequence	sentinel
IF-THEN structure	trailer number
logical IF statement	trailer record
logical expression	EOF condition
flag	AT END/END AT END statements
switch	infinite loop

41.   Forecasting Population Growth.   Modify the program and flowchart or pseudocode in Exercise 16 of Chapter 3 (page 100) as follows.

a. Use an LRC loop to output predicted population based on the different sets of data.

b. Let *N* be a counter in an "inner" UNTIL loop that lies entirely within the "outer" loop in part a. This inner loop increments *N* by 1, calculates predicted population, and prints *N*, corresponding year, and predicts population. Initialize *N* by defining an input variable called *N*1. Exit from the loop when the ratio of predicted population to current population exceeds a desired ratio (*R*). Run the program for the following three sets of values.

Current Population	Base Year	B	D	N1	R
4	1976	0.025	0.009	10	2
4	1976	0.025	0.009	25	3
4	1976	0.020	0.009	30	3

For example, your output for the first run should look like this.

YEARS INTO FUTURE	CORRESPONDING YEAR	PREDICTED POPULATION
10	1986	4.688
11	1987	4.763
.	.	.
.	.	.
.	.	.
43	2019	7.915
44	2020	8.042

Note that the counter is initialized by *N*1 and that this loop terminates when the predicted population *exceeds* (not equals) double (*R* has a value of 2) the current population. Comment on the number of years it takes the current world population to double and triple relative to changes in the birthrate.

42. **Area Problem.** Rework Exercise 24 in Chapter 4 (page 134) by using a WHILE or UNTIL structure in part a and an LRC loop in part b.

43. **Blood Bank Inventory Problem.** Rework Exercise 26 in Chapter 4 (page 135) by using WHILE and/or UNTIL structures (don't use DO-loops).

44. **Poisson Probability Function.** The function

$$p = \frac{a^x \cdot e^{-n}}{x!}$$

describes the probability (*p*) that a random or chance variable takes on a value equal to *x*, where *a* is the mean or average value of the random variable, *e* is the base of natural logarithms (see Section 2.6), and *x*! (*x* factorial) is the product $1 \cdot 2 \cdot 3 \cdot \ldots \cdot (x - 1) \cdot x$. For example, if the random variable "number of electronic failures per year" is distributed according to the Poisson function above and the average number of failures is known to be 5.2 per year (*a* = 5.2), then the probability of zero failures (*x* = 0) in a one-year period is

$$p = \frac{(5 \cdot 2)^0 \cdot e^{-5.2}}{0!}$$

$$= \frac{(1) \cdot (0.005516564)}{(1)}$$

$$= 0.0055 \text{ (or } 0.55\%)$$

and the probability of five failures per year is

$$p = \frac{(5.2)^5 \cdot e^{-5.2}}{5!}$$

$$= \frac{(3802.040) \cdot (0.005516564)}{120}$$

$$= 0.1747850 \text{ (or } 17.5\%)$$

Note that 0! is defined as 1.

The Poisson function is widely used to describe phenomena; hence published tables of probabilities for this function are common.

a. Design and run a program that inputs the average a and outputs a table of probabilities as follows:

```
A = xxx.xxx
X          PROBABILITY
---------------------------------
0          .xxxx
1          .xxxx
2          .xxxx
↓           ↓
```

Terminate this table when the probability drops below 0.0001.

b. Include an outer LRC loop that processes different values of a. Use the following input values: 2.0, 5.2, 6.0, 10.0, 20.0.

45. Factorials. The factorial of a number N (written $N!$) is a useful calculation in many problems in mathematics and statistics. By definition $N!$ is given by the product

$$N \cdot (N - 1) \cdot (N - 2) \cdot \cdots \cdot 2 \cdot 1$$

For example, if the value of N is 5, then

$$5! = 5 \cdot 4 \cdot 3 \cdot 2 \cdot 1 = 120$$

Note that 0! is defined to have a value of 1 and $N!$ is undefined if $N < 0$.

a. Run a program that inputs N and calculates and prints $N!$ What are the factorials of 1, 5, 10, 25, 50, and 100?

b. Did you get overflow in part a? By trial and error determine the maximum value of N whose factorial your computer can process. Then design your program to check each input of N to make sure it's within the allowable range of zero to the maximum value. If it's not, print a message to the user to this effect and then process the next input value.

c. Ensure that your program is capable of printing out the correct value of 0! should a user input zero for N.

d. Design an "outer" loop in your program for the purpose of processing K different values of *N*. For example, the data in part a would require six iterations of this loop.

e.   Instead of the outer loop in part d, design an outer loop that processes values of *N* from some initial value (*N1*) to some terminal value (*N2*) in increments of *N3*. Print a table of *N* values and their factorials. Try two test runs: the first processes *N* from 1 to 10 in increments of 1; the second processes *N* from 10 to 50 in increments of 5.

46.   **Quadratic Roots.**   A quadratic equation is defined by

$$y = ax^2 + bx + c$$

where *a*, *b*, and *c* are constants called parameters. Many mathematical applications require the "roots" of this equation. By definition, a root is a value of *x* that when substituted into the equation yields a value of zero for *y*. The following familiar *quadratic formula* determines the appropriate roots.

$$x = \frac{-b \pm (b^2 - 4ac)^{1/2}}{2a}$$

Run a program to calculate and print quadratic roots for the following input values of *a*, *b*, and *c*.

a	*b*	*c*
5	6	1.35
1	10	−1
1	2	1
7	4	2

Use a DO-loop to process these values. Your program should have three separate branches within the loop, depending on the value of the expression $b^2 - 4ac$. If this expression is negative, have the computer print "COMPLEX ROOTS"; if the expression equals zero exactly, evaluate the single root using $x = -b/(2a)$; if the expression is positive, use the above quadratic formula to calculate the two roots.

47.   **Computerized Matching: A File Search.**   The Placement Office on a college campus wants a program for the computerized matching of employers and graduating seniors looking for a job. Each student who registers with the Placement Office provides the following information.

Item
Name
Student ID
Address
Major (codes 1 to 10)
Grade point average (GPA)
Willing to relocate?
(1 = no, 2 = yes)
Willing to travel?
(1 = no, 2 = yes)

a. A firm is looking for a computer science major (code = 6) with a GPA of 3.25 or better who is willing to relocate and travel. Search the accompanying Placement Office file and print the name and address of each student who meets the criteria for this job.

Placement Office File

Name	ID	Address	Major	GPA	Relocate	Travel
Iris Abbot	2119	11 Estell Drive	6	3.45	1	2
Calvin Budnick	3112	Burnside Dorm	8	2.75	2	2
Susan Dent	4112	12 Upper College Rd.	3	2.50	2	2
Ken Driden	4819	RR3	4	2.85	1	1
Flo Further	5811	107 Ocean Rd.	1	3.00	1	2
Ben Lewis	6237	Heath Dorm	3	3.25	1	1
Bella Senate	6331	71 Boston Neck Rd.	6	3.75	1	2
Wally Tenure	6581	15 South Rd.	8	3.25	2	1
Alice Tillitson	8211	97 North Rd.	6	3.30	2	2
Martin Wiener	9112	10 Ballentine	6	3.70	2	1

**b. Generalize your program such that the Placement Office can output the name and address of each student who satisfies criteria which the firm specifies as part of the input. In other words, define variables in your program for (1) desired major, (2) desired minimum GPA, (3) relocation requirement, and (4) travel requirement. Thus, for the criteria in part a, the input for these variables would be 6, 3.25, 2, and 2, respectively. Assume that those students who are willing to relocate or travel would also be willing to accept a job that does not require relocation or travel. Test your program by running the following data for inquiries on the above four variables.

(1)	(2)	(3)	(4)
6	3.25	2	1
3	3.00	1	1
8	3.70	2	2

Are you capable of looping for these three inquiries? Or must you run the program again for each inquiry? Time-sharing users can accomplish the former by storing the Placement Office file on disk. Batch users, however, will have to wait until Chapter 8 or 11 to handle looping for this problem.

**c. Include an error routine to ensure that the major code is between 1 and 10 inclusive, GPA is 2.0 or above and 4.0 or less, relocate code is 1 or 2, and travel code is 1 or 2. If an error is found, print an appropriate error message and go on to the next student in the file. Add new data to test each of these possible errors.

48. **Credit Billing.**   Design a flowchart or pseudocode and write a program that prints monthly bills (statements) for Muster Charge, an internationally renowned credit card company. Use the following input data for three customers.

Name	Address	Credit Limit	Previous Balance	Payments	New Purchases
Napoleon B.	19 Waterloo St. Paris, France	$ 800	$ 300.00	$ 100.00	$700.00
Duke Welly	1 Thames Ave. London, UK	1500	1350.70	1320.70	645.52
Betsy Ross	1776 Flag St. Boston, MA USA	2000	36.49	36.49	19.15

Printout for each person should take up exactly 12 lines in order to conform to the size of the billing statement. In other words, ideally the printout should appear exactly as illustrated.

Output for these three customers would appear as follows.

```
NAPOLEON B.        PREVIOUS              FINANCE    NEW              NEW
19 WATERLOO ST     BALANCE  - PAYMENTS + CHARGE + PURCHASES = BALANCE
PARIS FRANCE
                   300.00  -   100.00 +   3.00 +   700.00 =   903.00

                                      MINIMUM PAYMENT DUE =   183.00
**WARNING**
YOU HAVE EXCEEDED YOUR CREDIT LIMIT
CONTROL YOURSELF, OR ELSE...


DUKE WELLY         PREVIOUS              FINANCE    NEW              NEW
1 THAMES AVE       BALANCE  - PAYMENTS + CHARGE + PURCHASES = BALANCE
LONDON GB
                   1350.70 -  1320.70 +    .45 +   645.52 =   675.97

                                      MINIMUM PAYMENT DUE =    67.60


BETSY ROSS         PREVIOUS              FINANCE    NEW              NEW
1776 FLAG ST       BALANCE  - PAYMENTS + CHARGE + PURCHASES = BALANCE
BOSTON MA USA
                   36.49   -    36.49 +    0.  +    19.15 =    19.15

                                      MINIMUM PAYMENT DUE =    19.15
```

Certain conditions must be reflected by the program.

1. The finance charge is 1.5 percent of the difference between the previous month's balance and the payments made since the previous month.
2. The minimum payment due is determined according to one of four results.
    a. If the new balance exceeds the credit limit, then the minimum payment is the difference between the new balance and the credit limit plus 10 percent of the credit limit. Thus, for the first statement $(903 - 800) + 10$ percent $\cdot$ (800) gives $183.
    b. If the new balance is $100 or more and does not exceed the credit limit, then the minimum payment is 10 percent of the new balance. Thus, for the second statement, 10 percent $\cdot$ (675.97) gives $67.60.
    c. If the new balance is less than $100, then the minimum payment is set to the new balance (see the third statement).
    d. If the new balance is negative, then the minimum payment is zero.
3. A warning is printed if the credit limit is exceeded by the new balance (Muster Charge doesn't fool around).

49. Police Car Replacement.   A police administrator would like to estimate the mileage at which a police cruiser should be replaced. Data analyses show that the *cost of operation* (gasoline, maintenance, and so on) is approximated by

$$c = f + v \cdot m + s \cdot m^2$$

where *f*, *v*, and *s* are called parameters, and *m* is the mileage reading (in thousands) on the odometer. For example, a cruiser that is driven for 30,000 miles and is characterized by $f = 1000$, $v = 200$, and $s = 2$ incurs an operating cost of approximately

$$c = 1000 + (200) \cdot (30) + (2) \cdot (30)^2$$
$$= \$8800.$$

The police department has an arrangement with the automaker for trade-ins of used police cruisers. The automaker has agreed to reduce the price of a new cruiser by the following amount.

$$r = pd^m$$

where *r* is the trade-in (salvage) value of a used cruiser, *p* is the original (new) car price, *d* is some depreciation factor, and *m* is defined as before. For example, if $p = \$10,000$, $d = 0.95$, and $m = 30$, then

$$r = (10,000) \cdot (0.95)^{30}$$
$$= \$2146.$$

This means that the police department pays $10,000 for a new cruiser, drives it for 30,000 miles, and gets $2146 on a trade-in. The *depreciation cost* in this case is $7854, or the difference between the new car price and the salvage price.

Thus, a cruiser driven for 30,000 miles costs $8800 to operate and $7854 in depreciation cost, for a total cost of $16,654. If this type of cruiser is replaced by a new cruiser of the same type at 30,000-mile intervals, then the total cost per 1000 miles is approximately $555 (that is, $16,654 $\div$ 30).

a. Run a program that determines the mileage (to the nearest thousand) at which cruisers should be replaced. Input for each cruiser should include the following.

1. Cruiser name
2. *f, v, s, p, d*

Output for each cruiser should appear as follows:

ANALYSIS FOR CRUISER NAME

m (1)	*c* (2)	*c* ÷ *m* (3) = (2) ÷ (1)	Depreciation Cost (4)	Depreciation Cost ÷ *m* (5) = (4)/(1)	Total Cost per 1000 Miles (6) = (3) + (5)
1					
2					
3					
.					
.					
.					
100					

Thus the best mileage at which to replace a cruiser is that which gives the smallest value in column (6). Note that 100,000 miles is the maximum replacement mileage that the police administrator is willing to consider. The police administrator is evaluating several types of cruisers, one of which must be selected. Their characteristics follow.

Cruiser Name	*f*	*v*	*s*	*p*	*d*
(Make these up)	1000	200	2·0	10,000	0.95
	800	300	2·5	8,000	0.93
	1200	225	1·6	13,000	0.98

At what mileage should each type be replaced and what is the total cost per 1000 miles? Which cruiser is the cheapest on the basis of total cost per 1000 miles?

**b. Design your program such that the program itself determines and outputs the best cruiser type and its associated total cost per 1000 miles.

**c. As you go down column (6) in this type of table, costs typically begin high, decrease to a minimum, and begin increasing again. Design your program to exit from the table loop once total cost begins to increase. Is this loop now a proper control structure? What is the advantage of this approach? Its disadvantage?

50. Personnel Benefits Budget. A budget officer for the State Agency of Education is in the process of preparing the personnel budget for the next fiscal year. One phase of this process is to prepare a budget of personnel expenditures paid by the state in addition to salaries. The additional expenditures include the following.

1. *Social Security.*   The state contributes 6.7 percent of an employee's salary up to $32,400. No deduction is made for earnings above that amount.
2. *Retirement.*   The state contributes 9.6 percent of total salary if the employee belongs to the state retirement plan; 9 percent is contributed by the state if the employee elects a private plan; and nothing is contributed by the state if the employee is not eligible for a retirement plan (for example, employees under 30 years of age are not eligible for a retirement plan).
3. *Group Life Insurance.*   The state contributes $1.30 for every $1000 of salary paid to the employee. For purposes of calculation, round every salary to the next highest $1000. For example, a yearly salary of $11,150 results in a $15.60 contribution (12 × 1.30).

The input for each employee consists of

1. Name
2. Social Security number
3. Annual salary
4. Code for retirement: NE = not eligible; SP = state plan; PP = private plan

Run a program that outputs each employee's name, Social Security number, salary, Social Security contribution, retirement contribution, group life contribution, and total contribution. After all employees have been processed, print the totals of each budget category (the four contribution columns) for all employees. Use the test data below to debug your program.

Name	Social Security Number	Salary ($)	Retirement Code
TEST 1	111-11-1111	17,000	2
TEST 2	222-22-2222	19,500	3
TEST 3	333-33-3333	21,300	2
TEST 4	444-44-4444	35,000	1
TEST 5	555-55-5555	32,400	2
TEST 6	666-66-6666	10,750	1
TEST 7	777-77-7777	24,375	2
TEST 8	888-88-8888	15,600	3

CHAPTER 6

Multiple Alternative Decision Structures

The solutions to many problems require choosing from several alternative courses of action to determine which block of statements is to be executed. In this chapter we illustrate three variations of these so-called **multiple alternative decision structures:** nested block-IF, ELSE IF, and DO CASE statements.

6.1
NESTED BLOCK IF STATEMENTS

A **nested decision structure** is a structure that contains one or more decision structures within another decision structure. A nested decision structure constructed from block IF statements is often called **nested IF-blocks.** The example below illustrates how two related decisions can be programmed by nesting one IF-THEN-ELSE structure within another IF-THEN-ELSE structure.

193

EXAMPLE 6.1   Sales Bonus Problem with Nested IF-THEN-ELSE Structures

Consider the following policy: If sales are *not above* $5000, we set the bonus to $0. If sales are *above* $5000, then we check the travel expenses. If travel expenses are *below* $600, then we award a bonus of $100; otherwise, we set the bonus to $0.

The flowchart, pseudocode, and FORTRAN segments on page 195 reflect this policy.

This program segment has two IF-THEN-ELSE structures, one nested within the other. The "inner" IF-THEN-ELSE structure in this case is within the IF-block of the "outer" IF-THEN-ELSE structure.

If the condition "SALES .GT. 5000" is true, a second condition "TRAVEL .LT. 600" is tested. If travel cost is less than $600, the statement that sets BONUS to 100 is executed; otherwise BONUS is set equal to zero. If the condition "SALES .GT. 5000" is false, the second ELSE-block is executed and bonus is set equal to zero.

Notice that there are two END IF statements in this program segment, *since each block IF statement requires its own END IF statement.* The first block IF statement is paired with the last END IF statement and the second block IF statement is paired with the next to last END IF statement. Thus the nesting scheme is similar to the nested DO-loop representation, as follows:

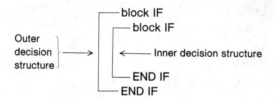

You should also notice the indentation in the pseudocode and FORTRAN versions, which facilitates an understanding of the nesting logic.

Alternatively, this particular nested decision structure is more simply represented by the following IF-THEN-ELSE structure with the logical operator .AND.:

```
IF (SALES .GT. 5000  .AND.  TRAVEL .LT. 600) THEN
   BONUS = 100
ELSE
   BONUS = 0
END IF
```

Thus, logical operators such as .AND. and .OR. can sometimes simplify nested logic.

EXAMPLE 6.1 (Continued)

Flowchart	Pseudocode	FORTRAN

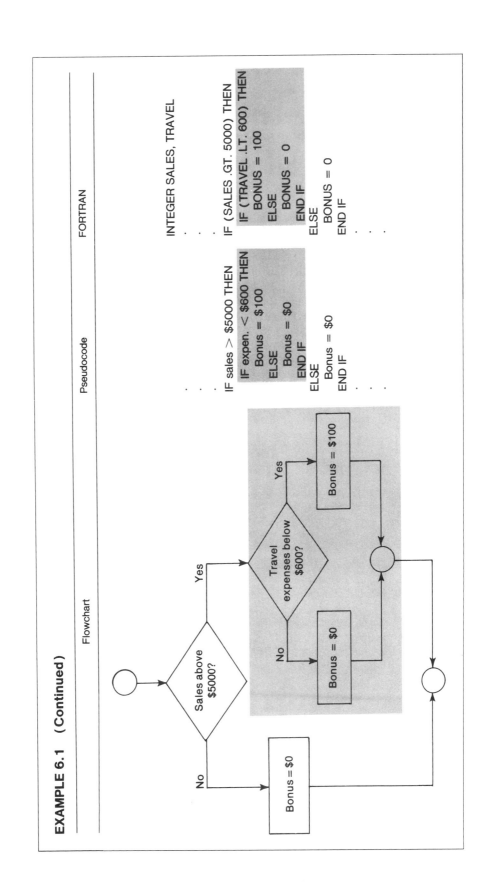

Flowchart:

```
    ○
    │
    ▼
  Sales above
    $5000?
   No│        │Yes
     │        ▼
     │    Travel
     │  expenses below
     │     $600?
     │   No│        │Yes
     │     ▼        ▼
  Bonus = $0   Bonus = $0   Bonus = $100
     │        │        │
     │        └───○────┘
     │            │
     └──────○─────┘
```

Pseudocode:

```
.  .  .
IF sales > $5000 THEN
    IF expen. < $600 THEN
        Bonus = $100
    ELSE
        Bonus = $0
    END IF
ELSE
    Bonus = $0
END IF
.  .  .
```

FORTRAN:

```
INTEGER SALES, TRAVEL
.  .  .
IF (SALES .GT. 5000) THEN
    IF (TRAVEL .LT. 600) THEN
        BONUS = 100
    ELSE
        BONUS = 0
    END IF
ELSE
    BONUS = 0
END IF
.  .  .
```

EXAMPLE 6.2   Tuition Schedule

The following table reflects the tuition schedule at a local college.

	Full-time Student	Part-time Student
In-state resident	$1500/term	$50/credit
Out-of-state resident	$3000/term	$125/credit

The logic for computing the tuition using nested IF blocks is illustrated on page 197.

Student records contain data on residence (RES), full-time/part-time status (STATUS) and number of credits (CREDIT). Each student's record is first tested for full-time (code FT) or part-time status. If the student is full-time then residence is checked using the "inner" IF-THEN-ELSE structure (label A). If residence is in-state (code IN), tuition (TUIT) is assigned the value $1500; otherwise $3000 is stored in TUIT. On the other hand, should the test for full-time student status be false, the IF-THEN-ELSE structure labeled B is used to determine residence and tuition.

Follow-up Exercises

1. Modify the logic in Example 6.1 according to the following two versions.
   a. Replace the inner IF-THEN-ELSE structure by a sequence structure followed by an IF-THEN structure.
   b. Replace both IF-THEN-ELSE structures by a sequence structure followed by nested IF-THEN structures.
2. Try simplifying the nested logic in Example 6.2 by using logical operators. Which approach do you prefer and why?
**3. Modify Example 6.1 to satisfy the following conditions.

   If sales > $5000 and travel cost < $300, bonus is $150.
   If sales > $5000 and travel cost ≥ $300 but < $600, bonus is $100.
   If sales ≤ $5000, bonus is $0.
   If travel cost ≥ $600, bonus is $0.

**4. In practice, the codes for STATUS (FT and PT) and RES (IN and OUT) may be mistyped and, therefore, stored incorrectly. Thus, a good defensive program would check both code values for each variable. Redesign the flowchart and FORTRAN code in Example 6.2 as follows.
   a. Print the message

      ***STATUS CODE IS INCORRECT

   whenever STATUS doesn't store either FT or PT.

EXAMPLE 6.2   (Continued)

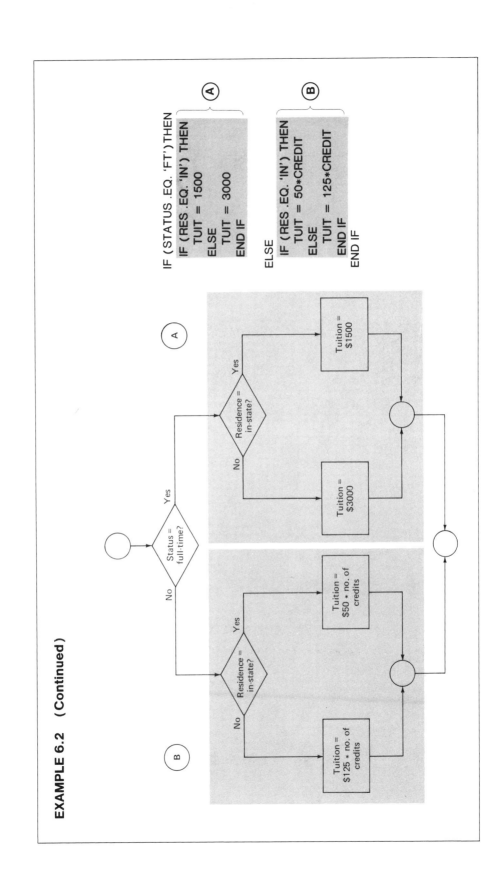

IF (STATUS .EQ. 'FT') THEN

Ⓐ
IF (RES .EQ. 'IN') THEN
    TUIT = 1500
ELSE
    TUIT = 3000
END IF

ELSE

Ⓑ
IF (RES .EQ. 'IN') THEN
    TUIT = 50*CREDIT
ELSE
    TUIT = 125*CREDIT
END IF

END IF

b. Print the message

   ***RESIDENCE CODE IS INCORRECT

   whenever RES doesn't store either IN or OUT.

5. Code the following flowcharts.

a.

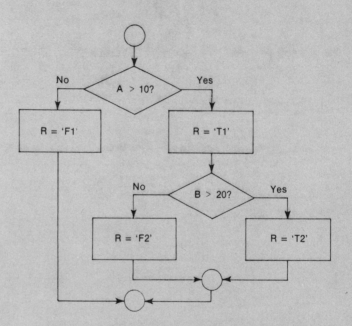

b.

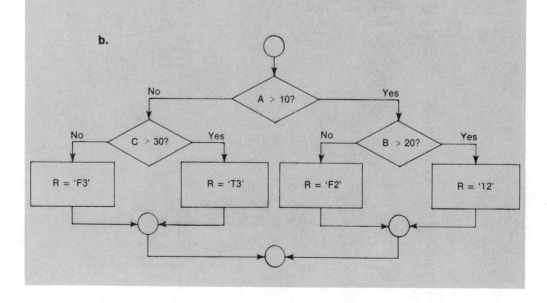

*c.

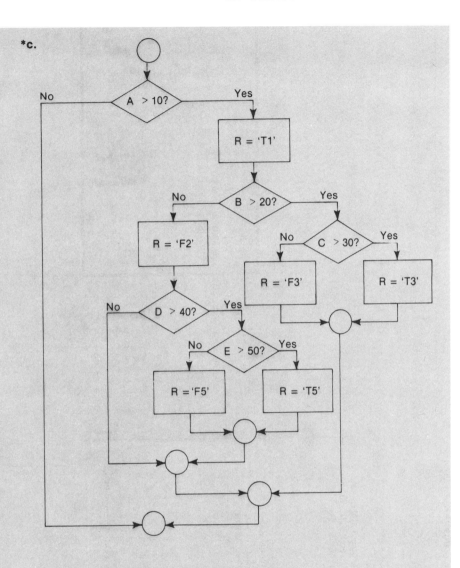

d. Fill in the final value in R if R initially stores the characters NULL and the following values are stored in A, B, C, D, E.

	A	B	C	D	E	Final Value in R Based on		
						Part a	Part b	Part c
i.	5	15	25	35	45			
ii.	20	15	25	35	45			
iii.	20	25	25	35	45			
*iv.	20	20	35	50	45			

FIGURE 6.1 *Generalized Multiple Alternative Decision Structure*

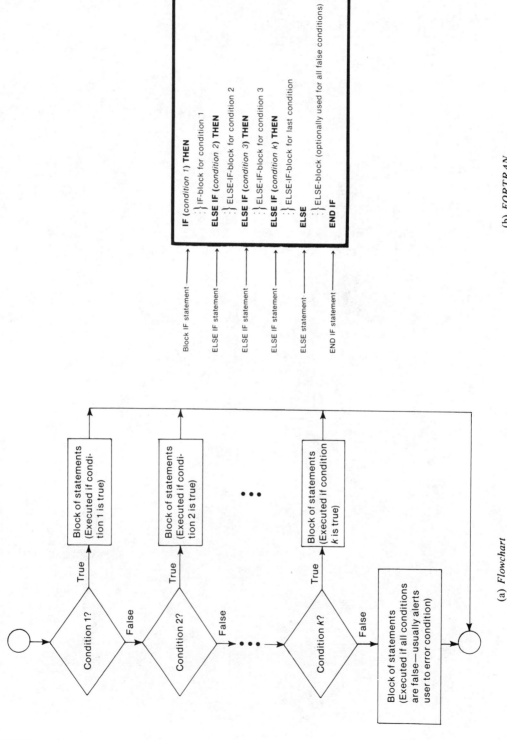

(a) *Flowchart*

```
IF (condition 1) THEN
  :} IF-block for condition 1
ELSE IF (condition 2) THEN
  :} ELSE-IF-block for condition 2
ELSE IF (condition 3) THEN
  :} ELSE-IF-block for condition 3
ELSE IF (condition k) THEN
  :} ELSE-IF-block for last condition
ELSE
  :} ELSE-block (optionally used for all false conditions)
END IF
```

Block IF statement
ELSE IF statement
ELSE IF statement
ELSE IF statement
ELSE statement
END IF statement

(b) *FORTRAN*

6.2
ELSE IF STATEMENTS

In Examples 6.1 and 6.2 we selected an outcome from among several possible alternatives using nested block IF statements. Here we present a **generalized multiple alternative decision structure** as illustrated in Figure 6.1a.

The ELSE IF statement given by

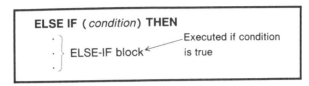

is used in combination with block IF, ELSE, and END IF statements to program this structure, as shown in Figure 6.1b.

The conditions are evaluated from top to bottom until one is true. The block of statements corresponding to the first true condition is executed, after which control passes to the first statement following the END IF statement. If all the conditions are false, the statements in the ELSE-block (optional) are executed, and control is then transferred to the END IF statement. This optional ELSE-block is often used to include error routines.

As you might recall from the last chapter, an *error routine* is a segment of the program that detects errors in either input data or computational results. Typically, an error routine prints a message that alerts the user to the problem and then either continues with the normal execution sequence or terminates program execution.

EXAMPLE 6.3   Microcomputer Discount Schedule

A computer store chain, Microland, is aggressively trying to penetrate the high school and college market for microcomputers. As part of this strategy it is offering the schools a discount on large orders of a popular microcomputer, as shown in Table 6.1.

TABLE 6.1   Discount Schedule

NUMBER OF MICROCOMPUTERS	COST PER MICROCOMPUTER
1–3	$1500
4–9	1350
10 or more	1200

The following program determines the amount owed by the customer.

```
C------------------------------------------------------------
C    MICROCOMPUTER DISCOUNT SCHEDULE PROGRAM
C
C    KEY:
C      PARAMETERS
C        MIN   = MINIMUM ORDER        (=1)
C        CUT1  = FIRST LEVEL CUTOFF   (=3)
```

```
C       CUT2  = SECOND LEVEL CUTOFF   (=9)
C       COST1 = FIRST COST PER UNIT   (=$1500)
C       COST2 = SECOND COST PER UNIT  (=$1350)
C       COST3 = THIRD COST PER UNIT   (=$1200)
C     VARIABLES
C      NAME  = NAME OF CUSTOMER
C      ORDER = NUMBER OF COMPUTERS ORDERED
C      AMT   = AMOUNT OWED
C-----------------------------------------------------------
       CHARACTER NAME*20
       INTEGER   AMT,ORDER,MIN,CUT1,CUT2,COST1,COST2,COST3
C-----------------------------------------------------------
       DATA MIN/1/, CUT1,CUT2/3,9/
       DATA COST1,COST2,COST3/1500,1350,1200/
C-----------------------------------------------------------
       READ, NAME,ORDER
C-----------------------------------------------------------
       WHILE (NAME .NE. 'END')
C
           IF (ORDER .LT. MIN) THEN
             PRINT, 'ORDER AMOUNT LESS THAN',MIN,'FOR',NAME
             AMT = 0
           ELSE IF (ORDER .LE. CUT1) THEN
             AMT = ORDER*COST1
           ELSE IF (ORDER .LE. CUT2) THEN
             AMT = ORDER*COST2
           ELSE
             AMT = ORDER*COST3
           END IF
C
       PRINT, '========================'
       PRINT, 'CUSTOMER    ',NAME
       PRINT, 'ORDER SIZE ',ORDER
       PRINT, 'AMOUNT OWED',AMT
       PRINT, '========================'
C
       READ, NAME,ORDER
C
       END WHILE
C-----------------------------------------------------------
       STOP
       END
```

Input

```
'PODUNK HIGH',0
'RYDELL HIGH',1
'FOREST HILLS',7
'MIAMI HIGH',50
'END',0
```

Output

```
ORDER AMOUNT LESS THAN           1 FOR PODUNK HIGH
========================
CUSTOMER    PODUNK HIGH
ORDER SIZE           0
AMOUNT OWED          0
========================
========================
CUSTOMER    RYDELL HIGH
ORDER SIZE           1
AMOUNT OWED       1500
========================
```

Output continues on next page

```
== == == == == == == == == == == == == ==
CUSTOMER      FOREST HILLS
ORDER SIZE             7
AMOUNT OWED         9450
== == == == == == == == == == == == == ==
== == == == == == == == == == == == == ==
CUSTOMER      MIAMI HIGH
ORDER SIZE            50
AMOUNT OWED        60000
== == == == == == == == == == == == == ==
```

First, notice that we treat the data in the discount schedule as parameters by assigning values through DATA statements. This facilitates subsequent program updates should we need to change the discount structure (a certainty in the real world). For example, to change the costs we need only change the second DATA statement, which avoids getting into program logic (the decision structure) to make changes.

Second, we use the generalized multiple alternative decision structure to determine the appropriate billing amount according to the discount schedule. For example, an order for seven microcomputers (ORDER = 7) yields the flowchart shown.

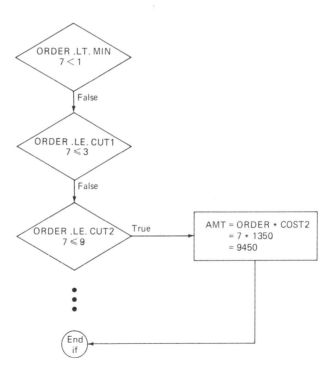

To make sure you understand this program, try processing the input data by role-playing computer and confirm the given output.

EXAMPLE 6.4   Class Report

Each term the vice president of academic affairs at a university receives a report of grade point averages for each undergraduate class. The following program processes a student file, where each input record contains the student's identification, class code (FR for freshman, SO for sophomore, etc.), and grade point average.

Study the program, its input and output. To make sure you understand the program, roleplay the given input and confirm the output. In particular, pay attention to the use of the generalized multiple alternative structure for controlling flow to each class block and the error block based on the student's code. Also, note the use of logical IF statements for calculating GPA averages, so as to avoid the possibility of the common execution error "division by zero."

```
C---------------------------------------------------------------
C    CLASS REPORT PROGRAM
C
C    KEY:
C      ID     = STUDENT'S ID
C      CLASS  = CODE REPRESENTING STUDENT'S CLASS
C               (FR = FRESHMAN,  SO = SOPHOMORE,
C                JR = JUNIOR,    SR = SENIOR)
C      GPA    = STUDENT'S GRADE POINT AVERAGE
C      NUMFR  = NUMBER OF FRESHMEN
C      NUMSO  = NUMBER OF SOPHOMORES
C      NUMJR  = NUMBER OF JUNIORS
C      NUMSR  = NUMBER OF SENIORS
C      AVEFR  = AVERAGE GPA FOR FRESHMEN
C      AVESO  = AVERAGE GPA FOR SOPHOMORES
C      AVEJR  = AVERAGE GPA FOR JUNIORS
C      AVESR  = AVERAGE GPA FOR SENIORS
C---------------------------------------------------------------
      CHARACTER CLASS*2
      INTEGER   ID,NUMFR,NUMSO,NUMJR,NUMSR
      REAL      GPA,SUMFR,SUMSO,SUMJR,SUMSR,AVEFR,AVESO,AVEJR,
     *          AVESR
C---------------------------------------------------------------
      DATA NUMFR,NUMSO,NUMJR,NUMSR/4*0/
      DATA SUMFR,SUMSO,SUMJR,SUMSR/4*0.0/
      DATA AVEFR,AVESO,AVEJR,AVESR/4*0.0/
C---------------------------------------------------------------
      LOOP
C
          READ, ID,CLASS,GPA
            AT END, QUIT
C
          IF (CLASS .EQ. 'FR') THEN
              NUMFR = NUMFR + 1
              SUMFR = SUMFR + GPA
          ELSE IF (CLASS .EQ. 'SO') THEN
              NUMSO = NUMSO + 1
              SUMSO = SUMSO + GPA
          ELSE IF (CLASS .EQ. 'JR') THEN
              NUMJR = NUMJR + 1
              SUMJR = SUMJR + GPA
          ELSE IF (CLASS .EQ. 'SR') THEN
              NUMSR = NUMSR + 1
              SUMSR = SUMSR + GPA
          ELSE
              PRINT, '==========================================='
              PRINT, 'ERROR IN CODE FOR ID NUMBER', ID
              PRINT, '==========================================='
          END IF
```

```
      C
             END LOOP
      C-- -- -- -- -- -- -- -- -- -- -- -- -- -- -- -- -- -- -- -- --
             IF (NUMFR .GT. 0) AVEFR = SUMFR/NUMFR
             IF (NUMSO .GT. 0) AVESO = SUMSO/NUMSO
             IF (NUMJR .GT. 0) AVEJR = SUMJR/NUMJR
             IF (NUMSR .GT. 0) AVESR = SUMSR/NUMSR
      C-- -- -- -- -- -- -- -- -- -- -- -- -- -- -- -- -- -- -- -- --
             PRINT, ' CLASS                  COUNT          AVE. GPA'
             PRINT, '-------------------------------------------------'
             PRINT, 'FRESHMEN   ',NUMFR,AVEFR
             PRINT, 'SOPHOMORES',NUMSO,AVESO
             PRINT, 'JUNIORS    ',NUMJR,AVEJR
             PRINT, 'SENIORS    ',NUMSR,AVESR
             PRINT, '-------------------------------------------------'
      C-- -- -- -- -- -- -- -- -- -- -- -- -- -- -- -- -- -- -- -- --
             STOP
             END
```

Input

```
250,'SO',3.20
403,'SR',2.75
420,'SR',2.93
222,'SO',3.58
196,'FR',4.00
555,'GR',3.40
276,'SO',2.05
```

Output

```
==================================================
ERROR IN CODE FOR ID NUMBER        555
==================================================
   CLASS             COUNT        AVE. GPA
-------------------------------------------------
FRESHMEN                1          4.0000000
SOPHOMORES              3          2.9433320
JUNIORS                 0          0.0000000
SENIORS                 2          2.8400000
-------------------------------------------------
```

Follow-up Exercises

6. Rewrite the logic in Example 6.3 by using the following.
   a. Nested IF-THEN-ELSE structures.
   b. Sequence of IF-THEN structures. (*Hint:* See Module E.)
   Discuss the pros and cons of each approach.
7. What would happen in Example 6.4 if:
   a. We were to remove the ELSE statement and ELSE-block?
   b. We were to remove the third DATA statement?
   c. We were to calculate the GPA averages straightaway (without the use of logical IF statements)?
8. Modify the generalized multiple-alternative structure in Example 6.4 as follows:
   a. Use nested IF-THEN-ELSE structures.
   b. Use a sequence of IF-THEN structures. (*Hint:* See Module E.)
   Which approach do you prefer, and why?

9. Modify the program in Example 6.4 as follows:
   a. Use the variable ERRCT to print the message

   ***NUMBER OF RECORDS WITH CODE ERRORS = xx

   just before the main report.
   b. Print the summary

   TOTAL NUMBER OF STUDENTS = xxxx
   OVERALL AVERAGE GPA   = x.xx

   following the main report.
*10. Flowchart the following codes.
   a. M = 5
      IF (J .LT. M) THEN
         J = J + 5
         M = M + 3
         IF (J .LT. 8) THEN
            M = M + 10
         ELSE
            M = M + 20
         END IF
      END IF

   b. M = 5
      IF (J .LT. M) THEN
         J = J + 5
         M = M + 3
      ELSE IF (J .LT. 8) THEN
         M = M + 10
      ELSE
         M = M + 20
      END IF

   c. What are the final values for J and M in parts a and b when initially J = 2? When initially J = 7? When initially J = 10?
*11. In Example 6.1, assume that the bonus is based on the following schedule, where travel expense does not play a role.

   Weekly sales under $4000   bonus is $0
   Weekly sales between $4000 and $5000 bonus is $50
   Weekly sales over $5000   bonus is $100

   Modify Example 6.1 to include this schedule.
*12. A student is assigned a grade A, B, C, D, or F according to the following rule.

   test score $\geq$ 90   grade is A
   80 $\leq$ test score $<$ 90   grade is B
   70 $\leq$ test score $<$ 80   grade is C
   60 $\leq$ test score $<$ 70   grade is D
   test score $<$ 60   grade is F

   Write a program segment that prints the student's name (NAME) and grade (GRADE) based on the test score (SCORE).

6.3
CASE STRUCTURE

The **CASE structure** is another variation of the multiple alternative decision structure. The need for this structure arises when the execution of one of many alternatives is selected on the basis of the value of a *numeric code*. For example, in a library circulation system we might

FIGURE 6.2 CASE Structure

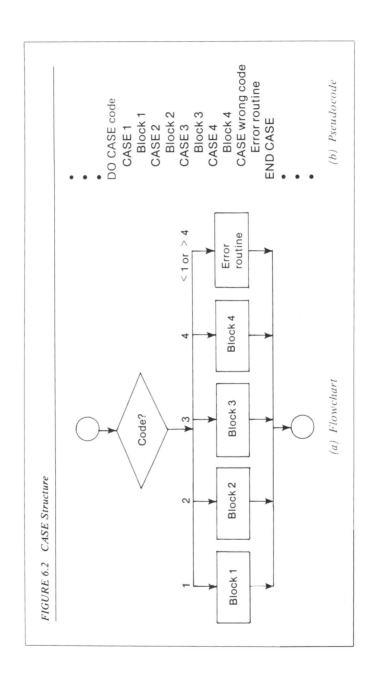

(a) Flowchart

DO CASE code
  CASE 1
    Block 1
  CASE 2
    Block 2
  CASE 3
    Block 3
  CASE 4
    Block 4
  CASE wrong code
    Error routine
END CASE

(b) Pseudocode

have the following "cases": (1) books checked out logic, (2) books returned logic, (3) new book acquisitions logic, and (4) books withdrawn from circulation logic. Figure 6.2 illustrates the CASE structure for this example, where the numeric codes 1 through 4 represent the described four cases.[1]

The CASE structure is implemented in WATFIV using the DO CASE, CASE, IF NONE, and END CASE statements as follows:

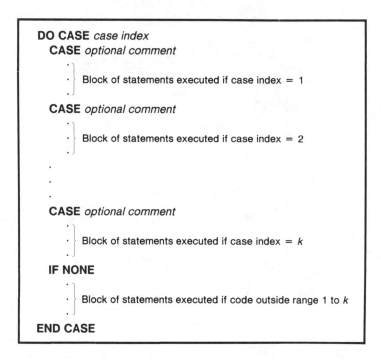

This structure allows *one* of a number of blocks of code (**case blocks**) to be executed by means of a **case index variable.** Each alternative block of statements is preceded by the word CASE. The value of the case index, *which must be stored in an integer variable,* determines which alternative case block is to be executed. The index must store integer values (1, 2, 3, ...) that fall within the range of 1 and the total number of cases. If the value of the case index is 1, then the statements in the block following the first case are executed, after which control passes to the statement following the END CASE statement. If the value of the index is 2, then the second case is executed, and so on.

The IF NONE segment is executed only if the value of the index is negative, zero, or greater than the number of cases provided. This segment typically contains an error routine. The IF NONE block, however, is optional. If this block is omitted and the value of the case index is out of the range 1 to *k*, control passes to statements following END CASE, and none of the case blocks is executed.

---

[1]Implementations of the CASE structure in certain languages (e.g., Pascal, ANS BASIC) include case selection based on character codes such as C for Checked, R for Returned, N for New and W for Withdrawn. (See Exercise 15.)

The *optional comment* following each CASE statement is ignored during execution. Its purpose is to document or identify each case block, as the next example illustrates.

EXAMPLE 6.5   Traffic Court Fines

Each week the clerk in traffic court summarizes the fines collected for traffic violations by major categories: moving violation, standing violation, and warning. The data on each violation include traffic violation type (1 = moving violation; 2 = standing violation; 3 = warning) and amount of fine.

   Figure 6.3 shows the algorithm for the program that summarizes the traffic violations data. In our example, we wish to accumulate the dollar amount (total fines) collected for moving violations and count the number of moving violations; to accumulate the total fines collected and number of fines for standing violations; and to count the number of warnings (warnings do not involve a fine).

FIGURE 6.3   *Algorithm for Traffic Court Fines Problem*

```
               Initialize summers and counters
               Start LRC loop
                  READ code, fine
                  Update ticket counter
                  DO CASE code
                     CASE 1 Moving
                        Accumulate total fines for moving violations
                        Count no. moving violations
                     CASE 2 Standing
                        Accumulate total fines for standing violations
                        Count no. standing violations
                     CASE 3 Warning
                        Count no. warnings
                     CASE wrong code
                        PRINT error message
                  END CASE
               End LRC loop
               PRINT summary report
               Stop
```

```
C-----------------------------------------------------------
C    TRAFFIC COURT FINES PROGRAM
C
C    KEY:
C      N      = TICKET NUMBER
C      CODE   = CODE FOR TYPE OF VIOLATION
C               (1 = MOVING, 2 = STANDING, 3 = WARNING)
C      FINE   = AMOUNT OF FINE
C      MOVFIN = TOTAL FINES FOR MOVING VIOLATIONS
C      MOVNUM = NUMBER OF MOVING VIOLATIONS
C      STDFIN = TOTAL FINES FOR STANDING VIOLATIONS
C      STDNUM = NUMBER OF STANDING VIOLATIONS
C      WARNUM = NUMBER OF WARNINGS
```

```
      C
      C-------------------------------------------------------------
            INTEGER N,CODE,FINE,MOVFIN,MOVNUM,STDFIN,STDNUM,WARNUM
      C-------------------------------------------------------------
            DATA N,MOVFIN,MOVNUM,STDFIN,STDNUM,WARNUM/6*0/
      C-------------------------------------------------------------
            LOOP
              READ, CODE,FINE
                AT END, QUIT
              N = N + 1
      C
      C
                DO CASE CODE
      C
                CASE 1  MOVING
                  MOVFIN = MOVFIN + FINE
                  MOVNUM = MOVNUM + 1
      C
                CASE 2  STANDING
                  STDFIN = STDFIN + FINE
                  STDNUM = STDNUM + 1
      C
                CASE 3  WARNING
                  WARNUM = WARNUM + 1
      C
                IF NONE
                  PRINT, '******************************************'
                  PRINT, ' ERROR IN CODE FOR TICKET-',N
                  PRINT, '******************************************'
                  PRINT, ' '
                END CASE
      C
      C
            ENDLOOP
      C-------------------------------------------------------------
            PRINT, '   TYPE            NUMBER        AMOUNT'
            PRINT, '-------------------------------------------'
            PRINT, ' MOVING  ',MOVNUM,MOVFIN
            PRINT, ' STANDING',STDNUM,STDFIN
            PRINT, ' WARNING ',WARNUM,0
      C-------------------------------------------------------------
            STOP
            END
```

Input	Output
1,50	**
2,15	ERROR IN CODE FOR TICKET 4
2,20	**
25,2	TYPE NUMBER AMOUNT
1,75	---
3,C	MOVING 2 125
2,10	STANDING 4 60
2,15	WARNING 1 0

Follow-up Exercises

13. Modify Example 6.5 to include the following summary whenever input errors are present:

```
         * ---------------------------------------------------- *
         *** NUMBER OF INPUT ERRORS  =  xx ***
         * ---------------------------------------------------- *
```

This should follow the main body of the report.

14. Rewrite Example 6.5 using:
    a. Series of block IF statements (sequence of IF-THEN structures).
    b. Nested block IF statements (nested IF-THEN-ELSE structures).
    c. ELSE IF statements (generalized multiple alternative decision structure).
    Which do you prefer and why?

*15. Suppose in Example 6.5 that we must use the character codes M, S, and W instead of 1, 2, and 3.
    a. Modify the example accordingly, but continue using the CASE structure. (*Hint:* You need decision structures to convert character codes to numeric codes.)
    b. Modify the example by using block IF, ELSE IF, ELSE, and END IF statements in place of the CASE structure.
    Which approach do you prefer and why?

*16. The affirmative action officer of a large corporation needs to determine statistics on employees within each of the following categories:

Category Designation (CAT)	Category Description
1	American Indian, Alaskan native
2	Asian, Pacific Islander
3	Black
4	Hispanic
5	White
6	Other

Design a CASE structure to (1) count the number of employees and (2) sum salaries within each category. Salary is stored under SAL. Use NUM1, NUM2, . . . for counts and SUM1, SUM2, . . . for sums.

6.4
THE GO TO MENACE

The GO TO statement causes the computer to interrupt the normal sequential execution of a program and branch (jump or transfer control) to some other executable instruction in the program that is not the next instruction in the normal sequence. Its basic form is

> **GO TO** *statement number*

For example, when the statement

    GO TO 10

is executed, control is transferred to the statement with label number 10.

In earlier versions of the FORTRAN language, some convenient control structures such as IF-THEN-ELSE were omitted. This promoted the widespread use of GO TO statements, as the next example illustrates.

EXAMPLE 6.6   GO TOs Go Wild

The following code is syntactically correct, but you must admit it's confusing. Although the program serves no real purpose, it should give a feel for the "jumping around" that occurs if we don't harness the use of the GO TO statement.

```
        .
        .
        .
        J = J + 1
        K = L*M
        IF (J .GT. K) GO TO 100
        GO TO 115
   85   PRINT, L
        STOP
  100   L = J + K
        J = J + 1
        GO TO 85
  115   L = J − K
        J = J − 1
        GO TO 85
        END
```

The problems caused by the excessive use of GO TO statements were one motivating factor in the development of structured programming concepts. Undisciplined use of this statement makes programs difficult to follow, hard to modify, and error prone. For example, the GO TO statement requires the numeric labeling of statements to which control is transferred. Subsequently, this opens the door to making mistakes with respect to mislabeling statements, forgetting labels, repeating labels as when two statements are numbered 50, and otherwise branching to the wrong statement.

Programs that eliminate the use of GO TO statements and statement labels also greatly reduce the likelihood of certain execution errors, as when control is transferred from outside into the body of a DO-loop or into an IF-block, ELSE-block, or ELSE-IF-block.

In the WATFIV version of FORTRAN, we need not use a single GO TO statement. Decision structures such as IF-THEN-ELSE, nested IF-blocks, CASE, and multiple alternative structures don't require explicit GO TO transfers of control. The same is true for the WATFIV versions of WHILE, UNTIL, and generalized (LOOP/END LOOP) loop structures.

In short, *we need not use any GO TO statements when writing WATFIV programs.* You should, however, be aware of the GO TO statement, since you're likely to come across "ancient" programs that use them liberally. Even the latest official version of the language (FORTRAN 77) does not completely do away with the need for GO TO statements.

Follow-up Exercises

17. What value gets printed in Example 6.6 if initially J stores 5, L stores 10, and M stores 2? What if J initially stores 50?
18. Flowchart the code in Example 6.6. Kind of a nightmare, isn't it?
19. Rewrite the code in Example 6.6 by entirely eliminating the GO TO statement.
*20. Rewrite the program in Example 5.12 on page 167 by using logical IF and GO TO statements in place of the block IF/END IF and WHILE/END WHILE statements. Now you would have a program in "old" FORTRAN. What do you think?

**6.5
ROOT BISECTION ALGORITHM**

In this section we illustrate the capability of an algebraic language such as FORTRAN to model intricate algorithmic logic.

Many mathematical applications, particularly in calculus, require values for the root(s) of a mathematical function. Given a general mathematical function of x, $f(x)$, a *root* of the function is a value of x that yields a value of zero for $f(x)$. For example, the linear function

$$f(x) = -1 + 2x$$

has a root at $x = 0.5$ since this value for x yields $f(0.5) = 0$. The quadratic function

$$f(x) = -2.25 - 4x + x^2$$

has two roots, one at $x = -0.5$ and another at $x = 4.5$. Figure 6.4 illustrates sketches of these functions. Note from the figure that real roots for the function

$$f(x) = 2^x$$

are not defined, since this function approaches the x-axis asymptotically (gets closer and closer to it) but does not cross it.

A number of analytic procedures have been developed for finding the roots of functions. In this section we illustrate the bisection method for finding a real root (if it exists) of any function; Exercise 32 at the end of the chapter describes another procedure.

To illustrate the root bisection procedure for the linear function in Figure 6.4, study Table 6.2 and Figure 6.5 together.

Make sure you understand the bisection procedure by reworking Table 6.2 and Figure 6.5 starting with, say, $L = -1$ and $R = 5$.

Step 1: Analysis

Root bisection program that calculates a real root of a function, provided it exists.

a. *Input data*
   Left end of interval
   Right end of interval
   Error tolerance
b. *Output data*
   A root (if it exists) or a message stating that a root can't be found for the given interval

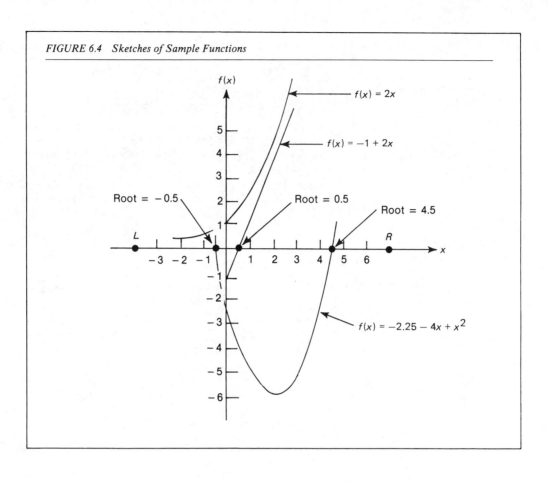

FIGURE 6.4   Sketches of Sample Functions

TABLE 6.2   Root Bisection Method for the Function $f(x) = -1 + 2x$

ITERATION	INTERVAL FROM LEFT TO RIGHT (L)	(R)	MIDPOINT (M) OR ROOT ESTIMATE	FUNCTION VALUES $f(L)$	$f(R)$	$f(M)$	HALF-INTERVAL OR MAX. ERROR	COMMENT
1	−3.0	1.0	−1.0	−7.0	1.0	−3.0	2.0	Root in right half-interval since $f(L)$ and $f(M)$ have same sign (both negative). Thus, set $L = M = -1.0$ to create new interval at iteration 2.
2	−1.0	1.0	0.0	−3.0	1.0	−1.0	1.0	Again root in right half-interval, so set $L = M = 0.0$ at iteration 3.
3	0.0	1.0	0.5	−1.0	1.0	0.0	0.5	Root found at $x = M = 0.5$ since $f(M) = 0.0$.

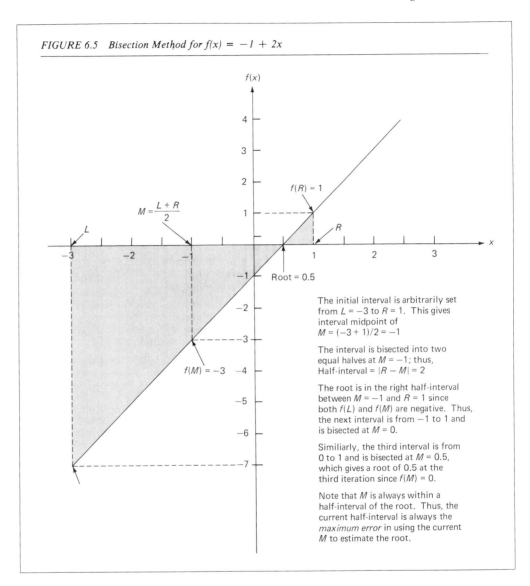

FIGURE 6.5   Bisection Method for $f(x) = -1 + 2x$

$M = \dfrac{L + R}{2}$

$f(R) = 1$

$f(M) = -3$

Root = 0.5

The initial interval is arbitrarily set from $L = -3$ to $R = 1$. This gives interval midpoint of
$M = (-3 + 1)/2 = -1$

The interval is bisected into two equal halves at $M = -1$; thus, Half-interval $= |R - M| = 2$

The root is in the right half-interval between $M = -1$ and $R = 1$ since both $f(L)$ and $f(M)$ are negative. Thus, the next interval is from -1 to 1 and is bisected at $M = 0$.

Similiarly, the third interval is from 0 to 1 and is bisected at $M = 0.5$, which gives a root of 0.5 at the third iteration since $f(M) = 0$.

Note that M is always within a half-interval of the root. Thus, the current half-interval is always the *maximum error* in using the current M to estimate the root.

c.   *Computations*
Midpoint $=$ (Left $+$ Right)/2
Half-interval $=$ absolute value of (Right $-$ Midpoint)
Values of $f(x)$ given values of x

Step 2: Design

Figure 6.6 illustrates exploded pseudocode (as in Module E) for this algorithm. Try to follow the root logic in this figure by relating the steps in Table 6.2 and Figure 6.5 to the pseudocode in Figure 6.6. Next, relate the pseudocode to the program in Step 3 and the input/output in Step 4, together with the discussion that follows Step 4. Note that line numbers in the pseu-

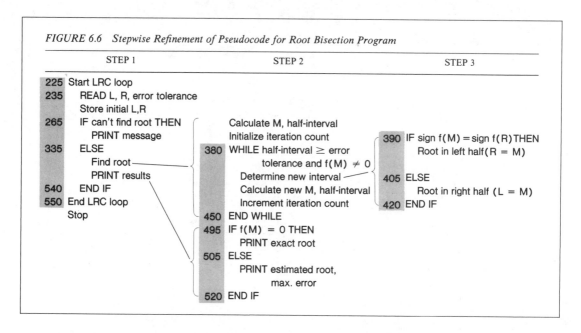

FIGURE 6.6   Stepwise Refinement of Pseudocode for Root Bisection Program

docode correspond to line numbers in the program so that you can better relate the pseudocode, program, and discussion. Are you up to it?

Step 3: Code

```
125 C------------------------------------------------------------
130 C    ROOT BISECTION PROGRAM
135 C
140 C    KEY:
145 C      ERROR  = ERROR TOLERANCE
150 C      F      = NAME OF STATEMENT FUNCTION
155 C      HALF   = WIDTH OF HALF-INTERVAL
160 C      INLEFT = INITIAL LEFT END OF INTERVAL
165 C      INRITE = INITIAL RIGHT END OF INTERVAL
170 C      IT     = ITERATION COUNT
175 C      LEFT   = LEFT END OF CURRENT INTERVAL
180 C      MID    = MIDDLE OF CURRENT INTERVAL
185 C      RIGHT  = RIGHT END OF CURRENT INTERVAL
190 C      X      = ABSCISSA IN STATEMENT FUNCTION F(X)
195 C------------------------------------------------------------
200       INTEGER IT
205       REAL    LEFT,RIGHT,MID,INLEFT,INRITE,X,F,HALF,ERROR
210 C------------------------------------------------------------
215       F(X) = -1.0 + 2.0*X
220 C------------------------------------------------------------
225       LOOP
230 C
235          READ, LEFT,RIGHT,ERROR
240             AT END, QUIT
245 C
250          INLEFT = LEFT
255          INRITE = RIGHT
260 C
```

```
265              IF ( F(LEFT)*F(RIGHT) .GT. 0.0 ) THEN
270 C
275 C---------CAN'T FIND ROOT
280 C
285              PRINT, '*******************************************'
290              PRINT, 'ROOT CAN''T BE FOUND WITHIN THE INTERVAL'
295              PRINT, LEFT,' TO',RIGHT
300              PRINT, 'POSSIBLE REASONS:'
305              PRINT, '  1.   NO ROOTS EXIST'
310              PRINT, '  2.   ROOT OUTSIDE INTERVAL ( EXPAND INTERVAL )'
315              PRINT, '  3.   MULTIPLE ROOTS WITHIN INTERVAL ( CONTRACT'
320              PRINT, '       INTERVAL )'
325              PRINT, '*******************************************'
330              PRINT, ' '
333 C
335          ELSE
340 C
345 C---------FIND ROOT BY BISECTION METHOD
350 C
355              MID  = (LEFT + RIGHT)/2.0
360              HALF = ABS(RIGHT - MID)
365              IT   = 1
370 C
375 C
380              WHILE (HALF .GE. ERROR  .AND.  F(MID) .NE. 0.0)
385 C
390                  IF ( F(MID)*F(RIGHT) .GT. 0.0 ) THEN
395 C---------------ROOT IN LEFT HALF-INTERVAL
400                      RIGHT = MID
405                  ELSE
410 C---------------ROOT IN RIGHT HALF-INTERVAL
415                      LEFT  = MID
420                  END IF
425 C
430                  MID  = (LEFT + RIGHT)/2.0
435                  HALF = ABS(RIGHT - MID)
440                  IT   = IT + 1
445 C
450              END WHILE
455 C
460 C
465              PRINT, '-------------------------------------------'
470              PRINT, 'INITIAL INTERVAL:'
475              PRINT, INLEFT,' TO',INRITE
480              PRINT, 'ERROR TOLERANCE =',ERROR
485              PRINT, 'ITERATIONS      =',IT
490 C
495              IF (F(MID) .EQ. 0.0) THEN
500                  PRINT, 'EXACT ROOT      =',MID
505              ELSE
510                  PRINT, 'ESTIMATED ROOT  =',MID
515                  PRINT, 'MAXIMUM ERROR   =',HALF
520              END IF
525 C
530              PRINT, '-------------------------------------------'
535 C
540          END IF
545 C
550      END LOOP
555 C-------------------------------------------------------
560      STOP
565      END
```

Step 4: Debugging

The following input/output shows part of the debugging process. Exercises 21, 22, and 23 complete the process.

Input

```
-3,1,0.001
-50,50,0.001
-50,50,0.00001
100,200,0.001
```

Output

```
---------------------------------------------------------
INITIAL INTERVAL:
              -3.0000000  TO            1.0000000
ERROR TOLERANCE =            0.0010000
ITERATIONS      =            3
EXACT ROOT      =            0.5000000
---------------------------------------------------------

---------------------------------------------------------
INITIAL INTERVAL:
              -50.0000000  TO           50.0000000
ERROR TOLERANCE =            0.0010000
ITERATIONS      =            17
ESTIMATED ROOT  =            0.4997253
MAXIMUM ERROR   =            0.0007629
---------------------------------------------------------

---------------------------------------------------------
INITIAL INTERVAL:
              -50.0000000  TO           50.0000000
ERROR TOLERANCE =            0.0000100
ITERATIONS      =            24
ESTIMATED ROOT  =            0.5000052
MAXIMUM ERROR   =            0.0000062
---------------------------------------------------------

*********************************************************
ROOT CAN'T BE FOUND WITHIN THE INTERVAL
              100.0000000  TO           200.0000000
POSSIBLE REASONS:
   1.   NO ROOTS EXIST
   2.   ROOT OUTSIDE INTERVAL ( EXPAND INTERVAL )
   3.   MULTIPLE ROOTS WITHIN INTERVAL ( CONTRACT
        INTERVAL )
*********************************************************
```

Discussion

Note the following items as they relate to the pseudocode, program, and input/output:

1. The program defines a **statement function** F(X) in line 215 to facilitate the calculation of F(LEFT) in line 265, F(RIGHT) in lines 265 and 390, and F(MID) in lines 380, 390, and 495. This statement function works pretty much like a programmer-defined library function. For example, F(MID) in line 495 is evaluated using F(X) in line 215 with X replaced by MID. This saves us the effort of having to use $-1.0 + 2.0*MID$ in place of F(MID) in lines 380, 390, and 495. The same goes for our use of F(LEFT) and F(RIGHT). The statement function also simplifies program changes for a new function, since we need only change line 215; otherwise, we would have to change lines 265, 380, 390, and 495. Chapter 9 presents statement functions in greater detail.

2. Input values for the initial interval and error tolerance are user-selected. Note that the LRC loop processes as many values as the user desires. We discuss the error tolerance in item 6 below.

3. The program can't find a root if the product F(LEFT)* F(RIGHT) is positive in line 265. This can happen if:

a. No root exists, as in the 2^x function in Figure 6.4. In this case, the interval from L to R gives $f(L) > 0$ and $f(R) > 0$, so $f(L)*f(R) > 0$.

b. The root is outside the interval. For example, the interval $L = -3$ to $L = 0$ in Figure 6.5 does not contain the root. In this case, $f(L) < 0$ and $f(R) < 0$, so $f(L)*f(R) > 0$.

c. Multiple roots are within the interval, as in Figure 6.4 for the function $f(x) = -2.25 - 4x + x^2$. Here we have $f(L) > 0$ and $f(R) > 0$, so $f(L)*f(R) > 0$.

In these cases, the message in lines 285 through 330 is printed.

4. The WHILE loop in lines 380 to 450 implements the bisection procedure for finding the root. This loop continues iterating either until the half-interval drops below the error tolerance or the exact root is found; that is, F(MID) = 0.

5. The test (F(MID)*F(RIGHT) .GT. 0.0) in line 390 is a slick way of determining whether the root lies in the left half-interval or the right half-interval. Take a look at Figure 6.5 again, which shows the root in the right half of the interval that runs from -3 to 1. In this case, we have F(MID) = -3 and F(RIGHT) = 1. Thus the test in line 390 is false, so LEFT gets set to MID in line 415. In general, if F(MID) and F(RIGHT) have the same sign (both negative or both positive) then the root is in the left half-interval; otherwise the root is in the right half-interval. You should confirm the generality of this approach by working Exercise 24.

6. The algorithm is not likely to find an exact root as in Table 6.1, for one of two reasons: Roundoff error may prevent locating the exact value, or the root may be an irrational number such as one-third (0.3333 . . .). For these reasons, we need to specify a certain error tolerance within which the precision of the computed root is acceptable. For example, we could terminate the algorithm and print the root whenever the half-interval is less than 0.001. The test in line 380 and the output logic in lines 495 to 520 handle both situations—an exact root and an approximate root.

Follow-up Exercises

21. Roleplay computer by processing the following data through the program:
    a. 0.0, 1.0, 0.001 (Note that M = root)
    b. 0.5, 1.0, 0.001 (Note that L = root)
    c. 0.0, 0.5, 0.001 (Note that R = root)
    You might want to fill in a table similar to Table 6.2 as you roleplay.

22. How would you change the program to process the function $f(x) = 2^x$? (See Figure 6.4.) Roleplay this function through the program, assuming the input data $-3, 1, 0.001$.

*23. How would you change the program to process the function $f(x) = -2.25 - 4x + x^2$? (See Figure 6.4.) Roleplay this function through the program for the following input data:
    a. 4, 6, 0.01
    b. -2, 1, 0.01
    c. 1, 3, 0.01
    d. -3, 6, 0.01

*24. Convince yourself that the test in line 390 for the location of the root in the left or right half-interval is perfectly general. Pick an interval in Figure 6.5 that locates the root in the left half and evaluate the test. Next, sketch a negatively sloped linear function and repeat the test for two different intervals—one that locates the root in the left half and the other in the right half.

*25. Improve the computational efficiency of the program by accounting for the possibility (as in Exercise 21b,c) that either F(LEFT) or F(RIGHT) is zero; that is, the initial *L* or *R* is at the root. (*Hint:* Make the IF-THEN-ELSE structure in lines 265–540 a multiple alternative structure that includes new "cases.")

6.6
COMMON ERRORS

Take note of the following possible errors.

END IF Omission

It's especially easy to forget an END IF statement when designing nested or multiple alternative decision structures. For example, the nested structure

```
IF (logical expression) THEN
    .
    .
    .
    IF (logical expression) THEN
        .
        .
        .
    ELSE
        .
        .
        .
    END IF
```

would give a syntax error since the outer structure is missing an END IF, that is, the single END IF is paired with the inner block IF statement. This nested decision structure should be written as follows.

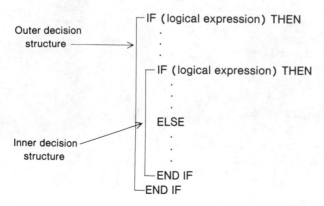

Note how indentation both helps to reduce the likelihood of forgetting an END IF statement and clarifies the nesting logic.

Logic Errors in Nested Decision Structures

You might construct a nested decision structure with a sequence of tests that you don't intend, thereby causing incorrect results. To avoid this, keep the following in mind: *Note the inner/outer nature of nested decision structures, take care in placing END IF statements, and indent accordingly,* as illustrated below.

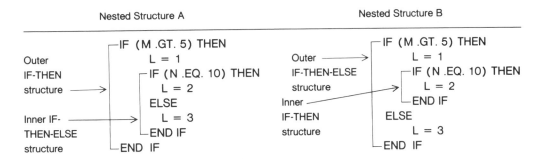

Nested structure A is an IF-THEN-ELSE structure nested within an IF-THEN structure, whereas version B is an IF-THEN structure nested within an IF-THEN-ELSE structure. Note that the placement of the first END IF statement is crucial in determining the nature of the nested structure. Also note how indentation helps to sort out the structure for us humans (it's irrelevant to the computer).

These two structures are quite different. In version A the IF-block for the outer structure includes the entire inner structure, as is the case in version B. The ELSE-block in version A, however, is part of the inner structure, which is not the case in version B. Thus the ELSE-block could be executed in version A when M .GT. 5 tests true (if N is unequal to 10), but could not possibly be executed in version B when M .GT. 5 tests true. To convince yourself, roleplay the following sets of values, where L initially stores a value of zero.

| | | Final Value Stored in L | |
M	N	Version A	Version B
8	10	2	2
8	15	3	1
3	10	0	3
3	15	0	3

Make sure you understand the above results, as well as Exercises 5 and 10 on pages 198–199 and page 206.

Many organizations avoid the nested decision structure when the number of levels exceeds three. They feel that the increasing complexity of the logic promotes the likelihood of coding error. Instead, they suggest using logical operators, a series of block IF statements, or ELSE IF statements to simplify the logic.

Algorithmic Logic Errors

Now that you are designing more complicated algorithms, you need to validate your programs carefully and systematically during the debugging phase. *The key to this procedure is the deliberate selection of test data.*

Always select test input data that validate all blocks or branches in your program. For example, the following test input values ensure that each of the three branches in Example 6.1 on page 194 is tested.

SALES	TRAVEL
4000	500
6000	500
6000	700

The output from the program can be checked against a set of "hand" calculations. *The use of trace (diagnostic PRINT) statements in each branch further facilitates this process for programs with complicated decision and loop structures.*

Where appropriate, "extreme" data values should be selected to test potential problems. For example, "boundary" values in IF tests should be checked to ensure intended results. Boundary values for SALES and TRAVEL in the preceding example are 5000 and 600, respectively. In Example 6.5 on page 209, values outside the range of 1 through 3 for CODE were tested by including the IF NONE (error) case. Another example of an extreme data value is one that causes division by zero. A common cause of this type of error is incorrect input data, as when mistakes are made in keying in data. In general, these situations are corrected by error routines, as demonstrated in Examples 5.12 (page 167) and 6.4 (page 204).

The test data we give in exercises at the ends of chapters are designed to push you in this debugging direction. You should always check the test data for thoroughness, and add your own when warranted. To complete the validation, confirm the correctness of computer output by parallel hand calculations.

ADDITIONAL EXERCISES

26.   Define or explain the following.

multiple alternative decision structure
nested decision structure
nested IF-blocks
generalized multiple alternative decision structure
ELSE IF statement
CASE structure
DO CASE, CASE, END CASE statements
IF NONE statement
case blocks
case index variable
GO TO statement
statement function

27. Property Tax Assessment. The property tax rate in a town is set at an increasing rate according to the following table.

Annual Property Tax Schedule

Value of Property	Tax Rate
Less than $10,000	3%
$10,000 and above	4%

a. Run a program to read in the value of the property, then determine and print the tax charge. Process the following test data.

Lot Number	Owner's Name	Property Value
613	A. Smith	$ 8,900
975	A. B. Smith	25,000
152	B. C. Smith	42,000
1642	C. B. Smith	37,000
1785	Deaf Smith	75,000

Sample Output

LOT NUMBER	OWNER	PROPERTY VALUE	TAX CHARGE
613	A. SMITH	8900	267
975	A. B. SMITH	25000	1000
152	B. C. SMITH	42000	2100
1642	C. B. SMITH	37000	1850
1785	DEAF SMITH	75000	3750

b. Modify the program in part a so that it prints the sum of property values, the total tax charge, the average property value, and the average tax charge.

**c. Instead of the tax schedule in part a use the following.

Value of Property	Tax Rate
Less than $10,000	3%
$10,000 or more but under $30,000	4%
$30,000 or more but under $60,000	5%
$60,000 and over	6%

**d. Check the input data for errors by ensuring that lot numbers are greater than zero and less than 5000 and property values are greater than $1 and less than $5 million. If an error is found, print an appropriate error message, bypass the tax charge calculation, and go on to the next property. Add new data to test each of these possible errors.

28. Mailing List. A professional group of computer specialists is planning a regional meeting in New Orleans. A subgroup of information system specialists within this professional group will have a well-known computer scientist as a guest speaker. The chairperson of this subgroup plans to send meeting notices to members in two regions—Southeast (code 3) and Southwest (code 5)—who have an interest in information systems (code 15) or computer science (code 18).

a. Design an algorithm and write a program that prepares mailing labels for members of the organization that satisfy the location and area of interest criteria.

The organization maintains the following data on each member.

(1) Last name
(2) First name
(3) Street address
(4) City
(5) State
(6) Zip
(7) Region code (one digit: there are nine regions overall)
(8) Interest code (two digits: there are 20 interest areas overall)

Sample Data File

(1)	(2)	(3)	(4)	(5)	(6)	(7)	(8)
Fastcode	Frank	11 Flower	Dallas	TX	75215	5	15
Burden	Kathy	193 West St	Warwick	RI	02886	1	18
Peripheral	Leslie	18 Grande	Slidell	LA	70808	5	20
Crowley	M. I. S.	1 Hope Rd	Atlanta	GA	30901	3	15
Deff	Doris	111 High St	Hartford	CT	06518	7	12
Aides	Clyde	963 Main St	Orlando	FL	32407	3	18
Frick	Ford	2 Rose Way	Boston	MA	01906	9	18

Sample Output (The First Mailing Label)

FRANK FASTCODE
11 FLOWER
DALLAS, TX 75215

Terminate input of the data file based on an EOF condition.

b. Include error detection for region and interest codes. If an error is found, print an appropriate error message and go on to the next member. Add new data with incorrect codes to debug your error logic.

c. Generalize your program so mailing labels can be prepared for any region and/or area of interest criteria. Specifically, design your program to provide the following options.

Option Code	Criteria
1	Specific region only
2	Specific interest area only
3	Specific region or interest area
4	Specific region and interest area

This version is more general than part a, but requires more computer runs to print labels for multiple regions and interest areas. For example, the run in part a requires four separate runs for option 4: region 3 and interest area 15; region 3 and interest area 18; region 5 and interest area 15; and region 5 and interest area 18.

29. **Telephone Company Billing.** "Flat rate service" charges for telephone service is a method of billing that includes some fixed amount for the main station (main telephone, switchboard, and so on) plus a variable amount per extension phone in service. Distinctions also are made between residential and business customers according to the table below. Private Branch Exchange (PBX) service uses a switchboard for the main station, off which extensions can be wired. Centrex service is for large-scale business firms and governmental agencies, which require such a large number of extensions that the telephone switching equipment is located on the customer's premises.

Customer Type	Code	Type of Service	Monthly Flat Rates Main Station	Each Extension
Residential	1	Main phone/extensions	$ 13	$ 3
Business	2	Main phone/extensions	50	10
Business	3	PBX/extensions	150	5
Business	4	Centrex/extensions	500	3

In actual practice, PBX and Centrex include many special features. For example, options include fully automatic equipment versus partly manual equipment, facilities for data transmission, private lines that ring at specific locations when the receiver is picked up (PLs), facilities for foreign exchange (FX), and many others.

To illustrate a calculation, consider a business customer with PBX equipment and 50 extensions. In this case, the monthly flat rate is $400 (or $150 + 50 × $5), which, of course, excludes long-distance charges, taxes, and charges due to special features.

a. Design and write a program that calculates flat rate service charges and outputs customer name, telephone number, and charge. Test your program with the following data.

Customer Name	Customer Phone Number	Code	Number of Extensions
Test 1	783-5123	2	5
Test 2	792-7541	4	400
Test 3	445-8162	4	550
Test 4	612-6148	3	75
Test 5	783-1235	1	0
Test 6	445-2164	1	3
Test 7	789-5849	2	7
Test 8	789-7812	4	730
Test 9	792-2674	1	1
Test 10	615-6513	3	50

Terminate customer read-in based on an EOF condition.

b. Modify the program in part a to include the calculation and output of the following.

1. Total number of customers by code category
2. Percent of customers by code category
3. Total charges by code category
4. Overall total charges

Try to design your output for easy readability.

c. Include error detection for code. If an error is found, print an appropriate error message and go on to the next customer. Do not include that customer's data in the output of part a or b. Add new data with incorrect codes to debug your error logic.

30. Checking Account Report.   Prepare pseudocode and write a program that produces a monthly checking account report for each customer. Checking charges are calculated on the basis of the following information.

1. If the ending balance is less than $200, the following service charges are assessed: a monthly fee of 80 cents plus a charge of 10 cents per honored check (withdrawal). No charges are assessed for deposits.
2. If the ending balance is $200 or more, no service charges are assessed.
3. If a check "bounces" (that is, if the balance becomes negative when the bank attempts to honor a check), a charge of $5 is assessed, and the current balance is reduced by this amount. This charge is made for each check that bounces. Checks that bounce are not honored. In other words, a withdrawal is not made from the account, since the person to whom the check was made out does not get paid. Also, the $200 limit does not apply to this bounce charge; that is, if a check bounces, the $5 charge is assessed regardless of the ending balance.

For each bank customer

1. The first line of data contains three items:
   Item 1—the bank account number
   Item 2—name
   Item 3—beginning balance
2. A variable number of lines follow the first line, each line representing a single transaction. If the value is negative, the transaction is a withdrawal; if the value is positive, the transaction is a deposit. A 0.0 entry in this line indicates the end of transactions for this customer.

Sample Input

```
614275, WENDY BRANDON, 741.62
50.75
-125
-260.50
0
```

216422, RICHARD R. WEEKS, 250.15
— 115
— 80.75
100
— 236.80
0

Sample Output

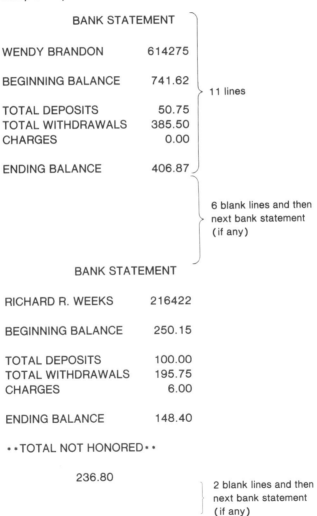

```
          BANK STATEMENT

WENDY BRANDON        614275

BEGINNING BALANCE    741.62

TOTAL DEPOSITS        50.75
TOTAL WITHDRAWALS    385.50
CHARGES                0.00

ENDING BALANCE       406.87
```

⎫
⎬ 11 lines
⎭

6 blank lines and then
next bank statement
(if any)

```
          BANK STATEMENT

RICHARD R. WEEKS     216422

BEGINNING BALANCE    250.15

TOTAL DEPOSITS       100.00
TOTAL WITHDRAWALS    195.75
CHARGES                6.00

ENDING BALANCE       148.40

**TOTAL NOT HONORED**

          236.80
```

2 blank lines and then
next bank statement
(if any)

Debug your program using the above data and the following additional data.

Account Number	Name	Beginning Balance	Transactions
(Make these up)		240.00	−50.00
			−35.00
			−175.00
			+200.00
(Make these up)		450.00	−300.00
			−125.00
			+200.00
			−75.00
			−35.00
			+150.00
			−66.00

Before designing your program, make sure you understand the logic by solving these problems by hand. Note that each bank statement takes up exactly 17 lines of input in order to conform to a standardized form. By the way, this is a good program to use diagnostic PRINT statements (traces) for current balance and charges during the debugging phase.

31. Crew Selection—A Combination Problem. An oceanographic food firm is planning extensive underwater experiments in aquaculture (sea farming). These experiments require people to live together in an isolated underwater environment for extended periods of time. To avoid problems associated with incompatibility, the firm has decided to run isolation tests for the purpose of judging compatibility. These tests require individuals to live together for two weeks under monitored conditions in an aboveground capsule that is cut off from the outside world.

As an example, suppose that four people are available for the experiments, but only two are required to live together underwater. How many subgroups of two persons are possible from among four? If we let $P1$ represent the first person, $P2$ the second person, and so on, we have the following six distinct subgroups of two persons each: $(P1, P2)$, $(P1, P3)$, $(P1, P4)$, $(P2, P3)$, $(P2, P4)$, $(P3, P4)$. Right? This means that six separate isolation tests would have to be conducted in the capsule to select the most compatible two persons.

This approach of listing groups works fine when we are dealing with small numbers, but becomes impractical when the numbers get large. For instance, if ten people are available and we need four for the experiments, then we have 210 distinct groups of four each. If you have had a course in statistics, you probably recognize this as a so-called *combination problem*.

Given that n people are available and k are needed, then the number of combinations of n taken k at a time is given by the formula

$$C = \frac{(n) \cdot (n-1) \cdot (n-2) \cdots (2) \cdot (1)}{[(n-k) \cdot (n-k-1) \cdots (2) \cdot (1)] \cdot [(k) \cdot (k-1) \cdots (2) \cdot (1)]}$$

For the first example above, $n = 4$ and $k = 2$, so

$$C = \frac{4 \cdot 3 \cdot 2 \cdot 1}{(2 \cdot 1) \cdot (2 \cdot 1)} = 6$$

For the second example, $n = 10$ and $k = 4$, so

$$C = \frac{10 \cdot 9 \cdot 8 \cdot 7 \cdot 6 \cdot 5 \cdot 4 \cdot 3 \cdot 2 \cdot 1}{(6 \cdot 5 \cdot 4 \cdot 3 \cdot 2 \cdot 1) \cdot (4 \cdot 3 \cdot 2 \cdot 1)} = 210$$

a. Design and write a program that calculates C, given n and k. Output should include C, and the total number of days required for all isolation experiments given that each experiment takes 14 days. Run the following data through your program.

n	k
6	2
10	4
10	6
10	10
20	4
40	4
40	6
60	6

Design your program such that the above data are processed by an LRC loop.

**b. Did you have numeric overflow when $n = 60$ and $k = 6$? Certain efficiencies can be realized in the calculation of C by dividing terms in the numerator by terms in the denominator. For example, for $n = 60$ and $k = 6$, we can write

$$C = \frac{60 \cdot 59 \cdot 58 \cdot 57 \cdot 56 \cdot 55}{6 \cdot 5 \cdot 4 \cdot 3 \cdot 2 \cdot 1}$$

Design your program to take advantage of this efficiency.

32. Newton's Approximation Method. This method describes a procedure for approximating the root of a function. Consider Figure 6.7, which reproduces a blown-up portion of the quadratic function in Figure 6.4. If we arbitrarily select the first root approximation at $x = 6.00$, then the second approximation is at $x = 4.78$. Graphically, the second approximation is found by constructing a tangent line on the function at $x = 6.00$ and extending this line to the x-axis. The intersection of the tangent line with the x-axis gives the next root approximation, which is 4.78 approximately. Next we construct a tangent at $x = 4.78$, and it intersects the x-axis at roughly 4.51. This process continues until a desired precision is achieved. Note that each successive approximation gets closer and closer to the root at $x = 4.50$.

Analytically, a tangent line is determined as the first derivative of the function, which we label y' (y prime). For the function

$$y = -2.25 - 4x + x^2$$

the first derivative is

$$y' = -4 + 2x$$

The next root approximation is determined from the following formula.

$$\text{Next } x = \text{current } x - \frac{y}{y'}$$

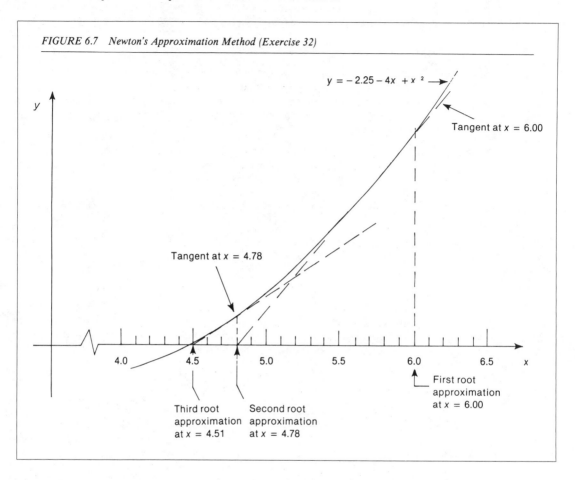

FIGURE 6.7   Newton's Approximation Method (Exercise 32)

The table below illustrates three iterations of this procedure.

Current x	$y = -2.25 - 4x + x^2$	$y' = -4 + 2x$	Next x
6.000000	9.750000	8.000000	4.781250
4.781250	1.485351	5.562500	4.514220
4.514220	0.0713022	5.028440	4.500040
.	.	.	.
.	.	.	.
.	.	.	.

a. Design and run a program that approximates roots by this method. Terminate iterations when the difference between two successive x's is less than 0.00001. Use the following test data.

y	y'	Initial x values
$-2.25 - 4x + x^2$	$-4 + 2x$	6.0; 4.0; 4.5
$-1 + 2x$	2	3.0; -2.0
2^x	$(2^x) \cdot (\ln 2)$ *	10
$-20 + 108x^2 - 4x^3$	$216x - 12x^2$	Make up your own. Try to find multiple roots.

*In 2 stands for the natural (base-e) logarithm of 2 (see Section 2.6).

**b.   Incorporate logic for finding multiple roots (if any).

33.   **Numerical Integration.**   A continuous monotonic function

$$y = f(x)$$

plots as a smooth curve (no breaks) and either continually rises (monotonically increases) or continually falls (monotonically decreases). Figure 6.8 illustrates two such functions in the interval $x = a$ to $x = b$. *Numerical integration* is the process of computing areas under curves of functions, a process that has widespread applicability in engineering and the sciences.[2] The procedure described below applies only to continuous monotonic functions.

The rectangles of width d in Figure 6.8 suggest one method of estimating area under $f(x)$ in the interval a to b. Focusing on Figure 6.8a, note that the leftmost rectangle is divided into a lower area given by the hatched portion and a triangular shaded area. The hatched area is calculated by

$$(\text{width}) \cdot (\text{height})$$

$$d \cdot f(a)$$

where $f(a)$ is the value of the function when $x = a$. The shaded area is the triangular lower half of the upper rectangle, or

$$(\tfrac{1}{2}) \cdot (\text{width of triangle}) \cdot (\text{height of triangle})$$

$$(\tfrac{1}{2}) \cdot (d) \cdot [f(a + d) - f(a)]$$

The estimated area under the curve from $x = a$ to $x = a + d$ is the sum of these two areas, or

$$\text{Area from } a \text{ to } a + d = d \cdot f(a) + \tfrac{1}{2} \cdot d \cdot [f(a + d) - f(a)]$$
$$= d/2 \cdot [f(a) + f(a + d)]$$

which is equivalent to the area of a trapezoid. Since the interval from a to b contains three of these trapezoids, each of width d, it follows that

$$
\begin{aligned}
\text{Area from } a \text{ to } b = \quad & d/2 \cdot [f(a) + f(a + d)] \\
+ \; & d/2 \cdot [f(a + d) + f(a + 2d)] \\
+ \; & d/2 \cdot [f(a + 2d) + f(b)] \\
= \quad & d/2 \cdot [f(a) + 2f(a + d) + 2f(a + 2d) + f(b)]
\end{aligned}
$$

[2] Those who have had calculus should recognize this as equivalent to evaluating the definite integral

$$\int_a^b f(x)\ dx$$

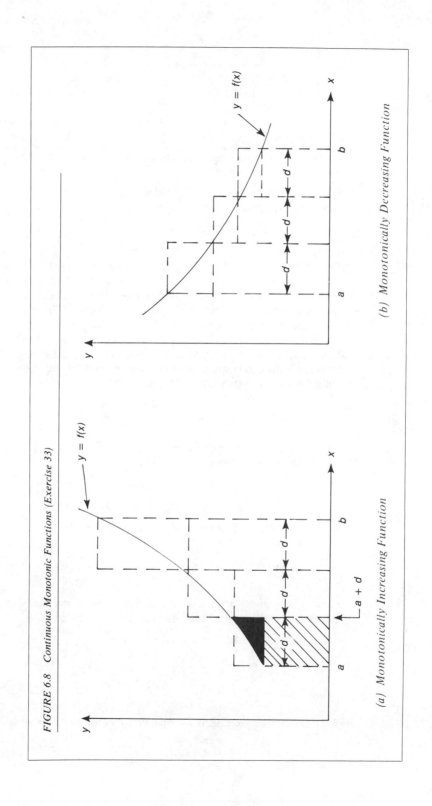

FIGURE 6.8 Continuous Monotonic Functions (Exercise 33)

(a) Monotonically Increasing Function

(b) Monotonically Decreasing Function

is an approximation to the actual area under $f(x)$ from a to b. It should make sense to you that the greater the number of trapezoids between a and b (that is, the smaller the width d), the better is the approximation to the actual area.

a. Suppose we wish to find the area under

$$y = 2^x$$

from $x = 1$ to $x = 4$. By hand, estimate this area by using three trapezoids. Next, double the number of trapezoids to six and compare results. The actual area is 20.19773. Which approximation has the least error?

b. Design and write a program that inputs a, b, and number of trapezoids, and outputs an approximation to the area. Use the following test data.

Function*	a	b	Number of Trapezoids
2^x	1.0	4.0	3; 6; 100; 211; 1000
$-1 + 2x$	1.0	10.0	100
	0.5	10.0	2; 10
$1 - e^{-x/8000}$	0.0	5000.0	100

*The symbol e is the base of natural logarithms.

c. The number of trapezoids needed for the approximation to be within a specified error (E) of the actual area is given by the formula

$$\text{Number of trapezoids} = \text{int}\left[\frac{(b - a) \cdot |f(a) - f(b)|}{2E}\right] + 1$$

where int stands for "integer part of" and $|f(a) - f(b)|$ is the absolute value of the difference. For example, if we want our estimated area for the first function in part b to be within 0.1 of the actual area, then we need 211 trapezoids.

$$\text{int}\left[\frac{(4 - 1) \cdot |2^1 - 2^4|}{2 \cdot (0.1)}\right] + 1 = 211$$

Was the estimated area within 0.1 of the actual area 20.19773 when you used 211 trapezoids in part b?

Modify your program to input E instead of number of trapezoids, and process the following data.

Function	a	b	E
$1 - e^{-x/8000}$	0.0	1000.0	0.001
	0.0	5000.0	0.001
	0.0	12000.0	0.001
	5000.0	12000.0	0.001

These data are consistent with the scenario outlined in Exercise 28 of Chapter 4 on page 136. What is the meaning of the area for the range 5000 to 12000?

One-Dimensional Arrays

Most of the programs you've written or studied up to this point have had this structure.

1. Read in a set of data.
2. Process the data.
3. Print the results.
4. Return to Step 1 if more data are available.

In some problems you may want to read and store large quantities of related data before you begin any computations. This was not possible in many earlier programs because reading in a new set of data automatically erased the values stored from the previous set, thus preventing access to the stored data of the previous set.

7.1
MOTIVATION

An array is a group of consecutive memory locations that have the same name. The use of arrays

1. Permits access to any data item that has been read previously.
2. Provides simple yet powerful capabilities to name and manipulate a large number of related storage locations.

To help you visualize this concept, the illustration below shows three storage locations for an array named DEPOS.

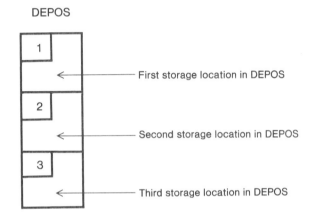

Just how we specify and manipulate arrays will become clear in the next two sections. First, however, we motivate their use through the following example.

EXAMPLE 7.1   Analysis of Bank Deposits

The vice-president of a bank wants to compare the percent of deposits that each branch contributes to the bank's total deposits. The number of deposits for each of three test branches is given below.

Branch	Number of Deposits
1	3500
2	5000
3	4000

Let's first try to solve this problem using the approach used in previous chapters. A program such as the following might be written in this way.

Version A

```
         INTEGER DEPOS,TOT,PER
   C
         TOT = 0
   C
         DO 10 I = 1,3
            READ, DEPOS
            TOT = TOT + DEPOS
   10    CONTINUE
   C
         DO 20 I = 1,3
            READ, DEPOS
            PER = DEPOS*100/TOT
            PRINT, DEPOS,PER
   20    CONTINUE
   C
         STOP
         END
```

Error occurs here during attempt to read fourth data line.

This program would not work if we use the following input data:

Test Input Data	Output
3500	***ERROR*** END OF FILE ENCOUNTERED ON UNIT
5000	
4000	

In the first loop, the three data items are read in and total deposits are accumulated for the bank; however, a problem occurs in the second loop when we try to *reinput* the data by executing the READ statement again, assuming we had only provided three input *records* or *lines*. The data already have been read in and an "END OF FILE ENCOUNTERED" error message occurs when we attempt to reread the data. This program would work only if we were to provide six input records, where the last three records are identical to the first three records.

	Test Input Data	Output	
	3500	3500	28
	5000	5000	40
	4000	4000	32
Repetition	3500		
of first	5000		
three records	4000		

This approach is not only conceptually unappealing but also inefficient, particularly if the program is used for a bank having many branches.[1]

Now, consider the program on the next page.

---

[1] Three input records would work with this approach if the data were stored on tape or sequential disk files. In this case, the file can be rewound right after loop 10. Chapter 11 discusses these concepts.

Version B

```
C
        INTEGER DEPOS1,DEPOS2,DEPOS3,TOT,PER
C
        READ, DEPOS1
        READ, DEPOS2
        READ, DEPOS3
C
        TOT = DEPOS1 + DEPOS2 + DEPOS3
C
        PER = DEPOS1*100/TOT
        PRINT, DEPOS1,PER
C
        PER = DEPOS2*100/TOT
        PRINT, DEPOS2,PER
C
        PER = DEPOS3*100/TOT
        PRINT, DEPOS3,PER
C
        STOP
        END
```

Test Input Data	Output	
3500	3500	28
5000	5000	40
4000	4000	32

This program works but . . . it's very rigid and inefficient. It works for three branches, but if you wish to add a fourth branch, the program will have to be rewritten. Worse yet, visualize this program written for the hundreds of Chase Manhattan branch banks in New York City. What a long and tedious program it would be for such a simple problem! A simpler solution to this problem is to use an array.

Version C

```
C
        INTEGER DEPOS(3),TOT,PER
C
        TOT = 0
C
        DO 10 I = 1,3
           READ, DEPOS(I)
           TOT = TOT + DEPOS(I)
    10  CONTINUE
C
        DO 20 I = 1,3
           PER = DEPOS(I)*100/TOT
           PRINT, DEPOS(I),PER
    20  CONTINUE
C
        STOP
        END
```

Test Input Data	Output	
3500	3500	28
5000	5000	40
4000	4000	32

In this program the first loop reads the number of deposits for each branch bank, storing them in an array called DEPOS, and accumulates the total deposits for all branches in TOT. The second loop references or recalls each element in the array DEPOS within the expression that calculates percentages and prints the number of deposits and the relative percent of total deposits for each branch bank. At this point, don't worry about the exact nature of the array. We discuss this topic next.

7.2
SUBSCRIPTS

An **array** is used to store a collection of related data items. The array is referenced by its **array name,** the symbolic name of an array. A number of unique memory locations is associated with an array name; each memory location in the array is an **array element,** which can be referenced by its relative position in the array through the use of a *subscript.*

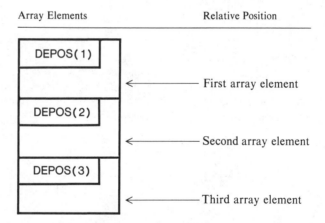

A **subscript** acts as an *index* or *pointer* to locate a specific array element. In FORTRAN, a subscript is a parenthetic expression following the array name, as follows:

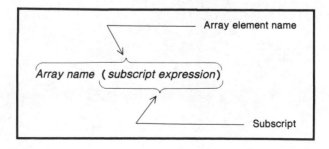

For example, the first array element in our sample program can be identified as

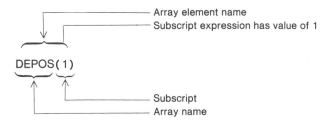

Thus an **array element name** is an array name followed by a subscript and is used to reference a specific location within the array. The subscript is a set of parentheses containing one or more subscript expressions.[2] A **subscript expression** is an *integer* expression which when evaluated has a *value*. In the above example, the array element name is DEPOS(1) and the subscript is (1); the subscript expression is the integer constant 1, which of course has a value of 1. The value of the subscript expression is used to identify an array element. In our example, the subscript value 1 identifies the first array element in the array named DEPOS. By the way, the same rules that apply to naming variable names (maximum of six characters, etc.) also apply to naming array names.

EXAMPLE 7.2 Subscripted Variables: Algebra vs. FORTRAN

The use of subscripts in FORTRAN gives the language great ease and flexibility in naming and manipulating a large number of *related* variables. This feature is "borrowed" from algebra, as the following illustrates.

Stock Number	Price of Stock ($)	Subscripted Variables in Algebra	Array Element Names (Subscripted Variables) in FORTRAN
1	75	x_1	X(1)
2	42	x_2	X(2)
3	24	x_3	X(3)
.	.	.	.
.	.	.	.
.	.	.	.
500	105	x_{500}	X(500)

For example, if we are dealing with a series of 500 numbers, where each number represents the price of a stock at the end of a given day on the New York Stock Exchange, then the algebraic notation x_3 refers to the price of the third stock and x_{75} refers to the price of the

---

[2] Subscripts with more than one subscript expression are considered in the next chapter.

75th stock. Similarly, in FORTRAN, X(3) refers to the storage location for the price of the third stock and X(75) identifies the storage location for the price of the 75th stock. Naming so many related variables would be quite tedious and impractical without the use of subscripts. For example, you wouldn't recommend a scheme such as A, B, C, . . . to name 500 variables, would you? These names are cumbersome, are difficult to manipulate, cause inefficient coding, and do not in themselves suggest contextual meaning. As you will see, the use of arrays overcomes each of these difficulties.

You should keep in mind the following additional points when working with subscripts.

1. A subscript having a single subscript expression references what is called a **vector** or **one-dimensional array.**
2. Subscript expressions must have *positive (nonzero) integer values.* Usually, they are either *positive integer constants* or integer variables that store positive (nonzero) integer values. For example,

```
INTEGER K
COST(K)
```

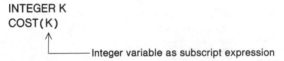

uses the *integer variable* K as a subscript. WATFIV, however, does allow a real subscript expression. The value of the expression simply gets truncated to its integer part.

When we use a variable as a subscript expression we may reference any element in the array on the basis of the value we assign that variable. For example, the program segment

```
REAL SALE (20)
    .
    .
    .
K = 3
SALE(K) = 500.0
```

results in the storage of 500.0 in the third location of the array SALE.

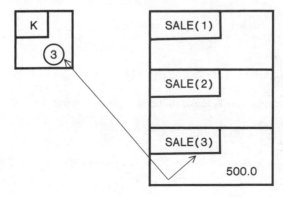

In Example 7.1, storage is accomplished as follows.

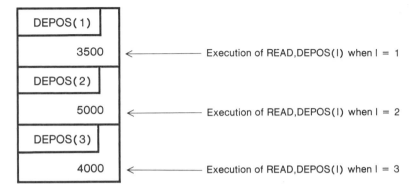

3. Generally the subscript expression is any integer expression. The computer determines which array element is referenced by evaluating the subscript expression and using this result to identify the specific array element. For example, if K stores 4 then LOAD(K + 3) and LOAD(2∗K + 1) are legitimate array element names that reference the seventh and ninth elements of the array LOAD.
4. The use of a positive, nonzero integer value for the subscript expression simplifies the relationship between this value and the array element. For example, if the value of the subscript expression is 3 in array SALE, then it simplifies our life if we can say that the array element name SALE(3) thus refers to the third array element (storage location) in the array, as in the above example.
5. We can use the same variable name as a subscript expression to reference corresponding elements in different arrays. For example, the program segment

```
K = 2
PROFIT(K) = SALE(K) − COST(K)
```

    subtracts the second array element in COST from the second array element in SALE and stores the result in the second array element of PROFIT.
6. Subscripts are not part of the array name; thus TAB(J) and TAB(I) both reference the array TAB. In addition, if I and J are equal, then TAB(J) and TAB(I) reference the same element in TAB.

7.3
ARRAY DECLARATION

Arrays must be *declared* in order for the computer to reserve multiple memory locations. Type statements with which you are familiar (CHARACTER, INTEGER, REAL, DOUBLE PRECISION) are a convenient means to this end. The general form of these statements when used to declare *one-dimensional* arrays[3] is

---

[3] These are generalized to multidimensional arrays in the next chapter.

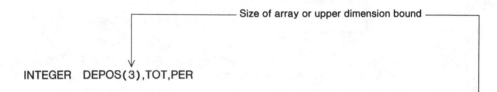

where *type keyword* is usually one of the following: CHARACTER, INTEGER, REAL, or DOUBLE PRECISION. These statements declare to the compiler which names are array names, their type, and their sizes (total number of array elements). In Example 7.1, the statement

INTEGER   DEPOS(3),TOT,PER

types DEPOS, TOT, and PER as integer and declares DEPOS a one-dimensional array with an *upper dimension bound* (on the value of the subscript expression) of 3. The *lower dimension bound* is always 1. Thus, array element names range from DEPOS(1) to DEPOS(3), which gives an array of *size* 3 in memory.

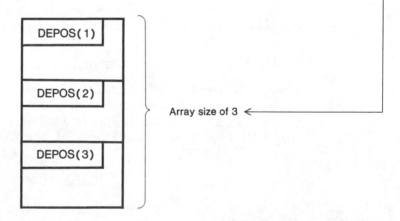

Note that the contents (stored values) of these locations are left blank; they are filled in with the appropriate values when the READ statement is executed three times in DO - loop 10 on page 237. If we had used

INTEGER DEPOS(5),TOT,PER

then five memory locations would have been reserved for DEPOS.

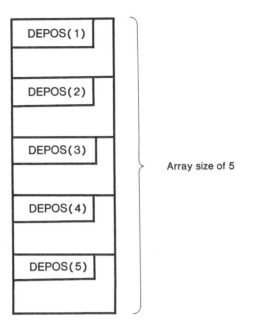

Loops 10 and 20, however, still would utilize only the first three of these locations.

More than one array can be declared in a single type statement by using commas to separate each array specification. For example,

```
REAL COST(80),REV(50),PROFIT(50)
```

reserves 80 locations for a real array named COST, another 50 locations for real array REV, and 50 more locations for real array PROFIT.

Here are some additional points to keep in mind when working with arrays.

1. Upper dimension bounds must be integer constants. For example,

   ```
   REAL LENGTH(N)
   ```

   would yield a syntax error, since a variable is not permitted for the array size, except within subprograms (Chapter 9).

2. If during execution the value of a subscript expression falls outside the range given by 1 and the upper dimension bound, then an execution error will occur.

3. The DIMENSION statement is an alternative to type statements for declaring arrays. The general form of this statement is

DIMENSION	*array name* (*array size*),	*array name* (*array size*) . . .

For example,

DIMENSION COST(80),REV(50),PROFIT(50)

reserves 80 locations for the array COST, 50 locations for REV, and 50 locations for PROFIT. Note, however, that this statement does not type the arrays. Good programing style, therefore, would dictate an explicit declaration of type as follows:

DIMENSION COST(80),REV(50),PROFIT(50)
REAL COST,REV,PROFIT

Since both operations (array declaration and type) can be combined in a type statement, we recommend that you do not use DIMENSION statements.

4. The declaration of *character arrays* usually requires a length declaration for elements in the array. For example, suppose the array LINE is to store lines of text on a page (such as a letter, notice, or document). If we assume 60 lines per page and a maximum of 70 characters per line, then we can declare LINE as a 60-element one-dimensional array with a length of 70 characters per element as follows:

```
                  ┌───── Size of array
                  ↙
CHARACTER*70 LINE(60)
```

Character arrays play an important role in what are called word-processing applications, a topic we take up in some detail in Chapter 10. In this chapter and the next we focus on *numeric arrays,* except for minor illustrations in Examples 7.9 and 7.12.

5. What size array should we declare? In general, the size of a declared array represents a trade-off between wasted storage costs and the software cost of updating the array declaration, taking into consideration actual and projected data needs. For example, if we currently have 75 branch banks and over the next 10 years expect at most 25 more branch banks, then it is reasonable to declare DEPOS as a 100-element array, since it is certain that the cost of updating the declaration in the program each time a branch bank is added far exceeds the cost of keeping at most 25 empty storage locations. However, if an array generally requires no more than 5000 elements, but once in a great while needs 100,000 elements, then it may be less costly to occasionally change the program itself by updating the array size from 5000 to 100,000 when needed.

Follow-up Exercises

1. How clear are you on the intricate terminology of the last two sections? For example, can you distinguish between
    a. An array and an array name?
    b. An array name and an array element name?
    c. An array element and an array element name?
    d. An array element and a storage location?
    e. A subscript and a subscript expression?
    f. The value of a subscript expression and the ith array element?
2. Can you reason why integer variables are not permitted in place of integer constants in defining the size of an array?

3. Indicate what is wrong, if anything, with each of the following program segments.

   a.   READ, K,X(K)
        REAL X(K),T(4 + 3)
        .
        .
        .

   b.   REAL A(50)
        DATA M,N/5,8/
        DATA A(0),A(15)/100.0,500.0/
        A(M + 10•N) = M•N
        .
        .
        .

   c.   DIMENSION D(10),E(10)
            INTEGER   D(10),E(10)
            DO 30 J = 1,20
              D(J) = J••2
        30 CONTINUE
            DO 40 J = 1,19
              E(J + 1) = D(J)•D(J + 1)
        40 CONTINUE
            .
            .
            .

   What would be stored in E(3) once the program is corrected?

4. Indicate the storage contents of specific array elements for the following, where a value of 4 is input for N.

   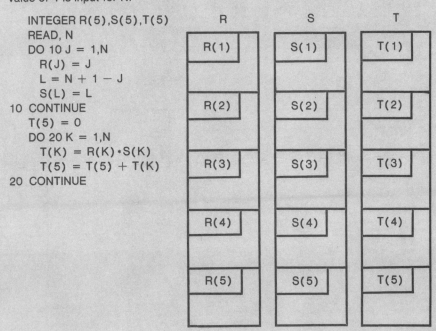

```
INTEGER R(5),S(5),T(5)
READ, N
DO 10 J = 1,N
  R(J) = J
  L = N + 1 - J
  S(L) = L
10 CONTINUE
T(5) = 0
DO 20 K = 1,N
  T(K) = R(K)•S(K)
  T(5) = T(5) + T(K)
20 CONTINUE
```

7.4
INPUT/OUTPUT

Essentially, we have three basic procedures for the efficient I/O of arrays. In the discussions that follow, assume that we wish to read or print every element in the array, beginning with the first element and moving sequentially through the array until the last element.

Using the DO Statement

The DO statement is a convenient device for performing I/O of arrays. In this case the DO-variable may be used as a subscript expression that takes on values that coincide with each element in the array.

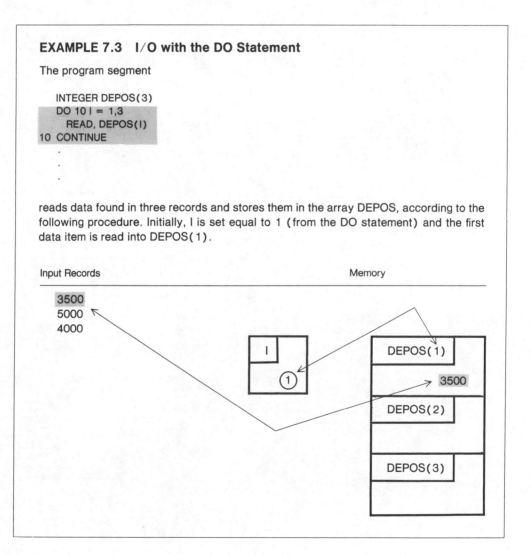

EXAMPLE 7.3   I/O with the DO Statement

The program segment

```
    INTEGER DEPOS(3)
      DO 10 I = 1,3
        READ, DEPOS(I)
10  CONTINUE
            .
            .
            .
```

reads data found in three records and stores them in the array DEPOS, according to the following procedure. Initially, I is set equal to 1 (from the DO statement) and the first data item is read into DEPOS(1).

Input Records   Memory

Then I is incremented to 2, the READ statement is executed a second time, the second input record is processed, and 5000 is stored in DEPOS(2).

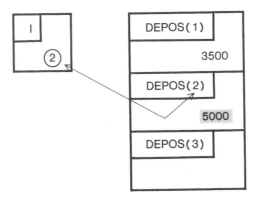

Finally, I is incremented to 3, and the third memory location for DEPOS is filled.

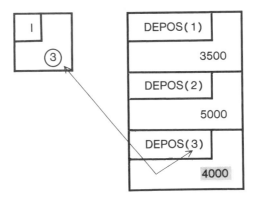

Note that a new input record is processed each time the READ statement in the DO-loop is executed.

In essence, DO-loop 10 is equivalent to the following.

```
READ, DEPOS(1)
READ, DEPOS(2)
READ, DEPOS(3)
```

In other words, identical results would be obtained if loop 10 were replaced with the above three statements. If we were reading in deposits for 200 banks, then you should readily appreciate the power of the DO-loop approach.

This looping technique using the DO statement also can be used for output. For example, the following statements result in the printout of the contents of array DEPOS.

```
        .
        .                        Output
        .
      DO 30 I = 1.3              3500
        PRINT, DEPOS(I)          5000
 30  CONTINUE                    4000
        .
        .
        .
```

Note that a new output line is written each time the PRINT statement is executed. In effect, DO-loop 30 is equivalent to the following.

```
    PRINT, DEPOS(1)
    PRINT, DEPOS(2)
    PRINT, DEPOS(3)
```

Follow-up Exercises

5. With respect to version C (the one using array DEPOS) in Example 7.1 on page 237:
    a. Change the program to process 100 branch banks. How many more statements would be needed in the version B program on page 237 to accomplish the same task? How about the length of the statement that calculates TOT? Do you now see why arrays give us a simple yet powerful means to name and manipulate a large number of related storage locations?
    b. Generalize the program so it can handle any number of branch banks up to 500.
6. Consider the following program segment for reading 50 values into an array named LOAD.

```
    REAL LOAD(50)
    READ, LOAD(1)  ⎫
    READ, LOAD(2)  ⎪
       .            ⎬  50 statements
       .            ⎪
       .            ⎪
    READ, LOAD(50) ⎭
```

Rewrite this segment using a DO-loop. Which approach is more code-efficient?
7. Describe output for the following.

	Input Data
`REAL A(100),B(100),SUMA,SUMB,SUMDIF`	
`DATA SUMDIF,SUMA,SUMB / 3 * 0.0 /`	
`READ, M`	4
`DO 50 J = 1,M`	1,5
`  READ, A(J),B(J)`	10,4
`  SUMA = SUMA + A(J)`	8,1
`  SUMB = SUMB + B(J)`	2,10
`  SUMDIF = SUMDIF + (A(J) − B(J))`	
`50 CONTINUE`	

```
        DO 75 J = 1,M
           PRINT, A(J),B(J),A(J) − B(J)
   75 CONTINUE
        PRINT,SUMA,SUMB,SUMDIF
        END
```

8. Given the following data

Cost	Sales
40	100
20	125
75	95

write an efficient program segment to read these data into the 500-element integer arrays COST and SALES. How would you place your input data?

9. **Formatted I/O.**   Answer the following regarding Example 7.1 on page 237 based on the material in Modules B, C, and D.

   a. Describe input records if we were to use the following code:

```
   2 FORMAT(I5)
        DO 10 I = 1,3
           READ 2,DEPOS(I)
   10 CONTINUE
```

   b. Same as part a except

```
   2 FORMAT(3I5)
```

   c. Describe output if we were to use the following code:

```
   4 FORMAT('0',I8,F7.1)
        DO 20 I = 1,3
           PER = REAL(DEPOS(I))/REAL(TOT)•100.0
           PRINT 4,DEPOS(I),PER
   20 CONTINUE
```

   d. Same as part c except

```
   4 FORMAT('0',I8/'b',F8.1)
```

Using the Implied-DO List

The combination of the DO statement with the READ or PRINT statement causes the processing of a new record (line) with each execution of the READ or PRINT statement. Thus, only one data value per record can be stored or output whenever the list of the READ or PRINT statement contains only one item. Often we want to store several values on a record or print a number of values on a line of output. For example, if the bank deposit data were stored on a single record in the following manner

```
3500,5000,4000
```

then the program segment

```
    DO 10 I = 1,3
        READ, DEPOS(I)
10  CONTINUE
```

would store the value 3500 in DEPOS(1), after which an "end of file encountered" error message would be printed.

The use of an implied-DO list *as an item within the list of a READ or PRINT statement* is a more flexible approach to reading and printing arrays. A general form of the implied-DO list is

$$
\begin{matrix}
\text{READ,} \\
\text{or} \\
\text{PRINT,}
\end{matrix}
\left(
\begin{matrix}
\textit{dlist,DO-variable} = & \textit{initial} & \textit{terminal} & \textit{incrementation} \\
& \textit{expression,} & \textit{expression,} & \textit{expression}
\end{matrix}
\right)
$$

Implied-DO list

where *dlist* refers to constants, variable names, array element names, array names, and expressions used in READ and PRINT statements. The *DO-variable, initial, terminal, and incrementation expressions* are subject to the same rules as the DO statement (see Section 4.5).

Typically, the items within an implied-DO list are array element names followed by indexing information that specifies the specific array elements that are to be processed, as we illustrate in the next example.

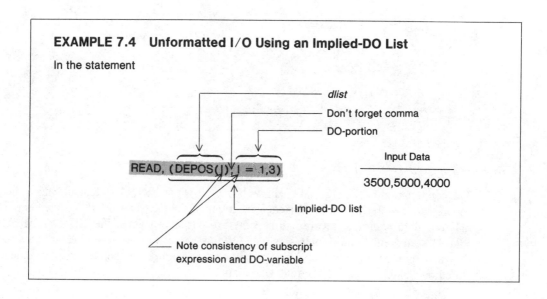

EXAMPLE 7.4   Unformatted I/O Using an Implied-DO List

In the statement

dlist

Don't forget comma

DO-portion

Input Data

READ, (DEPOS(J) I = 1,3)

3500,5000,4000

Implied-DO list

Note consistency of subscript expression and DO-variable

the list of the READ statement has a single item, an implied-DO list. The list within the implied-DO list itself (which we call *dlist*) has a single item, the array element name DEPOS(I). In this case the DO-variable I iterates from 1 to 3 in increments of 1 (the incrementation expression is given a value of 1 since it's omitted). The implied-DO list thus iterates three times, which means that DEPOS(I) is iterated three times with a different value in I each time. In other words, the array element name is repeated three times to yield an effect that is identical to the following.

    READ, DEPOS(1),DEPOS(2),DEPOS(3)

Now we can place all three data items on the same input record

Input Data

3500,5000,4000

since the list of the READ statement effectively has three separate items.

The implied-DO list also can be used to print data stored in arrays. For example,

    PRINT,(DEPOS(I),I = 1,3)

prints three values from array DEPOS on one line.

Output

| 3500 | 5000 | 4000 |

Moreover, we can label the output values as follows:

    PRINT,(I,I = 1,3)
    PRINT,(DEPOS(I),I = 1,3)

Output

| 1 | 2 | 3 |
| 3500 | 5000 | 4000 |

Note that DO parameters (I, 1, and 3 in the above examples) must be type integer when they are utilized by subscript expressions (I in the above examples).

There are many variations in using the implied-DO list, as we further illustrate with the examples shown on the next page.

Follow-up Exercises

10. Code a more efficient way of handling each of the following statements.
   a. READ,X(1),X(2),X(3),X(4),X(5),X(6),X(7),X(8)
   b. PRINT,X(1),X(2),X(3),X(4),X(5),X(6),X(7),X(8)
   c. READ,X(1),X(3),X(5),X(7),X(9),X(11)
   d. PRINT,A(1),B(1),A(2),B(2),A(3),B(3)
   e. PRINT,A(1),A(2),A(3),B(1),B(2),B(3),B(4),B(5)

EXAMPLE 7.4 (Continued)

Case	Implied-DO List Example	Equivalent to	Comment
a.	READ,(A(I),I = 2,6,2)	READ,A(2),A(4),A(6)	The DO-variable doesn't have to start at 1; it can start at any value. In addition, the increment can be any value.
b.	READ,(A(I),I = 1,2),(B(I),I = 1,2)	READ,A(1),A(2),B(1),B(2)	Read or print lists can contain more than one implied-DO list.
c.	READ (A(I),B(I),C(I),I = 1,2)	READ,A(1),B(1),C(1),A(2),B(2),C(2)	The list section within the implied-DO list (dlist) can contain more than one array element name.
d.	PRINT,X,Y,(A(I),I = 1,3),Z	PRINT,X,Y,A(1),A(2),A(3),Z	The implied-DO list may appear along with other items in the print list.
e.	PRINT,(I,A(I),I = 1,2)	PRINT,1,A(1),2,A(2)	Nonarray items inside the implied-DO list are also repeated.
f.	READ,N,(A(I),I = 1,N)	READ,N,A(1),A(2),A(3)	If the first data value in the record is 3, the implied-DO list is equivalent to what is shown. This approach should be used with caution since an error in data could cause a difficult debugging session. It's better to read N through a separate statement.

    f. READ,X(1),X(2),X(3),M,N

    g. PRINT,A,X(1),X(2),X(3),B

11. Suppose the values 10, 20, 30, and 40 are stored in the four-element integer array YES and the values 5, 10, 15, and 20 are stored in the four-element integer array NO. Indicate output for each case, where N stores a 4.

    a. PRINT, (YES(J),J = 1,N),(NO(J),J = 1,N)

    b. PRINT, (YES(J),NO(J),J = 1,N)

    c.   PRINT, (J,YES(J),NO(J),J = 1,N)

   ***d.**   DO 50 K = 1,2

            PRINT, K,(YES(J),J = 1,N)

       50 CONTINUE

12. Specify READ statements with implied-DO lists for each case below.

    a. Input Lines

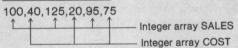

        100,125,95 ⟵ Integer array SALES

        40,20,75 ⟵ Integer array COST

    b. Input Lines

        100,40,125,20,95,75

                     — Integer array SALES

                     — Integer array COST

13. Do you see anything wrong with the following? Explain.

    a. READ, N,(X(J),J = 1,N)

    b. READ, (J,X(J),J = 1,N)

    c. PRINT, (X(P)**2,P = A,B,C/D)

EXAMPLE 7.5 Formatted I/O Using an Implied-DO List[4]

When we use the implied-DO list with format specifications, how the data are read or printed depends on how we code the format specification. For example,

        READ 1,(DEPOS(I), I = 1,3)

    1 FORMAT(3I6)

                     Input Record

             1 2 3 4 5 6 7 8 9 10 11 12 13 14 15 16 17 18

             3 5 0 0   5 0 0 0   4 0 0 0

stores three values from one record; however, if we change the FORMAT statement to

    1 FORMAT(I6)   Input Records

                       1 2 3 4 5 6 7 8

                     3 5 0 0

                     5 0 0 0

                     4 0 0 0

---

[4] This example requires knowledge of topics in Modules B, C, and D.

then three values would be read into the array DEPOS, but from three records (one value per record). This occurs because of *imbalance* between list and descriptors; that is, the input list has more variables (three) than the FORMAT statement has repeatable descriptors (one). If you're fuzzy about the imbalance rules, review Section D.2 at the end of the text.

The statements

        PRINT 3,(DEPOS(I),I = 1,3)
      3 FORMAT(1X,3I5)

print three values on one line as follows.

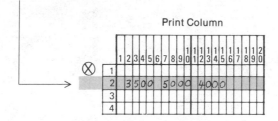

However, if we change the FORMAT statement to

      3 FORMAT (1X,I5)

then the imbalance rule causes the output to appear on three lines.

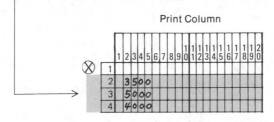

Follow-up Exercises

14. We wish to store the values 10, 20, 30, and 40 in the first four storage locations of the integer array MONEY. Indicate where you would place the data for each case.

                                                    Input Records
                                        1 2 3 4 5 6 7 8 9 10 11 12 13 14 15 16 17 18 19 20

    a.   READ 1, (MONEY(K), K = 1,4)
              1 FORMAT(4I3)
    b.   READ 1, (MONEY(K), K = 1,4)
              1 FORMAT(I3)

Input Records

1 2 3 4 5 6 7 8 9 10 11 12 13 14 15 16 17 18 19 20

   c.   READ 1, (MONEY(K), K = 1,4)
         1 FORMAT(2I3)
   d.   READ 1, (MONEY(K), K = 1,4)
         1 FORMAT(8I3)
   e.   1 FORMAT(I3)
           DO 10 K = 1,4
             READ 1, MONEY(K)
        10 CONTINUE

15. Suppose we wish to output the contents of MONEY as defined in the preceding exercise. Indicate how output would appear for each case.

   a.   PRINT 15,(MONEY(J), J = 1,4)
        15 FORMAT(1X,4I5)
   b.   PRINT 15,(MONEY(J), J = 1,4)
        15 FORMAT(1X,I5)
   c.   PRINT 15,(MONEY(J), J = 1,4)
        15 FORMAT(1X,2I5)
   d.   15 FORMAT(1X,I1,I5)
           DO 20 J = 1,4
             PRINT 15,J,MONEY(J)
        20 CONTINUE
   e.   PRINT 15,(J,MONEY(J), J = 1,4)
        15 FORMAT(1X,I1,I5)

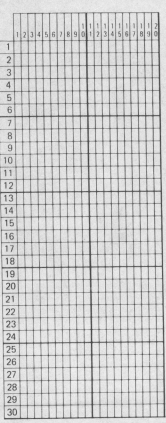

*16. Consider real array SAG with 99 declared array elements. For a given run, N represents the number of elements to be used in SAG.

   a. Write a complete program which inputs the single record given by

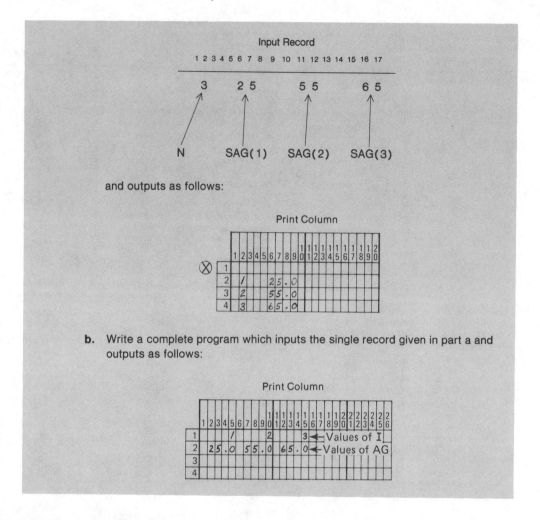

b. Write a complete program which inputs the single record given in part a and outputs as follows:

Using the Short-List Technique

Entire arrays may be read or written by placing the array name without subscripts in the input or output command. This is sometimes called the **short-list technique**. For example, in the program segment

    INTEGER DEPOS(3)

    READ, DEPOS   ← Equivalent to READ,(DEPOS(I), I = 1,3)

the computer reads in three values from *one* line, storing the first value in DEPOS(1), the second value in DEPOS(2), and the third value in DEPOS(3).

The presence of the array name without a subscript indicates that the values for *all the elements* in the array, *as specified in the type statement,* are to be read or written. Accordingly, this technique only can be used to read or write an *entire* array (as specified in the type statement); if only part of the array is to be processed, then the DO statement or implied DO must be used. To illustrate what we mean, the program segment

```
REAL PRESS( 10)
READ,PRESS
PRINT,PRESS
```

reads ten values on one line and prints ten values on one line. If we wish to input or output only five values of the array, but PRESS has been dimensioned to ten, then we can't use the short-list technique.

Follow-up Exercise

17. Describe I/O records for the following, where we wish to store 10 for N, the numbers 1, 2, ... , 8 for the array KIN, and the fractions 0.1, 0.2, ... ,1.5 for the array FRAC.
   a.
```
INTEGER KIN(8)
REAL     FRAC(15)
READ,N
READ,KIN
READ,FRAC
```
   b. Instead of the READ statements in part a use
```
READ, N,KIN,FRAC
```
   c.
```
1 FORMAT(I2)
2 FORMAT(8I1)
3 FORMAT( 15F4.1)
  READ 1,N
  READ 2,KIN
  READ 3,FRAC
```
How would output appear for each of the following?
   d.
```
PRINT 4,KIN,(FRAC(J), J = 1,N)
4 FORMAT( 1X,8I2,15F5.2)
```
   e.
```
PRINT 4,KIN,(FRAC(J), J= 1,N)
4 FORMAT( 1X,8I2/1X,10F5.2)
```
   **f.
```
PRINT 4,KIN,(FRAC(J), J = 1,N)
4 FORMAT( 1X,8(I2/1X)/(1X,F5.2))
```

7.5
MANIPULATING ARRAYS

This section presents four examples that illustrate techniques of manipulation for one-dimensional arrays.

EXAMPLE 7.6   Initialization

Often it is necessary to set each element in an array to some initial value. For example, to initialize all values in a 100-element real array to zero, we could write the following instructions.

```
      DO 10 I = 1,100
         SUM(I) = 0.0
   10 CONTINUE
```

As the value of I changes from 1 to 100, each of the 100 locations in the array SUM is set to zero.

The above procedure initializes the array during execution of the program. Alternatively, we can initialize the array during compilation using the *DATA statement* first discussed in Section 2.8.

```
      DATA SUM / 100 * 0.0 / ←──────────── Using the short-list technique
      DATA (SUM(I), I = 1,100) / 100 * 0.0 / ←── Using an implied-DO list.
```
　　　　　　　　　　　　　　　　　　　　　　　Note: DO-variable and DO expressions
　　　　　　　　　　　　　　　　　　　　　　　must be integer and entirely
　　　　　　　　　　　　　　　　　　　　　　　defined within the implied-DO list.

Use of the DATA statement is efficient if we only need to initialize the array once. If the array needs to be reinitialized during execution, then we must use the DO-loop approach, since the DATA statement is nonexecutable.

EXAMPLE 7.7   Accumulation of a Sum

Quite often it is necessary to perform arithmetic operations on all the elements in an array. The following segment from Example 7.1 illustrates the accumulation of a sum.

```
      TOT = 0.0
      DO 10 I = 1,3
         READ,DEPOS(I)
         TOT = TOT + DEPOS(I)
   10 CONTINUE
```

As the value of I changes from 1 to 3, each element of the array DEPOS is added to the accumulator TOT. When I = 1 we actually are executing

　　TOT = TOT + DEPOS(1)　　or　　TOT =　　0 + 3500;

when I = 2 we are executing

　　TOT = TOT + DEPOS(2)　　or　　TOT = 3500 + 5000;

and when I = 3 we are executing

　　TOT = TOT + DEPOS(3)　　or　　TOT = 8500 + 4000.

Thus, 12500 gets stored in TOT.

EXAMPLE 7.8 Correspondence Among Arrays

Sometimes we need to perform operations among corresponding elements of different arrays. For example, assume that a banking program has stored the current month's total dollar deposits in array DEPA and the total dollar withdrawals in array WITA. A third array can be used to accumulate the new balance (BAL), as follows.

```
      DO 30 I = 1,N
        BAL(I) = BAL(I) + DEPA(I) - WITA(I)
   30 CONTINUE
```

where N represents the number of customers to be processed. Note that the appearance of BAL(I) on the right side reflects the previous value of BAL(I), that is, last month's balance for the Ith account.

Sometimes we need not manipulate all the elements in an array. For example, the following logic updates specific accounts that are read in.

```
      REAL BAL(1000),DEPA(1000),WITA(1000)
      LOOP
        READ, J
          AT END, QUIT
        IF (J .GT. 0 .AND. J .LE. 1000) THEN
          BAL(J) = BAL(J) + DEPA(J) - WITA(J)
        ELSE
          PRINT,'ERROR IN DATA'
        END IF
      END LOOP
```

If J has a value of 8, the eighth array element in BAL is updated by adding the value in the eighth location of DEPA and subtracting the value in the eighth location of WITA.

EXAMPLE 7.9 Character Arrays

Character arrays are particularly useful when we need to store and manipulate a set of data with related character values, such as days of the week, months of the year, names of employees, and so on. In this example we retrieve a specific day from an array that stores names for all the days of the week.

```
C------------------------------------------------
C     CHARACTER ARRAY EXAMPLE
C
C     KEY:
C       K   = DAY NUMBER (1 TO 7)
C       DAY = ARRAY THAT STORES NAMES OF DAYS
C------------------------------------------------
      CHARACTER DAY*9(7)
      INTEGER   K
C------------------------------------------------
      READ, DAY  ←————————————————————— Short-list
                                         technique
```

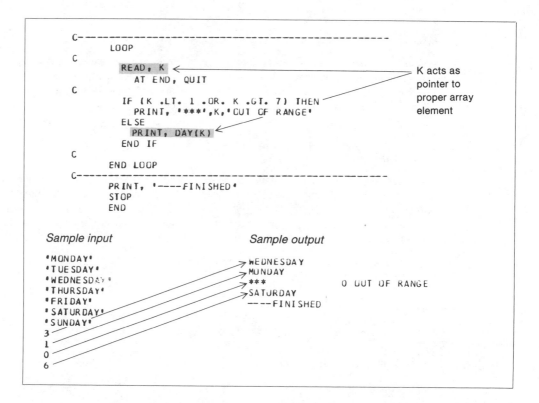

```
C- — — —————————————————————————————————— -
C      LOOP
          READ, K  <
            AT END, QUIT
C
          IF (K .LT. 1 .OR. K .GT. 7) THEN
            PRINT, '***',K,'OUT OF RANGE'
          ELSE
            PRINT, DAY(K)  <
          END IF
C
        END LOOP
C-————— —————————————————————————————————— -
        PRINT, '----FINISHED'
        STOP
        END
```

K acts as
pointer to
proper array
element

Sample input

```
'MONDAY'
'TUESDAY'
'WEDNESDAY'
'THURSDAY'
'FRIDAY'
'SATURDAY'
'SUNDAY'
3
1
0
6
```

Sample output

```
WEDNESDAY
MONDAY
***              0 OUT OF RANGE
SATURDAY
----FINISHED
```

Follow-up Exercises

18. With respect to Example 7.6, what would be wrong with the following?

    DATA (SUM(I),I = 1,N) /N*0.0/

19. A student, wishing to initialize an array with ten elements to zero, wrote the following.

    TOTAL (K) = 0.0

    On seeing this, his girlfriend (who also takes FORTRAN programming) says the above doesn't make sense because K is undefined. Perhaps, she reasons, we can try a short-list approach.

    TOTAL = 0.0

    Explain why each approach would provoke an error. Correct this segment of the program.

20. Sometimes, beginning programmers will try to use the implied-DO list for arithmetic operations. This is not possible. Correct the following attempt at summing the K elements in array REVEN.

    SUM = (SUM + REVEN(I),I = 1,K)

21. Suppose that before running the first program segment in Example 7.8, memory appears as follows:

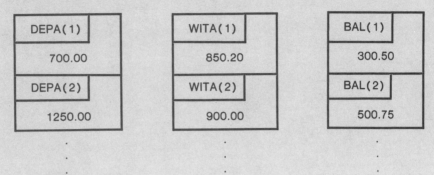

What changes would occur for the first two customer accounts following execution of the first program segment in Example 7.8?

22. Modify the loop body in the second program segment in Example 7.8 to print the account number, ACCNO(J), and new balance whenever the new balance is less than zero.

23. With respect to Example 7.9:
    a. What gets stored in DAY(1), DAY(2), . . . , DAY(7)?
    b. Indicate output for the numeric input

        5
        4
        10

    c. Can you think of a simpler alternative for defining values in array DAY?

*24. Write a short program such that the sample numeric input

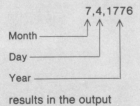

    results in the output

        JULY 4, 1776

    Terminate input if the year is zero or less. Print an error message if data input for either the month or the day is out of range.

25. Write code for the following manipulations of the 25-element integer array LIST.
    a. Input N values in reverse order; that is, the first value gets stored in LIST(N), the second in LIST(N − 1), and so on.
    b. Find and print the largest value in the array.
    c. Print locations of array elements (values of subscript expressions) that store values of zero.
    *d. Create a second array, LIST2, consisting of all nonzero elements in LIST.

*e. Move all values in the array up one position; that is, the value in LIST(1) gets eliminated, LIST(2) gets moved to LIST(1), LIST(3) to LIST (2), and so on. Insert −99 in the last array element.

26. Assume that the array VALUE has the following contents.

VALUE

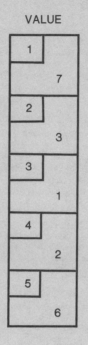

What values are stored in X, Y, and VALUE after the following segment is executed?

```
N = 1
M = 3
X = VALUE(M + N)
Y = VALUE(M) + VALUE(N)
VALUE(M) = M
VALUE(N + M) = N
```

7.6
APPLICATIONS

This section illustrates four common applications of one-dimensional arrays.

EXAMPLE 7.10   Direct Access to Array Element—SAT Scores

A more efficient method of utilizing arrays in some applications is to access or process values *directly* from one array location without moving sequentially through an entire array. To illustrate the direct-access concept, consider the following problem.

FIGURE 7.1   *Algorithm for Direct Access Problem*

```
            Initialize arrays
            LOOP while student needs processing
                READ class code, SAT verbal, SAT math
                IF class code out of range THEN
                    PRINT error message
                    STOP
                END IF
                Combine SAT verbal and math
                Update class count by direct access
                Update class SAT sums by direct access
            END LOOP
            DO-loop for classes
                PRINT class, count, average
            End DO-loop
            Stop
```

Every year State College prints a Fact Book that includes average SAT scores of students categorized as freshman, sophomore, junior, and senior. Figure 7.1 and the following program illustrate how an array can be used to accumulate these data.

```
C-------------------------------------------------------------------
C     SAT SCORES
C
C     KEY:
C       NOS    = NUMBER OF STUDENTS
C       CLASS  = CLASS CODE(1 = FRESHMAN,2 = SOPHOMORE,...)
C       SATVER = SAT VERBAL SCORE
C       SATMTH = SAT MATH SCORE
C       SATTOT = SAT COMBINED VERBAL AND MATH SCORE
C       COUNT  = ARRAY CONTAINING COUNT OF STUDENTS BY CLASS
C       SUMSAT = ARRAY CONTAINING SUM OF COMBINED SAT SCORES
C                BY CLASS
C-------------------------------------------------------------------
      INTEGER NOS,CLASS,SATVER,SATMTH,SATTOT
      INTEGER COUNT(4),SUMSAT(4)
C-------------------------------------------------------------------
      DATA COUNT,SUMSAT/8*0/
```

```
C-----------------------------------------------------------------
       LOOP
C
          READ,   CLASS,SATVER,SATMTH
             AT END, QUIT
C
          IF(CLASS .LT. 1 .OR. CLASS .GT. 4)THEN
             PRINT, 'ERROR IN CLASS CODE'
             PRINT, 'PROGRAM TERMINATED'
             STOP
          END IF
C
          SATTOT = SATVER + SATMTH
          COUNT(CLASS)  = COUNT(CLASS)  + 1
          SUMSAT(CLASS) = SUMSAT(CLASS) + SATTOT
C
       END LOOP
C-----------------------------------------------------------------
       PRINT,'            CODE      COUNT     AVERAGE'
       PRINT,'            ---------------------------'
C-----------------------------------------------------------------
       DO 20 J = 1,4
          IF (COUNT(J) .EQ. 0) THEN
             PRINT, J,COUNT(J),0
          ELSE
             PRINT, J, COUNT(J), SUMSAT(J)/COUNT(J)
          END IF
    20 CONTINUE
C-----------------------------------------------------------------
       STOP
       END
```

Direct-access logic

Input

```
2,580,640
3,720,680
2,610,560
1,560,590
2,580,420
4,495,505
```

Output

CODE	COUNT	AVERAGE
1	1	1150
2	3	1130
3	1	1400
4	1	1000

Note 1. The variable CLASS stores coded values 1 through 4, which represent 1 for freshman, 2 for sophomore, 3 for junior, and 4 for senior. The array COUNT is used to store the accumulated count of students in each class. For example, COUNT(1) represents number of freshmen, COUNT(2) represents number of sophomores, and so forth. The array SUMSAT stores the sum of combined SAT scores by class. For example, SUMSAT(1) will contain the sum of combined (math and verbal) SAT scores for all freshmen.

Note 2. If a student has a class standing of 2, then CLASS stores 2 and the statement

COUNT(CLASS) = COUNT(CLASS) + 1

increments by 1 the second storage location in COUNT. In other words, the equivalent statement given by

COUNT(2) = COUNT(2) + 1

is executed. Thus CLASS acts as a "pointer" (subscript expression) to the specific location in COUNT that is to be manipulated. The same approach is used to manipulate or update the array SUMSAT.

Note 3.   Notice that both COUNT(J) and COUNT(CLASS) are used in this program to access specific elements in COUNT. Our use of J rather than CLASS as the subscript expression of COUNT in loop 20 illustrates the fact that one should focus on the *value* taken on by the subscript expression rather than the subscript expression itself. We have no need to use CLASS as a subscript outside of the first loop; hence we use the simpler J.

Note 4.   In this particular example, the concept of "direct access" is illustrated by the fact that we need not loop through the entire array each time we wish to update (increment or sum) the contents of a specific location in COUNT or SUMSAT. The pointer CLASS conveniently serves to locate specific elements in COUNT and SUMSAT.

Follow-up Exercises

27.   For the program in Example 7.10:
   a.   Assume that a snapshot of memory is taken just before the execution of END LOOP. Indicate how the storage locations of COUNT and SUMSAT change as the program processes the sample input data

CLASS	SATVER	SATMTH	SATTOT	COUNT(1)	COUNT(2)	COUNT(3)	COUNT(4)	SUMSAT(1)	SUMSAT(2)	SUMSAT(3)	SUMSAT(4)
—				0	0	0	0	0	0	0	0

   b.   Indicate output if we were to delete the last input line.
   c.   Indicate output if the first class code were 5 instead of 2.
*28.   Suppose we wish to process data for each of N years in the same run. Appropriately modify the program in Example 7.10.

EXAMPLE 7.11   Table Look-up: Life Insurance Premium

The term **table look-up** refers to procedures for accessing data that are stored in a table. These procedures satisfy a very common need across a wide variety of professional fields and occupational areas. In this example we work with one-dimensional "tables"; in the next chapter, we discuss two-dimensional tables.

Suppose that a life insurance company uses the premium schedule below to bill its customers. In this case, the annual premium is based on the age of the policyholder. For example, a policyholder who is 47 years old would pay a premium of $327 per year.

Premium Schedule

Upper Age Limit	Annual Premium ($)
25	277
35	287
45	307
55	327
65	357

When looking up information in a table, three basic elements are required. First, there is the "search key," which is the item of information that helps you to locate the right place within the table. In the case of the life insurance company, each policyholder's age is the search key.

The table that is to be searched usually makes up the other two sets of elements needed for the search: (1) the set of "keys" used to access the proper location, and (2) the set of "function values." In the premium schedule the set of keys is the limits on the various age classes, and the corresponding premiums are the function values.

Figure 7.2 describes the algorithm that processes policyholders. The stepwise refinement procedure in Figure 7.2 is fully described in Module E. Study this figure before going on to the program and discussion that follow.

FIGURE 7.2   Stepwise Refinement of Pseudocode for Table Look-Up Problem

STEP 1	STEP 2	STEP 3
READ premium schedule	DO-loop for premium schedule READ age limit, premium End DO-loop	
PRINT header		

Process policyholders	LOOP to process
	        policyholders
	    READ name, age
	    Determine premium
	    PRINT name, premium
	END LOOP
		IF (age > 65) THEN
		    PRINT error message
		ELSE
		    Initialize index
		    DO WHILE age > age limit
		        Increment index
		    END WHILE
		END IF

Stop		

```
C--------------------------------------------------------
C   LIFE INSURANCE PREMIUMS
C
C   KEY:
C      NAME    = NAME OF POLICYHOLDER
C      AGE     = AGE OF POLICYHOLDER
C      AGELIM  = ARRAY CONTAINING UPPER AGE LIMITS
C      PREM    = ARRAY CONTAINING PREMIUMS
C      INDEX   = POINTER TO LOCATION WITHIN ARRAY
C
       CHARACTER NAME*20
       INTEGER   AGELIM(5),PREM(5),AGE,INDEX
C--------------------------------------------------------
       DO 10 I = 1,5
         READ, AGELIM(I),PREM(I)
   10  CONTINUE
C--------------------------------------------------------
       PRINT, '    NAME                    PREMIUM'
       PRINT, '===================================='
C--------------------------------------------------------
       LOOP
C
         READ, NAME,AGE
           AT END, QUIT
C
         IF (AGE .GT. AGELIM(5)) THEN
           PRINT, NAME, 'IS OVER',AGELIM(5),'--UNINSURABLE'
         ELSE
           INDEX = 1
           WHILE (AGE .GT. AGELIM(INDEX))
             INDEX = INDEX + 1               <-------- Table look-up
           END WHILE                                   logic
           PRINT, NAME, PREM(INDEX)
         END IF
C
       END LOOP
C--------------------------------------------------------
       PRINT, '===================================='
       STOP
       END
```

Input

```
25,277
35,287
45,307
55,327
65,357
'CLARK S. KENT',42
'LOIS S. LANE',28
```

Output

```
     NAME                    PREMIUM
 ====================================
 CLARK S. KENT                  307
 LOIS S. LANE                   287
 ====================================
```

The premium schedule is read into two one-dimensional arrays: AGELIM and PREM. Memory locations for these arrays appear as follows *after* loop 10 is completed:

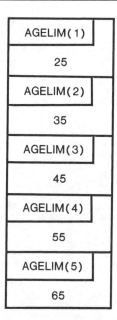

AGELIM(1)		PREM(1)
25		277
AGELIM(2)		PREM(2)
35		287
AGELIM(3)		PREM(3)
45		307
AGELIM(4)		PREM(4)
55		327
AGELIM(5)		PREM(5)
65		357

Next, the table header is printed and we enter the loop that processes policyholders. The first statement in the loop reads in the policyholder's name and age. If a policyholder's age is over 65, then a message to that effect is printed and we go on to the next policyholder.

The next segment contains the table look-up logic. In this case the "search key" is the value stored in AGE and the "set of keys" is the set of array elements in AGELIM. Starting with the first element (when INDEX = 1), the loop test sequentially evaluates each element of AGELIM until the proper age class is found; that is, until the age of the policyholder (search key) is less than or equal to an age limit value in array AGELIM. When this condition is satisfied (the WHILE-loop test gives a "false" result), the appropriate premium (function value) is identified as the array element of PREM that corresponds to the matching age class. For example, when 42 is stored in AGE, the WHILE loop operates as follows.

INDEX	Is AGE Greater than AGELIM(INDEX)?	Result
1	True; 42 is greater than 25	Continue looping
2	True; 42 is greater than 35	Continue looping
3	False; 42 is not greater than 45	Exit from loop

Thus, when loop exit is achieved, the statement

    PRINT,NAME,PREM(INDEX)

is executed, and the correct value of 3 in INDEX (age class) is used as the value of the subscript expression for PREM. In this case, the contents of PREM(3) are printed, which gives a premium of $307 for someone aged 42.

Follow-up Exercises

29. With respect to Example 7.11, what would the output look like if the last input record were as follows?

    'RIP VAN WINKLE', 99

30. Do you see anything wrong with the following table look-up logic?

    ```
    DO 15 I = 1,5
        IF (AGE .LE. AGELIM(I)) GO TO 20
    15  CONTINUE
    20  PRINT,NAME,PREM(I)
    ```

*31. Suppose the program were not to include the test for an upper age limit; that is, delete the IF, PRINT, ELSE, and END IF statements. What would happen if it were to process a policyholder aged 75?

EXAMPLE 7.12   Polynomial Plot

This example illustrates how we can use a one-dimensional array to plot the coordinates (x,y) of any polynomial function up to third degree,

$$y = b_0 + b_1x + b_2x^2 + b_3x^3$$

where the b_i are coefficients of the function and the values of x run from a lower limit to an upper limit in any desired increment.

Specifically, we plot the second-degree polynomial function

$$y = 20 + 10x - x^2$$

for values of x from 1 to 10 in increments of 1. In this case, $b_0 = 20$, $b_1 = 10$, $b_2 = -1$, and $b_3 = 0$; and y takes on values that range from 20.0 to 45.0.

Figure 7.3 illustrates the algorithm for the program on the next page.

FIGURE 7.3   *Algorithm for Polynomial Plot*

```
READ plot symbol
READ b0, b1, b2, b3, x-range
DO-loop for x-values
    Calculate y
    IF y-value within range THEN
        Place plot symbol in plot line vector
        PRINT x, y, plot line vector
        Eliminate plot symbol from plot line vector
    ELSE
        PRINT x, y, out-of-range message
    END IF
End DO-loop
Stop
```

```
C---------------------------------------------------------------
C     POLYNOMIAL PLOT PROGRAM
C
C     KEY:
C        LINE   = PLOT LINE VECTOR
C        BLANK  = STORES BLANK CHARACTER
C        SYMBOL = STORES PLOT SYMBOL
C        X      = INDEPENDENT VARIABLE
C        Y      = DEPENDENT VARIABLE
C        B0,... = POLYNOMIAL COEFFICIENTS
C        LOWLIM = LOWER LIMIT ON X
C        UPLIM  = UPPER LIMIT ON X
C        INC    = INCREMENT IN X
C        LOOP   = LOOP ITERATIONS FROM LOWLIM TO UPLIM
C---------------------------------------------------------------
      CHARACTER * 1 LINE(100),BLANK,SYMBOL
      REAL          X,Y,B0,B1,B2,B3,LOWLIM,UPLIM,INC
      INTEGER       LOOP,J
C---------------------------------------------------------------
      DATA LINE,BLANK /100*' ',' '/
C---------------------------------------------------------------
      READ,    SYMBOL
      READ,    B0,B1,B2,B3
      READ,    LOWLIM,UPLIM,INC
C---------------------------------------------------------------
      LOOP = INT((UPLIM - LOWLIM + INC)/INC + 0.5)
      X    = LOWLIM
      PRINT 15,B0,B1,B2,B3
C---------------------------------------------------------------
      DO 10 J = 1,LOOP
C
         Y = B0 + B1*X + B2*X**2 + B3*X**3
         K = INT(Y)
C
         IF (K .GT. 0 .AND. K .LE. 100) THEN
            LINE(K) = SYMBOL
            PRINT 20,X,Y,LINE
            LINE(K) = BLANK
         ELSE
            PRINT 25, X,Y
         END IF
C
         X = X + INC
C
   10 CONTINUE
C---------------------------------------------------------------
   15 FORMAT('1',T16,'POLYNOMIAL PLOT'/T16,15('-')/T18,'B0=',F10.2/
     +        T18,'B1=',F10.2/T18,'B2=',F10.2/T18,'B3=',F10.2/
     +        ' ',' X       Y'/
     +        ' ',' VALUE   VALUE'/3X,12('-'))
   20 FORMAT(1X,2F7.1,100A1)
   25 FORMAT(1X,2F7.1,' Y-VALUE OUTSIDE RANGE')
C---------------------------------------------------------------
      STOP
      END
```

Input

```
'*'
20,10,-1,0
1,10,1
```

Output

```
POLYNOMIAL PLOT
---------------
   B0=       20.00
   B1=       10.00
   B2=       -1.00
   B3=        0.00


     X       Y
   VALUE   VALUE
   ------------
    1.0     29.0                                        *
    2.0     36.0                                            *
    3.0     41.0                                              *
    4.0     44.0                                               *
    5.0     45.0                                                *
    6.0     44.0                                                *
    7.0     41.0                                              *
    8.0     36.0                                            *
    9.0     29.0                                        *
   10.0     20.0                            *
```

The program plots the function by placing the desired symbol (in this case *
according to data input) at the appropriate (x, y) coordinate. Values of x and y are
printed along the left margin.

The graph appears with the horizontal axis as the y-axis and the vertical axis as the
x-axis. Thus you should turn the page for conventional viewing.

Note how the 100-element character array LINE is used to print the function. First,
the entire array is initialized to blanks through the DATA statement. Then, once the value
of Y is determined, a corresponding location in the array LINE is set equal to the plot
symbol (all other elements in the array LINE remain blank). For example, at x = 6 we
have y = 44.0 so that LINE would appear as follows:

LINE(1)	LINE(2)	. . .	LINE(44)	. . .	LINE(99)	LINE(100)
b	b		*		b	b

Once a line of the graph is printed, the location containing the plot symbol is reinitialized
to blank, to get ready for the next value of y.

Finally, note that this program is restricted to y-values of at least 1 but 100 or less
since the integer part of the y-value is the subscript expression value for LINE, and these
values are limited to the range 1 to 100 inclusive according to the array size in the
CHARACTER statement. By the way, we could have omitted the length specification for
character variable and array names as follows:

    CHARACTER LINE(100),BLANK,SYMBOL

since a length of 1 is assumed when the length specification is omitted.

Follow-up Exercises

32. What change would you make to plot the X symbol instead of *?

33. Modify the program to plot any mathematical function (not just polynomials) whereby the user provides the appropriate line of code that represents the function.

*34. This program can be generalized to process any *n*-degree polynomial by storing the coefficients $b_0, b_1, \ldots, b_n$ in a one-dimensional array and using the subscript expression value to represent the exponent on *x*. Modify the program accordingly. *Hint:* Use a DO-loop to calculate values of *y*.

**35. A shortcoming of the current program is restrictions of *y* values in the range 1 to 100.

    a. Modify the program to handle any range of *y* values, so long as the integer difference between the minimum and maximum values doesn't exceed 100.

    b. Same as part a, except the range in *y* can exceed 100. *Hint:* Values of *y* must be proportionally scaled to between 1 and 100.

EXAMPLE 7.13   Sorting

One of the most common operations performed in data processing, called **sorting,** is arranging data either numerically or alphabetically into sequential order according to some criterion. For example, a student file contains a number of records, one for each student. Each record contains student name and identification number in addition to other data. We could sort the file either by ID number in ascending or descending order or we could arrange the file alphabetically using the student names. In either case, the item in the record that is used to sort the file is known as the "sort key."

Let's assume we want a listing of students in ascending numeric order according to their ID numbers. For simplicity, let's further assume we have only four students. The one-dimensional array called LIST is used to store and sort ID numbers, as shown below.

ID Number	Array LIST
8321	LIST(1)
	8321
3076	LIST(2)
	3076
2501	LIST(3)
	2501
7771	LIST(4)
	7771

For this problem, we use the **exchange method** of sorting. On each pass through the array, the first element is compared with the second: The smaller number is stored in the first position and the larger number is stored in the second position. Then the second element of the array is compared with the third: The smaller number is placed in the second position and the larger number is placed in the third position. This process of comparison and rearranging continues throughout the entire array. When this first pass through the array is complete, the array is processed again, from beginning to end. This procedure continues until no exchanges take place in a pass through the entire array. The exchange method is also called a **bubble sort** since items that are below their correct positions in the array tend to move upward to their proper places, like bubbles in a carbonated drink.

Figure 7.4 shows exploded pseudocode and Figure 7.5 illustrates the flowchart for the sorting program.

FIGURE 7.4   *Stepwise Refinement of Pseudocode for Sorting Problem*

STEP 1	STEP 2	STEP 3
READ no. items	IF array size exceeded THEN	
Error routine	PRINT error message	
READ list	STOP	
	END IF	
	WHILE sort incomplete	
	DO-loop for items in list	
	IF two items need exchanging THEN	Temporary location = current array element
Sort list	Exchange items	Current array element = previous array element
	END IF	Previous array element = temporary location
	End DO-loop	
	END WHILE	
PRINT sorted list		
Stop		

```
C-------------------------------------------------------------
C     SORT PROGRAM IN ASCENDING NUMERIC ORDER
C
C     KEY:
C        N      = NUMBER OF ITEMS
C        LIST   = INTEGER ARRAY TO BE SORTED
C        SWITCH = 0 IF SORT COMPLETE; 1 IF NOT COMPLETE
C        TEMP   = TEMPORARY STORAGE LOCATION
C-------------------------------------------------------------
       INTEGER N,LIST(1000),SWITCH,TEMP
C-------------------------------------------------------------
       DATA SWITCH/1/
C-------------------------------------------------------------
       READ, N
C
       IF (N .GT. 1000) THEN
          PRINT, N, ' EXCEEDS MAXIMUM NUMBER OF ITEMS'
          STOP
       END IF
C
       READ, (LIST(J),J=1,N)
```

Program continues on page 275

FIGURE 7.5   *Flowchart for Sorting Program*

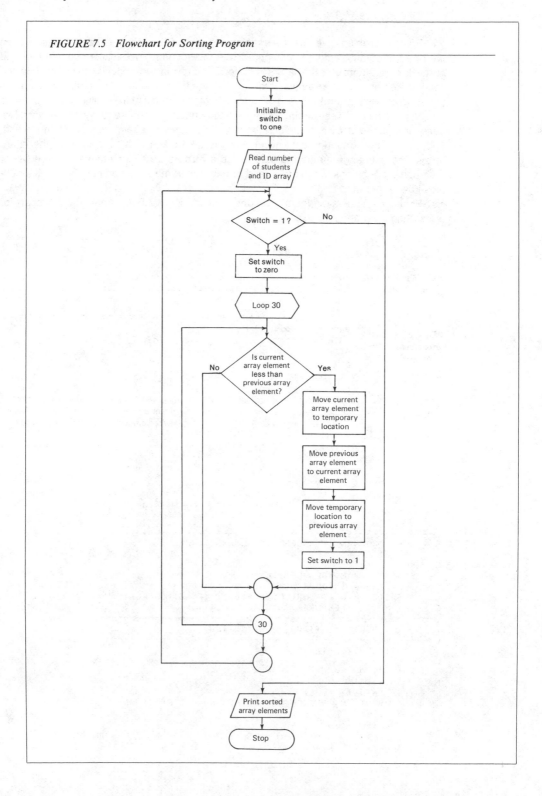

```
C--------------------------------------------------------
      WHILE (SWITCH .EQ. 1)
C
         SWITCH = 0
C
         DO 30 J=2,N
            IF (LIST(J) .LT. LIST(J-1)) THEN
               TEMP      = LIST(J)
               LIST(J)   = LIST(J-1)
               LIST(J-1) = TEMP
               SWITCH    = 1
            END IF
   30    CONTINUE
C
      END WHILE
C--------------------------------------------------------
      PRINT, 'SORT COMPLETED'
      PRINT, (LIST(J),J=1,N)
C--------------------------------------------------------
      STOP
      END
```

Input

```
4
8321,3076,2501,7771
```

Output

```
SORT COMPLETED
      2501           3076          7771          8321
```

The logic within loop 30 illustrates the bubble sort. The subscript expressions J and $J - 1$ are used to compare values stored in adjacent array elements. When an exchange takes place between two adjacent elements, a separate memory location (TEMP) serves as a temporary location to hold one of the values while the exchange takes place. To understand exactly what's happening, follow the diagram and steps below for the case $J = 2$ in loop 30.

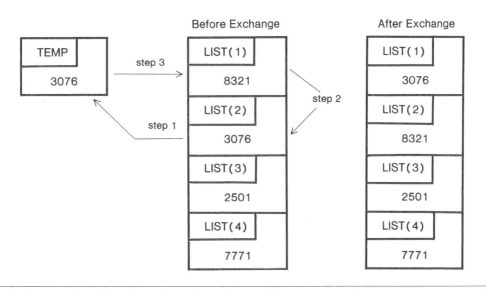

The variable SWITCH acts as a switch by storing either 0 or 1. If the value in SWITCH is 1 after a complete pass through the array LIST, then the sort is not complete and the entire array must be scanned again for the numbers out of sequence. If the value in SWITCH is 0 after a complete pass through the array LIST, then the sort is complete.

Follow-up Exercises

36. Fill in the following table based on the data in the example.

J	TEMP	LIST(1)	LIST(2)	LIST(3)	LIST(4)	SWITCH
			Contents When Control Is at 30 CONTINUE			
2	3076	3076	8321	2501	7771	1
3						
4						
2						
3						
4						
2						
3						
4						

How many passes through the entire array does it take to sort the array? How many passes does it take to terminate execution?

37. What would happen if we were to try a sort of 3000 items?

*38. Make appropriate changes in the program for a numeric sort in descending order. Test your program by tracing through the given data.

39. Is it possible to sort alphabetic data using the program in Example 7.13? Make necessary modifications to the program and run it on your system to sort the following data: SMITH,JONES,DAVIS,KELLY.

7.7
COMMON ERRORS

Arrays are great for giving a lot of practice in debugging. Often one "small" error will result in an "avalanche" of error messages. Pay attention to the following and you might avoid apoplexy.

1. **Declaration of array.**   Don't forget to declare your array by using a type or DIMEN-SION statement. If you forget to dimension an array, then you will get a *syntax* error message for *each* line containing an array element name. So, if you get an error message

such as "INVALID ELEMENT ..." or "ILLEGAL QUANTITY ..." for each line where the array element name appears, or "SUBPROGRAM ... MISSING" at the end of the listing, then check whether or not you dimensioned the array.

Also, don't forget to declare arrays before their use in the program. Place your DIMENSION or type statement before all other executable statements in the program.

Finally, you must use an integer constant to declare the size of your array. Don't try

```
REAL X(N)
```

if *N* is a variable name, unless you like to see syntax errors. A variable number of locations is not permitted, except for the material discussed in Chapter 9.

2. **Subscripts.** If you get an *execution* error message such as "SUBSCRIPT ... HAS THE VALUE 0," then a subscript value violates the bounds in your dimension declaration. Two kinds of mistakes are possible here: Either you reserved too few locations for your array or you made a logic error in assigning values to subscript expressions. In the latter case, you might want to diagnose the error by using a *trace* to print subscript expression values, as illustrated by the following program.

```
1              REAL X(5)
      C
2              DO 10 J = 1,5
3                 K = 5 - J
4                 PRINT, J,K
5                 X(K) = J**3          ←──────────  Execution error
6         10 CONTINUE                               when K = 0
      C
7              STOP
8              END
```

Output

```
1              4
2              3
3              2
4              1
5              0
```

```
***ERROR***  SUBSCRIPT NUMBER 1 OF X    HAS THE VALUE        0
PROGRAM WAS EXECUTING LINE 5 IN ROUTINE M/PROG WHEN TERMINATION OCCURRED
```

The error message is the result of a zero in the subscript K. If we wish K to take on the successive values 5, 4, 3, 2, 1, then the statement that defines K should read

```
K = 6 - J
```

Other common subscripting errors include using a real variable or constant for a subscript, and entirely forgetting the subscript for a variable that has been declared an array.

3. **Array names.** A common point of confusion among beginning programmers is exactly what represents the *array name*. For example, are B(J) and B(I) one and the same array? Yes. In this case, the array name is B, not B(J) or B(I). B(J) and B(I) are called *array element names,* which simply reference specific elements in array B.

A related problem is the following: Many students, thinking that the parentheses are part of the array name, believe it is all right also to use B as a *variable name* that is different from the array B. Not so. Once B is dimensioned, the variable B is treated as an array throughout the program, as the following illustrates.

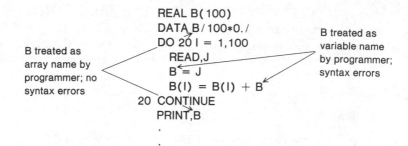

4. **Initialization.** If an array is to act as a summer or counter, then don't forget to initialize its contents to whatever values are required. (See Example 7.6.) Some compilers automatically initialize all storage locations to zero, but others don't. In WATFIV, you will get an execution error the first time your program attempts to use an uninitialized counter or summer. Sometimes during the same computer run you need to reinitialize your array. If so, don't use a DATA statement, as illustrated below for a 500-element array.

	Correct		Incorrect
	DO 20 J = 1,N		DO 20 J = 1,N
	DO 10 I = 1,500		DATA SUM/500*0.0/
	SUM(I) = 0.0		.
10	CONTINUE		.
	.		.
	.	20	CONTINUE
	.		
20	CONTINUE		

A DATA statement is nonexecutable, so it would not be possible to reinitialize an array by this method once the program begins executing.

5. **I/O.** Don't forget to coordinate the placement of data on the input record with the design of your input loop, as the following illustrates.

Input Record 1 2 3 4 5 6 7 8 9 . . .		Program Segment

10 2 5		1 FORMAT(3I2)
		  DO 10 I = 1,3
		    READ 1,LOAD(I)
		10 CONTINUE

An "end-of-file" execution error message would occur here, since loop 10 attempts to read three records. Don't forget that a new input record is processed each time a READ statement is executed. Also, the list in the foregoing READ statement contains only one array element, so the fact that 3I2 appears in the FORMAT statement is irrelevant according to the imbalance rules. For the given input record, we need to use an implied-DO list.

Finally, unless you use the short-list technique, don't forget to use a loop to output an array. We often see the following approach in an attempt to output the entire contents of an array:

```
PRINT 15,ARR(I)
```

This statement either prints one element (if an integer value within the bounds of the array is stored for I) or results in an execution error.

ADDITIONAL EXERCISES

40. Define or explain each of the following.

array	DIMENSION statement
array name	implied-DO list
array element	short-list technique
array element name	table look-up
subscript	sorting
subscript expression	exchange method
vector	bubble sort
one-dimensional array	

41. Property Tax Assessment Revisited. Solve Exercise 27 in Chapter 6 on page 223 as follows.

    a. Store the tax schedule, lot numbers, names, property values, and tax charges in one-dimensional arrays. Treat the number of rows in the rate schedule as an input variable. Nicely label your output. Following the output table print the sum of property values and the total tax charge. *Hint:* Let the numbers 10,000, 30,000, and 60,000 represent the "set of keys."

  **b. Following the output in part a, print a second table that shows tax charges (together with corresponding lot numbers, names, and property values) in descending order.

42. Crime Data Summary. The data below represent the number of arrests for felony crimes in a state over a three-year period.

	Arrest Data by Year		
	1	2	3
Homicide	1,000	1,000	1,000
Robbery	10,000	9,000	11,000
Burglary	27,000	24,000	28,000
Assault	13,000	15,000	16,000
Theft	19,000	20,000	23,000
Forgery	10,000	9,000	10,000

    a. Design an algorithm and write a program to read the data into several one-dimensional arrays. Print out the data in a table format that includes a new row for total arrests in each year and a new column for average arrests for each crime over the past three years. No need to label rows and columns here.

b. In the output of part a, label your columns 1, 2, 3, and AVERAGE. Label your rows according to the felony names in the above table; the last row being TOTALS. Preferably, the output of felony names should be handled through the use of arrays.

c. Print a second table that gives the percent of arrests for each crime to the total number of arrests in that year.

43. Support Facility for Oil-Drilling Platforms. Consider the coordinate system below, where the plotted points 1 through 5 represent the coordinate locations of offshore oil-drilling platforms and the plotted point labeled (x_0, y_0) is a possible

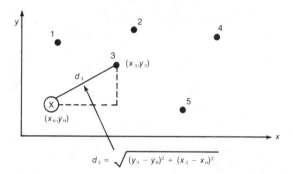

$$d_3 = \sqrt{(y_3 - y_0)^2 + (x_3 - x_0)^2}$$

location for a support facility. The figure also illustrates the distance d_3 between the support facility and platform 3. The formula for calculating d_3 is called the *Euclidian distance formula.* The coordinates in miles are given below.

Platform i	x_i	y_i
1	5	20
2	15	22
3	12	15
4	25	21
5	21	5

a. Design an algorithm and write a (preferably interactive) program that calculates and prints distance between each platform and the following proposed locations for the support facility.

x_0	y_0
4	6
20	14
20	18
23	20

Include the *total* distance $(d_1 + d_2 + \cdots + d_5)$ as part of your output.

b. Use your program (interactively) to determine the coordinate (to the nearest mile) for the support facility that minimizes total distance. In other words, by trial and error input a proposed location, and based on the output make a judgment regarding your next proposed coordinate. Repeat this procedure until you're satisfied you have converged on the coordinate that minimizes total distance.

c. Instead of the trial-and-error search in part b, design your program systematically to vary x_0 and y_0 between chosen ranges. Include x_0, y_0, and total distance in your output. Also, have the program print the coordinate, of the ones considered, that minimizes total distance.

44. **Revenue Sharing.** Consider the allocation program whereby the federal government apportions certain federal funds to the states on the basis of a ratio of each state's population to the total U.S. population. The table below provides population figures for all 50 states according to a recent census.

Population by State (in Thousands)

ME	1,059	NC	5,451
NH	808	SC	2,818
VT	468	GA	4,926
MA	5,199	FL	8,327
RI	938	KY	3,396
CT	3,080	TN	4,188
NY	18,101	AL	3,614
NJ	7,322	MS	2,364
PA	11,841	AR	2,068
OH	10,745	LA	3,762
IN	5,313	OK	2,681
IL	11,160	TX	12,017
MI	9,117	MT	748
WI	4,566	ID	820
MN	3,905	WY	374
IA	2,857	CO	2,534
MO	4,772	NM	1,147
ND	636	AZ	2,224
SD	681	UT	1,206
NB	1,541	NV	592
KS	2,266	WA	3,544
DE	577	OR	2,288
MD	4,089	CA	20,876
VA	4,967	AK	341
WV	1,803	HI	854

a. Write a program that uses one array for the names of the states and another array for the population figures. Read these arrays, calculate how much revenue should go to each state if $380 million is available for allocation, and output a table with appropriate labels that lists each state and its allocated amount. Include a flowchart or pseudocode.

b. Modify the preceding program to include a loop that processes more than one allocation. For example, if three allocation programs are to be run, then the output should appear as follows:

DOLLAR AMOUNTS ALLOCATED UNDER
EACH PROGRAM

STATE	1	2	3	TOTALS
ME	XXXXXXX	XXXXXXX	XXXXXXX	XXXXXXX
NH	XXXXXXX	XXXXXXX	XXXXXXX	XXXXXXX

The number of allocations to be made (three in the above example) should be a variable. Note that the total amount that is to be allocated to each state is given by row sums and output under the column labeled "TOTALS." Test your program by processing the following funds available for allocation under three programs: $380 million, $800 million, $500 million.

**c. Modify your output in either part a or part b such that the states are listed in alphabetical order. *Hint:* The bubble sort can be used for character data.

45. Sales Forecasts. Design and write a program that calculates and prints sales forecasts by quarters for future years based on current sales and projected annual growth rate. For example, if currently we are at the end of the second quarter in the year 1981 and sales this quarter were $1.2 million with a projected growth rate of 2 percent per quarter, then forecasts through 1983 should appear as follows:

· · SALES FORECAST FOR OUIJA BOARD · ·

CURRENT	YEAR	QUARTER	SALES
	1981	2	$ 1.2 M

YEAR	QUARTER	SALES
1981	3	1.224
1981	4	1.248
1982	1	1.273
1982	2	1.299
1982	3	1.325
1982	4	1.351
1983	1	1.378
1983	2	1.406
1983	3	1.434
1983	4	1.463

Note that the next forecast is always the last forecast increased by the growth rate.

a. Run your program for the following data.

Product Name	Current Sales	Growth Rate	Years Into Future
OUIJA BOARD	1.20	0.02	2
STAR TREK CHARM	0.85	0.05	4

Note that the sample output is based on the first set of data. Your program should allow input for a variable number of products.

b. *Graphical Output.* To the right of each sales forecast, print the asterisk character in a graph format. Do this as follows: Reserve columns 30 through 70 for graphical output. In this case, column 30 really represents 0 on a graph and column 70 represents 40 (that is, there are 40 print columns between 30 and 70). This means that all sales forecasts must be scaled to a range between 0 and 40; that is,

$$\text{Scaled forecast} = \left(\frac{\text{forecast}}{\text{maximum forecast}}\right) \cdot 40$$

For example, the scaled forecast for the fourth quarter in 1982 is (1.351/1.463) · 40, or 36.9. This means that we wish an asterisk printed in column 66 (or 30 + 36) of the print line where 1.351 is printed for sales.

c. Print a table that summarizes total sales over the next four quarters by product. Entries in this table should be arranged in descending order of total sales.

d. Same as part c, except that the table should list the results in alphabetical order by product name.

46. Exam Grading. Consider an *N*-question multiple choice exam, where only one answer is correct for each question.

a. Design an algorithm and write a program to grade the exam and print the student's name, the number right, the number wrong, and the final grade. The final grade is the percent number right. The data consist of

1. One line for *N*.
2. One line containing *N* integers representing the *N* correct answers (answer key).
3. One line indicating the number of students in the class who took the exam (*M*).
4. *M* lines, one for each student, containing the student's name and *N* answers.

Use two one-dimensional numeric arrays to store the answer key and a student's answers. Test your program with the following test data.

```
20
1,3,5,4,4,1,1,2,3,5,5,1,2,3,4,4,5,3,2,1
5
'PETROCELLI',1,3,4,4,4,1,1,2,3,3,5,1,2,3,4,4,5,1,1,1
'BAKER',1,3,5,4,3,2,1,2,3,4,3,2,2,3,3,3,5,1,2,1
'VALENTINO',1,3,5,4,4,1,1,2,3,5,5,1,2,3,4,4,4,3,2,1
'SIMPSON',1,2,5,4,4,2,2,3,3,1,2,1,3,3,3,5,5,3,1,1
'CARTER',2,3,5,4,4,1,1,3,3,5,4,1,5,4,4,4,5,2,1,3
```

b. Print the name and grade of the student with the highest grade.

c. Modify your output in part a such that the required output is in alphabetical order according to last name. *Hint:* The bubble sort can be used for character data.

**d. Print a frequency distribution of final grades for the exam, as follows.

90 or ABOVE	XX
80 BUT UNDER 90	XX
70 BUT UNDER 80	XX
60 BUT UNDER 70	XX
50 BUT UNDER 60	XX
BELOW 50	XX
	XX

AVERAGE GRADE FOR EXAM = XX.X

47. **Stock-Portfolio Valuation.**   Companies, universities, banks, pension funds, and other organizations routinely invest funds in the stock market. The set of stocks in which the organization invests its funds is called a *stock portfolio*. The table below illustrates a sample stock portfolio, including the number of shares owned of each stock, the purchase price per share, and the latest price per share quoted by the stock exchange.

Stock Portfolio

Stock	Number of Shares	Purchase Price ($/share)	Current Price ($/share)
Allegh Airls	40,000	$5\frac{7}{8}$	$7\frac{1}{4}$
Boeing	5,000	$61\frac{1}{2}$	56
EastmKo	10,000	60	$64\frac{1}{2}$
Hewlett P	15,000	80	$100\frac{1}{8}$
IBM	2,500	$77\frac{1}{8}$	$80\frac{3}{4}$
Texaco	8,000	$23\frac{1}{2}$	19
Tex Inst	12,000	80	$85\frac{7}{8}$

a. Design and run a program to calculate the initial (purchase) value of the portfolio, the current value of the portfolio, and the net change in the value. Store number of shares, purchase prices, and current prices in separate vectors. *Hint:* The value of the portfolio is found by multiplying shares by corresponding prices and summing, which is equivalent to multiplication of two vectors.

b. Include a loop in the program for processing more than one portfolio. Find two copies of a newspaper, where one copy is at least two weeks apart from the other. Select a portfolio, make up shares owned, and use the two sets of prices for purchase and current prices. Process the given portfolio and the new portfolio in one run, and include the output of combined value of all portfolios.

Multidimensional Arrays

In many situations it's convenient to store data in arrays with more than one dimension. FORTRAN allows up to seven dimensions, but here we focus on the more common two-dimensional arrays.

8.1 MOTIVATION

Generally, it's desirable to use two-dimensional arrays whenever we wish to store and manipulate data that are characterized by two attributes, as the following examples illustrate.

Occupied beds in a hospital are tabulated by *day* of the week and by *ward*.
Deposits for a major bank are recorded for all *branch banks* on a *monthly* basis.

Enrollments at a college are tabulated by *major* and *class standing*.

Five *exam scores* for a course are recorded for all *students*.

Ten *financial ratios* from the Fortune 500 list of major U.S. corporations are recorded for all 500 *corporations*.

8.2
SUBSCRIPTS

You will more easily understand a **matrix** or **two-dimensional array** (an array with two subscript expressions) if you visualize a group of memory locations as a grid of boxes (table) arranged in rows and columns.

3 × 5 Array

Column
	1	2	3	4	5
1					
Row 2					
3					

An array element within a two-dimensional array is referenced by specifying two subscript expressions: one for row number and one for column number. For example, in the three-row by four-column array below, the memory location that is marked with an X is found by looking at row 2, column 3; the memory location marked with XX is found in row 3, column 2.

3 × 4 Array DEPOS

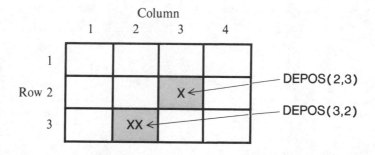

As you can see, two subscript expressions are needed when we use two-dimensional arrays. In FORTRAN, the *subscript* for a two-dimensional array has two *subscript expressions* separated by a comma within the parentheses following the array name. For example, if the above array is named DEPOS, then the location where the X is found is referenced as DEPOS(2,3) and the location where the XX is found is referenced as DEPOS(3,2). Notice that, in accordance with mathematical convention, the subscript expressions of the array element name are always given in the following order.

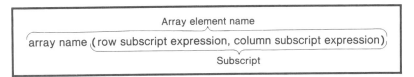

Except for the use of two-subscript expressions, according to the above convention, *subscripts for two-dimensional arrays are treated in the same manner as for one-dimensional arrays*. For example, subscript expressions must be integer arithmetic expressions.

Alternatively, the preceding table can be depicted by using *array element names* as follows:

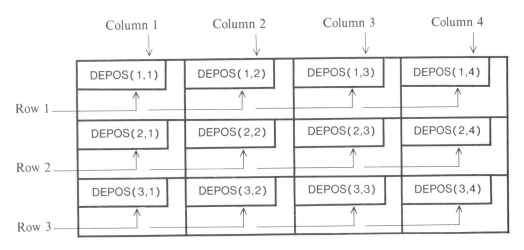

In actual practice, storage locations for two-dimensional arrays don't physically resemble a table in memory, but that need not concern us since the FORTRAN convention treats them like a table.

8.3
ARRAY DECLARATION

Just as with one-dimensional arrays, two-dimensional arrays must be declared in order to reserve memory locations that correspond to array elements. The same statements that declare one-dimensional arrays are used to declare multidimensional arrays, as follows:

$$
\begin{array}{llll}
\textit{type} & \textit{array} & \left(\begin{array}{c}\textit{dimension}\\ \textit{declarators}\end{array}\right) & \textit{array}\quad\left(\begin{array}{c}\textit{dimension}\\ \textit{declarators}\end{array}\right)\ \ldots\\
\textit{keyword} & \textit{name} & & \textit{, name}
\end{array}
$$

where *type keyword* is usually CHARACTER, INTEGER, REAL, or DOUBLE PRECISION. *Dimension declarators* in the list are separated by commas. The number of dimension declarators corresponds to the number of dimensions in the array: one dimension declarator for a one-dimensional array, two dimension declarators for a two-dimensional array, and so on.[1]

For example, we might store the number of deposits for three branch banks in each of four quarters in a three-row by four-column (3 $\times$ 4) two-dimensional integer array named DEPOS, where each row stores the quarterly data for one branch. The INTEGER statement would be specified as

    INTEGER DEPOS(3,4)

If we wanted DEPOS to store branch deposits for each month of the year, then we could set up an array with 3 rows and 12 columns. In this case, the INTEGER statement would be given by

    INTEGER DEPOS(3,12)

In the first case DEPOS has 12 elements in memory, whereas in the second case, 36 locations are reserved in memory.

Both one- and two-dimensional arrays can be dimensioned in a single type statement by using commas to separate each array specification. For example,

    REAL   LOAD(5,10),EXP(10,8),TOT(5)

This results in the reservation of 50 locations for the two-dimensional real array LOAD, 80 locations for the two-dimensional real array EXP, and 5 locations for the one-dimensional real array TOT.

As with one-dimensional arrays, dimension declarators must be integer constants, the value of a subscript expression must not fall outside the dimension bounds, and the declaration of character arrays usually requires a length declarator (see pages 241–244).

8.4
INPUT/OUTPUT

The same three methods for I/O that we illustrated for one-dimensional arrays can be used for two-dimensional arrays. For the examples that follow, we illustrate I/O for the two-dimensional integer array DEPOS, which is to store the following data on the number of deposits by branch and by quarter.

	Quarter			
Branch	1	2	3	4
1	1000	800	500	1200
2	500	2000	2000	500
3	1500	300	700	1500

[1] The DIMENSION statement introduced in Chapter 7 is also used to declare arrays; however, we don't recommend its use over type statements since type is not explicitly specified.

Using DO Statements

I/O of two-dimensional arrays with DO statements requires the use of two DO-loops, one "nested" within the other, as illustrated in the next example.

EXAMPLE 8.1   Unformatted I/O with Nested DO-Loops

Consider the following program segment for reading DEPOS:

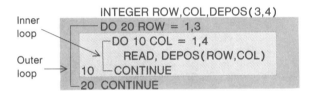

The flowchart in Figure 8.1 should help you visualize how the nesting of DO-loops works. The key concept that you need to understand here is the exact manner in which the subscript expressions change values. Carefully look at the program and the flow-chart to confirm that the subscript expressions of DEPOS change values as follows:

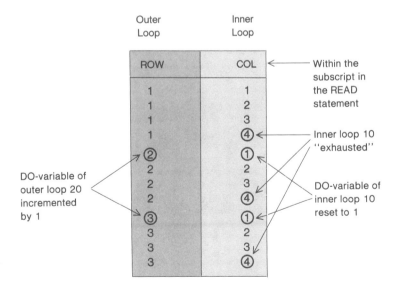

Suppose we have placed our data on input records as follows:

FIGURE 8.1   Nested DO-Loops for Input

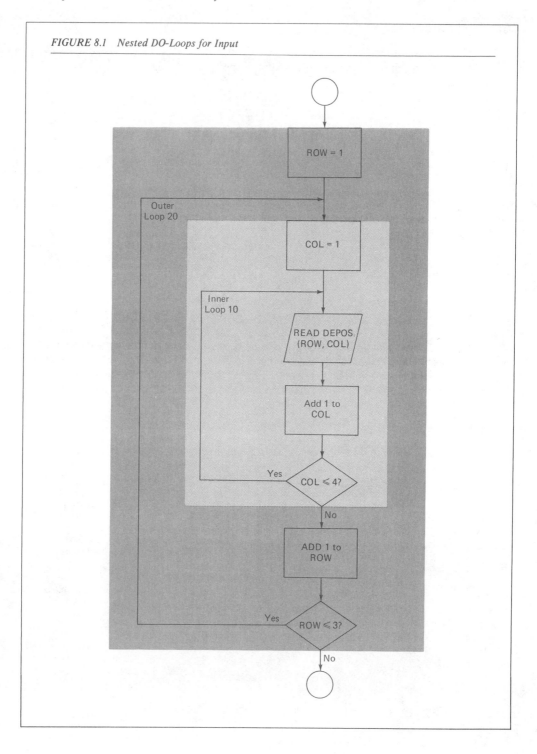

Data Input

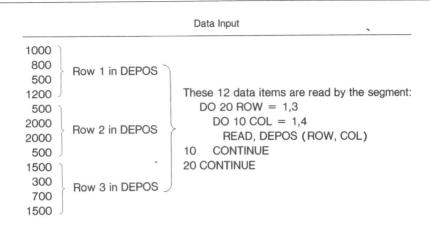

1000 ⎫
800 ⎬ Row 1 in DEPOS
500
1200 ⎭
500 ⎫
2000 ⎬ Row 2 in DEPOS
2000
500 ⎭
1500 ⎫
300 ⎬ Row 3 in DEPOS
700
1500 ⎭

These 12 data items are read by the segment:
```
      DO 20 ROW = 1,3
         DO 10 COL = 1,4
            READ, DEPOS (ROW, COL)
10    CONTINUE
20 CONTINUE
```

The first time through the loops, ROW = 1 and COL = 1, so the first data item is read into DEPOS(1,1).

After execution of READ, DEPOS(1,1)

DEPOS(1,1)	DEPOS(1,2)	DEPOS(1,3)	DEPOS(1,4)
1000			
DEPOS(2,1)	DEPOS(2,2)	DEPOS(2,3)	DEPOS(2,4)
DEPOS(3,1)	DEPOS(3,2)	DEPOS(3,3)	DEPOS(3,4)

The second time through the inner loop, ROW = 1 and COL = 2, so the second item is read into DEPOS(1,2).

After execution of READ, DEPOS(1,2)

DEPOS(1,1)	DEPOS(1,2)	DEPOS(1,3)	DEPOS(1,4)
1000	800		
DEPOS(2,1)	DEPOS(2,2)	DEPOS(2,3)	DEPOS(2,4)
DEPOS(3,1)	DEPOS(3,2)	DEPOS(3,3)	DEPOS(3,4)

The third time through the inner loop, ROW = 1 and COL = 3, so the third item is read into DEPOS(1,3).

After execution of READ, DEPOS(1,3)

DEPOS(1,1)	DEPOS(1,2)	DEPOS(1,3)	DEPOS(1,4)
1000	800	500	
DEPOS(2,1)	DEPOS(2,2)	DEPOS(2,3)	DEPOS(2,4)
DEPOS(3,1)	DEPOS(3,2)	DEPOS(3,3)	DEPOS(3,4)

The fourth time through the inner loop, ROW = 1 and COL = 4, so the fourth item is read into DEPOS(1,4).

After execution of READ, DEPOS(1,4)

DEPOS(1,1)	DEPOS(1,2)	DEPOS(1,3)	DEPOS(1,4)
1000	800	500	1200
DEPOS(2,1)	DEPOS(2,2)	DEPOS(2,3)	DEPOS(2,4)
DEPOS(3,1)	DEPOS(3,2)	DEPOS(3,3)	DEPOS(3,4)

At this point COL gets incremented to 5 and the inner loop tests false (see Figure 8.1). Then, ROW is incremented to 2 and again COL varies from 1 to 4 within the subscript. This results in the following sequence.

READ Operations for Second Row

ROW	COL	
2	1	READ, DEPOS(2,1)
2	2	READ, DEPOS(2,2)
2	3	READ, DEPOS(2,3)
2	4	READ, DEPOS(2,4)

Now the array appears as follows in memory.

After completion of inner DO-loop with ROW = 2 ⌐

DEPOS(1,1)	DEPOS(1,2)	DEPOS(1,3)	DEPOS(1,4)
1000	800	500	1200
DEPOS(2,1)	DEPOS(2,2)	DEPOS(2,3)	DEPOS(2,4)
500	2000	2000	500
DEPOS(3,1)	DEPOS(3,2)	DEPOS(3,3)	DEPOS(3,4)

Finally, ROW is set equal to 3 and COL varies from 1 to 4. This results in the sequence:

READ Operations for Third Row

ROW	COL	
3	1	READ, DEPOS(3,1)
3	2	READ, DEPOS(3,2)
3	3	READ, DEPOS(3,3)
3	4	READ, DEPOS(3,4)

At this point, read-in of the array is complete, yielding the following configuration in memory.

After completion of inner DO-loop with Row = 3 ⌐

DEPOS(1,1)	DEPOS(1,2)	DEPOS(1,3)	DEPOS(1,4)
1000	800	500	1200
DEPOS(2,1)	DEPOS(2,2)	DEPOS(2,3)	DEPOS(2,4)
500	2000	2000	500
DEPOS(3,1)	DEPOS(3,2)	DEPOS(3,3)	DEPOS(3,4)
1500	300	700	1500

Note that the READ statement is executed exactly 12 times. *Since there is only one item in the list of the READ statement, this means that 12 input records are required, each with a single value.*

We might note that typically I is used in place of ROW as the subscript expression for rows, and J is used instead of COL, as these are consistent with mathematical convention.

Finally, we cannot overemphasize the need for you to concentrate on the manner in which the subscript expressions change values. Again, *the inner loop must be exhausted (the DO-variable must exceed its terminal value) for each iteration of the outer loop. Once the inner loop is exhausted, then the DO-variable of the outer loop is incremented and the DO-variable of the inner loop is reset to its initial value.*

Follow-up Exercises

1. Write a program segment that utilizes nested DO-loops to output the contents of DEPOS. Indicate how the printout would appear.
2. Suppose the following program segment were executed using the same input records as the example.

```
        DO 20 J = 1,4
          DO 10 I = 1,3
            READ,DEPOS(I,J)
    10    CONTINUE
    20  CONTINUE
```

How would DEPOS appear in memory? Does the array in memory get filled in row by row or column by column? How should we place data on the input records so as to store the proper values in DEPOS using this program segment?

Using Nested Implied-DO Lists

Implied-DO lists are used with two-dimensional arrays for more flexible control of I/O than is possible with the nesting of DO-loops. A common form of the implied-DO list with two-dimensional arrays is given by

Nested Implied-DO Lists for Two-Dimensional Arrays

$$\left(\left(\begin{array}{l}\text{array} \\ \text{name}\end{array}\left(\begin{array}{cc}\text{row} & \text{column} \\ \text{subscript} & \text{subscript} \\ \text{expression,} & \text{expression}\end{array}\right), \begin{array}{l}\text{inner} \\ \text{DO-variable}\end{array} = \begin{array}{ccc}\text{initial} & \text{terminal} & \text{incrementation} \\ \text{expression,} & \text{expression,} & \text{expression}\end{array}\right),$$

$$\begin{array}{l}\text{outer} \\ \text{DO-variable}\end{array} = \begin{array}{ccc}\text{initial} & \text{terminal} & \text{incrementation} \\ \text{expression,} & \text{expression,} & \text{expression}\end{array}\right)$$

In this case one implied-DO list is an item in the *dlist*[2] of another implied-DO list; that is, one implied-DO list is nested within another implied-DO list—hence the term **nested implied-DO lists.**

Within the inner parentheses is the array name, followed by the two subscript expressions enclosed within parentheses, followed by a comma, followed by the DO portion of the inner implied-DO list, followed by a right parenthesis (which terminates the inner implied-DO list), followed by a comma, and finally followed by the DO portion of the outer implied-DO list and the closing parenthesis. As in the one-dimensional array case, the DO-variables also serve as subscript expressions.

EXAMPLE 8.2   Unformatted I/O with Nested Implied-DO Lists

To illustrate nested implied-DO lists, consider the following statement:

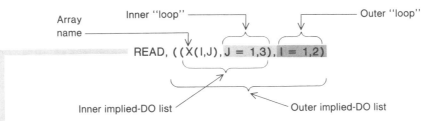

As you can see, the implied-DO lists are nested, and function in a way similar to the nesting of DO-loops. The inner loop (with the DO-variable closest to the array) is enclosed within the outer loop. As before, *the inner loop must be satisfied for each iteration of the outer loop.* In the above example, this is equivalent to the following statement.

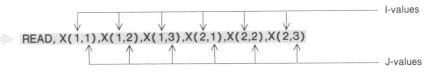

In effect, *the READ statement contains a list of six items, which allows us to input all six values for X on one input record.*

Did you pay attention to the manner in which subscript expression values (I and J) varied? The DO-variable of the inner loop (J subscript expression) varies from 1 to 3 while the DO-variable of the outer loop (I subscript) is held constant at 1. Then, expression I is incremented to 2 and the inner loop varies from 1 to 3 once more.

---

[2] You might want to review the terminology in Section 7.4, page 249.

If we wish to store the following in real array X,

X(1,1)	X(1,2)	X(1,3)
10.1	8.2	6.3
X(2,1)	X(2,2)	X(2,3)
4.4	2.5	0.6

then the following input record can be used with the above READ statement.

10.1, 8.2, 6.3, 4.4, 2.5, 0.6   ← Input data for two nested implied-DO lists

However, suppose we wish to prepare row-by-row input records. In other words, the input records are to be set up in a manner that is conceptually compatible with the table nature of a two-dimensional array, as follows:

10.1, 8.2, 6.3
4.4, 2.5, 0.6   ← Input data for implied-DO list nested within DO-loop

Then, the following *combination of the DO-loop and the implied-DO list* can be used to store these values into a two-dimensional array.

Inner loop

Outer loop
```
      DO 10 I = 1,2
         READ, (X(I,J),J = 1,3)
   10 CONTINUE
```

In this case, the *implied-DO list is the inner loop and the DO/CONTINUE statements define the outer loop.* You should carefully note that the READ statement is executed twice, once for each value of I (two input records are provided). Also, note that the list of the READ statement contains three items (which is why we have three values for each line of input). This is equivalent to the following statements.

```
READ, X(1,1),X(1,2),X(1,3)
READ, X(2,1),X(2,2),X(2,3)
```

Similarly, the statement

```
PRINT, ((X(I,J),J = 1,3),I = 1,2)
```

outputs all six values in X on one print line

10.1   8.2   6.3   4.4   2.5   0.6

whereas the statements

```
      DO 20 I = 1,2
         PRINT,(X(I,J),J = 1,3)
   20 CONTINUE
```

print X in a row-by-row manner:

10.1 8.2 6.3
 4.4 2.5 0.6

This latter approach is more desirable since it's consistent with the two-dimensional conceptualization of X.

Follow-up Exercises

3. Modify the PRINT statement in the last example such that rows in X are numbered

   1   10.1 8.2 6.3
   2   4.4 2.5 0.6

   Can you figure out how to number the columns as well?
4. Write the appropriate statement(s) such that DEPOS of Example 8.1 is printed out without FORMATs as follows:
   a. The entire array is printed on one line.
   b. The first row of the array appears on one line, the second row on the next line, and so on.
   c. The first column of the array appears on one line, the second column on the next line, and so on.

EXAMPLE 8.3   Formatted I/O with Nested Implied-DO Lists

Getting back to the banking problem in Example 8.1, suppose that the data are recorded on three input records as follows:

```
1 2 3 4 5 6 7 8 9 10 11 12 13 14 15 16 17 18 19 20 21 22 23 24 25
─────────────────────────────────────────────────────────────────
      1000      80 0      5 0 0      1 2 0 0
       500     200 0     2 0 0 0        5 0 0
      1500      30 0      7 0 0      1 5 0 0
```

Then the execution of

```
      READ 1,(DEPOS(I,J), J = 1,4),I = 1,3)
    1 FORMAT(4I6)
```

results in the following storage for DEPOS.

DEPOS(1,1)	DEPOS(1,2)	DEPOS(1,3)	DEPOS(1,4)
1000	800	500	1200
DEPOS(2,1)	DEPOS(2,2)	DEPOS(2,3)	DEPOS(2,4)
500	2000	2000	500
DEPOS(3,1)	DEPOS(3,2)	DEPOS(3,3)	DEPOS(3,4)
1500	300	700	1500

Carefully note that there is *imbalance* between the number of items (12) in the list of the READ statement and the number of edit descriptors (4) in the FORMAT statement. Thus, according to the procedure outlined in Module D on page 492, *the computer resets to the beginning of this format specification (and reads a new input record) after reading in each group of four values.* Do you realize why we selected a repeat specification of 4 in the FORMAT statement? Because we wish to input four values per line, which is consistent with the number of values found in each row of this table.

This array can be printed in table form using

```
    PRINT 9, ((DEPOS(I,J), J = 1,4),I = 1,3)
9 FORMAT ('0', 4I6)
```

which gives the following output.

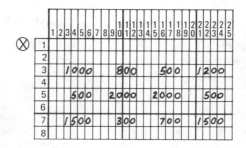

If we were to change the FORMAT statement to

```
9 FORMAT( 1X,I6)
```

the following would be printed.

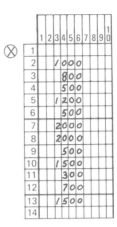

Finally, if the FORMAT statement is given by

9 FORMAT(1X,12I6)

then we have

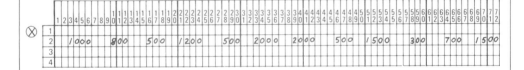

Follow-up Exercises

5. Specify the exact appearance of input records if DEPOS is read in using the nested implied-DO lists in the example and
   a. 1 FORMAT(I6)
   b. 1 FORMAT(16I5)
6. Consider the statements

   ```
   1 FORMAT(13I6)
     DO 30 I = 1,3
       READ 1, (DEPOS(I,J),J = 1,4)
   30 CONTINUE
   ```

   Would these statements properly process the input records in Example 8.3? What is the advantage of this combined DO-loop/implied-DO list approach to the nested implied-DO lists used in Example 8.3?
7. Write the appropriate READ and FORMAT statements if the data for DEPOS are recorded as follows:

```
1 2 3 4 5 6 7 8 9 10 11 12 13 14 15 16
```

```
1000    500    1 5 0 0
 800   2000    3 0 0
 500   2000    7 0 0
1200    500    1 5 0 0
```

Note that input records contain column entries rather than row entries in this case; however, we still wish to store the data as in Example 8.3.

8. Specify the exact appearance of output records for the program segment

```
      DO 70 I = 1,3
         PRINT 2, (DEPOS(I,J), J = 1,4)
   70 CONTINUE
```

using each of the following FORMAT statements.

a. 2 FORMAT(1X,I6)
b. 2 FORMAT(1X,4I6)
c. 2 FORMAT(1X,12I6)
d. 2 FORMAT('0', 'BANK DEPOSITS' / / '0', 4I6)
*e. What must you do to the statement in part d such that the label BANK DEPOSITS is printed once rather than three times?

9. Specify the exact appearance of output records for the following.

```
      DATA M,N/3,4/
```

```
   2 FORMAT( '1','BANK DEPOSITS' / '0',7X,16I7)
   4 FORMAT( 1X,'BANK',I3,16I7)
```

```
      PRINT 2,(J,J = 1,N)
```

```
      DO 30 I = 1,M
         PRINT 4, I,(DEPOS(I,J),J = 1,N)
   30 CONTINUE
```

What is the advantage of this combined DO-loop / implied-DO list approach to the nested implied-DO lists used in Example 8.3?

*10. Consider the following memory.

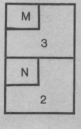

M		LOT(1,1)	LOT(1,2)		LOT(1,20)
3		10	50	. . .	
N		LOT(2,1)	LOT(2,2)		LOT(2,20)
2		4	320	. . .	
		LOT(3,1)	LOT(3,2)		LOT(3,20)
		15	8	. . .	

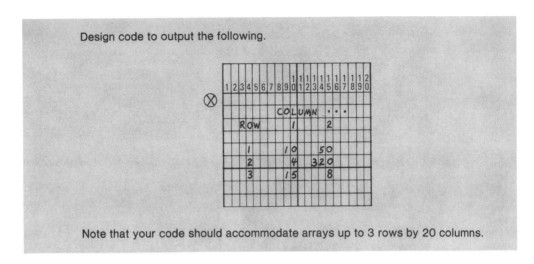

Design code to output the following.

Note that your code should accommodate arrays up to 3 rows by 20 columns.

Using the Short-List Technique

The short-list technique can be used with two-dimensional arrays to input or output entire arrays. In other words, the array name without subscripts can appear in a READ or WRITE statement.

```
INTEGER   DEPOS(3,4)
READ, DEPOS
```

The number of elements read in is equal to the number of rows times the number of columns that have been specified in the dimension declarators. In this case, there are 12 items (3 × 4 array elements) in the list of the READ statement.

One word of caution: *this technique requires that the data be arranged by column.* In other words, the above READ statement is equivalent to the following:

```
READ,   DEPOS(1,1),DEPOS(2,1),DEPOS(3,1),DEPOS(1,2),DEPOS(2,2),
        DEPOS(3,2),...., DEPOS(2,4),DEPOS(3,4)
```

The data would appear as follows on the input record.

```
1000,500,1500,800,2000,300,500,2000,700,1200,500,1500   ← Column-wise input
```

Also, the short-list technique can be applied only if the entire array, as specified by the dimension declarators, is to be read or written. If only part of the array is to be used, then you must use DO-loops or implied-DO lists.

Follow-up Exercises

11. Specify the appearance of input records for each of the following.

    INTEGER DEPOS(3,4)
    READ 1,DEPOS
    a. 1 FORMAT(I5)
    b. 1 FORMAT(12I5)
    c. 1 FORMAT(3I5)

12. Are the following PRINT statements equivalent?

    REAL Y(5,8)
    PRINT,Y
    PRINT,((Y(I,J),J = 1,8),I = 1,5)

13. Suppose we wish the following memory for arrays A and B.

    A

	1	2	3
1	5	10	15
2	35	45	55

    B

	1	2	3
1	75	76	77
2	78	79	80

    Specify input code if the data are to be input as follows.
    a. 5,10,15,75,76,77
       35,45,55,78,79,80
    b. 5,10,15,35,45,55
       75,76,77,78,79,80
    c. 5,35,10,45,15,55,75,78,76,79,77,80

14. Consider the real matrix X as stored in Example 8.2. Print X according to the following output layouts.

*15. Given memory as on page 288, print the values stored in DEPOS so the output appears as follows:

```
                    DEPOSITS AT BANK
                         1          2          3
QUARTER 1             1000        500       1500
QUARTER 2              800       2000        300
QUARTER 3              500       2000        700
QUARTER 4             1200        500       1500
```

8.5
MANIPULATING ARRAYS

Processing data stored in two-dimensional arrays normally involves nesting of DO-loops. The next example illustrates some common manipulations of two-dimensional arrays.

EXAMPLE 8.4   Row and Column Totals

One of the more common processing tasks is finding totals of each row or column in an array. The row or column totals can be stored either in one-dimensional arrays or in an extra row or column of the two-dimensional array. For example, to find the annual bank deposits in each branch for the data given on page 288, we need to sum the entries in each row. The following program segment would determine row sums.

```
      DO 30 I = 1,3
        SUM(I) = 0
        DO 25 J = 1,4
          SUM(I) = SUM(I) + DEPOS(I,J)
25      CONTINUE
30 CONTINUE
```

When I = 1, SUM(1) is initialized to zero; the inner loop 25 sums the values in the first row given by DEPOS(1,1), DEPOS(1,2), DEPOS(1,3), and DEPOS(1,4), and stores this sum in the first element of the array SUM.

SUM(1)	DEPOS(1,1)	DEPOS(1,2)	DEPOS(1,3)	DEPOS(1,4)
3500	1000	800	500	1200
SUM(2)	DEPOS(2,1)	DEPOS(2,2)	DEPOS(2,3)	DEPOS(2,4)
	500	2000	2000	500
SUM(3)	DEPOS(3,1)	DEPOS(3,2)	DEPOS(3,3)	DEPOS(3,4)
	1500	300	700	1500

After the DO-variable in the outer loop is incremented (I = 2), SUM(2) is initialized to zero, and the values in row 2 are accumulated and stored in the second element of array SUM.

SUM(1)	DEPOS(1,1)	DEPOS(1,2)	DEPOS(1,3)	DEPOS(1,4)
3500	1000	800	500	1200
SUM(2)	DEPOS(2,1)	DEPOS(2,2)	DEPOS(2,3)	DEPOS(2,4)
5000	500	2000	2000	500
SUM(3)	DEPOS(3,1)	DEPOS(3,2)	DEPOS(3,3)	DEPOS(3,4)
	1500	300	700	1500

Finally the outer loop iterates for the last time (I = 3) and the values of the third row are added to the third element in the array SUM.

SUM(1)	DEPOS(1,1)	DEPOS(1,2)	DEPOS(1,3)	DEPOS(1,4)
3500	1000	800	500	1200
SUM(2)	DEPOS(2,1)	DEPOS(2,2)	DEPOS(2,3)	DEPOS(2,4)
5000	500	2000	2000	500
SUM(3)	DEPOS(3,1)	DEPOS(3,2)	DEPOS(3,3)	DEPOS(3,4)
4000	1500	300	700	1500

Follow-up Exercises

16. Write a program segment that accumulates the bank's total deposits for each quarter. Store these totals in a one-dimensional array called TOT.

*17. Assume that DEPOS has been dimensioned to four rows and five columns. Instead of using SUM as in the example and TOT as in the preceding exercise, use the fourth row of DEPOS to store column totals and the fifth column to store row totals. Write program segments that accomplish this. Don't forget to initialize your summers to zero.

18. Write a program segment that calculates the percentage of each quarter's deposit to the annual number of deposits for each branch. Store these percentages in the two-dimensional array PER. After processing, PER should have the stored values shown. Can you fill in the third row? Note that, except for possible rounding error, rows of PER sum to 100.

PER(1,1)	PER(1,2)	PER(1,3)	PER(1,4)
28.57143	22.85714	14.28571	34.28571
PER(2,1)	PER(2,2)	PER(2,3)	PER(2,4)
10.00000	40.00000	40.00000	10.00000
PER(3,1)	PER(3,2)	PER(3,3)	PER(3,4)

19. Suppose an array has been dimensioned as follows:

    REAL WEIGHT(100,50)

    Write a program segment that initializes each element in WEIGHT to 100 using

    a. Two nested DO-loops.
    b. A DATA statement.
    Under what circumstances should you not use the approach in part b?

20. Write a program segment to initialize every element in the (5 × 6) real array D to the value 100.

21. Write a program segment that initializes the (4 × 4) integer array X in the following manner.

```
1  0  0  0
0  1  0  0
0  0  1  0
0  0  0  1
```

*22. Suppose a 10 × 20 real array X already exists in memory. Write code to
    a. Interchange the values of corresponding array elements in column 3 and column 1.
    b. Print out the smallest value in X and its location (row and column).

*23. Given a 5 × 5 integer array A, write code to
    a. Print the lower triangle and main diagonal as shown below.

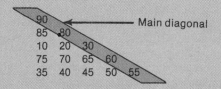

    b. Fill in the upper triangle symmetrically; that is, assuming only the lower triangle and main diagonal have been input as above, fill in the upper triangle to give the following symmetric matrix.

A

	1	2	3	4	5
1	90	85	10	75	35
2	85	80	20	70	40
3	10	20	30	65	45
4	75	70	65	60	50
5	35	40	45	50	55

**24. Vector Representation of a Matrix. A *symmetric matrix* is one whereby the triangle of elements above the main diagonal has values identical to the triangle of elements below the main diagonal (see the preceding exercise). Many applications, particularly in statistics, deal with very large symmetric matrices (which by definition have the same number of rows as columns). Often it's desirable to save storage by working with the lower triangle (including the main diagonal) and ignoring the upper triangle, since only one triangle is needed to represent all of the information. This is accomplished by using a vector (one-dimensional array) in place of the N $\times$ N matrix (two-dimensional array), with the following correspondences among subscript expression values.

Subscript Expression Values in 2-D Array (Main Diagonal and Lower Triangle)		Corresponding Subscript Expression Values in 1-D Array
I	J	K
1	1	1
2	1	2
2	2	3
3	1	4
3	2	5
3	3	6
.	.	.
.	.	.
.	.	.
N	1	
N	2	
.	.	.
.	.	.
.	.	.
N	N	$\dfrac{N \cdot (N+1)}{2}$

For example, the lower triangle and main diagonal of a 5 $\times$ 5 symmetric matrix (which requires a declaration of all 25 elements in the matrix) can be stored as a 15-element (5 $\times$ 6 $\div$ 2) vector, giving a saving of 10 storage locations (see the preceding exercise). A 500 $\times$ 500 symmetric array stored as a vector yields a substantial saving of 124,750 storage locations.

Write a complete program that (a) inputs N and a vector that stores the lower triangle/main diagonal of a symmetric matrix, (b) prints the lower triangle/main diagonal as shown in the preceding exercise, and (c) prints any two-dimensional A(I,J) element desired by the user. Use the matrix in the preceding exercise as test data. In part (c), use the following input:

Row Value	Column Value	
3	2	
2	2	
5	1	
1	5	←————— Note upper triangle element
0	0	←————— Terminate run

Hint: Given the scheme in the I-J-K table above, derive a formula that expresses K as a function of I and J.

8.6
INCOME TAX APPLICATION

After taking a tax course, you decide to earn some extra money (so that you can pay more taxes) by opening a computerized tax service for local accountants and individual taxpayers.

Given a taxpayer's wages (WAGES) from Form W-2, dividends (DIV), interest income (INTINC), income other than wages (OTHER), and adjustments (ADJ) such as moving expenses, the adjusted gross income (AGI) is given by

$$AGI = WAGES + DIV + INTINC + OTHER - ADJ$$

Taxable income (TI) is determined as adjusted gross income less excess itemized deductions (EXDED) less the product of number of exemptions (EXEM) and the allowance per exemption (APE).

$$TI = AGI - EXDED - EXEM*APE$$

EXDED is set equal to zero if a single taxpayer's itemized deductions (DED) are less than $2300; however, if DED is greater than $2300, then EXDED = DED − 2300. The income tax for single (unmarried) taxpayers is based on the taxable income according to the schedule below.

Tax Schedule for Single Taxpayers

		Column		
(1)	(2)	(3)	(4)	(5)
	But Not			of the Amount
Over—	Over—	Income Tax		Over—
$ 0	$2,300	$ 0 + 0%		—
2,300	3,400	0 + 12%		$ 2,300
3,400	4,400	132 + 14%		3,400
4,400	6,500	272 + 16%		4,400
6,500	8,500	608 + 17%		6,500
8,500	10,800	948 + 19%		8,500
10,800	12,900	1,385 + 22%		10,800
12,900	15,000	1,847 + 23%		12,900
15,000	18,200	2,330 + 27%		15,000
18,200	23,500	3,194 + 31%		18,200
23,500	28,800	4,837 + 35%		23,500
28,800	34,100	6,692 + 40%		28,800
34,100	41,500	8,812 + 44%		34,100
41,500	—	12,068 + 50%		41,500

To illustrate the computations, consider an individual who declares $19,700 in wages, $225 in dividends, $305.20 in interest income, $3200 in income other than wages, and no adjustments. This gives an AGI of $23,430.20. If itemized deductions amount to $4230 and one exemption is claimed at a $1000 allowance per exemption, then EXDED is $1930 and TI is $20,500.20. From the above tax schedule, the income tax (TAX) is determined as $3194 + (0.31) × (20,500.20 − 18,200), or $3907.06. If the taxpayer had paid taxes during the year that amounted to more than TAX, then the taxpayer would receive a welcome refund from the IRS; otherwise, a not-so-welcome balance due the IRS would have to be paid.

This is another example of a table look-up, this time using a two-dimensional array to store the table.[3] To solve this problem the data in columns 1, 3, and 4 of the tax schedule are stored in a two-dimensional array named TAXTAB. The "serach key" is the taxpayer's taxable income (TI); the "set of keys" is the upper limits of each income class (column 1 of TAXTAB, which is column 1 of the tax schedule) and the "function values" are in columns 3 and 4 of the tax schedule (columns 2 and 3 of TAXTAB).

Figure 8.2 shows exploded pseudocode for the income tax program that follows.

```
C------------------------------------------------------------
C     INCOME TAX PROGRAM
C
C     KEY:
C       NAME   = TAXPAYER'S NAME
C       WAGES  = WAGES
C       DIV    = DIVIDENDS
C       INTINC = INTEREST INCOME
C       OTHER  = INCOME OTHER THAN WAGES
C       ADJ    = ADJUSTMENTS TO INCOME
C       DED    = ITEMIZED DEDUCTIONS
C       EXEM   = NUMBER OF EXEMPTIONS
C       TAXPAY = TOTAL TAX PAID (OR WITHHELD)
C       AGI    = ADJUSTED GROSS INCOME
C       APE    = ALLOWANCE PER EXEMPTION ($1000)
C       EXDED  = EXCESS ITEMIZED DEDUCTIONS
C       TI     = TAXABLE INCOME
C       TAX    = INCOME TAX
C       BALDUE = BALANCE DUE IRS
C       REFUND = REFUND FROM IRS
C       DEDPAR = DEDUCTIONS PARAMETER ($2300)
C       TAXTAB = ARRAY WHERE COLUMNS 1,2,3 STORE
C                COLUMNS 1,3,4 OF TAX SCHEDULE
C       INDEX  = CORRECT ROW IN TAX SCHEDULE
C       FOUND  = .TRUE. IF CORRECT ROW IS FOUND
C
C------------------------------------------------------------
C
      CHARACTER NAME*20
      INTEGER   EXEM,MAXCOL,MAXROW,INDEX
      LOGICAL   FOUND
      REAL      WAGES ,DIV,INTINC,OTHER,ADJ,DED,TAXPAY,AGI,
     1          APE,EXDED,TI,TAX,BALDUE,REFUND,DEDPAR,
     2          TAXTAB(15,3)
C------------------------------------------------------------
      DATA APE,DEDPAR/1000.0,2300.0/
      DATA MAXROW,MAXCOL/15,3/
C------------------------------------------------------------
      READ, TAXTAB
C------------------------------------------------------------
      LOOP
C
         READ, NAME,WAGES,DIV,INTINC,OTHER,ADJ,DED,EXEM,TAXPAY
           AT END, QUIT
C
         AGI = WAGES + DIV + INTINC + OTHER - ADJ
C        --------------------------------
C        EXCESS DEDUCTIONS LOGIC
C        --------------------------------
         IF (DED .GT. DEDPAR) THEN
            EXDED = DED - DEDPAR
         ELSE
            EXDED = 0.0
         END IF
```

---
[3]Example 7.11 on page 265 illustrates a one-dimensional approach to table look-ups.

FIGURE 8.2 Stepwise Refinement of Pseudocode for Income Tax Program

STEP 1	STEP 2	STEP 3	STEP 4

Initial tasks	Initialize parameters
	READ tax schedule
		Allowance per exemption = $1000
		Deductions = $2300
		Rows in tax table = 15; columns = 3
		IF deductions > $2300 THEN
		  Excess item. ded. = ded. − $2300
		ELSE
		  Excess item. ded. = 0
		END IF	

Process taxpayer	LOOP
	  READ input data
	  Calculate adj. gross inc.
	  Calculate excess item. ded.
	  Calculate taxable income
	  Determine tax and print results
		Table look-up logic
		IF table look-up worked THEN
		  Calculate tax
		  PRINT name, adj. gross inc.,
		    tax, inc. tax
		  Refund/balance due logic
		ELSE
		  PRINT error message
		END IF
			DO-loop
			IF taxable inc. in table THEN
			  Found = .TRUE.
			  Index = DO-variable
			  END IF
			End DO-loop
			
			IF tax < tax withheld THEN
			  Calculate refund
			  PRINT refund
			ELSE
			  Calculate bal. due
			  PRINT bal. due
			END IF

Stop	END LOOP		

310

```
C         -------------------------------
          TI = AGI - EXDED - FLOAT(EXEM)*APE
C         -------------------------------
C         TABLE LOOK-UP LOGIC
C         -------------------------------
          FOUND = .FALSE.
          N = MAXROW - 1
          DO 10 I = 1,N
             IF (TI .GT. TAXTAB(I,1) .AND. TI .LE. TAXTAB(I+1,1)) THEN
                FOUND = .TRUE.
                INDEX = I
             END IF
   10     CONTINUE
C         -------------------------------
          IF (FOUND) THEN
C
             TAX = TAXTAB(INDEX,2) + (TI - TAXTAB(INDEX,1))
     *                                      *TAXTAB(INDEX,3)
             PRINT 90,NAME,AGI,TI,TAX
C         -------------------------------
C         REFUND/BALANCE DUE LOGIC
C         -------------------------------
             IF (TAX .LT. TAXPAY) THEN
                REFUND = TAXPAY - TAX
                PRINT 92,REFUND
             ELSE
                BALDUE = TAX - TAXPAY
                PRINT 94,BALDUE
             END IF
C         -------------------------------
          ELSE
C
             PRINT,'**************************************************'
             PRINT, TI,' TAXABLE INCOME NOT FOUND FOR ',NAME
             PRINT,'**************************************************'
C
          END IF
C
          END LOOP
C--------------------------------------------------------------------
          PRINT 96
C--------------------------------------------------------------------
   90     FORMAT (1X,38('=')/ ' NAME: ',A20/ 1X,38('=')/
     1                        ' ADJUSTED GROSS INCOME : $' ,F11.2/
     2                        ' TAXABLE INCOME        : $' ,F11.2/
     3                        ' INCOME TAX            : $' ,F11.2)
   92     FORMAT (              ' REFUND FROM IRS       : $' ,F11.2)
   94     FORMAT (              ' BALANCE DUE IRS       : $' ,F11.2)
   96     FORMAT (1X,38('='))
C
C--------------------------------------------------------------------
C
          STOP
          END
```

Input

```
0.0,2300.0,3400.0,4400.0,6500.0,8500.0,10800.0,12900.0,15000.0,
18200.0,23500.0,28800.0,34100.0,41500.0,1E30
0.0,0.0,132.0,272.0,608.0,948.0,1385.0,1847.0,2330.0,
3194.0,4837.0,6692.0,8812.0,12068.0,0.0
0.0,0.12,0.14,0.16,0.17,0.19,0.22,0.23,0.27,
0.31,0.35,0.40,0.44,0.50,0.0
'TEST 1',19700.0,225.0,305.20,3200.0,0.0,4230.0,1,3500.0
'TEST 2',12100.0,0.0,0.0,0.0,0.0,1900.0,1,2530.0
```

Output

```
=========================================
NAME: TEST 1
=========================================
    ADJUSTED GROSS INCOME : $    23430.20
    TAXABLE INCOME        : $    20500.20
    INCOME TAX            : $     3907.06
    BALANCE DUE IRS       : $      407.06
=========================================
NAME: TEST 2
=========================================
    ADJUSTED GROSS INCOME : $    12100.00
    TAXABLE INCOME        : $    11100.00
    INCOME TAX            : $     1451.00
    REFUND FROM IRS       : $     1079.00
=========================================
```

Follow-up Exercises

25. Identify what the following array element names represent in the program.
    a. TAXTAB(I,1)
    b. TAXTAB(I,2)
    c. TAXTAB(I,3)
    d. TAXTAB(I + 1,1)

26. Describe how the tax schedule is input. What entry is used for the last item in column 1 of TAXTAB? Why?

27. Given the following input data for a taxpayer:

    'TEST 3', 35000.0, 100.0, 500.0, 0.0, 150.0, 7500.0, 2, 6000.0

    a. Describe stored contents of the following memory locations for this taxpayer when the computer executes the END LOOP statement: WAGES,DIV, INTINC, OTHER, ADJ, DED, EXEM, TAXPAY, AGI, EXDED, TI, TAX, REFUND, BALDUE.
    b. Describe printout for this taxpayer.

*28. As the program stands, it has a minor bug whenever income tax exactly equals the total tax paid. Can you identify the problem? Modify the program to eliminate this bug.

*29. Modify the table look-up logic so that it conforms with our approach in Example 7.11 on page 267. Which approach do you prefer?

8.7
THREE OR MORE DIMENSIONS

FORTRAN allows arrays up to seven dimensions. In this section we focus mostly on the more common three-dimensional arrays.

If data are classified by three attributes, then three-dimensional arrays may be useful to store and manipulate these data. The following examples illustrate three-attribute data.

1. Ten financial ratios for each of the top 100 corporations on the Fortune 500 list for each of the last five years can be conceptualized as a 10 by 100 by 5 (10 × 100 × 5) array where the attributes (dimensions) are ratios, corporations, and years.

2. Enrollments at a college tabulated by 50 major subject areas, sex, and five class standings (first year, second year, . . . , graduate) imply a $50 \times 2 \times 5$ array with dimensions representing major subject area, sex, and class standing.

3. Airline reservations classified by 200 flight numbers, day of month, and type of ticket (first class, tourist, standby) suggests a $200 \times 31 \times 3$ array for the attributes flight number, day, and type of ticket.

Attributes beyond three simply add more dimensions. For example, if we further classify reservations by month in the airline example, we have a four-dimensional $200 \times 31 \times 12 \times 3$ array; if we additionally classify enrollments by residency (in-state, out-of-state, foreign) and by ten ethnic origins, we have a five-dimensional $50 \times 2 \times 5 \times 3 \times 10$ array.

Three-dimensional arrays are best visualized as a group of adjacent memory locations arranged in cube-like fashion by rows, columns, and depth, as illustrated in Figure 8.3.

An element within a three-dimensional array is referenced by specifying three subscript expressions: row number, column number, and depth number. For example, the memory location marked with an X in Figure 8.3 is referenced by A(1,1,3) since it is located in row 1, column 1, and depth 3; the XX locates A(2,3,2) in row 2, column 3, and depth 2.

You should carefully note the ordering of subscript expressions when using three-dimensional array element names.

$$\text{array name} \left(\begin{array}{ccc} \text{row} & \text{column} & \text{depth} \\ \text{subscript} & \text{subscript} & \text{subscript} \\ \text{expression,} & \text{expression,} & \text{expression} \end{array} \right)$$

Otherwise, all the rules that name, declare, reference, input, output, and manipulate two-dimensional arrays apply to three- (and greater) dimensional arrays.

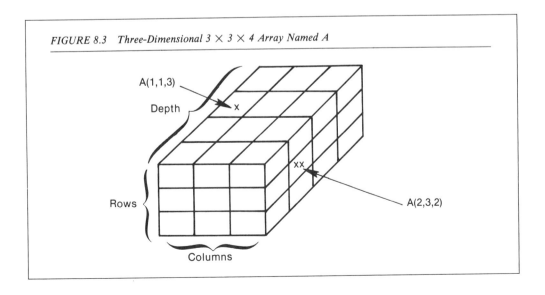

FIGURE 8.3   *Three-Dimensional 3 × 3 × 4 Array Named A*

EXAMPLE 8.5   Projected Enrollments

The administration of a small university has estimated enrollments for three years by college (Social Science, Physical Science, Humanities) and by level (lower, upper, graduate), as illustrated in Figure 8.4.

These data can be represented by a three-dimensional array named ENROLL, where the first dimension represents the colleges, the second dimension the levels, and the third dimension the years. Thus, ENROLL (I,J,K) references the enrollment in the Ith college, the Jth level, and the Kth year.

Looking at Figure 8.4, we can conceptualize ENROLL as a three-layered "sandwich" or "accordion," where the first layer is the first-year matrix, the middle layer is the second-year matrix, and the back layer is the third-year matrix. In other words, a three-dimensional array can be visualized as a cube with three layers, where each layer is a two-dimensional array. For example, ENROLL(3,1,1) references the value 600, ENROLL(1,3,1) references 100, and ENROLL(1,1,3) references 130.

The program below inputs the enrollment data, computes row and column totals, and prints the results.

FIGURE 8.4   *Projected Enrollments: 3 × 3 × 3 Array ENROLL*

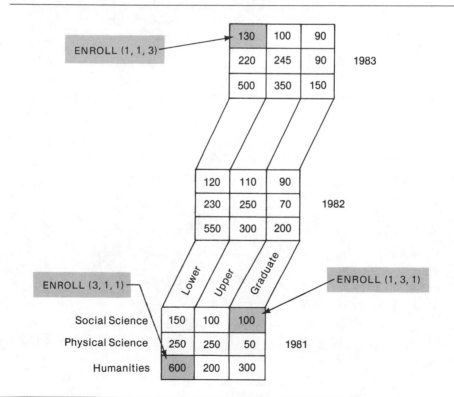

```
C----------------------------------------------------------------
C    PROJECTED ENROLLMENTS PROGRAM
C
C    KEY:
C       NOC    = NUMBER OF COLLEGES
C       NOL    = NUMBER OF LEVELS
C       NOY    = NUMBER OF YEARS
C       COL    = 1-D ARRAY STORING COLLEGE NAMES
C       LEVEL  = 1-D ARRAY STORING LEVEL NAMES
C       YEAR   = 1-D ARRAY STORING YEARS
C       ENROLL = 3-D ARRAY STORING ENROLLMENT DATA; ENROLL(I,J,K)
C                REFERENCES ITH COLLEGE, JTH LEVEL, KTH YEAR
C       COLTOT = 1-D ARRAY STORING TOTAL ENROLLMENT FOR EACH COLLEGE
C       LEVTOT = 1-D ARRAY STORING TOTAL ENROLLMENT FOR EACH LEVEL
C----------------------------------------------------------------
       CHARACTER*20 COL(6)
       CHARACTER*10 LEVEL(4)
       INTEGER NOC,NOL,NOY
       INTEGER YEAR(5),ENROLL(6,4,5),COLTOT(6),LEVTOT(4)
C----------------------------------------------------------------
       DATA NOC,NOL,NOY/3*3/
       DATA (COL(I),I = 1,NOC)/'SOCIAL SCIENCE','PHYSICAL SCIENCE',
      *                        'HUMANITIES'/
       DATA (LEVEL(J),J = 1,NOL)/'LOWER','UPPER','GRADUATE'/
C----------------------------------------------------------------
       DO 20 K = 1,NOY
          READ, YEAR(K)
          DO 10 I = 1,NOC
             READ, (ENROLL(I,J,K),J=1,NOL)
  10      CONTINUE
  20   CONTINUE
C----------------------------------------------------------------
       DO 100 K=1,NOY
C
          DO 40 I=1,NOC
             COLTOT(I) = 0
             DO 30 J = 1,NOL
                COLTOT(I) = COLTOT(I) + ENROLL(I,J,K)
  30         CONTINUE
  40      CONTINUE
C
          DO 60 J=1,NOL
             LEVTOT(J) = 0
             DO 50 I=1,NOC
                LEVTOT(J) = LEVTOT(J) + ENROLL(I,J,K)
  50         CONTINUE
  60      CONTINUE
C
          PRINT 910, YEAR(K)
          PRINT 920, (LEVEL(J), J=1,NOL)
          PRINT 900
C
          DO 70 I=1,NOC
             PRINT 930, COL(I),(ENROLL(I,J,K),J=1,NOL),COLTOT(I)
  70      CONTINUE
C
          PRINT 900
          PRINT 940, (LEVTOT(J), J=1,NOL)
C
 100   CONTINUE
```

```
C----------------------------------------------------------------
  900    FORMAT(1X,60('-'))
  910    FORMAT(19X,'ENROLLMENT DATA FOR',I5/)
  920    FORMAT(26X,A5,5X,A5,4X,A8,2X,'TOTALS')
  930    FORMAT(1X,A20,4I10)
  940    FORMAT(' TOTALS',14X,4I10///)
C----------------------------------------------------------------
        STOP
        END
```

Input

```
1981
150,100,100
250,250,50
600,200,300
1982
120,110,90
230,250,70
550,300,200
1983
130,100,90
220,245,90
500,350,150
```

Output

ENROLLMENT DATA FOR 1981

	LOWER	UPPER	GRADUATE	TOTALS
SOCIAL SCIENCE	150	100	100	350
PHYSICAL SCIENCE	250	250	50	550
HUMANITIES	600	200	300	1100
TOTALS	1000	550	450	

ENROLLMENT DATA FOR 1982

	LOWER	UPPER	GRADUATE	TOTALS
SOCIAL SCIENCE	120	110	90	320
PHYSICAL SCIENCE	230	250	70	550
HUMANITIES	550	300	200	1050
TOTALS	900	660	360	

ENROLLMENT DATA FOR 1983

	LOWER	UPPER	GRADUATE	TOTALS
SOCIAL SCIENCE	130	100	90	320
PHYSICAL SCIENCE	220	245	90	555
HUMANITIES	500	350	150	1000
TOTALS	850	695	330	

Follow-up Exercises

30. Describe input data if we declare three elements in YEAR, 3 × 3 × 3 elements in ENROLL, and replace DO-loops 10 and 20 with the short-list input

    READ,YEAR
    READ,ENROLL

31. With respect to the program:
    a. Up to how many years, levels, and colleges can it handle?
    b. What's stored in ENROLL(3,2,2), ENROLL(2,3,2), and ENROLL(3,3,4)?
32. Modify the program to input data as follows:

    150, 100, 100, 1981
    120, 110, 90, 1982
    130, 100, 90, 1983
    250, 250, 50, 1981
          .
          .
          .

33. Modify the program so that the total enrollment (TE) at the university is printed as the last item in the row labeled "TOTALS."
*34. Modify the program to print the following totals (TOTALS), once the other three matrices have been printed.

	1981	1982	1983
Social Science	350	320	320
Physical Science	550	550	555
Humanities	1100	1050	1000

*35. Can you think of a more efficient way of coding DO-loops 30, 40, 50, and 60, whereby the two totals vectors are summed within one nested DO-loop? What have you sacrificed by gaining some efficiency?

8.8
COMMON ERRORS

Errors associated with two-dimensional arrays are as likely to occur as errors associated with one-dimensional arrays. So review once more the common errors discussed on pages 276–279.

Errors associated with the I/O of two-dimensional arrays are perhaps the most common. If you use the short-list technique, then remember that I/O is column by column, not row by row. Otherwise, you must use nested loops for the I/O of two-dimensional arrays.

When using nested loops, keep in mind that the inner loop DO-variable varies faster than the outer loop DO-variable. Typically, we let the inner loop DO-variable represent the column subscript expression and the outer loop DO-variable the row subscript expression. This gives us row-by-row I/O, which is conceptually consistent with the usual way we treat tables.

If you want input records or printout to "look" like a table, then you must use an implied-DO list. In this case, the usual approach is to use the DO/CONTINUE pair for the outer loop (rows) and an implied-DO list for the inner loop (columns). Alternatively, a nested implied-DO list can be used, but this requires a FORMAT statement that sets the number of repeatable descriptors equal to the number of columns.

Figures 8.5 and 8.6 review some I/O procedures you should keep in mind.

ADDITIONAL EXERCISES

36. Mailing List Revisited.   Rewrite the program in part c of Exercise 28 in Chapter 6 on page 223 by storing columns (7) and (8) of the data file in a two-dimensional array. Store columns (1) to (6) in six one-dimensional arrays. Design your program to include a loop for processing multiple regions and interest areas. Thus one run can handle the four separate runs required by the old version.

37. Computerized Matching Revisited.   Rewrite the program in part b of Exercise 47 in Chapter 5 on page 187 by incorporating a loop to handle the different inquiries. Store the numeric portion of the placement office file in a two-dimensional array. Store name, ID, and address in three one-dimensional arrays.

FIGURE 8.5   Input Reminders

Input Records	Program Segment	Result
1 2 3 4 5 6 7 8 9 ... ——————— 10 20 30 40 50 60	1 FORMAT(3I3) 　　DO 20 I = 1,2 　　　　DO 10 J = 1,3 　　　　　　READ 1,KAT(I,J) 10　　CONTINUE 20 CONTINUE	"OUT OF DATA ERROR" condition during execution
	1 FORMAT(3I3) 　　DO 20 I = 1,2 　　　　READ 1,(KAT(I,J), J = 1,3) 20 CONTINUE *Note:* Repeat specification in the FORMAT 　　　　statement must be 3 or greater.	KAT | 10 | 20 | 30 | | 40 | 50 | 60 |
	1 FORMAT(3I3) 　　READ 1,((KAT(I,J), J = 1,3),I = 1,2) *Note:* Repeat specification in the FORMAT 　　　　statement must be exactly 3.	KAT | 10 | 20 | 30 | | 40 | 50 | 60 |

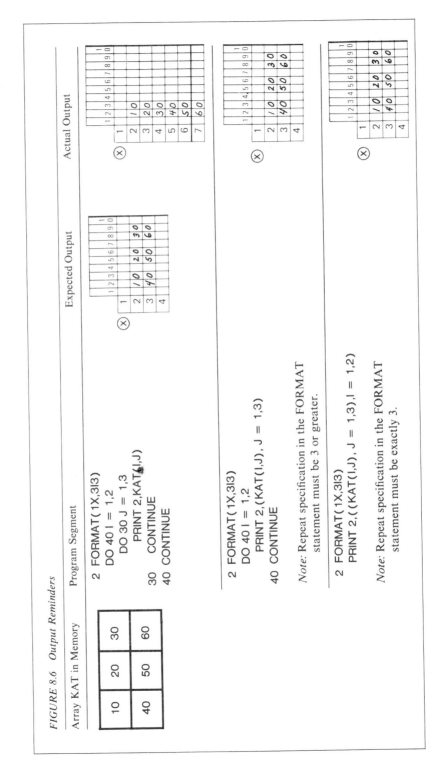

FIGURE 8.6 Output Reminders

38. Crime Data Summary Revisited.   Solve Exercise 42 in Chapter 7 on page 279 using two-dimensional arrays for numeric data.

39. Interactive Airline Reservation System.   All major airlines have automated their systems for handling seat reservations. A central computer keeps a record in storage of all relevant information describing the services being sold: flight numbers, flight schedules, seats available, prices, and other data.

A reservation clerk can request information on seat availability, can sell seats to passengers (providing they are available), can cancel reservations (which increases available seats), and, if a flight is full, can put individuals on a waiting list.

a. Develop an algorithm and an interactive program to incorporate the following menu options.

1. Update the accompanying flight information table. For example, if a customer requests one tourist reservation on flight number 4, the program should check for available tourist seats. Since one is available, it should then adjust the available tourist seats to zero and print a message such as RESERVATION ALLOWED. If the passenger had requested two seats, however, the program should print RESERVATION DISALLOWED. SORRY, OUR HIGH ETHICAL STANDARDS PREVENT OVERBOOKING.
2. Retrieve status on a particular flight by printing the appropriate row in the flight information table.
3. Print entire flight information table.
4. Terminate the run.

Remember to read the flight information data into arrays at the start of the program.

Current Table of Flight Information

Flight Number	Departing Airport	Arriving Airport	Time of Departure	Time of Arrival	Available Seats First Class	Available Seats Tourist	Seats Sold First Class	Seats Sold Tourist
1	BOS	CHI	0730	0855	20	8	10	75
2	BOS	CHI	1200	1357	20	20	10	50
3	BOS	TOR	0810	1111	30	10	0	120
4	ATL	SF	1145	1604	15	1	25	129
5	CHI	BOS	0645	0948	30	25	5	90
6	CHI	NY	0945	1237	30	8	0	120
7	CHI	LA	1530	1851	20	10	30	60
8	CHI	TOR	1955	2114	5	5	25	85
9	TOR	DEN	1025	1611	10	6	60	60
10	TOR	SF	1435	1556	20	10	10	89

Process the following requests in your computer run on an interactive basis.

Option Request	Flight Number	Seat Type	Number of Tickets	Reservation Request
1	4	Tourist	1	Reserve
1	6	Tourist	4	Reserve
2	3	—	—	—
1	9	Tourist	2	Cancel
1	9	1st Class	4	Cancel
1	4	Tourist	2	Reserve
3	—	—	—	—

   **b. Besides the options in part a, give your program the capability to retrieve and print flight information on all flights between two specified airports. Test your program for flights from Boston to Chicago and from Chicago to Los Angeles. In the first case, you should get a printout of the first two rows; in the second case, the seventh row should be printed.

40. Poisson-Distributed Electronic Failures. The likelihoods (probabilities) of failures for many electronic processes can be described by the Poisson probability function

$$f(x) = \frac{\lambda^x \cdot e^{-\lambda}}{x!}$$

where

$f(x)$ = probability of x failures per time period
λ = average number of failures per time period (lambda)
e = base of natural logarithm (the irrational number 2.71828 . . .)
x = number of failures per time period
$x!$ = x factorial, or the product $1 \cdot 2 \cdot 3 \cdots (x - 1) \cdot (x)$
     (*Note:* 0! is defined as 1.)

For example, suppose that malfunctions of onboard navigation systems for a large squadron of aircraft are Poisson-distributed with a failure rate of 20 per month (that is, $\lambda = 20$). In this case, the probability of 15 failures (that is, $x = 15$) in a month is

$$f(15) = \frac{(20)^{15} \cdot e^{-20}}{15!} = 0.0516$$

or about 5.16 percent.

   a. Print a table of Poisson probabilities where rows represent values of x from 0 to 40 in increments of 1 and columns represent values of λ from 10 to 20 in increments of 2. Use a two-dimensional array to store probabilities. *Note:* You might want to use the exponential function described in Section 2.6.

   b. Print a table of cumulative probabilities where again rows represent the same values of x and columns represent the same values of λ. The cumulative probability of x for a given λ is defined as the probability of x or less failures, or

$$F(x) = f(0) + f(1) + f(2) + \cdots + f(x)$$
$$= \sum_{i=0}^{x} f(i)$$

For example, the probability of three or *fewer* failures during a month when λ = 10 is

$$F(3) = f(0) \quad + f(1) \quad + f(2) \quad + f(3)$$
$$= 0.0000 + 0.0005 + 0.0023 + 0.0076$$
$$= 0.0104$$

or just over 1 percent.

c.   Use your tables to find the following probabilities.

1.   The probability of exactly 20 failures given λ = 20
2.   The probability of 20 or fewer failures given λ = 20
3.   The probability of exactly 0 failures given λ = 10
4.   The probability of exactly 10 failures given λ = 10
5.   The probability of exactly 20 failures given λ = 10
6.   The probability of 20 or fewer failures given λ = 10
7.   The probability of 20 or fewer failures given λ = 16
8.   The probability of more than 20 failures given λ = 16

41. Personnel Salary Budget.   The personnel office for a state government agency is in the process of developing a salary budget for the next fiscal year. The personnel file contains the following information on each employee.

1.   Employee name
2.   Social Security number
3.   Current annual salary
4.   Union code (1 = clerical, 2 = teachers, 3 = electrical)
5.   Current step in pay schedule (1 through 5)
6.   Year hired

The state agency deals with three labor unions: clerical, teachers, and electrical. Each union has negotiated a separate salary schedule that entitles each employee to an annual step increase. The salary schedules are listed in the table below. Each employee is hired at the lowest step in the salary schedule for his or her union, and moves up one step each year. The field "current step in pay schedule" indicates the employee's step prior to the new salary for the coming year; that is, "current annual salary" is consistent with this step. The salary for the upcoming year is to be based on the next highest step. Employees who have reached step 5 are at the maximum salary level for that job. Thus next year's step salary is the same as their current annual salary.

In addition to the salary step increase, employees who have been employed by the state for ten years or more are entitled to a longevity increase. A longevity increase represents a 5 percent increment added to the employee's *new* step salary.

a.   Design an algorithm and write a program that prints a budget report for the personnel office. Output from the report includes employee's name, current salary, increase in salary due to step, increase in salary due to longevity, and new salary. Following the output table, print totals for the four numeric columns. Treat the salary schedules as a two-dimensional (5 × 3) array that is to be read in. Data in the personnel file and in the output table need not be treated as arrays.

Salary Schedules

Step	Clerical	Teachers	Electrical
1	10176	9133	12170
2	10592	10433	14260
3	10956	11833	16668
4	11320	13333	19501
5	11921	14893	22801

Personnel File

SMYTHIE SMILE	032166789	10956	1	3	71
ALFRED ALFREDO	123454321	13333	2	4	68
MENDAL MICKEY	987654345	22801	3	5	67
FIELD FLORA	543297541	12170	3	1	76
CURRAN CURRENT	045811222	10176	1	1	76
HANDEL HALO	315791123	11320	1	4	70
UNKIND CORA	129834765	9133	2	1	75

b. Print a table that summarizes the salary budgets as follows:

```
                          SALARY
                          BUDGETS
          CLERICAL        $  xxxxxx
          TEACHERS        $  xxxxxx
          ELECTRICAL      $  xxxxxx
                          $ xxxxxxx
```

**c. Print the table of part b *prior* to the output in part a. *Hint:* Unlike part a, now you must subscript both the variables in the personnel file and the output in the report of part a. Do you see why? Use two-dimensional arrays.

42. Questionnaire Analysis. A university is conducting a survey to determine its undergraduates' "attitudes toward and experiences with the consumption of alcoholic beverages." The following questionnaire has been designed for this survey.

_____1.   What is your sex? 1. male _____ 2. female _____

_____2.   Where do you live? 1. on campus _____ 2. off campus with parents _____ 3. off campus alone / with roommates _____

_____3.   What is your class standing? 1. freshman ____ 2. sophomore ____ 3. junior _____ 4. senior _____ 5. other _____

_____4.   How often on the average do you drink alcoholic beverages? 1. never _____ 2. less than once a week _____ 3. 1–3 times per week _____ 4. 4–5 times per week _____ 5. more than 5 times per week _____

_____5.   Do you feel other people's drinking has any adverse effects on your life? 1. frequently _____ 2. occasionally _____ 3. rarely ____ 4. never _____

_____6.   Do your drinking habits affect your academic life? 1. frequently ____ 2. occasionally _____ 3. rarely _____ 4. never _____

_____7. Do you ever feel guilty about your drinking? 1. frequently _____
2. occasionally _____ 3. rarely _____ 4. never _____
_____8. Do you feel you drink primarily because of 1. boredom _____
2. peer pressure _____ 3. tension _____ 4. other _____
(specify)

Before conducting the full survey, it has been decided to pretest the question-naire on ten students. The results are shown in the table below.

Student	Answer to Question Number							
	1	2	3	4	5	6	7	8
1	1	1	3	3	4	4	2	3
2	1	1	3	1	2	2	1	1
3	2	2	2	2	1	3	3	2
4	2	3	1	4	3	1	3	3
5	1	1	4	4	1	1	2	3
6	1	2	2	2	1	1	2	3
7	2	3	4	1	3	2	1	2
8	2	1	1	2	4	4	2	1
9	1	2	3	3	1	1	1	1
10	2	2	1	4	2	3	2	1

a. Design an algorithm and write a program that reads questionnaire data into a two-dimensional array and outputs a frequency distribution for each question. For example, the frequency distribution for the first question and the above data would be

	Responses	
Question	1	2
1	5	5

For the second question, we have

	Responses		
Question	1	2	3
2	4	4	2

Label your output and try to make it as efficient as possible.

**b. Modify your program to provide cross-tabulation of responses for any two questions that are specified by the user. For example, if we wish to assess differences between the drinking frequencies of men and women, then our output might appear as follows:

		QUESTION 1	
		1	2
	1—	1	1
QUESTION 4	2—	1	2
	3—	2	0
	4—	1	2
	5—	0	0

To make sure you understand this cross-tabulation, confirm the numbers based on the data.

43. **Matrix Multiplication.** Let's define a matrix, **A**, as having dimensions (rows and columns) m_1 by n_1 or $(m_1 \times n_1)$. Another matrix, **B**, has dimensions $(m_2 \times n_2)$. Two matrices may be multiplied if and only if they are *compatible,* that is, the number of columns in the first matrix equals the number of rows in the second matrix. As an example, the multiplication of matrix **A** times matrix **B**, defined by **AB**, is possible if and only if $n_1 = m_2$. Similarly, the product **BA** is possible if and only if $n_2 = m_1$.

If two matrices are compatible, then the resulting matrix will have dimensions $(m \times n)$ where m equals the number of rows in the first matrix and n equals the number of columns in the second matrix. Referring to the matrices **A** and **B**, we see that if **AB** is possible and

$$\mathbf{AB} = \mathbf{C}$$

then the product matrix, **C**, will have dimensions $(m_1 \times n_2)$. Similarly, if **BA** is possible and

$$\mathbf{BA} = \mathbf{D}$$

then **D** will have dimensions $(m_2 \times n_1)$.

To compute the product matrix, consider the product

$$\mathbf{AB} = \mathbf{C}$$

Let c_{ij} be a generalized element that is located in row i and column j of the product matrix. To compute any c_{ij}, the elements in row i of matrix **A** are multiplied times the respective elements in column j of matrix **B** and are algebraically summed.

For example, if

$$\mathbf{A} = \begin{pmatrix} 1 & 4 \\ 5 & -3 \end{pmatrix}$$

and

$$\mathbf{B} = \begin{pmatrix} 1 \\ 4 \end{pmatrix}$$

then **A** is a (2×2) matrix and **B** is a (2×1) matrix. If we wish to find the product **AB**, then we must first examine the dimensions of the matrices. The product **AB** involves multiplying matrices with dimensions

Inner dimensions

$$(2 \times 2) \text{ times } (2 \times 1)$$

Outer dimensions

This product is defined because the "inner" dimensions are equal; that is, the number of columns of **A** equals the number of rows of **B.** The product matrix **C** will have dimensions equal to the "outer" dimensions indicated above, that is, (2×1). Thus the product will be of the form

$$\mathbf{AB} = \mathbf{C}$$

or

$$\begin{pmatrix} 1 & 4 \\ 5 & -3 \end{pmatrix} \begin{pmatrix} 1 \\ 4 \end{pmatrix} = \begin{pmatrix} c_{11} \\ c_{21} \end{pmatrix}$$

To compute the elements of **C**, we have

$$c_{11} = (1 \ 4) \begin{pmatrix} 1 \\ 4 \end{pmatrix} = (1)(1) + (4)(4)$$
$$= 17$$

and

$$c_{21} = (5 \ -3) \begin{pmatrix} 1 \\ 4 \end{pmatrix} = (5)(1) + (-3)(4)$$
$$= -7$$

or

$$\mathbf{C} = \begin{pmatrix} 17 \\ -7 \end{pmatrix}$$

The product **BA** is not defined because the inner dimensions do not match; that is, it involves multiplying a (2×1) matrix times a (2×2) matrix and the number of columns of **B** *does not equal* the number of rows of **A** $(1 \neq 2)$.

Design an algorithm and write a program to input two matrices and print the two matrices together with their matrix product (if defined). Process the following to debug your program.

a.   Find **AB** given **A** and **B** as in the example.
b.   Find **BA** given **A** and **B** as in the example.
c.   Find **AB** given

$$\mathbf{A} = \begin{pmatrix} 1 & 0 & 6 \\ 2 & -3 & 1 \end{pmatrix}$$

$$\mathbf{B} = \begin{pmatrix} 1 & 0 & 0 \\ 0 & 1 & 0 \\ 0 & 0 & 1 \end{pmatrix}$$

Subprograms

A **subprogram** is an independent section of code that's used for a specialized purpose. Typically a subprogram is designed to solve a part of the overall problem, such as input, error detection, output, sorting, or specialized computations. It is a complete program in itself, but plays a "subrole" in the total solution to the problem. The program that controls the overall program is usually termed the **main program.** Subprograms are combined with the main program to form the entire program. This design effectively conceptualizes a program as a set of distinct and independently compiled **program units** or **program modules** (main program plus subprograms).

Subprograms are an important feature of the FORTRAN language. Strictly speaking, however, they are not essential to writing complex programs. Rather, subprogramming capability is a sophisticated refinement of the language that permits a unique 'building-block' or *modular* approach to programming. This in turn promotes programs that are easier to code, debug, and maintain.

This chapter presents three types of subprograms—*subroutine subprogram, function subprogram* and *statement function*—and discusses a style of programming called *modular programming*.

9.1
SUBROUTINE SUBPROGRAMS

A **subroutine subprogram** (also called a **subroutine**) is a separate and complete program that accomplishes some particular task and may include such operations as input, output, computations, and decision and loop structures.

In fact, any of the statements we have used up to this point can be included in a subroutine. The subroutine is placed immediately following the main program. If additional subroutines are required, they are placed one after another following the main program. This arrangement of main program and subroutine subprograms is shown next. Note how this arrangement effectively subdivides a program into blocks or modules.

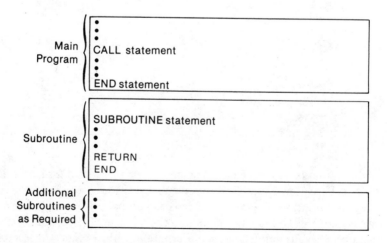

Subroutine subprograms represent the most powerful class of the subprograms. To illustrate their use, we first present a new problem.

EXAMPLE 9.1   Combinations

The number of combinations of *n* objects taken *k* at a time (where $n \geq k$) is a common calculation in many statistical and mathematical applications.[1] The formula is given by

$$C = \frac{n!}{(n-k)!k!}$$

where the exclamation point represents "factorial." For example, 5! reads "the factorial of 5" or "5 factorial," which is defined by the product $1 \cdot 2 \cdot 3 \cdot 4 \cdot 5$, or 120. The number of combinations of 5 taken 2 at a time ($n = 5$ and $k = 2$) is calculated from

$$C = \frac{5!}{(5-2)!2!} = \frac{5!}{3!2!} = \frac{1 \cdot 2 \cdot 3 \cdot 4 \cdot 5}{(1 \cdot 2 \cdot 3)(1 \cdot 2)} = \frac{120}{6 \cdot 2} = \frac{120}{12} = 10$$

Combinations are defined only if $n \geq k$, $n > 0$, and $k \geq 0$. Moreover, 0! is defined as 1.

The following program calculates and prints combinations given *n* and *k*.

```
C-------------------------------------------------------------
C     MAIN PROGRAM--CALCULATES AND PRINTS COMBINATIONS GIVEN N,K
C                BY REPEATEDLY CALLING SUBROUTINE FACTOR
C
C     KEY:
C        N     = AS IN FORMULA
C        K     = AS IN FORMULA
C        NFAC  = FACTORIAL OF N
C        NKFAC = FACTORIAL CF N-K
C        KFAC  = FACTORIAL OF K
C        COMB  = COMBINATIONS
C-------------------------------------------------------------
      INTEGER N,K,NFAC,KFAC,NKFAC,COMB
C-------------------------------------------------------------
      READ, N,K
      WHILE (N .GE. K .AND. N .GT. 0 .AND. K .GE. 0)
         CALL FACTOR(N,NFAC)
         CALL FACTOR(N-K,NKFAC)
         CALL FACTOR(K,KFAC)
         COMB= NFAC/(NKFAC*KFAC)
         PRINT, 'N =',N,'K =',K,'COMBINATIONS =',COMB
         READ, N,K
      END WHILE
C-------------------------------------------------------------
      STOP
      END
C==============================================
      SUBROUTINE FACTOR (NUMBER,FAC)
C==============================================
C
C     SUBROUTINE FACTOR--CALCULATES THE FACTORIAL OF A NUMBER
C                     GIVEN THE NUMBER
C
C     KEY:
C        NUMBER = NUMBER WHOSE FACTORIAL IS TO BE CALCULATED
C        FAC    = FACTORIAL OF NUMBER
C-------------------------------------------------------------
      INTEGER NUMBER,FAC
```

[1] For example, see page 228.

```
C- -- ------ -------------------------------------------- ----------
      FAC = 1
      IF(NUMBER .GE. 2) THEN
        DO 10 J=2,NUMBER
          FAC = FAC*J
   10   CONTINUE
      END IF
C- --------- ------------------------------------------ ----- ---
      RETURN
      END
```

Sample Input

```
5,2
10,4
5,0
0,0
```

Sample Output

```
N =          5  K =        2  COMBINATIONS =           10
N =         10  K =        4  COMBINATIONS =          210
N =          5  K =        0  COMBINATIONS =            1
```

At this time don't worry about exactly how this program works, as we explain the new statements in what follows next.

Calling the Subroutine

The execution of a subroutine is invoked from another program unit (referred to as the **calling program**) by using the CALL statement. The general form of this statement is

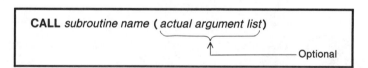

The *subroutine name* indicates the particular subroutine to be executed. Naming a subroutine follows the same rules as naming variables, for example, a subroutine name cannot have more than six characters.[2] The **actual argument list** passes values between the calling program and the subroutine, that is, data to the subroutine or results back to the calling program, or both. The argument list is made up of items (actual arguments) separated by commas. *Typical actual arguments include variable names, array names, array element names, constants, and expressions.*

For example, the statement

CALL FACTOR(N,NFAC)

[2] However, the first letter of the subroutine name has no effect on type.

in Example 9.1 is used to call subroutine FACTOR, and the contents of the variables N and NFAC are passed between the calling program and the subroutine. When this CALL statement is executed, control reverts to the subroutine, the subroutine utilizes the value in N to calculate its factorial, the value of the factorial is placed in NFAC, and control returns to the point of call in the calling program.

Now look at the main program on page 000. Next, the execution of

`CALL FACTOR(N − K,NKFAC)`

provides the value of the expression N − K to the subroutine, the subroutine calculates the factorial of this value, places the result in NKFAC, and returns control to the main program. The statement

`CALL FACTOR(K,KFAC)`

is executed next, which after execution yields the factorial of the value in K as the contents in KFAC. Finally, the number of combinations is calculated and stored in COMB, results are printed, the next set of N,K values is read in, and we loop back to the test in the WHILE loop.

The effect of calling the subroutine is similar to placing the set of statements in the subroutine at the point of call (sometimes referred to as the "point of invocation") in the calling program.

In general, the calling program can be the main program or another subprogram. Further, subroutines may include calls to other subprograms. However, a subroutine cannot call itself nor can two subroutines call each other.

Structure of the Subroutine

A subroutine has the following general structure.

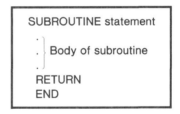

The subroutine *always begins* with a subroutine statement having the following general form.

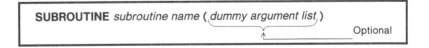

This statement identifies both the name of the subroutine and the variables in the argument list whose values are to be passed between the calling program and the subroutine. In Example 9.1 the subroutine statement is

In this case FACTOR is the name of the subroutine and NUMBER,FAC represents the **dummy argument list.** When the subroutine is called and control is transferred to the subroutine, *actual arguments are associated with corresponding dummy arguments,* as the following illustrates for the first call.

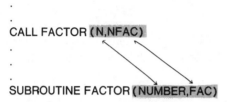

In effect, the value in N is associated with the value in NUMBER and the value in NFAC is associated with the value in FAC. Similarly, N − K is matched with NUMBER and NKFAC is matched with FAC during the second call; K is matched with NUMBER and KFAC with FAC during the third call. *Typical dummy arguments include variable names and array names.* Moreover, *dummy and actual argument lists must correspond with respect to number of arguments and their type.*

The "body" of the subroutine is sandwiched between the SUBROUTINE statement and the RETURN statement. In general, the body can include any statement except a SUBROUTINE or FUNCTION (see Section 9.3) statement. In Example 9.1, the shaded statements below

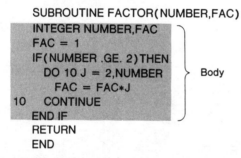

represent the body of the subroutine.

Now carefully note the following procedure. During the first call, 5 is stored in the actual argument N according to the sample input data. Since the dummy argument NUMBER is paired with N *during this call,* NUMBER utilizes the value 5 during execution of the body in the subroutine. Thus DO-loop 10 is processed in the subroutine and FAC emerges with a value of 120.

After the body is processed, the RETURN statement in the subroutine is executed, *at which time control returns to the calling program at the point of call.* Since the actual argument NFAC is paired with the dummy argument FAC, it follows that NFAC stores 120 at this time. Similarly, the value 3 for the expression N − K is utilized by NUMBER during the second call and the result 6 for FAC gets passed to NKFAC in the calling program; during the third call, 2 in K is used by NUMBER and 2 in FAC is returned to KFAC. We can represent this process as follows:

First Call	Second Call	Third Call
CALL FACTOR (N, NFAC) ↓5 ↑120 SUBROUTINE FACTOR(NUMBER, FAC)	CALL FACTOR (N − K, NKFAC) ↓3 ↑6 SUBROUTINE FACTOR(NUMBER, FAC)	CALL FACTOR (K, KFAC) ↓2 ↑2 SUBROUTINE FACTOR(NUMBER, FAC)

Thus *values in the calling program required by the subroutine are passed to the subroutine via the argument lists; similarly, computational results in the subroutine required by the calling program are returned to the calling program via the argument lists.*

The statement

$$\boxed{\textbf{RETURN}}$$

returns control from the subroutine to the point of call in the calling program. WATFIV subroutines must include at least one RETURN statement, usually placed just before the END statement. We discuss alternative placements of the RETURN statement in the next subsection.

The relationship between the calling program and the subroutine for the first call is illustrated in Figure 9.1.

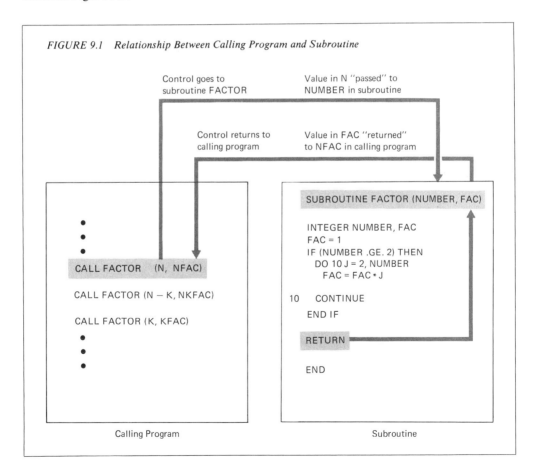

FIGURE 9.1   *Relationship Between Calling Program and Subroutine*

Additional Considerations

1. A subroutine is compiled independently from the main program and all other subprograms. Thus identical variable names and statement labels can be used in different program units without concern for syntax errors. For example, the label 10 was used in both the main program and subroutine of Example 9.1.

2. The actual and dummy argument lists must agree with respect to number of arguments, type correspondence (integer with integer, real with real, character with character, etc.), and kind correspondence (for example, a constant, variable name, or expression as an actual argument is usually matched with a variable name as the dummy argument and an actual array name is matched with a dummy array name). Also, note that constants or expressions are not allowed as dummy arguments.

3. You should ensure length correspondence between character actual and dummy arguments by declaring the character dummy argument the same length as the character actual argument. For example,

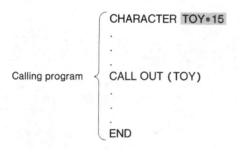

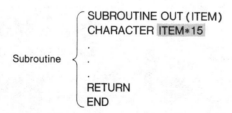

In this case, the character dummy argument ITEM has a declared length of 15 characters, the same as the character actual argument TOY.

4. Symbolic names for variables and arrays in the dummy argument list need not have the same names as corresponding actual arguments. In Example 9.1 real arguments N and K were matched with the dummy argument NUMBER during separate calls; the dummy argument FAC was matched in turn with the real arguments NFAC, NKFAC, and KFAC. This feature generalizes the subprogram for greater flexibility; that is, the same subprogram can be used by CALL statements having different actual

argument lists. More important, generalized subprograms can be designed for use by different programs altogether without the need to match identical symbolic names.

5. Example 9.1 illustrated a simple application whereby the argument lists effectively passed one value from the calling program to the subroutine and returned one value from the subroutine to the calling program. In general, multiple values may be passed in either direction, as illustrated below.

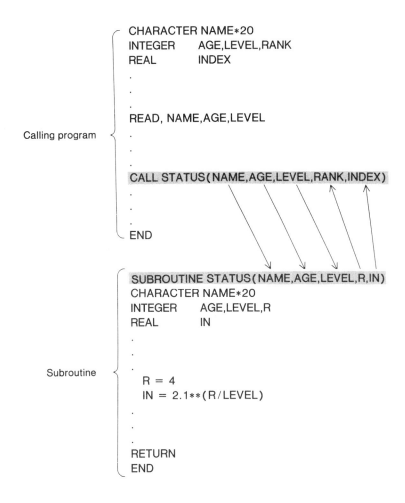

In this case, NAME, AGE, and LEVEL are passed to the subroutine and computational results for R and IN in the subroutine are returned to locations RANK and INDEX in the calling program. Note how the two argument lists match with respect to number, type, and kind.

6. Argument lists may be omitted altogether, either when the design does not require data communication between the calling program and the subroutine or when COMMON statements (discussed in the next section) are used to pass values. For example,

a subroutine that simply prints extensive titles and table headings might be treated as follows:

```
        .
        .
        .
    CALL HEADNG
        .
        .
        .
    STOP
    END
C
    SUBROUTINE HEADNG
    PRINT, 'WADSWORTH PUBLISHING COMPANY'
    PRINT, 'A DIVISION OF WADSWORTH INC.'
    PRINT, 'TEN DAVIS DRIVE'
    PRINT, 'BELMONT, CA 94002'
    RETURN
    END
```

7. Some designs may require a return to the calling program at points other than at the physical end of a subroutine. For example, the subroutine in Example 9.1 can be rewritten by using logical IF and RETURN statements as follows.

```
      SUBROUTINE FACTOR(NUMBER,FAC)
      INTEGER NUMBER,FAC
      FAC = 1
      IF(NUMBER .LT. 2) RETURN   ←——————————————— First exit
      DO 10 J = 2,NUMBER
        FAC = FAC*J
   10 CONTINUE
      RETURN                     ←——————————————— Second exit
      END
```

Convince yourself that this version is equivalent to the version on pages 329; that is, control is returned to the calling program either whenever NUMBER is zero or 1 (which gives a factorial of 1) or on completion of the DO-loop.

For reasons discussed in Section 9.4, *it's best to design a subroutine with one entry point and one exit point.* Consequently we prefer the original one-exit design in Example 9.1 to the two-exit design above.

**8. In our earlier descriptions of argument association we were purposely vague about the actual mechanics of just how values are passed and returned between corresponding actual and dummy arguments. (We decided to spare you the agony at that point.) Now that your subroutine knowledge is maturing, consider the following statement. Argument association between two symbolic names is usually implemented either by *value/result* or by *location/address.*

To illustrate argument association by value/result, consider the following scheme for the first call in Example 9.1.

Value/Result Association: The Call

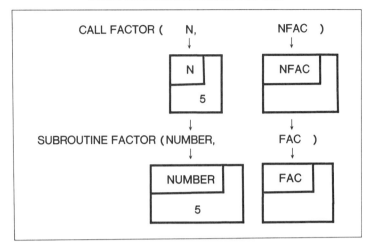

In this case dummy names have storage locations separate from corresponding actual names. When the CALL statement is executed, values in N and NFAC are copied into the storage locations for NUMBER and FAC. In the body of the subroutine, the value in NUMBER is used to calculate the factorial 120, which is then stored in FAC. When the RETURN statement in the subroutine is executed, we can visualize the following.

Value/Result Association: The Return

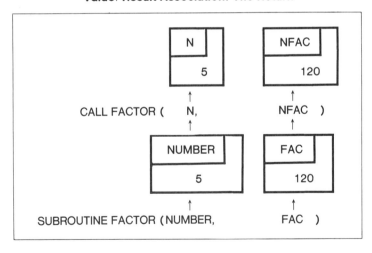

Now the flow is reversed as values in NUMBER and FAC are copied into N and NFAC, respectively.

Argument association between names by location/address does not assign separate storage locations for dummy names. In this case dummy names share the storage locations of corresponding actual names. Thus, rather than a flow of values or contents between separate memory locations, there is a transfer of addresses, so that the dummy name can utilize the same storage location as its "sister" actual name.

In either case, we have a word of caution: *If a dummy argument is assigned a new value in the subroutine, the value of the corresponding actual argument also is changed.* Make sure you don't inadvertently change the value in a dummy argument. In particular, never change the value in a dummy argument that corresponds to an expression or constant in the actual argument; otherwise either an execution error occurs (in WATFIV) or the error results are unpredictable (depending on the FORTRAN complier).

Follow-up Exercises

1. Roleplay the computer in Example 9.1 by processing the following data through the program (don't forget to specify the output).

    8,6
    4,4
    4,0
    4,1
    1,4

2. Would it be alright to initialize FAC in the subroutine of Example 9.1 by using a DATA statement? Would there be a problem if we had forgotten the INTEGER statement in the subroutine? Do you see any problem with using the name FACTOR in place of FAC in the subroutine?
3. Specify what's wrong, if anything, with each of the following.

Calling Program	Subroutine
a. INTEGER N,NFAC CALL FACTOR(N,NFAC)	SUBROUTINE FACTOR(N,NFAC) INTEGER N,NFAC
b. INTEGER N,NFAC CALL FACTOR(N,NFAC)	SUBROUTINE(NUMBER,FAC) INTEGER NUMBER,FAC
c. CALL ADD	SUBROUTINE ADD(A,B,C)
d. CHARACTER A*10 INTEGER B,C REAL D,E,F CALL SEARCH(A,B,C,D,E,F,100,'YES')	SUBROUTINE SEARCH(P,Q,R,S,T,U) CHARACTER Q*50 INTEGER P,T REAL R,S,U
e. REAL R,A CALL AREA(R,A)	SUBROUTINE AREA(RADIUS,AREA) REAL RADIUS,AREA,PI . . . AREA = PI*RADIUS**2

4. Specify output for the program below. Assume the following input: 1.1, 2.2, 3.3.

```
REAL A,B,C,SUM
CALL INPUT(A,B,C)
CALL ADD(A,B,C,SUM)
CALL OUTPUT(A,B,C,SUM)
END

SUBROUTINE INPUT(X,Y,Z)
REAL X,Y,Z
READ,X,Y,Z
RETURN
END

SUBROUTINE ADD(X,Y,Z,TOTAL)
REAL X,Y,Z,TOTAL
Y = X + Y
Z = Y + Z
X = Z + X
TOTAL = X + Y + Z
RETURN
END

SUBROUTINE OUTPUT(X,Y,Z,TOTAL)
REAL X,Y,Z,TOTAL
PRINT,'VALUES:',X,Y,Z
PRINT,'TOTAL:',TOTAL
RETURN
END
```

Have the original contents in A, B, C changed?

5. Write a subroutine named HEAD that inputs a character value up to a length of 25 characters (stored in DATE) and prints the following heading.

```
PERIODIC REPORT
DECEMBER 15, 1982   ←Sample input/output value
```

No data need be passed to and from this subroutine.

*6. Revise Example 5.5 on page 153 by finding minimum PCI through a subroutine.

9.2
ADDITIONAL TOPICS

In this section we cover some further topics on the use of subroutines: the design of flowcharts and pseudocode, the passing of arrays, an alternative method of passing values, and methods of sharing storage locations.

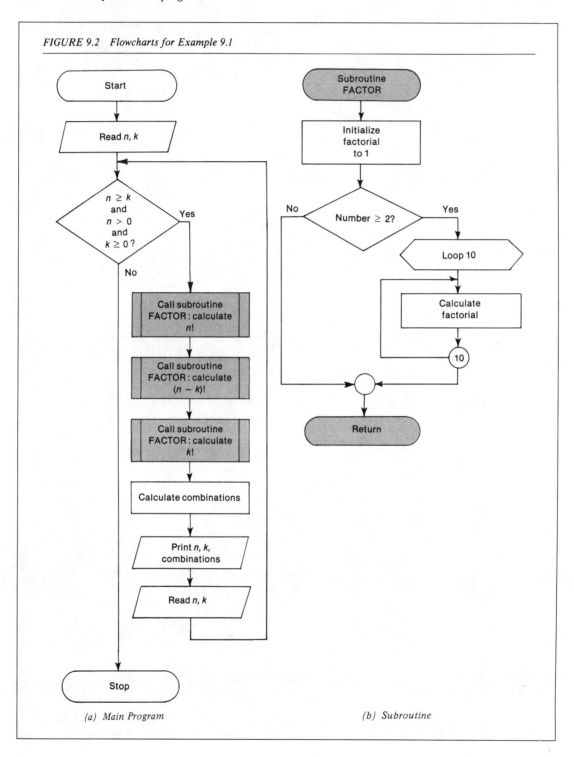

FIGURE 9.2   Flowcharts for Example 9.1

(a) Main Program

(b) Subroutine

Flowcharts/Pseudocode

Figure 9.2 illustrates the flowcharts for the main program and subprogram of Example 9.2. Note the following.

1. Each subprogram has a separate flowchart. Thus a program with one main program and four subprograms would have five distinct flowcharts.
2. The **predefined process symbol** can be used to indicate the call of the subprogram, as illustrated in Figure 9.2a. The exact nature of the writing within the symbol is a matter of personal preference.
3. The Start-Stop symbol is used to indicate entry and exit points in the subprogram. The entry point is labeled with the name of the subprogram and the exit point is labeled with the word return. Between these two symbols, the logic of the subprogram is illustrated using any of the legitimate symbols for main programs.

Figure 9.3 illustrates pseudocode for Example 9.1. Note how each program module begins with a "start" and ends with an "end," to identify program modules clearly. Moreover, this identification is further enhanced by indenting the module itself. Finally, note that the word "return" should be included in the subroutine to indicate the return point unambiguously (since return points can differ depending on the design).

FIGURE 9.3   *Pseudocode for Example 9.1*

```
Start main program
   READ n,k
   WHILE n ≥ k,n > 0,k ≥ 0
      CALL FACTOR to calculate n!
      CALL FACTOR to calculate (n − k)!
      CALL FACTOR to calculate k!
      Combinations = n!/(n − k)!/k!
      PRINT n,k, combinations
      READ n,k
   END WHILE
   Stop
End main program

Start subroutine FACTOR
   Factorial = 1
   IF no. ≥ 2 THEN
      DO-loop
         Recursively update factorial
      End DO-loop
   END IF
   RETURN
End subroutine FACTOR
```

Follow-up Exercises

7. **Crew Selection Revisited.**   Design flowchart or pseudocode and write a program to solve part a of Exercise 31 in Chapter 6 on page 228. Use the following modular design.

   Main program inputs all data, calls subroutine combinations, and outputs required results.
   Subroutine combinations calculates combinations by repeatedly calling subroutine factorial.
   Subroutine factorial calculates the factorial of a number.

*8. **Crew Selection Re-Revisited.**   Design flowchart or pseudocode and write a program to solve part b of Exercise 31 in Chapter 6 on page 228. Use the following modular design.

   Main program inputs all data, calls subroutine combinations, and outputs required results.
   Subroutine combinations calculates combinations based on the logic in part b of the original exercise in Chapter 6.

Passing Arrays

Up until now we have avoided the use of arrays in argument lists, in order for you to concentrate on the essentials of subroutines. Most analytical and statistical programming packages that are available commercially make use of subprograms that pass arrays, as the following example illustrates.

EXAMPLE 9.2   Mean of One-Dimensional Array

The following modular design illustrates one approach to calculating the mean (arithmetic average) of a set of test scores.

Main program reads number of scores and test score vector, calls subroutine mean, and prints the mean.
Subroutine mean calculates the mean of a vector given the size of the vector and the vector.

The program below reflects this design, where test scores are stored in the vector or one-dimensional array SCORE. The program handles up to 500 scores, but reads in the actual number of scores for a particular run under the variable N.

```
C-------------------------------------------------------
C    MEAN TEST SCORE PROGRAM
C
C    KEY:
C       ARRSIZ = MAXIMUM ARRAY SIZE (500)
C       AVE    = AVERAGE TEST SCORE
C       N      = NUMBER OF TEST SCORES
C       SCORE  = ONE-DIMENSIONAL ARRAY OF SCORES
C-------------------------------------------------------
         INTEGER N,ARRSIZ
         REAL     SCORE(500),AVE
C-------------------------------------------------------
         DATA     ARRSIZ/500/
C-------------------------------------------------------
         READ, N
C-------------------------------------------------------
         IF (N .GT. ARRSIZ) THEN
             PRINT, 'TOO MANY SCORES.  MAX =',ARRSIZ
             PRINT, 'PROGRAM TERMINATED.'
             STOP
         ELSE
             READ, (SCORE(J),J = 1,N)
             CALL MEAN(N,SCORE,AVE)
             PRINT, 'MEAN SCORE =',AVE
         END IF
C-------------------------------------------------------
         STOP
         END
C========================================================
         SUBROUTINE MEAN(N,X,XBAR)
C========================================================
C
C    THIS SUBROUTINE CALCULATES THE MEAN OF A REAL VECTOR
C
C    KEY:
C       N      = NUMBER OF ITEMS IN VECTOR
C       X      = VECTOR (ONE-DIMENSIONAL ARRAY)
C       XBAR   = MEAN OF N ITEMS
C-------------------------------------------------------
         INTEGER N
         REAL     X(N),XBAR,SUM
C-------------------------------------------------------
         SUM = 0.0
         DO 10 J = 1,N
             SUM = SUM + X(J)
      10 CONTINUE
C-------------------------------------------------------
         XBAR = SUM/N
C-------------------------------------------------------
         RETURN
         END
```

Input

```
5
85.0
77.0
82.0
95.0
91.0
```

Output

```
MEAN SCORE =          86.0000000
```

Note the following in Example 9.2:

1. The actual argument list passes to the subprogram both the number of storage locations (N, total number of exam scores) that are used in the array and the array itself (SCORE).
2. The dummy argument list pairs N with N, X with SCORE, and XBAR with AVE. The dummy array X merely utilizes the storage locations for the real array SCORE; however, X *must be dimensioned in the subprogram.* Otherwise the compiler has no way of knowing that X is an array.[3]
3. In the subroutine, the dummy array defined by the statement

makes use of an **adjustable array declarator** to define the size of the array in the subprogram. In this case N is called an **adjustable dimension,** which means that the dummy array X is assumed to have a size given by the value in N. For example, if N stores 75, the dummy array X is assumed to have 75 elements, which is exactly consistent with the number of elements *utilized* in the main program for array SCORE. The next time, N may have a value of 200, so the dummy array X would have 200 assumed elements. In general, *adjustable array declarators are specified by using integer variables.* The use of adjustable array declarators allows us to pair the same general subprogram with calling programs having varying array sizes, without concern for the size of the dummy array. In doing so, however, we should keep the following in mind.

a. An adjustable dimension must be an integer variable, must be included in the dummy argument list, and must take on values that are compatible with the dimension bounds that were declared for the corresponding actual array. In the example, N is an integer variable for the dimension bound of a one-dimensional dummy array X, it appears within the dummy argument list, and its value must not exceed 500 since this is the value of the dimension bound for the corresponding actual array SCORE.
b. When using adjustable dimensions for dummy arrays of two or more dimensions, the value of each *adjustable* dimension should equal exactly the corresponding *actual* dimension; otherwise the conceptual relations of array elements (for example, a table of numbers) would not be maintained. Thus the CALL statement in

---

[3] Systems invariably use argument association by location/address for arrays, which means that X does not have its own separate storage locations. Association by value/result for arrays would be storage and time inefficient.

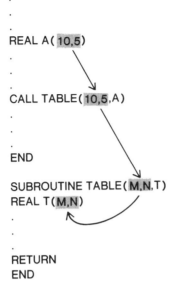

```
.
.
.
REAL A( 10,5)
.
.
.
.
CALL TABLE( 10,5,A)
.
.
.
END
SUBROUTINE TABLE( M,N,T)
REAL T( M,N)
.
.
.
RETURN
END
```

ensures that the arrays A and T are conceptually identical (that is, the first row of elements in T is the same as the first row in A, etc.). This is so because the number of rows and columns in T (given by M and N, respectively) is identical to the number of rows and columns reserved for A in the REAL statement (10 and 5, respectively); however, the statement

CALL TABLE(4,3,A)

would not preserve this row-by-row conceptual relationship.

4. Sometimes the number of needed array elements is either determined or input in the subprogram rather than the calling program. In this situation one could use the **constant array declarator** in the statement

REAL X(500)

Constant array declarator

to define the dummy array. This approach requires size consistency of 500 between the array declarations in the calling program and subroutine. Better yet, a generalized approach that makes the entire actual array available to the subroutine uses a 1 as the dimension bound on the dummy array. Thus, the **generalized array declarator** in

REAL X(1)

Generalized array declarator

defines the size of the dummy array X, at each call, to be the size of the corresponding actual array as defined in the calling program. Another term for this approach is **pseudovariable dimensioning**.

Follow-up Exercises

9. Indicate errors, if any, in the following.
    a. SUBROUTINE X(X,M,N,T)
        REAL X(M),Y(M,2*K + 1),T(N)
        .
        .
        .
        RETURN
        END

    b. INTEGER K,N,TOT(500),A(K,N)
        .
        .
        .
        CALL SUM(K,N,TOT(3))
        .
        .
        .
        END

        SUBROUTINE SUM(M,N,S)
        INTEGER M,N,S,POINT(M)
        .
        .
        .
        RETURN
        END

    c. INTEGER ROW,COL
        DATA ROW,COL / 100,50 /
        INTEGER DOT(ROW,COL), SUM(ROW)
        CALL MOD1(ROW,COL,DOT,SUM)
        .
        .
        .
        END

        SUBROUTINE MOD1(M,N,X,S)
        INTEGER M,N,X(200,50),S(*)
        .
        .
        .
        RETURN
        END

10. Given the following CALL statements for Example 9.2, identify which are illegal and why. Explain how the legal statements work.

     a. CALL MEAN(100,SCORE,AVE)
     b. CALL MEAN(300,SCORE,AVE)
     c. CALL MEAN(600,SCORE,AVE)
     d. CALL MEAN(SCORE,N,AVE)
     e. CALL MEAN(N,X,AVE)
     f. CALL MEAN(SCORE,AVE)

11. Modify Example 9.2 such that SUM, the sum of the scores, is output in the main program along with AVE.

12. Modify Example 9.2 such that N and the array are input and XBAR is output by the subroutine. Under what conditions can we input N through the subroutine?

*13. Add a second subroutine to Example 9.2 called SORT, which rearranges and outputs the scores in ascending order. Use a desirable array declarator. *Hint:* See Example 7.13 on page 272.

*14. **Data Editing.** Modify Example 9.2 by adding a new subroutine that edits scores for input errors right after the score array is read in by the main program. Specifically, if all scores are in the range 0 to 100, control is returned to the main program. Otherwise execution stops after printing all scores outside this range together with their positions in the array.

**15. Modify Example 9.2 as follows: Treat SCORE as a 100 × 10 array; treat AVE as a ten-element one-dimensional array that is to contain column averages from SCORE; read in N (number of students or rows used in SCORE), M (number of tests or columns used in SCORE), and SCORE (row by row); modify the subroutine such that dummy arrays are properly declared and AVE stores column averages from X.

COMMON Statement: Blank Common Block

Up until now, the only means of communication between the calling program and the subprogram has been through their arguments. An alternative means of communication between program units is through a common storage area that can be referenced by two or more program units that use COMMON statements. This is useful in programs with several subprograms that reference the same set of variables. There are two kinds of COMMON statements: blank (unlabeled) COMMON and named (labeled) COMMON. First we discuss the blank COMMON statement.

The **blank COMMON statement** has the general form

> **COMMON** *list of names*

where the *list of names* refers to variable names, array names, and array declarators, all separated by commas. The blank COMMON statement causes the compiler to establish an area of storage that is to be "shared in common" by all program modules using blank COMMON statements.

EXAMPLE 9.3   Mean of One-Dimensional Array Using a Blank COMMON Statement

The following is a rewrite of Example 9.2 on page 343. Note that the only differences are the elimination of argument lists, the insertion of two COMMON statements, and the use of a constant array declarator for the dummy array X, as shown in the shaded portions.

```
C----------------------------------------------------------
C   MEAN TEST SCORE PROGRAM (BLANK COMMON VERSION)
C
C   KEY:
C     ARRSIZ = MAXIMUM ARRAY SIZE (500)
C     AVE    = AVERAGE TEST SCORE
C     N      = NUMBER OF TEST SCORES
C     SCORE  = ONE-DIMENSIONAL ARRAY OF SCORES
C----------------------------------------------------------
      INTEGER N,ARRSIZ
      REAL    SCORE(500),AVE
C----------------------------------------------------------
      COMMON N,SCORE,AVE
C----------------------------------------------------------
      DATA    ARRSIZ/500/
C----------------------------------------------------------
      READ, N
C----------------------------------------------------------
      IF (N .GT. ARRSIZ) THEN
        PRINT, 'TOO MANY SCORES.   MAX =',ARRSIZ
        PRINT, 'PROGRAM TERMINATED.'
        STOP
      ELSE
        READ, (SCORE(J),J = 1,N)
        CALL MEAN
        PRINT, 'MEAN SCORE =',AVE           <----
      END IF                                         > Note elimination
C----------------------------------------------------------        of argument lists
      STOP
      END
C========================
      SUBROUTINE MEAN
C========================
C
C   THIS SUBROUTINE CALCULATES THE MEAN OF A REAL VECTOR
C
C   KEY:
C     N    = NUMBER OF ITEMS IN VECTOR
C     X    = VECTOR (ONE-DIMENSIONAL ARRAY)
C     XBAR = MEAN OF N ITEMS
C----------------------------------------------------------
      INTEGER N          <----- Must use either constant or
      REAL    X(500),XBAR,SUM      generalized array declarator
C----------------------------------------------------------
      COMMON N,X,XBAR
C----------------------------------------------------------
      SUM = 0.0
      DO 10 J = 1,N
        SUM = SUM + X(J)
   10 CONTINUE
C----------------------------------------------------------
      XBAR = SUM/N
C----------------------------------------------------------
      RETURN
      END
```

Conceptually, the memory for this program can be visualized as illustrated in Figure 9.4. The COMMON statement allocates 502 cells to the **blank common block.** Each program unit that includes a blank COMMON statement can use or alter any of the values stored in this blank common block. Note that the storage locations for J and ARRSIZ in the main program are *local* to the main program; the storage locations for J and SUM in the subroutine are local to the subroutine.

Here are some additional points concerning the use of blank COMMON statements.

1.   The association in a common block is by relative position rather than by name. This means that it is the order of names in COMMON statements that determines which variable names or array element names are associated among program units (as is the case with argument lists). In looking at the two COMMON statements in the example and at Figure 9.4, we see that N in the main program and N in the subroutine refer to the same storage location, as do SCORE(1) and X(1), SCORE(2) and X(2), and so on.

2.   Corresponding names among COMMON statements should be consistent with respect to type; that is, you should pair integer with integer, real with real, character with character, and so on.

3.   It should be noted that the COMMON statement is a nonexecutable statement that serves to declare certain information about storage, and hence must appear in the program before instructions that use common storage. *The COMMON statement must precede all DATA and executable statements in the program module.*

4.   The list of names in the COMMON statement can include array declarations. For example, in the main program of Example 9.3 we could have written

instead of

```
REAL      SCORE(500),AVE
COMMON N,SCORE,AVE
```

Similarly, in the subroutine we could have written

instead of

```
REAL      X(500),XBAR,SUM
COMMON N,X,XBAR
```

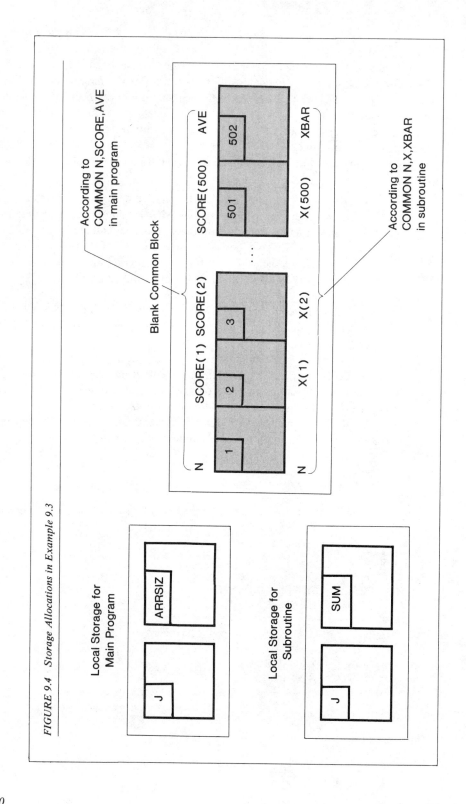

FIGURE 9.4 Storage Allocations in Example 9.3

We might note that *adjustable array declarators are not permitted in COMMON*. For example,

COMMON N, X(N) ,XBAR      Illegal

── Adjustable array declarator illegal
in COMMON statement

would give a syntax error. These array declarators are permitted only in type or DIMENSION statements and only if the array is a *dummy* array, that is, it appears in a dummy argument list. This is why we had to change the array declarator X(N) to X(500), since X no longer appears in a dummy argument list.

5. It's permissible to pass values among program modules by a mixture of argument lists and common blocks. For example, if other program modules were to be added to Example 9.3, each of which uses N and X (or SCORE) but not XBAR (or AVE), then it would make sense to place N and X (or SCORE) in a common block and to pass XBAR (or AVE) through an argument list. Thus in the main program of Example 9.3 we could write

        COMMON N,SCORE
        CALL MEAN(AVE)

and change the subroutine by writing

        SUBROUTINE MEAN(XBAR)
        COMMON N,X

A word of caution: Dummy arguments must not be part of a common block. For example, the following is illegal, since XBAR is both a dummy argument and in the common block.

        SUBROUTINE MEAN(XBAR)   Illegal
        COMMON N,X, XBAR

6. For convenience and efficiency, many programmers prefer the use of COMMON statements to argument lists whenever many of the same names are to be passed among several program modules. Argument lists are thus simplified or entirely eliminated. Note, however, that the inclusion of an array name in a COMMON statement (rather than in a dummy argument list) precludes the declaration of that array through adjustable array declarators.

7. In certain applications, common blocks also can substantially reduce storage requirements. For example, suppose that three program modules within the same executable program each use a very large local array of 100,000 elements. Further assume that these modules do not communicate with one another, and that once a module finishes executing its results need not be used by another module. These arrays thus take up

300,000 locations of local storage (100,000 in each of three local storage areas). If we use COMMON statements to associate these arrays, we can reduce storage requirements by two-thirds to 100,000 locations. Note, however, that in doing so we must make sure that the contents of a previously filled array are not needed once the next associated array starts utilizing the common block.

**8. Consider the following subtle point on how the use of a common block differs from the use of argument lists with respect to methods of storage and data "transfers." When using argument lists, the compiler must supply a special set of instructions in machine code that specifies the correspondence between actual and dummy argument lists. *Each time a subprogram is called, these instructions must be executed.* When using a common block, however, no special instructions are needed for "passing" values, since passing is eliminated due to the direct sharing of storage locations. To put it another way, the use of a common block results in the explicit sharing of storage locations whereas the use of argument lists results in implicit sharing. Thus the use of a common block promotes fewer machine code instructions (which is storage-efficient) and faster execution times (since there are fewer instructions to execute).

COMMON *Statement: Named* Common Blocks

In some programs the common area may be treated as a single block; in other programs the programmer may wish to subdivide the common area into smaller blocks, where each block has a name. We can accomplish this by using the following form of the COMMON statement.

COMMON	/	*name of* *common block*	/	*list of* *names*	/	*name of* *common block*	/	*list of . . .* *names*

The block name is formed in the same way as a variable name; however no type is associated with the common name. For example, the statement

```
COMMON/BLOCK1/A,B,C/BLOCK2/D,E
```

sets up two **named common blocks,** as illustrated below.

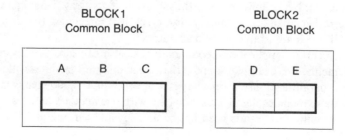

EXAMPLE 9.4   Named Common Blocks Illustration

```
C------------------------------------------------
C    NAMED COMMON BLOCKS EXAMPLE
C
C------------------------------------------------
      INTEGER A,B,C,D,E,F,G,H
C
      COMMON F,G,H
      COMMON /BLOCK1/A,B,C
      COMMON /BLOCK2/D,E
C
      READ,F,G,H,A,B,C,D,E
C
      CALL ONE
      CALL TWO
C
      STOP
      END
C=================
      SUBROUTINE ONE
C=================
      INTEGER A,B,C,F,G,H
C
      COMMON F,G,H
      COMMON /BLOCK1/A,B,C
C
      PRINT, 'SUBROUTINE ONE'
      PRINT, '  BLANK COMMON',F,G,H
      PRINT, '  BLOCK1      ',A,B,C
C
      RETURN
      END
C=================
      SUBROUTINE TWO
C=================
      INTEGER D,E,F,G,H
C
      COMMON F,G,H
      COMMON /BLOCK2/D,E
C
      PRINT, 'SUBROUTINE TWO'
      PRINT, '  BLANK COMMON',F,G,H
      PRINT, '  BLOCK2      ',D,E
C
      RETURN
      END
```

Input

```
5,10,15,20,25,30,35,40
```

Output

```
SUBROUTINE ONE
  BLANK COMMON      5       10      15
  BLOCK1           20       25      30
SUBROUTINE TWO
  BLANK COMMON      5       10      15
  BLOCK2           35       40
```

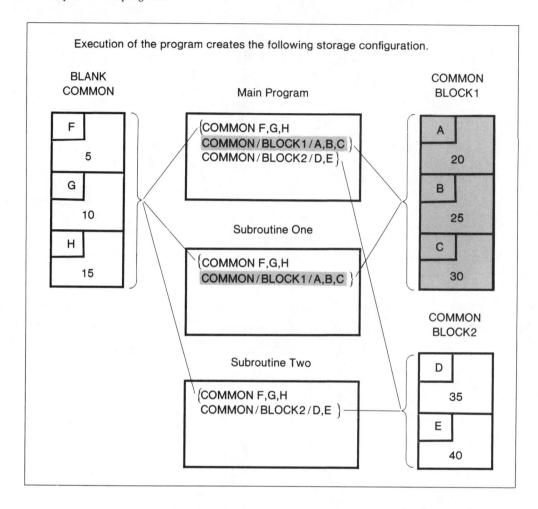

Execution of the program creates the following storage configuration.

Here are some additional points to consider regarding named common blocks.

1. Named common blocks are preferred to a blank common block when there are several program units, a few of which have a need to share data that are of no concern to other program units.

2. Note that references to the same *named* common block among different program modules must be consistent with respect to the size of the block, but references to a *blank* common block may imply different block sizes, as the following examples illustrate.

Main Program	Subprogram	Comment
COMMON /BLOCKA/A,B,C	COMMON /BLOCKA/D,E,F	Size consistency; three storage locations each
COMMON /BLOCKB/X,Y,Z	COMMON /BLOCKB/R,S	Not permitted, since first specifies three locations and second specifies two locations
COMMON M,N,A(500)	COMMON K,L,B(300)	Permitted in blank common; K with M, L with N, B(1) with A(1), . . . , B(300) with A(300); A(301) to A(500) are defined but not used by subprogram

Follow-up Exercises

16. If the statement

    PRINT,D,E

    were added to SUBROUTINE ONE in Example 9.4, what would happen?

17. Is it feasible to eliminate argument lists in Example 9.1 on page 329 by using COMMON statements? Explain.

18. Given the following program

    ```
    INTEGER X,A
    COMMON X(2),A
    X(1) = 10
    X(2) = 20
    A = 5
    CALL SUB
    PRINT, X(1),X(2),A
    END

    SUBROUTINE SUB
    INTEGER Y,B
    COMMON Y(2),B
    B = Y(1) + Y(2) + B
    RETURN
    END
    ```

    a. Schematically represent the blank common block and show how contents change as the program executes.
    b. Specify the output.

c. Indicate what happens if we use

COMMON B,Y(2)

in the subroutine.

19. For each of the following, identify what is wrong, if anything (assume implicit typing).

Calling Program	Subprogram
a. COMMON M,N,Y(1),Q	COMMON R,J,P,K
b. COMMON L,S(50),T	COMMON K,R(30)A
c. COMMON A,B,C	COMMON D,E

First subprogram (D,E,F are to be paired with A,B,C)

Calling Program	Subprogram
d. COMMON A,B,C,I,J	COMMON D,E,F
	COMMON M,N

Second subprogram (M,N are to be paired with I,J)

Calling Program	Subprogram
e. COMMON M,N,A(500,20)	COMMON M,N,A(500,20)
f. COMMON /B2/X(1000)	COMMON /B2/A(800)
*****g.** COMMON A,B,C CALL SUB(A)	SUBROUTINE SUB(R) COMMON S,T,U
**h. CHARACTER C*50 COMMON N,B(1000),C CALL SUB	SUBROUTINE SUB CHARACTER C*20 COMMON N,B(N),C DATA C/'TRUE'/

*20. Solve Exercise 13 using COMMON statements.
*21. Solve Exercise 14 using COMMON statements.
**22. Solve Exercise 15 using COMMON statements.

EQUIVALENCE Statement**

The COMMON statement specifies that storage locations are to be shared by items (variable names, array names, etc.) *in different program units.* If we wish items *within the same program unit* to share storage locations, then we can use

---

EQUIVALENCE (*list of associated names*) , (*list of associated names*) , . . .

---

where each list of associated names (variables, arrays, etc.) enclosed within the same parentheses shares the same memory locations.

** Can be skipped without loss of continuity.

For example, suppose that in a large program a programmer accidentally uses the variables LARGE and BIG for the same quantity. Instead of changing one of the names, the following EQUIVALENCE statement could be inserted.

    EQUIVALENCE(LARGE,BIG)

This results in the following storage configuration.

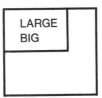

Whenever LARGE or BIG is referenced the same memory location is accessed.
    Note the following points.

1. The EQUIVALENCE statement specifies that the storage sequence of the associated names in the list is to have the same *first* storage location. For example, the statements

    REAL A(5),B(5),C(3), D(5),E(4),F(100000),G(100000)
    EQUIVALENCE (A(1),B(1)),(C(2),D,E(3)),(F,G)

result in the following storage configuration for the list (A(1),B(1)).

1	2	3	4	5
A(1)	A(2)	A(3)	A(4)	A(5)
B(1)	B(2)	B(3)	B(4)	B(5)

A(1) and B(1) share or reference the first storage location in the sequence. The relationships between A(2) and B(2), etc., are automatically equivalenced since array names imply a sequence of adjacent storage locations. Thus five locations instead of ten are needed.

For the list (C(2), D, E(3)) we have

1	2	3	4	5	6	7
E(1)	E(2)	E(3)	E(4)			
	C(1)	C(2)	C(3)			
		D(1)	D(2)	D(3)	D(4)	D(5)

E(2) and C(1) share; E(3), C(2), and D(1) share; E(4), C(3), and D(2) share. Seven instead of 12 locations used, so five locations saved.

For the list (F, G) we have

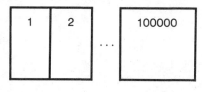

F and G totally share corresponding elements. One hundred thousand instead of 200,000 locations used, so 100,000 locations saved.

F(1)   F(2)   ···   F(100000)
G(1)   G(2)   ···   G(100000)

2.   Arrays C, D, and E are said to be *partially associated* whereas arrays A and B, and F and H, are *totally associated*.

3.   Names of type character can be equivalenced only with other names of type character. For example, the statements

        CHARACTER A*10,B*6
        EQUIVALENCE (A,B)

     equivalence the first six (of ten) *character storage units* in A with the six character storage units in B.

4.   The EQUIVALENCE statement is nonexcutable, but must precede executable statements in the program unit.

5.   Dummy arguments must not be equivalenced.

6.   Two names in one common block or in two different common blocks must not be equivalenced.

7.   Names having different numeric type may be equivalenced, but it's not suggested in practice as it may lead to unpredictable logic errors, depending on the hardware.

8.   Associations in the list of an EQUIVALENCE statement apply only within the program unit where the EQUIVALENCE statement resides, unless one of the equivalenced names is part of a common block (see Exercise 23f).

The primary justification for using EQUIVALENCE statements is that they can substantially reduce storage requirements. This is particularly desirable when several large arrays are used in one program, as illustrated by the 100,000 storage locations saved by equivalencing arrays F and G in the above example. Assuming that F and G have different meanings and purposes within the program unit, the act of equivalencing them is feasible only if we're through with one of the arrays before we begin manipulating the other. Otherwise logic errors may result.

Unless storage is critical, we don't recommend the use of EQUIVALENCE statements, as they reduce program readability and increase the likelihood of syntax, execution, and logic errors.

Follow-up Exercise

23. Specify storage configurations for each part, given the following type statements.

```
CHARACTER A*4,B*4,C(2)*3
INTEGER    D,E(5),F(4),G(5)
REAL       X(8),Y(6)
DOUBLE PRECISION Z (Note: A double-precision variable name takes up two adja-
                          cent storage locations.)
```

   a. EQUIVALENCE (E(1),G,F(4),D,E)
   b. EQUIVALENCE (A,D)
   c. EQUIVALENCE (Y(5),Z)
   d. EQUIVALENCE (X(8),Y(6))
   e. EQUIVALENCE (A,C(1)),(B,C(2))
**f. COMMON /ONE/D,E(5)
       EQUIVALENCE (E(4),F)

9.3
FUNCTION SUBPROGRAMS*

A **function subprogram** is another type of subprogram that looks very much like a subroutine. Unlike a subroutine, however, it is called in the manner of a library function such as SQRT, and returns a single value to the calling program.

EXAMPLE 9.5   Combinations Using Function Subprogram

The following program is a rewrite of the program in Example 9.1 on page 329, with the subroutine replaced by a function subprogram. Key differences between this version and the original version are shaded in. Make note of these differences and then read on.

```
C-------------- ----- --------------------------------------------
C    MAIN PROGRAM--CALCULATES AND PRINTS COMBINATIONS GIVEN N,K
C                  BY REPEATEDLY CALLING FUNCTION FACTOR
C
C    KEY:
C      N      = AS IN FORMULA
C      K      = AS IN FORMULA
C      FACTOR = FACTORIAL FUNCTION          Function name replaces
C      COMB   = COMBINATIONS                NFAC, NKFAC, KFAC
C------------------------------------------------------------------
       INTEGER N,K,FACTOR,COMB
C------------------------------------------------------------------
       READ, N,K
       WHILE (N .GE. K .AND. N .GT. 0 .AND. K .GE. 0)
```

---

* This section may be skipped without loss of continuity.

```
       C
       C                                                    ←————————  CALL statements
       C                                                                eliminated
             COMB = FACTOR(N)/(FACTOR(N-K)*FACTOR(K))  ←————————Function
             PRINT, 'N =',N,'K =',K,'COMBINATIONS =',COMB          references
             READ, N,K
             END WHILE
       C------------------------------------------------------
             STOP
             END
       C==========================                         Function statement
             FUNCTION FACTOR (NUMBER)  ←————————————————  replaces subroutine
       C==========================                         statement
       C
       C    FUNCTION FACTOR--CALCULATES THE FACTORIAL OF A NUMBER
       C                     GIVEN THE NUMBER
       C
       C    KEY:
       C        NUMBER = NUMBER WHOSE FACTORIAL IS TO BE CALCULATED
       C        FACTOR = FACTORIAL OF NUMBER
       C------------------------------------------------------
             INTEGER NUMBER, FACTOR  ←
       C------------------------------------------------------        Function name
             FACTOR = 1                                               replaces FAC
             IF(NUMBER .GE. 2)—THEN
               DO 10 J=2,NUMBER
                 FACTOR = FACTOR*J
        10     CONTINUE
             END IF
       C------------------------------------------------------
             RETURN
             END
```

Sample Input

```
5,2
10,4
5,0
0,0
```

Sample Output

```
N =          5  K =          2   COMBINATIONS =          10
N =         10  K =          4   COMBINATIONS =         210
N =          5  K =          0   COMBINATIONS =           1
```

Calling the Function Subprogram

A function subprogram is executed by referencing the function through another program termed the **calling program.** Any reference to a function in a calling program transfers control to the function subprogram. The **function reference** (or **call**) consists of the *function name* followed by the actual argument list enclosed in parentheses. Functions are named and typed in the same manner as variables. **Actual arguments** are usually names and expressions whose values are transferred to the function subprogram from the calling program and are treated the same as in subroutine calls.

In all cases the function subprogram is called by using its name and actual arguments in an expression. In Example 9.5 the assignment statement

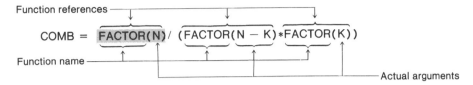

contains three function references to the function subprogram called FACTOR. The reference FACTOR(N) passes the value in N (5 for the first set of test data above) to the function subprogram. The subprogram then returns the value of the factorial (120 in this case) to the point of call. The other two references work in the same manner, as illustrated in Figure 9.5.

Note that the function name FACTOR is typed integer in the main program. It's a good programming practice to type explicitly all function names by using type statements (REAL, CHARACTER, etc.) in the calling program.

You should further note the fact that the mechanics of function subprogram references are essentially the same as references to statement functions (Section 9.4) or to library functions such as MAX and LOG. This type of reference is said to be *implicit,* as opposed to the *explicit* reference of a subroutine through a CALL statement.

In general, the calling program can be the main program, another function subprogram, or a subroutine. Also, a function subprogram can call other subprograms, but may not call itself.

Structure of the Function Subprogram

A function subprogram has the following general structure:

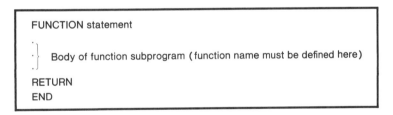

The function subprogram always begins with a function statement having the following general form.

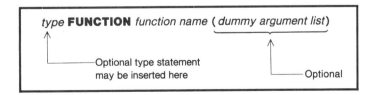

Naming the function subprogram follows the same rules as naming variables. This means that the first letter in the *function name* implicitly determines the type of the function (real

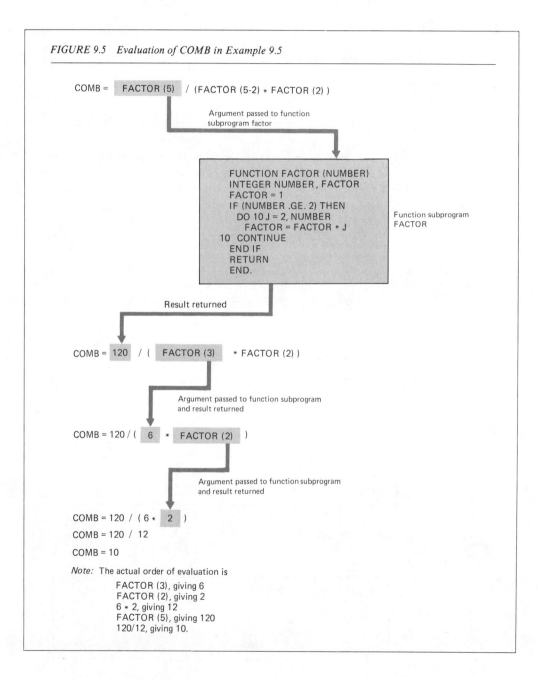

FIGURE 9.5   Evaluation of COMB in Example 9.5

or integer). As usual, however, we strongly recommend explicit typing by using a type statement such as CHARACTER, LOGICAL, INTEGER, REAL, or DOUBLE PRECISION. The **dummy argument list** is used in the same manner as subroutines, that is, when the function is called actual arguments are associated with corresponding dummy arguments. In Example 9.5 the statement

    FUNCTION FACTOR(NUMBER)

identifies the beginning of a function subprogram called FACTOR and NUMBER is a dummy argument.

    The body of the function subprogram follows the function statement and precedes the RETURN statement. In general, the body can include any statement except a SUBROUTINE or FUNCTION statement.

    When the function is called by the reference FACTOR(N), the dummy argument, NUMBER assumes the value in the actual argument N (5 in the first line of input data) and the body is executed.

    Within the body the name of the function must be defined (assigned a value), since the function name is the vehicle by which the result is transmitted back to the calling program. Normally this is accomplished by placing the function name on the left side of an assignment statement, as illustrated by

    FACTOR = 1

and

    FACTOR = FACTOR*J

in Example 9.5. The appearance of the name of the function, FACTOR, to the left of an equal sign ensures that the value of the function is returned to the calling program once a RETURN statement is executed, Thus, when the RETURN statement is executed in the function subprogram in Example 9.5, the value 120 in FACTOR is returned as the function value for the reference FACTOR(N) in the calling program (when 5 is in N).

Additional Considerations

1. Note that a function subprogram returns a *single* result to the calling program through the name of the function itself, unlike a subroutine that returns one or more results through the argument list.

2. If only a single result is needed from a subprogram, many programmers prefer to use a function subprogram rather than a subroutine. The program in Example 9.5, for example, is "cleaner" than the program in Example 9.1. If multiple results are needed, however, a subroutine is used.

3. Example 9.5 illustrates one argument, but as in the use of subroutines, we can pass multiple values to function subprograms in the argument lists.

4. As in subroutines, a change in the value of a dummy argument within the body of the function subprogram has corresponding effects on actual arguments. As a matter of style, a function subprogram should never be designed to change the value of a dummy argument, as this obscures the intended effect of a function—namely, to return a single result through the function name.

5. Don't forget to specify the type of the function, both in the calling program and in the subprogram. In the subprogram, we have a choice as to how we explicitly type the function. Either we can use a type statement in the body (as in Example 9.5) or we can insert the type statement in front of the keyword FUNCTION in the FUNCTION statement. For example, we could have written

```
INTEGER FUNCTION FACTOR(NUMBER)
INTEGER NUMBER
```

in place of

```
FUNCTION FACTOR(NUMBER)
INTEGER NUMBER,FACTOR
```

in Example 9.5.

6. The treatment of all other issues discussed under subroutines is the same in function subprograms as in subroutines. For example, there are no differences with respect to independent compilation, the treatment of actual and dummy arguments, use of RETURN statements, specification of flowcharts and pseudocode, the passing of arrays, or the use of common blocks.

Follow-up Exercises

24. Modify Figure 9.2 on page 340 and Figure 9.3 on page 341 to reflect the program in Example 9.4.

25. Solve the following using function subprograms in place of subroutines.
    a. Exercise 7 on page 342.
    *b. Exercise 8 on page 342.

26. Modify Example 9.2 on page 343 to use a function subprogram in place of the subroutine. Also, use adjustable dimensions in the function subprogram.

27. Is it possible to solve Exercise 11 on page 347 using a function subprogram? If so, is it recommended?

28. Modify Example 9.3 on page 348 to use a function subprogram in place of the subroutine. Can you use adjustable dimensions in this function subprogram?

29. Specify output for the program below, given the following input: 5, 10, 7, 15, 2, 4.

```
        INTEGER N,A(500),MAXVAL
        READ, N,(A(J),J = 1,N)
        PRINT, MAXVAL(N,A)
        STOP
        END

        FUNCTION MAXVAL(N,A)
        INTEGER N,A(N),MAXVAL
        MAXVAL = -9999999
        DO 50 J = 1,N
          MAXVAL = MAX0(MAXVAL,A(J))
     50 CONTINUE
        RETURN
        END
```

30. Design function subprograms to
    a. Round a real value to the nearest integer.
    b. Return the maximum of two real values.
*31. Design two versions of a real function called MINMAX that returns either the minimum or maximum value in an N-element one-dimensional array A, given that the calling program passes N,A, and either the character constant 'MIN' or 'MAX.'
    a. In the first version, use the type of logic illustrated in Exercise 29.
    b. In the second version, use the function subprogram to call subroutine SORT (see Exercise 13 on page 347).

9.4 STATEMENT FUNCTIONS

Subroutines and functions are the most commonly used subprograms. Another type of subprogram is the statement function. The statement function is a subprogram where the computations are specified in a single statement and placed within the calling program; otherwise, a statement function is similar to library or function subprograms with respect to how it is referenced and used. Example 9.6 illustrates the use of a statement function.

EXAMPLE 9.6 Exponential Statement Function

```
C-------------------------------------------------------------
C    EXPONENTIAL DECAY PROGRAM
C
C    KEY:
C      FIXED  = ACTUAL ARGUMENT PAIRED WITH DUMMY ARGUMENT A
C      DECAY  = ACTUAL ARGUMENT PAIRED WITH DUMMY ARGUMENT B
C      TIME   = ACTUAL ARGUMENT PAIRED WITH DUMMY ARGUMENT T
C      TLIMIT = UPPER LIMIT ON TIME
C      EXPO   = FUNCTION NAME
C      RESULT = PRINTED VALUE OF FUNCTION
C-------------------------------------------------------------
      INTEGER T,TIME,TLIMIT                          Dummy argument list
      REAL    FIXED,DECAY,A,B,EXPO,RESULT
C-------------------------------------------------------------
      EXPO(A,B,T) = A*B**T                           Statement function
C-------------------------------------------------------------
      READ, FIXED,DECAY,TLIMIT
      PRINT, '            TIME           RESULT'
      PRINT, '-----------------------------------'
C-------------------------------------------------------------
      DO 10 TIME=1,TLIMIT                            Function reference
        RESULT = EXPO(FIXED,DECAY,TIME)
        PRINT, TIME,RESULT
   10 CONTINUE                                       Actual argument list
C-------------------------------------------------------------
      PRINT, '-----------------------------------'
      STOP
      END
```

Input

50.0,0.8,5

Output

TIME	RESULT
1	40.0000000
2	31.9999800
3	25.5999900
4	20.4799900
5	16.3839800

This example illustrates a **statement function statement** or **statement function** of the general form

> function name (dummy argument list) = expression

where the *function name* is a symbolic name in FORTRAN, the **dummy argument list** is a list of variable names that are used in the expression to the right of the equal sign, and the *expression* is a legitimate FORTRAN expression (integer, real, character, etc.).

In our illustration, EXPO is the function name, A,B,T is the dummy argument list, and A*B**T is the expression. EXPO is typed real and represents an exponential function as given by the following algebraic representation.

$$f(x) = a \cdot b^t$$

The statement function statement thus defines a function that is to be used or referenced at one or more locations within the program. In our simple example, EXPO is referenced five times at its single location within the body of the DO-loop. In general, a function is referenced by using its **function reference** given by

> function name (actual argument list)

in an expression. For example, the function reference in Example 9.6 is

    EXPO(FIXED,DECAY,TIME)

When this function reference is executed, the following actions are taken.

a. The **actual argument list** is associated with the dummy argument list according to

        A   B   T   ←Dummy argument list
        ↑   ↑   ↑
      FIXED DECAY TIME   ←Actual argument list

Remember that based on the input data, FIXED stores 50.0, DECAY stores 0.8, and TIME successively stores 1, 2, ... , 5.

b. The first evaluation of the expression A*B**T uses 50.0 for A, 0.8 for B, and 1 for T.

c. The value of the expression is returned to the point where the function was referenced. In this case the value returned for EXPO at the first function reference is 40.0, which is then stored in RESULT.

d. In our example, the actions described by a–c above are repeated a total of five times, since the function is referenced each time the loop iterates.

When using statement functions, keep the following points in mind.

1. The statement function statement is not an executable statement; it is a declarative statement and must follow type statements and precede executable statements.

2. It's a good idea to type the name of a statement function, as done in our example.

3. Dummy arguments are *local* to the statement function statement (that is, have no meaning or effect anywhere else in the program) whereas actual arguments must be defined (have values) at points in the program that precede the function reference. For example, FIXED, DECAY, and TIME must be defined before each function reference.

4. Actual arguments must agree in order, number, and type with corresponding dummy arguments. For example, if the dummy argument list has five integer variables, then the actual argument list must have five integer arguments; if the dummy argument list consists of an integer variable followed by a real variable, then the actual argument list must have an integer argument followed by a real argument. *Note that dummy arguments must be variables but actual arguments can include expressions.*

5. Statement functions are useful or convenient when a particular function would otherwise recur at several different points in the program. Under these circumstances, their use can save code and improve the style of programs, as illustrated in Example 9.7.

EXAMPLE 9.7   Statement Function with Multiple References/Locations

The root bisection program in Section 6.5 on page 216 is a good illustration of the proper use of statement functions for saving code and improving program style. Below we reproduce the relevant portions of this program. Item 1 on page 218 explains the use of this function. You really need not understand the reasoning behind the logical expressions that reference this function. Instead, just focus on the advantages of using the statement function for multiple references in different locations within the program—and try solving Exercise 34.

```
125 C-------------------------------------------------------------
130 C    ROOT BISECTION PROGRAM
131 C        .
132 C        .
133 C        .
210 C------------------------------------------------------------
215        F(X) = -1.0 + 2.0*X
220 C------------------------------------------------------------
225        LOOP
230 C
235          READ, LEFT,RIGHT,ERROR
240           AT END, QUIT
245 C
250          INLEFT = LEFT
255          INRITE = RIGHT
260 C
265          IF ( F(LEFT)*F(RIGHT) .GT. 0.0 ) THEN
266 C          .
267 C          .
268 C          .
355          MID  = (LEFT + RIGHT)/2.0
360          HALF = ABS(RIGHT - MID)
365          IT   = 1
370 C
375 C
380            WHILE (HALF .GE. ERROR .AND. F(MID) .NE. 0.0)
385 C
390             IF ( F(MID)*F(RIGHT) .GT. 0.0 ) THEN
391 C             .
392 C             .
393 C             .
495            IF ( F(MID) .EQ. 0.0) THEN
500              PRINT, 'EXACT ROOT        =',MID
505            ELSE
510              PRINT, 'ESTIMATED ROOT  =',MID
515              PRINT, 'MAXIMUM ERROR   =',HALF
520            END IF
521 C        .
522 C        .
523 C        .
560        STOP
565        END
```

Statement function

Multiple (six) references to statement function

Follow-up Exercises

32. Specify a statement function to convert Fahrenheit to Celsius temperatures. (See Example 2.11 on page 55.)

33. Specify a statement function to evaluate any polynomial function up to the third degree, as given by the following:

$$f(x) = b_0 + b_1X + b_2X^2 + b_3X^3$$

34. Rewrite relevant portions of Example 9.7 as follows.
  a. Use a function subprogram instead of a function statement.
  b. Use a subroutine instead of a function statement.
  c. Don't use a subprogram at all.
  Compare these alternatives to the use of the statement function with respect to coding efficiency and programming style.

9.5
MODULAR PROGRAMMING

Subroutines and function subprograms are convenient vehicles for dividing programs into groups of related instructions called **modules.** This style of programming is called **modular programming,** and we fully discuss and illustrate it in Module F. If you have the stamina, it would be best that you study Module F at this time since the topic is strongly related to this chapter. Moreover, Module F describes a complete scenario that makes extensive use of subroutines and illustrates **nested subprograms** or the call of one subprogram by another.

9.6
COMMON ERRORS

Certain errors regarding subprograms seem to occur more commonly than others. Make note of these.

1. **Forgetting END or RETURN.** Don't forget the END statement following the main program and RETURN and END for each subprogram or a syntax error may result. Many beginning programmers figure they only need one END statement at the very end of the last subprogram. Not so. Since the main program and each subprogram are treated as independent program units, the END statement at the end of each program unit signals the compiler that the current program unit is over.

2. **Type of a function.** Logic and/or mixed type errors can result if you forget that the first letter of a function name implicitly determines the type of the value returned by that function. The best approach is to explicitly type the function name, as we have done with all other names. By the way, *don't forget to define the function name within the body of the function subprogram.*

3. **Mismatches in argument lists.** Pay close attention to the number, order, and type of actual and dummy arguments lists. In many cases, mismatches may not result in syntax or execution error messages. Instead, you may get unpredictable results (wrong answers) that are system dependent, as the following chart illustrates. (Assume that type is determined implicitly.)

Actual Argument	Corresponding Dummy Argument	Comment
IN	ON	Inconsistent mode.
X	J	Inconsistent mode.
2	COST	Inconsistent mode.
2.0	COST	OK, as long as the value of COST is not changed within the subprogram.
COST	2.0	Not allowed. Dummy arguments must be names.
M	N	OK, but if the subprogram redefines the value of N, then M changes accordingly. If you're not aware of this, you've committed a logic error.
A(3)	B(1)	OK when A and B are declared arrays.
A(3)	C	OK when A is declared an array.
6*K + 3	JOB	OK, as long as the value in JOB is not changed within the subprogram.

4. **Dummy argument pitfalls.** Take care in defining and using dummy arguments. For example, you get a syntax error if a dummy argument is used in a DATA, EQUIVALENCE, or COMMON statement. More insidiously, you commit execution and/or logic errors if you *unintentionally* define a dummy argument within the body of a subprogram. In particular, an execution error occurs if the corresponding actual argument is a constant or expression. If the corresponding actual argument is a name, remember that its contents are changed whenever the dummy argument is assigned a value.

5. **Common block pitfalls.** Use COMMON statements consistently across program units to avoid readability and error problems. For example, match array names with array names and take care that their sizes correspond. If global names must be used, try to use the same names in each program unit *so that COMMON statements across program units are duplicates of one another.* This avoids difficult-to-detect errors, such as misspelling a name or violating positional correspondence. When changing a COMMON statement in one program unit, take care that corresponding changes are made in all program units using the same common block.

6. **Mismatch in size between actual array and corresponding dummy array.** Reread item 3 on page 344. Consider the following program.

```
      REAL X(5)
      DO 10 J = 1,5
        X(J) = J
 10   CONTINUE
      CALL TRY(X)
      END

      SUBROUTINE TRY(A)
      REAL A(10)
      PRINT,(A(J),J = 1,5)
      RETURN
      END
```

In this case the size of the dummy array A (ten elements) exceeds the size of the actual array X (five elements). We ran this program and got the following execution error message when subroutine TRY was called: DECLARED SIZE OF ARRAY A EXCEEDS SPACE PROVIDED BY CALLING ARGUMENT. To be safe, specify the same sizes for actual and dummy arrays. Better yet, use either adjustable or generalized array declarators.

7. **Array declaration pitfalls.**   Don't forget to type and declare arrays in both the calling program and the subprogram. Remember to match array sizes either (a) by using identical constant array declarators or (b) by using generalized or adjustable array declarators. In the latter case, remember that they apply only to *dummy* arrays within subprograms. This means that adjustable declarators can't be used either to declare *actual* arrays or to declare arrays through the COMMON statement. When working with adjustable dimensions, don't forget that the variables that make up the adjustable dimensions must be passed from the calling program to the subprogram through either argument lists or COMMON statements.

ADDITIONAL EXERCISES

35. Define or explain the following

subprogram
main program
program units
program modules
subroutine subprogram
subroutine
calling program
CALL statement
actual argument list
SUBROUTINE statement
dummy argument list
RETURN statement
predefined process symbol
adjustable array declarator
adjustable dimensions

constant array declarator
generalized array declarator
pseudovariable dimensioning
COMMON statement
blank common block
named common block
EQUIVALENCE statement
function subprogram
function reference (call)
FUNCTION statement
statement function
modular programming
modules
nested subprograms

36. **Revisit.**   Modify a program in a previous chapter by using modular programming concepts. You might design modules as follows:
   a. A main program calls all modules.
   b. One module reads and edits the input data.
   c. Another module performs calculations.
   d. Another module outputs results.

37. **Electric Bill.**   Gotham City Electric Company wishes to redesign the computerized bills that it sends to commercial and residential customers. It has announced a city-wide contest to determine the best algorithm/FORTRAN program for this purpose.

a. Provided data *include the following.*

Initialization data

1. Month (three letters) and day (two digits) for beginning date of monthly billing cycle
2. Month and day for ending date of monthly billing cycle
3. Year (two digits)

Customer data

4. Previous meter reading in kilowatthours (up to seven digits)
5. New meter reading in kilowatthours
6. Customer rate code (one digit)
7. Past due amount (dollars and cents)
8. Payment since last bill (dollars and cents)
9. Name of customer (up to 20 characters)
10. Street address of customer (up to 20 characters)
11. City, state, and ZIP (up to 24 characters)
12. Account number of customer (up to eight digits)

Use the following sample data for the computer run.

	Billing Cycle	
From	To	Year
SEP 19	OCT 18	1981

Use the following sample data per customer.

Previous Reading	New Reading	Rate Code	Past Due Amount	Payment	Name	Street Address	City, State, Zip	Account Number
27648	28648	1	60.10	60.10	make these up			....
42615	45115	2	45.20	0.00	make these up			....
314625	354625	3	3110.00	3110.00	make these up			....
615700	695700	3	8000.00	8000.00	make these up			....
800500	1025500	3	3000.00	1000.00	make these up			....

Rate codes and their corresponding rates per kilowatthour (kWh) are explained by the following table.

Rate Code	Rate Per kWh(cents)	Comment
1	5.25	Residential, partly electric home
2	4.85	Residential, all electric home
3	8.50	Commercial, usage under 50,000 kWh
3	7.50	Commercial, usage between 50,000 kWh and 100,000 kWh
3	6.50	Commercial, usage above 100,000 kWh

If past due amount less payment is above zero, then a 1 percent per month charge on this difference is added to the customer's bill. For example, the last customer in the input data is commercial and used 225,000 kWh (1,025,500 − 800,500). Thus the customer is charged at 6.5 cents per kWh, which amounts to a current bill of $14,625.00. This customer, however, has a $3000 past due account and payments of only $1000. At an interest rate of 1 percent per month, the interest charge is $20, that is, (3000 − 1000) × 0.01; hence the total now due from this customer is $16,645.00, that is, 2000 + 20 + 14,625.

Output from your program should include the following.

1. Name of customer
2. Street address of customer
3. City, state, and ZIP
4. Account number
5. Billing cycle: from (month, day) to (month, day, year)
6. Kilowatthours
7. Current amount owed
8. Past due amount
9. Interest charge
10. Total amount due

Label your output and design it to fit within a 3- by 5-inch image, since these statements must fit in a standard size envelope.

b. Include error detection to ensure that the rate code is 1, 2, or 3 and the new meter reading is greater than the previous meter reading. If an error is encountered, print an appropriate error message that includes the customer's name, complete address, and account number; bypass the calculations and printout for this customer; space down to the next statement; and go on to the next customer. Add new data to test each of the possible input errors.

Use a modular design for your program. By the way, the winner of the contest gets to ride the Batmobile, which recently was retrofitted with an all-electric power plant.

38. Statistical Analysis Program. Large programs that give options for various statistical analyses are common in commercial applications. For example, IBM's STATPACK, UCLA's BMD, North Carolina State's SAS, and the University of Chicago's SPSS are all widely used packages for implementing a variety of statistical analyses across many disciplines.

a. *Measures of central tendency and dispersion.* Design and write a modular program that calculates and prints the statistics described below for analyzing a set of n data items given by $x_1, x_2, \ldots, x_n$. In the descriptions below, assume the following set of values for x: 7, 14, 10, 6, 3.

1. *Mean,* given by

$$\bar{x} = \frac{x_1 + x_2 + \cdots + x_n}{n} = \frac{\sum\limits_{i=1}^{n} x_i}{n} = \frac{40}{5} = 8$$

2. *Median,* a value such that one-half of the values are above it and one-half of the values are below it. First sort the data in ascending order, and then

find the *position* of the median using the formula $(n + 1)/2$. For example, if the sorted values of x are

3   6   7   10   14

————————————————— Location of median

then the median is found in position $(5 + 1)/2$, or third position. Thus the median is 7. If n is an even number, however, the median is defined as halfway between the two adjacent positions in the center. For example, in the six-item sequence

3   6   7   10   14   16

————————————————— Location of median in position $\dfrac{6 + 1}{2}$

the median is in position 3.5, or midway between the third item (7) and the fourth item (10). Thus the median is 8.5.

3. Minimum value of x, or 3 for the given data.
4. Maximum value of x, or 14 for the given data.
5. *Range*, the difference between max x and min x, or 11 for the given data.
6. *Mean absolute deviation (MAD)*, given by

$$MAD = \frac{\sum_{i=1}^{n} \left| x_i - \bar{x} \right|}{n} = \frac{16}{5} = 3.2$$

7. *Variance*, given by

$$s^2 = \frac{\sum_{i=1}^{n} (x_i - \bar{x})^2}{n - 1} = \frac{70}{4} = 17.5$$

8. *Standard deviation*, given by

$$s = \sqrt{s^2} = \sqrt{17.5} = 4.1833$$

b. *Frequency distribution.*   Add a second option to the program to print a frequency distribution. Let the user specify two suboptions here: (1) Enter number of classes and upper class limits, or (2) just enter number of classes and let the computer determine class limits. For example, in the first suboption we might want to group the data into four classes with upper limits 5, 10, and 15 for the first three classes.

In this case, the frequency distribution is given by

Class Limits	Frequency
Under 5	1
5 but under 10	2
10 but under 15	2
15 or above	0
	5

Thus, of the five data items, one was under 5, two were at least 5 but under 10, two were in the range 10 but under 15, and none were 15 or above. In the second suboption, a four-class frequency distribution would be given by

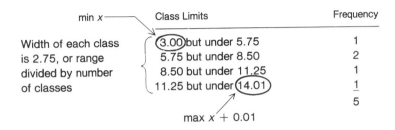

min x	Class Limits	Frequency
Width of each class is 2.75, or range divided by number of classes	3.00 but under 5.75	1
	5.75 but under 8.50	2
	8.50 but under 11.25	1
	11.25 but under 14.01	1
		5

max x + 0.01

c. *Bar chart.* Add a third option that prints a bar chart, as illustrated for the second frequency distribution in part b.

```
CLASS +              FREQUENCIES
-------------------------------------------------
 1 + *  1
 2 + **2
 3 + *  1
 4 + *  1
```

****d.** *Histogram.* Instead of the bar chart in part c, print a histogram as follows:

```
                    2
        1          ***        1          1
       ***         ***       ***        ***
       -------------------------------------------
       5.75       8.50      11.25      14.01
```

CHAPTER 10

Operations on Character Data

In earlier chapters we liberally used character constants, variables, and arrays to store, test, and print character data such as names, addresses, and descriptions. Simple character processing of the type we have described is used routinely in practice but is not suggestive of more sophisticated manipulative requirements in such applications as text editing, text analysis, linguistics analysis, and the encoding/decoding of secret messages. In this chapter, following a review of character-related terminology and statements, we describe how WATFIV can be used to manipulate character data.

10.1
REVIEW

A **character datum** or **character string** or simply **string** is a sequence of characters, including any blank characters. The **length** of a string is the number of characters in the string.

The form of a **character constant** is an apostrophe followed by a nonempty string followed by an apostrophe. The *value* of the character constant is the string. Thus 'I LOVE

FORTRAN!' is a character constant with a value given by the string I LOVE FORTRAN!, which has a length of 15 characters. Remember that an apostrophe within a string is represented as two successive apostrophes within the character constant. Thus 'I DON''T LOVE FORTRAN!' is a character constant having the value I DON'T LOVE FORTRAN!, with length 21 characters. *The length of a character constant must be greater than zero.*

The **CHARACTER statement** is used to type symbolic names that are to store character values, and to declare the length of stored strings. Its general form is

CHARACTER [∗*dl*] *item* [∗*dl*] [, *item* [∗*dl*]] . . .

where we use brackets to denote optional portions and where *dl* represents the **declared length** expressed as an unsigned, nonzero integer constant, and *item* is a variable name, or an array name, or an array declarator, or a function name.[1]

If the length is declared just after the keyword CHARACTER, then each item in the list without its own declared length assumes this length. If the length is not declared just after the keyword CHARACTER, then each item in the list without its own declared length assumes a length of 1. For example, the statements

```
CHARACTER A*10,B,C*80(100)
CHARACTER*20 D,E*10,F,G(80)
```

specify that the names A, B, C, D, E, F, and G store character strings, where A and E store strings of length 10, B stores one character, each element in the 100-element vector C stores 80 characters, D and F each store 20 characters and each element in the 80-element array G stores 20 characters.

We can use DATA statements to *initialize* character variables. For example, the statements

```
CHARACTER  TITLE*20
DATA   TITLE/'ENGINEERING REPORT'/
```

define the following storage.

```
                    T I T L E
       1  2  3  4  5  6  7  8  9  10  11 12 13  14  15  16  17  18  19  20
     | E | N | G | I | N | E | E | R | I | N | G |   | R | E | P | O | R | T |   |   |
```

Note that TITLE has a declared length of 20 characters and the character constant 'ENGINEERING REPORT' has a length of 18 characters. Thus the last two character positions in storage are "padded" with blanks.

---

[1] This list also includes a dummy procedure name, that is, a dummy argument that corresponds to the name of a procedure such as a function subprogram.

We can also read a character value into a **character variable name.** Thus the segment

```
CHARACTER ITEM*15
      .
      .
      .
DO 50 J = 1,N
    READ, ITEM
      .
      .
      .
 50  CONTINUE
```

results in the following storage sequence for the given input records.

J   Input Record   Value in ITEM

1 'BARBIE DOLL'

1	2	3	4	5	6	7	8	9	10	11	12	13	14	15
B	A	R	B	I	E		D	O	L	L				

2 'POCKET MICROPROCESSOR'

1	2	3	4	5	6	7	8	9	10	11	12	13	14	15
P	O	C	K	E	T		M	I	C	R	O	P	R	O

Declared length in CHARACTER statement

In the above example, note the following.

1. Character strings on input records processed by *list-directed* input statements must be enclosed in apostrophes. Apostrophes are not used if processing is by *format-directed* input (as described in Modules B and C).
2. We have numbered the 15 *character positions* within the *storage location* identified by ITEM to get you to focus on individual characters within a string and to realize that these positions are numbered sequentially (are adjacent to one another). However, ITEM is not an array.
3. If the length of the input string is less than the declared length of the character variable, then the rightmost unused character positions in storage are "padded" with blanks, as illustrated when J = 1.
4. If the length of the input string is greater than the declared length of the character variable, then the input string is "truncated" on the right before storage occurs, as illustrated when J = 2.

Character array names store a string for each array element, where each array element (location) stores the number of character positions defined by the declared length. For example, if the one-dimensional array DAY is to store the names of days in the week, then the statements

```
CHARACTER*9 DAY(7)
DATA DAY/'MONDAY', 'TUESDAY', 'WEDNESDAY', 'THURSDAY',
+           'FRIDAY', 'SATURDAY', 'SUNDAY'/
```

store as follows:

	1	2	3	4	5	6	7	8	9
DAY(1)	M	O	N	D	A	Y			
DAY(2)	T	U	E	S	D	A	Y		
DAY(3)	W	E	D	N	E	S	D	A	Y
DAY(4)	T	H	U	R	S	D	A	Y	
DAY(5)	F	R	I	D	A	Y			
DAY(6)	S	A	T	U	R	D	A	Y	
DAY(7)	S	U	N	D	A	Y			

Recall that DAY(3), for example, is called a **character array element name;** it references the third element in array DAY.

Character function names are symbolic names that store character values defined in either *statement functions* (Section 9.4) or *function subprograms* (Section 9.3).

A **character expression** expresses a character string and has one of the following forms.

1. A character constant
2. A character variable name
3. A character array element name
4. A character function name

For example, if ANS is a variable typed character, then the block IF statement

    IF (ANS .EQ. 'YES') THEN

illustrates a logical expression that compares two simple character expressions. The character expression to the left of the relational operator is the character variable ANS; the character expression to the right is the character constant 'YES'. We illustrate more complicated character expressions in the next two sections.

A **character assignment statement** has the following general form

$$\boxed{v = \textit{character expression}}$$

where v is the name of a character variable or character array element. For example, the following illustrates character assignment statements and the resulting storage.

CHARACTER∗9 DAYOFF,DAY(7),ANS∗5

.
.
.

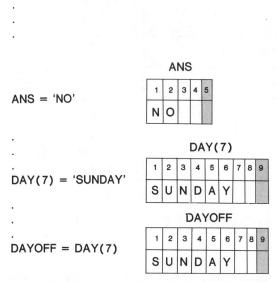

ANS

ANS = 'NO'

1	2	3	4	5
N	O			

DAY(7)

DAY(7) = 'SUNDAY'

1	2	3	4	5	6	7	8	9
S	U	N	D	A	Y			

DAYOFF

DAYOFF = DAY(7)

1	2	3	4	5	6	7	8	9
S	U	N	D	A	Y			

Finally, keep in mind that the blank character takes up a character position in the internal representation of a string. In particular, note how blank characters are placed into the rightmost unused positions in storage. For example, when the 11-character string BARBIE DOLL is input into the 15-character variable ITEM (page 378), the rightmost four positions within ITEM each stores a blank character; when the six-character string SUNDAY is assigned to the nine-character array element DAY(7), positions 7 through 9 store blanks. *The computer pads blanks into the string before the string is placed in the memory location. It accomplishes this by increasing the length of the string with as many blanks as necessary to make the length of the string equal to the declared length of the name.*

This blank-padding procedure also has implications when strings within logical expressions are being compared. For example, if ANS has a declared length of 5 and stores

ANS

1	2	3	4	5
Y	E	S		

then the logical expression

ANS .EQ. 'YES'

has the value true, since the character constant 'YES' is converted to 'YESƀƀ' before the logical expression is evaluated.

That ends a somewhat lengthy, but reasonably complete, review of character-related topics scattered throughout the text. In the next several sections we show, among other things, WATFIV's capability to replace or remove part of a string, insert a string within a string, search a string for the occurrence of another string, and compare strings.

10.2
TWO COMMON FUNCTIONS

Text-editing programs are widely used to create, modify, and print textual material such as letters, notices, computer programs, articles, manuscripts, and books. These programs involve the manipulation of character data. FORTRAN 77 has special functions and commands to manipulate character data. In WATFIV, however, these functions and commands are not available. Thus it's necessary to develop function or subroutine subprograms to accomplish these tasks.

Preliminaries

The usual approach to manipulating character data starts with the storage of a line of text (assume 80 characters) in a one-dimensional character array with 80 array elements, where *each array element stores one character*. For example, we can store the character string

I LOVE FORTRAN

in an 80-element, one-dimensional array named TEXT as

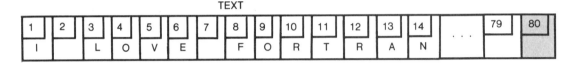

where TEXT is declared by

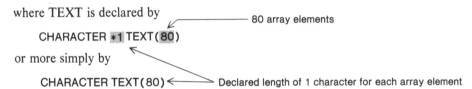

or more simply by

CHARACTER TEXT(80) ← Declared length of 1 character for each array element

Again, notice that each element in TEXT stores a single character. Also, notice that it's useful to visualize TEXT as a "line of text" on a page that fits 80 characters per line.

The most convenient way of storing a line of text utilizes READ/FORMAT statements. Thus, for the example above, we would use

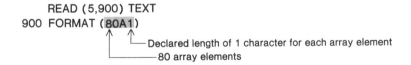

and the input data line

I LOVE FORTRAN

LENGTH Function

One basic operation with character data is to determine the **length** (number of characters) of a character string. One approach is to end each string with a special character that indicates the end of the string. Such a character is called a **delimiter.** For example, a slash (/) might act as a delimiter in the following string

In this case, the slash is in position 15, which indicates a string length of 14. The function subprogram LENGTH in Example 10.1 determines the length of any string stored in an array, where the slash acts as a delimiter.

EXAMPLE 10.1   Function LENGTH

First you should study the pseudocode for function LENGTH, then try to roleplay the input / output through the program.

```
Start Main Program to test LENGTH
    Initialize maximum length to 80
    READ line of text
    Determine length of text (LENGTH function)
    PRINT LENGTH
End Main Program

Start LENGTH Function
    Initialize slash and found flag
    DO-loop while pointer ≤ maximum length of text
       IF text (pointer) = slash THEN
          LENGTH = pointer − 1
          Found = 'yes'
       END IF
    End DO-loop
    IF slash not found THEN
       PRINT error message
    END IF
    RETURN
End LENGTH function
```

```
C-----------------------------------------------------------------
C       PROGRAM TO TEST FUNCTION LENGTH
C
C       KEY:
C          TEXT   = ARRAY CONTAINING STRING
C          LEN    = LENGTH OF STRING
C          MAXLEN = MAXIMUM LENGTH OF STRING
C-----------------------------------------------------------------
        CHARACTER * 1 TEXT(80)
        INTEGER       LEN,LENGTH,MAXLEN  ←———— Type declaration
C-----------------------------------------------------------------
        DATA  MAXLEN/80/
C-----------------------------------------------------------------
        READ(5,90) TEXT
```

```
          LEN   = LENGTH(TEXT,MAXLEN) <─────── Function call
          PRINT, 'LENGTH = ',LEN
          STOP
C-------------------------------------------------------------------
   90 FORMAT(80A1) <─────── Note use of (80A1) format specification for input
C-------------------------------------------------------------------
          END
C-------------------------------------------------------------------
C-------------------------------------------------------------------
          FUNCTION LENGTH(LINE,MAXLEN)
C
C     RETURNS LENGTH OF STRING
C
C     KEY:
C        LINE   = ARRAY CONTAINING STRING
C        MAXLEN = MAXIMUM LENGTH OF STRING
C        FOUND  = FLAG (YES=DELIMITER FOUND; NO= DELIMITER NOT FOUND)
C        LENGTH = NUMBER OF CHARACTERS IN STRING
C-------------------------------------------------------------------
          CHARACTER * 1 LINE(1),SLASH
          CHARACTER * 3 FOUND
          INTEGER       MAXLEN, LENGTH
C-------------------------------------------------------------------
          DATA          SLASH/'/'/
C-------------------------------------------------------------------
          FOUND = 'NO'
C-------------------------------------------------------------------
          DO 10 J=1,MAXLEN
             IF (LINE(J) .EQ. SLASH) THEN
                LENGTH = J - 1 <─────── Length is one less
                FOUND = 'YES'                  than position of slash
             END IF
   10 CONTINUE
C-------------------------------------------------------------------
          IF (FOUND .EQ. 'NO') THEN
             PRINT, 'END OF STRING MARK NOT FOUND'
             PRINT, 'STRING IMAGE : ',LINE
             STOP
          END IF
C-------------------------------------------------------------------
          RETURN
          END
```

Input	Output
I LOVE FORTRAN/	LENGTH = 14

In this example, the input string is 14 characters, so function LENGTH returns a value of 14. Note that the DO-loop searches array LINE character by character, where the DO-variable J is a *pointer* that indicates the current character position in the string. If a slash is found, then LENGTH is set to one less than the value of J. If no slash is found, then an error message is printed.

Follow-up Exercises

1. Indicate the output from function LENGTH for each input string below. Roleplay computer (especially in DO-loop 10) to get your answer.
   a. BIG APPLE!/
   b. I LOVE FORTRAN$
   c. /
   d. VELOCITY = DISTANCE/TIME/
2. Suppose the calling program in Example 10.1 were to read in TEXT as follows:

   READ, TEXT

   How should the input data appear? Tedious, isn't it?
3. Write a calling program that inputs 50 lines of text through a DO-loop and prints the average length of a line. Utilize function LENGTH in Example 10.1.

INDEX Function

A portion of a string is called a substring. A **substring** can be a single character, a group of characters, a word, a phrase, or an entire string. For example, LOVE, FORTRAN, LO, I, TRAN, and I LOVE are all illustrations of substrings within the string

   I LOVE FORTRAN

The program in Example 10.2 illustrates the function INDEX, which searches the specified *string* for the occurrence of a given *substring*. If the string contains the substring, INDEX returns an integer value corresponding to the character position where the substring begins. If the substring is not found within the string, INDEX returns a value of zero. If the substring appears more than once, INDEX returns the starting position of the *leftmost* substring. This function, for example, can be used to find specific characters within words, specific words within sentences, and specific phrases within text.

EXAMPLE 10.2   Function INDEX

```
Start Main Program to test INDEX
    Initialize maximum length to 80
    READ string
    READ substring
    Calculate length of string (LENGTH function)
    Calculate length of substring (LENGTH function)
    Find starting position of substring (INDEX function)
    PRINT string
    PRINT substring
    IF substring found THEN
        PRINT index
    ELSE
        PRINT error message
    END IF
End Main Program

Start LENGTH function
    ↓   (As in Example 10.1)
End LENGTH function

Start INDEX function
    DO-loop to scan string character by character
        Initialize counter
        LOOP
          Increment counter
        UNTIL counter reaches substring length
              or
              substring character different from string character
        IF counter = length of substring
           and
           substring character same as string character THEN
                    Set INDEX to starting position of substring
                    RETURN
        END IF
    End DO-loop
    Set INDEX = 0 since substring not found
    RETURN
End INDEX function
```

```
122 C--------------------------------------------------------
125 C       PROGRAM TO TEST FUNCTION INDEX
130 C
135 C       KEY:
140 C         STRING = ARRAY CONTAINING STRING
145 C         SUBSTR = ARRAY CONTAINING SUBSTRING
150 C         LENSTR = LENGTH  OF STRING
155 C         LENSUB = LENGTH OF SUBSTRING
160 C         MAXLEN = MAXIMUM LENGTH OF STRING
165 C         IND    = STARTING POSITION OF SUBSTRING WITHIN STRING
170 C         LENGTH = LENGTH FUNCTION
175 C         INDEX  = INDEX FUNCTION
180 C--------------------------------------------------------
185         CHARACTER * 1 STRING(80),SUBSTR(80)
190         INTEGER    LENSTR,LENSUB,IND,MAXLEN,INDEX,LENGTH
195 C--------------------------------------------------------
200         DATA      MAXLEN/80/
205 C--------------------------------------------------------
210         READ 90, STRING
215         READ 90, SUBSTR
220 C
225         LENSTR = LENGTH(STRING,MAXLEN)
230         LENSUB = LENGTH(SUBSTR,MAXLEN)
235 C
240         IND  = INDEX(STRING,SUBSTR,LENSTR,LENSUB)   <──── Function call
245 C
250         PRINT 91, (STRING(J),J=1,LENSTR)
255         PRINT 92, (SUBSTR(J),J=1,LENSUB)
260 C
265         IF (IND .GT. 0) THEN
270           PRINT 93, IND
275         ELSE
280           PRINT 94
285         END IF
290 C
295         STOP
300 C--------------------------------------------------------
305      90 FORMAT(80A1)
310      91 FORMAT(' STRING IS          :',80A1)
315      92 FORMAT(' SUBSTRING IS       :',80A1)
320      93 FORMAT(' BEGINS IN POSITION :',I2)
325      94 FORMAT(' SUBSTRING NOT FOUND')
330 C--------------------------------------------------------
335         END
340 C--------------------------------------------------------
345 C--------------------------------------------------------
350         FUNCTION LENGTH(LINE,MAXLEN)


                        (As in Example 10.1)


510         END
515 C--------------------------------------------------------
```

```
520 C------------------------------------------------------------
525       FUNCTION INDEX(STRING,SUBSTR,LENSTR,LENSUB)
530 C
535 C     RETURNS STARTING POSITION OF SUBSTRING WITHIN STRING
540 C     (OR ZERO IF SUBSTRING NOT PRESENT)
545 C
550 C     KEY:
555 C        STRING = ARRAY CONTAINING STRING
560 C        SUBSTR = ARRAY CONTAINING SUBSTRING
565 C        LENSTR = LENGTH OF STRING
570 C        LENSUB = LENGTH OF SUBSTRING
575 C        INDEX  = STARTING POSITION OF SUBSTRING WITHIN STRING
580 C------------------------------------------------------------
585       CHARACTER * 1 SUBSTR(1),STRING(1)
590       INTEGER       LENSTR,LENSUB, INDEX
595 C------------------------------------------------------------
600       N = LENSTR - LENSUB + 1
605       DO 5 K = 1,N
610 C
615         J = 0
620         LOOP
625           J = J + 1
630         UNTIL ( J .EQ. LENSUB  .OR.  SUBSTR(J) .NE. STRING(K+J-1) )
635 C
640         IF ( J .EQ. LENSUB  .AND.  SUBSTR(J) .EQ. STRING(K+J-1) ) THEN
645           INDEX = K                          Substring found starting
650           RETURN                             in position K
655         END IF
660 C
665    5 CONTINUE
670 C------------------------------------------------------------
675       INDEX = 0                              Substring not found
680       RETURN
685 C------------------------------------------------------------
690       END
```

Input
```
I LOVE FORTRAN/
LOVE/
```

Output
```
STRING IS          :I LOVE FORTRAN
SUBSTRING IS       :LOVE
BEGINS IN POSITION : 3
```

The string I LOVE FORTRAN and substring LOVE are read into STRING and SUBSTR in lines 210–215. Next, the length of each is determined using the LENGTH function in lines 225–230. Then the INDEX function is referenced in line 240 to find the starting position of the substring (3 for our example). Finally, the indicated output is printed by lines 250, 255, and 270.

Within function subprogram INDEX, DO-loop 5 scans STRING from character position 1 (K = 1) until the substring is found. If the substring is not present, then K reaches its terminal value of N (N = 14 − 4 + 1 = 11 in this case), DO-loop 5 is exhausted, and INDEX is set to zero in line 675. Note that we need not scan STRING beyond N since the substring would not fit within the remaining character positions. For example, if the string I LOVE FORTRAN is 14 characters and the substring HATE is 4 characters, and if we haven't found the beginning of the substring by the 11th character (the value in N), then we need not check the 12th through the 14th position since HATE doesn't fit within the last 3 characters in the string.

The UNTIL loop in lines 620–630 looks for the substring match, character by character. Looping continues either until the entire substring is scanned (J reaches LEN-SUB) or until a character mismatch is detected. If a character mismatch is found, then control goes from line 630 to line 640 to line 665; however, if characters match for all values of J (the substring match is found), then J reaches LENSUB, the first relational expression in line 630 tests true, line 640 tests true, and INDEX is set to K in line 645.

If you're reeling from all this good logic, then try roleplaying our computer run by following Table 10.1. Study this table from left to right, row by row as you ''execute'' the program. It's really the best way to understand what's happening.

TABLE 10.1   Roleplay for Example 10.2

STRING	SUBSTR	LENSTR	LENSUB	N	K	J	(K + J − 1)	Test Line 630	Test Line 640	INDEX	Comment
I LOVE FORTRAN	LOVE	14	4	11	1	0					
						1	1	True	False		$L \neq I$
					2	0					
						1	2	True	False		$L \neq \flat$
					3	0					
						1	3	False			$1 \neq 4; L = L$
						2	4	False			$2 \neq 4; 0 = 0$
						3	5	False			$3 \neq 4; V = V$
						4	6	True	True	3	$4 = 4; E = E$

Follow-up Exercises

4. Roleplay the following input data through Example 10.2 according to Table 10.1, and indicate output:
   a. string: MAKE MINE COORS/
      substring: COOR/
   b. string: Where did he go?/
      substring: didhe/
5. What happens in Example 10.2 if the length of the substring is greater than the length of the string?
*6. Design a routine that inputs and scans N lines of text (where array TEXT stores one line at a time) to replace as often as necessary a specific substring of given length (OLD) by another specific substring of the *same length* (NEW). Assume that the substring to be replaced never appears more than once within a single line. For example, we might want to replace HATE with LOVE in a text of 1000 lines.

Print the entire revised text. Also, count and print the number of replacements. If the length of OLD and NEW don't match, print UNEQUAL LENGTHS and stop processing. Just fill in the missing portion below. (*Hint:* Use INDEX to locate OLD, and then insert NEW into TEXT through an assignment statement like TEXT(M) = NEW(K) where K runs from 1 to the length of NEW and M starts at IND.)

```
      CHARACTER*1 TEXT(80),OLD(80),NEW(80)
      INTEGER COUNT,LENGTH,INDEX,LENOLD,LENNEW,LENTXT,IND
      COUNT = 0
      READ(5,900) OLD
      READ(5,900) NEW
      .
      . } ← We leave the "easy" part for you
      .
      PRINT, 'NUMBER REPLACED =', COUNT
  900 FORMAT(80A1)
      STOP
      END
      Function LENGTH
      ↓
      END
      Function INDEX
      ↓
      END
```

*7. Design a routine that inputs lines of text (where array TEXT stores one line at a time) through an LRC loop; scans each line for illegitimate characters; and prints each line of text, where lines with illegitimate characters are preceded by an asterisk. Also, count and print the number of lines having illegitimate characters. Legitimate characters only include the following 71 characters:

    ABC →Zabc → z012 →9ø( ),.'$:;

Just fill in the missing portion below. (*Hint:* Input the legitimate characters into array LEGIT and compare each character in TEXT to all characters in LEGIT. Let L represent the number of legitimate characters in a line. Thus, if L = 80 then the entire line is legitimate; else, the line contains at least one illegitimate character.)

```
      CHARACTER*1 TEXT(80),LEGIT(71)
      INTEGER COUNT, L
      COUNT = 0
      .
      . } ← This is for you
      .
      PRINT,'ILLEGITIMATE LINES = ',COUNT
  900 FORMAT(80A1)
      STOP
      END
```

10.3
TEXT-EDITING ILLUSTRATION

Text editing includes, among other things, the ability to move and change substrings within character strings. This requires input of the original string, the substring to be replaced, and the new substring replacement. For example, suppose TEXT stores the string

> I LOVE FORTRAN

and we wish to change the string to

> I AM CRAZY OVER FORTRAN

The routine below edits TEXT on the basis of the following input:

Original text:	I LOVE FORTRAN /
Substring to be replaced:	LOVE /
Replacement substring:	AM CRAZY OVER /

The text-editing program below inputs data as above, determines string lengths using the LENGTH function, searches for the substring to be replaced using INDEX, and inserts the replacement substring within the string using a new subroutine called INSERT. First you should study the pseudocode, then relate the program to the pseudocode, and finally roleplay the input/output with the help of the discussion.

Pseudocode

```
Start Main Program
    Initialize maximum length to 80
    READ original text
    READ substring to be replaced
    READ replacement substring
    Determine length of strings (LENGTH function)
    IF revised text length exceeds maximum length THEN
        PRINT error message
        STOP
    END IF
    PRINT strings
    Search for substring within original text (INDEX function)
    IF substring found THEN
        Change text (INSERT subroutine)
    ELSE
        PRINT error message
    END IF
End Main Program

Start LENGTH function
↓    (As in Example 10.1)
End  LENGTH function
```

Start INDEX function
↓   (As in Example 10.2)
End   INDEX function

Start INSERT subroutine
    Calculate ending position within text of substring being removed
    Calculate ending position within text of replacement substring
    Calculate number of positions of text remaining after the substring being replaced
    Move remaining text following substring being replaced to temporary location
    Insert replacement substring into text
    Move remaining text back into string immediately following replacement substring
    Calculate revised length of text
    PRINT revised text
    RETURN
End INSERT subroutine

Program

```
125  C-------------------------------------------------------------
130  C      TEXT REPLACEMENT PROGRAM
135  C
140  C      KEY:
145  C        TEXT   = ARRAY CONTAINING ORIGINAL STRING
150  C        OLD    = SUBSTRING BEING REPLACED
155  C        NEW    = REPLACEMENT SUBSTRING
160  C        MAXLEN = MAXIMUM LENGTH OF STRING
165  C        LENTXT = LENGTH OF ORIGINAL STRING
170  C        LENOLD = LENGTH OF SUBSTRING BEING REPLACED
175  C        LENNEW = LENGTH OF REPLACEMENT SUBSTRING
180  C        IND    = STARTING POSITION OF OLD WITHIN TEXT
185  C        LENGTH = LENGTH FUNCTION
190  C        INDEX  = INDEX FUNCTION
195  C-------------------------------------------------------------
200         CHARACTER * 1 TEXT(80),OLD(80),NEW(80)
205         INTEGER        LENTXT,LENOLD,LENNEW,MAXLEN,IND,LENGTH,INDEX
210  C-------------------------------------------------------------
215         DATA    MAXLEN/80/
220  C-------------------------------------------------------------
225         READ(5,90) TEXT
230         READ(5,90) OLD
235         READ(5,90) NEW
240  C-------------------------------------------------------------
245         LENTXT = LENGTH(TEXT,MAXLEN)
250         LENOLD = LENGTH(OLD,MAXLEN)
255         LENNEW = LENGTH(NEW,MAXLEN)
260  C-------------------------------------------------------------
265         IF (LENTXT + (LENNEW - LENOLD) .GT. MAXLEN) THEN
270            PRINT, 'DECLARED LENGTH OF STRING EXCEEDED'
275            STOP
280         END IF
285  C-------------------------------------------------------------
290         PRINT 91, (TEXT(J),J=1,LENTXT)
295         PRINT 92, ( OLD(J),J=1,LENOLD)
300         PRINT 93, ( NEW(J),J=1,LENNEW)
305  C-------------------------------------------------------------
310         IND = INDEX(TEXT,OLD,LENTXT,LENOLD)
315  C-------------------------------------------------------------
```

```
320         IF (IND .GT. 0) THEN
325            CALL INSERT(TEXT,NEW,OLD,IND,LENTXT,LENOLD,LENNEW)
330         ELSE
335            PRINT, 'OLD STRING NOT FOUND IN TEXT'
340            PRINT, 'OLD STRING WAS : ',( OLD(J),J=1,LENOLD)
345            PRINT, 'TEXT        WAS : ',(TEXT(J),J=1,LENTXT)
350         END IF
355 C-------------------------------------------------------------
360         STOP
365 C-------------------------------------------------------------
370      90 FORMAT(80A1)
375      91 FORMAT(' CURRENT TEXT        :',80A1)
380      92 FORMAT(' REPLACE SUBSTRING   :',80A1)
385      93 FORMAT(' WITH NEW SUBSTRING  :',80A1)
390 C-------------------------------------------------------------
395         END
400 C-------------------------------------------------------------
405 C-------------------------------------------------------------
410         FUNCTION LENGTH(LINE,MAXLEN)

                     (As in Example 10.1)

570         END
575 C---------------------------------------------------------------
580 C---------------------------------------------------------------
585         FUNCTION INDEX(STRING,SUBSTR,LENSTR,LENSUB)
590 C
                     (As in Example 10.2)

750         END
755 C---------------------------------------------------------------
760 C---------------------------------------------------------------
765         SUBROUTINE INSERT(TEXT,NEW,OLD,IND,LENTXT,LENOLD,LENNEW)
770 C
775 C       INSERTS NEW SUBSTRING IN PLACE OF OLD SUBSTRING WITHIN TEXT
780 C
785 C       KEY:
790 C          TEXT   = ARRAY CONTAINING ORIGINAL AND REVISED STRING
795 C          OLD    = SUBSTRING BEING REPLACED
800 C          NEW    = REPLACEMENT SUBSTRING
805 C          IND    = STARTING POSITION OF OLD SUBSTRING IN TEXT
810 C          LENTXT = LENGTH OF ORIGINAL AND REVISED STRING
815 C          LENOLD = LENGTH OF SUBSTRING BEING REPLACED
820 C          LENNEW = LENGTH OF REPLACEMENT SUBSTRING
825 C          TEMP   = TEMPORARY ARRAY
830 C          ENDOLD = ENDING POSITION OF SUBSTRING BEING REMOVED
835 C          ENDNEW = ENDING POSITION OF REPLACEMENT SUBSTRING
840 C          REMAIN = NUMBER OF POSITIONS OF TEXT REMAINING AFTER
845 C                   SUBSTRING BEING REPLACED
850 C-------------------------------------------------------------
855         CHARACTER * 1 TEXT(1),NEW(1),OLD(1),TEMP(80)
860         INTEGER       IND,LENTXT,LENOLD,LENNEW,ENDOLD,ENDNEW,REMAIN
865 C-------------------------------------------------------------
870         ENDOLD = IND + LENOLD - 1
875         ENDNEW = IND + LENNEW - 1
880         REMAIN = LENTXT - ENDOLD
885 C--------------------------------REMAINING TEXT TO TEMP. LOC.---
890         DO 50 J=1,REMAIN
895            TEMP(J) = TEXT(ENDOLD + J)
900      50 CONTINUE
905 C--------------------------------INSERT NEW INTO TEXT-----------
910         DO 60 J=1,LENNEW
915            TEXT(IND -1 + J) = NEW(J)
920      60 CONTINUE
925 C--------------------------------TEMP BACK INTO TEXT-----------
930         DO 70 J=1,REMAIN
935            TEXT(ENDNEW + J) = TEMP(J)
940      70 CONTINUE
```

```
945 C-------------------------------------------------------------
950         LENTXT = LENTXT + (LENNEW - LENOLD)
955         PRINT 90, (TEXT(J),J=1,LENTXT)
960      90 FORMAT(' NEW TEXT              :',80A1)
965 C-------------------------------------------------------------
970         RETURN
975         END
```

Input/Output

The input

```
I LOVE FORTRAN/
LOVE/
AM CRAZY OVER/
```

gives the output

```
CURRENT TEXT          :I LOVE FORTRAN
REPLACE SUBSTRING     :LOVE
WITH NEW SUBSTRING    :AM CRAZY OVER
NEW TEXT              :I AM CRAZY OVER FORTRAN
```

Discussion

To really understand the text replacement program, you must understand each item in Table 10.2. The parenthetic numbers under each variable name and DO-loop refer to lines in the program. First, note the following character positions for each input array, and the length and position values calculated within the main program and subroutine INSERT as shown in Table 10.2.

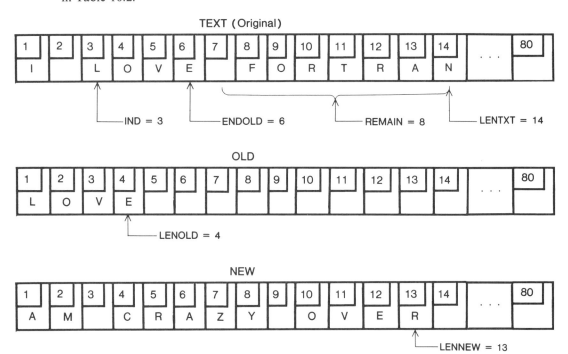

TEXT (Revised)

1	2	3	4	5	6	7	8	9	10	11	12	13	14	15	16	17	18	19	20	21	22	23		80
I		A	M		C	R	A	Z	Y		O	V	E	R		F		O	R	T	R	A	N	

ENDNEW = 15   LENTXT = 23

Finally, relate the execution of DO-loops 50, 60, and 70 to the results in Table 10.2. This should give you a detailed understanding of how we shift and insert textual material.

We might conclude by saying that our text replacement program represents a single text-editing task from among many that would be available in a comprehensive text-editing or word-processing package of the types available commercially. Other tasks include line, paragraph, and page displays; word, line, paragraph, and page inserts and deletes; movement of text within documents stored on disk files; and so on. Can you appreciate why these packages are so expensive?

Follow-up Exercises

8. Roleplay the following changes according to Table 10.2, but first indicate how you would input the substrings OLD and NEW. (Be careful!)

   a. Original TEXT: I AM HAPPY
        Revised TEXT: I AM VERY HAPPY

   b. Original TEXT: I AM HAPPY
        Revised TEXT: I AM HAPPY FOR YOU

   c. Original TEXT: I AM HAPPY
        Revised TEXT: THEY THINK I AM HAPPY

   d. Original TEXT: I AM VERY HAPPY
        Revised TEXT: I AM HAPPY

   e. Original TEXT: I AM HAPPY
        Revised TEXT: I AM

*9. Design a program that deletes OLD from TEXT, as in part d of the preceding exercise. You could just indicate necessary changes to our own sample program.

10.4
COMMON ERRORS

Logic errors are the most common errors in string processing, so it pays to devote special attention to test data selection and output validation during the debugging phase. In particular, take care when using the INDEX function that you account for a returned value of zero. For example, it's best to design an error routine if substring mismatches are possible (see lines 320–350 on page 392).

TABLE 10.2 Roleplay for Text Replacement Run

TEXT (225)	OLD (230)	NEW (235)	LENTXT (245)	LENOLD (250)	LENNEW (255)	IND (310)
I LOVE FORTRAN	LOVE	AM CRAZY OVER	14	4	13	3

ENDOLD (870)	ENDNEW (875)	REMAIN (880)	DO-loop 50 (890–900)	DO-loop 60 (910–920)	DO-loop 70 (930–940)	LENTXT (950)
6	15	8	TEMP(1) = TEXT(7) = b	TEXT(3) = NEW(1) = A	TEXT(16) = TEMP(1) = b	23
			(2) = (8) = F	(4) = (2) = M	(17) = (2) = F	
			(3) = (9) = O	(5) = (3) = b	(18) = (3) = O	
			(4) = (10) = R	(6) = (4) = C	(19) = (4) = R	
			(5) = (11) = T	(7) = (5) = R	(20) = (5) = T	
			(6) = (12) = R	(8) = (6) = A	(21) = (6) = R	
			(7) = (13) = A	(9) = (7) = Z	(22) = (7) = A	
			(8) = (14) = N	(10) = (8) = Y	(23) = (8) = N	
				(11) = (9) = b		
				(12) = (10) = O		
				(13) = (11) = V		
				(14) = (12) = E		
				(15) = (13) = R		

If we expect to find a substring within a string and no match is found, then (assuming the string is correct) it could be due to any one of the following logic errors.

1. The wrong substring is used.
2. The string and substring are reversed in the INDEX function.
3. Declared length instead of string length was used in the INDEX function for the name that contains the substring.

To illustrate all three errors, consider the following memory.

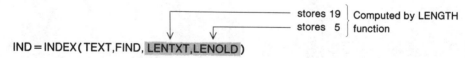

If the user inputs 'NEVAR' when

```
   READ(5,90)FIND
90 FORMAT(80A1)
```

is executed, the first error is committed.

If the programmer uses

        IND = INDEX(FIND,TEXT,LENTXT,LENOLD)

the second error is committed. In this case TEXT is not a substring within FIND, which implies IND = 0. Moreover, LENTXT is greater than LENOLD, which results in either IND = 0 or an execution error (see Exercise 5).

If we were to use

                                    ┌── Declared lengths in CHARACTER statement
      IND = INDEX(TEXT,FIND,50,10)   for TEXT and FIND

instead of

                                    ── stores 19 ┐ Computed by LENGTH
                                    ── stores 5 ┘ function
      IND = INDEX(TEXT,FIND, LENTXT,LENOLD)

then possibly (depending on the system) the third error is committed. In this case the substring is taken to be NEVER/ƀƀƀƀ, which is not present in TEXT.

ADDITIONAL EXERCISES

10. Define or explain the following.

       character datum   string
       character string   length (of a string)

character constant	character function name
CHARACTER statement	character expression
declared length	character assignment statement
character variable name	length (of string)
character array name	delimiter
character array element name	substring

11. **Form Letter Revisited.** Solve Exercise 29 in Chapter 4 on page 137 on the basis of the following additional considerations.

   a. Suppress trailing blanks following the output of names and addresses by using the LENGTH function.

   b. Appropriately use lowercase and uppercase letters (if your system allows it).

   **c. Preliminary to the loop that prints a form letter for each person, input the constant portions of the form letter into either vectors or an array that store each line of the form letter. In this version, PRINT statements don't have character constants in their lists.

The following texts are used as test data by Exercises 12 to 15.

⎡— Column 1

Text 1

Jack and Jill went up the hill
  To fetch a pail of water;
Jack fell down and broke his crown,
  And Jill came tumbling after.

Text 2

   Among other duties, a regional office of the Environmental
Protection Agency (EPA) is charged with investigating complaints
regarding industrial pollution, when "warranted." A complaint is
investigated by sending a panel of three experts, collectively
called the "proboscis patrol," to the site of the alleged offender.
By consensus, the proboscis patrol then renders one of three opin-
ions: low level, medium level, or high level of pollution. (We
might note that the human nose has yet to find an electronic "equal"
in detecting offending odors.) Following an opinion, the regional
director of the EPA then has the option of issuing or not issuing a
citation to the offender. Alternatively, the EPA may choose not to
investigate the complaint and then make a decision regarding issuance
of a citation.

12. **Character Frequency Text Analysis I.**   Write a program that processes *any number* of separate texts and prints the following for *each* text.
    a.   Number of characters
    b.   Number of letters and proportion of characters that are letters
    c.   Number of vowels and proportion of letters that are vowels
  **d.   Number of lowercase letters and proportion of letters that are lowercase
    Process each text one line at a time (maximum line length is 80 characters) and ignore trailing blanks in a line. Process the two given texts in your run.

13. **Character Frequency Text Analysis II.**   Write a program that processes *any number* of separate texts and prints the number and proportion of *each* letter in the alphabet for each text. Make no distinction between lowercase and uppercase letters for purposes of the count. Process each text one line at a time, where the maximum line length is 80 characters. Process the two given texts in your run.

14.   **Word Frequency Text Analysis.   Write a program that processes *any number* of separate texts and prints the following for *each* text.
    a.   Number of words (take care in defining a "word.")
    b.   Number and proportion of words specified by the user (use "the" or "The" and "and" or "And" as test input)
    c.   Number and proportion of words that end in a substring specified by the user (use "ing" as test input)
    d.   Number and proportion of words that begin with a letter (or more generally any substring) specified by the user (use the letters "a" or "A" and "e" or "E" as test input)
    Process each text one line at a time, where the maximum line length is 80 characters. Process the two given texts in your run.

15.   **Keyboard Text Analysis.   A typing textbook contains numerous exercises consisting of paragraphs for students to type. These exercises vary in their level of difficulty according to the following criteria.

    1.   *Number of strokes* in the exercise. A stroke is any keyboard act, such as typing a letter, typing a space, and returning the carriage to the next line (except for the last line in the exercise), and so on.
    2.   *Number of words* in the exercise. Words can include a single letter. For example, the phrase "I love computers" has three words.
    3.   *Average word length* in the exercise. This is defined as the number of strokes divided by the number of words.

    The usual approach to developing these exercises is for someone manually to count strokes, words, and word length for each proposed exercise, to ensure that exercises having various levels of difficulty are selected—a tedious task. This is where you come in. You are to computerize this task.
    Write a program that processes *any number* of separate exercises and outputs each line of the exercise followed by a count of the number of strokes and words for that line. For example, the first two lines of Exercise 1 (Text 1) might be printed as follows:

	STROKES	WORDS
Jack and Jill went up the hill	31	7
To fetch a pail of water;	28	6

At the end of each exercise print summary values for the three criteria discussed earlier. Process each exercise one line at a time, where the maximum line length is 80. Use the two given texts as test data.

**16. Text Processing. Write a program that inputs and stores lines of text (80 characters per line) as a two-dimensional array, and then processes this text as follows.

a. Prints *n* copies of the text, where each copy begins on a new page (*n* is input by the user).

b. Prints no more than *m* lines on a page. If the text exceeds *m* lines, continue printing lines on subsequent pages. Subsequent pages should be numbered at the bottom center. (*m* is input by the user.)

c. Starts text at line *k* of each page, where *k* is input by the user.

**d. Right-justifies text to *max* print characters per line, where *max* is the character position of the line that has the rightmost nonblank character. The program determines *max* by processing each line of text, and then right-justifies text by appropriately placing blank characters in all lines of text whose rightmost nonblank characters are less than *max*. For example, if *max* = 70, a line having its last nonblank character at position 65 needs to have five blanks inserted. The program should select five reasonably spaced words in this line (never the *first* word) and insert a *single* blank in *front* of each. Make sure you don't right-justify the last line in a paragraph. The first line of each paragraph is indented. (Programs that set computerized type for books must handle this feature.)

Use the first five paragraphs of the Preface in this text (ignoring headings) as test data. Use *n* = 3, *m* = 10, and *k* = 20.

17. Cryptography I. Cryptography is the encoding and decoding of messages in secret code, a task well suited for the character processing capabilities of computers. To illustrate a straightforward procedure called "increment coding" consider the following coding scheme for letters.

```
                    |←— increment = 10—→|
Actual letter:   A B C D E F G H I J K L M N O P Q R S T U V W X Y Z
Encoded letter:  K L M N O P Q R S T U V W X Y Z A B C D E F G H I J
```

In this case the encoded letter is obtained by displacing the actual letter by an increment of 10; that is, K is the tenth letter from A, L is the tenth letter from B, and so on. Once an encoded letter reaches the end of the alphabet, the next encoded letter starts at the beginning of the alphabet.

It follows that messages are encoded by using encoded letters in place of actual letters, as illustrated below.

> Actual message: HELP IS ON THE WAY
> Encoded message: ROVZ SC YX DRO GKI

a. Write an encoding program that inputs an actual message and an increment and prints the actual message together with an encoded message.

b. Write a decoding program that inputs an encoded message and outputs the encoded message together with a decoded message. Include the option of not knowing the increment, in which case the program outputs 25 "decoded" messages, or one for each possible increment. In your test runs include the message encoded in part a and the following additional encoded message: A DGNW XGJLJSF.

c. Include the blank character and the ten digits 0 through 9 as part of the character set. Place these 11 additional characters just after the actual letter Z.

18. Cryptography II. Another, more cunning, variation on the increment coding described in Exercise 17 is "keyword" coding, whereby letters in a keyword are used to establish variable increments, as illustrated below.

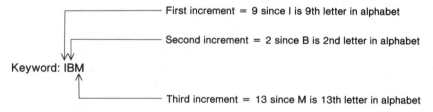

First increment = 9 since I is 9th letter in alphabet

Second increment = 2 since B is 2nd letter in alphabet

Keyword: IBM

Third increment = 13 since M is 13th letter in alphabet

Actual Message	Increment Used	Encoded Message
H	9	Q
E	2	G
L	13	Y
P	9	Y
I	2	K
S	13	F
O	9	X
N	2	P
T	13	G
H	9	Q
E	2	G
W	13	J
A	9	J
Y	2	A

Increments are repeated in sequence as often as necessary.

a. Write an encoding program that inputs a keyword of up to ten characters and an actual message and outputs the actual message together with an encoded message. In your test runs, use the above message and the keywords IBM and DIGITAL.

b. Write a decoding program that inputs an encoded message and keyword and outputs the encoded message together with the decoded message.

External Files

Up until now, we have processed small amounts of input data, either from punched cards or from the terminal, and have printed output data at either the printer or a terminal. Moreover, we physically have represented a file (as described in Module C) by either a set of data cards or a set of data input lines at the terminal.

Many applications, particularly those with large amounts of data, require the processing of files that reside in external or secondary storage on media other than punched cards. For example, customer files for a telephone company are placed on either magnetic disk or magnetic tape for processing by either disk drives or tape drives that are online to the CPU.

This chapter is an introduction to the processing of external files on media such as magnetic tape or magnetic disk.

11.1
FIELDS, RECORDS, AND FILES

Let's first define what we mean by a field, record, and file within our present context.

Field. A data item (fact or attribute) about some entity such as a person, place, thing, or event. For example, an employer might maintain data on employees' name, Social Security number, rate of pay, number of deductions, and other items. Each of these attributes is considered a field.

Record. A collection of related fields grouped together and retrievable as a unit. For example, all of the data items relating to a single employee represent a record.

File. A collection of related records. Each record is a logical part of the file because it contains the same data items as all the other records in the file. For example, an "employee file" contains all employee records.

Figure 11.1 illustrates this relationship among fields, records, and a file. In this case, the file is made up of three records, and each record contains four fields.

11.2
FILES IN FORTRAN

Any file that is used in a FORTRAN program has the following characteristics.

1. The file is either external or internal.
2. The file is either formatted or unformatted.
3. Access to the file is either sequential or direct.

External versus Internal Files

An **external file** is a collection of records stored on an I/O medium such as paper tape, punched cards, cassette, magnetic tape, or magnetic disk. The data are stored on a storage medium external to primary memory, and so the file is called an "external" file.

Punched cards technically can store external files. However, the use of punched cards for large external files is costly, unwieldy, and functionally limited compared with media such as tape and disk. In this chapter we implicitly assume the use of tape or disk as the relevant external storage media.

FIGURE 11.1   Relationship Among Fields, Records, and File

		Fields		
	Name	Employee ID	Salary	Sex
Record 1	ABATAR JANE A.	1	20000	F
File Record 2	BOMBERG BO B.	3	15800	M
Record 3	DRURY DAVID D.	6	18000	M

An **internal file** is a collection of records stored within an area of main memory. Internal files allow the transfer of data among different portions of primary memory for specialized uses that are not considered in this text.

Unformatted versus Formatted Files

An **unformatted file** consists strictly of unformatted records. An **unformatted record** contains data in a form that's identical to the machine's internal representation of data (in binary form). Unformatted records are read or written only by *unformatted* input/output statements, as defined in the next section.

A **formatted file** is made up entirely of formatted records. A **formatted record** contains data in "external" form as characters (numeric, alphabetic, or special). Formatted records are read or written only by *formatted* input/output statements, as defined in the next section.

Unformatted files are processed more rapidly than formatted files because it's not necessary to convert internal/external representations. When the computer inputs a formatted record from an external file into primary memory, it first must convert data from external representation (as stored in the file) to internal representation (as stored within primary memory). Similarly, when the computer writes a formatted record onto an external file, it first must convert data from internal representation to external representation. If the external file is unformatted, however, then there's no need for time-consuming (by computer standards) conversion operations, since all data are represented using the "internal" form.

Unformatted files save storage space on disk and tape, and speed up the processing of data. Unformatted files, however, are processor-dependent. Thus, if a particular file is likely to be used by more than one type of computer, it is then necessary to use formatted files.

Sequential Access versus Direct Access

We can process a file in either of two ways—by sequential access or by direct access. File processing by **sequential access** writes or reads records one after the other in serial or "sequential" fashion. For example, if a personnel file contains 1000 records (employees), sequential processing means that we can read the 900th record if and only if we first read or process the first 899 records.

Figure 11.2a illustrates the file in Figure 11.1 as a file set up for sequential access. The last record in this file is called an **endfile record.** It signals the processor that the physical end of this file has been reached. An endfile record is used only as the *last* record in a *sequential-access file*.

We might note that

1. *All* records in a sequential-access file must be either formatted or unformatted, except for the endfile record.
2. Sequential-access files are processed only by *sequential-access* input/output statements, as described in Section 11.3.

File processing by **direct access** writes or reads a record without the need to process any other record in the file. For example, if there are 1000 records in a direct-access personnel file, we can "directly" read the 900th record without having to read the previous 899 records.

In direct-access files the storage locations are numbered from 1 to n (where n is the maximum number of records in the file). For example, if the direct-access file is to hold 1000

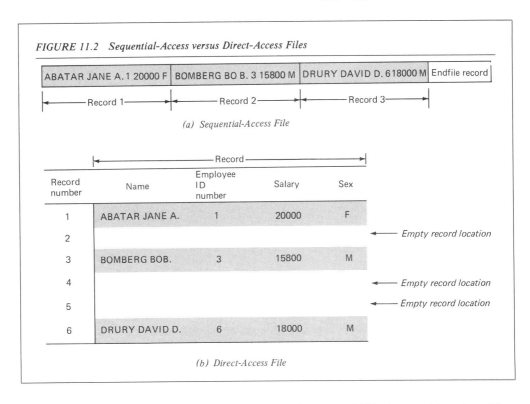

FIGURE 11.2 Sequential-Access versus Direct-Access Files

ABATAR JANE A. 1 20000 F	BOMBERG BO B. 3 15800 M	DRURY DAVID D. 6 18000 M	Endfile record

|←——Record 1——→|←——Record 2——→|←——Record 3——→|

(a) Sequential-Access File

|←—————————————Record—————————————→|

Record number	Name	Employee ID number	Salary	Sex	
1	ABATAR JANE A.	1	20000	F	
2					←—— *Empty record location*
3	BOMBERG BOB.	3	15800	M	
4					←—— *Empty record location*
5					←—— *Empty record location*
6	DRURY DAVID D.	6	18000	M	

(b) Direct-Access File

records, then the record locations on disk use numbers 1 to 1000. A record location either stores a record or is empty (no record currently stored). The storage and retrieval of a record is based on its **record number,** which is a positive integer that uniquely identifies a record.

Figure 11.2b depicts our sample file as a file that is compatible with direct access. You should keep the following points in mind with regard to *direct-access files.*

1. All records must be either formatted or unformatted.
2. All records have the same *length.* For example, all records in a formatted, direct-access file have the same number of characters.
3. Reading and writing of records are accomplished only by *direct-access* input/output statements, as described in Section 11.4.
4. Record numbers are placed on a file when the file is "defined." Once established, a record number cannot be changed.
5. The order of the records is the order of their record numbers; however, records may be read or written in any order. For example, it's permissible to write record 5 without having written records 1 through 4.
6. *List-directed* input/output statements are not permissible for processing direct-access files. (More on this in the next section.)

By the way, files stored on magnetic tape can be processed only by sequential access whereas files stored on magnetic disk can be processed by either sequential access or direct access. In general, the access method allowed depends on both the file medium and the processor. Issues regarding which medium to use and which access method to implement relate to factors such as speed, cost, application, and processing environment. For example, time-shared processing invariably uses magnetic disk and airline reservation inquiry systems process direct-access files.

Follow-up Exercises

1. Briefly describe the possible makeup of records in a "student grade" file for your course. Would you expect this file to be processed by sequential access or by direct access? Would you expect it to be formatted or unformatted?
2. Add G. W. CLARK, ID = 2, salary = 24000, sex = M to both sequential- and direct-access files in Figure 11.2.
3. Is it possible to process a direct-access file sequentially? Why or why not? Is it possible to process a sequential-access file by direct access? Why or why not?

11.3
SEQUENTIAL-ACCESS FILES

In this section we define and illustrate commonly used statements for processing sequential files.

Sequential-Access READ/WRITE Statements

A sequential file first must be defined through the system's control language (your instructor should give you the appropriate control cards). Then the file can be processed by **sequential-access READ/WRITE statements.** The READ statement transfers (copies) a record from a file to primary memory. The WRITE statement transfers data stored in primary memory to a file.

The general forms of these statements are given by

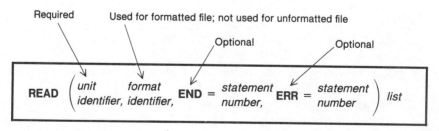

and

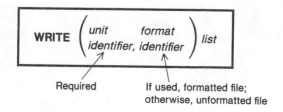

where

1. **Unit identifier** for an external file identifies the specific I/O unit that is to be used (such as tape drive). It must be an integer variable, an integer constant, or a character variable. A value of, say, 10 for a unit identifier might refer to a specific tape drive. The relationship of specific values to specific I/O units is system-dependent, so ask your instructor.
2. **Format identifier** identifies the *format specification* to be used. It can be an integer constant that's the same as the statement label of the FORMAT statement, or an integer variable storing a value that's the same as the statement label of the FORMAT statement, or a character array name that stores the format specification, or a character expression whose value is the format specification, or an asterisk for list-directed formatting. (See Section D.3 if you're "fuzzy" on these terms.) If the format identifier is omitted, the file is unformatted.
3. **END = statement number** is the statement label of an executable statement that appears in the same program unit as this **end-of-file specifier.** Execution of the READ statement terminates, and control is transferred to this statement number whenever the processor encounters an endfile record. This specifier is used only when reading a sequential-access file; it cannot be used either with a direct-access file or within a WRITE statement. If the END = specifier is omitted, then AT END, QUIT should follow the READ statement.
4. **ERR = statement number** is the statement label of an executable statement that appears in the same program unit as this optional **error specifier.** Control is transferred to this statement number whenever an error condition is encountered during the execution of this READ statement.

EXAMPLE 11.1 Formatted Sequential Files

Layout of Each Record

Column	Data Type	Field
1–5	Integer	ID
6–20	Character	Name
21–24	Real	Rate

a. *Read record from tape drive 1*

```
      READ(1,100)ID,NAME,RATE
100 FORMAT(I5,A15,F4.2)
```

    or

```
      UNIT = 1
      READ(UNIT,100)ID,NAME,RATE
```

    or

```
      READ(UNIT,100,END=90,ERR=95)ID,NAME,RATE
```

b.   *Write record to disk drive 3*

          WRITE(3,100)ID,NAME,RATE

   or

          READ,UNIT
          WRITE(UNIT,100)ID,NAME,RATE

   where 3 is input for UNIT.

EXAMPLE 11.2   Unformatted Sequential Files

For purposes of illustration, we assume that three fields make up each record.

a.   *Read data from unit (drive) 10*

          READ(10)X,Y,Z

   or

          UNIT = 10
          READ(UNIT)X,Y,Z

   or

          READ,UNIT
          READ(UNIT,END = 999)X,Y,Z

   where the first read statement inputs the 10 for UNIT.

b.   *Write record to unit 15*

          WRITE(15)X,Y,Z

   or

          DATA UNIT/15/
          WRITE(UNIT)X,Y,Z

END FILE *Statement*

Execution of an END FILE statement places an endfile record as the next record in a *sequential*-access file. The general form of this statement is

$$\boxed{\textbf{END FILE } \textit{unit identifier}}$$

where the *unit identifier* is an integer variable or constant indicating the I/O unit-number associated with disk or tape files.

To illustrate, suppose we have just finished writing an entire sequential file on unit 2. If we wish an endfile record, we should next use

END FILE 2

When a program attempts to read this record, the end-of-file mark indicates that the end of data on the file was reached.

REWIND *Statement*

If we need to process the same *sequential* file more than once during a run, we must start over at the beginning of the file—that is, the file must be rewound. Execution of the REWIND statement repositions the file at its initial point (the first record).

The general form of this statement is

> **REWIND** *unit identifier*

where the *unit identifier* is an integer variable or constant indicating the device number associated with disk or tape files.

On magnetic tape the REWIND statement activates the tape drive to rewind the tape physically. On magnetic disk the REWIND statement repositions the read/write arms of the disk drive to the first record of the file.

To illustrate, suppose we have just finished writing a complete sequential file on unit 10. If we next wish to read all records in the file for the purpose of printing (displaying) its contents, we must first specify that the file is to be rewound by using the statement

REWIND 10

Many programmers also prefer to use REWIND statements at the beginning of programs to ensure that sequential files are properly positioned and at the end of programs to ensure that sequential files are properly repositioned for subsequent use in other runs.

Follow-up Exercises

4. In Example 11.1a what happens in each READ statement if the processor encounters:
   a. An error condition?
   b. An endfile record?
5. Describe the nature of the statement

   WRITE(15)A

6. Construct the following statements:
   a. Rewind a tape on unit 12.
   b. Write an end-of-file record on unit 4.
7. For each part assume unit identifier number 2, and the following record layout:

Column	Field	Type
1–20	Student Name	Character
21–36	Street Address	Character
37–49	City	Character
50–51	State Code	Character
52–56	Zip Code	Integer
57–66	Phone Number	Integer
67–69	Major Code	Character
70–80	Unused	

410   Chapter 11   External Files

a. Construct the appropriate statement(s) to create (write to) a formatted sequential file.

b. How would part "a" differ if the file were an unformatted file?

c. Assume many records are on punched cards in list-directed format. Write a program that inputs all cards and writes the data to a formatted sequential file according to the following pseudocode:

```
Start LRC loop
    READ record from card
    WRITE record to sequential file
End loop
PRINT "file created"
Stop
```

*d. Suppose the given data are in a formatted file on unit 2 and we wish to create a "backup copy" on unit 3. Write FORTRAN code given the following pseudocode:

```
Start LRC loop
    READ record from unit 2
    WRITE record to unit 3
End loop
PRINT "backup complete"
Stop
```

*e. Modify the preceding part so that the message "READ ERROR AT RECORD xxxx" is printed should we encounter an error condition on unit 2.

EXAMPLE 11.3   Sequential-Access Personnel File-Creation/Display Logic

Now that we have the necessary "tools," let's illustrate the creation and display of the formatted sequential-access personnel file in Figure 11.2a on page 405, based on the following record layout.

TABLE 11.1   Record Layout for Personnel File

FIELD DESCRIPTION	SYMBOLIC NAME	TYPE	COLUMNS
Employee name	NAME	Character	1–20
Employee ID	ID	Integer	21–23
Salary (nearest dollar)	SAL	Integer	24–28
Sex code (M or F)	SEX	Character	29

The pseudocode below describes the algorithm.

READ unit identifier from card / terminal

File-creation logic
- Start LRC loop
    - READ record from card / terminal
    - WRITE record to sequential file
- End loop
- Create endfile record

REWIND file

File-display logic
- PRINT header at printer / terminal
- Initialize record count
- Start LRC loop
    - READ record from file
    - Increment record count
    - PRINT record at printer / terminal
- End loop

PRINT message at printer / terminal

Stop

The file-creation logic first inputs a record into primary memory from the card reader or terminal; then the record is transferred from primary memory to the file medium (tape or disk). Finally, after all records have been written to the file, an endfile record is written.

The file-display logic first reads a record from the file and stores this record in primary memory; then this record is transferred from primary memory to printer paper or terminal paper / screen.

Figure 11.3 illustrates the data flows for both file creation and display. Make sure you understand these record transfers. The program on pages 412–413 reflects this pseudocode design. You should note the following.

1. The inputting of values for unit identifier from a card reader or terminal for greater generality.
2. Use of the END FILE statement to place an endfile record on the file.
3. Use of the REWIND statement before the file is displayed, to reinitialize the file to the first record.
4. Use of AT END, QUIT after the READ statement together with LOOP / END LOOP statements, a convenient approach to establishing a last-record-check loop when processing external files.
5. The fact that a record resides in three media. For example, in the file creation portion each record first resides on a punched card (or data line following the program, for those of us using remote batch), then temporarily resides in memory locations (NAME, ID, SAL, SEX), and finally resides "permanently" on tape in the personnel file.

FIGURE 11.3   *Record Transfers to and from Sequential-Access Personnel File*

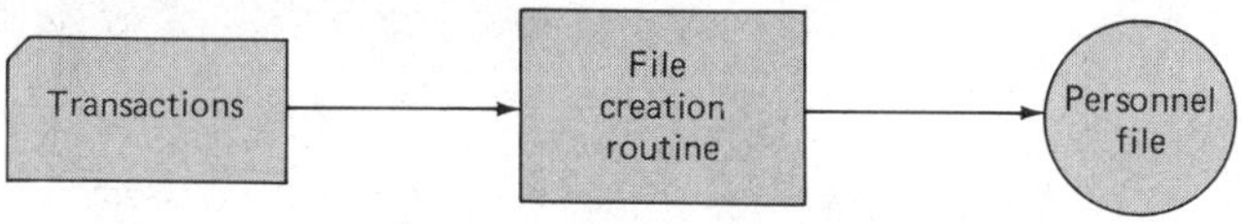

(a) File-creation logic

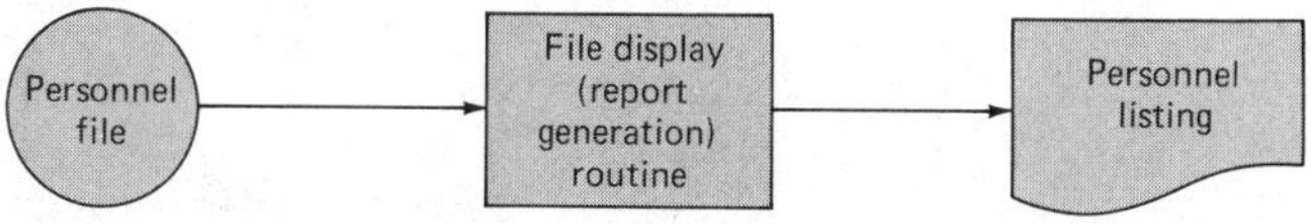

(b) File display logic

Symbol Key

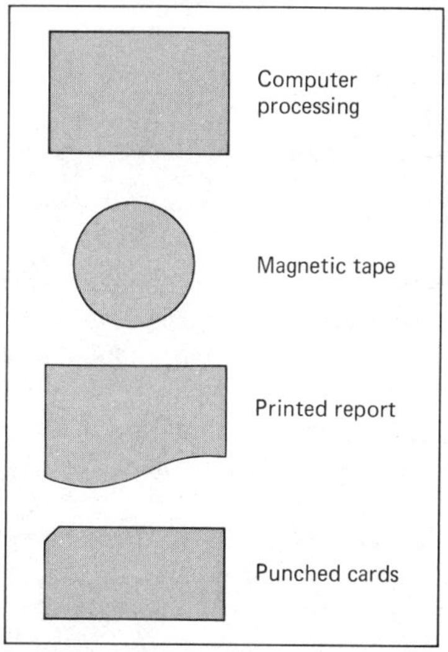

▢	Computer processing
◯	Magnetic tape
▱	Printed report
▭	Punched cards

```
C-- -- -- --- --- -- -- --- -- --- --- -- -- ----- -- --- --- -- --- --- --- --
C      PERSONNEL FILE CREATION/DISPLAY PROGRAM
C
C      FORMATTED SEQUENTIAL-ACCESS FILE
C
C      KEY:
C        NAME   = EMPLOYEE NAME
C        ID     = EMPLOYEE IDENTIFICATION NUMBER
C        SAL    = SALARY
C        SEX    = SEX CODE (M OF F)
C        U      = UNIT IDENTIFIER
C        COUNT  = RECORD COUNT
C
C      RECORD LAYOUT:
C        NAME      TYPE CHARACTER      COLUMNS  1-20
```

```
C        ID         TYPE INTEGER      COLUMNS 21-23
C        SAL        TYPE INTEGER      COLUMNS 24-28
C        SEX        TYPE CHARACTER    COLUMNS 29
C-------------------------------------------------------
      CHARACTER NAME*20,SEX
      INTEGER   ID,SAL,U,COUNT
C-------------------------------------------------------
      READ, U
C-------------------------------------------------------
C  FILE-CREATION LOGIC
C-------------------------------------------------------
      LOOP
        READ, NAME,ID,SAL,SEX
          AT END, QUIT
        WRITE(U,10) NAME,ID,SAL,SEX
      END LOOP
C-------------------------------------------------------
      END FILE U
C
      REWIND U
C-------------------------------------------------------
C  FILE-DISPLAY LOGIC
C-------------------------------------------------------
      PRINT, '        NAME                    ID    SALARY SEX'
      PRINT, '-------------------------------------------------'
C
      COUNT = 0
C
      LOOP
        READ(U,10)NAME,ID,SAL,SEX
          AT END, QUIT
        PRINT ,NAME,ID,SAL,SEX
        COUNT = COUNT + 1
      END LOOP
C-------------------------------------------------------
      PRINT, '-------------------------------------------------'
      PRINT, 'FILE CREATION-DISPLAY TERMINATED'
      PRINT, 'RECORDS PROCESSED =',COUNT
C-------------------------------------------------------
      STOP
C-------------------------------------------------------
  10  FORMAT(A20,I3,I5,A1)
C-------------------------------------------------------
      END
```

Input

```
1
'ABATAR    JANE A.',1,20000,'F'
'BOMBERG   BO B.',3,15800,'M'
'DRURY     DAVID D.',6,18000,'M'
```

Output

```
        NAME                    ID    SALARY SEX
-------------------------------------------------
ABATAR    JANE A.               1      20000  F
BOMBERG   BO B.                 3      15800  M
DRURY     DAVID D.              6      18000  M
-------------------------------------------------
FILE CREATION-DISPLAY TERMINATED
RECORDS PROCESSED =             3
```

Follow-up Exercises

8. With respect to Example 11.3:
    a. What unit identifier did we use in our sample run?
    b. How would you change the program to create/display an unformatted sequential-access file?
9. Modify Example 11.3 to use the END = specifier instead of the AT END, QUIT option. Which approach do you prefer and why?
10. Modify Example 11.3 to print the error message

    ERROR IN FILE READ IN AT RECORD xxxx

*11. Write a program that reads the personnel file and performs an analysis to print the number of females and their average salary and the number of males and their average salary.

11.4
DIRECT-ACCESS FILES

In many cases it's desirable to create direct-access rather than sequential-access files. For example, direct-access files are normally used for "on-line/real-time" systems such as those implemented by airlines to schedule flights and provide flight information and those used by credit card companies to check credit status.

Direct-access files allow us to go directly to the desired record instead of having to search for the record sequentially. These files must be created and processed using direct-access I/O statements, which differ slightly from the sequential-access I/O statements discussed in the previous section.

Define File Statement

The DEFINE FILE statement is used to specify the characteristics of a direct-access file. The general form of this executable statement is

$$\textbf{DEFINE FILE}\ \begin{matrix}unit\\identifier\end{matrix}\ \left(\ number,\ size,\ mode,\ next\ \right)$$

where

1. **Unit identifier** specifies the I/O *disk* device number that is associated with the file. This must be an integer constant.
2. **Number** is the maximum number of records stored on the file. This also must be an integer constant.
3. **Size** is either the number of characters in each record of a formatted file or the number of words (characters/4) in a record of an unformatted file.
4. **Mode** is a code (E, U, or L) indicating whether the record is formatted (**E**), unformatted (**U**) or a combination of the two forms (**L**).

5. **Next** is an integer variable that points to the "next" record to be read/written from the file. This variable, called an **associated variable,** is automatically incremented by the system after the execution of each direct-access I/O statement.

EXAMPLE 11.4   **DEFINE FILE Examples**

The statements below illustrate the DEFINE FILE statement under varying conditions.

a. A formatted direct-access file that is referenced on unit 10 contains 1000 records of 50 characters each.

DEFINE FILE 10(1000,50,E,NEXT)

b. An unformatted direct-access file referenced on unit 1 contains 500 records of 25 words (100 characters).

INTEGER POINT

.

.

.

DEFINE FILE 1(500,25,U,POINT)

Direct-Access READ/WRITE Statements

Direct-access files are read/written by a special variation of the READ/WRITE statement used with sequential files. **Direct-access READ/WRITE statements** have the following general forms:

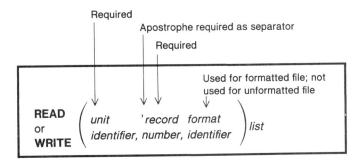

where

1. **Unit identifier,** as before, specifies the I/O unit number that is associated with the file.
2. **Record number** is a constant integer expression or associated variable which specifies the location of the record to be read or written.
3. **Format identifier** as before identifies the format specification to be used with formatted direct-access files. If the file is unformatted, the format identifier is omitted.

EXAMPLE 11.5   Direct-Access I/O Examples

a. Read the 25th record from unit 10 of a direct-access file formatted according to FORMAT statement 100.

```
        READ(10'25,100)NAME,ID,SAL,SEX
100    FORMAT(A20,I3,I5,A1)
```

or

```
        ID=25
        READ(10'ID,100)NAME,ID,SAL,SEX
100    FORMAT(A20,I3,I5,A1)
```

b. Read list-directed record from card reader or terminal and write to record number 30 in the above file

```
        READ,NAME, ID ,SAL,SEX
        WRITE(10' ID ,100)NAME, ID ,SAL,SEX
```

where 30 is input for ID. Note how ID represents both the record number and a field within the record, which is a convenient way of identifying records in a direct-access file.

c. Write to an unformatted direct-access file on unit 3.

```
        WRITE(U'ID)A,B,C
```

where U is typed integer and stores 3.

Follow-up Exercises

12. Write code to:

Define a formatted direct-access file that gets connected to unit 20 and has record lengths of 30 characters and a maximum of 5000 records.

Read from a card reader or terminal the integer variable student identification (ID), the character variable student name (NAME), and the character variable final letter grade (GRADE).

Write to the file student name (25 characters), ID (4 characters), and final grade (1 character) using ID as the record number.

*13. Write FORTRAN code for the flowchart on the opposite page where we have an unformatted direct-access file with 1000 records and 60 characters per record.

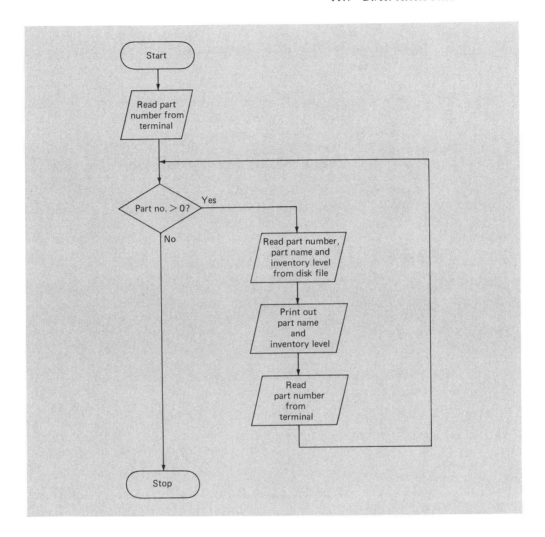

EXAMPLE 11.6   Direct-Access Personnel File-Creation/Display Logic

To illustrate the creation and display of a direct-access file, let's return to our personnel example. The file design is the same as that shown in Figure 11.2b on page 405. The record layout is identical to that shown in Table 11.1 on page 410.

In our example we use employee ID number to represent the record number, which serves as a convenient "key" for writing and reading specific records. That is, to access any record in the file directly, we need only specify the ID of that employee.

The pseudocode below describes the algorithm.

READ unit identifier from card / terminal
Define the file

File-creation logic

READ employee record from card / terminal
WHILE ≠ trailer record
    WRITE record on file
    READ employee record from card / terminal
END WHILE

File-display logic

PRINT header at printer / terminal
READ ID from card / terminal
WHILE ID ≠ −99
    READ record from file
    PRINT employee record at printer / terminal
    READ ID from card / terminal
END WHILE

PRINT "file display terminated"
Stop

The file-creation logic first inputs the employee record into primary memory from the terminal; then the record is transferred from primary memory to the file medium (magnetic disk) using ID as the record number.

The file display logic illustrates random retrieval from a direct-access file. Any ID can be entered from a terminal. The ID is then used as the record number to locate the appropriate record on the file. Next, the record is read from the file and stored in primary memory. Finally, the record is transferred from primary memory to terminal paper / screen. This type of file-display logic is the basis of computerized direct-access inquiry systems.

The program below reflects the pseudocode design and systems flowchart logic of Figure 11.4.

```
C---------------------------------------------------------------
C      PERSONNEL FILE CREATION/DISPLAY PROGRAM
C
C      FORMATTED DIRECT-ACCESS FILE
C
C      KEY:
C        NAME    = EMPLOYEE NAME
C        ID      = EMPLOYEE IDENTIFICATION NUMBER
C        SAL     = SALARY
C        SEX     = SEX CODE (M OF F)
C        U       = UNIT IDENTIFIER
C        NEXT    = ASSOCIATED VARIABLE
C
C      RECORD LAYOUT:
C        NAME       TYPE CHARACTER     COLUMNS  1-20
C        ID         TYPE INTEGER       COLUMNS 21-23
C        SAL        TYPE INTEGER       COLUMNS 24-28
C        SEX        TYPE CHARACTER     COLUMNS 29
```

```
C-----------------------------------------------------------
      CHARACTER NAME*20,SEX
      INTEGER   ID,SAL,U,NEXT
C-----------------------------------------------------------
      READ, U
C
      DEFINE FILE 1 (100,29,E,NEXT)
C-----------------------------------------------------------
C  FILE-CREATION LOGIC
C-------------------
      READ, NAME,ID,SAL,SEX
C
      WHILE (NAME .NE. 'EOF')
        WRITE(U'ID,10) NAME,ID,SAL,SEX
        READ, NAME,ID,SAL,SEX
      END WHILE
C
      PRINT, 'FILE CREATION COMPLETED'
C-----------------------------------------------------------
C  FILE-DISPLAY LOGIC
C------------------
      PRINT, '-----------------------------------------------'
      PRINT, '      NAME                      ID    SALARY SEX'
      PRINT, '-----------------------------------------------'
C
      READ, ID
C
      WHILE (ID .NE. -99)
        READ(U'ID,10)NAME,ID,SAL,SEX
        PRINT, NAME,ID,SAL,SEX
        READ, ID
      END WHILE
C
      PRINT, '-----------------------------------------------'
      PRINT, 'FILE DISPLAY TERMINATED'
C-----------------------------------------------------------
      STOP
C-----------------------------------------------------------
   10 FORMAT(A20,I3,I5,A1)
C-----------------------------------------------------------
      END
```

Input

```
1
'ABATAR   JANE A.',1,20000,'F'
'BOMBERG  BO B.',3,15800,'M'
'DRURY    DAVID D.',6,18000,'M'
'EOF',0,0,'U'
6
3
-99
```

Output

```
FILE CREATION COMPLETED
-----------------------------------------------
      NAME                      ID    SALARY SEX
-----------------------------------------------
DRURY    DAVID D.               6     18000 M
BOMBERG  BO B.                  3     15800 M
-----------------------------------------------
FILE DISPLAY TERMINATED
```

FIGURE 11.4   Record Transfer to and from Direct-Access Personnel File

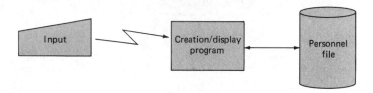

Symbol Key

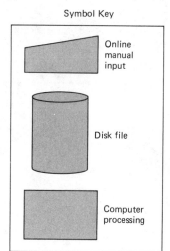

Online
manual
input

Disk file

Computer
processing

EXAMPLE 11.7   Direct-Access Personnel File-Automatic Display Logic

We can use the associated variable within the DEFINE FILE statement to conveniently process all or part of a direct-access file, as illustrated in the next program.

Study the program together with its input/output, and note that:

1. *The associated variable NEXT is automatically incremented by one* within DO-loop 5 each time a record is processed.
2. NEXT is initialized to 1 through the input data.
3. NEXT is used as the record number pointer in the READ statement within DO-loop 5.
4. Given that J runs from 1 to NUM (10 in our example), NEXT is initialized to 1, and NEXT is incremented by 1 for each value in J, it follows that NEXT will run from 1 to 10 (that is, the first 10 records are retrieved). If NEXT were initialized to k and NUM to n, then you should convince yourself that the retrieved records would have the numbers k through $k + n - 1$.

```
C------------------------------------------------------------------
C       PERSONNEL FILE AUTOMATIC DISPLAY PROGRAM
C
C       FORMATTED DIRECT-ACCESS FILE
C
C       KEY:
C         NAME    = EMPLOYEE NAME
C         ID      = EMPLOYEE IDENTIFICATION NUMBER
C         SAL     = SALARY
C         SEX     = SEX CODE (M OF F)
C         U       = UNIT IDENTIFIER
C         NEXT    = ASSOCIATED VARIABLE
C         NUM     = NUMBER OF RECORDS RETRIEVED
C
C       RECORD LAYOUT:
C         NAME       TYPE CHARACTER       COLUMNS  1-20
C         ID         TYPE INTEGER         COLUMNS 21-23
C         SAL        TYPE INTEGER         COLUMNS 24-28
C         SEX        TYPE CHARACTER       COLUMNS 29
C------------------------------------------------------------------
        CHARACTER NAME*20,SEX
        INTEGER   ID,SAL,U, NEXT,NUM
C------------------------------------------------------------------
        DEFINE FILE 1 (100,29,E, NEXT)
C------------------------------------------------------------------
        READ, U
C
        READ, NEXT,NUM
C------------------------------------------------------------------
        PRINT, '-----------------------------------------------'
        PRINT, '          NAME                   ID     SALARY SEX'
        PRINT, '-----------------------------------------------'
C
        DO 5 J=1, NUM
          READ(U'NEXT,10)NAME,ID,SAL,SEX
          PRINT, NAME,ID,SAL,SEX
      5 CONTINUE
C
        PRINT, '-----------------------------------------------'
        PRINT, 'FILE RETRIEVAL TERMINATED'
C------------------------------------------------------------------
        STOP
C------------------------------------------------------------------
     10 FORMAT(A20,I3,I5,A1)
C------------------------------------------------------------------
        END
```

Input

```
1
1, 10
```

Output

```
---------------------------------------------
          NAME                ID    SALARY  SEX
---------------------------------------------
ABATAR    JANE A.              1     20000  F  ⎫
                               0         0     ⎬
BOMBERG   BO B.                3     15800  M  ⎭        Records
                               0         0     ⎫        2, 4, 5,
                               0         0     ⎬        7-10
DRURY     DAVID D.             6     18000  M  ⎭        are empty.
                               0         0     ⎫
                               0         0     ⎬
                               0         0     
                               0         0     ⎭
---------------------------------------------
FILE RETRIEVAL TERMINATED
```

Note: Ten records were retrieved, starting with record number 1.

Follow-Up Exercises

14. With respect to Example 11.6:
    a. Why can't we replace "1" with "U" in the DEFINE FILE statement? Why would it be desirable to do so?
    b. At most, how many records can be processed by this program?
    c. Why can't we use the AT END LRC loop for the file-creation logic (as we did in Example 11.3)?
    d. Specify input for retrieving records 1, 6, and 10.

15. With respect to Example 11.7:
    a. What records would get retrieved if we were to input 3,6 for NEXT and NUM?
    b. Specify input for NEXT and NUM if we wish to retrieve records 6 through 10.

16. What can be done if a mistake is made in entering an employee's identification number and the record already has been written on the direct-access file?

*17. Solve Exercise 11 on the basis of the direct-access file. Supply record numbers as card/terminal input. Which file is more convenient for this type of processing?

18. **Index File**   Modify the program in Example 11.6 according to the following.
    a. Assume the ID field is the nine-digit Social Security number. Modify the program accordingly. Can you think of a practical problem regarding the use of SS number in place of our simpler ID number?
    **b. To overcome the storage problem in part a, we set up an "index" (sequential-access) file that contains SS numbers in the same order as SS numbers in the personnel file. Thus, the first SS number in this sequential file is found in record number 1 of the personnel file; the second SS number in the sequential file is in record number 2 of the direct-access file; and so on. Assume the index file has been created as an unformatted sequential file and it resides on tape unit 8. Now make the following changes:

       1. Modify the file-creation logic to use the associated variable for record numbers.
       2. Modify the file-display logic to find the position of ID (SS no.) within the index file and then use this position (index) as the record number. Note that this approach requires us to process the index file on unit 8 for *each* requested ID. If the ID is incorrect, print an error message and go on to the next ID. Can you think of a shortcoming with this approach?

    **c. Same as part b, except store the index file within primary memory as the one-dimensional array INDEX. Then perform a table look-up procedure to find the proper record number as the subscript value of the requested ID. Compare pros and cons of this approach to that in part b.

19. **Hashing Algorithm.   Hashing is a common technique used to access records in a direct-access file where the record key has more digits than the number of records (storage positions) in the file. For example, the direct use of SS number as a record number would require a file of the order of one billion records, since SS number is a nine-digit number.

The hashing algorithm converts the record key to a "relative record number" having a value within the range of the number of records reserved for the file. The location of each record is determined as follows:

1. Convert the record key, via a hashing algorithm, to a relative record number that is within the range 1 to *n*, where *n* is the number of records stored in the file. One hashing algorithm divides the record key by the *prime number*[1] closest to *n*, and uses the remainder from the division as the relative record number (the quotient is ignored).[2]
2. Use the relative record number to write the record to (or read the record from) the direct-access file.

Modify the program in Example 11.6 using a hashing algorithm. Assume the employee file contains no more than 100 employees and the Social Security number is the record key. (*Hint:* Convert the Social Security number to a two-digit record number using the hashing algorithm described above. The prime number closest to 100 is 97.)

**20. Assuming that a direct-access personnel file already has been created (as in the example), write a complete program to update the file according to the following options.

1. Display a record.
2. Add a new record to the file.
3. Change an existing record in the file.
4. "Delete" a record from the file by replacing character fields with blanks and numeric fields with zeros.
5. No more options (stop processing).

11.5
DATA PROCESSING APPLICATIONS

Data processing applications such as payroll, inventory control, and accounts receivable routinely use external files to process large amounts of data. In these types of applications it's useful to make a distinction between two file types called master files and transaction files.

A **master file** contains data items that are central to continued operation of the organization. These files are relatively permanent collections of records containing informational, historical, and current-status items. For example, the master file for bank checking accounts

---

[1] For you mathematical wizards, a prime number is a positive integer that is *not* evenly divisible by any positive integer except 1 and itself. For example 2, 3, 5, 7, and 11 are the first five prime numbers.
[2] Remaindering in FORTRAN for integer values is best accomplished by the library function MOD(N,K), which gives the remainder when N is divided by K. For example, MOD(100,97) has the value 3.

might contain a record for each customer account that includes the customer's name, account number, address, telephone, and last month's ending balance.

A **transaction file** is a relatively temporary collection of records containing data about transactions that have occurred during the most recent operating period of time. This type of file is used to process data against the master file. For example, a transaction file for bank checking accounts might contain data on all checks processed during the current month. At the end of the current month, data from both the transaction file and the master file are processed into a new master file that updates the current status of ending balance for each account.

Records within a file (transaction or master) are typically organized for easy access based on a record key. A **record key** is one field (sometimes more) in each record that uniquely distinguishes one record from another. For example, in the banking illustration, the customer account number might serve as the record key. Data on the bank file would be arranged (sorted) by customer account number; the customer record with the lowest account number is first, followed by the customer with the next account number, and so on until the last record is the customer with the highest account number.

EXAMPLE 11.8   Computerized Blood Donor System

A local hospital is developing a computerized blood donor system. This system will be used to contact donors when certain types of blood are needed and develop statistics about donor usage.

A blood donor master file consisting of one record for each donor has been created. Among the fields in each record are the following:

Donor number
Donor name
Address
Phone
Date of last donation
Blood type

·
· } Other data items
·

One approach for updating the blood donor file is **periodic (batch) processing.** Using this approach, every time a donor gives blood, the donor's ID and date of donation are recorded in a transaction file. Periodically, weekly perhaps, the records in the transaction file are used to update (change) the "date of last donation" field in the blood donor master file.

The process of updating is illustrated by the system flowchart in Figure 11.5. A **system flowchart** presents a general overview of an entire system, the sequence of major processing operations, and the data flow to and from files. The type of flowchart you have been drawing in this course is technically called a **program flowchart.**

FIGURE 11.5   *Systems Flowchart for Batch Processing Blood Donor System (Sequential File)*

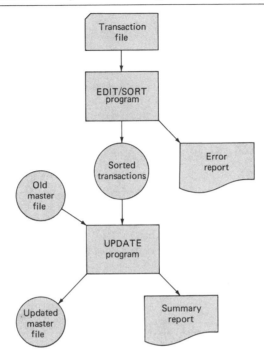

In our blood donor illustration each donor contribution is recorded on cards. This transaction file is first processed under control of an EDIT/SORT program. For example, at the end of a week the following transactions might represent the transaction file:

Transaction File

Donor ID	Date of Blood Donation	
4	061183	
1	140683 ←——————— Incorrect month
3	061483	
6	061583	
Endfile record		

The EDIT/SORT program in Figure 11.5 checks the validity of the date (note the mistake in the second entry), rejecting any transactions with invalid dates, and sorts only the valid records according to donor ID. Then it places these data on a temporary "sort" file. The data on this file appear as follows:

Sorted Transaction File

Donor ID	Date of Blood Donation
3	061483
4	061183
6	061583
Endfile record	

Note that only three records were sorted, as one record was rejected and printed on the error report because of an incorrect date.

The UPDATE program next utilizes the sorted transaction file and the master file to create an updated master file. The purpose of the program is to update the "date of last donation" field. Additionally, the UPDATE program prints a report showing the donor name, date, and blood type for each donor during that week. If the "old" master file contains the data shown below before the update

Old Master File

1	Smith, A.	125 Halpern Ave.	Kingston, RI	7924091	A+	010383
2	Jones, J.	25 Elmire Rd.	Cranston, RI	7312067	B+	111281
3	Nagel, T.	Estelle Rd.	Warwick, RI	3316022	O+	052283
4	Bosworth, B.	106 Broad St.	Westerly, RI	3489021	A−	100782
5	Bobick, D. D.	1 Main St.	Woonsocket, RI	8612221	AB+	081782
6	Regae, J.	97 Sinker Dr.	Kingston, RI	4011111	O+	071682
7	Myer, B.	2 Fort St.	Wakefield, RI	7891702	O−	031183
8	Fips, B. B.	1036 Indian Rd.	Narragansett, RI	7832173	B+	021282
Endfile record						

the processing of the transaction file against the master file would result in the following "updated" master file.

Updated Master File

1	Smith, A.	· · ·	A+	010383
2	Jones, J.	· · ·	B+	111281
3	Nagel, T.	· · ·	O+	061483
4	Bosworth, B.	· · ·	A−	061183
5	Bobick, D. D.	· · ·	AB+	081782
6	Regae, J.	· · ·	O+	061583
7	Myer, B.	· · ·	O−	031183
8	Fips, B. B.	· · ·	B+	021282
Endfile record		· · ·		

A program flowchart for the UPDATE program is illustrated in Figure 11.6. The "transaction key" is the blood donor ID read from a record of the transaction file and the "master key" is the blood donor ID from a record of the master file. In the discussion that follows keep in mind that records in both the transaction and master files are in ascending order according to blood donor ID. Also, we assume that both files are processed by sequential access.

The update program compares the key of the transaction record with the corresponding data item (key) in the master record. If a match occurs (keys of both files are equal) the transaction data are used to update the "date of last donation" field for that master record as illustrated by the middle branch in Figure 11.6.

When the transaction key tests greater than the master key, it follows that processing of the current blood donor on the master file has been completed. Thus, the updated record for this blood donor now can be written onto the new master file. For example, when the second record in the sorted transaction file on page 426 is processed, the transaction key will test greater than the master key ($4 > 3$). At this time the updated record for Nagel (ID $= 3$) on the new master file can be written, as depicted in the third (rightmost) branch of Figure 11.6.

A transaction key greater than the master key may also indicate that no transaction (activity) occurred for that record. This is particularly common when master files have many records. In such cases, the master record is copied unchanged onto the new master file, as done in the third branch. For example, the first two records of the master file are copied unchanged, since the first transaction ID is 3.

Depending on the situation, however, an error may be indicated by the mismatch of keys. In this case, an error message is printed, as illustrated by the first branch in Figure 11.6.

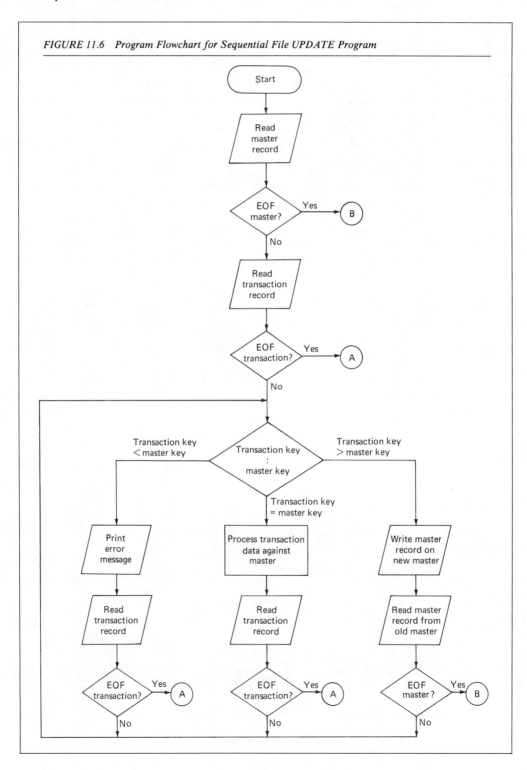

FIGURE 11.6   *Program Flowchart for Sequential File UPDATE Program*

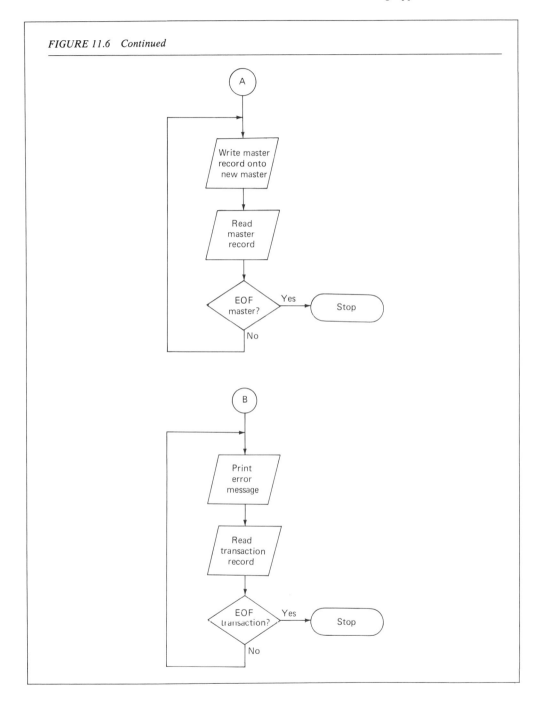

FIGURE 11.6 *Continued*

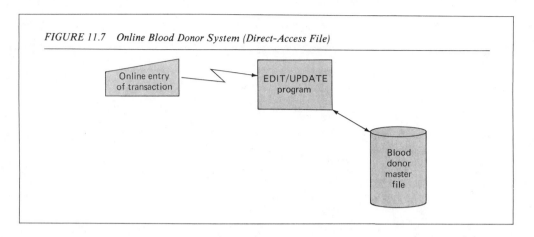

FIGURE 11.7   Online Blood Donor System (Direct-Access File)

The above description is typical of a batch processing system. Alternatively, and more simply, we could design an **online processing** system that updates a direct-access master file as transactions are keyed in, as illustrated in the systems flowchart of Figure 11.7. In this case, transactions are usually entered from a terminal under the control of an EDIT/UPDATE program. This program edits the input data for a valid date and record number. If valid, it then directly updates the proper record in the direct-access master file. If invalid, it prompts the user for a correct entry.

11.6
COMMON ERRORS

Don't forget the following when working with files.

1. Use the necessary file-related control cards (batch processing) or system commands (time-shared processing) for your system. Mistakes in preparing these non-FORTRAN instructions are frequent (and very frustrating). Pay careful attention to your instructor, or carefully read the system's manual, or befriend a file expert at the computer center.
2. Double-check the logic that terminates the processing of sequential-access files. For example, a common error is attempting to read in beyond the last record in the file. This execution error is possible when an endfile record is missing from the file. A possible logic error is forgetting to use either the END = specifier or AT END,QUIT in a sequential-access READ statement. In this case processing simply stops when the endfile record is encountered, which means that execution never enters any postprocessing logic to which control might have been transferred.

ADDITIONAL EXERCISES

21. Define or explain the following:

field	internal file
record	unformatted file
file	unformatted record
external file	formatted file

formatted record	direct-access READ / WRITE statement
sequential access	sequential-access READ / WRITE statement
endfile record	END FILE statement
format identifier	REWIND statement
unit identifier	DEFINE FILE statement
end-of-file specifier	master file
error specifier	transaction file
direct access	record key
record number	system flowchart
associated variable	program flowchart
READ statement	periodic (batch) processing
WRITE statement	online processing

22. **Computerized Matching: A File Search Revisited.** Design the program of Exercise 47 in Chapter 5 on page 187 or Exercise 37 in Chapter 8 on page 318 so that input of the placement office file is from an external sequential-access file.

23. **Mailing List Revisited.** Design the program of Exercise 28 in Chapter 6 on page 223 so that input of the data file is from an external sequential-access file.

24. **Revenue-Sharing Revisited.** Design the program of Exercise 44 in Chapter 7 on page 281 so that input of the state population file is from an external sequential-access file.

25. **Blood Donor System I.** Use the system in Figure 11.7 so that the master blood donor file is a direct-access file with 10,000 records. Transactions are entered from a terminal or card reader and processed by an EDIT / UPDATE program that edits the input data for valid date and record number, and updates records in the master file. If input is by terminal, prompt the user for a correct entry whenever it's invalid. If input is by card reader, ignore updates for invalid data but include a printout of invalid input records as part of the summary report. Use the data from Example 11.8.

26. **Blood Donor System II.** As in the preceding exercise, except that the transaction file is a sequential-access file on a medium such as tape.

27. **Blood Donor System III.** Write and run the following programs for the system described in Example 11.8:
     a. EDIT / SORT. Don't forget to design the error routine for dates.
     b. UPDATE.
     **c. Add other useful features. For example, UPDATE could include an option to echo print all records in the transaction and master files, an option to provide summaries by blood type following the first table, etc.

28. **Interactive Airline Reservation System Revisited.** Modify Exercise 39 of Chapter 8 on page 320 as follows.
     a. Use a direct-access file instead of an array for the current table of flight information. Each table (file) of flight information is based on a specific week for the coming year. Use flight number as the record number.
     b. Instead of the record numbers in part a, use a record number based on the sum of flight number and day code. Assuming the ten flights in the table are numbered 240, 250, 260, 810, 100, 110, 120, 130, 950, and 960, and days in the week (Monday, Tuesday, . . . , Sunday) are coded 1, 2, . . . , 7, a request for flight 950 on Wednesday would access record number 953 whereas the same flight on Sunday would access record number 957.
     **c. Add other useful features. For example, you might want to allow 1 percent overbooking of seats (a common practice); create a file that stores reser-

vations information such as customer's name, address, telephone number, etc.; create a waiting list file that periodically gets processed against the flight table (master) file.

29. **Credit Billing Revisited.**   Design the program of Exercise 48 in Chapter 5 on page 188 so that master and transaction files are used. The master file contains name, address, credit limit, and last billing period's ending (previous) balance for each customer. The transaction file contains name, payments, and new purchases.
    a. Run your program for the data given in the problem such that bills are printed and the master file is updated.
    **b. Include the following action codes in the transaction file and program logic.

    1. Change in address
    2. Change in credit limit
    3. Delete customer from master file
    4. Add customer to master file

    Make up data to test each of these action codes.
30. **Electric Bill Revisited.**   Design the program of Exercise 37 in Chapter 9 on page 371 so that master and transaction files are used. The master file contains previous reading, rate code, past due amount, name, street address, city, state, zip code, and account number for each customer. In addition to dates, the transaction file contains account number, name, new meter reading, and payments since last bill.
    a. Run your program for the data given in the problem such that bills are printed and the master file is updated.
    **b. Include the following action codes in the transaction file and program logic.

    1. Change of address
    2. Delete customer from master file
    3. Add customer to master file

    Make up data to test each of these action codes.
31. **Payroll.**   Each week a small firm processes its weekly payroll for hourly employees. The following input is necessary to process the payroll.

Master Employee File
___

Employee ID
Name
Hourly rate of pay
Number of dependents
Cumulative gross pay thus far this year
Cumulative FICA tax thus far this year
Cumulative withholding (income) tax thus far this year
Cumulative group health contribution thus far this year

Transaction File
___

Date
Employee ID
Number of hours worked

Develop a program that

a. Generates a "wage summary report" consisting of a line for each employee: the line contains employee name, employee number, hourly rate, hours worked, gross pay, FICA, income tax, group health, and net pay. After individual figures are printed, the program is to print totals for gross pay, each deduction, and net pay. Include appropriate report and column headings.

b. Updates cumulative gross pay, cumulative FICA tax, cumulative withholding tax, and cumulative group health contribution for each employee in the master file.

To determine the pay for each employee, the following facts must be included in your program:

1. Gross pay is defined as pay for regular time plus pay for overtime. Overtime pay is 1.5 times the regular rate for each hour above 40.
2. Social Security tax (FICA) is 6.65 percent of gross pay. The deduction is made until the employee's cumulative earnings are above $29,700, after which there is no deduction.
3. Deduction for withholding tax and group health plan are tied to the number of dependents as follows.

Dependents	Income Tax (% of gross pay)	Group Health ($ per week)
1	22	2.50
2	20	3.60
3	18	5.10
4	16	6.00
5 or more	13	6.50

4. Net pay is defined as gross pay less FICA deduction less income tax deduction less group health deduction. Use the data below to test your program.

Master File

1940	Bella Bitta, Al	2.50	4	1500.00	99.75	240.00	180.00
1942	Budget, Frank	8.25	5	30000.00	1975.05	3900.00	195.00
2001	Manicotti, Diane	6.00	1	12300.00	817.95	2706.00	75.00
2542	Saintvi, Arun	8.00	3	29600.00	1968.40	5328.00	153.00

Transaction file for (date, which you supply)

1940	60
1942	40
2001	45
2542	35

c. Run parts a and b again for the next week using the data below.

Transaction file for (date one week after preceding transaction file)

1940	32
1942	45
2001	35
2542	42

d. Design a routine that edits the input data for errors. Specifically it ensures that

1. Number of dependents is greater than zero and less than 15.
2. Rate of pay is greater than $2.30 and less than $10.00.
3. Number of hours worked is greater than zero and less than 65.
4. Total earnings thus far this year is zero or greater and less than $40,000.

If an error is detected, print an appropriate error message that includes the employee's name and number, bypass the calculations and printout for this employee, and go on to the next employee. Add new input data to test each of these four possible input errors.

**e. Design your program to include the processing of the following action codes in the transaction file.

1. Change in hourly rate of pay
2. Change in number of dependents
3. Delete employee from master file
4. Add employee to master file

Make up data to test each of these action codes.

**32. Class Grades.   Design a comprehensive program that maintains and processes student grades for an academic course. You might include features such as file creation, file modifications (e.g., change a grade, add a grade, delete a grade, delete a record, add a record, etc.), file display, calculation of final numeric grade based on weights for individual grades (including the assignment of a letter grade if applicable), ... If a student is added to the file, make sure this student is placed in the correct alphabetic position. Once your program is debugged, hire yourself a marketing major and pedal your program to faculty members for an exorbitant software fee.

Modules

Structured Charts

> A.1 SEQUENCE, DECISION, AND LOOP STRUCTURES
>
> A.2 NESTED AND MULTIPLE ALTERNATIVE DECISION STRUCTURES
>
> A.3 A COMPLETE STRUCTURED CHART

Another approach to developing the algorithm besides a flowchart or pseudocode is what is variously called the **structured chart, structured diagram, structured flowchart,** or **Nassi-Schneiderman chart,** the latter in honor of its developers. These charts show the logic of the program inside a series of boxes that represent sequence, decision and loop structures. The box can be any size necessary to describe the logic. Inside the box pseudocode-like syntax is used.

A.1
SEQUENCE, DECISION, AND LOOP STRUCTURES

The representation of sequence, decision, and loop structures within structured charts is best shown by example.

EXAMPLE A.1 Control Structure Examples

The examples on this and the next page take pseudocode examples from Chapter 4 and illustrate the structured chart equivalents.

Structure	Pseudocode	Structured Chart
Sequence	READ name, ID, no. credits Calculate tuition Balance due = tuition + fees PRINT output for this student Stop	READ name, ID, no. credits Calculate tuition Balance due = tuition + fees PRINT output for this student Stop

---

* This module is best covered following Chapters 4, 5, or 6.

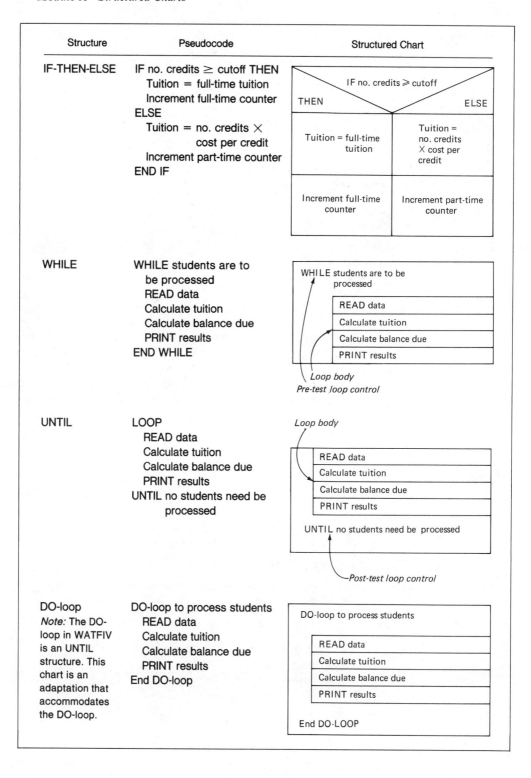

EXAMPLE A.2 Multiple Alternative Decision Structure

In this example we show pseudocode and structured chart versions of the class report program of Example 6.4 on page 204. Note that the structured chart essentially describes a nested decision structure.

Pseudocode

IF Class = Freshman THEN
    Add 1 to Freshman count
    Add GPA score to Freshman sum
ELSE IF Class = Sophomore
    Add 1 to Sophomore count
    Add GPA score to Sophomore sum
ELSE IF Class = Junior
    Add 1 to Junior count
    Add GPA score to Junior sum
ELSE IF Class = Senior
    Add 1 to Senior count
    Add GPA score to Senior sum
ELSE
    PRINT error message
END IF

Structured Chart (at right)

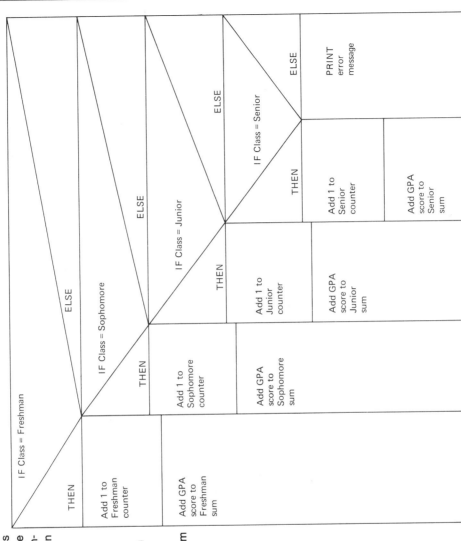

A.2
NESTED AND MULTIPLE ALTERNATIVE
DECISION STRUCTURES

The multiple alternative (including CASE) decision structures are special cases of nested decision structures, as presented in Chapter 6. See Example A.2 on page 439.

A.3
A COMPLETE STRUCTURED CHART

A complete structured chart describes all of the sequence, decision, and loop structures that make up the entire algorithm, as illustrated in Example A.3.

To summarize, we have three tools to design and document programs: the flowchart, pseudocode, and the structured chart. Compared to a flowchart, the structured chart is more compact and emphasizes structured design, since the design of boxes conforms to sequence, IF-THEN-ELSE, pre-test, and post-test structures. The flowchart, however, better describes logic flows when used as an introductory description of a particular structure, such as pre-test loop or multiple alternative. Moreover, the flowchart itself is "structured" if it strictly describes the control structures presented in Chapters 4 through 6.

Flowcharts and structured charts must be redrawn whenever programs change, whereas pseudocode can be changed easily using the computer's text editor. Pseudocode describes control structures just as clearly as a structured chart and has the maintenance advantage of easy revision whenever programs get changed (which can be quite often in practice).

Personally, we prefer pseudocode both for design and documentation of programs, as long as control structures are strictly adhered to. Flowcharts we find useful as a means to introduce a new structure (as in Figures 4.3 and 4.4 on pages 106 and 107). A growing number of writers, however, have a preference for the structured chart, especially because it imposes structured methodology on the programmer.

Follow-up Exercises

1. Define or explain the following:
    structured chart
    structured diagram
    Nassi-Schneiderman chart
    structured flowchart

2. Does our definition of "structured flowchart" include the method of flowcharting used in Chapter 4? Explain.
*3. Develop a structured chart for each of the following, and support an opinion for which approach (flowchart, pseudocode, or structured chart) you prefer.
    a. Bank savings program in Section 4.8, page 127.
    b. Minimum value program in Example 5.5, page 153.
    c. Inflation curse program in Example 5.12, page 167.
    d. Inflation curse program in Example 5.13, page 171.
    e. Sales bonus program in Example 5.16, page 179.
    f. Example 6.1 on page 194.
    g. Microcomputer discount schedule program in Example 6.3, page 201.
    h. Traffic court fines program in Example 6.5, page 209.

EXAMPLE A.3   Structured Chart for Sales Bonus Algorithm

This example shows a comparison of the complete pseudocode and structured chart for the Sales Bonus Program (LRC/trailer number version) of Example 5.15 on page 175.

Pseudocode

```
PRINT column headings
Base pay = $350
READ name, SSN, sales
WHILE SSN ≠ −99
    IF sales ≤ $5000 THEN
        Bonus = $0
    ELSE
        Bonus = $100
    END IF
    Total pay = base pay + bonus
    PRINT name, SSN, total pay
    READ name, SSN, sales
END WHILE
Stop
```

Structured Chart (at right)

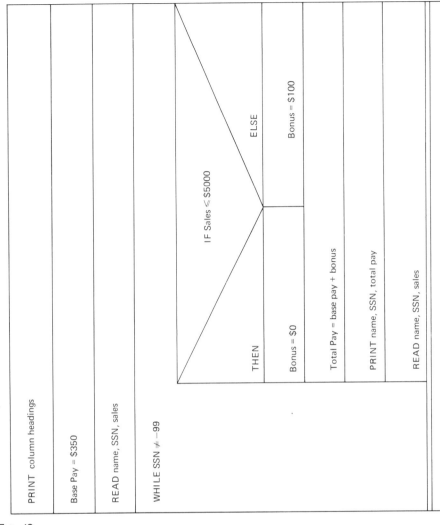

MODULE B*

Output with Formats

Up to now we have used **list-directed output.** This is convenient for beginning programmers and for problems requiring simple output. You may, however, have felt frustrated over your inability to control the exact positioning of output, over the untidiness of E-notation for numeric output, and over excessive time spent trying to align appropriate values under column headings.

Frustrations aside, many applications require rather extensive and precisely positioned output. For example, an elaborate report with many labels, column headings, and extensive character and numeric data requires careful output design to enhance communication with the reader. In other cases precise output is required, as in the printing of invoices and bills on standardized preprinted forms.

In this module you'll learn how to arrange data precisely on a printed page, called **format-directed output,** thereby (in theory) becoming master of your output. First, however, we motivate your interest by presenting a familiar example using format-directed output.

---

* Can be assigned anytime after Chapter 4.

EXAMPLE B.1   Student Billing Program with Format-Directed Output

Consider the following version of the student billing program.

```
C-----------------------------------------------
C    STUDENT BILLING PROGRAM WITH OUTPUT FORMATS
C
C    KEY:
C       CPC    = COST PER CREDIT
C       FEES   = STUDENT FEES
C       NAME   = STUDENT NAME
C       ID     = STUDENT ID NUMBER
C       CREDIT = NUMBER OF CREDITS
C       TUIT   = TUITION
C       BALDUE = AMOUNT OWED BY STUDENT
C       CUMBAL = AMOUNT OWED TO INSTITUTION
C       N      = NUMBER OF STUDENTS
C-----------------------------------------------
      CHARACTER NAME*15
      INTEGER   ID,N
      REAL      CPC,FEES,CREDIT,TUIT,BALDUE,CUMBAL
C-----------------------------------------------
      CUMBAL = 0.0
C-----------------------------------------------
      READ, CPC,FEES
      READ, N
C-----------------------------------------------
      PRINT 30
  (A) PRINT 40
      PRINT 50
C-----------------------------------------------
      DO 5 J = 1,N
         READ, NAME,ID,CREDIT
         TUIT   = CREDIT*CPC
         BALDUE = TUIT + FEES
         CUMBAL = CUMBAL + BALDUE
  (B)    PRINT 60,NAME,ID,BALDUE
    5 CONTINUE
C-----------------------------------------------
      PRINT 50
  (C) PRINT 80,CUMBAL
      PRINT 70
      PRINT 70
C-----------------------------------------------
   30 FORMAT('1','           **TUITION REPORT**')
   40 FORMAT('0','      NAME          SS NUMBER    BALANCE DUE')
   50 FORMAT(' ','-------------------------------------------')
  (D) 60 FORMAT(' ',A15,I12,F14.2)
   70 FORMAT(' ',31X,'-----------')
   80 FORMAT(18X,'**TOTALS**    $',F10.2)
C-----------------------------------------------
      STOP
      END
```

For the input data

```
100.0,250.0
3
'W. MITTY',206612463,15.0
'X. MITTY',206612464,18.5
'Y. MITTY',206612465,12.0
```

the program would print the following output.

```
                    **TUITION REPORT**
            NAME         SS NUMBER      BALANCE DUE
        ----------------------------------------------
        W. MITTY           266612463        1750.00
        X. MITTY           266612464        2100.00
        Y. MITTY           266612465        1450.00
        ----------------------------------------------
                         **TOTALS**    $     5300.00
                                             ----------
                                             ----------
```

Labels that precede body of report. Printed by statements in box A, which reference statements 30, 40, and 50 in box D.

Body of report. Printed by repeated execution of PRINT statement in box B, which references statement 60 in box D.

Labels and summary that follow body of report. Printed by statements in box C, which reference statements 70 and 80 in box D.

At this point, don't worry about understanding the mechanics of the above output. Just look at the "big picture," realizing that we are now controlling exactly how and where data are to appear on the printed lines.

B.1
PRINT AND FORMAT STATEMENTS

Output from the computer often requires precise column-by-column and line-by-line control. The precise control of printing usually is accomplished by pairing the PRINT statement with a FORMAT statement.

The general form of the PRINT statement is

> **PRINT** *format identifier, list*

In previous programs the *format identifier* was omitted, which meant we desired list-directed output. For format-directed output the format identifier is a statement label (number) that identifies the FORMAT statement to be used by the PRINT statement. As before, the *list* is a sequence of variable names, constants, or expressions separated by commas.[1]

To illustrate, the statement

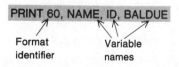

PRINT 60, NAME, ID, BALDUE

Format identifier   Variable names

---

[1] The output list may also include an array element name (Chapters 7 and 8), an array name (Chapters 7 and 8), and implied-DO lists (Chapters 7 and 8).

in box B of Example B.1 specifies the variables whose values are to be printed (NAME, ID, and BALDUE) and identifies the FORMAT statement to use (statement number 60) for positioning these values on the print page.

The **FORMAT statement** for output is used to describe exactly how printed matter is to appear on the output medium. A general form of the FORMAT statement is given by

> *format*
> *statement* **FORMAT** *(list of edit descriptors)*
> *label*

where the *format statement label* is any unsigned, nonzero integer constant up to five digits that uniquely identifies the FORMAT statement and *edit descriptors* are codes that specify the editing necessary to print the desired output (or read the desired input as described in Module C). These edit descriptors indicate the position, type (integer, real, etc.), size, and decimal point location (if applicable) of the values to be output.[2]

For example, the statement

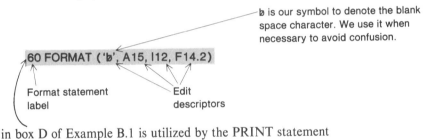

in box D of Example B.1 is utilized by the PRINT statement

> PRINT 60,NAME,ID,BALDUE

to print the body of the output table on page 444. Note how the format identifier 60 in the PRINT statement corresponds to the format statement label in the FORMAT statement.

The following points are worth remembering as you use format-directed output.

1. A new line is printed each time a PRINT statement is executed. For example, the PRINT statement that outputs NAME, ID, and BALDUE in Example B.1 is executed three times within the loop; hence the body of the table on page 444 has three printed lines of new output. Note that the repeated execution of a PRINT statement within a loop, as illustrated by box B in the program, results in a "table-like" appearance of printed output.

2. Look once more at the output on page 444. Note that PRINT statements that are to print headings must precede the loop that creates the body of the table, as illustrated by

---

[2] Technically, the portion (list of edit descriptors) following the keyword FORMAT is called the *format specification*. More complicated format specifications include nested sets of parentheses, as discussed in Module D.

box A in the program. Similarly, PRINT statements that summarize data in a report must follow the loop that prints the body of the report, as illustrated by box C in the program.

3. The maximum length of a printed line varies. Typical sizes for printers are 80 and 133 characters. Video display terminals usually have maximum print line lengths of 80 characters. Make a note of the maximum print line length on your system.

4. The FORMAT statement is a *nonexecutable statement* that serves as a reference for a PRINT statement. Since the FORMAT statement is nonexecutable, it can be placed virtually anywhere in the program prior to the END statement. In fact, many programmers prefer to place all FORMAT statements in a group, either at the beginning or the end of a program. This improves the readability of programs by "getting them out of the way" of the execution logic.[3]

5. A FORMAT statement may be referenced by more than one PRINT statement. For example, the FORMAT statement labeled 70 on page 443 is referenced by two PRINT statements in box C.

Follow-up Exercise

1. **WRITE Statement.** An alternative statement for processing format-directed output is

$$\text{WRITE} \left(\begin{array}{cc} output & format \\ unit & statement \\ number, & label \end{array} \right) list$$

The *output unit number* is an integer variable or constant that specifies the output unit to be used. In many systems this number is "6" for either the line printer in batch processing or the terminal in time-shared processing, although it varies depending on what computer you're using. The *format statement label* identifies the FORMAT statement to be used by this WRITE statement. As before, the typical *list* is a sequence of variable names separated by commas.

The WRITE statement is more versatile than the PRINT statement since, among other things, it allows us to specify specific output units such as printer, disk drive, tape drive, and card punch (as described in Chapter 11).

Replace PRINT statements in Example B.1 with appropriate WRITE statements.

B.2
SELECTED EDIT DESCRIPTORS

The full version of WATFIV includes numerous distinct edit descriptors for input/output editing. In this section we discuss the most commonly used edit descriptors; additional edit descriptors and options are presented in Module D.

---

[3] FORMAT statements cannot precede the statements that identify the beginning of a subprogram (FUNCTION and SUBROUTINE in Chapter 9) when used within subprograms.

The Apostrophe Edit Descriptor

The apostrophe edit descriptor is a character constant that is used either for carriage control or for textual matter.

Carriage Control. If you are using a line printer or a terminal, carriage control is the first item of information that you need to communicate through your FORMAT statement. To illustrate what we mean, consider what happens when you're typing a term paper. Suppose you have just finished typing the last character on some line. You need to make a decision as to what to do next. In other words, should the carriage stay on the present line (as when you underscore words)? Should the carriage go down the page one line before typing (single space) or two lines (double space)? Should it go to the top of a new page? Just as you must make these simple decisions when you type, so too must you inform the printer how the vertical spacing is to appear.

In FORTRAN we control the carriage or line by using the **carriage control characters** indicated in Table B.1. We communicate our carriage control desires to the computer by enclosing one of these characters within apostrophes as the first edit descriptor of each FORMAT statement (just after the left parenthesis).[4]

TABLE B.1 *Control of Carriage**

CARRIAGE CONTROL CHARACTER	EFFECT ON CARRIAGE
+	Do not advance before printing (hold the line).
Blank space	Advance one line before printing (single space).
0	Advance two lines before printing (double space).
1	Go to the top of a new page.

*Some time-sharing systems may not utilize all of these characters; others may use different characters. Ask your instructor.

EXAMPLE B.2

Consider the following statements from Example B.1.

```
      PRINT 30
   30 FORMAT ('1', '              **TUITION REPORT**')
                 ↑
                 └── Carriage control character
```

When the PRINT statement is executed, FORMAT "30" is used as a reference. The '1' after the left parenthesis instructs the carriage to "go to the top of a new page" before printing the report title.

Other examples of carriage control are illustrated below.

---

[4] Other means of providing carriage control characters are discussed later in this module.

Textual Matter.   Textual matter such as report titles, column headings, and messages can be output by using the apostrophe edit descriptor. The character constant is printed exactly as it appears in the FORMAT statement.

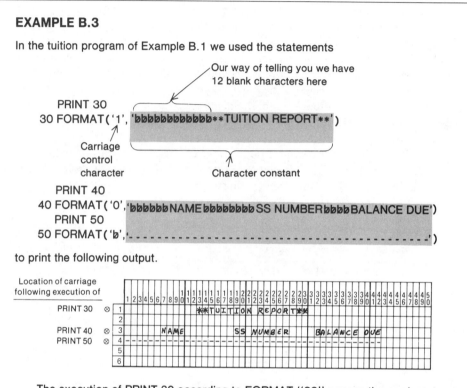

EXAMPLE B.3

In the tuition program of Example B.1 we used the statements

to print the following output.

The execution of PRINT 30 according to FORMAT "30" causes the carriage to go to the beginning of *print line* 1 at the top of a new page, after which the printer outputs 12 blanks followed by the title ∗∗TUITION REPORT∗∗. *The carriage now returns to the beginning of the current print line* (that is, print line 1), awaiting the next carriage control instruction.

Next the statement PRINT 40 is executed. The '0' carriage control in FORMAT "40" tells the carriage to advance two lines (from print line 1, its current location, to print line 3) before printing the character constant exactly as shown by the second edit descriptor in FORMAT "40." After printing the word DUE, the carriage returns to the beginning of print line 3. Note that line 2 is blank.[5]

Finally, the execution of PRINT 50 tells the carriage to advance one line to print line 4 before printing 42 dashes.

You should note the following points regarding this example.

[5] See Exercise 2 in this section and the slash edit descriptor in Module D for other methods of printing blank lines.

1. The list of a PRINT statement can be left empty. In this case we're simply printing a report title and column headings, without the need to print contents within storage locations.
2. Use a comma to separate adjacent edit descriptors in the list within parentheses.
3. The apostrophe edit descriptor that controls the carriage at the beginning of each FORMAT statement is itself a character constant, since it's enclosed in apostrophes. If a carriage control apostrophe edit descriptor is followed by another apostrophe edit descriptor, both apostrophe edit descriptors can be combined into one. For example, FORMAT ''30'' could be written as

   30 FORMAT('1ƀƀƀƀƀƀƀƀƀƀƀƀ**TUITION REPORT**')

Follow-up Exercises

2. On the basis of your work in Chapter 3, how else could you print a blank line following the report heading in Example B.3? Can you think of a simple way of printing, say, 15 blank lines?
3. Suppose that the printer has just finished printing line 20 and that the statement

   PRINT 15

is to be executed next. Write the appropriate FORMAT statement to print the label HAL SPEAKS:
   a. At the beginning of line 20.
   b. At the beginning of line 21.
   c. At the beginning of line 22.
   d. Starting in the fifth print position (column) of line 22.
   e. Starting at the beginning of the first line on the next page.
4. Indicate exactly how the output would appear when the following is executed while the carriage is at the beginning of line 1.

    9 FORMAT('ƀSTUDENT')
   10 FORMAT('ƀID')
   11 FORMAT('+ƀƀƀNUMBER')
     PRINT 9
     PRINT 10
     PRINT 11

5. Write the necessary statements in such a way that, at the beginning of a line that is double-spaced from the preceding line of output, the computer prints

   THE ANSWER =
        ⌃——————Minus character

The A Edit Descriptor

The output of character values based on character expressions is accomplished by using the A edit descriptor. The general form is

$$\boxed{\textbf{A}w}$$

where *w* is the *field width* or number of characters to be output for the corresponding character value. The portion of the print line allocated to the output value is called a **field.**

EXAMPLE B.4

In Example B.1 we used the statements

PRINT 60,NAME,ID,BALDUE

60 FORMAT('b',A15,I12,F14.2)

to produce the following portion of the output.

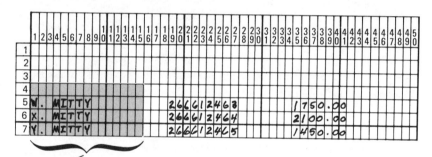

Field for NAME is 15
columns wide according
to A15 descriptor

For now, ignore the variables ID and BALDUE and the descriptors I12 and F14.2. When this PRINT statement is executed, the carriage of the printer first goes down the page one line from its current position (from print line 4 to print line 5), as specified by 'b'. Then the character value stored in NAME is printed, *left-justified,* in the field given by columns 1 to 15. Thus NAME in the print list is paired with A15 in the list of edit descriptors.

Note that, in Example B.1, the statement

CHARACTER NAME*15 ←────── Declared length of 15 equals
field width of 15 in A15
within FORMAT "60"

identifies NAME as a character variable with *a declared length* of 15 characters. Thus, during the first iteration of the loop, the first value stored in NAME is internally represented as follows based on the input data.

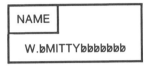

Seven blanks are padded in after the name because the input value was represented by the eight characters in 'W. MITTY'. The use of A15 to output the character value in NAME specifies a *field width* of 15, the same as the declared length in NAME. Conveniently, the output of NAME in print line 5 exactly corresponds to its internal representation. In effect, *the output of a character value is identical to its internal representation when the field width w equals the declared length l in the CHARACTER statement.*

In general, the field width w may differ from the declared length l of the character variable. In some instances (for example, right-justifying character output) you might find it convenient to select a field width w different from the declared length l, in which cases the following rules apply.

Rule 1: If the field width w is less than or equal to the declared length l of the character variable ($w \le l$), then the *leftmost w* characters in storage are output.

Rule 2: If the field width w exceeds the declared length l of the character variable ($w > l$), then all l characters in storage are printed *right-justified* within the field.

EXAMPLE B.5

Study the two examples below and relate them to the two rules above.

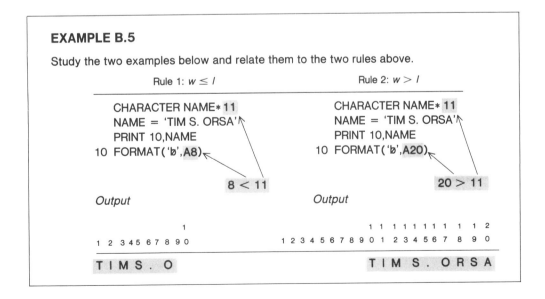

Follow-up Exercises

6. Assume the character constant 'RHODE ISLAND' is stored in the character variable STATE as follows:

    CHARACTER STATE*20
    STATE = 'RHODE ISLAND'

    How would the output appear in each of the following situations?
    a.   PRINT 50,STATE
        50 FORMAT('ɓɓɓɓɓ',A20)
    b.   PRINT 50,STATE
        50 FORMAT('ɓTHE OCEAN STATE IS ɓ',A20)
    c.   PRINT 50,STATE
        50 FORMAT('ɓ',A10)
    d.   PRINT 50,STATE
        50 FORMAT('ɓ',A25)
    e.   PRINT 50,STATE
        50 FORMAT('ɓ',A20,'IS THE SMALLEST STATE')
    f.   PRINT 50,STATE,'IS THE SMALLEST STATE'
        50 FORMAT('ɓ',A20,A21)

7. Rewrite the statements in Example B.3 on page 448 such that apostrophe edit descriptors in the FORMAT statements are replaced by A edit descriptors, except for carriage control.

The I Edit Descriptor

Integer values can be output using the descriptor

$$I w$$

where w is the width of the field. The integer output is automatically *right-justified* when it appears on the line. If the value to be output does not fill the field, the left position of the field is padded with blanks. Also, you should note that the output of a negative integer requires a print position for the negative sign, which means that you should take this into consideration in specifying the field width. The plus sign for a positive integer is not printed, however.

EXAMPLE B.6

Continuing Example B.4, the statements

        PRINT 60,NAME,ID,BALDUE

    60 FORMAT('ɓ',A15,I12,F14.2)

yield the following output.

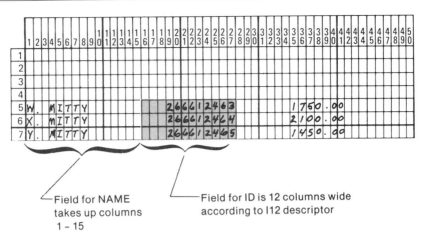

Field for NAME takes up columns 1 – 15

Field for ID is 12 columns wide according to I12 descriptor

Note that I12 is paired with ID, since A15 is paired with NAME and, of course, 'b' is used for carriage control. Following the output of NAME in the field given by columns 1 through 15, the integer value in ID is printed *right-justified* in the next 12 columns according to *w* in I12. Thus columns 16–27 are reserved as the field for the value in ID. Note that these values are printed to the extreme right of this field (columns 19–27), with blanks in the unused portion of the field (columns 16–18).

EXAMPLE B.7

Study the following program and its output.

```
INTEGER DAY,YEAR
DAY = 24
YEAR = 1942
PRINT 10,DAY,YEAR
10 FORMAT('bMY BIRTHDAY IS MARCH',I3,',',I5,'.')
END
```

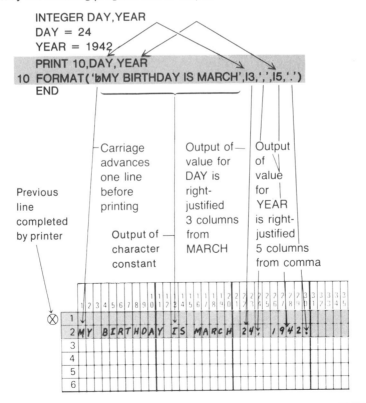

Previous line completed by printer

Carriage advances one line before printing

Output of character constant

Output of value for DAY is right-justified 3 columns from MARCH

Output of value for YEAR is right-justified 5 columns from comma

EXAMPLE B.8

Consider the statements

```
    PRINT 3,K
  3 FORMAT(' ',I4)
```

and the following variations.

	Output Columns
Contents of K	1 2 3 4 5 ...
705	7 0 5
−705	− 7 0 5
7050	7 0 5 0
−7050	* * * *
215305	* * * *

Both of the last two cases indicate that **format overflow** has occurred; that is, the field I4 is of insufficient width to handle the five characters in −7050 and the six characters in 215305. If K is not expected to exceed six characters, including a negative sign, then I6 should be used here.

In the above examples of format overflow, asterisks (*) were printed in the field that overflowed. Not all systems, however, print asterisks when overflow occurs. Some systems simply print the rightmost characters that fit in the field (7050 and 5305 in the above illustrations), whereas other systems print some other character to indicate overflow.

Follow-up Exercises

8. Test out how format overflow occurs in your system by writing a short program that causes the overflow conditions illustrated in Example B.8.

9. Indicate the exact output for the following program.

```
    INTEGER L,M,N
    .
    .
    .
    PRINT 15,M,N
    PRINT 20,L
 15 FORMAT ('1','M=',I4,'bN=',I5)
 20 FORMAT ('0','bbbbL=',I3)
    END
```

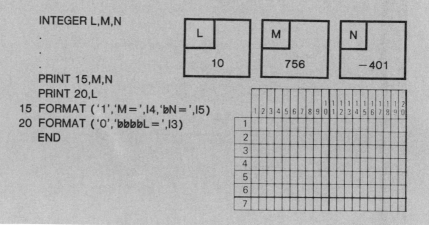

*10. Indicate the appropriate PRINT and FORMAT statements for the following desired output.

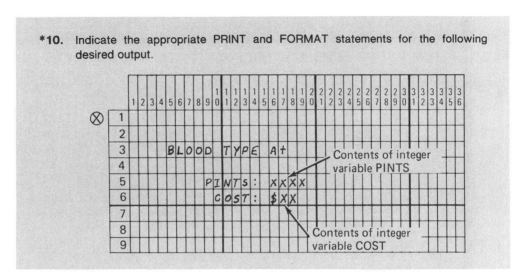

The F Edit Descriptor

Real values can be output in decimal form using F edit descriptors. The general form is

$$\boxed{\textbf{F}w.d}$$

where *w* is the width of the field and *d* is the number of digits in the fractional part of the value (the number of digits to the right of the decimal point). For example, F10.2 means *round* the real value to two decimal places and output the contents of the real variable right-justified within the ten-column field, as follows:

xxxxxxx.xx

To reduce the likelihood of format overflow, care must be taken in specifying widths of sufficient size. A rule of thumb to keep in mind is that the width of the field to be used for printing the contents of a real variable must be large enough to include positions for the decimal point and the sign (only the minus sign is printed), in addition to the digits. For example, if -52.1 is stored in ANS, then the field specification F5.1 uses the smallest field width that will avoid format overflow. We illustrate these situations by the examples that follow.

EXAMPLE B.9

To conclude Examples B.4 and B.6, consider once more the statements

    PRINT 60,NAME,ID, BALDUE

    60 FORMAT('b',A15,I12, F14.2)

---

and the resulting output when PRINT 60 is executed three times within the loop illustrated in Example B.1 on page 443.

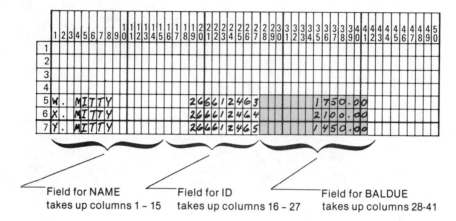

Field for NAME
takes up columns 1 – 15

Field for ID
takes up columns 16 – 27

Field for BALDUE
takes up columns 28-41

Note that commas separate the items in the list of descriptors and that F14.2 is paired with BALDUE. According to the F14.2 descriptor the value in BALDUE is printed to two decimal places right-justified in a 14-column field immediately to the right of the field for ID, as illustrated.

EXAMPLE B.10

Consider the variations shown below for output of various values for the real variable B using different F edit descriptors and the statements

```
     PRINT 8,B
   8 FORMAT('0',Fw.d)
```

Case	Contents in Memory for B	F*w.d*	1	2	3	4	5	6	7	8	9	...
a	735.	F6.0			7	3	5	.				
b	735.	F6.2	7	3	5	.	0	0				
c	735.	F5.2	*	*	*	*	*					
d	−735.	F6.0		−	7	3	5	.				
e	66.318	F8.3			6	6	.	3	1	8		
f	66.318	F8.2				6	6	.	3	2		
g	66.318	F8.1					6	6	.	3		
h	.14	F7.2				0	.	1	4			
i	.14	F4.2	0	.	1	4						
j	.14	F3.2	*	*	*							
k	−.14	F4.2	*	*	*	*						
l	−.14	F5.2	−	0	.	1	4					
m	−.14	F5.3	*	*	*	*	*					
n	−.14	F6.3	−	0	.	1	4	0				
o	0.	F7.2				0	.	0	0			

These cases illustrate some points worth remembering.

1. If the number is negative, the negative sign appears immediately to the left of the number (cases d and l); however, positive numbers usually do not appear with a plus sign.
2. For fractional numbers less than 1, most computers print a leading zero, as in cases i, l, and o.
3. Format overflow occurs when the field width is of insufficient size; see cases c, j, k, and m. These conditions are respectively corrected by cases b, i, l, and n. Overflow would not occur for cases k and m if the computer suppresses the leading zero.
4. The computer *rounds the output* to the specified number of decimal positions when the number of decimal positions in the F descriptor is less than the actual number of decimal digits stored in the variable. See cases f and g.
5. When the number of decimal positions specified in F$w.d$ is greater than the decimal digits stored in the variable, the trailing positions are filled with zeros. See cases b and n.

Follow-up Exercise

11. Fill in the following table for the output of a real variable.

Case	Contents	F$w.d$	Printed Output 1 2 3 4 5 6 7 8 9
a	3.105		3 . 1
b	3.105		3 . 1 0 5 0
c	−.1074	F6.4	
d	−.1074	F7.4	
e	−.1074	F9.4	
f	.1074	F6.4	
g	3764.	F9.1	
h	3764.16	F9.1	
i	3764.16	F9.0	
j	3764.16	F9.3	
k	3764.16	F6.3	

The E Edit Descriptor

The E edit descriptor allows the output of real values in exponential form. A general form of the E descriptor is given by

$$\boxed{\text{E}w.d}$$

where w is the field width and d represents the number of significant digits to be output. The usual exponential form of the output field is

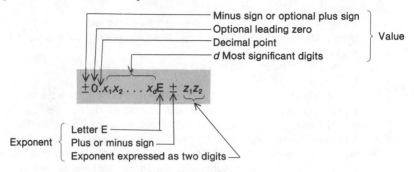

In other words, values are printed as a number between 0.1 and 1.0 or -0.1 and -1.0 followed by the appropriate exponent ($E \pm z_1z_2$).

EXAMPLE B.11

If 3.14159 is stored in PI, then the statements

```
    PRINT 5,PI
  5 FORMAT('ᵇᵇPIᵇ=',E15.5)
```

generally would print the following.

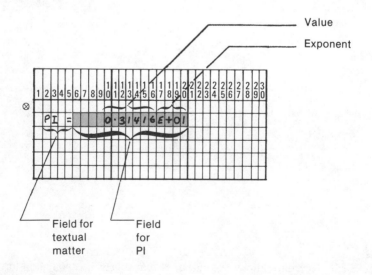

The computer thus rounds the value to five digits (since $d = 5$) and right-justifies the value in the 15-column field (since $w = 15$) given by columns 6–20.

To avoid format overflow, field width w should be at least seven more than significant digits d ($w \geq d + 7$) since we have to allow four columns for the exponent ($E \pm z_1 z_2$) and three columns for the sign, leading zero, and decimal point ($\pm 0.$).[6]

In the example for PI, if we wish d to be 5, then we should specify $w \geq 12$ to avoid format overflow. For example, if we had used E9.5, the field width would have been insufficient to output the value in PI.

EXAMPLE B.12

Consider the variations below.

			Printed Output															
	Contents in											1	1	1	1	1	1	
Case	Memory	Ew.d	1	2	3	4	5	6	7	8	9	0	1	2	3	4	5	
a	38.716	E15.5					0	.	3	8	7	1	6	E		0	2
b	38.716	E15.4						0	.	3	8	7	2	E		0	2
c	38.716	E15.3							0	.	3	8	7	E		0	2
d	38.716	E15.0									0	.		E		0	2
e	−38.716	E15.5				−	0	.	3	8	7	1	6	E		0	2
f	0.000617	E12.5	0	.		6	1	7	0	0	E	−	0	3			
g	0.000617	E12.3			0	.	6	1	7	E	−	0	3				
h	0.000617	E12.2			0	.	6	2	E	−	0	3					
i	0.268	E12.4		0	.	2	6	8	0	E		0	0				
j	3.268	E9.4	*	*	*		*	*	*	*	*	*					
k	3.268	E12.4		0	.	3	2	6	8	E		0	1				

The following points may be worth remembering.

1. If the number is negative, the negative sign appears immediately to the left of the number (case e); however, positive numbers usually do not appear with a plus sign.
2. We show a leading zero for each output value, but its inclusion depends on the system.
3. Format overflow occurs when the field width is of insufficient size; see case j. This condition is corrected by case k.
4. The computer rounds the output to the specified number of decimal positions given by d when d is less than the actual number of digits stored in the variable. See cases b, c, and h.
5. When d in Ew.d is greater than the digits stored in the variable, the trailing positions are filled with zeros. See cases f and i.
6. The d portion of the descriptor Ew.d must be greater than zero if any value is to be written (case d).

---

[6] The rule of thumb is $w \geq d + 6$ for systems that suppress the leading zero.

Follow-up Exercise

12.   Fill in the following table for the output of a real variable.

			Printed Output														
Case	Contents	E*w.d*	1	2	3	4	5	6	7	8	9	1 0	1 1	1 2	1 3	1 4	1 5
a	3.105						0	.	3	1	0	5	E		0	1	
b	3.105							0	.	3	1	E		0	1		
c	−.1074	E15.5															
d	−.1074	E15.4															
e	−.1074	E15.2															
f	−.1074	E15.9															
g	3764.	E14.5															
h	3764.16	E14.5															
i	3764.16	E14.6															
j	3764.16	E10.4															
k	3764.16	E12.3															

The D Edit Descriptor

The D edit descriptor is used to output double-precision values. Its general form is

$$\boxed{\text{D}w.d}$$

where w is the field width and d is the number of significant digits to be output. The D descriptor is treated identically to the way the E descriptor is treated, except that E is replaced by D.

EXAMPLE B.13

If 3.1415926536 is stored in the double-precision variable PI, the statements

        PRINT 5,PI
    5 FORMAT('ⴆⴆPIⴆ=',D20.11)

generally would print

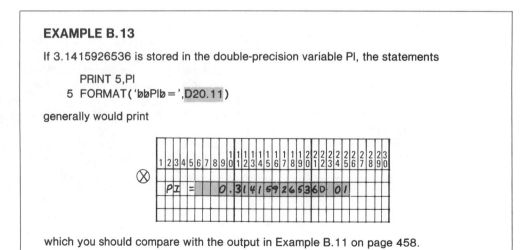

which you should compare with the output in Example B.11 on page 458.

Follow-up Exercise

13. Describe the output of PI in Example B.13 based on the cases below.

		Printed Output
		1 1 1 1 1 1 1 1 1 1 2 2 2 2 2 2
Case	FORMAT Statement	1 2 3 4 5 6 7 8 9 0 1 2 3 4 5 6 7 8 9 0 1 2 3 4 5
a	5 FORMAT('ƀ',D20.11)	
b	5 FORMAT('ƀ',D15.8)	
c	5 FORMAT('ƀ',D15.11)	

The X Edit Descriptor

The X edit descriptor is used to insert blanks in the printed line. The general form is

$$nX$$

where *n* represents the number of blanks to be inserted. For example, 5X means to print five blank spaces. This descriptor also can be used to single-space the carriage.

EXAMPLE B.14

The statements

        PRINT 70
    70 FORMAT('ƀ', 31X,'– – – – – – – – – – –')

are used in Example B.1 to "dress up" the output shown on page 444. In this case the carriage advances one line according to 'ƀ', prints 31 blank characters according to 31X, and prints 11 minus signs in columns 32–42 according to the apostrophe edit descriptor.

    Alternatively, carriage control can be incorporated into the X descriptor as

    70 FORMAT(32X,'– – – – – – – – – – –')

where it is understood that the first X transmits a blank for carriage control and the remaining 31 X's are used to print 31 blanks.

    You should appreciate that use of the X edit descriptor represents a more efficient and less painful approach than the "brute force" approach given by

32 blank characters instead of 32X

    70 FORMAT('ƀƀƀƀƀƀƀƀƀƀƀƀƀƀƀƀƀƀƀƀƀƀƀƀƀƀƀƀƀƀƀƀ– – – – – – – – – – –')

Follow-up Exercises

14. Rewrite FORMATs "30" and "40" in Example B.1 on page 443 to use the X edit descriptor. Which approach do you prefer and why?

*15. Indicate the appropriate PRINT and FORMAT statements for the following desired output. Use the X descriptor for four or more consecutive blanks.

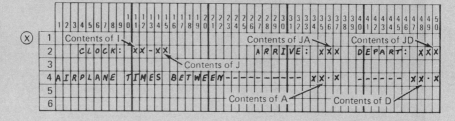

The T Edit Descriptor

The T edit descriptor controls horizontal spacing, as does the X edit descriptor. Its general form is given by

$$\boxed{\text{T}n}$$

where *n* is the output column where the next output character is to be printed. Whereas the *n*X descriptor is used to skip the next *n* output columns, the T*n* descriptor is used to "tab" to the *n*th output column. *Caution:* The first output column is taken to be carriage control; hence T*n* actually tabs to the $(n - 1)$th *print* column.

EXAMPLE B.15

Convince yourself that the following two FORMAT statements are equivalent.

    10 FORMAT('0',19X,'ITEM',16X,'RESULT')
    10 FORMAT('0',T21,'ITEM',T41,'RESULT')

In each case ITEM is in print columns 20–23 and RESULT is in print columns 40–45. Which approach to use is simply a matter of preference. Which do you prefer?

Follow-up Exercises

16. Use the T descriptor in FORMAT "80" of Example B.1 on page 443.

17. Rework the following exercises using the T descriptor.

    a. Exercise 14 above.

  *b. Exercise 15 above.

B.3
COMMON ERRORS

In our years of teaching FORTRAN, and in our own early efforts in learning FORTRAN "long" ago, we have witnessed time and again certain output errors that occur commonly.

1. **Unaligned output.** Output that is other than trivial involves careful planning. For example, if you have to output table headings and values for several variables, then *before writing your FORMAT statements you can save yourself some grief by outlining your output on a sheet of plain paper, quadrille paper, or print chart.* To illustrate, consider the following layout:

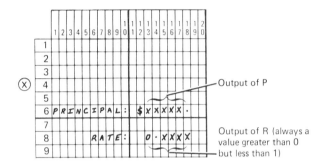

This layout was done *before* the following PRINT/FORMAT statements were written.

```
35  FORMAT('0PRINCIPAL:$',F6.0)
40  FORMAT('0',5X,'RATE:',F8.4)
    PRINT 35,P
    PRINT 40,R
```

You should confirm that these two FORMATs exactly correspond to this output plan.

2. **Forgetting about carriage control in output FORMATs.** If your output is to either a line printer or a terminal, the computer expects a carriage control character whether you like it or not. If you remember to specify carriage control in your output FORMAT, then you are in charge. Otherwise the printer will "rip off" a column from your first edit descriptor. For example, the statements

```
    PRINT 3
 3  FORMAT('RESULT')
    PRINT 4,J
 4  FORMAT(I3)
```

where 23 is stored for J in memory would yield the following output.

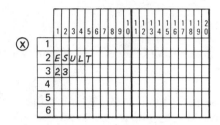

Carriage control was not specified before the character constant 'RESULT'; hence the printer uses the R for carriage control and prints out "ESULT." Again, carriage control is omitted in the second FORMAT. So the printer takes the first column of the descriptor I3 and prints the 23 right-justified in column 2 instead of column 3.

3. **Inconsistency of type between variables in the print list and edit descriptors in the format list.**   Do you see anything wrong with the following?

```
     REAL Q
     INTEGER K
     PRINT 7,K,Q
   7 FORMAT( 1X,F5.0,I10)
```

In this case the integer variable K is type mismatched with the real descriptor F5.0. Also, the real variable Q is mismatched with the integer descriptor I10. This type of error is insidious, as many compilers will not identify the error. Instead of getting either a syntax error or an execution error, you get a "junk" number printed; that is, the number that is printed will be in the proper form according to the specification, but its value will be incorrect.

Try writing and submitting a short program that assigns, say, 15 to K and 6.5 to Q, and use the PRINT and FORMAT statements above. What happens on your system?

4. **Insufficient field width for numeric output.**   Some students misinterpret the way in which the F descriptor determines the width of a field. For example, a beginning student may use F5.2 to output a value such as 1059.25. The student adds the width of the field (5) and the number of decimal digits (2) and concludes, erroneously, that seven characters can be printed. Not so. Only five characters can be printed. Thus 99.99 is the largest value and −9.99 the smallest value that can be printed with a F5.2 descriptor. Values larger than this would cause format overflow (see Examples B.10 and B.12). What does your computer print when format overflow occurs?

5. **Memory lapses in using the F and E descriptors.**   The only form of the F descriptor is F$w.d$. When students use a real variable to store values with no decimal digits, they sometimes incorrectly use Fw instead of F$w.0$ to output these values. Another error occurs when the field width (w) and decimal digits (d) in E and F descriptors are reversed. For example, E15.6 and F9.3 are written incorrectly as E6.15 and F3.9.

6. **Incorrect character output.**   Pay careful attention to Rules 1 and 2 on page 451 when the field width w in your A descriptor differs from the declared length l of your character variable. The example for Rule 1 shows a common error.

7. **"Falling off" the print line.**   Check the maximum number of characters that can be printed on a print line of your terminal or printer. Make sure the format specification

does not exceed that amount. When it does, either the next print line is used to complete the current print line, which plays havoc with your (presumably) carefully designed output, or you get an error message.

Follow-up Exercise

18. Define or explain the following.

list-directed output	A edit descriptor
format-directed output	I edit descriptor
general form of PRINT statement	F edit descriptor
FORMAT statement	E edit descriptor
apostrophe edit descriptor	D edit descriptor
carriage control	X edit descriptor
carriage control characters	T edit descriptor
field	format overflow

Input with Formats

Up until this point we have used **list-directed input,** which is free of FORMAT statements. You probably found this method of data entry easy and felt little motivation to change. Many situations, however, require the precise arrangement of input data whereby each value is placed in certain columns of an input medium such as punched card or disk. To read in such values we must use **format-directed input** statements, which we explain in this module.

EXAMPLE C.1   Student Billing Program with Format-Directed Input/ Output

To illustrate the use of formatted input, we have revised the student billing program once again, this time substituting format-directed input statements for list-directed input statements. The shaded segments indicate the changes introduced in this version from the version on page 443.

---

* Can be assigned anytime after Chapter 4 and Module B.

Review the program briefly now, and as you read this module the details will become clear.

```
C-----------------------------------------------------------
C    STUDENT BILLING PROGRAM WITH INPUT/OUTPUT FORMATS
C
C    KEY:
C      CPC    = COST PER CREDIT
C      FEES   = STUDENT FEES
C      NAME   = STUDENT NAME
C      ID     = STUDENT ID NUMBER
C      CREDIT = NUMBER OF CREDITS
C      TUIT   = TUITION
C      BALDUE = AMOUNT OWED BY STUDENT
C      CUMBAL = AMOUNT OWED TO INSTITUTION
C      N      = NUMBER OF STUDENTS
C-----------------------------------------------------------
      CHARACTER NAME*15
      INTEGER   ID,N
      REAL      CPC,FEES,CREDIT,TUIT,BALDUE,CUMBAL
C-----------------------------------------------------------
      CUMBAL = 0.0
C-----------------------------------------------------------
      READ 10, CPC,FEES
      READ 15, N
C-----------------------------------------------------------
      PRINT 30
      PRINT 40
      PRINT 50
C-----------------------------------------------------------
      DO 5 J = 1,N
        READ 20, NAME,ID,CREDIT
        TUIT   = CREDIT*CPC
        BALDUE = TUIT + FEES
        CUMBAL = CUMBAL + BALDUE
        PRINT 60,NAME,ID,BALDUE
    5 CONTINUE
C-----------------------------------------------------------
      PRINT 50
      PRINT 80,CUMBAL
      PRINT 70
      PRINT 70
C-----------------------------------------------------------
   10 FORMAT(F5.2,F5.2)
   15 FORMAT(I5)
   20 FORMAT(A15,I9,F4.1)
   30 FORMAT('1','          **TUITION REPORT**')
   40 FORMAT('0','     NAME        SS NUMBER    BALANCE DUE')
   50 FORMAT(' ','-------------------------------------------')
   60 FORMAT(' ',A15,I12,F14.2)
   70 FORMAT(' ',31X,'-----------')
   80 FORMAT(18X,'**TOTALS**    $',F10.2)
C-----------------------------------------------------------
      STOP
      END
```

The circled labels A, B, C appear beside: READ statements (A), the READ 20 inside the DO loop (B), and the FORMAT statements block (C).

Formatted Input

```
100 250
  3
W. MITTY    266612463 150
X. MITTY    266612464 185
Y. MITTY    266612465 120
```

Formatted Output

```
              **TUITION REPORT**
        NAME        SS NUMBER    BALANCE DUE
        -------------------------------------
        W. MITTY       266612463      1750.00
        X. MITTY       266612464      2100.00
        Y. MITTY       266612465      1450.00
        -------------------------------------

                    **TOTALS**    $   5300.00
                                   -----------
                                   -----------
```

C.1
ON FIELDS, RECORDS, AND FILES

You may find the following classification scheme useful in helping you understand the mechanics of input with FORMATs.

Field.   A data item. For example, an employer might maintain data on the employee's name, Social Security number, rate of pay, number of deductions, and other items. Each of these data items is considered a field. In the input data for the student billing example, name is a field, ID number is a field, and number of credits is another field. In the printed output, name is a field, ID number is a field, and the balance due is another field.

Record.   A collection of related fields. For example, all of the data items relating to a single employee represent a single record. In the student billing example, the data items pertaining to a single student make up a record. Typically, a single data card or a single line of print represents a record.

File.   A collection of related records. For example, a "payroll file" contains all the employee pay records; a "student file" contains data on all students.

Figure C.1A illustrates the relationship among fields, records, and files for the student billing data. Notice that these records are processed by the READ statement in box B of the program, which is associated with FORMAT "20" in box C.

When designing the placement of input data, it's best first to design a layout similar to that in Figure C.1B. The **record layout** is a drawing and/or narrative that indicates the arrangement of data on an I/O record. In this type of documentation you might find some or all of the following.

Description of the field
Variable name assigned to the field
Type of data in the field
Location of the field on the record
Edit descriptor associated with the field

Notice that the record layout is consistent with both Figure C.1A and the input data in Example C.1.

C.2
READ AND FORMAT STATEMENTS

The input of data from specific columns of an input record requires format-directed input for precise control. This usually is accomplished by pairing the READ statement with a FORMAT statement.

The general form of the READ statement is

READ *format identifier, list*

In earlier programs the *format identifier* was omitted, which meant list-directed input. For format-directed input the format identifier is usually a statement label (number) that iden-

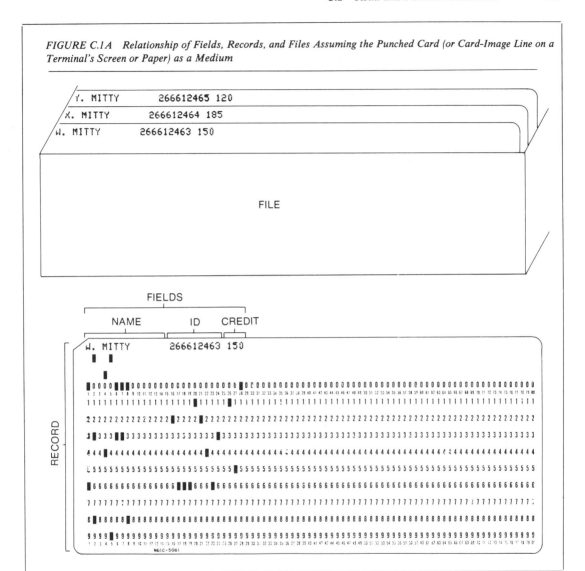

FIGURE C.1A   Relationship of Fields, Records, and Files Assuming the Punched Card (or Card-Image Line on a Terminal's Screen or Paper) as a Medium

FIGURE C.1B   Record Layout

Field Description	Variable Name	Type of Data	Columns	Edit Descriptor
Student name	NAME	Character	1–15	A15
Social Security no.	ID	Integer	16–24	I9
Credit hours	CREDIT	Real	25–28	F4.1

tifies the FORMAT statement that is to be used by the READ statement.[1] As before, the *list* is a sequence of variable names.[2]

To illustrate, the statement

in box B of Example C.1 specifies the variables whose values are to be input (NAME, ID, and CREDIT) and identifies the FORMAT statement to use (statement 20) for selecting these values from the input record.

The FORMAT statement for input is used to describe the location of data on the input record. A general form of the FORMAT statement is given by

format
statement **FORMAT** *(list of edit descriptors)*
label

where the *format statement label* is any unsigned, nonzero integer constant up to five digits that uniquely identifies the FORMAT statement and *edit descriptors* are codes that specify the editing necessary to process the I/O records. These edit descriptors indicate the position, type (integer, real, etc.), size, and decimal point location (if applicable) of the values to be input.[3]

For example, the statement

in box C of Example C.1 is utilized by the READ statement

READ 20,NAME,ID,CREDIT

to convert data values in the input record for storage in the variables NAME, ID, and CREDIT. Note how the format identifier 20 in the READ statement corresponds to the format statement label in the FORMAT statement.

The following points are worth remembering.

1.   The READ statement directs the reading of a new record from the data file each time the READ statement is executed. For example, the READ statement in box B of Exam-

---

[1] We can also use a character variable name (see Module D, Section D.3) as a format identifier.
[2] The input list may also include an array element name (Chapters 7 and 8), an array name (Chapters 7 and 8), and implied-DO lists (Chapters 7 and 8).
[3] As also mentioned in Module B, the portion (list of edit descriptors) following the key word FORMAT is called the *format specification.* More complicated format specifications include nested sets of parentheses, as discussed in Module D. Format specifications also can be provided without the use of a FORMAT statement, as illustrated in Section D.3.

ple C.1 is executed three times. Thus three new records are processed from the student file in Figure C.1A.

2. Since FORMAT statements are nonexecutable, the input FORMATs are often placed in a group out of the way of the execution logic, as was done with output FORMATs to improve readability.

3. The maximum length of an input record may depend on the processor and/or the input medium. For example, if punched-card image is considered a complete input record, then 80 characters is the maximum length of this input record.

Follow-up Exercise

1. An alternative READ statement for processing format-directed input is

$$\textbf{READ}\left(\begin{array}{ll}\textit{input} & \textit{format} \\ \textit{unit} & \textit{statement} \\ \textit{number,} & \textit{label}\end{array}\right)\textit{list}$$

The *input unit number* is an integer variable or constant that specifies the type of input unit that is to be used to read in your data, such as a card reader or a terminal. In our system we use the number "5" to identify either the card reader or the terminal, although this number varies depending on which computer system your institution is using. The *format statement label* references the FORMAT statement that is to be used by this READ statement. As before, the typical *list* is a sequence of variable names separated by commas.

This READ statement is more versatile than the other since, among other things, it allows us to specify specific input units such as card reader, disk drive, and tape drive (as in Chapter 11).

Replace the READ statements in Example C.1 with this version.

C.3
SELECTED EDIT DESCRIPTORS

The same edit descriptors discussed in Module B, except for the apostrophe edit descriptor, are applied in the current section to format-directed input. Note that carriage control and textual matter (as discussed in pages 447–448) are not relevant to input data.

The A Edit Descriptor

The input of a character value that is to be stored in a character variable is accomplished by using the A edit descriptor. The general form is

$$A w$$

where *w* is the width of the field used to input the character value.

EXAMPLE C.2

In Example C.1 the following statements were used to read in a student's record.

        READ 20,NAME,ID,CREDIT

    20 FORMAT(A15,I9,F4.1)

For now, ignore the variables ID and CREDIT and the descriptors I9 and F4.1. In effect, the READ statement tells the computer "to read the value of NAME according to the statement labeled 20." Format "20" tells the computer "the input value for NAME is to be found in a character field which is 15 columns wide." In other words, the first descriptor, A15, has been paired with the first variable in the list, NAME.

   In the program of Example C.1, NAME is declared a character variable with a length of 15 characters according to the statement

    CHARACTER NAME*15 ←—— Declared length of 15 equals
                              field width of 15 in A15 within
                              FORMAT "20"

Thus, to simplify the rules associated with character input, we used A15 to edit the input value for NAME. In other words, we selected the *field width w* equal to the *declared length l,* or 15 characters.

   Now look at the first input record that's processed by this READ/FORMAT pair.

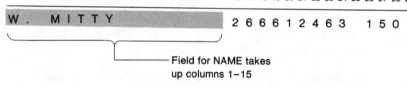

Field for NAME takes
up columns 1–15

The character value to be stored in NAME is found in columns 1–15 since A15 is the first edit descriptor in FORMAT "20." After this input record is processed, the first value stored in NAME is internally represented as follows:

Note that seven blank characters are stored as the last seven characters in NAME, since columns 9–15 of the input record are blank and NAME has a declared length of 15 characters. Also note that *apostrophes are not placed around character data in formatted input records.* In fact, if we were to use the formatted input record

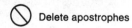

       Delete apostrophes

NAME would appear incorrectly as

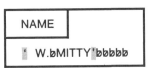

As we advised for format-directed output, we suggest that under most circumstances you set the field width *w* in A edit descriptors equal to the declared length *l* in the CHAR-ACTER statement.

In general, the field width *w* may differ from the declared length *l*. In some instances you might find it convenient to select *w* unequal to *l*, in which case the following rules would apply.

Rule 1: If $w \leq l$, the internal representation will be *w* characters *left-justified* followed by $l - w$ trailing blanks.

Rule 2: If $w > l$, the internal representation will consist of the *rightmost l* characters in the input field.

EXAMPLE C.3

Study the two examples below and relate them to the two rules above, given the input record:

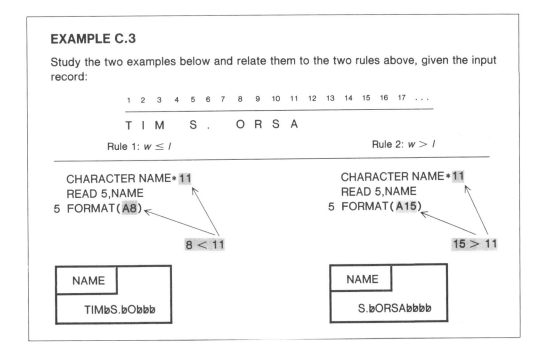

Follow-up Exercises

2. Suppose an input record contains an employee's first name in columns 1–8, second name in columns 9–16, and last name in columns 17–28. Using

    CHARACTER FIRST∗8,MIDDLE∗8,LAST∗12

   a. Specify READ/FORMAT statements to enter these data.
   b. Specify PRINT/FORMAT statements to give an output line at the top of a new page having last name in columns 50–61 followed by a comma, blank space, first name in columns 64–71, blank space, and middle name in columns 73–80.

3. Given the input record

   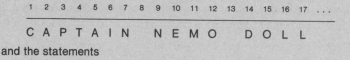

1	2	3	4	5	6	7	8	9	10	11	12	13	14	15	16	17	...
C	A	P	T	A	I	N		N	E	M	O		D	O	L	L	

   and the statements

   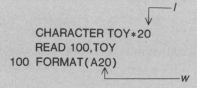

   ```
             CHARACTER TOY∗20
             READ 100,TOY
       100   FORMAT(A20)
   ```

   specify storage contents for each variation below.

Part	Declared Length, *l*	Field Width, *w*	Contents in TOY
a	20	20	
b	20	10	
c	20	25	
d	15	20	
e	15	10	

The I Edit Descriptor

The input of integer values for storage within integer variables requires the descriptor

$$I w$$

where *w* is the field width.

EXAMPLE C.4

Consider the following statements from Example C.1

            READ 15,N
        15 FORMAT (I5)

and the associated input record

        123456789...

        3 ⟵————— Right-justify in the field

which give the storage result

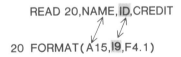

The descriptor I5 in FORMAT "15" tells the computer "the value for N is type integer in a field 5 columns wide." Note that N is an integer variable; hence the I edit descriptor must be used.

Now look at the input record. The value that is to be stored in N is found in the first five columns of the record—specifically in column 5. In general, *leading blanks for numeric input are ignored;* hence the integer value 3 is stored in the integer variable N.

Embedded and trailing blanks in format-directed numeric input are treated as zeros. For example, a 3 in column 1 of the above input record would be stored as 30000. *Make sure you right-justify* numeric input in the field, as shown above.

Have you wondered why we chose a field width of 5 to input number of students (N)? We assumed that this program is to be used by universities with student enrollments up to 99,999. In general, *select a field width that's compatible with the width of the largest foreseeable input value.*

Finally, consider the following statements in Examples C.1 and C.2.

        READ 20,NAME,ID,CREDIT

        20 FORMAT(A15,I9,F4.1)

Note that A15 is paired with the character variable NAME and I9 is paired with the integer variable ID. The first input record in the student file is edited as follows:

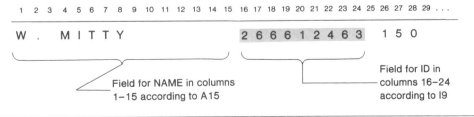

Field for NAME in columns
1–15 according to A15

Field for ID in
columns 16–24
according to I9

Thus the "9" in I9 tells the computer that the input field for ID is the next nine positions following the field for NAME. Since the first field takes up columns 1–15, it follows that the second field is in columns 16–24.

EXAMPLE C.5

Consider the statements

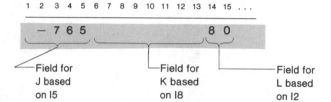

and the input record

```
1  2  3  4  5  6  7  8  9  10 11 12 13 14 15 ...

   – 7 6 5                          8 0
```

Field for J based on I5

Field for K based on I8

Field for L based on I2

In this case −765 is stored in J, zero is stored in K, and 80 is stored in L. *Note that a numeric null field, one containing all blanks, is edited as having a value of zero.*

Follow-up Exercises

4. For the statements

```
INTEGER JACK,JILL,UP,HILL
READ 3,JACK,JILL,UP,HILL
```

and the input record

```
1  2  3  4  5  6  7  8  9  10 11 12 13 14 ...

5        6 2 4 1 9 8 4     7 5
```

determine the stored values for each case below.
   a. 3 FORMAT(I1,I3,I4,I2)
   b. 3 FORMAT(I1,I8,I2,I3)

5. Given the input record

```
1  2  3  4  5  6  7  8  9 ...

6 1 3 0 4 2     1
```

write the appropriate statements that result in the storage of 613 for K, 42 for M, and 1 for N.

6. Appropriately fill in the input record below if 35 for J, 600 for K, and −3 for L are to be stored using

> READ 25,J,K,L
> 25 FORMAT(I4,I4,I4)
> 1 2 3 4 5 6 7 8 9 10 11 12 13 14 . . .

The F Edit Descriptor

The F edit descriptor is used to input values for either real or double-precision variables. The general form is

$$\boxed{\mathbf{F}w.d}$$

where w is the field width and d is the number of digits in the fractional part of the value. The corresponding input field in the input record typically consists of an optional sign followed by a string of digits optionally containing a decimal point.[4] If the decimal point is omitted, the rightmost d digits of the string represent the fractional part of the value. If the decimal point is included in the input field, d has no effect on the value stored.

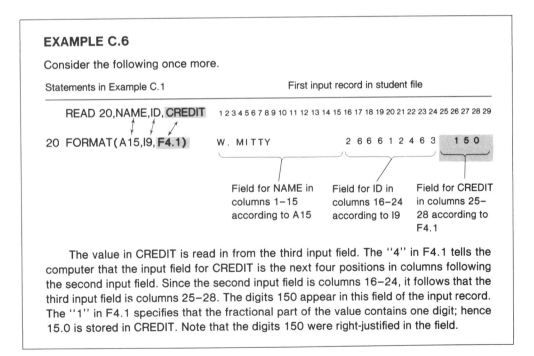

EXAMPLE C.6

Consider the following once more.

Statements in Example C.1   First input record in student file

       READ 20,NAME,ID, CREDIT   1 2 3 4 5 6 7 8 9 10 11 12 13 14 15 16 17 18 19 20 21 22 23 24 25 26 27 28 29

20 FORMAT(A15,I9, F4.1)   W . MI TTY   2 6 6 6 1 2 4 6 3   1 5 0

Field for NAME in   Field for ID in   Field for CREDIT
columns 1–15   columns 16–24   in columns 25–
according to A15   according to I9   28 according to
                                             F4.1

The value in CREDIT is read in from the third input field. The "4" in F4.1 tells the computer that the input field for CREDIT is the next four positions in columns following the second input field. Since the second input field is columns 16–24, it follows that the third input field is columns 25–28. The digits 150 appear in this field of the input record. The "1" in F4.1 specifies that the fractional part of the value contains one digit; hence 15.0 is stored in CREDIT. Note that the digits 150 were right-justified in the field.

---

[4] The string of digits can be followed by an optional exponent, which we illustrate in the next subsection.

Alternatively, we could have included the decimal point as part of the input field, in which case the "1" in F4.1 is ignored. For example, we could place the value in any of the following ways.

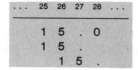

In other words, by directly using the decimal point ourselves, the computer does not need to "figure out" where the decimal point is to be placed.

Finally, note that CREDIT and the F descriptor agree with respect to type; that is, CREDIT is a real variable and the F descriptor edits real values.

EXAMPLE C.7

Make sure you understand the variations below based on the statements

    REAL HEIGHT,WEIGHT
    READ 7,HEIGHT,WEIGHT

and the input record

```
1  2  3  4  5  6  7  8  9  10 11 12 13 14 15 16 17 18 19...
   7  5  5  3              1  3  4  6
```

Case	FORMAT Statement	Values Stored in HEIGHT	WEIGHT
a	7 FORMAT(F6.2,F9.1)	75.53	134.6
b	7 FORMAT(F6.3,F9.1)	7.553	134.6
c	7 FORMAT(F6.4,F9.3)	0.7553	1.346
d	7 FORMAT(F6.5,F9.3)	0.07553	1.346

Follow-up Exercises

7. In Example C.1, page 467, what gets stored in CPC and FEES? What are the maximum values that can be stored in these variables?

8. For the statements

    REAL JACK,JILL,UP,HILL
    READ 3,JACK,JILL,UP,HILL

and the input record

```
1  2  3  4  5  6  7  8  9  10 11 12 13 14 ...
5        6  2  4  1  9  8  4     7  5
```

determine the stored values for each case below.

   a. 3 FORMAT(F1.0,F3.0,F4.1,F2.2)

   b. 3 FORMAT(F1.0,F8.3,F2.0,F3.3)

9. Consider Example C.6.

   a. What's the maximum number of credits that a student can take assuming no decimal point is used in the input field? Assuming a decimal point is used?

   b. Suppose fractional credits are not allowed by the university. Why would it be wrong to use the following?

        READ 20,NAME,ID,CREDIT
       20 FORMAT(A15,I9,I4)

10. Given the input record

1	2	3	4	5	6	7	8	9	...
6	1	3	0	4	2		1		

write appropriate statements that result in the storage of 6.13 for X, 42.0 for Y, and 0.1 for Z.

11. Appropriately fill in the input records below for storage of the indicated values using

        READ 1,COST,NUM,QUANT
      1 FORMAT(F5.2,I5,F5.0)

Part	Values Stored in			Columns in Input Record
	COST	NUM	QUANT	1 2 3 4 5 6 7 8 9 10 11 12 13 14 15 16 17 18 19 20
a	15.25	45	507.0	
b	152.50	450	5070.0	
c	1525.00	50	507.4	
d	105.0	5	−300.0	

12. Consider the following statements, which replace those in Example C.6.

      19 FORMAT(A15)
      20 FORMAT(I9)
      21 FORMAT(F4.1)
         READ 19,NAME
         READ 20,ID
         READ 21,CREDIT

Describe input records for the first student. How many input records are needed for each student?

13. More than one READ statement can reference a single FORMAT statement, since the latter is a nonexecutable statement that simply provides information to the control unit. To illustrate, consider the following.

      10 FORMAT(F5.1,I5)
         READ 10,X,J
         READ 10,R,K

Indicate how the values 73.4 for X, 100 for J, 607.0 for R, and 3 for K should be placed on input records.

*14.   Consider the following layout for an input record.

Column	Variable	Type	Contents
1–11	SSN	Character	Social Security number (for example, 267-61-9814)
12–31	NAME	Character	Name
32–33	AGE	Integer	Age (for example, 37)
34	MS	Character	Marital status (M = married, S = single, O = other)
35	SEX	Character	Sex (M = male, F = female)
36–42	SAL	Real	Salary (to two decimal places; for example, 1534275 would be a salary of $15,342.75)
43–80	Blank		

Develop READ and FORMAT statements to enter these data. Include type statements for these variables.

The E Edit Descriptor

Real values in exponential form are usually input using the E edit descriptor

$$\boxed{\textsf{E}w.d}$$

where w is the field width and d is the number of digits in the fractional part of the value. The corresponding input field in the input record consists of (1) an optional sign, (2) a string of digits optionally containing a decimal point, and (3) an exponent. The exponent can be denoted by either (a) a signed integer constant or (b) E followed by zero or more blanks, followed by an optionally signed integer constant. If the decimal point is included in the input field, d has no effect on the value stored. If the exponent is omitted from the input field, the E descriptor is equivalent to the F descriptor. In fact, *there is no distinction between E and F descriptors for input fields,* since exponents also can be used for input fields edited by F descriptors (see footnote 4 on page 477).

EXAMPLE C.8

Suppose we wish to input the value 6.6254×10^{-27} using the statement

```
REAL PLANCK
READ 9,PLANCK
```

Study the following variations.

Case	FORMAT Statement	Input Record (1 2 3 4 5 6 7 8 9 10 11 12 13 14 15 16 17 18 19 . . .)
a	9 FORMAT(E10.4)	6 6 2 5 4 E – 2 7
b		6 6 2 5 4 – 2 7
c		6 · 6 2 5 4 E – 2 7
d		6 · 6 2 5 4 – 2 7
e		· 6 6 2 5 4 E – 2 6
f	9 FORMAT(E15.1)	6 6 2 5 4 E – 3 0
g		6 6 2 5 4 – 3 0
h		6 · 6 2 5 4 E – 2 7
i		6 · 6 2 5 4 – 2 7
j		· 6 6 2 5 4 E – 2 6

Note that inclusion of the decimal point (cases c, d, e, h, i, and j) overrides the d portion of the descriptor. Also, make sure that your field width is large enough to accommodate the exponent. For example, E8.4 would be sufficient only for case b, since cases a and d take up nine columns and cases c and e take up ten columns. Finally, we could have used F10.4 in place of E10.4 and F15.1 in place of E15.1, since E and F descriptors are equivalent for input fields.

Follow-up Exercise

15. Given the statements

```
READ 5,V1,V2,V3
5 FORMAT(E10.2,E10.3,E9.2)
```

What values are stored in V1, V2, and V3 for each input record below?

	1 2 3 4 5 6 7 8 9 10 11 12 13 14 15 16 17 18 19 20 21 22 23 24 25 26 27 28 29 . . .
a	– 1 2 . 1 E + 2 5 . 5 5 5 E + 3 . 3 3 E 0 4
b	– 1 2 E + 2 5 5 5 5 . E 3 3 3 E – 0 4
c	– 1 2 + 2 5 5 5 . 3 3

The D Edit Descriptor

Double-precision values are usually input using the D edit descriptor

$$\boxed{\text{D}w.d}$$

where w is the field width and d is the number of digits in the fractional part of the value. Alternatively, the F descriptor can be used to input double-precision values. The D descriptor is treated identically to the E descriptor, except that E is replaced by D.

EXAMPLE C.9

If we wish to input the value 3.1415926536 using the statements

```
    READ 7,PI
 7  FORMAT(D15.11)
```

where PI is typed double precision, any of the following input field variations will serve the purpose.

```
1  2  3  4  5  6  7  8  9  10 11 12 13  14  15 ...
_____
          3 . 1 4 1 5 9 2 6 5  3  6
3 1 4 1 5 9 2 6 5 3 6 D + 0 1
    3 1 4 1 5 9 2 6 5 3 6 + 1
```

The X Edit Descriptor

The X descriptor is used to skip columns in an input record. Its general form is

$$n\,X$$

where *n* is the number of columns to skip.

EXAMPLE C.10

Suppose that FORMAT "20" in Example C.1 is changed as follows:

```
    READ 20,NAME,ID,CREDIT
 20 FORMAT(A15,5X,I9,1X,F4.1)
```

The input unit finds the value of NAME in columns 1–15 of the input record, skips the next five columns (16–20), finds the value for ID in columns 21–29, skips column 30, and finds the value for CREDIT in columns 31–34. The input record would look like this.

```
1  2  3  4  5 6 7 8 9 10 11 12 13 14  15  16  17  18 19 20 21 22 23 24 25 26 27 28 29 30 31 32 33 34 ...
_____
W .    M I T T Y                                   2 6 6 6 1 2 4 6 3      1 5 0
```

You might ask why columns 16–20 would contain blanks in the first place. Why not begin the next field in column 16? If you have room on an input record such as a card, then spacing between fields (or alternatively using wide fields) improves readability (for us humans). Otherwise blank fields in input records represent wasted space and effort. You should design input records efficiently. Generally, the X descriptor is used within input format specifications to skip fields that contain data not needed in the current analysis, as the following exercises illustrate.

Follow-up Exercises

17. In Example C.10 suppose that the input record contains ID in columns 1–9, the student's name in a field given by columns 10–24, the home address in columns 25–71, and the value of CREDIT in columns 72–75. We wish to read in only ID and CREDIT. Appropriately change the READ and FORMAT statements.

*18. You're given an input record with the following layout.

Column	Contents	Variable Name	Type
1–9	Social Security number	SSN	Integer
22–45	Name	NAME	Character
46–47	Age	AGE	Integer
48	Marital status	MAR	Character
49	Sex	SEX	Character
50–57	Salary (to two decimal places)	SALARY	Real
58–80	Blank	— — —	— — —

Construct the READ and FORMAT statements necessary to read AGE, SEX, and SALARY.

The T Edit Descriptor

The T edit descriptor indicates the location of the first position of the next field to be read in. The general form of this specification is

$$\boxed{\text{T}n}$$

where n indicates the starting position of the next input field.

EXAMPLE C.11

In Example C.10 the field for NAME is in columns 1–15, for ID in columns 21–29, and for CREDIT in columns 31–34. Alternatively, the following statements can be used to enter the data.

```
      READ 20,NAME,ID,CREDIT
   20 FORMAT(A15,T21,I9,T31,F4.1)
```

This is equivalent to

    20 FORMAT(A15,5X,I9,1X,F4.1)

which was used in the previous example.

Notice that the T descriptor indicates the starting position of the next input field and the X descriptor indicates the number of spaces to skip to reach the next input field.

EXAMPLE C.12

The first three digits of the five-digit ZIP code are used to determine to which of eight postal zones in the United States a package is to be sent. This postal zone also determines the cost of mailing a package. Suppose that ZIP code is stored in columns 10–14. First we'll read the entire ZIP code into an integer variable called ZIP and then we'll read the first three digits into an integer variable called ZONE.

1	2	3	4	5	6	7	8	9	10	11	12	13	14	...
									0	2	8	8	2	

    READ 5,ZIP,ZONE
  5 FORMAT(T10,I5,T10,I3)

Thus 02882 is stored in ZIP and 028 is stored in ZONE.

Interesting feature, isn't it? The T descriptor allows us to rescan data on the current record.

Follow-up Exercises

19. Rework Exercise 17 using the T descriptor instead of the X descriptor.
*20. Rework Exercise 18 using the T descriptor instead of the X descriptor.

C.4
COMMON ERRORS

Take care to avoid the following input errors.

1. **Type inconsistency.**   This error is perhaps the most common. Make sure that the variable type in the list of the READ statement matches the descriptor in the format specification and that both in turn match the value in the input field. Thus we require three-way agreement with respect to type. For example, use an F or E descriptor for a real variable and an input field containing a value in real form; use an I descriptor for an integer variable and an input field having an integer value; and use an A descriptor for a character variable and an input field containing a character value without enclosing apostrophes.

2. **Incorrect character input.** Pay careful attention to Rules 1 and 2 on page 473 when your field width *w* in the A descriptor differs from your declared length *l* for the character variable. Also remember that, unlike list-directed input, format-directed input character fields do not include enclosing apostrophes, as illustrated on page 472.

Follow-up Exercise

21. Define or explain the following.

list-directed input	A edit descriptor
format-directed input	I edit descriptor
field	F edit descriptor
record	E edit descriptor
file	D edit descriptor
record layout	X edit descriptor
general form of READ statement	T edit descriptor
FORMAT statement	

ADDITIONAL FORMATTED I/O

This module completes your introduction to format-directed input/output by discussing the following features: additional options within FORMAT statements, situations where the number of items in the PRINT or READ list is different from the number of corresponding edit descriptors, and format specifications without the use of FORMAT statements.

D.1 OTHER FORMAT SPECIFICATIONS

The **format specification** is the portion of the FORMAT statement that follows the key word FORMAT, that is,

> *statement label* **FORMAT** *format specification*

In Modules B and C we simplified the format specification by omitting certain features that are useful. In this section we illustrate the repeat specification, the slash edit descriptor, and embedded format specifications.

---

* Can be assigned anytime after Chapter 4 and Module C.

Repeat Specification

A **repeat specification** is a nonzero, unsigned integer constant that appears immediately in front of a repeatable edit descriptor. A **repeatable edit descriptor** (are you ready for this?) is an edit descriptor that can be repeated. In practice, repeatable edit descriptors are those that edit input/output fields that correspond to items in READ/PRINT lists. Of the descriptors we have discussed, A, I, F, E, and D are repeatable edit descriptors; the apostrophe, X, and T descriptors, for example, are called **nonrepeatable edit descriptors.**

EXAMPLE D.1

Given the statements

```
      INTEGER JAY,KAY
      REAL     A,B,C
      PRINT 10,A,B,C,JAY,KAY
   10 FORMAT('0',F10.2,F10.2,F10.2,I5,I5)
```

it follows that A, B, and C are to be output with each using the repeatable descriptor F10.2, and JAY and KAY each using the repeatable descriptor I5. This FORMAT statement can be simplified by using repeat specifications, as follows:

```
   10 FORMAT('0',3F10.2,2I5)
```

Repeat
specifications

Slash Edit Descriptor

The **slash edit descriptor** is a nonrepeatable descriptor that terminates a record. For example, it terminates a line of printed output when using a line printer and terminates the reading of a data card when using a card reader.

A series of consecutive slashes within format specifications used for output has the effect of producing blank lines on the page. The number of blank lines will be one less than the number of consecutive slashes if the slashes are in the middle of the format specification, but will be equal to the number of slashes appearing at the very beginning or end of the format specification.

EXAMPLE D.2

Suppose we wish to output the contents in memory given by

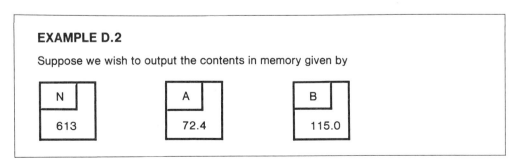

using the statement

    PRINT 10,N,A,B

Study each FORMAT statement and its corresponding output on page 489. Note that a comma need not separate a slash from other edit descriptors.

To summarize the use of slashes for output: n slashes between two other edit descriptors cause $n - 1$ blank lines to be printed, where *the first slash is used to return the carriage to the beginning of the current line*. When n slashes are used at the beginning or the end of the format specification, however, n blank lines are printed. In the case where slashes appear at the end, the first slash is again used to return to the beginning of the current line, after which $n - 1$ blank lines by the remaining slashes plus one additional blank line by the right parenthesis are printed. Note that, in general, *the right outer parenthesis causes the identical behavior of a slash.* The same conclusions can be drawn about records on input. Note, however, that *on output the control unit looks for carriage control following the last slash in a sequence of slashes at the beginning or middle of the format specification.*

Embedded Format Specifications

A format specification may be *embedded* within another format specification for greater efficiency. This is equivalent to saying that inner parentheses may be used within the outer parentheses. The inner parentheses and their items make up what we call a *group*. The combination of pairing repeat specifications with groups is a powerful feature in output formats, which we illustrate next.

EXAMPLE D.3

In part d of Example D.2 the statement

    10 FORMAT ('ᑲ',I5 / 'ᑲ',F8.1 / 'ᑲ',F8.1)

could have been written as

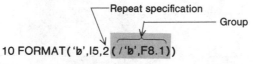

    10 FORMAT('ᑲ',I5,2 (/ 'ᑲ',F8.1))

If the repeat factor had been 15, for example, then you should really appreciate the efficiency of this approach.

    To illustrate another convenience due to grouping, try to determine what the following statements accomplish before reading on:

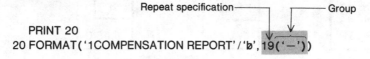

    PRINT 20
    20 FORMAT('1COMPENSATION REPORT' / 'ᑲ', 19('−'))

EXAMPLE D.2 Continued

Case	FORMAT Statement	Output	Comment
a	10 FORMAT('ƀ',I5/'0',2F8.1)	Line 2: `613` Line 4: `72.4  115.0`	The 'ƀ' brings carriage to line 2 for printing of N. The slash terminates line 2, *which brings carriage back to beginning of line 2.* The '0' brings carriage to line 4 to print A and B.
b	10 FORMAT('ƀ',I5/'ƀ'/'ƀ',2F8.1)	Line 2: `613` Line 4: `72.4  115.0`	The first slash terminates line 2 and the second slash terminates line 3. The 'ƀ' brings the carriage to line 4. Result identical to case a.
c	10 FORMAT('ƀ',I5////'ƀ',2F8.1)	Line 2: `613` Line 6: `72.4  115.0`	Compared with case b, the two additional slashes cause lines 4 and 5 to be terminated as well.

d	10 FORMAT('ƀ',I5/'ƀ',F8.1/'ƀ',F8.1)	Line 2: `613` Line 3: `72.4` Line 4: `115.0`	This case is identical to but more efficient than
			```PRINT 10,N```
			```10 FORMAT('ƀ',I5)```
			```PRINT 11,A```
			```PRINT 11,B```
			```11 FORMAT('ƀ',F8.1)```

e	10 FORMAT(//5X,'PAYROLL REPORT'/ 'ƀ', 'IDENTIFICATIONƀƀPAY'/)	Line 4: `PAYROLL REPORT` Line 5: `IDENTIFICATION   PAY`	The first slash brings carriage to line 2 and the second slash to line 3. The first X out of 5X brings carriage to line 4. The last slash brings carriage to beginning of line 5. *The right parenthesis brings carriage to line 6.*

First, the carriage goes to the top of a new page. Next, the heading, COMPENSATION REPORT is printed in columns 1–19 of line 1. The slash then instructs the carriage to return to the beginning of line 1. The 'ƀ' causes the carriage to go to line 2, after which 19 underscore (dash or minus sign) characters are printed immediately under the heading. Do you realize what would be required without the use of the repeat specification and inner parentheses? An apostrophe edit descriptor with 19 underscore characters.

Follow-up Exercises

1. Improve the program of Example B.1 on page 443 as follows.
   a. Make FORMAT "50" more efficient.
   b. Eliminate PRINT 50 and FORMAT "50" by appropriately modifying FORMAT "40" and FORMAT "80."
2. Can you think of two reasonably efficient ways of printing, say, 15 blank lines?
*3. Rework Exercise 15 in Module B on page 462 using options in this section.
*4. Rework Exercise 10 in Module B on page 455 using options in this section. Underscore the heading BLOOD TYPE A$^+$.
5. Indicate an appropriate FORMAT statement for

   READ 25,A,B,C,D,E

   where three input fields for A, B, and C of ten columns each are on the first input record and two input fields for D and E of five columns each are on the next input record. Each value is to be entered to two decimal places.
6. Determine the FORMAT statement for

   PRINT 30,A,I,B,J,C,K,D,L

   which results in output of 12-column field widths all on one print line at the top of a new page. Output real variables to one decimal place and insert a percent sign (%) immediately after the output of each real variable. Use inner parentheses.
7. Describe output for each of the following.

   PRINT 3,M,N

   In each case the carriage is currently on line 20.

   a. 3 FORMAT(1X,I5,10(/) 1X,I5)
   b. 3 FORMAT(10(/) 1X,2I5)
   c. 3 FORMAT(1X,2I5,10(/))
   d. 3 FORMAT(1X,6('*'),2I5,2X,6('*'))
   **e.   PRINT 3,K,L,M,N
        3 FORMAT(1X,2(/ 1X,2(10X,I5)))

where the contents of M and N are given above and

8.   Indicate what is wrong with each of the following.

    a. 3 FORMAT(1X,I5/ /I5)
    b. 3 FORMAT(/ / /2I5)
    c. 3 FORMAT(1X,I523X,I5)

D.2
IMBALANCE BETWEEN LIST AND DESCRIPTORS

In our work thus far, the number of items in the list of a READ or PRINT statement has equaled (balanced) the number of repeatable edit descriptors in the format specification. FORTRAN allows imbalance between these two numbers for greater flexibility.

Fewer Items in List than Repeatable Descriptors

In this case the following procedure is adopted by the processor.

> **Each item in the list is processed according to its corresponding repeatable edit descriptor. Format control then terminates at the first repeatable descriptor not having a corresponding item in the list.**

EXAMPLE D.4

Given the statements

```
    READ 8,A,B
  8 FORMAT(F5.1,F10.2,I5)
```
                           └────── Unused repeatable descriptor

F5.1 is used to read in A, F10.2 is used to read in B, and I5 is simply ignored. Then why have I5 in the first place? Perhaps because some other READ statement such as

```
    READ 8,X,Y,J
```

also is used in the program, which allows us to get by with one FORMAT statement.

More Items in List than Repeatable Descriptors

For this situation the procedure states:

> Items in the list are processed until the descriptors in the format specification are exhausted, after which the record is terminated; the scan of the format specification is repeated as many times as needed until all items in the list are processed. If inner parentheses are present, repeat scans begin with the rightmost group, including the repeat specification that may be present.

EXAMPLE D.5

Suppose we wish to output the contents in memory given by

```
 _____     _____     _____
|  I     |  |   |  J    |  |   |  K    |  |  |
|_____|  |   |_____|  |   |_____|  |  |
|           |   |          |   |          |  |
|    5      |   |   10     |   |   15     |  |
|_____|   |_____|   |_____|  |
```

using the statement

    PRINT 10,I,J,K

Study each FORMAT statement on page 493 and its corresponding output.

Follow-up Exercises

9. Describe input records.

           READ 12,A,B,L,C,D
        12 FORMAT(2F5.0,I10)

10. Fill in the output.

```
 _____     _____     _____     _____
|  A     |  |   |  B    |  |   |  C    |  |   |  D    |  |  |
|_____|  |   |_____|  |   |_____|  |   |_____|  |  |
|           |   |          |   |          |   |          |  |
|   5.2     |   |   7.1    |   |   10.4   |   |   6.3    |  |
|_____|   |_____|   |_____|   |_____|  |
```

        PRINT 20,A,B,C,D

Case	FORMAT Statement	Output
a	20 FORMAT('0',2F5.1)	

EXAMPLE D.5 Continued

Case	FORMAT Statement	Output	Comment
a	10 FORMAT(1X,I5)		Format specification is scanned three times from the beginning. Note the use of carriage control for each scan.
b	10 FORMAT(1X,2I5)		First scan prints contents of I and J. Second scan prints contents of K.
c	10 FORMAT('bCODES',I5)		Three scans.
**d	10 FORMAT('bCODES'/(1X,I5))		Three scans. First prints label and contents of I. Second and third print J and K, respectively. Note how scans beyond the first reset to rightmost group, or nearest left parenthesis from end of scan.
**e	10 FORMAT('bCODES'/2(1X,I5))		Two scans. First prints label, I, and J. Second prints K. Note reset at repeat specification.
**f	10 FORMAT('bCODES',2(1X,I5))		Two scans.

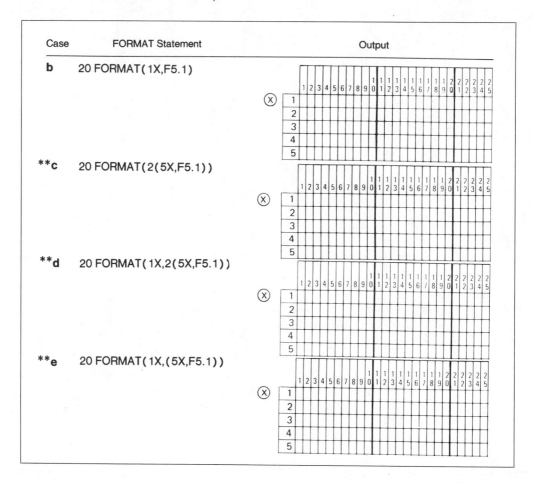

D.3
EXECUTION-TIME FORMAT SPECIFICATIONS

Any given format specification can be provided in one of two ways.

1. Through a FORMAT statement, for example,

```
     PRINT 75,X
 75  FORMAT ( 10X,F11.4)
```

2. Through a character array as a format identifier, for example,

```
 CHARACTER * 80 FM( 1 )
 FM( 1 ) = '( 10X,F11.4)'
 PRINT FM,X
```

This approach actually stores the format specification within the character array FM *during execution of the program,* rather than during compilation. For this reason, this alternative is called **execution-time** (or **variable**) **format specifications.**

In actual practice, variable format specifications are almost always implemented by reading in the character values, as the following illustrates.

```
    CHARACTER * 80 FM( 1 )
    READ 2,FM
  2 FORMAT(A80)
    PRINT FM,X
```

In this case the format specification (10X, F11.4) is provided as data input during execution.

This flexibility of providing format specifications as part of the input data is quite important in certain commercial applications, as it allows complete independence between the programmer and the user with respect to specific formatting requirements. The following example illustrates this advantage.

EXAMPLE D.6   Execution-Time Format Specifications

Statistical packages widely available in the software libraries of computer installations often make use of execution-time format specifications. Motivations for doing so include flexibility, convenience, and lower costs in preparing large amounts of data input.

In many commercial and research environments, input data are often in formatted form on cards, tape, or disk for use by a variety of different programs. Without the variable formatting feature, either each program would have to have identical input formats consistent with the input data file or the data file would have to be modified for consistency with each program. Either approach would be costly, which is why FORTRAN has the option of using variable format specifications.

To illustrate, suppose that the program below is designed for a software library available to many different users.

```
C----------------------------------------------------------------
C     PROGRAM THAT CALCULATES THE ARITHMETIC
C     MEAN OF N REAL VALUES
C
C     KEY:
C        FM    = VARIABLE FORMAT SPEC.
C        N     = NUMBER OF VALUES
C        VALUE = REAL VALUE
C        MEAN  = ARITHMETIC MEAN (AVERAGE)
C----------------------------------------------------------------
       CHARACTER*80 FM( 1)
       INTEGER   N
       REAL      VALUE,SUM,MEAN
C----------------------------------------------------------------
       READ 1,FM
       READ 3,N
C----------------------------------------------------------------
       SUM = 0.C
C
       DO 50 I = 1,N
       READ FM,VALUE
       SUM = SUM + VALUE
  50 CONTINUE
```

```
C----------------------------------------------------------
       MEAN = SUM/N
   C
       PRINT 5,MEAN
C----------------------------------------------------------
     1 FORMAT(A80)
     3 FORMAT(I5)
     5 FORMAT(T10,22('=')/T10,'MEAN = ',F15.4/T10,22('='))
C----------------------------------------------------------       '
       STOP
       END
```

I/O First User	I/O Second User
(F5.1)	(10X,F2.0)
3	5
75.0	RED 80
45.0	WHITE 50
85.5	BLUE 20
	BLUE 25
	GREEN 5
==========================	
MEAN = 68.5000	==========================
==========================	MEAN = 36.0000
	==========================

Note that the shaded portions of the program identify the variable format specification logic, and that the single program accommodates two (or any number of) users with differently formatted input files. However, each set of data is run separately.

Follow-up Exercise

11. Answer the following with respect to Example D.6.
   a. Why do you think we declared the length of FM as 80?
   b. Specify the input file for a user that has 115 numbers to two decimal places, one value per record in columns 16 to 25.
   c. Suppose that a user's 98 values are placed five at a time on an input record, where each value is to three decimal places in a field 15 columns wide. The 98 values are thus placed on 20 input records. Explain why the program can't handle this data file.
   **d. Modify the program so that it also handles files of the type described in part c. *Hint:* You need to store values in an array (Chapter 7).

D.4
COMMON ERRORS

Pay close attention to the effect of slashes in format specifications. Remember that n slashes at the beginning or the end cause the printing of n blank lines; however, n slashes between two other descriptors cause the printing of $n - 1$ blank lines. Moreover, n slashes by themselves in a format specification result in $n + 1$ blank lines (see the answer to Exercise 2 in this module).

Also, *don't forget to specify carriage control following the last slash in a sequence that appears at the beginning or the middle of output FORMATs.* For example, suppose 3 is stored in J and 500 is stored in K and we use the following statements.

```
    PRINT 1,J,K
  1 FORMAT( 1X,I1//I3)
```
Missing carriage control

We would get the following output.

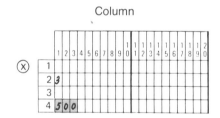

In this case carriage control was not specified following the second slash, so the printer "rips off" the first position in the field for carriage control, effectively leaving 00 for the output of 500. The statement

```
  1 FORMAT( 1X,I1//1X,I3)
```
Includes carriage control

would give the desired output.

Column

Follow-up Exercise

12.   Define or explain the following.

   format specification
   repeat specification
   repeatable edit descriptor
   nonrepeatable edit descriptor
   slash edit descriptor
   embedded format specifications
   imbalance between list and descriptors (two rules)
   execution-time format specifications
   variable format specifications

MODULE E*

Top-Down Design and Stepwise Refinement

E.1 MOTIVATION

E.2 ILLUSTRATION: GOVERNMENT PRINTING OFFICE ORDERS
Analysis
Design
Code
Debugging

E.3 LOOSE ENDS
Top-Down Structured Programming
Top-Down Design and the Four-Step Procedure
Top-Down Testing

Recent programming trends indicate a growing use of certain design techniques collectively called top-down design. This module motivates and illustrates the top-down philosophy.

E.1
MOTIVATION

The term **top-down design** refers to a process for simplifying and systematizing the design and development of complex programs. Strictly speaking, it is not a specific technique, but rather a philosophy that translates into a personalized process for writing programs. As such, the manner of implementing top-down design will vary from programmer to programmer or organization to organization.

Top-down design starts with an overall "look" at the entire problem, that is, a look from the "top." Subsequently the problem is refined further by working "down" through successive levels of greater detail. To illustrate what we mean, consider the process of writing a textbook. First we decide the topic of the book. This is the least level of detail and the highest level of

* This module is best assigned at Section 5.7, but can be assigned anytime after Chapter 5.

abstraction. Next we write down the titles of chapters, which gives us the next level of detail. Next we specify the main headings within each chapter, which represents a further refinement in the level of detail. Next we state the subheadings within each main heading. Finally, we provide the greatest level of detail: each word in the body of the text.

The *implementation* of top-down design at the programming stage is often carried out by a process called **stepwise refinement,** which is an iterative (stepwise) procedure that successively refines the problem at each step. In other words, stepwise refinement is a step-by-step process that continually expands or refines the flowchart, pseudocode, or program, starting at a low level of detail and working toward a high level of detail.

In addition to the guidelines and techniques illustrated in Chapters 2 through 9 and in Module F, top-down design is an effort to control exploding software costs by promoting better organization and development of complex programs. In effect, top-down techniques promote lower costs with respect to program development, debugging, reliability, and maintenance.

E.2
ILLUSTRATION: GOVERNMENT
PRINTING OFFICE ORDERS

Let's design a simplified program that prints billing information for publications produced by the Government Printing Office. Stepwise refinement is illustrated under "Design," following the analysis of the problem.

Analysis

This program determines the charge for an order of publications, prints the charge together with other data regarding the order, and finally prints summary statistics once all orders are processed. The basic charge is the unit price of the publication multiplied by the quantity ordered. This basic charge is then modified to include a 10 percent discount for orders between 50 and 100 copies of a single publication; a 25 percent discount is given if more than 100 copies are ordered. In addition, a surcharge of 25 percent is added to any order mailed to a non-U.S. address.

The data obtained from the order blank include (1) customer name, (2) customer address, (3) whether or not from a foreign country, (4) title of publication, (5) unit price of publication, and (6) quantity ordered.

At the end of each day a report is printed that lists the individual orders. In addition, a summary of the day's activities is printed that includes (1) number of orders for the day, (2) average order size, and (3) total amount billed for the day.

a. *Input data*
   1. Customer name
   2. Customer address
   3. Foreign country, yes or no
   4. Title of publication
   5. Unit price of publication
   6. Quantity ordered

b. *Output data*
  For each customer:
  1. Customer name
  2. Title of publication
  3. Quantity ordered
  4. Charge
    Summary:
  5. Number of orders
  6. Average order size
  7. Total amount billed

c. *Computations*
  1. Charge = unit price × quantity ordered
  2. Discount according to the following schedule:

Size of Order	Percent Discount
49 or less	0
50–99	10
100 or more	25

  3. Surcharge of 25 percent if mailed to foreign address, after any discount

Design

We now illustrate stepwise refinement, first through flowcharts and then through pseudocode. Figure E.1 is an example of stepwise refinement through the "explosion" of flowcharts. Step 1, the first level of detail, describes the nature of the program. Step 2, the next level of refinement, divides the program's tasks into three segments: initial tasks, order processing, and concluding tasks. Step 3 provides a greater level of detail for each segment in Step 2. Note that the task "process order" is actually a pre-test/LRC loop. Step 4 further elaborates Step 3 by specifying the nature of the charge and identifying the specific variables to be accumulated. Finally, Step 5 gives the "nitty-gritty" of the discount and surcharge logic, based on decision structures in Chapter 5.

Figure E.2 illustrates the same procedure by exploding the pseudocode. The flowchart and pseudocode approaches are essentially equivalent, although the use of flowcharts is more tedious and more difficult to modify than the use of pseudocode. In practice only one of the two is needed, according to the preference of the programmer or the organization. (A third alternative, structured charts, is discussed in Module A.)

Regardless of which approach you might prefer, you should note that each iteration in stepwise refinement describes the logic of the problem in greater detail. Moreover, this very process of starting with the "big picture" followed by progressive "fine tuning" is conceptually appealing and consistent with the way the human mind most effectively solves complex problems.

You should also remember that the specifics for each step in stepwise refinement are apt to vary from programmer to programmer. We ask you to consider variations of Figures E.1 and E.2 in Exercises 1 and 2.

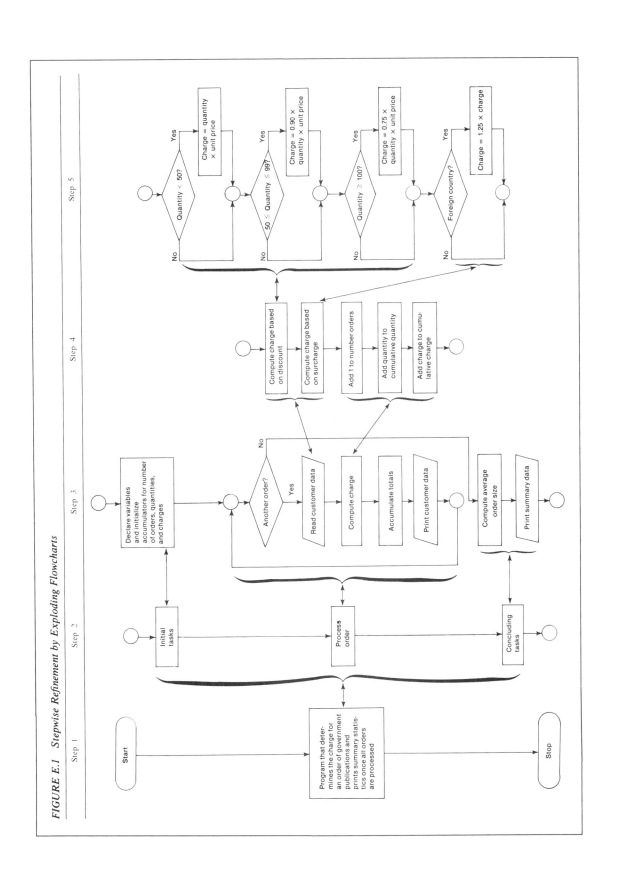

FIGURE E.1 Stepwise Refinement by Exploding Flowcharts

FIGURE E.2 *Stepwise Refinement by Exploding the Pseudocode*

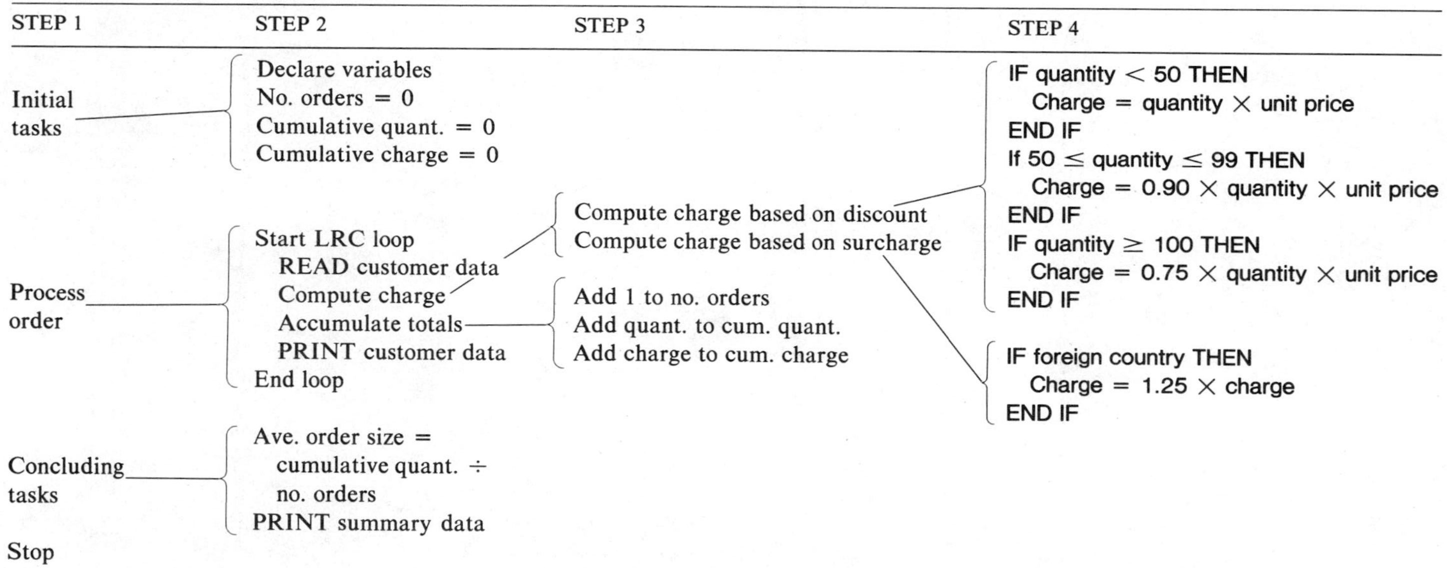

STEP 1	STEP 2	STEP 3	STEP 4
Initial tasks	Declare variables No. orders = 0 Cumulative quant. = 0 Cumulative charge = 0		

Process order	Start LRC loop
	READ customer data
	Compute charge
	Accumulate totals
	PRINT customer data
	End loop
		Compute charge based on discount
		Compute charge based on surcharge
		
		Add 1 to no. orders
		Add quant. to cum. quant.
		Add charge to cum. charge
			IF quantity < 50 THEN
			  Charge = quantity × unit price
			END IF
			If 50 ≤ quantity ≤ 99 THEN
			  Charge = 0.90 × quantity × unit price
			END IF
			IF quantity ≥ 100 THEN
			  Charge = 0.75 × quantity × unit price
			END IF
			
			IF foreign country THEN
			  Charge = 1.25 × charge
			END IF

Concluding tasks	Ave. order size =
	  cumulative quant. ÷
	  no. orders
	PRINT summary data		

Stop			

As your algorithms have become more elaborate, particularly beginning with some of the problems at the end of Chapter 5, we advise that you practice stepwise refinement as a means of programming more effectively.[1]

Code

FORTRAN code readily follows from either the flowchart or pseudocode version in Figures E.1 and E.2, as illustrated in Figure E.3. You should confirm that the code is consistent with

FIGURE E.3 WATFIV Code

```
C-------------------------------------------------------------
C   GOVERNMENT PRINTING OFFICE PROGRAM
C
C   VERSION:  GOP.1     DATE:   JANUARY, 1984
C
C   PROGRAMMERS:   R. AGELOFF/R. MOJENA
C                  UNIVERSITY OF RHODE ISLAND
C
C-------------------------------------------------------------
C   STATEMENT
C-----------
C     THIS PROGRAM PROCESSES ORDERS FOR PUBLICATIONS.
C     IT INPUTS ORDER DATA, CALCULATES THE CHARGE, PRINTS
C     SELECTED ORDER INFORMATION, AND PRINTS SUMMARIES
C     ONCE ALL ORDERS ARE PROCESSED.
C-------------------------------------------------------------
C   INPUT VARIABLES
C-----------------
C     NAME    = CUSTOMER'S NAME
C     ADDRES  = CUSTOMER'S ADDRESS
C     FOR     = YES IF FOREIGN; OTHERWISE DOMESTIC
C     TITLE   = TITLE OF PUBLICATION
C     PRICE   = UNIT PRICE OF PUBLICATION
C     QUANT   = QUANTITY ORDERED
C
C     NOTE:  ALL INPUT LIST-DIRECTED
C-------------------------------------------------------------
C   OUTPUT DATA
C-------------
C     PER ORDER:
C     NAME, TITLE, QUANT
C     CHARGE = CHARGE IN DOLLARS
C
C     PER RUN:
C     NUMORD = NUMBER OF ORDERS
C     AVERAGE ORDER SIZE, CUMQTY/NUMORD WHERE CUMQTY
C        IS CUMULATIVE QUANTITY
C     TOTBIL = TOTAL AMOUNT BILLED
C-------------------------------------------------------------
C   OTHER VARIABLES (AS PARAMETERS)
C-------------------------------
C     BREAK1 = FIRST BREAK IN DISCOUNT SCHEDULE (=50)
C     BREAK2 = SECOND BREAK IN DISCOUNT SCHEDULE (=100)
C     DISC1  = DISCOUNT FOR FIRST BREAK (=0.10)
C     DISC2  = DISCOUNT FOR SECOND BREAK (=0.25)
C     SURC   = SURCHARGE (=0.25)
C-------------------------------------------------------------
```

[1] The explosion process takes up a lot of room, so we suggest you use printer paper. Try using the back of discarded paper, which then gives you claim to being an ecologically conscious programmer.

FIGURE E.3 *Continued*

```
C    DECLARATIONS
C--------------
      CHARACTER NAME*15,ADDRES*20,FOR*3,TITLE*20
      INTEGER   NUMORD,CUMQTY,QUANT,BREAK1,BREAK2
      REAL      PRICE,CHARGE,TOTBIL,DISC1,DISC2,SURC
C----------------------------------------------------------
C    INITIALIZATIONS
C--------------
      DATA BREAK1,BREAK2/50,100/
      DATA DISC1,DISC2,SURC/0.10,0.25,0.25/
      DATA NUMORD,CUMQTY,TOTBIL/2*0,0.0/
C----------------------------------------------------------
C    START LRC LOOP TO PROCESS ORDERS
C--------------------------------
      LOOP
C
C    PROCESS NEXT ORDER
C--------------------
C      READ ORDER DATA
C-------------------
        READ, NAME,ADDRES,FOR,TITLE,PRICE,QUANT
C
C        EXIT LOOP WHEN OUT OF DATA
C-------------------------------
        AT END,QUIT
C
C      DISCOUNT LOGIC
C-------------------
      IF (QUANT .LT. BREAK1) THEN
         CHARGE = QUANT*PRICE
      END IF
      IF (QUANT .GE. BREAK1 .AND. QUANT .LT. BREAK2) THEN
        CHARGE = (1.0 - DISC1)*QUANT*PRICE
      END IF
      IF (QUANT .GE. BREAK2) THEN
        CHARGE = (1.0 - DISC2)*QUANT*PRICE
      END IF
C
C      SURCHARGE LOGIC
C--------------------
      IF (FOR .EQ. 'YES') THEN
         CHARGE = (1.0 + SURC)*CHARGE
      END IF
C
C      ACCUMULATE TOTALS
C----------------------
      NUMORD = NUMORD + 1
      CUMQTY = CUMQTY + QUANT
      TOTBIL = TOTBIL + CHARGE
C
C      PRINT ORDER DATA
C--------------------
      PRINT, 'NAME        :',NAME
      PRINT, 'TITLE       :',TITLE
      PRINT, 'QUANTITY    :',QUANT
      PRINT, 'CHARGE      :',CHARGE
      PRINT, '-------------------------'
C
      END LOOP
C----------------------------------------------------------
C    CONCLUDING TASKS
```

FIGURE E.3   Continued

```
C ----------------------
      PRINT, ' '
      PRINT, 'SUMMARY'
      PRINT, '-------'
      PRINT, ' '
      PRINT, 'NUMBER OF ORDERS        :',NUMORD
      PRINT, 'AVERAGE ORDER SIZE      :',FLOAT(CUMQTY)/FLOAT(NUMORD)
      PRINT, 'TOTAL AMOUNT BILLED     :',TOTBIL
C --------------------------------------------------------------
      STOP
      END
```

the flowchart/pseudocode versions, except for the fact that discount and surcharge parameters in the program have been generalized and initialized through DATA statements.

Debugging

Processing the test data through the program in Figure E.3 gave the results shown in Figure E.4. You should confirm that the output is correct by roleplaying the computer.

FIGURE E.4   Test Input/Output

```
'ADAM SMITH','WASHINGTON D.C.','NO','WEALTH OF NATIONS',10.00,40
'THE RED BRIGADE','ITALY SOMEWHERE','YES','CIA TACTICS',10.00,40
'J. APPLESEED','U.S. OF A.','NO','PLANTING TREES',8.00,80
'BENEDICT ARNOLD','WEST POINT','NO','DEVIL MADE ME DO IT',1.00,500


NAME      : ADAM SMITH
TITLE     : WEALTH OF NATIONS
QUANTITY  :        40
CHARGE    :        400.0000000
--------------------------------
NAME      : THE RED BRIGADE
TITLE     : CIA TACTICS
QUANTITY  :        40
CHARGE    :        500.0000000
--------------------------------
NAME      : J. APPLESEED
TITLE     : PLANTING TREES
QUANTITY  :        80
CHARGE    :        575.9997000
--------------------------------
NAME      : BENEDICT ARNOLD
TITLE     : DEVIL MADE ME DO IT
QUANTITY  :        500
CHARGE    :        375.0000000
--------------------------------

SUMMARY
-------

NUMBER OF ORDERS       :              4
AVERAGE ORDER SIZE     :       165.0000000
TOTAL AMOUNT BILLED    :      1850.9990000
```

E.3
LOOSE ENDS

In this section we tie up some loose ends by relating top-down design to structured programming, our four-step procedure, and modular programming.

Top-Down Structured Programming

You should realize that *structured programming is related to the stepwise refinement process in top-down design.* The billing problem illustrated in Figure E.2 on page 502 begins with a sequence structure and successively builds into the design additional sequence, loop, and decision structures. This approach to designing programs is often called **top-down structured programming.** Moreover, the execution of structured programs proceeds from the top down to the bottom; that is, transfers of control to upper parts of the program are not possible (except for the loop structure, of course).

Also note that execution enters each control structure from the top and exits from the bottom, which is clearly evident from the diagrams in Sections 4.1 to 4.3, pages 104–107.

Top-Down Design and the Four-Step Procedure

The four-step procedure first introduced in Chapter 2 and used as the subheadings in Section E.2 of this module also utilizes top-down design ideas. The problem analysis in Step 1 is the first level of detail. Once the nature of the problem is fully defined in words, the process can be refined further by working "down" through successive levels of greater detail. The specification of the design through exploded flowcharts or pseudocode in Step 2 is the next level of detail. Step 3, specification of code, is a further refinement of the flowchart/pseudocode versions. Finally, the debugging process in Step 4 is the final level of detail.[2]

Top-Down Testing

Another aspect of top-down design relates to the method of testing or debugging a modular program of the type described in Figure F.1 on page 510. **Top-down testing** is a debugging procedure that systematically tests each module as it works its way from the top to the bottom of the type of chart shown in Figure F.1. We illustrate this procedure in Module F.

Follow-up Exercises

1. Discuss how the process in Figures E.1 and E.2 might explode differently. In other words, can you think of legitimate variations in these explosions that still would be consistent with the program in Figure E.3?
2. An alternative to the explosion scheme in Figure E.2 is to label each task in the first step as 1, 2, . . . , *n*, where *n* is the number of tasks in the first step (4 in Figure E.2); thus, in place of Figure E.2 we would write:

   1. Initial tasks
   2. Process order

---

[2] The description of modules in modular programming (Chapter 9 and Module F) can be incorporated under Step 2.

3. Concluding tasks
4. Stop

Successive refinements then build on this numbering scheme by adding further digits. For example, item 3 is further refined by

3.1   Ave. order size = cumulative quant. ÷ no. orders
3.2   PRINT summary data

Complete this stepwise refinement scheme for the problem illustrated in Figure E.2. Which approach do you prefer?

3. Modify Figure E.3 by using either
   a. three logical IF statements (Section 5.1) or
   b. block IF, ELSE IF, and ELSE statements (Chapter 6) to represent the multiple alternative decision structure for the discount logic. Which approach seems clearest to you?

*4. Modify the program in Figure E.3 to express the following output to two decimal places: Charge, Average Order Size, and Total Amount Billed. Place the dollar sign symbol ($) in front of each monetary value.

*5. Modify Figure E.3 to include the fact that a given order can include more than one publication. For example, one order might include a quantity of 10 for a first title, 700 for a second title, and 200 for a third title.

6. Define or explain the following.

top-down design
stepwise refinement
top-down structured programming
top-down testing

MODULE F*

Modular Programming

F.1 FUNDAMENTALS
Properties
Implementation
Advantages

F.2 SUBROUTINES AS MODULES
Analysis
Design
Code
Debugging

F.3 REMOTE BLOCKS AS MODULES

Another approach to the organization and development of complex programs is modular programming. This approach divides a program into groups of related instructions called modules. Each module within a program typically performs one function related to the overall purpose of the program. For example, in a telephone billing program separate modules might be developed for the following purposes.

1. Data input and error routine
2. Calculation of bills
3. Printing of bills
4. Management report, which includes statistical summaries of billing information—for example, sums, averages, frequency distributions (Exercise 38 in Chapter 9)
5. Bills sorted by ZIP codes (for the purpose of simplifying mailings)

* This module is best assigned at Section 9.5.

F.1
FUNDAMENTALS

Before presenting an illustration, we first discuss the properties, implementation, and advantages of modular programming.

Properties

In theory there is no general agreement on either the exact meaning of modular programming or the exact definition of a module. For our purposes let's say that **modular programming** decomposes a program into distinct modules, and then let's focus on certain properties of modules. A growing concensus in the field defines the following properties of a **module.**

1. **A module has a single entry point and a single exit point.**   In essence, a module is like a "black box" that is uniquely activated (entered at a specific point), performs some assigned function, and is uniquely deactivated (exited at a specific point).
2. **A module is "independent" from other modules.**   Essentially this means that we should be able to change or modify a module without affecting other modules. In reality, absolute independence may not be achievable in many cases; however, modules should at least exhibit the type of functional independence described in the five modules of the telephone billing example. Independence is further enhanced by certain design considerations. For example, data overlap among modules should be minimized. A module should access memory only to achieve its designated function. In the context of subprograms this means that we should try to minimize the use of common blocks. Independence is also promoted by carefully designing the hierarchical relationships among modules, which we illustrate in the next subsection.
3. **A module is "not too large."**   The industry rule of thumb says that a module should not exceed 50 to 100 lines of code, which is one or two pages of listing. The basic idea here is that the size of a module should not become so unwieldy that the programmer loses "intimacy" (understanding in depth) with this portion of the code. Needless to say, this property is subjective but well meaning.

Implementation

How can we represent modules within a program? A *control structure* (sequence, decision, or loop) is a good candidate for a module because it can come close to the three properties described earlier. In this case the independence property is the most easily violated whereas the single entry/exit property is exactly adhered to. In effect, a structured program can be decomposed into its separate control structures (building blocks or modules). On the basis of this perspective, control structures are not unlike modules that together make up the whole. Structured programs thus utilize modular programming concepts.

Subprograms are also obvious candidates for modules. In this case the main program, called the **control module,** directs the entire program by calling modules (subprograms) as required. We illustrate the use of subroutines as modules in Section F.2.

Modules can be created not only by subroutines and function subprograms but also by *remote blocks.* We describe this approach in Section F.3.

A **hierarchy chart** is a useful way to express the relationships among modules. This chart is similar in appearance to an organization chart, with each box representing a module. For example, the telephone billing modules might be related as shown in Figure F.1. In this case the control module (main program) not only calls modules (subroutines) 1, 2, and 3 as required but also might perform certain "housekeeping" chores such as documentation (features of programs, definition of variables, and so forth) and initializations.

Notice that module 2 successively calls modules 4 and 5 in Figure F.1. This illustrates **nested subprograms,** where modules 4 and 5 are said to be separately nested within module 2. In the spirit of promoting independence among modules, *no module should call another module at the same or higher level in the hierarchy chart.* Otherwise, the compromising of the top-down look of the hierarchy chart degrades readability and complicates debugging.

A hierarchy chart, together with a description of each module, is an early step in good program design. In effect, the hierarchy chart allows the programmer to focus on defining *what* needs to be done before deciding *how* it is to be done.

Advantages

The use of modular programming concepts results in several well-established advantages in the writing of long, complicated programs.

1. **Facilitates design, coding, and debugging process.** The design process is simplified because a large problem is decomposed into simpler, more manageable tasks. For example, the hierarchy chart gives the "big picture" and shows interrelationships among programming tasks. At the programming level, we can view a module as a fourth control structure, within which are found the three other control structures (sequence, decision, and loop). Moreover, a modular design is consistent with **top-down programming** principles (as described in Module E). As we design pseudocode or main code, we need not refine the subprogram at the point of call. In addition, execution of a module proceeds from the top down to the bottom. Debugging is facilitated by the fact that experience

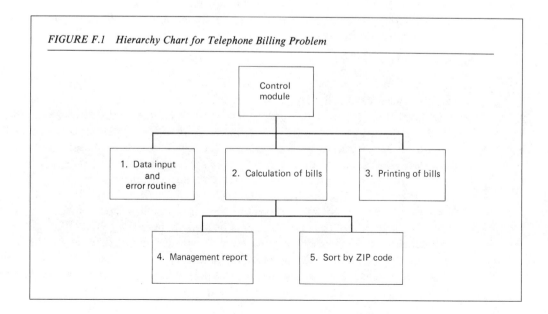

FIGURE F.1   *Hierarchy Chart for Telephone Billing Problem*

now shows that structured, modular, top-down programs are coded with fewer errors than programs that don't utilize these principles. **Top-down testing** also simplifies the debugging process because the independence of modules better isolates bugs for their diagnosis and correction. One popular way of implementing top-down testing is first to code and test the control module before coding the other modules. In this case **dummy modules** (also called **program stubs**) are used in place of modules 1–5. For example, these dummy modules might be nothing more than a PRINT statement for tracing execution and either STOP or RETURN and END statements. Once the control module is debugged, we proceed to the next level of detail (modules 1, 2, and 3) and repeat the coding and testing procedure. Now modules 4 and 5 are the dummy modules. Finally, we code and test modules 4 and 5. Variations on this modular, top-down procedure are common, depending on the programmer and the problem. For example, we could: first, code and test the control module and module 2, with modules 1, 3, 4, and 5 as dummies; second, code and test modules 4 and 5, with modules 1 and 3 remaining as dummies; and third, code and test modules 1 and 3. We illustrate top-down testing in Example F.1 of this module.

2. **Provides flexibility in a dynamic environment.**   Most applications programs evolve over time, which means that they are changed either to reflect new conditions or to incorporate improvements. The use of modules simplifies this evolutionary process by minimizing the effort required in making changes: that is, modules can be changed, added, or deleted with greater independence and ease. Additionally, **general-purpose** or **utility modules** (for example, statistical and sort routines) can be written for use in more than one program, thereby reducing overall programming effort. The importance of this advantage is underscored by the fact that as much as 50 percent of entire data processing budgets is allocated to maintaining, modifying, and improving existing programs.[1]

3. **Allows specialization and division of labor.**   Specific modules can be assigned to specific programmers, which can promote greater productivity and more effective programs. For example, programmer A might be better at designing I/O features than programmer B, but the latter is better at designing efficient calculating procedures. The assignment of modules should reflect these specializations. You might be interested to know that sizeable programs in commercial environments are invariably developed by teams of programmers and systems analysts, which dovetails nicely with the assignment of specific modules to individuals within the team.

F.2
SUBROUTINES AS MODULES

In our next program we illustrate how subroutines can be used to structure a program into modules, whereby each module accomplishes a set of related tasks. Additionally, we illustrate *nested subroutines,* that is, the call of one subroutine by another subroutine.

Analysis

Hartz Rent-Some-Wheels, the largest and most progressive car rental company, has decided to improve customer service by designing a computer program that would be used by its

---

[1] Edward Yourdon, *Techniques of Program Structure and Design,* Englewood Cliffs, N.J.: Prentice-Hall, 1975, page 97.

agents to quote projected rental fees. Basically, the program computes projected total cost for each of its two rental plans: the daily plan and the weekly plan. A customer who rents a car under the daily plan pays a fixed cost per day plus a charge per mile but does not pay for gasoline expenses. Under the weekly plan, the customer pays both a fixed cost per week and buys gasoline, but does not pay a mileage charge. Which plan is cheaper for a customer depends on factors such as the various costs for the specific type of automobile, the projected number of miles to be driven, the number of days that the car is to be rented, the price of gasoline, the efficiency of the automobile, and (of course) the driving habits of the customer.

Table F.1 defines the required variables and illustrates sample data. Thus, for the first request the best plan is the weekly plan, since the total cost of the daily plan ($364.00) is greater than the total cost of the weekly plan ($330.00); however, for the second request the daily plan is best ($175.00 versus $224.50).

Before going on, you should confirm these cost calculations. Note that the fixed cost under the weekly plan is incurred for any part of a week; that is, the fixed cost in car group 1 for 12 days is the same as for two weeks, or $290.00 (2 × 145); the fixed cost in car group 2 for five days is the same as for one week, or $199.00.

Note that the first request specifies a car from group 1 (the "compact" group) and the

TABLE F.1   Variable Descriptions and Computations

			TEST VALUES	
VARIABLE DESCRIPTION		NAME	REQUEST 1	REQUEST 2
a.	Run input			
	Number of customer requests	NUM		
b.	Customer request input			
	Name of customer	NAMEC	TEST 1	TEST 2
	Car group	GROUP	1	2
	Projected miles of driving	MILES	800	300
	Number of days in rental	DAYS	12	5
c.	Car group initializations			
	Daily fixed cost ($/day)	DFC	17.00	20.00
	Charge per mile ($/mile)	CPM	0.20	0.25
	Weekly fixed cost ($/week)	WFC	145.00	199.00
	Price of gasoline ($/gallon)	PRICE	1.50	1.70
	Miles per gallon (EPA rating)	MPG	30	20
d.	Output per customer request			
	Total cost of daily plan ($)	COST(1)	364.00	175.00
	Total cost of weekly plan ($)	COST(2)	330.00	224.50
	Best plan	BEST	WEEKLY	DAILY
e.	Computations			

$$\text{COST}(1) = \text{DFC} \cdot \text{DAYS} + \text{CPM} \cdot \text{MILES}$$

$$\text{COST}(2) = \text{WFC} \cdot \left(\text{int} \left[\frac{\text{DAYS} - 1}{7} \right] + 1 \right) + \frac{\text{MILES} \cdot \text{PRICE}}{\text{MPG}}$$

$$\text{Minimum cost} = \min_{i} \text{COST}(i)$$

second request specifies a car from group 2 (the "luxury" group). At this time, the company offers cars in only two groups, but plans to add a "superluxury" group in the future. Other rental plans are also under consideration. Finally, the number of days in a rental is limited to 90. Rentals for more than 90 days are treated as leases under a leasing plan not considered by this program.

Design

The primary programming tasks are divided into the eight modules described in Table F.2. The hierarchy chart in Figure F.2 clearly shows the relationships described in Table F.2. Note that subroutines DAILY, WEEKLY, and MINVAL are each nested within subroutine PLANS.

Figure F.3 illustrates the pseudocode for these eight modules. Note how the design is upward-compatible for (easily accommodates) new car groups within subroutine CARDAT: Each new car group simply represents a new case in the CASE structure. The design of the algorithm also facilitates the subsequent addition of new rental plans: We simply nest new modules within module 4 (PLANS).

Code

The program beginning on page 516 reflects the design in Figure F.3. As you read through the program and relate it to the design, you should note the following.

1. The design of any module requires decisions regarding its
    a. *Purpose within the overall program.* What activities is this module to perform?

TABLE F.2 Description of Modules

MODULE	DESCRIPTION
1	Main program inputs number of customer requests and processes these requests by iteratively calling modules 2, 3, 4, and 5.
2	Subroutine INPUT reads the data for a specific customer request (see part b in Table F.1) and tests for maximum limit on days in rental.
3	Subroutine CARDAT initializes data for the given car group (group 1 or group 2 as in part c of Table F.1).
4	Subroutine PLANS calls modules 6 and 7, stores results in the vector COST, calls module 8, and determines the name of the best rental plan.
5	Subroutine OUTPUT prints the name of the customer, the name and cost of each rental plan, and the name of the best rental plan.
6	Subroutine DAILY calculates the total cost of the daily plan.
7	Subroutine WEEKLY calculates the total cost of the weekly plan.
8	Subroutine MINVAL determines the minimum total cost plan by finding the smallest element in COST.

FIGURE F.2   *Hierarchy Chart for Automobile Rental Decision Program*

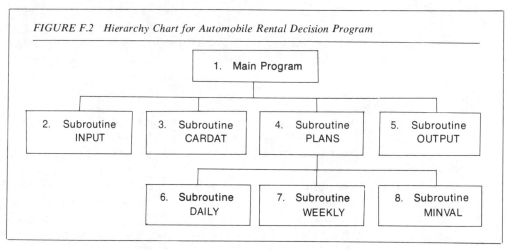

FIGURE F.3   *Pseudocode for Automobile Rental Decision Program*

```
Start main program
   READ no. customers
   Start DO-loop
     CALL INPUT
     CALL CARDAT
     CALL PLANS
     CALL OUTPUT
   End DO-loop
   Stop
End main program
```

a.   Module 1

```
Start subroutine INPUT
     READ customer request data
     IF no. days > limit THEN
        PRINT error message
        STOP
     END IF
     Return
End subroutine INPUT
```

b.   Module 2

```
Start subroutine CARDAT
   IF group no. < 1 or > max THEN
     Set group no. to error code
   END IF
   DO CASE group no.
     CASE 1
        Initialize car group 1 data
     CASE 2
        Initialize car group 2 data
     CASE wrong group
        PRINT error message
        STOP
   END CASE
   Return
End subroutine CARDAT
```

c.   Module 3

```
Start subroutine PLANS
     Initialize no. plans
     Initialize plan names
     CALL DAILY
     CALL WEEKLY
     CALL MINVAL
     Assign name of best plan
     Return
End subroutine PLANS
```

d.   Module 4

FIGURE F.3 *Continued*

Start subroutine OUTPUT
  PRINT customer's name
  Start DO-loop
    PRINT plan name, cost
  End DO-loop
  PRINT name of best plan
  Return
End subroutine OUTPUT

Start subroutine DAILY
  Calculate total cost daily plan
  Return
End subroutine DAILY

e. **Module 5**

f. **Module 6**

Start subroutine WEEKLY
  Calculate no. weeks in rental
  Calculate total cost weekly plan
  Return
End subroutine WEEKLY

Start subroutine MINVAL
  Initialize min. value
  Start DO-loop
    IF element < min. value THEN
      Update min. value
      Update associated subscript
        expression value
    END IF
  End DO-loop
  Return
End subroutine MINVAL

g. **Module 7**

h. **Module 8**

---

    b. *Specific needs or requirements.* Exactly what data are to be input by the module and/ or passed to the module from some other module?

    c. *Specific results.* Exactly what data are to be output by the module and/or returned to the calling program?

2. Pay attention to style, particularly documentation, as programs become more complex. Look at the car rental program and note that

    a. Modules are identified and summarized at the beginning of the program.

    b. The beginning and end of each module are clearly visible.

    c. Within each module we document its purpose, needs, and results, and describe the names relevant to this module (if not described previously).

    d. As a matter of style in the argument lists, we first list items that are to be passed and then list items that are to be returned. For example, in the argument list of subroutine PLANS, the items MILES, DAYS, DFC, CPM, WFC, PRICE, and MPG are "passed" to the module (which coincide with its described "needs") and the items NOP, NAMEP, COST, and BEST are "returned" from the module (which coincide with its described "results").

3. It pays to double-check actual and dummy argument lists for agreement with respect to number, type, and kind, as mismatches here are common sources of error. Don't forget to type explicitly names in argument lists and COMMON statement lists.

4. Module 8 (MINVAL) illustrates the use of a general-purpose (utility) module for finding the location and value of the minimum-valued element in a vector. This same module can be used exactly as is by any other program or module that has the same need for a minimum value.

```
1050  C-----------------------------------------------------------------
1060  C-----------------------------------------------------------------
1070  C                     AUTOMOBILE RENTAL DECISION PROGRAM
1080  C
1090  C     PROGRAM COMPUTES AND PRINTS THE TOTAL COST OF ALTERNA-
1100  C     TIVE RENTAL PLANS AND PRINTS THE NAME OF THE LOWEST
1110  C     COST PLAN
1120  C
1130  C     MODULES IN PROGRAM:
1140  C          1.   MAIN PROGRAM-------ESTABLISHES PROCESSING LOOP AND
1150  C                                  REPEATEDLY CALLS MODULES 2,3,4,5
1160  C          2.   SUBROUTINE INPUT---READS CUSTOMER REQUEST DATA AND
1170  C                                  PERFORMS ERROR CHECK
1180  C          3.   SUBROUTINE CARDAT--INITIALIZES CAR-GROUP DATA AND
1190  C                                  PERFORMS ERROR CHECK
1200  C          4.   SUBROUTINE PLANS---DETERMINES NAME OF BEST RENTAL
1210  C                                  PLAN BY CALLING MODULES 6,7,8
1220  C          5.   SUBROUTINE OUTPUT--PRINTS CUSTOMER NAME, NAME AND
1230  C                                  COST OF EACH PLAN, AND NAME OF
1240  C                                  BEST PLAN
1250  C          6.   SUBROUTINE DAILY---CALCULATES COST OF DAILY PLAN
1260  C          7.   SUBROUTINE WEEKLY--CALCULATES COST OF WEEKLY PLAN
1270  C          8.   SUBROUTINE MINVAL--UTILITY TO FIND MINIMUM-VALUED
1280  C                                  ELEMENT IN VECTOR
1290  C-----------------------------------------------------------------
```

```
1300 C-----------------------------------------------------------------
1310 C                  BEGIN MODULE 1:   CONTROL MODULE
1320 C
1330 C        PURPOSE--PROCESSES CUSTOMER REQUESTS BY ITERATIVELY
1340 C                      CALLING MODULES 2,3,4,5
1350 C
1360 C        NEEDS----INPUTS NUM
1370 C
1380 C        RESULTS--NONE
1390 C
1400 C        KEY------NUM   = NUMBER OF CUSTOMER REQUESTS
1410 C                 NAMEC = NAME OF CUSTOMER
1420 C                 GROUP = CAR GROUP NUMBER
1430 C                 MILES = PROJECTED MILES OF DRIVING
1440 C                 DAYS  = NUMBER OF DAYS IN RENTAL
1450 C                 DFC   = DAILY FIXED COST ($/DAY)
1460 C                 CPM   = CHARGE PER MILE ($/MILE)
1470 C                 WFC   = WEEKLY FIXED COST ($/WEEK)
1480 C                 PRICE = PRICE OF GASOLINE ($/GALLON)
1490 C                 MPG   = MILES PER GALLON (EPA RATING)
1500 C                 NOP   = NUMBER OF RENTAL PLANS (=2)
1510 C                 NAMEP = VECTOR THAT STORES NAME OF EACH
1520 C                         PLAN:  1=DAILY, 2=WEEKLY
1530 C                 COST  = VECTOR THAT STORES TOTAL COST OF
1540 C                         EACH PLAN:  1=DAILY, 2=WEEKLY
1550 C                 BEST  = NAME OF BEST PLAN
1560 C
1570 C-----------------------------------------------------------------
1580 C
1590       CHARACTER * 10 NAMEP(6),BEST,NAMEC*20
1600       INTEGER    NUM,GROUP,MILES,DAYS,NOP
1610       REAL       DFC,CPM,WFC,PRICE,MPG,COST(6)
1620 C
1630 C-----------------------------------------------------------------
1640 C
1650       READ, NUM
1660 C
1670 C-----------------------------------------------------------------
1680 C
1690       DO 50 J=1,NUM
1700         CALL INPUT (NAMEC,GROUP,MILES,DAYS)
1710         CALL CARDAT(GROUP,DFC,CPM,WFC,PRICE,MPG)
1720         CALL PLANS (MILES,DAYS,DFC,CPM,WFC,PRICE,MPG,
1730      *              NOP,NAMEP,COST,BEST)
1740         CALL OUTPUT(NAMEC,NOP,NAMEP,COST,BEST)
1750    50 CONTINUE
1760 C
1770 C-----------------------------------------------------------------
1780 C
1790       STOP
1800       END
1810 C
1820 C                  END CONTROL MODULE
1830 C-----------------------------------------------------------------
```

```
1840 C --------------------------------------------------------------
1850 C                        BEGIN MODULE 2
1860 C
1870        SUBROUTINE INPUT (NAMEC,GROUP,MILES,DAYS)
1880 C
1890 C          PURPOSE—READS CUSTOMER REQUEST DATA AND TESTS INPUT
1900 C                    LIMIT ON DAYS. ERROR MESSAGE PRINTED AND
1910 C                    PROCESSING STOPS IF LIMIT EXCEEDED
1920 C
1930 C          NEEDS----INPUTS NAMEC, GROUP, MILES, DAYS
1940 C
1950 C          RESULTS—RETURNS NAMEC, GROUP, MILES, DAYS TO MODULE 1
1960 C
1970 C          KEY-----DLIMIT = LIMIT ON DAYS (=90)
1980 C                  SEE MODULE 1 FOR OTHER NAMES
1990 C
2000 C --------------------------------------------------------------
2010 C
2020        CHARACTER NAMEC * 20
2030        INTEGER   GROUP,MILES,DAYS,DLIMIT
2040 C
2050 C --------------------------------------------------------------
2060 C
2070        DATA DLIMIT/90/
2080 C
2090 C --------------------------------------------------------------
2100 C
2110        READ, NAMEC,GROUP,MILES,DAYS
2120 C
2130 C --------------------------------------------------------------
2140 C
2150        IF(DAYS .GT. DLIMIT) THEN
2160          PRINT,  NAMEC
2170          PRINT, 'NUMBER OF DAYS IN RENTAL EXCEEDS',DLIMIT
2180          PRINT, 'TRY OUR LEASING PLAN...'
2190          PRINT, 'IT''S AN OFFER YOU CAN''T REFUSE.'
2200          STOP
2210        END IF
2220 C
2230 C --------------------------------------------------------------
2240 C
2250        RETURN
2260        END
2270 C
2280 C                        END MODULE 2
2290 C --------------------------------------------------------------
```

```
2300 C-----------------------------------------------------------------
2310 C
2320 C                         BEGIN MODULE 3
2330       SUBROUTINE CARDAT(GROUP,DFC,CPM,WFC,PRICE,MPG)
2340 C
2350 C          PURPOSE--INITIALIZES CAR-GROUP DATA; IF WRONG GROUP,
2360 C                   ERROR MESSAGE PRINTED AND PROCESSING STOPS
2370 C
2380 C          NEEDS----RECEIVES GROUP FROM MODULE 1
2390 C
2400 C          RESULTS--RETURNS DFC, CPM, WFC, PRICE, MPG TO MODULE 1
2410 C
2420 C          KEY------NOG     = NUMBER OF CAR-GROUP CATEGORIES (=2)
2430 C                   SEE MODULE 1 FOR OTHER NAMES
2440 C
2450 C-----------------------------------------------------------------
2460 C
2470       INTEGER GROUP,NOG
2480       REAL    DFC,CPM,WFC,PRICE,MPG
2490 C
2500 C-----------------------------------------------------------------
2510 C
2520       DATA NOG/2/
2530 C
2540 C-----------------------------------------------------------------
2550 C
2560       IF (GROUP .LT. 1 .OR. GROUP .GT. NOG) GROUP = NOG+1
2570 C
2580 C-----------------------------------------------------------------
2590 C
2600       DO CASE GROUP
2610 C
2620          CASE 1
2630 C
2640             DFC   =  17.00
2650             CPM   =   0.20
2660             WFC   = 145.00
2670             PRICE =   1.50
2680             MPG   =  30.00
2690 C
2700          CASE 2
2710 C
2720             DFC   =  20.00
2730             CPM   =   0.25
2740             WFC   = 199.00
2750             PRICE =   1.70
2760             MPG   =  20.00
2770 C
2780          IF NONE
2790 C
2800             PRINT, 'GROUP NUMBER INCORRECT.'
2810             STOP
2820 C
2830       END CASE
2840 C
2850 C-----------------------------------------------------------------
2860 C
2870       RETURN
2880       END
2890 C
2900 C                         END MODULE 3
2910 C-----------------------------------------------------------------
```

```
2920 C-------------------------------------------------------------------
2930 C
2940 C                      BEGIN MODULE 4
2950 C
2960       SUBROUTINE PLANS (MILES,DAYS,DFC,CPM,WFC,PRICE,MPG,
2970      *                  NOP,NAMEP,COST,BEST)
2980 C
2990 C         PURPOSE--INITIALIZES NOP AND NAMEP, CALLS MODULES 6
3000 C                  AND 7, STORES RESULTS IN VECTOR COST, CALLS
3010 C                  MODULE 8, AND DETERMINES NAME OF BEST PLAN
3020 C
3030 C         NEEDS----RECEIVES MILES, DAYS, DFC, CPM, WFC, PRICE,
3040 C                  MPG FROM MODULE 1
3050 C
3060 C         RESULTS--RETURNS NOP, NAMEP, COST, BEST TO MODULE 1
3070 C
3080 C         KEY------MINJ = ELEMENT IN COST STORING MIN VALUE
3090 C                  MINX = MINIMUM VALUE IN COST
3100 C                  SEE MODULE 1 FOR OTHER NAMES
3110 C
3120 C-------------------------------------------------------------------
3130 C
3140       CHARACTER * 10 NAMEP(6),BEST
3150       INTEGER   MILES,DAYS,NOP,MINJ
3160       REAL      DFC,CPM,WFC,PRICE,MPG,COST(6),MINX
3170 C
3180 C-------------------------------------------------------------------
3190 C
3200       NOP = 2
3210       NAMEP(1) = 'DAILY'
3220       NAMEP(2) = 'WEEKLY'
3230 C
3240 C-------------------------------------------------------------------
3250 C
3260       CALL DAILY (MILES,DAYS,DFC,CPM,COST(1))
3270       CALL WEEKLY(MILES,DAYS,WFC,PRICE,MPG,COST(2))
3280       CALL MINVAL(NOP,COST,MINJ,MINX)
3290 C
3300 C-------------------------------------------------------------------
3310 C
3320       BEST = NAMEP(MINJ)
3330 C
3340 C-------------------------------------------------------------------
3350 C
3360       RETURN
3370       END
3380 C
3390 C                      END MODULE 4
3400 C-------------------------------------------------------------------
```

```
3410  C--------------------------------------------------------------------
3420  C                          BEGIN MODULE 5
3430  C
3440        SUBROUTINE OUTPUT (NAMEC,NOP,NAMEP,COST,BEST)
3450  C
3460  C          PURPOSE--PRINTS ALL OUTPUT, EXCEPT ERROR MESSAGES
3470  C
3480  C          NEEDS----RECEIVES NAMEC, NOP, NAMEP, COST, BEST FROM
3490  C                      MODULE 1
3500  C
3510  C          RESULTS--PRINTS NAMEC, NAMEP, COST, BEST
3520  C
3530  C          KEY------SEE MODULE 1
3540  C
3550  C--------------------------------------------------------------------
3560  C
3570        INTEGER   NOP
3580        REAL      COST(NOP)
3590        CHARACTER * 10 NAMEP(NOP),BEST,NAMEC * 20
3600  C
3610  C--------------------------------------------------------------------
3620  C
3630        PRINT 10,NAMEC
3640        DO 5 J=1,NOP
3650          PRINT 20,NAMEP(J),COST(J)
3660     5  CONTINUE
3670        PRINT 30,BEST
3680  C
3690  C--------------------------------------------------------------------
3700  C
3710    10  FORMAT(///'0','RENTAL COSTS FOR ',A20/
3720       1          '0','RENTAL PLAN   PROJECTED COST'/
3730       2          ' ',28('-'))
3740    20  FORMAT(' ',A10,7X,'$',F8.2)
3750    30  FORMAT(' ',28('-')/
3760       1          '0','THE BEST PLAN IS ',A10//)
3770  C
3780  C--------------------------------------------------------------------
3790  C
3800        RETURN
3810        END
3820  C
3830  C                          END MODULE 5
3840  C--------------------------------------------------------------------
```

```
3850 C-----------------------------------------------------------------
3860 C
3870 C                        BEGIN MODULE 6
3880 C
3890       SUBROUTINE DAILY (MILES,DAYS,DFC,CPM,TCDP)
3900 C
3910 C          PURPOSE--CALCULATES TOTAL COST OF DAILY PLAN
3920 C
3930 C          NEEDS----RECEIVES MILES, DAYS, DFC, CPM FROM MODULE 4
3940 C
3950 C          RESULTS--RETURNS TCDP TO MODULE 4
3960 C
3970 C          KEY------TCDP   = TOTAL COST OF DAILY PLAN
3980 C                   SEE MODULE 1 FOR OTHER NAMES
3990 C
4000 C-----------------------------------------------------------------
4010 C
4020       INTEGER MILES,DAYS
4030       REAL    DFC,CPM,TCDP
4040 C
4050 C-----------------------------------------------------------------
4060 C
4070       TCDP = DFC*DAYS + CPM*MILES
4080 C
4090 C-----------------------------------------------------------------
4100 C
4110       RETURN
4120       END
4130 C
4140 C                        END MODULE 6
4150 C-----------------------------------------------------------------
```

```
4160 C-----------------------------------------------------------------
4170 C
4180 C                        BEGIN MODULE 7
4190       SUBROUTINE WEEKLY(MILES,DAYS,WFC,PRICE,MPG,TCWP)
4200 C
4210 C          PURPOSE--CALCULATES TOTAL COST OF WEEKLY PLAN
4220 C
4230 C          NEEDS----RECEIVES MILES, DAYS, WFC, PRICE, MPG FROM
4240 C                   MODULE 4
4250 C
4260 C          RESULTS--RETURNS TCWP TO MODULE 4
4270 C
4280 C          KEY------TCWP   = TOTAL COST OF WEEKLY PLAN
4290 C                   WEEKS  = NUMBER OF WEEKS IN RENTAL
4300 C                   SEE MODULE 1 FOR OTHER NAMES
4310 C
4320 C-----------------------------------------------------------------
4330 C
4340       INTEGER MILES,DAYS,WEEKS
4350       REAL    WFC,PRICE,MPG,TCWP
4360 C
4370 C-----------------------------------------------------------------
4380 C
4390       WEEKS = (DAYS - 1)/7 + 1
4400       TCWP = WFC*WEEKS + MILES*PRICE/MPG
4410 C
4420 C-----------------------------------------------------------------
4430 C
4440       RETURN
4450       END
4460 C
4470 C                        END MODULE 7
4480 C-----------------------------------------------------------------
```

```
4490  C ----------------------------------------------------------------
4500  C                      BEGIN MODULE 8
4510  C
4520        SUBROUTINE MINVAL(N,X,MINJ,MINX)
4530  C
4540  C        PURPOSE--UTILITY THAT FINDS MIN VALUE IN VECTOR AND
4550  C                 CORRESPONDING SUBSCRIPT EXPRESSION VALUE
4560  C
4570  C        NEEDS----RECEIVES N, X FROM CALLING PROGRAM
4580  C
4590  C        RESULTS--RETURNS MINJ AND MINX TO CALLING PROGRAM
4600  C
4610  C        KEY------N     = NUMBER OF ELEMENTS IN VECTOR
4620  C                 X     = VECTOR
4630  C                 MINJ  = SUBSCRIPT EXPRESSION VALUE CORRES-
4640  C                         PONDING TO ELEMENT WITH MIN VALUE
4650  C                 MINX  = MINIMUM VALUE IN X
4660  C                   .
4670  C ----------------------------------------------------------------
4680  C
4690        INTEGER N,MINJ
4700        REAL    X(N),MINX
4710  C
4720  C ----------------------------------------------------------------
4730  C
4740        MINX = 1.E30
4750        DO 10 J=1,N
4760          IF(X(J) .LT. MINX) THEN
4770             MINX = X(J)
4780             MINJ = J
4790          END IF
4800   10 CONTINUE
4810  C
4820  C ----------------------------------------------------------------
4830  C
4840        RETURN
4850        END
```

Debugging

Sample Input

```
3
'TEST1',1,800,12
'TEST2',2,300,5
'TEST3',1,1200,91
```

Sample Output

```
RENTAL COSTS FOR TEST1

RENTAL PLAN    PROJECTED COST
-----------------------------
DAILY                $  364.00
WEEKLY               $  330.00
-----------------------------

THE BEST PLAN IS WEEKLY


RENTAL COSTS FOR TEST2

RENTAL PLAN    PROJECTED COST
-----------------------------
DAILY                $  175.00
WEEKLY               $  224.50
-----------------------------

THE BEST PLAN IS DAILY


TEST3
NUMBER OF DAYS IN RENTAL EXCEEDS    90
TRY OUR LEASING PLAN...
IT'S AN OFFER YOU CAN'T REFUSE.
```

Follow-up Exercises

1. Answer the following with respect to the algorithm/program.
    a. What happens if 100 is input for DAYS?
    b. What happens if 4 is input for GROUP?
    c. In module 7 why do we subtract the constant 1 in the calculation for WEEKS? Could we subtract some other value?
    d. Why does Module 8 use an adjustable array declarator?
    e. Roleplay the computer and indicate the exact output for the following input data.

        3
        'B. HOLLY',2,1000,21
        'R. VALENS',0,500,7
        'F. DOMINO',1,5000,100

2. Modify the program to print the following.

    .
    .
    .

    THE BEST PLAN IS ccccccccc WITH A PROJECTED COST OF $xxxxx.xx
                     ‾‾‾‾‾‾‾‾‾   ‾‾‾‾‾‾‾‾‾
                     Character field   Real field

3. Modify the program to print the following at the end of the run.

    .
    .
    .

    THE SUM OF COST MINIMA IS $xxxxxxx.xx
                              ‾‾‾‾‾‾‾‾‾‾
                              Real field

4. Describe the changes needed in the program to add a "superluxury" car group.
5. Modify the program to make all relevant names global through common blocks. Discuss pros and cons of this approach.
6. Eliminate modules DAILY and WEEKLY and include the cost calculations in PLANS. Discuss pros and cons of this design.
7. Which subroutines are naturally convertible to function subprograms? Make the necessary changes to do so. Which approach do you prefer in this case?
8. Modify subroutine CARDAT as follows.
    a. Declare a 7 × 5 real array PAR that stores the five car-group parameters for up to seven car-group categories. Input this array at the beginning of the run just before the input of NUM. CARDAT is called as before, checks the group number, and assigns values to DFC, CPM, WFC, PRICE, and MPG by using PAR. What's the advantage of this approach with respect to car-group parameter updates?

    b. Use array PAR as in part a but eliminate the use of module CARDAT alto-gether. Incorporate the error check on GROUP in module INPUT. Which version do you prefer and why?

9. Modify the program as follows.

    a. If the limit on DAYS is exceeded, print the error message and go on to the next customer's request.

    b. If the input item for GROUP is in error, print the error message and go on to the next customer's request.

    Roleplay the data in Exercise 1.

*10. Modify the program to add module SORT, so that the output shows the plans in ascending order of cost. Eliminate the use of module MINVAL.

*11. Modify the program to include subroutine HYBRID, which calculates the total cost of the following new plan: The customer pays an extra $1.95 over the daily fixed cost ($18.95 per day for car group 1 data), pays for gasoline expenses, and pays a charge of 35 cents for each mile over an allotment given by 100 times the number of days in the rental.

12. Modify the program as follows.

    *a. Eliminate subroutine OUTPUT. Modify subroutine PLANS to print the customer's name, table headings, and best plan. Modify subroutines DAILY and WEEKLY to print their respective plan names and costs.

    **b. *Sensitivity analysis.* Elaborate the output in subroutines DAILY and WEEKLY as follows: Each subroutine has a nested DO-loop, where MILES1 (projected miles of driving) is the DO-variable of the outer loop and MPG1 (miles per gallon) is the DO-variable of the inner loop. Use the same data as in the example, except let MILES1 run from 50 to 150 percent of MILES in steps of 10 percent of MILES (all expressed as integers) and let MPG1 run from MPG − 4 to MPG + 4 in steps of 1. (*Note:* DAILY need not have a loop for MPG1.) The purpose of each nested loop is to print a cost table, where rows represent projected miles of driving and columns represent miles per gallon. Do a nice job of labeling your output. Conduct four runs so as to vary the number of days in the rental as follows: 2, 5, 12, 23. What factors favor each plan?

F.3
REMOTE BLOCKS AS MODULES

Subroutine and function subprograms are two methods for building modules in FORTRAN programs. WATFIV offers another approach via REMOTE BLOCK/END BLOCK and EXECUTE statements.

A **remote block** is like a subprogram in that it's an identifiable block of code that performs specialized tasks such as input, editing, or output. The major difference between a remote block and a subprogram is that the subprogram is a complete program unit; that is, it's a complete and separate program, whereas the remote block is within (only a part of) a program unit. Since the remote block is like a "subprogram" within the same program unit, there is no need to pass values between the "calling program" and the remote block, as you will see.

   A comparison of the subroutine subprogram and remote block is illustrated in Figure F.4.

   The execution of a remote block is invoked (from within the same program unit) by using the EXECUTE statement. The general form of this statement is

EXECUTE   *remote block name*

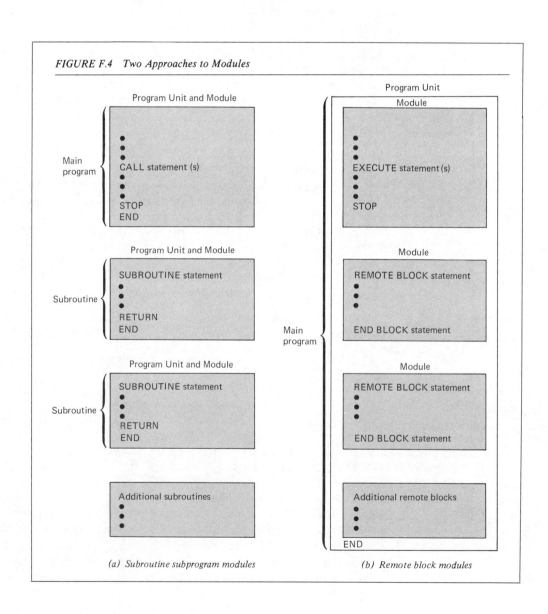

FIGURE F.4   Two Approaches to Modules

(a) Subroutine subprogram modules   *(b) Remote block modules*

The remote block name indicates the particular remote block to be executed. Naming the remote block follows the same rules as naming subroutines. For example, the statement

    EXECUTE INPUT

is used to invoke a remote block named INPUT. When the statement is executed, control transfers to the remote block and the statements within the named block are executed.

The remote block always begins with a REMOTE BLOCK statement having the general form

> **REMOTE BLOCK**   *remote block name*

and ends with an END BLOCK statement having the general form

> **END BLOCK**

The END BLOCK statement acts as a transfer of control from the remote block to the statement following the EXECUTE statement which invoked it.

EXAMPLE F.1   Automobile Rental Program with Remote Blocks

The program listed below is a rewrite of our earlier Automobile Rental Program, where modules are now expressed as remote blocks instead of subroutines. Key differences from the earlier version are highlighted by shading.

```
1050 C------------------------------------------------
1060 C------------------------------------------------
1070 C                 AUTOMOBILE RENTAL DECISION PROGRAM
1080 C                        REMOTE BLOCK VERSION
1090 C
1100 C      NOTE:  DOCUMENTATION IS NOT INCLUDED TO SAVE TEXT SPACE
1105 C             SEE EARLIER VERSION WITHIN THIS MODULE FOR VARIABLE KEY
1560 C
1570 C------------------------------------------------
1580 C                                                      Previously local
1590        CHARACTER * 10 NAMEP(6),BEST,NAMEC*20            to subroutines
1600        INTEGER    NUM,GROUP,MILES,DAYS,NCP,DLIMIT,NCG,MINJ
1610        REAL       DFC,CPM,WFC,PRICE,MPG,COST(6),MINX
1620 C
1630 C------------------------------------------------
1640 C
1650        READ, NUM
1660 C
1670 C------------------------------------------------
1680 C
1690        DO 50 J=1,NUM
1700           EXECUTE INPUT         ------ Replace CALL statements
1710           EXECUTE CARDAT
1720           EXECUTE PLANS
1730           EXECUTE OUTPUT
1750     50 CONTINUE
```

```
1760  C
1770  C-----------------------------------------------------
1780  C
1790        STOP                        ← END statement deleted
1800  C
1810  C-----------------------------------------------------
1820  C-----------------------------------------------------
1830  C                                 ← Replaces SUBROUTINE statement. (Note that
1870        REMOTE BLOCK INPUT            typing within modules is deleted. See lines
2040  C                                   2020–2030 in earlier version.)
2050  C-----------------------------------------------------
2060  C
2070        DATA DLIMIT/90/
2080  C
2090  C-----------------------------------------------------
2100  C
2110        READ, NAMEC,GROUP,MILES,DAYS
2120  C
2130  C-----------------------------------------------------
2140  C
2150        IF(DAYS .GT. DLIMIT) THEN
2160          PRINT,  NAMEC
2170          PRINT, 'NUMBER OF DAYS IN RENTAL EXCEEDS',DLIMIT
2180          PRINT, 'TRY OUR LEASING PLAN...'
2190          PRINT, 'IT''S AN OFFER YOU CAN''T REFUSE.'
2200          STOP
2210        END IF
2220  C
2230  C-----------------------------------------------------
2240  C                                 ← Replaces RETURN and END
2250        END BLOCK
2260  C
2270  C-----------------------------------------------------

2280  C-----------------------------------------------------
2290  C                                  ← Remaining modules are dummy modules.
2300        REMOTE BLOCK CARDAT
2310  C
2320          PRINT, 'CARDAT IS NOT READY.
2330  C
2340        END BLOCK
2350  C
2360  C
2370  C-----------------------------------------------------
2380  C-----------------------------------------------------
2390  C
2400        REMOTE BLOCK PLANS
2410  C
2420          PRINT, 'PLANS   IS NOT READY.'
2430  C
2432          EXECUTE DAILY
2434          EXECUTE WEEKLY
2436          EXECUTE MINVAL
2438  C
2440        END BLOCK
2441  C
2442  C-----------------------------------------------------
2443  C-----------------------------------------------------
2444  C
2450        REMOTE BLOCK OUTPUT
2460  C
2470          PRINT, 'OUTPUT IS NOT READY FOR ',NAMEC
2480  C
2490        END BLOCK
```

```
2491 C
2492 C ------------------------------------------------------------
2493 C ------------------------------------------------------------
2494 C
2500      REMOTE BLOCK DAILY
2510 C
2520         PRINT, 'DAILY  IS NOT READY.'
2530 C
2540      END BLOCK
2541 C
2542 C ------------------------------------------------------------
2543 C ------------------------------------------------------------
2544 C
2550      REMOTE BLOCK WEEKLY
2560 C
2570         PRINT, 'WEEKLY IS NOT READY.'
2580 C
2590      END BLOCK
2591 C
2592 C ------------------------------------------------------------
2593 C ------------------------------------------------------------
2594 C
2600      REMOTE BLOCK MINVAL
2610 C
2620         PRINT, 'MINVAL IS NOT READY.'
2630 C
2640      END BLOCK
2641 C
2642 C ------------------------------------------------------------
2643 C ------------------------------------------------------------
2644 C
2650         END
```

Input

```
3
'TEST1',1,800,12
'TEST2',2,300,5
'TEST3',1,1200,91
```

Output

```
CARDAT IS NOT READY.
PLANS  IS NOT READY.
DAILY  IS NOT READY.
WEEKLY IS NOT READY.
MINVAL IS NOT READY.
OUTPUT IS NOT READY FOR   TEST1
CARDAT IS NOT READY.
PLANS  IS NOT READY.
DAILY  IS NOT READY.
WEEKLY IS NOT READY.
MINVAL IS NOT READY.
OUTPUT IS NOT READY FOR   TEST2
TEST3
NUMBER OF DAYS IN RENTAL EXCEEDS          90
TRY OUR LEASING PLAN...
IT'S AN OFFER YOU CAN'T REFUSE.
```

← Output from dummy modules

Note the following regarding the use of remote blocks.

1. The remote blocks INPUT, CARDAT, PLANS, OUTPUT, DAILY, WEEKLY, and MINVAL are part of one program unit and can be invoked only from within this program unit. In this case the one program unit is the main program. Remote blocks also can be placed within program units given by subroutines and function subprograms.

2. All variables within this program unit are shared. Thus, there is no need to pass values using arguments or common blocks as is done with subroutine and function subprograms. The previously local variables DLIMIT in INPUT, NOG in CARDAT, and MINJ and MINX in MINVAL are now global to the program unit. These are now typed at the beginning of the program in lines 1600 and 1610.

3. Remote blocks can call (execute) other remote blocks within the same program unit, as illustrated in remote block PLANS. However, a remote block can be executed from within a given program unit only if it is local to the program unit. For example, if PLANS were to remain a subroutine as in the original version, then it could not execute remote block DAILY unless DAILY were to be placed within subroutine PLANS. This is because subroutine PLANS would be a separate program unit from the main program.

4. As the program now stands, remote blocks CARDAT, PLANS, OUTPUT, DAILY, WEEKLY, and MINVAL are incomplete modules called *dummy modules,* as described earlier in this module on page 511. This allows us to write and debug modules one at a time within long, complicated programs. We ask you to complete the top-down testing procedure in Exercise 13.

5. Compared to subprograms, remote blocks have the advantage of "less overhead"; that is, programs using remote block modules use less object code and less execution time than programs using subprogram modules. However, subroutines are more flexible with respect to both their use as utility programs and the definition of local versus global variables.

Follow-up Exercises

13. Finish the program in Example F.1 as follows:
    a. Complete module CARDAT and either execute the program or roleplay the expected output.
    b. Complete module PLANS and either execute the program or roleplay the expected output.
    c. Complete module DAILY and either execute the program or roleplay the expected output.
    d. Complete module WEEKLY and either execute the program or roleplay the expected output.
    e. Complete module MINVAL (take care with variable names!) and either execute the program or roleplay the expected output.
    f. Complete module OUTPUT and either execute the program or roleplay the expected output.
    Why is it best to test OUTPUT last in the sequence?

14. How would you change the program in Example F.1 (and the preceding exercise) to treat MINVAL as a subroutine module? What's the advantage of this approach?

*15. Redesign the Automobile Rental Program as follows:

Module 1   Processing loop as before (main program)
     2   Remote block INPUT within main program
     3   Remote block CARDAT within main program
     4   Subroutine PLANS
     5   Remote block OUTPUT within main program
     6   Remote block DAILY within PLANS
     7   Remote block WEEKLY within PLANS
     8   Subroutine MINVAL

Which approach do you prefer and why?

*16. Rewrite subprogram modules as remote block modules for each of the following:
a. Example 9.1 on page 329.
b. Example 9.2 on page 343.
c. Example 9.3 on page 348.

*17. Select an end-of-chapter exercise from Chapters 5–9 and write a modular program that uses remote blocks (or redesign a program you previously wrote).

18. Define or explain the following.

modular programming	dummy modules
module	program stubs
control module	general-purpose or utility modules
hierarchy chart	remote block
nested subprograms	EXECUTE statement
control structures	REMOTE BLOCK statement
top-down programming	END BLOCK statement
top-down testing	

On Designing
Better Programs

G.1   MOTIVATION

G.2   STRUCTURED, TOP-DOWN, MODULAR PROGRAMMING

G.3   DOCUMENTATION
Staff Documentation
User Documentation

G.4   OTHER STYLE CONSIDERATIONS

G.5   SYMBOLIC PROGRAMMING: GENERAL VERSUS
SPECIFIC PROGRAMS

G.6   TRANSPORTABILITY

G.7   EFFICIENCY

G.8   DEBUGGING

G.9   RELIABILITY

G.10 MANAGEMENT PRACTICES

By now you have studied and put into practice the key features of the FORTRAN language. As you probably realize, the act of writing good programs for solving specific problems requires not only knowledge of FORTRAN and an understanding of the problem, but also practice, skill, judgment, thought, and art. This module reviews principles and techniques *used throughout this text* to improve the design of programs.

* This module can be assigned anytime after Chapter 9 and Modules E and F. Except for some material in Sections G.2 and G.7, this module could be assigned as early as Chapter 6.

G.1
MOTIVATION

Most computer applications in business, government, education, and other organizations require complex programs. For instance, an application such as a company's payroll may include dozens of programs with hundreds of instructions within each program.

A programmer's ability to organize and develop a program becomes considerably more important as the complexity of the task increases. Unfortunately, many applications programs have been planned inadequately, which makes them difficult to follow, hard to debug, and time-consuming to modify. The result is low software productivity and higher costs. In fact, *industry estimates now place the total cost of software well above the total cost of hardware.*

In an effort to control software costs, guidelines and new techniques have evolved for improving the design of programs. In all cases their aim is to produce readable, well-organized, easy-to-debug, reliable, easy-to-update programs. The remainder of this module summarizes a number of these guidelines and techniques, many of which you will recognize. The page references within boxes in the margin indicate earlier discussions of these issues.

G.2
STRUCTURED, TOP-DOWN, MODULAR PROGRAMMING

See pages 103–108

We should strictly use *control structures—sequence structure, decision structure* (IF-THEN, IF-THEN-ELSE, nested, multiple alternative, CASE), *loop structure* (WHILE, UNTIL)— to enhance the readability and reliability of programs.

See pages 143, 170, 211

We should *use GO TO statements sparingly,* to reduce the likelihoods of inadvertently writing *un*structured programs and of transferring control to wrong statements. WATFIV allows the elimination of the GO TO statement altogether by having statements that directly reflect all control structures. For example, the block IF, ELSE, and END IF statements exactly reproduce the IF-THEN-ELSE structure; the LOOP and UNTIL statements implement the UNTIL structure.

See pages 498–506

When designing complex programs, we can reduce development and maintenance costs by incorporating *top-down* principles. *Stepwise refinement* at the pseudocode/flowchart stage facilitates development of the algorithm. Remember that structured and top-down programming are related. Each control structure has a single entry point at the top and a single exit point at the bottom. Thus structured programs execute from the top down to the bottom.

See pages 508–530

We should break elaborate programs down into *modules* to enhance program development, improve readability, facilitate subsequent modifications, and allow specialization and division of labor. Remote block modules and subprogram modules can be viewed as a fourth control structure, within which are found the other three control structures (sequence, decision, and loop). Also note that structured programming utilizes modular programming principles, since control structures can be viewed as modules which together make up the whole. Moreover, modular programming is consistent with top-down design, since the process of designing a hierarchy chart, followed by a simplified main program, followed by more refined modules all suggest a top-down process.

G.3
DOCUMENTATION

Programs that are *actually* used for scientific and data processing should be carefully documented. Documentation can be subdivided into two broad categories, depending on the intended reading audience: documentation to be read by programming staff and documentation to be read by users of the program.

Staff Documentation

Staff documentation is to be read by other programming staff for the purpose of updating the program either to incorporate improvements and new circumstances or to debug newly found errors. Staff documentation is found in two places: within the program and in a manual separate from the program. **Program documentation** appears within the program as comment lines. Generally, it includes

See
pages
503, 516
1. A block of comments at the beginning of the program that usually includes the title of the program, version and/or date of the program, name of programmer, a short narrative summary describing the scope and purpose of the program, a description of input/output, the names and definitions of key variables, and other useful information such as subprograms used and specific system-dependent features.

See
pages
503, 516
2. A liberal use of comment lines within the program that identify major tasks, explain logic, describe modules, and otherwise improve the appearance and facilitate the readability of the program.

A **program manual** is a piece of documentation separate from the program itself, but meant for use by maintainers of programs within the programming staff. This piece of documentation is essentially an elaboration of problem analysis, design, and debugging (Steps 1, 2, and 4 in our four-step procedure). It often includes a description of the problem, input/output, definitions of key variables, descriptions of modules, the calling sequence of modules and/or a *hierarchy chart,* a *system flowchart* (see Figure 11.5), a *program flowchart* or *pseudocode* (ideally showing *stepwise refinement*), test data used to debug the program together with sample runs of the program, and other useful features such as system-dependent peculiarities and suggestions for incorporating additional tasks.

See
pages
425, 514

User Documentation

User documentation is to be read by users of the program. It is typically called a **user's manual** or **user's guide,** and is meant to acquaint users with the features and implementation of a specific program. A user's manual typically includes a description of the program's features, ways to implement these features, instructions on the preparation of input data, sample computer runs showing input/output, actions to take in the event of program error messages, and other useful features such as formulas, references, and (particularly in scientific, mathematical, and statistical applications) descriptions, assumptions, and limitations of underlying theory.[1]

---

[1] Next time you're at the computer center look up a user's manual for any of the widely available statistical computer packages such as BMD, SPSS, and SAS.

G.4
OTHER STYLE CONSIDERATIONS

Readability is further enhanced by incorporating the following familiar features.

1. **Indentation.** Indentation of loop bodies and decision blocks clearly identifies loop and decision logic.

2. **Selecting names.** The effective selection of symbolic names requires paying attention to meaning. If names reflect what they represent, a programmer can follow programming logic without constantly referring to a key that defines names. For example, the variable COST has more meaning than the variable X if we wish to represent the cost of an item.

3. **Data structure.** The data structure that the symbolic name is to represent also should be considered. For example, a table of numbers is better represented by a two-dimensional array name than by a series of one-dimensional array names or by an "army" of unsubscripted variable names. In other situations, the use of array names promotes shorter programs.

4. **Type statements.** Use type statements to declare the type of all key symbolic names in your program, particularly since we recommend suppression of the I-N typing convention as it interferes with the selection of meaningful names. For example, if we wish to store the mean of a set of numbers as a real value, then we prefer the variable name MEAN together with the explicit typing

   REAL MEAN

   to the implicitly typed XMEAN. Minor variables in the program such as I and J can be typed implicitly according to the I-N convention. Also, consider the issue of typing a numeric name integer versus real versus double precision. For example, if a name such as AGE is to store an employee's age, then it's meaningful to type this variable integer.

5. **Statement numbers.** Select statement numbers with care, in a manner that promotes readability and reduces the likelihood of error. For example, a round number such as 100 is more readable than a number such as 57. Use sequential numbering by consistently increasing the magnitude of numbers as you go down the program, since we tend to associate higher numbers with statements further down in the listing. Finally, associate groups of numbers with logical segments in the program. For example, FORMAT statements might be numbered sequentially in the 900s. By the way, the use of statement numbers is a source of bugs that it is best to avoid. Statements in FORTRAN that directly reflect control structures altogether eliminate the use of direct transfers to labeled statements.

See pages 443, 504

6. **Nonexecutable statements.** Enhance the readability of executable code by placing nonexecutable statements "out of harm's way." For example, place all FORMAT statements in a group either at the beginning or end of a program. And design comment lines to make them easily distinguishable from executable code—by liberal vertical spacing, underlining, or indenting to the right of executable code.

See pages 444, 523

7. **Output formats.** Take care in designing output formats. Keep the user in mind by providing labeled, unambiguous, attractive, concise, informative output.

8. **Block programming.**   Break programs down into identifiable *blocks* of code, where each program block performs a set of related tasks. For example, the program in Module E is broken down into the following *program blocks.*

See
page
504

Declarations
Initializations
Initial order read-in
Order processing
Concluding tasks

In effect, *block programming* is a simple implementation of *modular programming.*

G.5
SYMBOLIC PROGRAMMING: GENERAL VERSUS SPECIFIC PROGRAMS

A general program requires less upkeep than a specific program for applications where certain data items may change. To illustrate what we mean, consider a program that calculates the mean (average) of a set of numbers or items. A general program would treat the number of items as an input variable (say, N), whereas a specific program would calculate the mean for, say, 100 items. Thus the general program can calculate the mean for any number of items whereas the specific program is restricted to 100 items. If the number of items is likely to change from one application to the next, then the general program is best since the specific program would require frequent changes. The principle behind the development of general programs is called **symbolic programming,** since most values are referenced by "symbolic" names rather than constants.

Some estimates now place the cost of designing and maintaining software above the cost of purchasing or leasing hardware. Thus *it is good programming practice to treat all required data as either input data or parameters given values through DATA or assignment statements, rather than as constants.* This practice reduces the cost of updating programs in situations where data may change.

See
page
504
For example, the program in Section E.2 generalizes the discount and surcharge parameters by specifying symbolic names through the variables BREAK1, BREAK2, DISC1, DISC2, and SURC and initializing them through DATA statements. Should these values change in the future, it would be easier to update DATA statements than to update statements in the discount and surcharge decision structures. Alternatively, we could have input the values through a READ statement or assigned values through assignment statements.

See
pages
68–69
If parameters change often in a program (for example, weekly or daily as in international currency exchange rates), then rather than initializing through assignment or DATA statements, it might be best to read in parameters as input data.

G.6
TRANSPORTABILITY

A **transportable program** is one that can be used by different installations with little or no modification. If a particular program either is to be run on different computer systems or the system on which it is to be used is likely to change in the future (a virtual certainty), then software costs will be reduced if the program is designed with transportability in mind. Thus, as much as possible, transportable programs maximize the use of statements in the ANSI standard and simultaneously minimize the use of statements based on local enhancements. The WATFIV version of FORTRAN is less transportable than the official FORTRAN 77 version, as WATFIV is restricted to systems supported by the WATFIV compiler.

G.7
EFFICIENCY

A good program, in addition to being readable, is one that accomplishes its objective efficiently with respect to computer time and storage. Here are a few suggestions to help you write more efficient programs.

1. **Integer arithmetic is faster than real arithmetic.**   On some machines 25 or more integer computations can be performed in the time it takes to execute one real computation. Thus use integer expressions in place of real expressions whenever the expected value of the expression is a whole number. Moreover, if a numeric variable is to store strictly whole numbers and is not used in real arithmetic expressions (except as an exponent), it should be typed as an integer variable. For example, the variable TIME should be typed integer in the expression RATE**TIME if TIME is to store whole-number values, since this avoids time-consuming logarithmic routines for evaluating real expressions raised to real powers. Finally, avoid the indiscriminate use of mixed-type arithmetic expressions, since the required type conversions are costly.

2. **Library functions are usually faster and more accurate than using alternative codes.**   For example,

        B = SQRT(A)

    is preferred to

        B = A**0.5

    and

        C = ABS(X − Ẏ)

    is preferred to

        C = X − Y
        IF(C .LT. 0.0)THEN
          C = −C
        END IF

3. **When possible avoid unnecessary loops since time is spent in incrementing and testing loop termination.**   For example, the segment

        SUM = 0.0
        DO 100 J = 1,N
        READ,VOLUME(J)
        SUM = SUM + VOLUME(J)
    100 CONTINUE

is more efficient than

```
       DO 100 J = 1,N
       READ,VOLUME(J)
100  CONTINUE
       SUM = 0.0
       DO 150 J = 1,N
       SUM = SUM + VOLUME(J)
150  CONTINUE
```

4. **Constant computations should be removed from within a loop.** For example, the segment

```
       DO 200 J = 1,M
       READ, X(J)
       Y(J) = (A + B**2/C)*X(J)
200  CONTINUE
```

unnecessarily recomputes the expression $(A + B**2/C)$ a total of $M - 1$ times more than needed. A more efficient design is

```
       D = A + B**2/C
       DO 200 J = 1,M
       READ, X(J)
       Y(J) = D*X(J)
200 CONTINUE
```

5. **Nest long loops within short loops.** Each time an outer loop iterates, the inner-loop parameters get reinitialized, which takes time. Thus, it's best to place the "long" loop (the one with more iterations) inside the "short" loop whenever possible, as this reduces the number of loop reinitializations.

See pages 200, 207

6. **Use ELSE IF statements for extensive multiple alternative decision structures** rather than a sequence of block IF statements, since the former avoids the unnecessary testing of conditions once the "true" condition is found. Similarly, use the CASE structure in place of nested IF-THEN-ELSE structures where appropriate.

See pages 351, 358

7. **To save space in primary memory,** avoid unnecessarily large arrays and use COMMON and EQUIVALENCE statements to share space among large arrays. These statements, however, must be applied with care as their use increases the likelihood of errors.

8. **A poorly designed algorithm is a primary factor that contributes to excessive computer time.** This factor is so important in certain applications that professionals in applied mathematics, statistics, and computer science have devoted extensive research efforts to improving the time efficiency of many algorithms. More often than not, this involves the development of an entirely new algorithm that achieves the same end result. For example, sorting algorithms have been developed that significantly reduce the cost of sorting by traditional methods such as the bubble sort described in Chapter 7.

In general, programmers should *look for economies that make a significant difference, but without degrading the readability of the program.* In commercial applications, an esoteric, obscure code that saves CPU time is generally not preferred to a less efficient version that is readable, understandable, and easy to change.

G.8
DEBUGGING

See page 95

See page 222

See pages 511, 530

The process of testing and correcting programs for errors is time-consuming and costly. In fact, an industry rule of thumb states that *debugging consumes on the average between one-third and one-half of the total project time.* The incorporation of good design principles as discussed in this module, the use of classic debugging techniques as discussed in Section 3.3, and familiarity with common programming errors as discussed at the end of Chapters 3 through 11 all serve to promote an efficient debugging phase. In particular, great care must be exercised in designing test data to ensure that all branches, combinations of branches, and boundary values of data are tested, as discussed in Section 6.6.

If you're working with lengthy modules, then top-down testing as discussed in Section F.1 is a good aid for breaking a large debugging job down into smaller components.

G.9
RELIABILITY

See pages 168, 201, 202, 208, 210, 518, 519, 523

A program should reliably operate as intended once it is implemented on an ongoing basis. A process called **defensive programming** means that the design of a program should antici-pate "unforeseen circumstances" as much as feasible. For example, good commercial pro-grams anticipate errors in the input data through programmed error routines, as emphasized in Chapters 5, 6, and 9. Generally, programmers should anticipate what might go wrong operationally, thereby designing their programs to react accordingly. At the same time the temptation to make programs "overreliable" must be tempered by judgments regarding the benefits versus the costs. In other words, reliable program design requires assessments regard-ing the nature of potential difficulties, their likelihood of occurrence, the cost of incorporating programmed reactions to these difficulties, and the benefits (or cost savings) realized when these difficulties are avoided through program design.

G.10
MANAGEMENT PRACTICES

It can be argued that "all the tools, techniques, and subprograms (utilities) needed to properly develop the successful advanced commercial applications in the 1980s are already here today—everything except the discipline, the training, and the understanding." Generally, there "is a combination of poor technical training, lack of leadership at the top management level, strong resistance to change, and short-term fire fighting instead of long-term planning."[2]

---

[2] Martin A. Goetz, "Advanced Commercial Applications in the '80s," *DATAMATION*, Vol. 25, No. 13, Novem-ber 1979, pp. 104–108.

In effect, problems regarding poor productivity (that is, costly software development, implementation, and maintenance) are attributable to personnel and their management, not to the state of the art in the technology. Among the solutions are the following.

1. Massive training and retraining of programming personnel with respect to improving the design of programs
2. Recognition that programming is more a science than an art by requiring, for example, the use of top-down design, structured programming, and modular programming
3. Encouragement of group processes in programming, which brings individuals together as a group for specific tasks such as evaluating program design and code[3]
4. Improvement in the organizational structure of a data processing department (a) by unambiguously specifying relationships among managers, chief programmers, programmers, project directors, and group leaders, and (b) by clarifying the relationships that relate personnel to projects and functions[4]

Follow-up Exercises

1. Define or explain the following.

   staff documentation
   program documentation
   program manual
   user documentation
   user's manual (guide)
   symbolic programming
   transportable program
   defensive programming

2. What are the three key characteristics of modules? Do control structures have the same characteristics?
3. How is modular programming related to top-down design?
4. How is modular programming related to structured programming?
5. How is top-down design related to structured programming?
*6. Select one of the programs that you have completed and perform and answer the following.
   a. Improve its program documentation.
   b. Improve its style both in ways discussed in Sections G.2 and G.4 and through possible ideas of your own.
   c. Improve its generality through symbolic programming.
   d. Can you improve its efficiency without degrading its readability?
   e. Incorporate defensive programming, specify modules, and draw a hierarchy chart. Include the description of modules within the program documentation. In describing a module, state its data needs, its purpose, and its results. Explode the pseudocode before writing code.
   f. Select a thorough set of test data to debug your program.

---

[3] See, for example, Ben Shneiderman, *Software Psychology: Human Factors in Computer and Information Systems,* Cambridge, Mass.: Winthrop Publishers, 1980.
[4] See, for example, Edward B. Daly, "Organizing for Successful Software Development," *DATAMATION,* Vol. 25, No. 14, December 1979, pp. 106–120.

**7.   Electric Bill Revisited.   The following poorly written program is a technically correct solution to Exercise 37 in Chapter 9 on page 371.

```
          K = 0
        2 K = K + 1
          IF (K.GT.5)GO TO 38
          READ,A,B,C,D,E,F,G,H,I,J,K,L
          IF(C.NE.1)GO TO 13
          M1 = B*.0525 − A*.0525
          N1 = 1.01*D − 1.01*E + M1
          PRINT,F,G,H,I
          PRINT,J,K,L
          PRINT,'FROM SEP 19 TO OCT 18, 1981'
          PRINT,B − A,M1,D − E,(D − E)*0.1,D − E + (D − E)*0.01 + M1
          GO TO 2
       13 IF(C.NE.2) GO TO 10
          M2 = B*0.0485 − A*0.0485
          N2 = 1.01*D − 1.01*E + M2
          PRINT,F,G,H,I
          PRINT,J,K,L
          PRINT,'FROM SEP 19 TO OCT 18, 1981'
          PRINT,B − A,M2,D − E,(D − E)*0.01,D − E + (D − E)*0.01 + M2
          GO TO 2
       10 IF(C.EQ.3) GO TO 15
       22 PRINT,F,G,H,I
          PRINT,J,K,L
          PRINT,'FROM SEP 19 TO OCT 18, 1981'
          PRINT,B − A,M3,D − E,(D − E)*0.01,D − E + (D − E)*0.01 + M3
          GO TO 2
       15 IF(B − A.GE.50000)GO TO 31
          M3 = B*0.085 − A*0.085
          N3 = 1.01*D − 1.01*E + M3
          GO TO 22
       31 IF(B − A.LE.100000)GO TO 35
          M3 = B*0.065 − A*0.065
          N3 = 1.01*D − 1.01*E + M3
          GO TO 22
       35 M3 = B*0.075 − A*0.075
          N3 = 1.01*D − 1.01*E + M3
          GO TO 22
       38 STOP
          END
```

   a.   Briefly describe aspects of this program that illustrate poor style and design.
   b.   Flowchart this program. Kind of a nightmare, isn't it?
   c.   Redesign the program (from scratch) by following the steps described in Exercise 6.
   d.   Incorporate part b of Exercise 37 in Chapter 9.

MODULE H

Selected Differences between WATFIV and FORTRAN 77

The table in this module highlights some chapter-by-chapter key differences between WAT-FIV and FORTRAN 77, as established by the American National Standard Institute in ANSI X3.9-1978.

In general, compared to the current version of WATFIV, FORTRAN 77 includes powerful string commands, more modern external file commands, greater flexibility with respect to Do-loop parameters and array declarations, and simplified library functions. WATFIV, however, is superior from a structured programming point-of-view. For example, WATFIV explicitly supports WHILE, UNTIL, CASE, and GO-TO-less LRC loops, while FORTRAN 77 implements these structures only through the use of GO TO statements (which is painful to structured enthusiasts). Moreover, the WATFIV compiler is "friendlier" with respect to identifying the sources of syntax and execution errors.

FORTRAN 77, of course, is the "official" FORTRAN dialect; hence, you are more likely to encounter it than WATFIV outside of academic environments. We expect that reading or writing a FORTRAN 77 program would be reasonably straightforward for you, after finishing the WATFIV course and noting differences in the following table.[1]

---

[1] See Roy Ageloff and Richard Mojena, *Applied FORTRAN 77* (Belmont, Calif.: Wadsworth Publishing Company, 1981) for FORTRAN 77 details within a chapter-by-chapter organization that's very similar to this textbook.

Chapter or Module	Topic/Statement	WATFIV	FORTRAN 77
2	STOP Statement	STOP must be included in program to terminate execution.	STOP statement optional. END statement serves same purpose.
	Library Functions	Generic names for library functions are not supported.	Generic library functions are supported. That is, the type of arguments determines the type of value supplied by function. MAX(X,Y,10.5) MAX(J,K,1)
	List-Directed I/O		List-directed READ/PRINT statements require an * before first comma.
		READ,list PRINT,list	READ *,list PRINT *,list
	Initialization of Parameters	PARAMETER statement is not supported.	Reference to a constant by a symbolic name is defined via a PARAMETER statement. PARAMETER(PI = 3.141593)
		Initialization through type statements. REAL SUM/0.0/,AGE	Not supported. REAL SUM,AGE DATA SUM/0.0/
3	Multiple Statements	Supported. SUMA = 0 ; SUMB = 0 SUMA = SUMB = 0	Not supported. SUMA = 0 SUMB = 0
4	Do-Loop	Negative incrementation not supported.	Do-loop can have negative incrementation. DO 100 J = 5,1,−1
		Real parameters not supported.	Do-loops can have real loop-control parameters. DO 200 X = 0.5,1.5,0.1
		Parameter expressions not supported.	Do-loops can have expressions for loop-control parameters. DO 300 L = 1,N + 1
		Do-loop is a post-test loop. The loop DO 400 K = 10,9 . . } Loop body . 400 CONTINUE executes the loop body once.	Do-loop is a pre-test loop. The loop DO 400 K = 10,9 . . } Loop body . 400 CONTINUE does not execute the loop body.

Chapter or Module	Topic/Statement	WATFIV	FORTRAN 77

5	WHILE Structure	WHILE (condition)
		
		· ⎤
		· ⎬ Loop body
		· ⎦
		
		END WHILE
			Not supported directly
			Must use block IF paired with GO TO

	UNTIL Structure	LOOP · ⎤ · ⎬ Loop body · ⎦ UNTIL (condition)	Not supported directly. Must use logical IF and GO TO.
	LOOP/END LOOP	LOOP · ⎤ · ⎬ Loop body · ⎦ END LOOP	Not supported.

	AT END	End of file check using AT END statement is supported.
		  READ . . .
		    AT END, . . .
			Not supported.

	QUIT	Exit from loop or block via QUIT statement. Especially useful in LRC loops when combined with LOOP, END LOOP, and AT END statements. (See next example.)	Not supported.

	Generalized LRC loop	LOOP
		  READ . . .
		    AT END, QUIT
		
		· ⎤
		· ⎬ Loop body
		· ⎦
		
		END LOOP
		. . .
			10 READ(. . . END = 20)
			
			· ⎤
			· ⎬ Loop body
			· ⎦
			
			GO TO 10
			
			20 . . .

6	CASE Structure	Variation of multiple alternative decision structure.
		  DO CASE
		    CASE
		    ⋮
		    CASE
		    ⋮
		    IF NONE
		    ⋮
		  END CASE
			Not supported directly. Must use computed GO TO and GO TO statements.

Chapter or Module	Topic/Statement	WATFIV	FORTRAN 77
7,8	Array Declarations	Lower dimension bound of array is always 1. Only upper dimension bound is specified. Array name (20) └─Upper dimension bound	Lower dimension bound of array can be specified by programmer. Upper dimension bound┐ Array name (− 10:20) └─Lower dimension bound
	Subscript Values ≤ 0	Not supported.	Supported, but must be within dimension bounds.
	Character Array Declarations	Variation in syntax: CHARACTER DAY*9(7)	CHARACTER DAY(7)*9
9	RETURN Statement	RETURN statement is required in each subprogram.	RETURN statement is not required in each subprogram. END statement serves same purpose.
	Assumed-size Array Declarator	Not supported.	Asterisk can be used to declare size of dummy array equal to size of actual array. REAL X(*) └─Dummy array
10	Concatenation	Not supported.	Two or more strings can be combined to form longer string using the concatenation operator //. character / / character expression / / expression
	Substrings	Not supported.	Substrings can be referenced within any character variable or array using substring notation. The substring TEXT(3:6) references character positions 3 through 6 within the string value stored in character variable TEXT.

Chapter or Module	Topic/Statement	WATFIV	FORTRAN 77
	String Library Functions	Not supported.	Eight library functions that process character data are included. For example, LEN—determines length of character string INDEX—searches string for occurrence of substring ICHAR—converts string of length 1 to integer value CHAR—reverse of ICHAR
11	OPEN Statement	Not supported.	OPEN statement is used to define properties and links among I/O units, the external file and FORTRAN program. OPEN (UNIT = 10,FILE = 'SALES', STATUS = 'OLD', ACCESS = 'SEQUENTIAL')
	Sequential-Access Files	Variations in syntax: READ(10,900, END= 90, ERR= 95) list	READ(UNIT = 10, FMT = 900, END = 90, ERR = 95) list
	Direct-Access Files	Variations in syntax: DEFINE FILE 10 (100,30,E,NEXT) READ(10'ID,900) list	OPEN(ACCESS = 'DIRECT',FORM= 'FORMATTED',RECL = 30, UNIT = 10,STATUS = 'NEW') READ(UNIT = 10,FMT = 900, REC = ID) list
	CLOSE Statement	Not supported.	CLOSE statement is used to disconnect file from I/O unit. CLOSE(UNIT = 10,STATUS = 'KEEP')
B,C,D	Format Identifiers	Not supported.	Format specification can be incorporated in READ or PRINT statement. PRINT '("0", I10,F15.4)',J,X

Chapter or Module	Topic/Statement	WATFIV	FORTRAN 77
	Execution-Time Format Specifications	Requires use of character array.	Allows use of character variable.
		CHARACTER*80 FM(1)	CHARACTER*80 FM
		.	.
		.	.
		.	.
		READ FM, list	READ FM, list
	A Edit Descriptor Without Field Width	Not supported.	CHARACTER NAME*20
			.
			.
			.
			PRINT 10,NAME
			10 FORMAT ('0',A)
			Same as A20
F	Remote Blocks	Division of complex programs into modules within same program unit by using REMOTE BLOCK/END.	Not supported.

Answers to Selected Follow-up Exercises

CHAPTER 2

1. **(a)** Acceptable. **(b)** Acceptable. **(c)** Unacceptable; begins with number. **(d)** Acceptable. **(e)** Unacceptable; special character. **(f)** Acceptable. **(g)** Acceptable. **(h)** Unacceptable; more than six characters. **(i)** Acceptable. **(j)** Unacceptable; special character, more than six characters. **(k)** Acceptable. **(l)** Acceptable.

2. **(a)** Unacceptable constant; comma. **(b)** Integer constant. **(c)** Real constant. **(d)** Real constant. **(e)** Real constant. **(f)** Real constant. **(g)** Real constant. **(h)** Unacceptable; comma. **(i)** Integer constant.

3. **(a)** Real variable. **(b)** Integer variable. **(c)** Integer variable. **(d)** Real variable. **(e)** Real variable. **(f)** Integer variable. **(g)** Unacceptable variable. **(h)** Real variable.

4. **(a)** $-6.142E15$ or $-0.6142E16$ etc. **(b)** $-6142E12$ or $-0.6142E16$ etc. **(c)** $0.7E-9$ or $7E-10$ etc. **(d)** $7E-10$ etc. **(e)** $0.167E125$ *Note:* May exceed maximum value of the machine.

5. **(a)** 123×10^4 **(b)** 0.123×10^7 or 123×10^4
   (c) 456×10^{-8} **(d)** 0.456×10^{-5} or 456×10^{-8}

6. **(a)** Missing right apostrophe.
   (b) Quotation marks not part of the ANSI standard; use apostrophes.
   (c) Use double apostrophes for apostrophes embedded within outer apostrophes: 'YOU''RE OK, I''M OK'. Otherwise the computer can't distinguish between legitimate apostrophes within the character constant and the outer apostrophes that enclose the character constant. The double apostrophe is internally represented (stored) correctly as a single apostrophe.

7. CHARACTER NAME*20
    NAME = 'CLARK S. KENT'

```
┌─────────────────────────────┐
│  NAME                       │
│                             │
│  CLARKɓS.ɓKENTɓɓɓɓɓɓɓ       │
└─────────────────────────────┘
```

If we had used

    CHARACTER NAME*15

there would be only two trailing blanks in storage instead of seven. If the length specification had been ten, storage would appear as follows.

```
┌──────────────────┐
│  NAME            │
│                  │
│  CLARKɓS.ɓK      │
└──────────────────┘
```

8. **(a)** Variable must appear to left of the equal sign.

    A = B + C

    (b) Two operation symbols next to each other.

    (c) Variable must appear to left of the equal sign.

    AGE = 5.

    (d) Permissible in WATFIV for *numeric* (but not character) assignment statements. Equivalent to:

    X = 5.3
    Y = 5.3
    Z = 5.3

    (e) Not permissible to raise a negative value to a decimal (real) power since the computer attempts to take the logarithm of a negative number.

    (f) OK to raise a negative integer value to an integer power since integer arithmetic in this example is performed as follows.

    J*J*J

9.
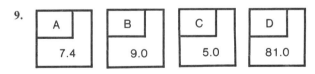

10.
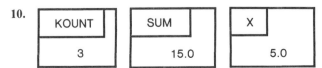

11.

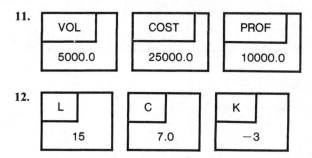

VOL	COST	PROF
5000.0	25000.0	10000.0

12.

L	C	K
15	7.0	−3

13. (a) STRESS − 100.0 (b) 5*K − 1 (c) 7.0**Q (d) Undefined; execution error because base is negative. See Example 2.5. (e) OK. Not considered mixed type. Y**2 computes faster than Y**2.0, since the latter uses logs. (f) 0.217182183D0l*Y.

14. (a) Integer result; 0 (b) Real result; 0.4 (c) Integer result; will cause integer overflow. (d) Real result; 8E120 (May cause real overflow.) (e) Double-precision result; 8D120 (Note that the expression here is mixed type, since A is double precision and B is real; the pairwise computation upgrades the result to double precision, although the magnitude of the result may cause overflow.)

15. No, since expressions appear only to the right of the equal sign. The computer stores 15.0 in CREDIT and copies the integer value in MONEY for storage in COST as a real value.

16. 132.0; AVG = (EXAM1 + EXAM2)/2.0

17. (a) 85.77778 (b) 100 (c) 0

18. 0; ENG*100/UNIV gives 20

19. (a) 116.0 (b) 28.0 (c) 28.0 (d) 8.5 (e) 4.0 (f) 4.0

20. (a) X**(K + 1)   (e) SQRT(7.0 − X)
     (b) X**K + 1   (f) (Y − 5.0/(X*T) + 2.0)*(−4.0)
     (c) (X − A)**2/(S + 4.0)   (g) (Y − 3.0**(X − 1.0) + 2.0)**5
     (d) SQRT((X − A)**2/(S + 4.0))

21. (a) 1.875 (b) 0.2625

22. (a) Z = 0.6, Z = 1.8, K = 20
     (b) P = 0.1609438, T = 0.3010300
     (c) 0.1680668E−01
     (d) In both cases, to avoid mixing mode in the arithmetic expressions.
     (e) S = 7.0
     (f) L = 10

23. (a) 4.000000 (b) 4.000000 (c) 2.000000 (d) 5.399999 with roundoff error (e) 5.399999 with roundoff error (f) 3.699999 with roundoff error (g) 3.699999 (h) 3.199999 with roundoff error (i) 3.199999

24. INTEGER ID,CREDIT,TUIT,BALDUE

.
.
.

CREDIT = 15
TUIT = CREDIT*100
BALDUE = TUIT + 250

.
.
.

END

Output values for these variables now expressed as integers.
Advantages: Improves visual look of output: integer arithmetic faster, more precise.
Disadvantages: Can't process fractional credits; financial data can't be expressed to the nearest cent.

27. (a) PRINT,(−6.5 + SQRT(6.5**2 − 4.0*(−3.4)*50.0))/(2.0*(−3.4))
   (b) PRINT,100.56**2,100.56**3,SQRT (100.56),100.56**(1.0/3.0)
   (c) PRINT,ALOG10(100.0),10.0**ALOG10(100.0)
   (d) PRINT,EXP(6.21461),ALOG(50.0),ALOG(EXP(6.21461))

28. For an IBM 370 system,

   WRITE(6,*)CREDIT,TUIT,BALDUE

30. For an IBM 370 system,

   READ(5,*)NAME,ID,CREDIT

31. (a) DATA A,B,C,D,E,F,R1,R2,R3/5*0.0,100.0, 3*'YES'/
   (b) REAL A,B,C,D,E,F/5*0.0, 100.0/
       CHARACTER*3 R1,R2,R3/3*'YES'/

32. Otherwise the program has to be changed each time we wish to process different values.

33. PRINCIPAL = 1000.0000000
   RATE   =   0.0200000
   QUARTERS =   2
   AMOUNT   = 1040.3980000

34. CHARACTER NAME*20,STREET*20,CSZ*30
   INTEGER NUM
   REAL   PRIN,RATE,ACCUM
   READ,NAME,STREET,CSZ
   READ,PRIN,RATE,NUM
   ACCUM = PRIN*(1.0 + RATE)**NUM
   PRINT,NAME
   PRINT,STREET
   PRINT,CSZ
   PRINT,' '
   PRINT, ' '

   .
   .
   .

   END

CHAPTER 3

1. (a) Confirmed by student.
   (b) CHARACTER NAME*15,ID*11
       INTEGER   CPC,FEES,CREDIT,TUIT,BALDUE
       .
       .
       .
       END
       See answer to Exercise 24 in Chapter 2 for advantages and disadvantages of typing integer.

2. Confirmed by student.   5. System-dependent.

3. Same as Exercise 1.   6. Varies for each student.

4. Confirmed by student.

CHAPTER 4

1. (a)

   (b) WHILE students are to be
       processed

          READ data
          IF no. credits ≥ cutoff THE
             Tuition = full-time tuition
             Increment full-time counte
          ELSE
             Tuition = no. credits ×
                       cost per credit
             Increment part-time coun
          END IF
          Calculate balance due
          PRINT results
       END WHILE

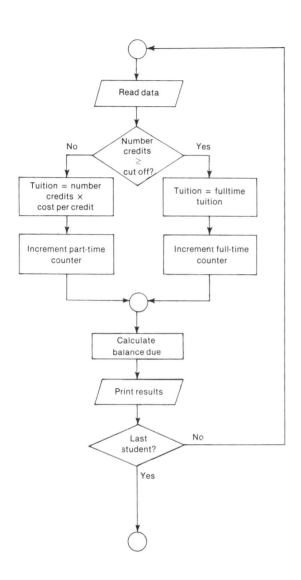

LOOP
    READ data
    IF no. credits ≥ cutoff THEN
        Tuition = full-time tuition
        Increment full-time counter
    ELSE
        Tuition = no. credits × cost per credit
        Increment part-time counter
    END IF
    Calculate balance due
    PRINT results
UNTIL no students need be processed

2. (a) 1 ⎫
         2 ⎪
         3 ⎪
         4 ⎬ 7 iterations
         5 ⎪
         6 ⎪
         7 ⎭

(b) 1 ⎫
       4 ⎬ 3 iterations
       7 ⎭

(c) 2 ⎫
       3 ⎪
       4 ⎬ 4 iterations
       5 ⎭

(d) 5} 1 iteration
(e) 6} 1 iteration

3. No changes in program. In the input data replace the 3 by 4562 and add the remaining data lines for all students.

4. These column headings would be printed just before each output line in the table, which would be a logic error.

```
STUDENT NAME   IDENTIFICATION    BALANCE DUE
W. MITTY             266612463    1750.0000000
STUDENT NAME   IDENTIFICATION    BALANCE DUE
X. MITTY             266612464    2100.0000000
etc.
```

5. Syntactically no, but it's not good programming style to align the body left and to place the statement number at the last statement in the body.

6. (a) Real parameters are not permitted. (b) Missing statement number in both DO and CONTINUE statements. (c) Check logic; initial value greater than terminal value. (d) DO-variable redefined within loop; negative incrementation value.

8. (a) No. (b) Yes. First time through BALDUE is undefined; results in an execution error.

(c)
```
STUDENT NAME        IDENTIFICATION   BALANCE DUE
W. MITTY                266612463    1750.0000000
TOTAL BALANCE DUE:$              1750.0000000
X. MITTY                266612464    2100.0000000
TOTAL BALANCE DUE:$              3850.0000000
Y. MITTY                266612465    1450.0000000
TOTAL BALANCE DUE:$              5300.0000000
```

(d)
```
STUDENT NAME     IDENTIFICATION           BALANCE DUE
-----------------------------------------------------
W. MITTY                266612463           1750.0000000
***ERROR***   VALUE OF SUM      IS UNDEFINED
```

9.

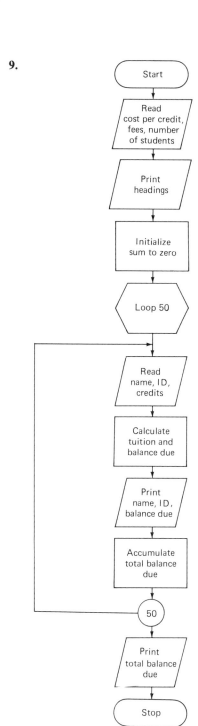

10. .

.

.

```
REAL CPC,FEES,CREDIT,TUIT,BALDUE,SUM,AVE
```
.

.

.

```
PRINT,'TOTAL BALANCE DUE: $',SUM
AVE = SUM/N
PRINT,'AVERAGE BALANCE DUE:$',AVE
STOP
END
```

11. **(a)** Eliminate SUM = 0.0 and place the following just after the REAL statement.

```
DATA SUM/0.0/
```

Note: Caution must be exercised when using DATA statements to initialize sums. We're getting ahead of ourselves, but see Exercise 15.

13.

M	N	I	J	SCORE	SUM	AVE
2	3	1	1	90.0	90.0	—
			2	70.0	160.0	—
			3	80.0	240.0	—
			—	80.0	240.0	80.0
	2	2	1	50.0	50.0	80.0
			2	90.0	140.0	80.0
			—	90.0	140.0	70.0

Note 1: The placement of the snapshot does not record the fact that SUM gets initialized to zero before it contains 90.0 and again gets initialized to zero between values of 240.0 and 50.0.
Note 2: AVE is undefined in the first three rows of the table; J may become undefined after the J-loop gets exhausted, depending on the system.

14.

Input	Output		
3			
2			
20.0	MEAN SCORE FOR SECTION	1 =	55.0000000
90.0			
4	MEAN SCORE FOR SECTION	2 =	72.5000000
40.0			
100.0	MEAN SCORE FOR SECTION	3 =	70.0000000
70.0			
80.0			
3			
60.0			
80.0			
70.0			

15. SUM would not get reinitialized to zero before each new section is to be processed, since the DATA statement is nonexecutable. The mean for the second section would be calculated incorrectly as 190.0. In general, we don't recommend using a DATA statement to initialize sums, unless you're sure that the sums need not be reinitialized.

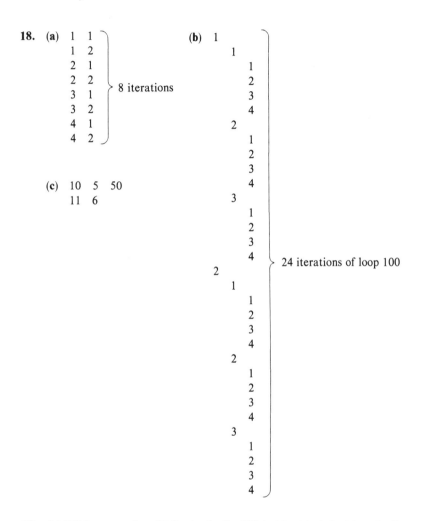

18. **(a)**

1	1
1	2
2	1
2	2
3	1
3	2
4	1
4	2

} 8 iterations

(b)

1
  1
    1
    2
    3
    4
  2
    1
    2
    3
    4
  3
    1
    2
    3
    4

} 24 iterations of loop 100

2
  1
    1
    2
    3
    4
  2
    1
    2
    3
    4
  3
    1
    2
    3
    4

(c)

10	5	50
11	6	

19. **(a)** DO-loops overlap. **(b)** Syntactically OK, but best to indent loop bodies.

20. **(a)**

PRIN	NUM	LOOPS	RATE	ACCUM
1000.0	20	5	0.020	1485.932
			0.025	1638.604
			0.030	1806.101
			0.035	1989.782
			0.040	2191.121

(b)
PRINCIPAL =	1000.0000000
QUARTERS =	20
RATE	ACCUM. FUNDS

RATE	ACCUM. FUNDS
0.0100000	1220.1710000
0.0120000	1269.4110000
0.0140000	1320.5600000
0.0160000	1373.6370000
0.0180000	1428.7370000
0.0200000	1485.9320000

CHAPTER 5

1. (a) True. (b) False. (c) True. (d) True. (e) Invalid. (f) True. (g) True. (h) False. (i) Invalid.

2. (a) HELP. (b) O'HARE.

3.

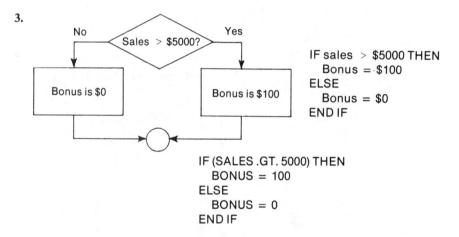

```
IF sales > $5000 THEN
    Bonus = $100
ELSE
    Bonus = $0
END IF
```

```
IF (SALES .GT. 5000) THEN
    BONUS = 100
ELSE
    BONUS = 0
END IF
```

4. Define

    COUNTN = NO. SALES PEOPLE WHO DON'T RECEIVE BONUS
    COUNTY = NO. SALES PEOPLE WHO DO RECEIVE BONUS

Add COUNTN and COUNTY to list of INTEGER statement.
Between the INTEGER statement and loop 50 insert

    COUNTN = 0
    COUNTY = 0

In the IF-block insert

    COUNTN = COUNTN + 1

and in the ELSE-block insert

    COUNTY = COUNTY + 1

After loop 50 insert

```
PRINT,'b'
PRINT,'NON-BONUS COUNT = ',COUNTN
PRINT,'BONUS COUNT      = ',COUNTY
```

6. (a) IF credits ≥ 12 THEN
       Tuition = $1200
   ELSE
       Tuition = $100 × credits
   END IF

              IF (CREDIT .GE. 12.0) THEN
                TUIT = 1200.0
              ELSE
                TUIT = 100.0*CREDIT
              END IF

(b) IF fixed cost + var. cost < revenue THEN
       Profit = revenue − (fixed + variable costs)
       PRINT profit
   ELSE
       Loss = fixed cost + variable cost − revenue
       PRINT loss
   END IF

              IF (FIXED + VAR .LT. REV) THEN
               PROF = REV − FIXED − VAR
               PRINT,'PROFIT = ',PROF
              ELSE
               LOSS = FIXED + VAR − REV
               PRINT,'LOSS = ',LOSS
              END IF

(c) IF balance < $50 THEN
       Payment = balance
   ELSE
       Payment = $50 + 10% (balance − $50)
   END IF

              IF (BAL .LT.50.0) THEN
               PAYS = BAL
              ELSE
               PAYS = 50.0 + 0.10*(BAL − 50.0)
              END IF

(d) IF sex = male THEN
       PRINT ''sex = male''
   ELSE
       PRINT ''sex = female''
   END IF

              IF (SEX .EQ. 'MALE') THEN
               PRINT,'SEX = MALE'
              ELSE
               PRINT,'SEX = FEMALE'
              END IF

7. (a) IF (CUME .GT. 32400.0) THEN
       FICA = 0.0
   ELSE
       FICA = 0.067*SAL
   END IF

  (b) IF (A*C .LT. B/D) THEN
       C = D/E
       F = F − 1.0
   ELSE
       X = A + B
       D = B − A
   END IF
```
```

8.

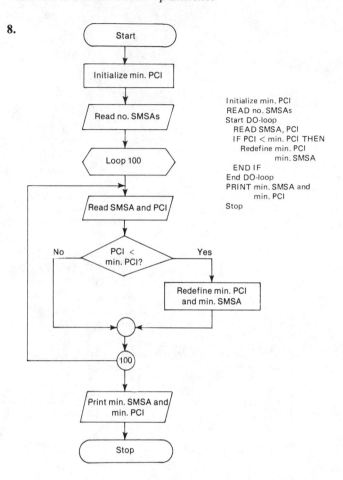

Initialize min. PCI
READ no. SMSAs
Start DO-loop
  READ SMSA, PCI
  IF PCI < min. PCI THEN
    Redefine min. PCI
              min. SMSA
  END IF
End DO-loop
PRINT min. SMSA and
        min. PCI
Stop

N	I	SMSA	PCI	MINPCI	MINSMS
5	1	147	5165.0	5165.0	147
	2	56	7860.0	5165.0	147
	3	75	6350.0	5165.0	147
	4	41	4293.0	4293.0	41
	5	105	5415.0	4293.0	41

9. Modify the flowchart in the preceding exercise as follows, where corresponding program segments are shown to the right.

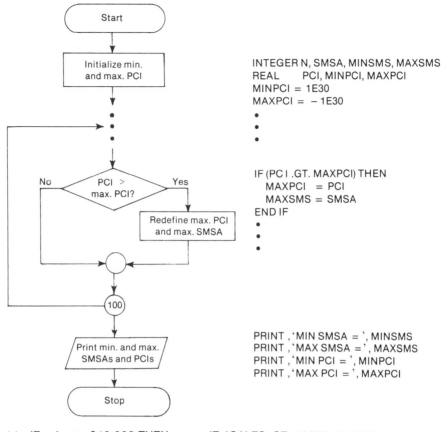

INTEGER N, SMSA, MINSMS, MAXSMS
REAL   PCI, MINPCI, MAXPCI
MINPCI = 1E30
MAXPCI = −1E30
•
•
•

IF (PCI .GT. MAXPCI) THEN
    MAXPCI = PCI
    MAXSMS = SMSA
END IF
•
•
•

PRINT , 'MIN SMSA = ', MINSMS
PRINT , 'MAX SMSA = ', MAXSMS
PRINT , 'MIN PCI = ', MINPCI
PRINT , 'MAX PCI = ', MAXPCI

10. **(a)** IF sales > $10,000 THEN   IF (SALES .GT. 10000.0) THEN
                Add $150 to pay   PAY = PAY + 150.0
              END IF   END IF

      (b) IF part name = wrench THEN   IF (PART .EQ. 'WRENCH') THEN
                PRINT quantity on hand   PRINT,QOH
              END IF   END IF

11. IF (M .EQ. N) THEN
            I = I + 3
            J = J + 2
            K = K + 1
         END IF

12. **(a)** END is not a legal statement following the relational expression.
      (b) Valid.
      (c) LT should be .LT.

13. READ, NAME, PHONE
         IF(NAME .EQ. 'SMITH') PRINT,'NAME:',NAME
         IF(NAME .EQ. 'SMITH') PRINT,'PHONE NUMBER:',PHONE

14. **(a)** Correct. **(b)** Incorrect. A+B is not a relational expression. **(c)** Correct. **(d)** Incorrect.

15. IF(CODE .LT. 'A'   .OR.   CODE .GT. 'E') ERROR = .TRUE.

16. **(a)** IF(VAL .GT. 100 .AND. VAL .LT. 200) THEN
    (b) IF(MAJOR .EQ. 'ECN' .OR. MAJOR .EQ. 'MATH') THEN
    (c) Use .OR. instead of OR

17. **(a)** No.
    (b) Yes, since (false) .OR. (true) gives true.
    (c) No, since (false) .AND. (true) .AND. (true) is followed by (false) .AND. (true), which is false.
    (d) Yes, since (true) .AND. (true) gives true.

18. **(a)**

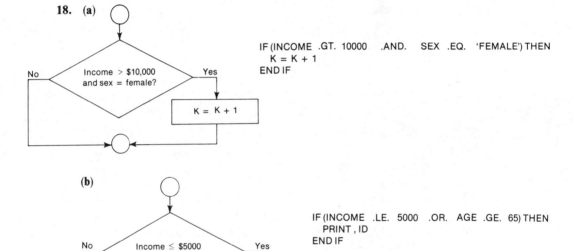

IF (INCOME .GT. 10000   .AND.   SEX .EQ.   'FEMALE') THEN
    K = K + 1
END IF

(b)

IF (INCOME .LE. 5000   .OR. AGE .GE. 65) THEN
    PRINT , ID
END IF

19. **(a)** (LFORT .EQ. .TRUE.) .AND. (LCOBOL .EQ. .TRUE.)
    (b) (LPASCL .EQ. .TRUE.) .OR. (LFORT .EQ. .TRUE.)
    (c) (LPASCL .EQ. .TRUE.) .AND. (LFORT .EQ. .TRUE.) .AND. (LCOBOL .EQ. .TRUE.)
    (d) LPASCL .NE. .TRUE.

21.

COSTC	RATE	YEAR	COSTF
60000.0	0.1	1	65999.93
		2	72599.87
		.	.
		.	.
		.	.
		8	128614.50

22. **(a)** We get an execution error at the WHILE statement since COSTF is undefined.

(b) COSTF would always store 66000.0, which gives us an infinite loop.

(c) The output for YEAR would be one year too high. If YEAR is initialized to 1, place the counter for YEAR just before the END WHILE statement.

(d) Just before the WHILE statement use

```
RATE = 1.0 + RATE
```

Then replace the assignment statement for COSTF with

```
COSTF = COSTF*RATE
```

Since 1.0 + RATE remains constant within the loop, we need only calculate it once before the loop instead of repeatedly within the loop.

23.   .
.
.
```
REAL COSTC,COSTF,RATE,PRI,M
READ,COSTC, PRI,M
```
.
.
.
```
WHILE (COSTF .LT. M*COSTC)
```
.
.
.

24.   WHILE (COSTF .LT. 2*COSTC   .OR.   YEAR .LE. 9)

25. **(a)** Insert

```
READ,N
DO 20 J = 1,N
```

just after the REAL statement and

```
20 CONTINUE
```

just after the END WHILE statement.

(b)

Data Set	Year when Doubling Achieved
1	15
2	8
3	5
4	8

Note that the original cost makes no difference as to when there's a doubling. Only the inflation rate makes a difference.

27.

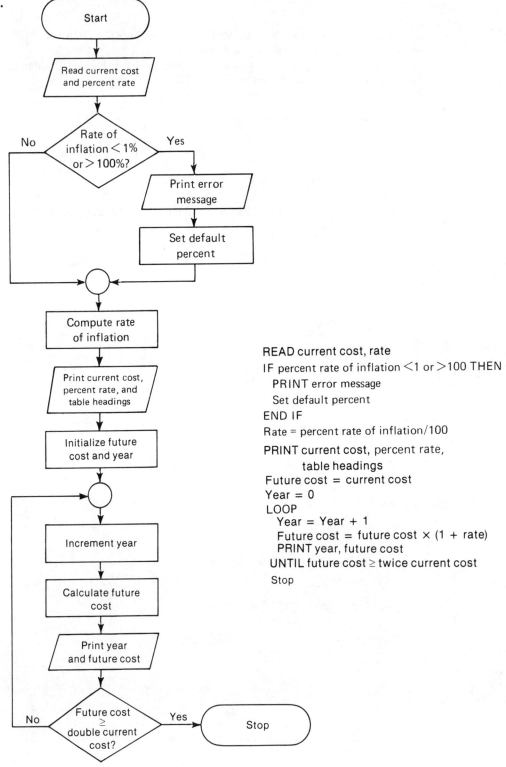

READ current cost, rate
IF percent rate of inflation <1 or >100 THEN
  PRINT error message
  Set default percent
END IF
Rate = percent rate of inflation/100
PRINT current cost, percent rate,
      table headings
Future cost = current cost
Year = 0
LOOP
  Year = Year + 1
  Future cost = future cost × (1 + rate)
  PRINT year, future cost
UNTIL future cost ≥ twice current cost
Stop

28. (a)
```
LOOP
    YEAR = YEAR + 1
    COSTF = COSTF*(1.0 + RATE)
UNTIL(COSTF .GE. 2.0*COSTC)
PRINT,'COST HAS AT LEAST DOUBLED',YEAR,'YEARS FROM NOW'
```
(b) Just after the REAL statement insert

```
READ,N
DO 50 J = 1,N
```

Just before the STOP statement insert

```
50 CONTINUE
```

31. (a) The line for the last (eighth) year would not be printed.
(b) We would get the same output as before.
(c) The body of the loop would not get executed; only the table headings would be output.

33. (a) The trailer record becomes

```
'LRC',0,0
```

Change WHILE statement to

```
WHILE (SSN .NE. 0)
```

There should be no danger in using zero as a trailer number since Social Security numbers are never zero.
(b) Yes, otherwise we get an "out of data" execution error when the READ statement is executed. No, they can be any string value and integer value, respectively, since they're not utilized following the READ statement.

34. We would end up processing the trailer record as if it were a salesperson.

35. WHILE statement changes to

```
WHILE(NAME .NE. 'EOF')
```

and the trailer record changes to

```
'EOF',0,0
```

36. Change the AT END block as follows:

```
.
.
.
READ,NAME,SSN,SALES
    AT END
        PRINT,'END OF DATA'
        QUIT 2 or STOP
    END AT END
IF (SALES .LE. 5000) THEN
.
.
.
```

37. **(a)**

```
                    10
                    20
                    30
EOF
LOOP EXIT
```

(b)

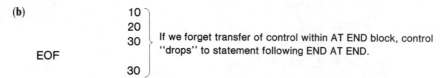

```
                    10
                    20
                    30    If we forget transfer of control within AT END block, control
EOF                       "drops" to statement following END AT END.

                    30
***ERROR***    ATTEMPT TO READ ON UNIT 5 AFTER IT HAS HAD END-OF-FILE
```

(c) Same output as part b. This is because control would be transferred to the end of the current or inner block (AT END block) instead of to the end of the second outer block (LOOP block).

CHAPTER 6

1. **(a)**

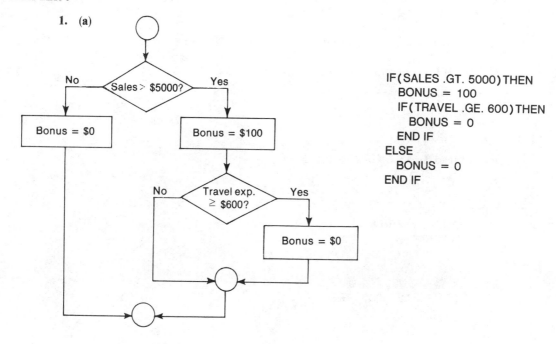

```
IF(SALES .GT. 5000)THEN
    BONUS = 100
    IF(TRAVEL .GE. 600)THEN
        BONUS = 0
    END IF
ELSE
    BONUS = 0
END IF
```

(b)

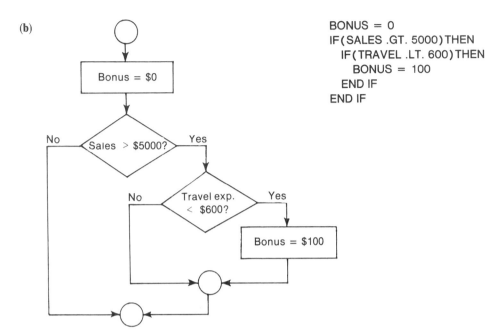

```
BONUS = 0
IF(SALES .GT. 5000)THEN
    IF(TRAVEL .LT. 600)THEN
        BONUS = 100
    END IF
END IF
```

The original version has the "cleanest" logic but the longest code. The logic in part (b) is reasonably clear, and it has the shortest code. We prefer the original version.

2.  ```
    IF(STATUS .EQ. 'FT' .AND. RES .EQ. 'IN')   TUIT = 1500
    IF(STATUS .EQ. 'FT' .AND. RES .EQ. 'OUT')TUIT = 3000
    IF(STATUS .EQ. 'PT' .AND. RES .EQ. 'IN')   TUIT = 50•CREDIT
    IF(STATUS .EQ. 'PT' .AND. RES .EQ. 'OUT')TUIT = 125•CREDIT
    ```

    The use of logical operators simplifies the logic.

5. (a)
    ```
    IF (A .GT. 10) THEN
        IF (B .GT. 20) THEN
            R = 'T2'
        END IF
    ELSE
        R = 'F1'
    END IF
    ```

    (b)
    ```
    IF (A .GT. 10) THEN
        IF (B .GT. 20) THEN
            R = 'T2'
        ELSE
            R = 'F2'
        END IF
    ELSE
        IF (C .GT. 30) THEN
            R = 'T3'
        ELSE
            R = 'F3'
        END IF
    END IF
    ```

    (d)

	Part	
	a	b
i.	F1	F3
ii.	F2	F2
iii.	T2	T2
    ```

6. **(a)**
```
IF(ORDER .LT. MIN)THEN
    PRINT,'ORDER AMOUNT LESS THAN',MIN,'FOR',NAME
    AMT = 0
ELSE
  IF(ORDER .LE. CUT1)THEN
    AMT = ORDER*COST1
  ELSE
    IF(ORDER .LE. CUT2)THEN
      AMT = ORDER*COST2
    ELSE
      AMT = ORDER*COST3
    END IF
  END IF
END IF
```

The nested approach is more difficult to follow than the ELSE IF approach.

(b)
```
IF(ORDER .LT. MIN)THEN
    PRINT,'ORDER AMOUNT LESS THAN',MIN,'FOR',NAME
    AMT = 0
END IF

IF(ORDER .GE. MIN .AND. ORDER .LE. CUT1)THEN
    AMT = ORDER*COST1
END IF

IF(ORDER .GT. CUT1 .AND. ORDER .LE. CUT2)THEN
    AMT = ORDER*COST2
END IF

IF(ORDER .GT. CUT2)THEN
    AMT = ORDER*COST3
END IF
```

The sequence of IF-THEN structures is easy-to-follow logic, but CPU inefficient compared to the ELSE-IF approach, which is also easy to follow.

7. **(a)** No error message would be printed whenever ID is out of range.
(b) An execution error would result when the computer attempts to output AVEJR, which would have undefined contents.
(c) An execution error would result when the computer attempts to divide by zero in the calculation of AVEJR.

8. **(a)**
```
IF(CLASS .EQ. 'FR')THEN
    NUMFR = NUMFR + 1
    SUMFR = SUMFR + GPA
ELSE
  IF(CLASS .EQ. 'SO')THEN
    NUMSO = NUMSO + 1
    SUMSO = SUMSO + GPA
```

```
        ELSE
          IF(CLASS .EQ. 'JR')THEN
            NUMJR = NUMJR + 1
            SUMJR = SUMJR + GPA
          ELSE
            IF(CLASS .EQ. 'SR')THEN
              NUMSR = NUMSR + 1
              SUMSR = SUMSR + GPA
            ELSE
              PRINT,'======================================='
              PRINT,'ERROR IN CODE FOR ID NUMBER',ID
              PRINT,'======================================='
            END IF
          END IF
        END IF
      END IF
```

This approach is more difficult to read than the original. Agree?

(b)
```
    IF(CLASS .EQ. 'FR')THEN
      NUMFR = NUMFR + 1
      SUMFR = SUMFR + GPA
    END IF

    IF(CLASS .EQ. 'SO')THEN
      NUMSO = NUMSO + 1
      SUMSO = SUMSO + GPA
    END IF

    IF(CLASS .EQ. 'JR')THEN
      NUMJR = NUMJR + 1
      SUMJR = SUMJR + GPA
    END IF

    IF(CLASS .EQ. 'SR')THEN
      NUMSR = NUMSR + 1
      SUMSR = SUMSR + GPA
    END IF

    IF(CLASS .NE. 'FR' .AND. CLASS .NE. 'SO' .AND. CLASS .NE. 'JR'
                             .AND. CLASS .NE. 'SR')THEN
      PRINT,'======================================='
      PRINT,'ERROR IN CODE FOR ID NUMBER',ID
      PRINT,'======================================='
    END IF
```

This approach is easy enough to read, but it's cumbersome and CPU inefficient.

9. (a) Add ERRCT to integer list.
Initialize ERRCT to zero in first DATA list.
Insert the following statement into ELSE-block.

```
ERRCT = ERRCT + 1
```

Insert the following statement before first PRINT statement in report.

```
PRINT,'***NUMBER OF RECORDS WITH CODE ERRORS =',ERRCT
```

(b) Add TOTSTU to integer list and SUMGPA to real list.
Initialize TOTSTU and SUMGPA to zero.
Insert the following statements after the AT END statement.

```
TOTSTU  = TOTSTU + 1
SUMGPA = SUMGPA + GPA
```

Insert the following statements before the STOP statement.

```
PRINT, 'TOTAL NUMBER OF STUDENTS =', TOTSTU
PRINT, 'OVERALL AVERAGE GPA       =', SUMGPA / TOTSTU
```

Note: This design would include students with error codes as part of the summary statistics. To avoid this, then either place the counter and summer within each class block or delete these altogether and use

```
TOTSTU  = NUMFR + NUMSO + NUMJR + NUMSR
SUMGPA = SUMFR + SUMSO + SUMJR + SUMSR
```

just before the new PRINT statements.

13. Add ERRCNT to integer list.
Before LOOP statement add the following statement.

```
ERRCNT = 0
```

Within error case add

```
ERRCNT = ERRCNT + 1
```

Just before STOP statement add

```
PRINT,'*-------------------------------------------*'
PRINT,'***NUMBER OF INPUT ERRORS = ',ERRCNT,'***'
PRINT,'*-------------------------------------------*'
```

17. −14; 71

18.

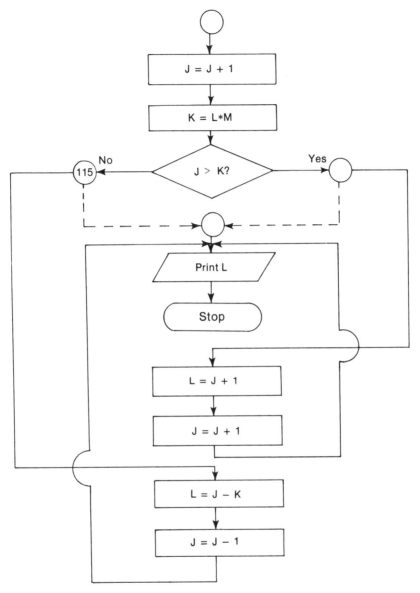

Note how control structures are obscured (is that really an IF-THEN-ELSE structure?) and how top-down execution of a program is violated (going back to statement 85 doesn't establish a loop, which is the only legitimate flow reversal).

19.

```
J = J + 1
K = L*M
IF (J .GT. K)THEN
   L = J + K
   J = J + 1
```

```
    ELSE
      L = J − K
      J = J − 1
    END IF
    PRINT,L
    STOP
    END
```

21.
```
-----------------------------------------------------
INITIAL INTERVAL:
            0.0000000   TO              1.0000000
ERROR TOLERANCE =        0.0010000
ITERATIONS       =       1
EXACT ROOT       =       0.5000000
-----------------------------------------------------
-----------------------------------------------------
INITIAL INTERVAL:
            0.5000000   TO              1.0000000
ERROR TOLERANCE =        0.0010000
ITERATIONS       =       9
ESTIMATED ROOT   =       0.5009766
MAXIMUM ERROR    =       0.0009766
-----------------------------------------------------
-----------------------------------------------------
INITIAL INTERVAL:
            0.0000000   TO              0.5000000
ERROR TOLERANCE =        0.0010000
ITERATIONS       =       9
ESTIMATED ROOT   =       0.4990234
MAXIMUM ERROR    =       0.0009766
```

22. Change line 215 to

$$F(X) = 2.0**X$$

In line 265 we have

$$F(\text{LEFT}) \quad = F(-3) = 0.125$$
$$F(\text{RIGHT}) = F(1) \quad = 2.000$$

Thus, the test in line 265 is "true" and the message gets printed. In reality, this function has no root.

CHAPTER 7

1. **(a)** The array is conceptualized as the (physical) group of memory locations whereas the array name identifies this group by name. In mathematics, the array is the list of items or values.

(b) The array name depicts or implies the entire array whereas the array element name (i.e., the array name with attached subscript) identifies a specific element of the array.

(c) The array element suggests a specific (physical) storage location (the box), whereas the array element name gives a name to this storage location (identifies the box by name).

(d) No distinction in our terminology.

(e) The subscript is a subscript expression enclosed in parentheses. The subscript expression takes on a value, not the subscript. In mathematics, no distinction is made between these two.

(f) These are identical.

2. Arrays are allocated memory during compilation, not during execution. Values in variables are not available until the execution phase.

3. (a) Array declarations must precede use of the arrays, so the REAL statement must precede the READ statement. In general, type statements must precede executable statements. The expression 4 + 3 cannot be used as an upper dimension bound. Also, K cannot be used as an upper dimension bound in declaring the array X (see Exercise 2). If we wish 50 elements in X, we write

      REAL X(50),T(7)

(b) M + 10*N evaluates as 85. Thus the value of the subscript expression in A(85) exceeds the upper dimension bound in the array declarator A(50). We must declare at least 85 elements in A.

(c) Arrays D and E have only ten elements. As soon as J reaches 11, an execution error occurs. Also, we cannot dimension D and E twice, so either eliminate the DIMENSION statement or change the INTEGER statement to INTEGER D, E. E(3) would store 36.

4.

S	S	T
1	1	1
2	2	4
3	3	9
4	4	16
		30

5. (a) INTEGER DEPOS (100),TOT,PER

    .
    .
    .

DO 10 I = 1,100

    .
    .
    .

DO 20 I = 1,100

The second program would require 291 new statements. One hundred variables would appear to the right of the equal sign in the calculation of TOT.

(b) INTEGER DEPOS (500),TOT,PER
    READ,N

    .
    .
    .

```
        DO 10 I = 1,N
          .
          .
          .
        DO 20 I = 1,N
          .
          .
          .
```

6.   REAL LOAD (50)
       DO 10 J = 1,50
         READ,LOAD(J)
   10 CONTINUE

7.

1	5	−4
10	4	6
8	1	7
2	10	−8
21	20	1

8.

```
      INTEGER COST(500),SALES(500)     Input Data
      READ,N                           3
      DO 50 J = 1,N                    40,100
        READ,COST(J),SALES(J)          20,125
   50 CONTINUE                         75,95
```

9. **(a)**   1 2 3 4 5 6 7 8 9 ...
_____

     3500
     5000
     4000

(b)   Same as part (a).

(c)

(d)

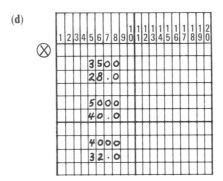

10. (a) READ,(X(J),J = 1,8)   (e) PRINT,(A(J),J = 1,3),(B(J),J = 1,5)
    (b) PRINT,(X(J),J = 1,8)   (f) READ,(X(J),J = 1,3),M,N
    (c) READ,(X(J),J = 1,11,2)   (g) PRINT,A,(X(J),J = 1,3),B
    (d) PRINT,(A(J),B(J),J = 1,3)

11. (a)
10 20 30 40 5 10 15 20
   (b)
10 5 20 10 30 15 40 20
   (c)
1 10 5 2 20 10 3 30 15 4 40 20

12. (a) READ,(SALES(J),J = 1,3)   (b) READ,(SALES(J),COST(J),J = 1,3)
         READ,(COST(J),J = 1,3)

13. (a) OK. (b) J can't be an input item and a DO-variable, since values of the DO-variable would be redefined. (c) OK, as long as P, A, B, C, and D are declared type integer.

14.

| 1 2 3 4 5 6 7 8 9 10 11 12 13 14 15 16 17 18 19 20 ... |

(a) and (d)   1 0 2 0 3 0   4 0
(b) and (e)   1 0
            2 0
            3 0
            4 0
(c)   1 0 2 0
            3 0 4 0

15. (a)

(b)

	1 2 3 4 5 6 7 8 9 0	1 1 1 1 1 1 1 1 1 2 / 1 2 3 4 5 6 7 8 9 0
1		
2	1 0	
3	2 0	
4	3 0	
5	4 0	
6		

(c)

	1 2 3 4 5 6 7 8 9 0	1 1 1 1 1 1 1 1 1 2 / 1 2 3 4 5 6 7 8 9 0
1		
2	1 0	2 0
3	3 0	4 0
4		

(d) and **(e)**

	1 2 3 4 5 6 7 8 9 0	1 1 1 1 1 1 1 1 1 2 / 1 2 3 4 5 6 7 8 9 0
1		
2	1 1 0	
3	2 2 0	
4	3 3 0	
5	4 4 0	
6		

17. **(a)** 10
      1,2,3,4,5,6,7,8
      .1,.2,.3,.4,.5,.6,.7,.8,.9,1.,1.1,1.2,1.3,1.4,1.5
   (b) 10,1,2,3,4,5,6,7,8,.1,.2,.3,.4,.5,.6,.7,.8,.9,1.,1.1,1.2,1.3,1.4,1.5
   (c)

1 2 3 4 5 6 7 8 910111213141516171819202122232425262728293031323334353637383940414243444546474849505152535455565758 5960

10
12345678
  1   2   3   4   5   6   7   8   9   10   11   12   13   14   15

(d)

⊗	
1	
2	1 2 3 4 5 6 7 8 0.10 0.20 0.30 0.40 0.50 0.60 0.70 0.80 0.90 1.00
3	

(e)

⊗	
1	
2	1 2 3 4 5 6 7 8
3	0.10 0.20 0.30 0.40 0.50 0.60 0.70 0.80 0.90 1.00
4	

18. Can't use variables as either DO expressions or repeat factors in DATA statements.

19. The first approach either gives an execution error, if K is undefined, or stores zero in location TOTAL(0), if the system initializes K to zero. The second approach simply sets the variable (not the array) TOTAL to zero.

    Use either

```
    DO 10 K = 1,10
      TOTAL(K) = 0.0
  10 CONTINUE
```

or

```
  DATA TOTAL / 10*0.0 /
```

or

```
  DATA (TOTAL(K),K = 1,10) / 10*0.0 /
```

20.
```
    SUM = 0.0
    DO 10 I = 1,K
      SUM = SUM + REVEN(I)
  10 CONTINUE
```

21.

BAL(1)
150.30

BAL(2)
850.75

22. Immediately after the assignment statement for BAL(J) insert:

Or use a logical IF statement
```
  IF (BAL(J) .LT. 0.0) THEN
    PRINT, 'ACCT. NO. =',ACCNO(J), 'BALANCE =',BAL(J)
  END IF
```

23. (a) MONDAY,TUESDAY, . . . , SUNDAY

    (b) FRIDAY
        THURSDAY
        ***10   OUT OF RANGE
        - - - - FINISHED

    (c)
```
  DATA DAY / 'MONDAY','TUESDAY', 'WEDNESDAY','THURSDAY',
  *              'FRIDAY', 'SATURDAY', 'SUNDAY' /
```

25. (a)
```
      INTEGER LIST (25)
      READ, N
      J = N + 1
      DO 10 I = 1,N
      J = J - 1
      READ,LIST(J)
  10 CONTINUE
```

(b)
```
        MAXI = −999999
        DO 20 J = 1,N
            IF (LIST(J) .GT. MAXI) THEN        Or use logical IF
                MAXI = LIST(J)                 statement
            END IF
    20  CONTINUE
        PRINT, MAXI
```
(c)
```
        DO 30 J = 1,N
            IF (LIST(J) .EQ. 0) THEN           Or use logical IF
            PRINT,J                            statement
            END IF
    30  CONTINUE
```

26.

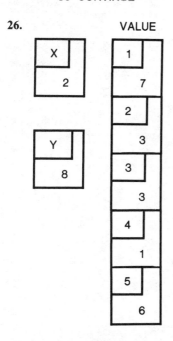

27. (a)

SATTOT	COUNT(1)	COUNT(2)	COUNT(3)	COUNT(4)	SUMSAT(1)	SUMSAT(2)	SUMSAT(3)	SUMSAT(4)
—	0	0	0	0	0	0	0	0
1220	0	1	0	0	0	1220	0	0
1400	0	1	1	0	0	1220	1400	0
1170	0	2	1	0	0	2390	1400	0
1150	1	2	1	0	1150	2390	1400	0
1000	1	3	1	0	1150	3390	1400	0
1000	1	3	1	1	1150	3390	1400	1000

(b)
```
1   1   1150
2   3   1130
3   1   1400
4   0     0
```

(c) ERROR IN CLASS CODE
PROGRAM TERMINATED

29. Just after the output line for Lois insert:

RIP VAN WINKLE IS OVER 65— —UNINSURABLE

30. This traditional approach works in the sense that it gives correct results; however, it's an illustration of undesirable and ambiguous structure, since there are two possible exits from this loop structure:

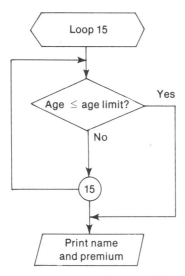

Note: In Exercise 29 we would exit through statement 15, which would give an incorrect premium of $357 for Rip.

32. Change the first input record to 'X'.

33. Eliminate the second READ statement and the variables B0, B1, B2, and B3 from the REAL statement. In loop 10, the user must insert the appropriate assignment statement for Y.

36.

J	TEMP	LIST(1)	LIST(2)	LIST(3)	LIST(4)	SWITCH
2	3076	3076	8321	2501	7771	1
3	2501	3076	2501	8321	7771	1
4	7771	3076	2501	7771	8321	1
2	2501	2501	3076	7771	8321	1
3	2501	2501	3076	7771	8321	1
4	2501	2501	3076	7771	8321	1
2	2501	2501	3076	7771	8321	0
3	2501	2501	3076	7771	8321	0
4	2501	2501	3076	7771	8321	0

Two passes; three passes.

37. The message

3000 EXCEEDS MAXIMUM NUMBER OF ITEMS

would be printed and then execution would stop.

39. Yes, since the internal computer coding of alphabetic data is expressed in numeric code. This means, for example, that the alphabetic character A is represented by a coded value that is "numerically" less than the code for the alphabetic character B. Try it.

CHAPTER 8

1.

Program Segment	Output
DO 40 I = 1,3	1000
DO 30 J = 1,4	800
PRINT,DEPOS(I,J)	500
30 CONTINUE	1200
40 CONTINUE	500
	2000
	2000
	500
	1500
	300
	700
	1500

2. DEPOS

1000	1200	2000	300
800	500	500	700
500	2000	1500	1500

Array is filled column by column. Input data should be in the following order.
1000
500
1500
800
2000
300
500
2000
700
1200
500
1500

3. To number rows:

PRINT,I,(X(I,J),J = 1,3)

To number columns place the following before loop 20.

PRINT,(J,J = 1,3)

4. **(a)**   PRINT,((DEPOS(I,J),J = 1,4),I = 1,3)
(b)   DO 30 I = 1,3
            PRINT,(DEPOS(I,J),J = 1,4)
    30 CONTINUE
(c)   DO 40 J = 1,4
            PRINT,(DEPOS(I,J),I = 1,3)
    40 CONTINUE

5. **(a)** 1 2 3 4 5 6 ...   **(b)** 1 2 3 4 5 6 7 8 9 10 11 12 ... 56 57 58 59 60

1000	1000 800 ... 1 5 0 0
800	
500	
.	
.	
.	
700	
1500	

6. Yes. The advantage here is that the repeat specification in the new FORMAT statement (13) allows up to 13 columns of input versus exactly 4 in the earlier version. Moreover, the fact that each row of input begins on a new input record is now explicit since DO-loop 30 processes rows (that is, the READ statement is reexecuted for each new value of I). In the earlier version it was necessary to use a repeat specification of *exactly* 4 to accomplish the same desirable "table" appearance of input data.

7.   READ 1,((DEPOS(I,J),I = 1,3),J = 1,4)
    1 FORMAT(3I5)
In this case the array in memory gets filled in column by column, ending up the same as in Example 8.3.

8. **(a)**

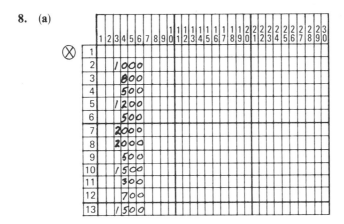

(b)   and   **(c)**

	1000	800	500	1200
2	1000	800	500	1200
3	500	2000	2000	500
4	1500	300	700	1500

(d)

3	BANK DEPOSITS			
6	1000	800	500	1200
8	BANK DEPOSITS			
11	500	2000	2000	500
13	BANK DEPOSITS			
16	1500	300	700	1500

9.

BANK DEPOSITS

	1	2	3	4
BANK 1	1000	800	500	1200
BANK 2	500	2000	2000	500
BANK 3	1500	300	700	1500

Two advantages: greater flexibility and clearer design. The new repeat specification (16) allows up to 16 columns of output versus exactly 4 in the earlier version, which reduces program maintenance should the number of columns change. Moreover, the fact that each row of the matrix is printed on a new output record is now explicit since DO-loop 30 processes rows (that is, the PRINT statement is reexecuted for each new value of I). In the earlier version it was necessary to use a repeat specification of *exactly* 4 to accomplish the same desirable "table" appearance of output data. Additionally, the labeling of rows and columns improves the appearance of output. Finally, the use of variables M and N to generalize the loop iterations simplifies subsequent program maintenance should these values change.

11. (a) 12 records, each with one item within the first 5 columns.
    (b) 12 items on one record, with fields of 5 columns.
    (c) 4 records, each with 3 items, with fields of 5 columns.

    Remember: Data are read
    column by column in the
    sequence 1000,500,1500, . . . ,
    500,1500.

12. No. The first prints column by column and the second prints in the usual row-by-row manner.

13. (a)
```
        DO 10 I = 1,2
          READ,(A(I,J),J = 1,3),(B(I,J),J = 1,3)
    10 CONTINUE
```
    (b)
```
        READ,((A(I,J),J = 1,3),I = 1,2)
        READ,((B(I,J),J = 1,3),I = 1,2)
```

    (c) `READ,A,B`   (provided A and B have been dimensioned as 2 × 3 arrays)

14. (a)
```
        PRINT 90
        DO 50 I = 1,2
          PRINT 92,(X(I,J),J = 1,3)
    50 CONTINUE
    90 FORMAT ('1',38X,'MATRIX X:'/)
    92 FORMAT (36X,3F5.1)
```
    (b) `PRINT 2,X`   (provided X is dimensioned as a 2 x 3 array)
```
     2 FORMAT ('0',35X,'ELEMENTS IN X:'/(1X,F45.1))
```

16.
```
        DO 40 J = 1,4
          TOT(J) = 0
          DO 35 I = 1,3
            TOT(J) = TOT(J) + DEPOS(I,J)
    35    CONTINUE
    40    CONTINUE
```

18.
```
        REAL PER(3,4)
           .
           .
           .
        DO 80 I = 1,3
          DO 75 J = 1,4
            PER(I,J) = FLOAT(DEPOS(I,J))/FLOAT(SUM(I))*100.0
    75    CONTINUE
    80 CONTINUE
```

    Third row in PER: 37.5   7.5   17.5   37.5

19. (a)
```
        DO 10 I = 1,100
          DO 5 J = 1,50
            WEIGHT(I,J) = 100.0
     5    CONTINUE
    10 CONTINUE
```

(b)   DATA WEIGHT /5000*0.0/

The alternative in (b) should not be used if there's a need to reinitialize to zero during execution.

20.   DATA D /30*100.0/

21.
```
     DO 10 I = 1,4
        DO 5 J = 1,4
           IF (I .EQ. J)X(I,J) = 1
           IF (I .NE. J)X(I,J) = 0
   5    CONTINUE
  10 CONTINUE
```

Or, more simply,

```
     DATA X /16*0/
     DO 10 K = 1,4
        X(K,K) = 1
  10 CONTINUE
```

25.   TAXTAB(I,1) = Lower limit of taxable income (column 1 in Tax Schedule)
TAXTAB(I,2) = Fixed amount of tax within a class (column 3 in Tax Schedule)
TAXTAB(I,3) = Variable percent amount of tax within a class (column 4 in Tax Schedule)
TAXTAB(I + 1,1) = Upper limit of taxable income, which is the same as lower limit in next class (column 2 in Tax Schedule)

26. Column by column: 0.0,2300.0, ... 1E30 0.0,0.0,132.0, ... 12068.0,0.0 0.0,0.12, ... 0.50,0.0. The last entry in column 2 of the Tax Schedule theoretically is infinity. In practice, any large value would do, so long as it would never be exceeded by the value in TI. We used 1E30. Note that this requires a matrix of 15 rows instead of the 14 rows in the Tax Schedule.

27. **(a)**

WAGES	= 35000.0	DED	=	7500.0	TI	=	28250.0
DIV	= 100.0	EXEM	=	2	TAX	=	6499.5
INTINC	= 500.0	TAXPAY	=	6000.0	REFUND	=	
OTHER	= 0.0	AGI	=	35450.0	BALDUE	=	499.5
ADJ	= 150.0	EXDED	=	5200.0			

(b)

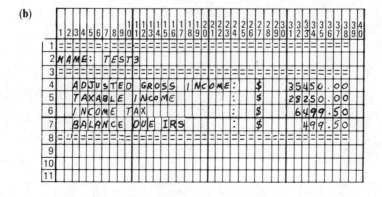

30. 1981, 1982, 1983

150, 250, 600, 100, . . . , 300, 120, 230, . . . , 200, 130, 220, . . . , 150

        1981   1982   1983

Thus ENROLL gets input column by column from lowest to highest depth level. This is equivalent to

READ,(((ENROLL(I,J,K),I = 1,NOC),J = 1,NOL),K = 1,NOY)

31. **(a)** Five years, four levels, and six colleges according to the array declarations. Note that changes up to these limits must be reflected in the first DATA statement. **(b)** 300, 70, and undefined.

32. Replace DO-loops 10 and 20 with

```
        DO 20 I = 1,NOC
          DO 10 K = 1,NOY
            READ,(ENROLL(I,J,K),J = 1,NOL),YEAR(K)
  10      CONTINUE
  20    CONTINUE
```

33. To describe one alternative among several: Add TE to the list in the INTEGER statement, insert

TE = 0

just before DO-loop 70, insert

TE = TE + COLTOT(I)

within DO-loop 70, place TE as the last item in the list of PRINT 940 following DO-loop 70, and change the repeat factor in FORMAT 940 from 4 to 5.

CHAPTER 9

1. Assume snapshot, just before execution of END WHILE, and argument association by value/result.

N	K	NFAC	NKFAC	KFAC	COMB	NUMBER	FAC
8	6	40320	2	720	28	6	720
4	4	24	1	24	1	4	24
4	0	24	24	1	1	0	1
4	1	24	6	1	4	1	1

Execution terminates when 1 and 4 are read in for N and K, respectively.

Output

N =	8 K =	6 COMBINATIONS =	28
N =	4 K =	4 COMBINATIONS =	1
N =	4 K =	0 COMBINATIONS =	1
N =	4 K =	1 COMBINATIONS =	4

2. No, since FAC needs to be reinitialized to 1 for each new call. Yes, there would be a type mismatch between real FAC and integers NFAC, NKFAC, and KFAC. Yes, FACTOR is the name of the subroutine and FAC is the name of a variable local to that subroutine. We can't use the same name for both purposes.

3. **(a)** OK.
(b) SUBROUTINE statement is missing the name of the subroutine, FACTOR.
(c) Either add (A,B,C) to the CALL statement or delete it from the SUBROUTINE statement.
(d) Incorrectly matched argument lists by number and type. There are eight actual arguments and only six dummy arguments. Moreover, character A is paired with integer P, integer B is paired with character Q, integer C is paired with real R, and real E is paired with integer T. Rewrite the dummy arguments as (Q,P,T,R,S,U,V,W) and declare as follows:

```
CHARACTER Q*10,W*3
INTEGER    P,T,V
REAL       R,S,U
```

(e) The name AREA has two meanings in the subroutine. Either change the name of the subroutine in both the CALL and SUBROUTINE statements or change the dummy variable AREA to, say, A in the subroutine.

4. VALUES: 7.7   3.3   6.6
TOTAL: 17.6
Yes, the original contents in A, B, and C have changed. Often this is an unintended effect (logic error).

5.
```
SUBROUTINE HEAD
CHARACTER DATE*25
READ,DATE
PRINT,'PERIODIC REPORT'
PRINT,DATE
END
```

7.

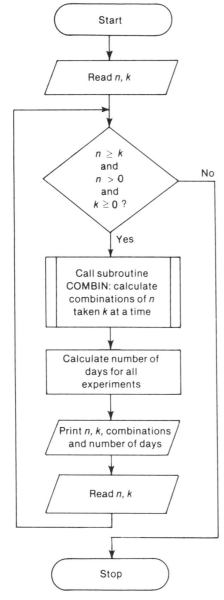

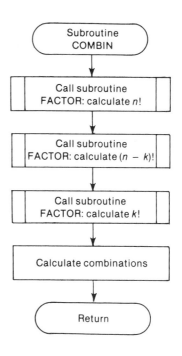

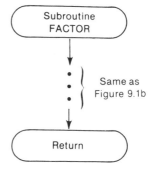

Start main program
  READ *n,k*
  WHILE *n* ≥ *k,n* ≥ 0,*k* ≥ 0
    CALL COMBIN to calculate *C*
    No. days = 14 × *C*
    PRINT *n,k,C*, no. days
    READ *n,k*
  END WHILE
  Stop
End main program

Start subroutine COMBIN
  CALL FACTOR to calculate *n*!
  CALL FACTOR to calculate (*n* − *k*)!
  CALL FACTOR to calculate *k*!
  Combinations = *n*!/(*n* − *k*)!/*k*!
  Return
End subroutine COMBIN

Start subroutine FACTOR ⎫
  ⋮   ⎬ As in Figure 9.2
End subroutine FACTOR ⎭

```
     INTEGER N,K,C,DAYS,DAYPER
     DATA DAYPER/14/
     READ,N,K
     WHILE (N .GE. K .AND. N .GT. 0 .AND. K .GE. 0) THEN
         CALL COMBIN (N,K,C)
         DAYS = DAYPER*C
         PRINT,'N =',N,'K =',K,'C =',C,'DAYS =',DAYS
         READ,N,K
     END WHILE
     STOP
     END


     SUBROUTINE COMBIN(N,K,C)
     INTEGER N,K,C,NFAC,NKFAC,KFAC
     CALL FACTOR(N,NFAC)
     CALL FACTOR(N - K,NKFAC)
     CALL FACTOR(K,KFAC)
     C = NFAC/(NKFAC*KFAC)
     RETURN
     END


     SUBROUTINE FACTOR (NUMBER,FAC)
     .
     .                                        As in Example 9.1
     .
     END
```

Note: Subroutine FACTOR is said to be *nested* within subroutine COMBIN, since COMBIN calls FACTOR. Also, note the generality of subroutine FACTOR as a module that simply calculates factorials. This means it can be used unchanged in different programs, as done here and in Example 9.1.

9. (a) X can't be both a subroutine name and an array name. K must appear in the dummy argument list since it's an adjustable dimension.
    (b) Adjustable dimensions for array A are not allowed in the calling program. In the subroutine, POINT is not a *dummy* array, which means we can't give it an adjustable dimension. If POINT is local to the subroutine, use a *constant* dimension; otherwise place POINT in the dummy argument list and give it a corresponding actual argument.
    (c) In the dummy array declarator X(200,50), the size of the dummy array (200 × 50 = 10,000) exceeds the size of the corresponding actual array (100 × 50 = 5000). Use X(M,N). Also, use S(M) instead of S(*).

10. (a) Valid; array X has 100 locations. However, the use of 100 requires program changes for array size instead of simpler input data changes.
    (b) Valid; array X has 300 locations. (See criticism in part a.)
    (c) Invalid; array X is dimensioned too large (above 500).
    (d) Invalid; order or actual arguments does not match order of dummy arguments.
    (e) Invalid; X is not defined in the calling program.
    (f) Invalid; too few arguments.

11. Make the following changes in the main program.

```
REAL SCORE(500),AVE,SUM
CALL MEAN(N,SCORE,AVE,SUM)
PRINT,AVE,SUM
```

Make the following change in the subroutine.

```
SUBROUTINE MEAN(N,X,XBAR,SUM)
```

12. Main program:

```
CALL MEAN
STOP
END
```

Subroutine:

```
SUBROUTINE MEAN
INTEGER N
REAL X(500),XBAR,SUM
READ,N
READ,(X(J),J = 1,N)
SUM = 0.0
DO 10 J = 1,N
    SUM = SUM + X(J)
10 CONTINUE
XBAR = SUM/N
PRINT,XBAR
RETURN
END
```

Note that the main program has no function other than to call the subroutine. N can be input through the subroutine only if it's not used as an adjustable dimension. If N is to be an adjustable dimension for X, it will be necessary to input N in the main program and to have argument lists that contain both N and X.

16. Execution error; D and E are undefined.

17. No, since the unique identities of N, K, NFAC, NKFAC, and KFAC could not be preserved.

18. **(a)**

X(1) Y(1)	X(2) Y(2)	A B
10	20	5
		35

(b) 10 20 35

(c) The common block changes to:

Contents change as follows:

X(1) B	X(2) Y(1)	A Y(2)
10 35	20	5

The output changes to:

35 20 5

19. (a) N and J, Y(1) and P match-ups OK, but integer M must not be paired with real R; real Q must not be paired with integer K.

(b) Missing comma after R(30); dimension of S should coincide with dimension on R. Either change the 50 to 30 or the 30 to 50. If this dimension change is not made, then A will share storage with S(31).

(c) OK. D shares with A, and E shares with B.

(d) COMMON D,E,F, is OK, but COMMON for the second subprogram should be changed to:

    COMMON A,B,C,M,N

in order to align M with I and N with J.

(e) OK.

(f) Named common must be size-consistent. Use A(1000).

23. (a)

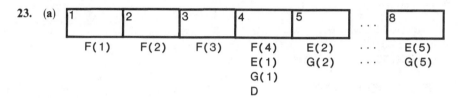

(b) Not allowed. Character values can't be mixed with numeric values.

(c)

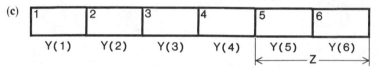

Numeric type mixing is not generally recommended. Above, Y is real and Z is double precision.

(d)

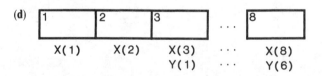

(e)

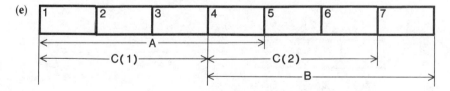

24. In Figure 9.2a, eliminate the three CALL boxes and rewrite the next box as follows:

> Calculate combinations
> using function FACTOR

In Figure 9.2b, replace the start symbol with

Function
FACTOR

In Figure 9.3, eliminate the three CALL lines in the main program and replace the combinations line with

Combinations = function FACTOR(n) / (function FACTOR($n - k$)∗function FACTOR(k))

and replace the word "subroutine" with the word "function."

25. **(a)** Make the following changes to the answer beginning on page 000. In the flowcharts, eliminate all "call" boxes and replace the word "subroutine" with the word "function" in the start symbols. Replace corresponding boxes with the following.

| Calculate number of days for all experiments using function COMBIN | Calculate combinations using function FACTOR |

In the pseudocode, eliminate the four CALL lines and use

No. days = 14 $\times$ function COMBIN(n,k)

and

Combinations = function FACTOR(n) / (function FACTOR($n - k$)∗function FACTOR(k))

and replace the word "subroutine" with the word "function." In the main program, eliminate the CALL statement, use

DAYS = DAYPER∗COMBIN(N,K)

and replace "C" with "COMBIN" in the INTEGER statement and "C" with "COMBIN(N,K)" in the PRINT statement.

In the first subprogram, replace the SUBROUTINE statement with

FUNCTION COMBIN(N,K)

replace "C" with "COMBIN' in the INTEGER statement, eliminate the three CALL statements, and use

COMBIN = FACTOR(N) / (FACTOR(N − K)∗FACTOR(K))

In the second subprogram, replace the SUBROUTINE statement with

FUNCTION FACTOR(NUMBER)

and replace "FAC" with "FACTOR."

26. In the main program, eliminate the CALL statement and use the following in place of the originals.

REAL SCORE(500),MEAN
PRINT,MEAN(N,SCORE)

In the subprogram, replace the SUBROUTINE statement with

    FUNCTION MEAN(N,X)

replace the REAL statement with

    REAL X(N),MEAN,SUM

and replace the assignment statement for XBAR with

    MEAN = SUM/N

27. Yes, we could make SUM a dummy argument by using

    FUNCTION MEAN(N,X,SUM)

However, as a matter of style, we don't recommend doing this, since functions are expected to return a single value (not the two values in SUM and MEAN as would be the case here).

28. In the main program, eliminate the CALL statement and use the following in place of the originals.

    REAL SCORE(500),MEAN
    COMMON N,SCORE
    PRINT,MEAN( )

In the subprogram, replace the subroutine statement with

    FUNCTION MEAN( )

the REAL statement with

    REAL X(500),MEAN,SUM

the COMMON statement with

    COMMON N,X

and the assignment statement for XBAR with

    MEAN = SUM/N

We can't use the adjustable dimension N for X in this subprogram because X is not part of a dummy argument list.

29. 15

30. (a)
    FUNCTION RND(VALUE)
    REAL VALUE
    INTEGER RND
    RND = INT(VALUE + 0.5)
    RETURN
    END

(b)
    FUNCTION MAX(A,B)
    REAL A,B,MAX
    MAX = MAX0(A,B)
    RETURN
    END

32. CEL(FAHREN) = 5.0/9.0∗(FAHREN − 32.0)

33. POLY(B0,B1,B2,B3,X) = B0 + B1 + B2∗X∗∗2 + B3∗X∗∗3

34. **(a)** Delete line 215 and add this FUNCTION at the end of the program.

```
FUNCTION F(X)
REAL X,F
F = −1.0 + 2.0∗X
RETURN
END
```

(b) Delete line 215. Add the following:

```
262   CALL FOX(LEFT, FL)
263   CALL FOX(RIGHT, FR)
265   IF(FL∗FR .GT. 0.0)THEN
377   CALL FOX(MID,FM)
380   Replace F(MID) by FM
390   IF(FM∗FR .GT. 0.0)THEN
495   Replace F(MID) by FM
```

Add FL, FR, and FM to the REAL statement. Add the following right after the END statement:

```
SUBROUTINE FOX(X,F)
REAL X,F
F = −1.0 + 2.0∗X
RETURN
END
```

(c) Delete line 215.
Use (−1.0 + 2.0∗LEFT) in place of F(LEFT) in line 265.
Use (−1.0 + 2.0∗RIGHT) in place of F(RIGHT) in lines 265 and 390.
Use (−1.0 + 2.0∗MID) in place of F(MID) in lines 380, 390, and 495.

The statement function approach in Example 9.7 is much preferred to these other alternatives with respect to coding efficiency and style. The subroutine approach in part b is especially cumbersome.

CHAPTER 10

1. **(a)** LENGTH =   10
(b) END OF STRING MARK NOT FOUND
STRING IMAGE: I LOVE FORTRAN$
(c) LENGTH =   0
(d) LENGTH =   24

67 total

2. 'I', 'L', 'O', 'V', 'E', 'F', 'O', 'R', 'T', 'R', 'A', 'N', '/', 'ᵬ', 'ᵬ', . . . , 'ᵬ'

3.
```
        CHARACTER*1  TEXT(80)
        INTEGER      LENGTH,MAXLEN,SUM
        REAL         AVE

        DATA MAXLEN/80/

        DO 50 I = 1,50
          READ (5,90) TEXT
          SUM = SUM + LENGTH(TEXT,MAXLEN)
    50  CONTINUE

        AVE = FLOAT (SUM)/50.0
        PRINT, 'AVERAGE LENGTH = ',AVE
        STOP

    90  FORMAT(80A1)
        END

        FUNCTION LENGTH(LINE,MAXLEN)
        .
        .
        .
        END
```

4. (a)
```
    STRING IS          : MAKE MINE COORS
    SUBSTRING IS       : COOR
    BEGINS IN POSITION : 11
```
   (b) SUBSTRING NOT FOUND

5. N will be zero or negative. If the substring doesn't match at least one character, then DO-loop 5 is processed once and INDEX = 0, which is OK; if the first LENSTR characters of the substring match the string, then the UNTIL test in line 630 may give an execution error when $K + J - 1$ exceeds LENSTR. It's best to insert the following error routine:

```
    601  IF(N .LE. 0)THEN
    602     PRINT,'LENGTH OF SUBSTRING EXCEEDS LENGTH OF STRING'
    603     INDEX = 0
    604     RETURN
    605  END IF
    606  DO 5 K = 1,N
```

8. Try the following input. (There are other possibilities as well.)
   (a) OLD: AM
        NEW: AM VERY
   (b) OLD: PY
        NEW: PY FOR YOU
   (c) OLD: I
        NEW: THEY THINK I
   (d) OLD: ḃVERYḃ
        NEW: ḃ
   (e) OLD: M HAPPY
        NEW: M

CHAPTER 11

1. The record might have fields such as name of student, identification number, grade on assignment 1, . . . , grade on assignment *n,* grade on exam 1, . . . , grade on exam *m.* Most likely it would be a sequential-access file, since this type of file is generally processed in its entirety for the purpose of calculating final grades. It's likely to be an unformatted file since this reduces processing time and there's not likely to be a change in processor during the school term.

2. In part a, insert

   CLARK G.W. 2   24000   M

   as the new Record 2 and renumber Records 2 and 3 as 3 and 4. This assumes that records are in sequential order alphabetically by last name.
   In part b, insert the same data as above in the slot for Record Number 2. This assumes that record numbers are based on the ID numbers.

3. Yes, by sequentially specifying all record numbers. No, since the file doesn't have record numbers.

4. (a) Execution terminates for each of the first two READ statements and control gets transferred to statement number 95 for the third READ statement.
   (b) Same as part a, except control goes to statement 90 in the third case.

5. Writes an *unformatted* record to a *sequential* file on unit 15.

6. (a) REWIND 12
   (b) END FILE 4

7. (a)   WRITE (2,90) NAME, STREET, CITY, STATE, ZIP, PHONE, MAP
       90 FORMAT (A20, A16, A13, A2, I5, I10, A3)
   (b)   WRITE (2) NAME, STREET, CITY, STATE, ZIP, PHONE, MAP
   (c)   CHARACTER NAME*20, STREET*16,CITY*13,STATE*2,MAP*3
          INTEGER   ZIP, PHONE
          LOOP
             READ, NAME, STREET, CITY, STATE, ZIP, PHONE, MAP
               AT END, QUIT
             WRITE (2,90) NAME, STREET, CITY, STATE, ZIP, PHONE, MAP
          END LOOP
          PRINT, 'FILE CREATED'
       90 FORMAT (A20, A16, A13, A2, I5, I10, A3)
          STOP
          END

8. (a) 1 (see first item in input data)
   (b) Eliminate format 10.
       Change WRITE (U, 10) to WRITE (U).
       Change READ (U, 10) to READ (U).

   Note: Most likely the specifications that set up the file within the control cards will have to be changed.

9. Change READ(U, 10) to READ(U, 10,END = 5).
Delete AT END,QUIT.
Label the PRINT statement following END LOOP as statement 5.

We prefer the approach in the example to the traditional END = approach because it avoids the use of a statement label.

10. Change READ(U, 10) to READ (U,10,ERR = 99).
Move COUNT = COUNT + 1 to just after LOOP.
Just after the FORMAT statement insert

```
99  PRINT,'ERROR IN FILE READ IN AT RECORD',COUNT
    STOP
```

12.
```
    DEFINE FILE 20(5000,30,E,NEXT)
    READ,ID,NAME,GRADE
    WRITE (20'ID,900)NAME,ID,GRADE
900 FORMAT(A25,I4,A1)
```

14. **(a)** Syntax error since the unit identifier in *this* statement must be a constant. The use of U here would generalize this identifier to facilitate changing unit numbers, as done in the READ/WRITE statements.
(b) 100 according to the DEFINE FILE statement.
(c) Because we need to process the file display data in the input data file. Without the 'EOF' terminal record we would get an execution error as

```
    READ, NAME, ID, SAL, SEX
```

attempts to process the 6.
(d) Replace 6   with   1
              3   6
                           10

15. **(a)** Records 3 through 8. **(b)** 6,5.

16. We can neither change a record number nor delete a record once a direct-access file is created. We could, however, proceed as described in item (iv) of Exercise 20.

18. **(a)** The record length changes to 35 characters. This means we have to change the DEFINE FILE statement by replacing 100 with, say, 999999999 and 29 with 35. Also, the format specification changes to:

```
    (A20, I9, I5,A1)
```

Two practical problems here:

1. The disk file would have to be impossibly huge at about 3.5×10^{10} bytes (999,999,999 $\times$ 35), or 35,000 megabytes or 35 gigabytes.
2. An incredible number of records would be unused (i.e., 3.5×10^{10} less the number of employees)

See part b for the solution.

MODULE A

1. Reread the module.

2. Yes, if it strictly describes the control structures presented in Chapters 4–6.

MODULE B

1. First you should find out the appropriate "output unit number" for your system. We use 6.

    ```
    WRITE (6,30)
    WRITE (6,40)
    WRITE (6,50)
    WRITE (6,60) NAME,ID,BALDUE
    WRITE (6,50)
    WRITE (6,80) CUMBAL
    WRITE (6,70)
    WRITE (6,70)
    ```

2. Change the carriage control character in FORMAT "40" from '0' to 'ƀ' and use either

    ```
        PRINT 35
    35 FORMAT ('ƀ')
    ```

    or

    ```
        PRINT, 'ƀ'
    ```

    immediately after PRINT 30. From Chapter 4 we can easily print 15 blank lines using a DO-loop.

    ```
        DO 3 K = 1,15
            PRINT,'ƀ'
    3 CONTINUE
    ```

3. (a) `15 FORMAT('+','HAL SPEAKS')`   (d) `15 FORMAT('0','ƀƀƀHAL SPEAKS')`
    (b) `15 FORMAT('ƀ','HAL SPEAKS')`   (e) `15 FORMAT('1','HAL SPEAKS')`
    (c) `15 FORMAT('0','HAL SPEAKS')`

4.
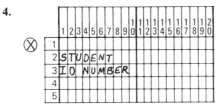

5.
    ```
    PRINT 90
    PRINT 95

        .
        .
        .

    90 FORMAT('0THE ANSWER = ')
    95 FORMAT('ƀ ————————— ')
    ```

6.

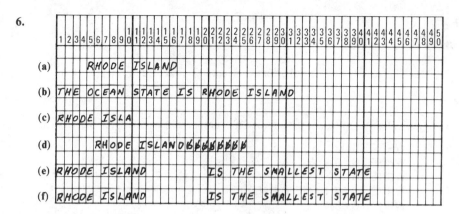

7.   PRINT 30, 'bbbbbbbbbbbb∗∗TUITION REPORT∗∗'
   30 FORMAT('1',A30)
       PRINT 40, 'bbbbbbNAMEbbbbbbbbbSS NUMBERbbbbBALANCE DUE'
   40 FORMAT('0',A42)

8. System dependent.

9.

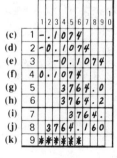

11. **(a)** F5.1 **(b)** F8.4

	1	2	3	4	5	6	7	8	9	0
(c) 1	-	.	1	0	7	4				
(d) 2	-	0	.	1	0	7	4			
(e) 3			-	0	.	1	0	7	4	
(f) 4	0	.	1	0	7	4				
(g) 5			3	7	6	4	.	0		
(h) 6			3	7	6	4	.	2		
(i) 7				3	7	6	4	.		
(j) 8	3	7	6	4	.	1	6	0		
(k) 9	∗	∗	∗	∗	∗	∗				

(Overflow if computer inserts leading zero.)

12.

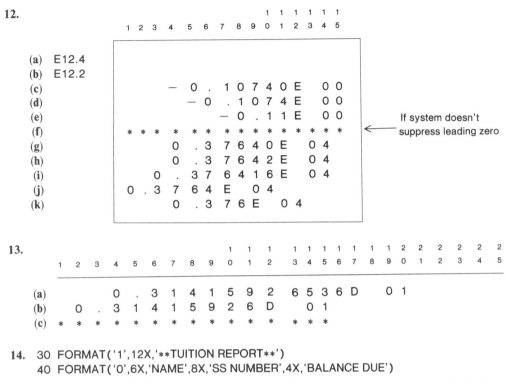

(a) E12.4
(b) E12.2
(c)   −0.10740E 00
(d)   −0.1074E 00
(e)   −0.11E 00
(f)   * * * * * * * * * * * * * * *
(g)   0.37640E 04
(h)   0.37642E 04
(i)   0.37 6416E 04
(j)   0.3764E 04
(k)   0.376E 04

If system doesn't suppress leading zero

13.

(a)   0.314159 2 6536 D 01
(b)   0.3141592 6 D 01
(c)   * * * * * * * * * * * * * * *

14. 30 FORMAT('1',12X,'**TUITION REPORT**')
40 FORMAT('0',6X,'NAME',8X,'SS NUMBER',4X,'BALANCE DUE')

The advantage of the X edit descriptor is questionable here, since we lose alignment by sight as in the original version.

16. 80 FORMAT(T19,'**TOTALS**',T32,'$',F10.2)

17. (a) 30 FORMAT('1',T14,'**TUITION REPORT**')
40 FORMAT('0',T8,'NAME',T20,'SS NUMBER',T33,'BALANCE DUE')

18. Look up those you're not sure of.

MODULE C

1. First you should find out the appropriate "input unit number" for your system. We use 5.

```
READ(5,10)CPC,FEES
READ(5,15)N
READ(5,20)NAME, ID,CREDIT
```

2. (a)   READ 900,FIRST,MIDDLE,LAST
900 FORMAT(A8,A8,A12)
(b)   PRINT 950,LAST,FIRST,MIDDLE
950 FORMAT('1',49X,A12',b',A8,'b',A8)

3.   <u>TOY</u>
- (a) CAPTAIN NEMO DOLLƀƀƀ
- (b) CAPTAIN NEƀƀƀƀƀƀƀƀƀ
- (c) IN NEMO DOLLƀƀƀƀƀƀƀƀ
- (d) IN NEMO DOLLƀƀƀ
- (e) CAPTAIN NEƀƀƀƀƀ

4.

	JACK	JILL	UP	HILL
(a)	5	0	6241	98
(b)	5	62419	84	75

5.   READ 1,K,M,N
      1 FORMAT(I3,I3,I2)

6.

1	2	3	4	5	6	7	8	9	10	11	12	13	14	...
		3	5		6	0	0				−	3		

7. 100.0 and 250.0; 9999.0 and 9999.0

8.

	JACK	JILL	UP	HILL
(a)	5.0	0.0	624.1	0.98
(b)	5.0	62.419	84.0	0.075

9. (a) 999.9; 999.0 (b) A real variable (CREDIT) is paired with an integer edit descriptor (I4). Retype CREDIT as integer.

10.   READ 1,X,Y,Z
       1 FORMAT(F3.2,F3.0,F2.1)
          or   (F4.3,F2.0,F2.1)

11.

	1	2	3	4	5	6	7	8	9	10	11	12	13	14	15	...
(a)	1	5	.	2	5				4	5		5	0	7	.	
	1	5	2	5					4	5			5	0	7	
(b)	1	5	2	.	5			4	5	0	5	0	7	0	.	
	1	5	2	5	0			4	5	0		5	0	7	0	
(c)	1	5	2	5	.				5	0	5	0	7	.	4	

Need field width of 6 to input
COST without decimal point.

	1	2	3	4	5	6	7	8	9	10	11	12	13	14	15	...
(d)	1	0	5	.						5	−	3	0	0	.	
	1	0	5	0	0				5			−	3	0	0	

12.   1 2 3 4 5 6 7 8 9 10 11 12 13 14 15 ...

W .   M I T T Y
2 6 6 6 1 2 4 6 3
   1 5 0

Three input records are needed per student.

13.   1 2 3 4 5 6 7 8 9 10 ...

      7 3 4   1 0 0
   6 0 7 0   3

15.

	V1	V2	V3
(a)	-12.1×10^2	5.555×10^3	0.33×10^4
(b)	-0.12×10^2	$5555. \times 10^3$	0.33×10^{-4}
(c)	-0.12×10^2	0.555	0.33

16. (a) Right-justify in column 20.
 (b) Use D-05 in the second record and -5 in the third record.
 (c) Insufficient field width for this edit descriptor.
 (d) No changes.

17.   READ 20,ID,CREDIT
     20 FORMAT(I9,62X,F4.1)

Also see Exercise 19.

19. 20 FORMAT(I9,T72,F4.1)

21. Look up those you're not sure of.

MODULE D

1. (a) 50 FORMAT(' ',42('-'))
 (b) Just before right parenthesis in FORMAT 40 insert /' ',42('-')
     Just before 18X in FORMAT 80 insert ' ',42('-')/

2.   DO 50 J = 1,15
       PRINT,'ƀ'
     50 CONTINUE
       PRINT 10
     10 FORMAT(14(/))
Note: n slashes alone in a format specification print $n + 1$ blank lines.

5. 25 FORMAT(3F10.2/2F5.2)

6. 30 FORMAT('1',4(F12.1,'%',I12))

7. **(a)**

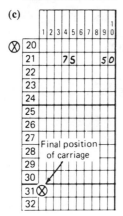

(b)

(c)   Final position of carriage

(d)

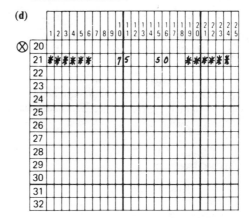

8. **(a)** No explicit carriage control after //. **(b)** No explicit carriage control after ///. **(c)** Do we mean I52,3X or I5,23X?

9.

	Columns	Variable
First record	1–5	A
	6–10	B
	11–20	L
Second record	1–5	C
	6–10	D

10. **(a)**

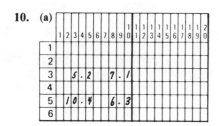

(b)

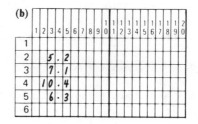

11. **(a)** Assuming card or card image input, it allows use of the entire card for entering the format specification.

(b)

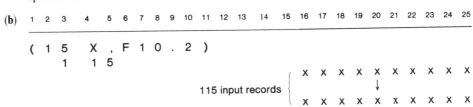

(c) The statement

    READ FM,VALUE

reads only a single value per input record. We would need to store values in an array (Chapter 7), as done in part (d).

12. Look up those you're not sure of.

MODULE E

1. For example, in Figure E.2 we could have placed within Step 2 the initial and concluding tasks shown within Step 3. There are many such permutations for long, complicated programs, especially with respect to how much detail we show within each step.

2.
    1.1 Declare variables
    1.2 No. orders = 0
    1.3 Cumulative quant. = 0
    1.4 Cumulative charge = 0
    1.5 READ customer data

    2.1 WHILE more orders
        2.1.1 Compute charge
        2.1.2 Accumulate totals
        2.1.3 PRINT customer data
        2.1.4 READ customer data
    2.2 END WHILE

    2.1.1.1 Compute charge based on discount
    2.1.1.2 Compute charge based on surcharge

    2.1.2.1 Add 1 to no. orders
    2.1.2.2 Add quant. to cum. quant.
    2.1.2.3 Add charge to cum. charge

2.1.1.1.1   IF quant. < 50 THEN
  2.1.1.1.1.1   Charge = quant. × unit price
2.1.1.1.2   END IF
2.1.1.1.3   IF 50 ≤ quant. ≤ 99 THEN
  2.1.1.1.3.1   Charge = 0.9 × quant. × unit price
2.1.1.1.4   END IF
2.1.1.1.5   IF quant. ≥ 100 THEN
  2.1.1.1.5.1   Charge = 0.75 × quant. × unit price
2.1.1.1.6   END IF

2.1.1.2.1   IF foreign country THEN
  2.1.1.2.1.1   Charge = 1.25 × charge
2.1.1.2.2   END IF

The numbering scheme gets a bit tedious, don't you think?

3. (a)   IF (QUANT .LT. BREAK1) CHARGE = QUANT*PRICE
          IF (QUANT .GE. BREAK1 .AND. QUANT .LT. BREAK2) CHARGE =
          +   (1.0 − DISC1)*QUANT*PRICE
          IF (QUANT .GE. BREAK2) CHARGE = (1.0 − DISC2)*QUANT*PRICE

    (b) IF (QUANT .LT. BREAK1) THEN
           CHARGE = QUANT*PRICE
         ELSE IF (QUANT .GE. BREAK1 .AND. QUANT .LT. BREAK2) THEN
           CHARGE = (1.0 − DISC1)*QUANT*PRICE
         ELSE
           CHARGE = (1.0 − DISC2)*QUANT*PRICE
         END IF

6. Look up those you're not sure of.

MODULE F

1. (a) Module 2 prints a default message, since 100 > 90, and execution stops. See TEST3 output.
    (b) Module 3 prints an error message, since 4 > 2, and execution stops.
    (c) To obtain the correct number of weeks when any of the values 7, 14, 21 . . . is stored in DAYS. Otherwise, for example, 7 in DAYS would give 2 in WEEKS. We could subtract any real constant between 0 and 1, but then the entire expression to the right of the equal sign would be evaluated using real arithmetic and the resulting value would be truncated to integer for storage in WEEKS. We would get correct results but with inefficient processing.
    (d) To improve the generality of the module with respect to matching the sizes of real and dummy arrays.

(e)

```
    27
    28
    29
    30
    31
    32  RENTAL COSTS FOR B. HOLLY
    33
    34  RENTAL PLAN    PROJECTED COST
    35  ---------------------------------
    36  DAILY             $  670.00
    37  WEEKLY            $  682.00
    38  ---------------------------------
    39
    40  THE BEST PLAN IS DAILY
    41
    42
    43  GROUP NUMBER INCORRECT.
    44
    45
    46
    47
    48
```

2. Add MINX to the dummy argument lists in modules 4 and 5, to the actual argument lists in CALL PLANS and CALL OUTPUT in module 1, and to the REAL statements in modules 1 and 5. In module 5 use

    PRINT 30,BEST,MINX

and in format 30 replace A10// with

    A10,'WITH A PROJECTED COST OF $',F8.2//

3. Add MINX to the dummy argument list in module 4, to the actual argument list in CALL PLANS in module 1, and to the REAL statement in module 1. Add MINSUM to the REAL statement in module 1. Just after the REAL statement in module 1 insert

    MINSUM = 0.0

Just before the CONTINUE statement in module 1 insert

    MINSUM = MINSUM + MINX

Just before the STOP statement in module 1 insert

    PRINT 40,MINSUM
    40 FORMAT(//'0THE SUM OF COST MINIMA IS $',F10.2)

4. Only changes in module 3 are required. Initialize NOG to 3 and add a new third case to initialize data for the new group.

5. Module 8 remains unchanged. In *each* of modules 1–7 use the following statements for *global* names.

```
CHARACTER   NAMEC*20,NAMEP*10(6),BEST*10
INTEGER     GROUP,MILES,DAYS,NOP
REAL        DFC,CPM,WFC,PRICE,MPG,COST(6)
COMMON      /NAMES/NAMEC,NAMEP,BEST
COMMON      GROUP,MILES,DAYS,NOP,DFC,CPM,WFC,PRICE,MPG,COST
```

Note that all character data reside in a named common block.

In modules 6 and 7 replace TCDP and TCWP by COST(1) and COST(2), respectively.

In each of the modules below, add the indicated type statements for local variables.

Module	Type Statement	
1	INTEGER NUM	
2	INTEGER DLIMIT	
3	INTEGER NOG	
4	INTEGER MINJ	Actually, MINJ and MINX are
	REAL MINX	localized to modules 4 and 8
7	INTEGER WEEKS	

Remove all argument lists in modules 1–7, except for the actual argument list that calls MIN-VAL in module 4.

This approach is slightly more efficient, perhaps more convenient, and forces us to think in terms of global and local names. However, it de-emphasizes the needs/results of (or which variables get passed to and from) modules. Since we can't use generalized and adjustable array declarators, this approach is slightly less convenient for array size and character length updates. It's basically a matter of the programmer's preferences.

6. Replace the first two CALL statements in module 4 with

```
COST(1)= DFC*DAYS + CPM*MILES
WEEKS  = (DAYS − 1)/7 + 1
COST(2)= WFC*WEEKS + MILES*PRICE/MPG
```

This design is more code efficient but less explicitly modular from the standpoint of adding and/or deleting car plans. Those who prefer the approach in this exercise can claim with good reason that the small size of modules 6 and 7 is a case of *overmodularization*. Exercises 11 and 12 better justify plans as separate modules.

7. Modules 6 and 7 are naturals for function subprograms, since they each return a single value to the calling program.

Module 4 changes
Add DAILY and WEEKLY to the REAL statement
Replace the first two CALL statements with

```
COST(1) = DAILY(MILES,DAYS,DFC,CPM)
COST(2) = WEEKLY(MILES,DAYS,WFC,PRICE,MPG)
```

Module 6 changes
Replace the SUBROUTINE statement with

```
FUNCTION DAILY(MILES,DAYS,DFC,CPM)
```

Replace TCDP with DAILY in the REAL and assignment statements.

Module 7 changes
Replace the SUBROUTINE statement with

```
FUNCTION WEEKLY(MILES,DAYS,WFC,PRICE,MPG)
```

Replace TCWP with WEEKLY in the REAL and assignment statements.
We have a slight preference for the approach in this exercise, as it's more direct with respect to defining elements in COST.

8. (a)
```
SUBROUTINE CARDAT(GROUP,PAR,DFC,CPM,WFC,PRICE,MPG)
        .
        .
        .
REAL PAR(7,5)
        .
        .
 DFC   = PAR(1,1)
 CPM   = PAR(1,2)
 WFC   = PAR(1,3)
 PRICE = PAR(1,4)
 MPG   = PAR(1,5)
        .
        .
 DFC   = PAR(2,1)
 CPM   = PAR(2,2)
 WFC   = PAR(2,3)
 PRICE = PAR(2,4)
 MPG   = PAR(2,5)
        .
        .
        .
        .
        .
        .
END
```

Module 1 must be changed by adding NOG to the INTEGER statement, PAR(7,5) to the REAL statement, and

```
READ, NOG
READ, ((PAR(I,J),J = 1,5),I = 1,NOG)
```

just before the READ statement.

This approach simplifies data updates for the five car-group parameters. It's worthwhile if these values change often. How close is our price per gallon of gasoline?

9. **(a)** *Module 1 changes*
Add the type statement

      LOGICAL FLAG

Change DO-loop 50 as follows:

```
DO 50 J = 1,NUM
  FLAG = .TRUE.
  CALL INPUT (add FLAG to this list)
  IF (FLAG) THEN
    CALL CARDAT (as before)
    CALL PLANS (as before)
    CALL OUTPUT (as before)
  END IF
50 CONTINUE
```

Module 2 changes
Add FLAG to the dummy argument list.
Add the type statement

      LOGICAL FLAG

Replace the STOP statement with

      FLAG = .FALSE.

(b) Here we assume that the changes in part (a) have been made.

Module 1 changes
Same changes as part (a).
Modify the DO-loop body in part (a) as follows:

```
IF (FLAG) THEN
  CALL CARDAT (add FLAG to this list)
  IF (FLAG) THEN
    CALL PLANS (as before)
    CALL OUTPUT (as before)
  END IF
END IF
50 CONTINUE
```

Module 3 changes
Same changes that were made in module 2.
Given the input data in Exercise 1(e), processing now continues through the third customer, rather than stopping after the second customer. Besides the output shown in the answer to Exercise 1(e), we get the following output for the third customer.

```
F. DOMINO
NUMBER OF DAYS IN RENTAL EXCEEDS 90
TRY OUR LEASING PLAN . . .
IT'S AN OFFER YOU CAN'T REFUSE.
```

13. **(a)–(f)**
Replace SUBROUTINE statements with REMOTE BLOCK statements.
Delete RETURN statements and replace END statements with END BLOCK statements.
Replace CALL statements with EXECUTE statements.

Eliminate all typing statements (REAL, etc.) within modules.

Don't forget to replace N by NOP and X by COST within Module 8.

OUTPUT should be tested last because it requires the calculated values from all other modules to give the correct output report.

14. Let remote block PLANS call MINVAL as done in line 3280 of the original version, and design module MINVAL as done in the subroutine (lines 4490–4850) of the original version. This approach is best if MINVAL is an "off-the-shelf" utility subroutine.

18. Look up those you're not sure of.

MODULE G

1. Look up those you're not sure of.

2. (a) Single entry and single exit point. (b) Independence. (c) Not too large. Control structures exactly satisfy characteristic (a), usually satisfy characteristic (c), and often satisfy characteristic (b).

3. Reference to a module represents an unrefined level of detail, whereas the module itself is a more refined level of detail. Also, modules such as subroutines facilitate top-down testing.

4. Structured programming exclusively utilizes the three basic control structures; each control structure, in turn, can be viewed as a module based on the three main characteristics of modules (as summarized in Exercise 2). Moreover, subprogram and remote block modules are best treated as a fourth type of control structure. In this view the module is a "mega" control structure that contains the three other control structures.

5. Execution of control structures is from top to bottom, except for the loop structure, which *cycles* from top to bottom.

Index

A edit descriptor, *see* Edit descriptors
ABS, 58
Accumulating a sum, *see* Loops
Actual argument list, 330
Address, 13
Adjustable dimension, 344 (*see also* Sub-
routines)
Algorithm, 27
ALOG, 58
ALOG10, 58
Alphanumeric array, *see* Character array
Alphanumeric data, *see* Character datum
Alphanumeric variables, *see* Character
variable name
American National Standards Institute, *see*
ANSI
AMIN0, 58
AMIN1, 58
.AND., 159
ANSI, 19
Apostrophe edit descriptors, *see* Edit de-
scriptors
Applications of the computer
management information systems, 5
decision support systems, 6
Applications software, *see* Software
Arithmetic expression, *see* Expressions
Arithmetic hierarchy, 51
left-to-right rule, 52
parentheses, 54

Arithmetic-logic unit, *see* Central proces-
sing unit
Arithmetic operators, 43
Arithmetic statement function, *see* State-
ment function
Argument, 57, 330, 332, 342, 360, 366
Array, *see* One-dimensional arrays; Two-
dimensional arrays; Three-dimen-
sional arrays; Character array
Array declaration, 241
Array element, 238
Array element name, 239
Array name, 238
Artificial intelligence, 7
Assembly language, 18
Assignment statement
arithmetic, 41
character, 41, 379
logical, 156
(*see also* Expressions)
AT END statement, 178
Auxiliary storage, *see* Secondary storage
Assumed-size array declarator, *see* Sub-
routines

Batch, *see* Batch environment
Batch environment
card deck, 76
comment cards, 80
control cards, 80

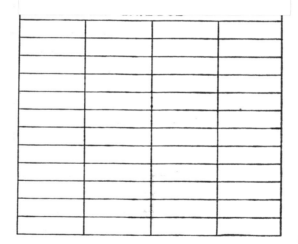

SUMMARY OF WATFIV STATEMENTS AND FUNCTIONS USED IN THIS TEXT

STATEMENT	DESCRIPTION (TEXT PAGE)	EXECUT-ABLE?	EXAMPLES
IF NONE	Defines error case in CASE structure; see DO CASE (208)	Yes	IF NONE
INTEGER	Types integer names; can declare arrays and initialize (38)	No	INTEGER CODE,D(200) INTEGER COUNT/0/
LOGICAL	Types logical names; can declare arrays and initialize (39)	No	LOGICAL FLAG,F(50)

LOOP	Defines beginning of generalized, LRC, and UNTIL loop structures (170, 173, 178)	Yes	LOOP
			   READ . . .
			      AT END, QUIT
			   .
			   .
			   .
			END LOOP
			LOOP
			   .
			   .
			   .
			UNTIL (A .GT. B)

PRINT	Transfers data from primary memory to output medium (60, 250, 444)	Yes	PRINT, 'ANSWER' = ,ANS PRINT 15,A,B,A•B PRINT 90,(NAME(J),J = 1,N)
QUIT	Transfers control to end of structured block; see LOOP (173, 180)	Yes	QUIT QUIT 2
READ	Transfers data from input medium to primary memory (64, 66, 178, 250, 406, 415, 468, 471)	Yes	READ,A,B READ 92,M,N,D,E,F READ (10,95,END = 99)NAME,ID READ (10'ID,100)NAME, ID
REAL	Types real names; can declare arrays and initialize (39)	No	REAL LIST(500),COST,LOAD REAL SUM/0.0/

REMOTE BLOCK	Defines beginning of remote block (527)	Yes	REMOTE BLOCK PLANS
			   .
			   .
			END BLOCK

RETURN	Returns execution to calling program (333)	Yes	RETURN
REWIND	Rewinds sequential-access file (409)	Yes	REWIND 10